MODERN LITERARY THEORY

A READER

Third Edition

**Edited by
Philip Rice
and
Patricia Waugh**

ARNOLD

A member of the Hodder Headline Group

LONDON • NEW YORK • SYDNEY • AUCKLAND

First published in Great Britain in 1989
Second edition published in 1992
Third edition published in 1996 by
Arnold, a member of the Hodder Headline Group
338 Euston Road, London NW1 3BH
175 Fifth Avenue, New York, NY 10010
Second impression 1997

Distributed exclusively in the USA by
St Martin's Press Inc.
175 Fifth Avenue, New York, NY 10010

British Library Cataloguing in Publication Data
A catalogue record for this book is available from the British Library

Library of Congress Cataloging-in-Publication Data
Modern literary theory: a reader / [edited by Philip Rice and
Patricia Waugh]. — 3rd ed.
    p.   cm.
Includes bibliographical references and index.
ISBN 0-340-64585-7 (pbk.)
1. Literature — History and criticism — Theory, etc.   I. Rice,
Philip.   II. Waugh, Patricia.
PN81.M54   1996
801'.95'09045 — dc20   96–17312

ISBN 0 340 64585 7

Typeset in 10/12 Palatino by Anneset, Weston-super-Mare, Somerset
Printed and bound in Great Britain by J W Arrowsmith Ltd, Bristol

MODERN LITERARY THEORY

CONTENTS

Acknowledgements   vii
Preface   ix

PART ONE   1
Introduction   1
Section One: Saussure   6
  1 Ferdinand de Saussure, From *Course in General Linguistics*
    (1915)   8

Section Two: Russian Formalism   16
  2 Victor Shklovsky, From 'Art as Technique' (1917)   17

Section Three: Structuralism   22
  3 David Lodge, 'Analysis and Interpretation of the Realist
    Text' (1980)   24
  4 Roland Barthes, 'To Write: An Intransitive Verb?' (1966) 41

Section Four: Marxism   51
  5 Louis Althusser, From 'Ideology and the State' (1969)   53
  6 E. Balibar and P. Macherey, From 'Literature as an
    Ideological Form' (1978)   61
  7 Terry Eagleton, From *Criticism and Ideology* (1976)   69

Section Five: Reader Theory   73
  8 Wolfgang Iser, From 'The Reading Process' (1974)   76
  9 H.R. Jauss, From 'Literary History as a Challenge to
    Literary Theory' (1967)   82
10 Paul Ricoeur, 'Phenomenology and Theory of
    Literature: An Interview with Paul Ricoeur' (1981) 89
11 Harold Bloom, From *The Anxiety of Influence* (1973)   95

Section Six: Feminism   98
12 Elaine Showalter, 'Towards a Feminist Poetics' (1979)   99
13 The Marxist-Feminist Collective, From 'Women Writing:
    Jane Eyre, Shirley, Villette, Aurora Leigh' (1978) 109

PART TWO   **114**
Introduction   **114**
14 Roland Barthes, 'The Death of the Author' (1968)   118

Section One: The Subject   **123**
15 Jacques Lacan, 'The Mirror Stage as Formative of
the Function of the I as Revealed in Psychoanalytic
Experience' (1949)   126
16 Julia Kristeva, 'A Question of Subjectivity – an Interview'
(1986)   131
17 Hélène Cixous, 'Sorties' (1975)   137
18 Judith Butler, 'Variations on Sex and Gender: Beauvoir,
Wittig and Foucault' (1987)   145
19 Jonathan Dollimore, From *Radical Tragedy: Religion,
Ideology and Power in the Drama of Shakespeare and his
Contemporaries* (1984)   159

Section Two: Language and Textuality   **173**
20 Jacques Derrida, 'Structure, Sign and Play in the
Discourse of the Human Sciences' (1966)   176
21 Roland Barthes, 'From Work to Text' (1971)   191
22 Paul de Man, 'The Resistance to Theory' (1982)   198
23 Barbara Johnson, 'Gender Theory and the Yale School'
(1985)   215

Section Three: History and Discourse   **226**
24 M.M. Bakhtin, From 'Discourse in the Novel' (1934)   230
25 Michel Foucault, From 'The Order of Discourse' (1971)   239
26 Jerome J. McGann, 'The Text, the Poem, and the Problem
of Historical Method' (1985)   251
27 Stephen Greenblatt, 'Resonance and Wonder' (1990)   268

Section Four: Postmodernism and Postcolonialism   **289**
28 Fredric Jameson, 'Periodizing the 60s' (1984)   292
29 Patricia Waugh, 'Stalemates?: Feminists, Postmodernists
and Unfinished Issues in Modern Aesthetics' (1991)   322
30 bell hooks, 'Postmodern Blackness' (1991)   341
31 Edward Said, From *Culture and Imperialism* (1993)   348
32 Homi BhaBha, 'Of Mimicry and Man: The Ambivalence of
Colonial Discourse' (1983)   360

Section Five: Looking Back on the States of Theory   **368**
33 Jacques Derrida, 'Some Statements and Truisms about
Neo-Logisms, Newisms, Postisms, Parasitisms, and other
Small Seismisms' (1990)   368

Select Bibliography   **379**
Index   **384**

ACKNOWLEDGEMENTS

The editors and publishers would like to thank the following for permission to use copyright material in this book:

Louis Althusser: 'Ideology and the State' from *Lenin and Philosophy and Other Essays*, translated by Ben Brewster (New Left Books, 1977). Reprinted by permission of Verso.

Etienne Balibar and Pierre Macherey: 'Literature as an Ideological Form', in *Untying the Text* by Robert Young (Routledge & Kegan Paul, 1978). Reprinted by permission of Associated Book Publishers (UK).

M.M. Bakhtin: 'Discourse in the Novel', from Michael Holquist ed., *The Dialogic Imagination: Four Essays by M.M. Bakhtin* translated by Carl Emerson and Michael Holquist (University of Texas Press, 1981). Copyright © 1981 by the University of Texas Press. Reprinted by permission of the University of Texas Press.

Roland Barthes: 'To Write: An Intransitive Verb?' in R. Macksey and E. Donato, eds, *The Structuralist Controversy*. Reprinted by permission of the Johns Hopkins University Press. 'The Death of the Author' and 'From Work to Text', by Roland Barthes, from S. Heath ed. and trans., *Image-Music-Text*. Reprinted by permission of Editions du Seuil and Collins.

Homi BhaBha: 'Of Mimicry and Man: The Ambivalence of Colonial Discourse' by Homi BhaBha, *October*, 28 (1984), pp. 125–33. Reprinted by permission of the MIT Press.

Harold Bloom: Selection from *The Anxiety of Influence: A Theory of Poetry*, by Harold Bloom. Copyright © 1973 by Oxford University Press, Inc. Reprinted by permission.

Judith Butler: 'Variations on Sex and Gender; Beauvoir, Wittig and Foucault' in S. Benhabib and D. Cornell, eds, *Feminism as Critique* (Polity, 1987), pp. 128–42. Reprinted by permission of Blackwell Publishers.

Hélène Cixous: 'Sorties', by Hélène Cixous. Reprinted by permission of the author.

Jacques Derrida: 'Some Statements and Truisms About Neo-Logisms, Newisms, Postisms, Parasitisms and Other Small Seismisms', from David Carroll ed, *The State of Theory*. Copyright © 1989 by Columbia University Press. Reprinted with permission of the publisher. 'Structure, Sign and Play in the Discourse of the Human Sciences', from *Writing and Difference* by Jacques Derrida, translated by Alan Bass (Routledge & Kegan Paul and the University of Chicago Press, 1966). Reprinted by permission of Associated Book Publishers (UK) and the University of Chicago Press.

Jonathan Dollimore: Selection from *Radical Tragedy: Religion, Ideology and Power in the Drama of Shakespeare and His Contemporaries* by Jonathan Dollimore (Harvester, 1984). Reprinted by permission of Prentice Hall.

Terry Eagleton: 'Criticism and Ideology'. Reprinted by permission of Verso.

Stephen Greenblatt: 'Resonance and Wonder' by Stephen Greenblatt. First published in *Bulletin of the American Academy*, January 1990. Reprinted by permission of the author.

bell hooks: 'Postmodern Blackness' by bell hooks from *Yearning: Race Gender and Cultural Politics Turnaround*. Reprinted with permission of the publisher, South End Press, 116 Saint Botolph Street, Boston, MA 02115.

Wolfgang Iser: Selection from *The Implied Reader* by Wolfgang Iser. Reprinted by permission of the Johns Hopkins University Press.

Fredric Jameson: 'Periodizing the 60s' by Fredric Jameson, published in *The Sixties Without Apology*, eds S. Saynes et al. (1984). Reprinted by permission of the University of Minnesota Press.

Hans Robert Jauss: 'Literary History as a Challenge to Literary Theory', by Hans Robert Jauss reprinted from *New Literary History*, (1970), pp. 7–37. Reprinted by permission of the Johns Hopkins University Press.

Barbara Johnson: 'Gender Theory and the Yale School' in Robert Con Davis and Ronald Schleifer, eds, *Rhetoric and Form; Deconstruction of Yale* (University of Oklahoma Press). Reprinted by permission of the University of Oklahoma Press.

Jacques Lacan: 'The Mirror Stage as Formative of the Function of the I as Revealed in Psychoanalytic Experience', from *Ecrits* by Jacques Lacan, translated by Alan Sheridan (Tavistock Publications and W.W. Norton & Company). Copyright © 1977 by Tavistock Publications Ltd. Reprinted by permission of Associated Book Publishers (UK).

David Lodge: 'Analysis and Interpretation of the Realist Text', from *Working with Structuralism* (Routledge & Kegan Paul, 1980). Reprinted by permission of Associated Book Publishers (UK). 'Cat in the Rain' by Ernest Hemingway. Reprinted by permission of Jonathan Cape, Macmillan Publishing Company and the Executor of the Estate of Ernest Hemingway.

Paul de Man: 'The Resistance to Theory' by Paul De Man, *Yale French Studies*, 63 (1982). Reprinted by permission of Yale French Studies.

Jerome J. McGann: 'The Text, the Poem, and the Problem of Historical Method'. © Jerome J. McGann 1985. Reprinted from *The Beauty of Inflections*, by Jerome J. McGann (1985) by permission of the Oxford University Press.

Paul Ricoeur: 'Phenomenology and Theory of Literature: an Interview with Paul Ricoeur', *Modern Language Notes*, 96. Reprinted by permission of Modern Language Notes.

Edward Said: Selection from *Culture and Imperialism* by Edward Said (Chatto & Windus, 1993). Copyright © 1993 by Edward Said. Reprinted by permission of Random House UK Ltd and Wylie, Aitken & Stone, Inc.

Ferdinand de Saussure: Selection from Charles Bally and Albert Sechehaye, eds, *Course in General Linguistics*, translated by Wade Baskin (Peter Owen Ltd). Reprinted by permission of Peter Owen Ltd.

Victor Shklovsky: 'Art as Technique' from *Russian Formalist Criticism: Four Essays*, translated by Lee T. Lemon and Marion Reiss. Copyright © 1965 by the University of Nebraska Press. Reprinted by permission of the University of Nebraska Press.

Elaine Showalter: 'Towards a Feminist Poetics' by Elaine Showalter in *Women Writing About Women* by Mary Jacobus. Reprinted by permission of Croom Helm Ltd.

To the best of our knowledge all copyright holders of material reproduced in this book have been traced. Any rights not acknowledged here will be noted in subsequent printings if notice is given to the publisher.

PREFACE

The success of the first two editions of this anthology has fulfilled original hopes that it would form the basis for a pedagogic introduction to and clarification of the immense volume and diversity of theoretical writing that, over the past 25 years, has so radically questioned our understanding and construction of literature as an object of critical study and the methods and presuppositions of criticism itself. When we wrote the first preface (in 1988), it was evident that the rapid growth of literary theory since the mid-1960s and the mass of work devoted to the theoretical discussion of literature had transformed literary study by the 1980s. Critics and philosophers have always theorized about literature and literary criticism, but the recent erosion of boundaries between philosophy, political theory, psychoanalysis, social theory and literary criticism would seem to represent something of a 'paradigm shift' in literary studies. The very foundations of the Anglo-American literary tradition have been challenged. Since then, all foundations of Western thought and representation have increasingly been held up to critical gaze: the concept of criticism born with modern scepticism was always poised to turn introspective. Sceptical doubt was bound eventually to turn on the instruments of its own articulation and analysis, so that objects of knowledge may come to seem not so much entities on which language reflects than artefacts actually constructed through and within language. In literary criticism the notion of the text as an 'object' to be analysed methodically by the empiricist critic has given way to a situation where distinctions between truth and rhetoric, literature and philosophy, history and text, have become increasingly obscure. As Jacques Derrida has written in the essay which concludes this anthology, English literature has become the site of a new multidisciplinarity which has challenged the methods and assumptions not only of literary critics, but of philosophers and scientists too.

The crisis in epistemology has brought with it a crisis in value: for there can hardly be agreement about the value of literary works when there cannot be agreement about the constitution of literature itself. The postmodern critique of 'grand narratives' has spread its nets over the controversial issue of the canon and the idea that aesthetic value is essential and universal and self-evidentially reflected in a broadly stable tradition of great works of art. Recent developments in feminist criticism, in Cultural Materialism, New Historicism and Postcolonialism, have further 'exploded' English and challenged earlier assumptions about aesthetic value and meaning. There has been a visible retreat from totalities: in the postmodern resistance to universalization; in New Historical method – an eclectic mix of theories which avoids any single paradigm; in the postcolonialist resistance to the universalizing thrust of colonialist discourses. There is a new emphasis on reading, on the dialectics of interpretation, as opposed to the search for a systematic model which might 'explain' the text. Many of the newest schools of criticism, such as the New Historicism, are more practices of reading than 'theories of literature', but they draw extensively, if loosely, on shifting combinations of many of the theoretical models represented throughout this anthology.

In compiling this third edition the aim has been to retain those essays and documents which now seem to have a canonical place in the history of modern literary theory and to include more recent material which reflects some of the critical issues emerging from the retreat from theoretical holism. Earlier sections have been expanded, revised and updated and new essays selected which represent the current debate in Postmodernism, Postcolonialism, New Historicism and Cultural Materialism. Derrida's retrospective essay on the state of theory has been included to indicate how any reflection upon Postmodernism or New Historicism inevitably raises questions about the compatibility or otherwise of different theoretical models and about their epistemological presuppositions. It seems likely that these are issues which will continue to be central to literary theoretical debates in the future, a tendency reflected in the growing interest of literary theorists in philosophies of science.

The task of selection for this anthology has not been an easy one, for the field which has to be mapped continuously changes its boundaries as new relations and combinations move in and out of the foreground. A book which attempted to be totally inclusive would be well beyond the means of the readers we hope to reach. Our aims, therefore, have been modest rather than ambitious: to introduce a broad and diverse selection of works which might be seen as conceptual 'keys' to the theoretical revolution; to draw out some of the implications of the theoretical positions represented and, in particular, to offer an anthology through which the reader can get a foothold on the map of contemporary theory and become acquainted with some of the principal theories and theorists involved.

The book is organized into two parts which are subdivided into sections, each one representing a major area in contemporary literary theory. In most sections we have tried to include an extract which gives an account of the theory and, where appropriate, a contribution which uses that theoretical paradigm as a critical approach to literary texts. Editorial commentary has been kept to a minimum in order to devote as much space as possible to the source material, but commentary is nevertheless required for the field only partially organizes itself, and then more on the basis of history than of nature. If contemporary theory teaches us anything it is that the orders of the world are not 'natural' but constructed. Our commentary is thus offered more as an attempt to rationalize the organization of the material rather than to provide an exhaustive critical explanation of it. Indeed the anthology might usefully be seen as a supplement to the various critical accounts of literary theory that have appeared in the last few years (Eagleton's *Literary Theory: An Introduction* (1983), Jefferson and Robey's *Modern Literary Theory: A Comparative Introduction* (1982) and Selden's *A Reader's Guide to Contemporary Literary Theory* (1985)). Again, to save space, the bibliography is selective and indicative only, though it should prove an adequate starting point for further research.

We hope that the experience of reading the book will stimulate further interest and help to clarify the major theoretical positions and their relations to each other. But beyond that (and in the spirit of contemporary theory) we hope that it will encourage readers to contest and challenge the very structures of knowledge and understanding we have used in compiling this book.

PART ONE
INTRODUCTION

Though literary theory is not a recent phenomenon it often appears that way. Its rapid growth since the mid-1960s, and the mass of work devoted to theoretical discourse about and around literature has produced what can only be described as a radical transformation. If literary theory seems new it is not because theorizing about literature is new, but because of the quantitative and qualitative difference of contemporary work. What characterizes contemporary theory is, on the one hand, its heterogeneity and on the other, its unprecedented attack on the grounding assumptions of the Anglo-American critical tradition.

Literary studies has always been a pluralistic discipline. The various practices that constituted the Anglo-American tradition, such as literary history, literary biography, moral-aesthetic criticism and even the New Criticism had, until recently, managed to coexist in a state of fairly 'stable disequilibrium' based on a broad consensus about the author, the nature of the literary work, and the purpose of criticism. Critics might have argued about the inclusion of this or that piece of writing in the canon of literature, but the notion that something called 'literature' existed was never in doubt nor was the sense that the author was the originator of the work, or that the act of criticism was subordinate to the literature it studied. All of this and more has come in for rigorous interrogation and re-evaluation from a theoretical discourse no longer consigned to the margins.

Contemporary critical theory has asserted itself in the everyday life of literary studies, refusing to accept its marginalization as a peripheral concern more akin to philosophy. It sees itself as existing at the heart of the critical enterprise, insisting that there is no critical act that can transcend theory. As numerous theorists have pointed out, the traditional forms of criticism through which literature is and has been studied are not 'theory free' responses to great literary works, nor are they pure scholastic endeavours. All forms of criticism are founded upon a theory, or an admix of theories, whether they consciously acknowledge that or not. Theoretical writings have recognized that what are often taken to be 'natural' and 'commonsensical' ways of studying literature actually rest upon a set of theoretical injunctions which have been naturalized to the point at which they no longer have to justify their own practices.

The way that theory has been inflected into the everyday workings of the literary discipline has often proved a source of passionate debate. Responses have taken many different forms, from irate dismissal to enthusiastic development. If theory seems to some critics to be deeply implicated in the everyday pursuits and routines of the discipline, to others it seems not to be addressing the object of study directly and to be operating in the realms of the abstract and the abstruse, divorced from that close reading and intimate study of literary works that has so characterized the discipline. Much of the theory *is* abstract, and does not offer a method for approaching literary texts directly, however, it has important implications for the way we study literature, implications that cannot be dismissed simply because the theory is of no immediate pragmatic value. The discipline of literary criticism is largely founded on the basis of an immediate relation with its objects of study, but this is historically determined, not inevitable or natural. Part of the attack on the critical orthodoxy has been concerned with the undermining of that sense of a 'natural' way to study literature. And if literary theory sometimes appears to caricature the tradition it attacks, and to make it seem more singular than it actually is, that is because its attack has often been targeted not at the manifest plurality of critical practices that constitute the tradition but at its roots, at that set of founding assumptions which traditional criticism often obdurately refuses to acknowledge as anything other than the 'natural' and 'sensible' way of criticism.

The critical orthodoxy is undoubtedly a plurality of practices; from literary history and literary biography, to myth criticism and psycho-analytic/criticism, to the New Criticism and moral-aesthetic criticism. But this plurality is grounded in a broad consensus focused on an epistemological and ontological certainty regarding the nature of the relation between the author, the text and the reader, and upon the definition of the text itself. Each form of criticism leans in a different direction: psychoanalytic/biographical emphasizes the author; historical/sociological emphasizes the context; New Criticism emphasizes the text-in-itself; moral-aesthetic criticism the relation between the text and the reality it portrays. However, they all accept a broadly mimetic view of literature where literature in some way or other, reflects and delivers up 'truths' about life and the human condition (even if, as in the case of New Criticism, the mimetic view is not foregrounded). The task of literature is to render life, experience and emotion in a potent way; the job of criticism is to reveal the true value and meaning of the rendition – a rendition at once contained within the literary work and yet, paradoxically, needing the critical act to reveal it.

The mimetic perspective depends upon a view of language as a transparent medium, a medium through which reality can be transcribed and re-presented in aesthetic form, and reality, self-contained and coherent, transcends its formulation in words. This view of language is, in turn, related to a general conception of the world which is 'man-centred', and to an epistemology that Catherine Belsey has characterized as 'empiricist-idealist'.

> common sense urges that 'man' is the origin and source of meaning, of action and of history (*humanism*). Our concepts and our knowledge are held to be the product of experience (*empiricism*), and this experience is preceded and interpreted by the mind, reason or thought, the property of a transcendent human nature whose essence is the attribute of each individual (*idealism*).[1]

The grounding assumptions of humanism presuppose that experience is prior to its expression in language and conceive of language as a mere tool used to express the way that experience is felt and interpreted by the unique individual. The existence of the unique individual is the cornerstor? of the humanist ideology and provides the grid on which traditional ?erary criticism enacts its particular studies of the literary text. Inscribed in this ideology is the notion that literature is the collective product of especially gifted individuals who are able to capture the elusive universal and timeless truths of the human condition through the sensuous and sensitive use of the tool of language. Contemporary literary theory addresses and interrogates this set of founding assumptions in various ways and from a number of different perspectives. Through its interrogation the consensus around literary studies, and the ideological grid which underwrites it, has fragmented.

One of the principal focuses for the attack on Anglo-American critical practices has centred on language and derives largely from the linguistic theory of Ferdinand de Saussure. Language, according to Saussure, is not a mere tool devised for the re-presentation of a pre-existent reality. It is rather, a constitutive part of reality, deeply implicated in the way the world is constructed as meaningful. According to this view language cannot be regarded as transparent, as it has to be if the mimetic tradition is to sustain its validity. Saussure's theory offers the possibility of a different perspective and gives rise to a wholly different epistemology. This perspective has been referred to as 'post-Saussurean'; it generally includes Structuralist and/or Post-Structuralist theories.

However, initial challenges to the orthodoxy did not come only from Structuralism. Other perspectives had an important influence – Feminism brought a cultural politics to literary studies, as did the particular mode of Marxism dominant in the 1960s/70s (though this mode of Marxism is closely related to Structuralism). Reader theory also disturbed the orthodoxy by shifting the object of study from the author/text to the text/reader nexus (again some of this work was closely allied to Structuralist thought). In general the critical perspectives that emerged strongly in the post-1960s period exhibited a much more self-conscious and reflexive tendency, and a more rigorous and coherent attitude to the study and analysis of literature. However, the more radical versions of theory, usually Post-Structuralist, took the issue further. They posed not just a new set of approaches and/or a revised understanding of literature and the world, but also a profoundly different mode of existence for the text, for discourse, for the individual and for the discipline of literary studies and literary criticism itself.

Part One of this book deals with the initial break with the orthodoxies of literary studies. The material for this part has been selected to exemplify its less radical questioning and undermining of the literary studies enterprise. But while it is less radical it does prepare the ground for the work represented in Part Two which generally adopts a more interrogative and disrupting perspective. It is in this sense that the book has been divided into two parts – but this division is not meant to imply an historical progression from, for instance, the inadequacies of Structuralism to a more satisfactory Post-Structuralism. This is not a matter of simple causal development or progression through the gradual accretion of knowledge. It is, rather, a matter of different trajectories and different directions that have been taken or refused.

This third edition of the Reader includes new material on Reader Theory, on 'The Subject' and on 'Language and Textuality', and two new sections entitled 'History and Discourse' and 'Postmodernism and Postcolonialism'. It is interesting that in the most recent critical developments, theory as coherent 'grand narrative' begins to break down. In its place, a hybrid and shifting mix of models and insights from earlier, often more 'totalizing' theoretical systems are brought together in a new practice of textual criticism or analysis of cultural meaning. In New Historicism and Postmodernism, there is a shift away from the pleasures of pure and coherent theory to an engagement with contingency, plurality, the fragment, and a loss of clear distinction between text and context, depth and surface. Postcolonialism draws on the Post-Structuralist critique of the centred Subject, on the Gramscian understanding of the concept of hegemony, on Lacanian psychoanalysis, narrative theory, Foucauldian analyses of power and knowledge, feminist critiques of difference and Postmodernist challenges to the discourses of Enlightenment. In all of these critical movements, there is a new emphasis on situatedness, on the provisional and perspectival nature of knowledge, on Constructivism: the transcendental theoretical 'view from nowhere' has largely disappeared as the object of theoretical enquiry is seen increasingly to be a discursive construction arising out of specific cultural and institutional practices.

The field of literary studies is currently a heterogeneous configuration of competing practices and epistemologies ranging from the traditional forms of literary criticism such as New Criticism and moral-aesthetic criticism, to the more recent Structuralism, Reader Theory, Feminism, and various Post-

Structuralisms. Within this configuration individuals do not always align themselves with one or other of the theoretical positions, rather, they often debate, support, argue against, believe in, deny and utilize a number of them; readers and critics, in other words, occupy multiple, and sometimes contradictory positions in relation to the theories. It is up to the reader of this book to evaluate the various positions represented here and though we have our own preferences our job is not to foist these on others. We would urge, though, a critical assessment of the various theories on the basis of the arguments they offer and an openness to the more radical positions offered in Part Two.

Note

1 C. Belsey, *Critical Practice* (London, Methuen, 1980), p. 7.

SECTION ONE
SAUSSURE

The work of the Swiss linguist Ferdinand de Saussure has played a crucial and formative role in the recent transformation in literary theory. Saussure's influence rests on a single book which records his seminal theory of language, the *Course in General Linguistics*. This was compiled by students and colleagues, after his death in 1913, from notes taken at lectures he delivered between 1907 and 1911 when he taught at the University of Geneva.

Though not as well known as Marx or Freud, Saussure has been ranked with them in terms of the influence he has had on systems of thought developed in the twentieth century. Like Freud and Marx, Saussure considered the manifest appearance of phenomena to be underpinned and made possible by underlying systems and structures; for Marx, it was the system of economic and social relations; for Freud, the unconscious; for Saussure, the system of language. The most radical implications of their work profoundly disrupt the dominant, humanist conception of the world for they undermine the notion that 'man' is the centre, source and origin of meaning. Saussure's influence on literary theory came to the fore in Structuralism and Post-Structuralism, though his work had had significant influence prior to that, notably on the structural linguistics of the Prague Circle and on the structural anthropology of Lévi-Strauss.

It is worth reviewing the main tenets of Saussurean theory since they form the necessary grounding for much of the theory represented in this book. Saussure argued that the object of study for linguistics is the underlying system of conventions (words and grammar) by virtue of which a sign (word) can 'mean'. Language is a system of signs, the sign being the basic unit of meaning. The sign comprises a signifier and signified, the signifier is the 'word image' (visual or acoustic) and the signified the 'mental concept'. Thus the signifier *tree* has the signified *mental concept of a tree*. It is important to note that Saussure is not referring here to the distinction between a name and a thing but to a distinction between the *word image* and the *concept*. The signifier and signified, however, are only separable on the analytic level, they are not separable at the level of thought – the word image cannot be divorced from the mental concept and vice versa.

The first principle of Saussure's theory is that the sign is arbitrary. It is useful to consider this at two levels: firstly at the level of the signifier, secondly at the level of the signified. At the level of the signifier, the sign is arbitrary because there is no *necessary* connection between the signifier *tree* and the signified *concept of tree*; any configuration of sounds or written shapes could be used to signify *tree* – for instance, *arbre, baum, arbor* or even *fnurd*.[1] The relation between the signifier and the signified is a matter of convention; in the English language we conventionally associate the word 'tree' with the concept 'tree'. The arbitrary nature of the sign at this level is fairly easily grasped, but it is the arbitrary nature of the sign at the level of the signified that is more difficult to see and that presents us with the more radical implications of Saussure's theory.

Not only do different languages use different signifiers, they also 'cut up' the phenomenal world differently, articulating it through language-specific concepts – that is, they use different signifieds. The important point to grasp here is that language is not a simple naming process, language does not operate by naming things and concepts that have an independently meaningful existence. Saussure points out that 'if words stood for pre-existing entities they would all have exact equivalents in meaning from one language to the next, but this is not true'.[2] One of the most commonly referred-to illustrations of this is the colour spectrum. The colours of the spectrum actually form a continuum; so, for instance, that part of the spectrum which runs from blue through to red does not consist of a series of different colours – blue, green, yellow, orange, red – existing independently of each other. The spectrum is, rather, a continuum which our language divides up in a particular way.

Just as there is nothing 'natural' about the way we divide up the colour continuum (indeed, other languages divide it up differently), so there is nothing natural or inevitable about the way we divide up and articulate our world in other ways. Each language cuts up the world differently, constructing different meaningful categories and concepts. It is sometimes difficult to see that our everyday concepts are arbitrary and that language does not simply name pre-existing things. We tend to be so accustomed to the world our language system has produced that it comes to seem natural – the correct and inevitable way to view the world. Yet the logic of Saussure's theory suggests that our world is constructed for us by our language and that 'things' do not have fixed essences or cores of meaning which pre-exist linguistic representation.

Returning to the colour spectrum, we can see that orange is not an independently existing colour, not a point on the spectrum but a range on the continuum: we can also see how the colour orange depends, for its existence, on the other colours around it. We can define 'orange' only by what it is not. There is no essence to the colour, only a differentiation. We know that it is orange because it is not yellow and not red. Orange depends for its meaning on what it is not, i.e. orange is produced by the system of difference we employ in dividing up the spectrum.

For Saussure the whole of our language works in this way. It is a system of difference where any one term has meaning only by virtue of its differential place within that system. If we consider the sign 'food', it could not mean anything without the concept of *not* food. In order to 'cut up' the world, even at this crude level, we need a system of difference, i.e. a basic binary system – food/not food. Language is a far more complex version of this simple binary system. This led Saussure to emphasize the *system* of language, for without the system the individual elements (the signs) could not be made to mean.

An important distinction follows from this: that between *langue* and *parole*. Langue is the system of language, the system of forms (the rules, codes, conventions), and parole refers to the actual speech acts made possible by the langue. Utterances (paroles) are many and varied and no linguist could hope to grasp them all. What linguists could do was to study what made them all possible – the latent, underlying system or set of conventions. Saussure then adds a further distinction, that between synchronic and diachronic aspects. The synchronic is the structural aspect of language, the system at a particular moment; the diachronic relates to the history of the language – the changes in its forms and conventions over time. Because signs do not have any essential core of meaning they are open to change, however, in order to 'mean' the sign must exist within a system that is complete at any one moment. This led Saussure to assert that the proper object of study for linguistics was langue (the system which made any one act of speech possible), in its synchronic aspect.

The extract we have chosen to represent the work of Saussure deals, for the most part, with the arbitrary nature of the signified and with that aspect of a sign's meaning which is given by virtue of its place in the system.

Notes

1 T. Hawkes, *Structuralism and Semiotics* (London, Methuen, 1977).
2 F. de Saussure, *Course in General Linguistics* tr. W. Baskin (London, Fontana/Collins), p. 116.

1   Ferdinand de Saussure,

From *Course in General Linguistics* (1915), pp. 111–19, 120–1

1 Language as Organized Thought Coupled with Sound

To prove that language is only a system of pure values, it is enough to consider the two elements involved in its functioning: ideas and sounds.

Psychologically our thought – apart from its expression in words – is only a shapeless and indistinct mass. Philosophers and linguists have always agreed in recognizing that without the help of signs we would be unable to make a clear-cut, consistent distinction between two ideas. Without language, thought is a vague, unchartered nebula. There are no pre-existing ideas and nothing is distinct before the appearance of language.

Against the floating realm of thought, would sounds by themselves yield predelimited entities? No more so than ideas. Phonic substance is neither more fixed nor more rigid than thought; it is not a mold into which thought must of necessity fit but a plastic substance divided in turn into distinct parts to furnish the signifiers needed by thought. The linguistic fact can therefore be pictured in its totality – i.e. language – as a series of contiguous subdivisions marked off on both the indefinite plane of jumbled ideas (*A*) and the equally vague plane of sounds (*B*). The following diagram gives a rough idea of it:

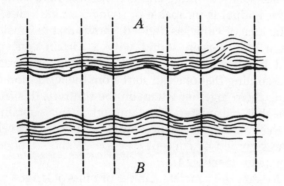

The characteristic role of language with respect to thought is not to create a material phonic means for expressing ideas but to serve as a link between thought and sound, under conditions that of necessity bring about the reciprocal delimitations of units. Thought, chaotic by nature, has to become ordered in the process of its decomposition. Neither are thoughts given material form nor are sounds transformed into mental entities; the somewhat mysterious fact is rather that 'thought sound' implies division and that language works out its units while taking shape between two shapeless masses. Visualize the air in contact with a sheet of water; if the atmospheric pressure changes, the surface of the water will be broken up into a series of divisions, waves; the waves resemble the union or coupling of thought with phonic substance.

Language might be called the domain of articulations, using the word as it was defined earlier. Each linguistic term is a member, an *articulus* in which an idea is fixed in a sound and a sound becomes the sign of an idea.

Language can also be compared with a sheet of paper: thought is the front and the sound the back; one cannot cut the front without cutting the back at the same time; likewise in language, one can neither divide sound from thought nor thought from sound; the division could be accomplished only abstractedly, and the result would be either pure psychology or pure phonology.

Linguistics then works in the borderland where the elements of sound and thought combine; *their combination produces a form, not a substance.*

These views give a better understanding of what was said before about the arbitrariness of signs. Not only are the two domains that are linked by the linguistic fact shapeless and confused, but the choice of a given slice of sound to name a given idea is completely arbitrary. If this were not true, the notion of value would be compromised, for it would include an externally imposed element. But actually values remain entirely relative, and that is why the bond between the sound and the idea is radically arbitrary.

The arbitrary nature of the sign explains in turn why the social fact alone can create a linguistic system. The community is necessary if values that owe their existence solely to usage and general acceptance are to be set up; by himself the individual is incapable of fixing a single value.

In addition, the idea of value, as defined, shows that to consider a term as simply the union of a certain sound with a certain concept is grossly misleading. To define it in this way would isolate the term from its system; it would mean assuming that one can start from the terms and construct the system by adding them together when, on the contrary, it is from the interdependent whole that one must start and through analysis obtain its elements.

To develop this thesis, we shall study value successively from the viewpoint of the signified or concept (Section 2), the signifier (Section 3), and the complete sign (Section 4).

Being unable to seize the concrete entities or units of language directly, we shall work with words. While the word does not conform exactly to the definition of the linguistic unit, it at least bears a rough resemblance to the unit and has the advantage of being concrete; consequently, we shall use words as specimens equivalent to real terms in a synchronic system, and the principles that we evolve with respect to words will be valid for entities in general.

2 Linguistic Value from a Conceptual Viewpoint

When we speak of the value of a word, we generally think first of its property of standing for an idea, and this is in fact one side of linguistic value. But if this is true, how does *value* differ from *signification*? Might the two words by synonyms? I think not, although it is easy to confuse them, since the confusion results not so much from their similarity as from the subtlety of the distinction that they mark.

From a conceptual viewpoint, value is doubtless one element in signification, and it is difficult to see how signification can be dependent upon value and still be distinct from it. But we must clear up the issue or risk reducing language to a simple naming-process.

Let us first take signification as it is generally understood. As the arrows in the drawing show, it is only the counterpart of the sound-image. Everything that occurs concerns only the sound-image and the concept when we look upon the word as independent and self-contained.

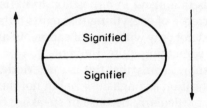

But here is the paradox: on the one hand the concept seems to be the counterpart of the sound-image, and on the other hand the sign itself is in turn the counterpart of the other signs of language.

Language is a system of interdependent terms in which the value of each term results solely from the simultaneous presence of the others, as in the diagram:

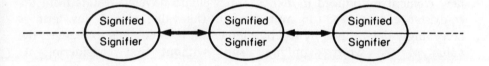

How, then, can value be confused with signification, i.e. the counterpart of the sound-image? It seems impossible to liken the relations represented here by horizontal arrows to those represented above by vertical arrows. Putting it another way – and again taking up the example of the sheet of paper that is cut in two (see p. 9) – it is clear that the observable relation between the different pieces A, B, C, D, etc. is distinct from the relation between the front and back of the same piece as in A/A', B/B', etc.

To resolve the issue, let us observe from the outset that even outside language all values are apparently governed by the same paradoxical principle. They are always composed:

1. of a *dissimilar* thing that can be *exchanged* for the thing of which the value is to be determined; and
2. of *similar* things that can be *compared* with the thing of which the value is to be determined.

Both factors are necessary for the existence of a value. To determine what a five-franc piece is worth one must therefore know: (1) that it can be exchanged for a fixed quantity of a different thing, e.g. bread; and (2) that it can be compared with a similar value of the same system, e.g. a one-franc piece, or with coins of another system (a dollar, etc.). In the same way a word can be exchanged for something dissimilar, an idea; besides, it can be compared with something of the same nature, another word. Its value is therefore not fixed so long as one simply states that it can be 'exchanged' for a given concept, i.e. that it has this or that signification: one must also compare it with similar values, with other words that stand in opposition to it. Its content is really fixed only by the concurrence of everything that exists outside it. Being part of a system, it is endowed not only with a signification but also and especially with a value and this is something quite different.

A few examples will show clearly that this is true. Modern French *mouton* can have the same signification as English *sheep* but not the same value, and this for several reasons, particularly because in speaking of a piece of meat ready to be served on the table, English uses *mutton* and not *sheep*. The difference in value between *sheep* and *mouton* is due to the fact that *sheep* has beside it a second term while the French word does not.

Within the same language, all words used to express related ideas limit each other reciprocally; synonyms like French *redouter* 'dread', *craindre* 'fear', and *avoir peur* 'be afraid' have value only through their opposition: if *redouter* did not exist, all its content would go to its competitors. Conversely, some words are enriched through contact with others: e.g. the new element introduced in *décrépit* (un vieillard *décrépit*) results from the co-existence of *décrépi* (un mur *décrépi*). The value of just any term is accordingly determined by its environment; it is impossible to fix even the value of the word signifying 'sun' without first considering its surroundings: in some languages it is not possible to say 'sit in the *sun*'.

Everything said about words applies to any term of language, e.g. to grammatical entities. The value of a French plural does not coincide with that of a Sanskrit plural even though their signification is usually identical; Sanskrit has three numbers instead of two (*my eyes, my ears, my arms, my legs*, etc. are dual);[1] it would be wrong to attribute the same value to the plural in Sanskrit and in French; its value clearly depends on what is outside and around it.

If words stood for pre-existing concepts, they would all have exact equivalents in meaning from one language to the next; but this is not true. French uses *louer* (*une maison*) 'let (a house)' indifferently to mean both 'pay for' and 'receive payment for', whereas German uses two words, *mieten* and *vermieten*; there is obviously no exact correspondence of values. The German verbs *Schätzen* and *urteilen* share a number of significations, but that correspondence does not hold at several points.

Inflection offers some particularly striking examples. Distinctions of time, which are so familiar to us, are unknown in certain languages. Hebrew does not recognize even the fundamental distinctions between the past, present, and future. Proto-Germanic has no special form for the future; to say that the future is expressed by the present is wrong, for the value of the present is not the same in Germanic as in languages that have a future along with the present. The Slavic languages regularly single out two aspects of the verb: the perfective represents action as a point, complete in its totality; the imperfective represents it as taking place, and on the line of time. The categories are difficult for a Frenchman to understand, for they are unknown in French; if they were predetermined, this would not be true. Instead of pre-existing ideas then, we find in all the foregoing examples *values* emanating from the system. When they are said to correspond to concepts, it is understood that the concepts are purely differential and defined not by their positive content but negatively by their relations with the other terms of the system. Their most precise characteristic is in being what the others are not.

Now the real interpretation of the diagram of the signal becomes apparent. Thus

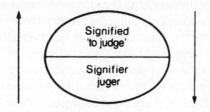

means that in French the concept 'to judge' is linked to the sound-image *juger*; in short, it symbolizes signification. But it is quite clear that initially the concept is nothing, that it is only a value determined by its relations with other similar values, and that without them the signification would not exist. If I state simply that a word signifies something when I have in mind the associating of a sound-image with a concept, I am making a statement that may suggest what acually happens, but by no means am I expressing the linguistic fact in its essence and fullness.

3 Linguistic Value from a Material Viewpoint

The conceptual side of value is made up solely of relations and differences with respect to the other terms of language, and the same can be said of its material side. The important thing in the word is not the sound alone but the phonic differences that make it possible to distinguish this word from all others, for differences carry signification.

This may seem surprising, but how indeed could the reverse be possible? Since one vocal image is no better suited that the next for what it is commissioned to express, it is evident, even *a priori*, that a segment of language can never in the final analysis be based on anything except its noncoincidence with the rest. *Arbitrary* and *differential* are two correlative qualities.

The alteration of linguistic signs clearly illustrates this. It is precisely because the terms *a* and *b* as such are radically incapable of reaching the level of consciousness – one is always conscious of only the *a/b* difference

– that each term is free to change according to laws that are unrelated to its signifying function. No positive sign characterizes the genitive plural in Czech *žen*; still the two forms *žena: žen* function as well as the earlier forms *žena: ženb; žen* has value only because it is different.

Here is another example that shows even more clearly the systematic role of phonic differences: in Greek, *éphēn* is an imperfect and *éstēn* an aorist although both words are formed in the same way; the first belongs to the system of the present indicative of *phēmí* 'I say', whereas there is no present *stēmi; n*ow it is precisely the relation *phēmí: éphēn* that corresponds to the relation between the present and the imperfect (cf. *déiknūmi: edéikūn*, etc.). Signs function, then, not through their intrinsic value but through their relative position.

In addition, it is impossible for sound alone, a material element, to belong to language. It is only a secondary thing, substance to be put to use. All our conventional values have the characteristic of not being confused with the tangible element which supports them. For instance, it is not the metal in a piece of money that fixes its value. A coin nominally worth five francs may contain less than half its worth of silver. Its value will vary according to the amount stamped upon it and according to its use inside or outside a political boundary. This is even more true of the linguistic signifier, which is not phonic but incorporeal – constituted not by its material substance but by the differences that separate its sound-image from all others.

The foregoing principle is so basic that it applies to all the material elements of language, including phonemes. Every language forms its words on the basis of a system of sonorous elements, each element being a clearly delimited unit and one of a fixed number of units. Phonemes are characterized not, as one might think, by their own positive quality but simply by the fact that they are distinct. Phonemes are above all else opposing, relative, and negative entities.

Proof of this is the latitude that speakers have between points of convergence in the pronunciation of distinct sounds. In French, for instance, general use of a dorsal *r* does not prevent many speakers from using a tongue-tip trill; language is not in the least disturbed by it; language requires only that the sound be different and not, as one might imagine, that it have a invariable quality. I can even pronounce the French *r* like German *ch* in *Bach, doch*, etc., but in German I could not use *r* instead of *ch*, for German gives recognition to both elements and must keep them apart.

. . . .

4 The Sign Considered in its Totality

Everything that has been said up to this point boils down to this: in language there are only differences. Even more important: a difference generally implies positive terms between which the difference is set up; but in language there are only differences *without positive terms*. Whether we take the signified or the signifier, language has neither ideas nor sounds that existed before the linguistic system, but only conceptual and phonic differences that have issued from the system. The idea or phonic substance that a sign contains is of less importance than the other signs that surround it. Proof of this is that the value of a term may be modified without either its meaning or its sound being affected, solely because a neighboring term has been modified (see p. 11).

But the statement that everything in language is negative is true only if the signified and the signifier are considered separately; when we consider the sign in its totality, we have something that is positive in its own class. A linguistic system is a series of differences of sound combined with a series of differences of ideas; but the pairing of a certain number of acoustical signs with as many cuts made from the mass of thought engenders a system of values; and this system serves as the effective link between the phonic and psychological elements within each sign. Although both the signified and the signifier are purely differential and negative when considered separately, their combination is a positive fact; it is even the sole type of facts that language has, for maintaining the parallelism between the two classes of differences is the distinctive function of the linguistic institution.

Note

1 The use of the comparative form for two and the superlative for more than two in English (e.g. *may the* better *boxer win: the* best *boxer in the world*) is probably a remnant of the old distinction between the dual and the plural number. [Tr.]

SECTION TWO
RUSSIAN FORMALISM

Terry Eagleton has suggested that 'if one wanted to put a date on the beginnings of the transformation which has overtaken literary theory in this century, one could do worse that settle on 1917, the year in which the young Russian Formalist Viktor Shklovsky published his pioneering essay "Art as Device" '.[1] Though formalist work predates the recent theoretical revolution by some 40 years, its stress on the systematic study of literature links it with the work which initially broke with the traditional critical orthodoxy in the 1960s. Indeed, Formalist work only became more widely available and influential in the post-60s period.

Russian Formalism is the name now given to a mode of criticism that emerged from two groups. The Moscow Linguistic Circle (1915) and the *Opojaz* group (standing for The Society for the Study of Poetic Language) (1916). The main figures in the movement were Roman Jakobson, Viktor Shklovsky, Boris Eichenbaum, Boris Tomashevsky and Yuri Tynyanov. Jakobson was also involved in the later Prague Linguistic Circle (1926–39), which developed some of the Formalist's concerns. Influenced by Futurism and Futurist poetry, and reacting against Symbolism's mystification of poetry (though not against its emphasis on form), they sought to place the study of literature on a scientific basis; their investigation concentrated on the language and the formal devices of literary works.

Although Russian Formalism is often likened to the American New Criticism of the 1950s because of a similar emphasis on close critical attention to the text, the Russian Formalists were, in fact, more interested in method and a scientific approach. Russian Formalism emphasized a differential definition of literature, as opposed to the New Criticism's isolation and objectification of the single text; they also rejected the mimetic/expressive function of literature more strongly. The New Criticism, while challenging some of the views of the traditional orthodoxy, remained within the humanist problematic.[2] Russian Formalism moves away from the view of the text as reflecting an essential unity which is ultimately one of moral or humanistic significance. The central focus of the movement was not literature *per se*, but *literariness*, that which makes a given work a 'literary' work. In this sense they sought to uncover the system of the literary discourse, the system that made literature possible. Their interests in texts centred on the functioning of literary devices rather than on content; literariness was to do with a special use of language.

Shklovsky's essay 'Art as Technique' was one of the first important contributions to the Russian Formalist movement. In it he develops the key notion of 'defamiliarization' (*ostranenie* – making strange). What literary language does is to 'make strange' or defamiliarize habituated perception and ordinary language. The key to defamiliarization is the literary device, for the 'device' impedes perception, draws attention to the artifice of the text and dehabituates automatized perception. (Formalists tend to be more interested in texts which 'lay bare the device' and which eschew realistic motivation, hence their privileging of difficult or modernist works.)

One of the most important implications of this is that logically it must lead to a view of literature as a *relational* system rather than an absolute one, and a system that is bound to change through history. Literary devices cannot remain strange for all time, they too become automatized, so that new literature has to produce new defamiliarizational devices to avoid habituated perception. Such a view must see the literary tradition not as a seamless continuity, but as discontinuity, where breaks and reformations in form and formal devices continually renew the system.

The work of the Russian Formalists has proved fertile ground for later transformations in critical practice. In defining the object of inquiry as that of 'literariness' they gave a systematic inflection to the study of literature, one that went beyond intrinsic study of the individual text.

Notes

1 T. Eagleton, *Literary Theory: An Introduction* (Oxford, Basil Blackwell, 1983).
2 C. Belsey, *Critical Practice* (London, Methuen, 1980).

---

2 Victor Shklovsky,

From 'Art as Technique', in L. T. Lemon and M. J. Reis, tr. and ed. *Russian Formalist Criticism: Four Essays* (1917), pp. 11–15, 18

If we start to examine the general laws of perception, we see that as perception becomes habitual, it becomes automatic. Thus, for example, all of our habits retreat into the area of the unconsciously automatic; if one remembers the sensations of holding a pen or of speaking in a foreign language for the first time and compares that with his feeling at performing the action for the ten thousandth time, he will agree with us. Such habituation explains the principles by which, in ordinary speech, we leave phrases unfinished and words half expressed. In this process, ideally realized in algebra, things are replaced by symbols. Complete words are not expressed in rapid speech; their initial sounds are barely perceived. Alexander Pogodin offers the example of a boy considering the sentence 'The Swiss Mountains are beautiful' in the form of a series of letters: *T, S, m, a, b.*[1]

This characteristic of thought not only suggests the method of algebra, but even prompts the choice of symbols (letters, especially initial letters). By this 'algebraic' method of thought we apprehend objects only as shapes with imprecise extensions; we do not see them in their entirety but rather recognize them by their main characteristics. We see the object as though it were enveloped in a sack. We know what it is by its configuration, but we see only its silhouette. The object, perceived thus in the manner of prose perception, fades and does not leave even a first impression; ultimately even the essence of what it was is forgotten. Such perception explains why we fail to hear the prose word in its entirety (see Leo Jakobinsky's article[2]) and, hence, why (along with other slips of the tongue) we fail to pronounce it. The process of 'algebrization', the overautomatization of an object, permits the greatest economy of perceptive effort. Either objects are assigned only one proper feature – a number, for example – or else they function as though by formula and do not even appear in cognition:

> I was cleaning a room and, meandering about, approached the divan and couldn't remember whether or not I had dusted it. Since these movements are habitual and unconscious, I could not remember and felt that it was impossible to remember – so that if I had dusted it and forgot – that is, had acted unconsciously, then it was the same as if I had not. If some conscious person had been watching, then the fact could be established. If, however, no one was looking, or looking on unconsciously, if the whole complex lives of many people go on unconsciously, then such lives are as if they had never been.[3]

And so life is reckoned as nothing. Habitualization devours works, clothes, furniture, one's wife, and the fear of war. 'If the whole complex lives of many people go on unconsciously, then such lives are as if they had never been.' And art exists that one may recover the sensation of life; it exists to make one feel things, to make the stone *stony*. The purpose of art is to impart the sensation of things as they are perceived and not as they are known. The technique of art is to make objects *'unfamiliar'*, to make forms difficult, to increase the difficulty and length of perception because the process of perception is an aesthetic end in itself and must be prolonged. *Art is a way of experiencing the artfullness of an object; the object is not important.*

The range of poetic (artistic) work extends from the sensory to the cognitive, from poetry to prose, from the concrete to the abstract: from Cervantes' Don Quixote – scholastic and poor nobleman, half consciously bearing his humiliation in the court of the duke – to the broad but empty Don Quixote of Turgenev; from Charlemagne to the name 'king' (in Russian 'Charles' and 'king' obviously derive from the same root, *korol*). The meaning of a work broadens to the extent that artfulness and artistry diminish; thus a fable symbolises more than a poem, and a proverb more than a fable. Consequently, the least self-contradictory part of Potebnya's theory is his treatment of the fable, which, from his point of view, he investigated thoroughly. But since his theory did not provide for 'expressive' works of art, he could not finish his book. As we know, *Notes on the Theory of Literature* was published in 1905, thirteen years after Potebnya's death. Potebnya himself completed only the section on the fable.[4]

After we see an object several times, we begin to recognize it. The object is in front of us and we know about it, but we do not see it[5] – hence we cannot say anything significant about it. Art removes objects from the automatism of perception in several ways. Here I want to illustrate a way used repeatedly by Leo Tolstoy, that writer who, for Merezhkovsky at least, seems to present things as if he himself saw them, saw them in their entirety, and did not alter them.

Tolstoy makes the familiar seem strange by not naming the familiar object. He describes an object as if he were seeing it for the first time, an event as if it were happening for the first time. In describing something he avoids the accepted names of its parts and instead names corresponding parts of other objects. For example, in 'Shame' Tolstoy 'defamiliarizes' the idea of flogging in this way: 'to strip people who have broken the law, to hurl them to the floor, and to rap on their bottoms with switches', and, after a few lines, 'to lash about on the naked buttocks'. Then he remarks:

> Just why precisely this stupid, savage means of causing pain and not any other – why not prick the shoulders or any part of the body with needles, squeeze the hands or the feet in a vice, or anything like that?

I apologize for this harsh example, but it is typical of Tolstoy's way of pricking the conscience. The familiar act of flogging is made unfamiliar both by the description and by the proposal to change its form without changing its nature. Tolstoy uses this technique of 'defamiliarization', constantly. The narrator of 'Kholstomer', for example, is a horse, and it is the horse's point of view (rather than a person's) that makes the content of the story seem unfamiliar. Here is how the horse regards the institution of private property:

> I understood well what they said about whipping and Christianity. But then I was absolutely in the dark. What's the meaning of 'his own', 'his colt'? From these phrases I saw that people thought there was some sort of connection between me and the stable. At the time I simply could not understand the connection. Only much later, when they separated me from the other horses, did I begin to understand. But even then I simply could not see what it meant when they called me 'man's property'. The words 'my horse' referred to me, a living horse, and seemed as strange to me as the words 'my land', 'my air', 'my water'.
>
> But the words made a strong impression on me. I thought about them constantly, and only after the most diverse experiences with people did I understand, finally, what they meant. They meant this: In life people are guided

by words, not by deeds. It's not so much that they love the possibility of doing or not doing something as it is the possibility of speaking with words, agreed on among themselves, about various topics. Such are the words 'my' and 'mine', which they apply to different things, creatures, objects, and even to land, people, and horses. They agree that only one may say 'mine' about this, that, or the other thing. And the one who says 'mine' about the greatest number of things is, according to the game which they've agreed to among themselves, the one they consider the most happy. I don't know the point of all this, but it's true. For a long time I tried to explain it to myself in terms of some kind of real gain, but I had to reject that explanation because it was wrong.

Many of those, for instance, who called me their own never rode on me – although others did. And so with those who fed me. Then again, the coachman, the veterinarians, and the outsiders in general treated me kindly, yet those who called me their own did not. In due time, having widened the scope of my observations, I satisfied myself that the notion 'my', not only in relation to us horses, has no other basis than a narrow human instinct which is called a sense of or right to private property. A man says 'this house is mine' and never lives in it; he only worries about its construction and upkeep. A merchant says 'my shop', 'my dry goods shop', for instance, and does not even wear clothes made from the better cloth he keeps in his own shop.

There are people who call a tract of land their own, but they never set eyes on it and never take a stroll on it. There are people who call others their own, yet never see them. And the whole relationship between them is that the so-called 'owners' treat the others unjustly.

There are people who call women their own, or their 'wives', but their women live with other men. And people strive not for the good in life, but for goods they can call their own.

I am now convinced that this is the essential difference between people and ourselves. And therefore, not even considering the other ways in which we are superior, but considering just this one virtue, we can bravely claim to stand higher than men on the ladder of living creatures. The actions of men, at least those with whom I have had dealings, are guided by *words* – ours, by deeds.

The horse is killed before the end of the story, but the manner of the narrative, its technique, does not change:

Much later they put Serpukhovsky's body, which had experienced the world, which had eaten and drunk, into the ground. They could profitably send neither his hide, nor his flesh, nor his bones anywhere.

But since his dead body, which had gone about in the world for twenty years, was a great burden to everyone, its burial was only a superfluous embarrassment for the people. For a long time no one had needed him, for a long time he had been a burden on all. But nevertheless, the dead who buried the dead found it necessary to dress this bloated body, which immediately began to rot, in a good uniform and good boots; to lay it in a good new coffin with new tassels at the four corners, then to place this new coffin in another of lead and ship it to Moscow; there to exhume ancient bones and at just that spot, to hide this putrefying body, swarming with maggots, in its new uniform and clean boots, and to cover it over completely with dirt.

Thus we see that at the end of the story Tolstoy continues to use the technique even though the motivation for it (the reason for its use) is gone.

. . . .

The technique of defamiliarization is not Tolstoy's alone. I cited Tolstoy because his work is generally known.

Now, having explained the nature of this technique, let us try to determine the approximate limits of its application. I personally feel that defamiliarization is found almost everywhere form is found. In other words, the difference between Potebnya's point of view and ours is this: An image is not a permanent referent for those mutable complexities of life which are revealed through it; its purpose is not to make us perceive meaning, but to create a special perception of the object – *it creates a 'vision' of the object instead of serving as a means for knowing it.*

Notes

1 Alexander Pogodin, *Yazyk, kak tvorchestvo (Language as Art)* (Kharkov, 1913), p. 42. (The original sentence was in French, *'Les montaignes de la Suisse vent belles'*, with the appropriate initials.)

2 Jakubinsky, *Sborniki*, I (1916).

3 Leo Tolstoy's *Diary*, entry dated 1987 February 29. (The date is transcribed incorrectly; it should read 1897 March 1.)

4 Alexander Potebnya, *Iz lektsy po teorii slovesnosti (Lectures on the Theory of Language)* (Kharkov, 1914).

5 Victor Shklovsky, *Voskresheniye slova (The Resurrection of the Word)* (Petersburg, 1914).

SECTION THREE
STRUCTURALISM

Though Structuralism developed out of Saussure's pioneering work on language, it was not until the 1960s and 1970s that it found its most widespread influence and application. Generally recognised as 'arriving' in France in the mid-1960s, it gradually made an impact on Anglo-American investigation in the human sciences, including literature. This mode of investigation has been called semiotics as well as Structuralism and though these terms are virtually synonymous some difference in orientation is apparent.[1] Literary Structuralism of this period finds its most powerful advocates in such figures as Roland Barthes, Umberto Eco, Tzvetan Todorov, A.J. Greimas and Gérard Gennette. Saussure's influence is readily apparent in the terms and concepts literary Structuralism deploys, however, the impetus for its development was also provided by such work as the structural anthropology of Lévi-Strauss and Roman Jakobson's studies of language.[2]

In the *Course in General Linguistics*, Saussure had proposed, in a couple of programmatic statements, a 'general science of signs' based on his theory of language. He called this putative science 'semiology' and suggested that the method it inaugurates could be applied to more than just the language system. Recognizing that verbal language, although the most important, was only one among many sign systems, semiology would be widely applicable. Indeed, Saussure's suggestions are taken up in Structuralism, where his theory of language is used as the basis for a critical model which investigates a diverse range of cultural phenomena.

However, Structuralism is more than a methodology; its debt to Saussure goes beyond an analytic model, for inscribed in his theory is the potential for a radical epistemology. Saussure, as we have seen in section 1, viewed the linguistic sign as arbitrary and as having meaning only because it participates in a system of conventions. Meaning is dependent upon differential relations among elements within a system, i.e. it is *diacritical* not *referential*. In fact, structuralism is not particularly interested in meaning *per se*, but rather in attempting to describe and understand the conventions and modes of signification which make it possible to 'mean'; that is, it seeks to discover the *conditions* of meaning. So *langue* is more important than *parole*

– system is more important than individual utterance. Concentration on the system led Todorov to advocate a 'poetics' which would provide a general grammar of literature, or a 'langue' of which the individual work is a 'parole'. Barthes, in *Elements of Semiology* (1964) and *Système de la Mode* (1967), working on broader cultural phenomena, assumes that an individual utterance – whether the wearing of clothes or the articulation of verbal sounds in a conversation – presupposes a system (of fashion or of language) which generates the possibility of meaning for those utterances. The first task of Structuralism is to describe and analyse that system so Structuralists usually begin their analysis by seeking general principles in individual works, though there is also a tendency to explain/interpret individual works by referring to those general principles.

Like Russian Formalism, Structuralism believes in the possibility of a 'science' of literature, one based on form rather than content. For Structuralism, such a science means it could potentially master and explain the world of signs through exhaustive detailing and analysing of the systems that allowed those signs to speak. Though this science would itself have to be carried out in language (the dominant sign system) the language of criticism was deemed to be a 'metalanguage' – that is, a language that can speak about and explain the workings of 'object' languages (languages that seem to speak directly about the world). Structuralism's claim to be operating through a metalanguage cannot, however, overcome the criticism that it is actually no more than a powerful interpretive schema for analysing texts. Moreover, while rejecting the idea of a unified meaning occupying the text, Structuralism still seeks unity or unification in the literary system as a whole, recourse to which can then 'explain' the individual work. It also tends to treat the text as a function of the system of literature, divorcing it from historical and social context.

In the initial break with orthodox critical practice Structuralism tended to be caught between being used simply as a method for analysing literature and the literary text, and being adopted as an epistemology – as a way of understanding the mode of existence of literature and the text. The two essays reprinted here illustrate, through their different inflections, the two sides of this moment of Structuralism. Roland Barthes's essay dates from 1966; this was the beginning of the period when his work was undergoing transformation from a Structuralist to a Post-Structuralist orientation, and elements of both can be traced in this article. We have included it here for that reason and because it outlines the grounds on which the epistemological break with traditional criticism was made. Though David Lodge's essay dates from 1980, we have placed this before the Barthes piece since it provides a clear and concise summary of the methods and approaches that Structuralist and Formalist-Structuralist work offered and because it quite explicitly assesses the usefulness of those methods as interpretive tools.

3   David Lodge,

'Analysis and Interpretation of the Realist Text', *Poetics Today*,
Vol. 1: 4 (1980)[1], pp. 5–22

I

It is a commonplace that the systematic study of narrative was founded by
Aristotle, and scarcely an exaggeration to say that little of significance was
added to those foundations until the twentieth century. Narrative theory in
the intervening period was mainly directed (or misdirected) at deducing from
Aristotle's penetrating analysis of the system of Greek tragedy a set of
prescriptive rules for the writing of epic. The rise of the novel as a distinctive
and eventually dominant literary form finally exposed the poverty of
neoclassical narrative theory, without for a long time generating anything
much more satisfactory. The realistic novel set peculiar problems for any
formalist criticism because it worked by disguising or denying its own
conventionality. It therefore invited – and received – criticism which was
interpretative and evaluative rather than analytical. It was not until the late
nineteenth and early twentieth centuries that something like a poetics of
fiction began to evolve from the self-conscious experiments of novelists
themselves, and was elaborated by literary critics. At about the same time,
developments in linguistics, folklore and anthropology stimulated a more
broad-ranging study of narrative, beyond the boundaries of modern literary
fiction. For a long time these investigations were pursued on parallel tracks
which seldom converged. In the last couple of decades, however, the Anglo-
American tradition of formalist criticism, essentially empirical and text-based,
theoretically rather underpowered but critically productive, has encountered
the more systematic, abstract, theoretically rigorous and 'scientific' tradition
of European structuralist criticism. The result has been a minor 'knowledge
explosion' in the field of narrative theory and poetics of fiction.

The question I wish to raise in this paper is whether progress in theory
and methodology means progress in the critical reading of texts.[2] Is it
possible, or useful, to bring the whole battery of modern formalism and
structuralism to bear upon a single text, and what is gained by so doing?
Does it enrich our reading by uncovering depths and nuances of meaning
we might not otherwise have brought to consciousness, help us to solve
problems of interpretation and to correct misreadings? Or does it merely
encourage a pointless and self-indulgent academicism, by which the same
information is shuffled from one set of categories to another, from one jargon
to another, without any real advance in appreciation or understanding? The
analysis offered here of a short story by Ernest Hemingway is intended to
support a positive answer to the first set of questions, a negative answer to
the second set. But first it may be useful to remind ourselves of the range

and variety of theories, methodologies and 'approaches' now available to the critic of fiction. I would group them into three categories, according to the 'depth' at which they address themselves to narrative structure.

I *Narratology and Narrative Grammar* – i.e., the effort to discover the *langue* of narrative, the underlying system of rules and possibilities of which any narrative *parole* (text) is the realisation. With a few arguable exceptions[3] this enterprise has been almost exclusively dominated by European scholars – Propp, Bremond, Greimas, Lévi-Strauss, Todorov and Barthes, among others. Crucial to this tradition of enquiry are the ideas of function and transformation. In the theory of Greimas for instance, all narrative consists essentially of the transfer of an object or value from one actant to another. An actant performs a certain function in the story which may be classified as Subject or Object, Sender or Receiver, Helper or Opponent, and is involved in doing things which may be classified as performative (tests, struggles, etc.), contractual (establishment and breaking of contracts) and disjunctional (departure and returns). These functions are not simply identifiable from the structure of a narrative text: for instance, several characters may perform the function of one actant, or one character may combine the functions of two actants. All concepts are semantically defined by a binary relationship with their opposites (e.g., Life/Death) or negatives (e.g., Life : Death::Non-Life : Non-Death), so that all narrative can be seen as the transformation into actants and actions of a thematic four-term homology.[4]

It is often said that this kind of approach is more rewarding when applied to narratives of a traditional, formulaic and orally transmitted type, rather than sophisticated literary narratives; and the exponents of narratology themselves frequently remind us that their aim is not the explication of texts but the uncovering of the system that allows narrative texts to be generated and competent readers to make sense of them Narratology does however bring to the attention of the literary critic factors involved in reading narrative that are important, but in a sense so obvious that they tend to be overlooked. Roland Barthes[5] (1975, 1977) has very fruitfully applied to the analysis of literary fictions the idea, derived from structuralist narratology, that narrative is divisible into sequences that open or close possibilities for the characters, and thus for the reader. The interest of these openings and closures may be either retrospective, contributing to the solution of some enigma proposed earlier in the text (the hermeneutic code) or prospective, making the audience wonder what will happen next (the proairetic code). Suspense and curiosity are therefore the two basic 'affects' aroused by narrative. A story of any sophistication will also, as Kermode points out,[6] make use of what Aristotle called peripeteia, or reversal, when a possibility is closed in a way that is unexpected and yet plausible and instructive. The reversal tends to produce an effect of irony, especially if it is anticipated by the audience.

Two problems arise in applying this kind of approach to realistic fiction.

If we segment a text into its smallest units of information, how do we identify those which are functional on the basic narrative level, and what do we do with those units (the majority) which are not? Roland Barthes suggests one solution in his 'Introduction to the Structural Analysis of Narratives' where, drawing his illustrations mainly from Ian Fleming's *Goldfinger*, he classifies the narrative units as either *nuclei* or *catalyzers*. Nuclei open or close alternatives that are of direct consequence for the subsequent development of the narrative and cannot be deleted without altering the story. Catalyzers are merely consecutive units which expand the nuclei or fill up the space between them. They can be deleted without altering the narrative, though not, in the case of realistic narrative, without altering its meaning and effect, since segments which connect not, or not only, with segments at the same level, but with some more generalized concept such as the psychological make-up of the characters, or the atmosphere of the story, function as *indices*, or (if merely factual) *informants*. Jonathan Culler has suggested that our ability to distinguish nuclei from catalyzers intuitively and to rank them in order of importance is a typical manifestation of reader-competence, verified by the fact that different readers will tend to summarize the plot of a given story in the same way. The intuitive recognition or ranking of nuclei is 'governed by readers' desire to reach an ultimate summary in which plot as a whole is grasped in a satisfying form'.[7] In short, the structural coherence of narratives is inseparable from their meaning, and reading them is inseparable from forming hypotheses about their overall meaning.

2 *Poetics of Fiction*   Under this head I include all attempts to describe and classify techniques of fictional representation. The great breakthrough in this field in the modern era was undoubtedly the Russian Formalists' distinction between *fabula* and *sjuzhet*: on the one hand the story in its most neutral, objective, chronological form – the story as it might have been enacted in real time and space, a seamless continuum of innumerable contiguous events; and on the other hand, the actual text in which this story is imitated, with all its inevitable (but motivated) gaps, elisions, emphases and reorderings. Work along these lines in Europe, culminating in Gérard Genette's 'Discours du Récit',[8] established two principal areas in which *sjuzhet* significantly modifies *fabula*: time, and what is generally called 'point of view' in Anglo-American criticism – though Genette correctly distinguishes here between 'perspective' (who sees the action) and 'voice' (who speaks the narration of it). He also distinguishes most suggestively three different categories in the temporal organisation (or deformation) of the *fabula* by the *sjuzhet*: order, duration and frequency.

The choices made by the narrative artist at this level are in a sense prior to, or 'deeper' than, his stylistic choices in composing the surface structure of the text, though they place important constraints upon what he can achieve in the surface structure. They are also of manifest importance in the realistic novel which, compared to other, earlier narrative forms, is characterized by a carefully discriminated, pseudo-historical treatment of temporality, and a remarkable depth and flexibility in its presentation of consciousness.

A good deal of Anglo-American critical theorising about the novel, from Percy Lubbock's *The Craft of Fiction* (1921) to Wayne Booth's *The Rhetoric of Fiction* (1961) was implicitly, if unconsciously, based on the same distinction between *fabula* and *sjuzhet*, between 'story' and 'way of telling it'. The cross-fertilization of the two critical traditions has produced much interesting and illuminating work, analyzing and classifying tying novelistic techniques and covering such matters as tense, person, speech and indirect speech in fictional narrative; and we are now, it seems to me, within sight of a truly comprehensive taxonomy of fictional form at this level. Two recent books which have made particularly valuable contributions in this respect are Seymour Chatman[9] and the more narrowly focused work of Dorrit Cohn.[10]

3 *Rhetorical Analysis*   By this I mean analyzing the surface structure of narrative texts to show how the linguistic mediation of a story determines its meaning and effect. This is a kind of criticism in which the Anglo-American tradition is comparatively strong, because of the close-reading techniques developed by New Criticism. Mark Shorer's essays are classic statements of this approach.[11] The stylistics that developed out of Romance Philology, represented at its best by Spitzer and Auerbach, also belongs in this category. When I wrote my first book of criticism, *Language of Fiction*[12], this seemed the best route by which to achieve a formalist critique of the realistic novel.

The underlying aim of this criticism was to demonstrate that what looked like redundant or random detail in realistic fiction was in fact functional, contributing to a pattern of motifs with expressive and thematic significance. Much of this criticism was therefore concerned with tracing symbolism and keywords in the verbal texture of novels. Though very few of the New Critics were aware of the work of Roman Jakobson, he provided a theoretical justification for this kind of criticism in his famous definition of literariness, or the poetic function of language, as 'the projection of the principle of equivalence from the axis of selection to the axis of combination'.[13] What the New Critics called 'spatial form'[14] was precisely a pattern of paradigmatic equivalences concealed in the narrative syntagm. Furthermore, as I tried to show in my book *The Modes of Modern Writing*,[15] in his distinction between metaphor and metonymy, Jacobson[16] provided a key to understanding how the realistic novel contrives to build up a pattern of equivalences without violating its illusion of life.

The argument is briefly as follows: metaphor and metonymy (or synecdoche) are both figures of equivalence, but generated by different processes, metaphor according to similarity between things otherwise different, metonymy according to continuity or association between part and whole, cause and effect, thing and attribute, etc. Thus, if I transform the literal sentence 'Ships sail the sea' into 'Keels plough the deep', *plough* is equivalent to 'sail' because of the similarity between the movement of a plough through the earth and/or a ship through the sea, but *keel* is equivalent to 'ship' because it is part of a ship (synecdoche) and *deep* equivalent to 'sea' because it is an attribute of the sea (metonymy). In fact, metonymy is a non-logical (and therefore foregrounded or rhetorical) condensation achieved by transformations of kernel sentences by deletion (*the keels of the ships* condensed to *keels* rather than *ships*, deep sea to *deep* rather than *sea*). Metonymy thus plays with the combination axis of language as metaphor plays with the selection axis of language, and together they epitomize the two ways by which any discourse connects one topic with another: either because they are similar or because they are contiguous. Jackobson's distinction thus allows the analyst to move freely between deep structure and surface structure.

Realistic fiction is dominantly metonymic in a double sense: it connects actions that are contiguous in time and space and connected by cause and effect, but since it cannot describe exhaustively, the narrative *sjuzhet* is always in a metonymic relation to the *fabula*. The narrative text necessarily selects certain details and suppresses or deletes others. The selected details are thus foregrounded by being selected, and their recurrence and interrelation with other selected details in the text become aesthetically significant (what the Prague School calls systematic internal foregrounding). If these selected details are rhetorically mediated, through the use of the actual figures of metonymy and synecdoche, or of metaphor and simile, a denser and more overt pattern of equivalences is generated, but such rhetoric is not essential to the process, which is usually called symbolism in Anglo-American criticism. Barthes defined it as connotation, the device by which one signified acts as the signifier of another signified. Jakobson's distinction enables us to distinguish four different ways in which it operates:

A. Metonymic Signified I metonymically evokes Signified II (e.g., hearth fires in Charlotte Bronte's *Jane Eyre* symbolize domestic comfort, intimacy, security, etc.).
B. Metonymic Signified I metaphorically evokes Signified II (e.g., mud and fog at the beginning of *Bleak House* symbolize obfuscation and degradation of goodness and justice by the law).
C. Metaphoric Signified I metonymically evokes Signified II (e.g., the description of the night in Llaregyb in Dylan Thomas's *Under Milk Wood* as 'bible-black' symbolizes the Protestant chapel-going religious culture of the community).
D. Metaphoric Signified II metaphorically evokes Signified I (e.g., in the opening lines of Yeats's poem, 'The Second Coming'):

Turning and turning in the widening gyre
The falcon cannot hear the falconer

the metaphor *gyre* applied to the spiraling movement of the falcon also symbolizes the cyclical movement of history.

Realistic fiction relies principally upon symbolism types A and B.

II

No choice of a text for illustrative purposes is innocent, and no analysis of a single text could possibly provide universally valid answers to the questions posed at the beginning of this paper. These questions will not be settled until we have a significant corpus of synthetic or pluralistic readings of narrative texts of various types. Two distinguished achievements of this kind come to mind: Barthes' *S/Z* and Christine Brooke-Rose's study of *The Turn of the Screw*.[17] The following discussion of Hemingway's short story 'Cat in the Rain'[18] is necessarily much more modest in scope and scale. Two considerations prompted the choice of this story, apart from its convenient brevity: (1) A staff seminar on it in my own Department at Birmingham revealed that it presents certain problems of interpretation, though without being quite so heavily encrusted with the deposits of previous readings and misreadings as *The Turn of the Screw*. (2) It is both realistic and modern, cutting across that historicist and tendentious distinction between the *lisible* and the *scriptible* which I personally find one of the less helpful features of the work of Barthes and his disciples. The implied notion of *vraisemblance* on which Hemingway's story depends, the assumed relationship between the text and reality, is essentially continuous with that of classic bourgeois realism, yet in the experience of readers it has proved ambiguous, polyvalent and resistant to interpretative closure.

This is what Carlos Baker, in the standard critical work on Hemingway, had to say about 'Cat in the Rain' (he discusses it in the context of a group of stories about men–women relationships):

'Cat in the Rain', another story taken in part from the woman's point of view, presents a corner of the female world in which the male is only tangentially involved. It was written at Rapallo in May, 1923. From the window of a hotel room where her husband is reading and she is fidgeting, a young wife sees a cat outside in the rain. When she goes to get it, the animal (which somehow stands in her mind for comfortable bourgeois domesticity) has disappeared. This fact is very close to tragic because of the cat's association in her mind with many other things she longs for: long hair she can do in a knot at the back of her neck; a candle-lighted dining table where her own silver gleams; the season of spring and nice weather; and of course, some new clothes. But when she puts these wishes into words, her husband mildly advises her to shut up and find something to read. 'Anyway', says the young wife, 'I want a cat. I want a cat. I want a cat now. If I can't have long hair or any fun, I can have a cat.' The poor girl is the referee in a face-off between the actual and the possible. The actual is made of rain, boredom, a preoccupied husband and irrational yearnings. The possible is made of silver, spring, fun, a new coiffure, and new dresses. Between the actual

and the possible stands the cat. It is finally sent up to her by the kindly old inn-
keeper, whose sympathetic deference is greater than that of the young husband.[19]

There are several things to quibble with in this account of the story. Most
important perhaps is Baker's assumption that the cat sent up by the hotel
keeper at the end is the same as the one that the wife saw from her window.
This assumption is consistent with Baker's sympathy with the wife as a
character, implied by his reference to her as 'the poor girl' and his
description of the disappearance of the cat as 'very close to tragic'. The
appearance of the maid with a cat is the main reversal, in Aristotelian terms,
in the narrative. If it is indeed the cat she went to look for, then the reversal
is a happy one for her, and confirms her sense that the hotel keeper
appreciated her as a woman more than her husband. In Greimas's terms,
the wife is the subject of the story and the cat the object. The hotel keeper
and the maid enact the role of helper and George is the opponent. The story
is disjunctive (departure and return) and concerns the transfer of the cat to
the wife.

The description of the tortoiseshell cat as 'big', however, suggests that it
is not the same as the one the wife referred to by the diminutive term 'kitty',
and which she envisaged stroking on her lap. We might infer that the
padrone, trying to humor a client, sends up the first cat he can lay hands
on, which is in fact quite inappropriate to the wife's needs. This would make
the reversal an ironic one at the wife's expense, emphasising the social and
cultural abyss that separates her from the padrone, and revealing her quasi-
erotic response to his professional attentiveness as a delusion.

I shall return to this question of the ambiguity of the ending. One more
point about Baker's commentary on the story: he says that the cat 'somehow
stands in [the wife's] mind for comfortable bourgeois domesticity', and
speaks of its 'association in her mind with many other things she longs for'.
In other words, he interprets the cat as a metonymic symbol of type A
above. Indeed he sees the whole story as turning on the opposition between
two groups of metonymies. 'The actual is made of rain, boredom, a
preoccupied husband, and irrational yearnings. The possible is made of
silver, spring, fun, a new coiffure, and new dresses.'

John V. Hagopian gives a very different reading of this story. It is,
he says, about 'a crisis in the marriage . . . involving the lack of fertility, which
is symbolically foreshadowed by the public garden (fertility) dominated by
the war monument (death)' in the first paragraph. These again are metonymic
symbols of type A, effect connoting cause; but Hagopian's reading of the
story hinges on the identification of the cat as a symbol of a wanted child,
and of the man in the rubber cape (lines 32–3) as a symbol of contraception
– symbolism of type B. in which a metonymic signified evokes a second
signified metaphorically, i.e., by virtue of similarity.

As [the wife] looks out into the wet empty square, she sees a man in a rubber
cape strolling to the café in the rain . . . The rubber cape is a protection from rain,

and rain is a fundamental necessity for fertility and fertility is precisely what is lacking in the American wife's marriage. An even more precise interpretation is possible but perhaps not necessary here.[20]

What Hagopian is presumably hinting at is that 'rubber' is an American colloquialism for contraceptive sheath, and that the wife notices the man in the rubber cape because of the subconscious association – a piece of classic Freudian 'symbolism'. It is an ingenious interpretation and all the more persuasive because there seems to be no very obvious reason for introducing the man in the cape into the story – he is not an actant in the narrative but an item of the descriptive background[21] and his appearance does not tell us anything about the weather or the square that we do not know already. Admittedly, the cape does signify, by contrast, the wife's lack of protection from the rain, thus emphasising the padrone's thoughtfulness in sending the maid with the umbrella. But if we accept Hagopian's reading then the umbrella itself, opening with almost comical opportuneness and effort-lessness behind her, becomes a symbol of how the wife's way of life comes between her and a vital, fertile, relationship with reality. Her later demands for new clothes, a new hairstyle, a candlelit dining table are, according to Hagopian plan, expressions of a desire that never reaches full consciousness, for 'motherhood, a home with a family, an end to the strictly companionate marriage with George'. And the cat, he says, is by this stage in the story 'an obvious symbol for a child'.[22]

Unlike Baker, Hagopian sees the final reversal in the story as ironic:

> The girl's symbolic wish is grotesquely fulfilled in painfully realistic terms. It is George, not the padrone, by whom the wife wants to be fulfilled, but the padrone has sent up the maid with a big tortoise-shell cat, a huge creature that swings down against her body. It is not clear whether this is exactly the same cat as the one the wife had seen from the window – probably not; in any case, it will most certainly not do. The girl is willing to settle for a child-surrogate, but the big tortoise-shell cat obviously cannot serve that purpose.[23]

The reason why this story is capable of providing these two very different interpretations might be expressed as follows: although it is a well-formed narrative, with a clearly defined beginning, middle and end, the primary action is not the primary vehicle of meaning. This can be demonstrated by testing upon the story Jonathan Culler's hypothesis that competent readers will tend to agree on what is and is not essential to the plot of a narrative test. Before the seminar at Birmingham University participants were invited to summarize the action of the story in not more than 30 words of continuous prose.[24] All the contributors mentioned the wife, the cat, the rain, and the hotel manager; most mentioned the nationality of the wife and her failure to find the cat under the table; about half mentioned the husband, located the story in Italy, and made a distinction between the two cats. None mentioned the maid, or the bickering between husband and wife.

These omissions are particularly interesting. The non-appearance of the maid is easily explained: on the narrative level her function is indistinguishable from that of the manager – both are 'helpers' and the narrative would not be significantly altered *qua* narrative if the maid were deleted from the story and her actions performed by the manager himself. She does contribute to the symmetry of the story both numerically and sexually: it begins by pairing husband and wife, then pairs wife and manager, then wife and maid, then (in the wife's thoughts) maid and manager, then wife and manager again, then wife and husband again, and ends by pairing husband and maid. But this seems to be a purely formal set of equivalences with no significance in the hermeneutic or proairetic codes (such as would obtain if, for instance, there were some intrigue linking the husband with the maid and the manager, the kind of plotting characteristic of the *lisible* text). The main function of the maid in the story is to emphasise the status of the wife as a client and expatriate, and thus to act as a warning or corrective against the wife's tendency to attribute to the padrone a deeply personal interest in herself.

Both Baker and Hagopian agree that the rift between husband and wife is what the story is essentially about, even if they disagree about the precise cause. That none of the synopses should make any allusion to the bickering between the couple is striking evidence that the meaning of the story does not inhere in its basic action. In trying to preserve what is essential to that action in a very condensed summary – the quest for the cat, the failure of the quest, the reversal – one has to discard what seems most important in the story as read: the relationship between husband and wife. Adopting Barthes' terminology in 'The Structural Analysis of Narratives', there are only four nuclei in the story, opening possibilities which might be closed in different ways: will the wife or the husband go to fetch the cat? will the wife get the cat? will she get wet? who is at the door?[25] The rest of the story consists of catalysers that are indexical or informational, and since most of the information is given more than once, these too become indexical of mood and atmosphere (for instance, we are told more than once that it is raining). One might indeed describe the story generically as indexical: we infer its meaning indexically from its non-narrative components rather than hermeneutically or teleologically from its action. Another way of putting it would be to invoke Seymour Chatman's distinction between the resolved plot and the revealed plot:

> In the traditional narrative of resolution, there is a sense of problem solving . . . of a kind of ratiocinative or emotional teleology . . . 'What will happen?' is the basic question. In the modern plot of revelation, however, the emphasis is elsewhere, the function of the discourse is not to answer the question or even to pose it . . . It is not that events are resolved (happily or tragically) but rather that a state of affairs is revealed.[26]

Chatman offers *Pride and Prejudice* and *Mrs. Dalloway* as examples of each kind of plot. 'Cat in the Rain' seems to share characteristics of both: it is, one might say, a plot of revelation (the relationship between husband and wife) disguised as a plot of resolution (the quest for the cat). The ambiguity of the ending is therefore crucial. By refusing to resolve the issue of whether the wife gets the cat she wants, the implied author indicates that this is not the point of the story.

There are several reasons why this ending is ambiguous. One, obviously, is that the story ends where it does, for if it continued for another line or two, or moment or two, it would become apparent from the wife's response whether the cat was the one she had seen from the window, whether she is pleased or disconcerted by its being brought to her, and so on. What I am doing here is comparing the *fabula* with the *sjuzhet*. The *sjuzhet* tantalisingly stops just short of that point in the *fabula* where we should, with our readerly desire for certainty, wish it to. In other respects there is nothing especially striking about the story's treatment of time, though we may admire the smooth transition in the first paragraph from summary of a state of affairs obtaining over a period of days or weeks to the state of affairs obtaining on a particular afternoon, and the subtle condensation of durational time in the final scene between husband and wife, marked by changes in the light outside the window. The order of events is strictly chronological (characteristic, Chatman observes, of the resolved plot (1978:48)). As regards what Genette calls frequency (the number of times an event is narrated), the story tends toward reiteration rather than summary, telling *n* times what happened *n* times or *n* times what happened once rather than telling once what happened *n* times. This is important because it reinforces the definition of the characters according to a very limited repertoire of gestures. Thus the wife is frequently described as looking out of the window, the husband as reading, the manager as bowing (and the weather as raining).

The story of the quest for the cat involves four characters, and in theory could be narrated from four points of view, each quite distinct and different in import. The story we have is written from the point of view of the American couple rather than that of the Italian hotel staff, and from the wife's point of view rather than the husband's. We must distinguish here between what Genette calls voice and perspective. The story is narrated throughout by an authorial voice which refers to the characters in the third person and uses the past tense. This is the standard mode of authorial narration and by convention the narrator is authoritative, reliable and within the fictional world of the discourse, omniscient. The authorial voice in this story, however, renounces the privilege of authorial omniscience in two ways: firstly, by abstaining from any comment, judgement or explanation of motive regarding the behaviour of the characters, and secondly by restricting itself to the perspective of only two of the characters, and, for part of the story, to the perspective of only one. By this I mean that the narrator describes nothing that is not seen by either husband or wife or both. Yet it is not quite true to say that the narrator has no independent angle of vision; he has. As in a film, we sometimes see the wife from the husband's angle, and the husband sometimes from the wife's angle, but much of the time we see them both from some independent, impersonal angle.

The first paragraph adopts the common perspective of the American couple, making no distinction between them. With the first sentence of the second paragraph, 'The American wife stood at the window looking out', the narrative adopts her perspective but without totally identifying with it. Note the deictic difference between '*her* husband' in line 18, which closely identifies the narration with her perspective, and '*the* husband' in line 20, '*the* wife' in line 23, which subtly reasserts the independence of the authorial voice. From this point onwards, however, for the next 50 lines the narration identifies itself closely with the wife's perspective, following her out of the room and downstairs into the lobby, and reporting what she thinks as well as what she sees. The anaphoric sequence of sentences beginning 'She liked' (lines 29–31) affects us as being a transcription rather than a description of her thoughts because they could be transposed into monologue (first person/present tense) without any illogicality or stylistic awkwardness. Sentences in free indirect speech, 'The cat would be round to the right. Perhaps she could go along under the eaves' (33–4) and 'of course, the hotel-keeper had sent her' (37–8), mark the maximum degree of identification of the narration with the wife's point of view. When she returns to the room the narration separates itself from her again. There is a lot of direct speech from now on, no report of the wife's thoughts, and occasionally the narration seems to adopt the husband's perspective alone, e.g., 'George looked up and saw the back of her neck, clipped like a boy's' (71), and – very importantly:

> Someone knocked at the door.
> 'Avanti', George said. He looked up from his book.
> In the doorway stood the maid. She held a big tortoise-shell cat . . . (93–5)

We can now fully understand why the ending of the story is so ambiguous: it is primarily because the narration adopts the husband's perspective at this crucial point. Since he did not rise from the bed to look: out of the window at the cat sheltering from the rain, he has no way of knowing whether the cat brought by the maid is the same one – hence the non-committal indefinite article 'a big tortoise-shell cat'. If, however, the wife's perspective had been adopted at this point and the text had read

> 'Avanti,' the wife said. She turned round from the window. In the doorway stood the maid. She held a big tortoise-shell cat . . .

then it would be clear that this was not the cat the wife had wanted to bring in from the rain (in which case the definite article would be used). It is significant that in the title of the story, there is no article before 'Cat', thus giving no support to either interpretation of the ending.

Carlos Baker's assumption that the tortoise-shell cat and the cat in the rain are one and the same is therefore unwarranted. Hagopian's reading of the ending as ironic is preferable but his assumption that the wife's desire for the cat is caused by childlessness is also unwarranted. Here, it seems to me, the structuralist notion of language as a system of differences and of meaning as the product of structural oppositions can genuinely help to settle a point of interpretation.[27] Hagopian's interpretation of the man in the rubber cape as a symbol of contraception depends in part on the association of rain with fertility. Now rain *can* symbolise fertility, when defined by opposition to drought. In this story, however (and incidentally, throughout Hemingway's work) it is opposed to 'good weather' and symbolises the loss of pleasure and joy, the onset of discomfort and ennui. Hagopian's comments on the disappearance of the artists, 'The rain, ironically, inhibits creativity,[28] is a strained attempt to reconcile his reading with the text: there is no irony here unless we accept his equation, rain = fertility.

The cat as a child-surrogate is certainly a possible interpretation in the sense that it is a recognised cultural stereotype, but again Hagopian tries to enlist in its support textual evidence that is, if anything, negative. He comments on the description of the wife's sensations as she passes the hotel keeper for the second time: ' "very small and tight inside . . . really important . . . of supreme importance" all phrases that might appropriately be used to describe a woman who is pregnant'.[29] But not, surely, to describe a woman who merely *wants* to be pregnant. Indeed, if we must have a gynecological reading of the story it is much more plausible to suppose that the wife's whimsical craving for the cat and for other things like new clothes and long hair is the result of her *being* pregnant. There is in fact some extratextual support for this hypothesis. In his biography of Hemingway, Carlos Baker states quite baldly that 'Cat in the Rain' was about Hemingway, his wife Hadley and the manager and chambermaid at the Hotel Splendide in Rapallo, where the story was written in 1923. He also states, without making any connection between the two items, that the Hemingways had left the chilly thaw of Switzerland and gone to Rapallo because Hadley had announced that she was pregnant.[30]

At about the same time, Hemingway was evolving 'a new theory that you could omit anything if you knew what you omitted, and the omitted part would strengthen the story and make people feel something more than they understood'.[31] This is, I think, a very illuminating description by Hemingway of his application of the metonymic mode of classical realism to modernist literary purposes. Metonymy, as I said earlier, is a device of non-logical deletion. Hemingway's word is 'omission'. By omitting the kind of motivation that classical realistic fiction provided, he generated a symbolist polysemy in his deceptively simple stories, making his readers 'feel more than they understood'. It would be a mistake, therefore, to look for a single clue, whether pregnancy or barrenness, to the meaning of 'Cat in the Rain'. That the wife's (and, for that matter, the husband's) behaviour is equally intelligible on either assumption is one more confirmation of the story's indeterminacy.

Hemingway's stories are remarkable for achieving a symbolist resonance without the use of rhetorical figures and tropes. Not only does 'Cat in the Rain' contain no metaphors and similes – it contains no metonymies and synecdoches either. The story is 'metonymic' in the structural sense defined above: its minimal semantic units are selected from a single context, a continuum of temporal and spatial contiguities, and are foregrounded simply by being selected, repeated and related to each other oppositionally. Consider, for example, the opening paragraph, which establishes the story's setting in diction that is apparently severely denotative, with no metaphors or metonymies, similes or synecdoches, no elegant variation or pathetic fallacies, yet is nevertheless highly charged with connotative meaning.

> *There were only two Americans stopping at the hotel.* Americans opposed to other nationalities: index of cultural isolation.
> *They did not know any of the people they passed on the stairs on their way to and from their room.* Index of social isolation and mutual dependence - vulnerability to breakdown in relationship.
> *Their room was on the second floor facing the sea.* Culture faces nature.
> *It also faced the public garden and the war monument.* Culture paired with nature (public: garden) and opposed to nature (monument: garden). Pleasure (garden) opposed to pain (war).
> *There were big palms and green benches in the public garden.* Culture and nature integrated. Benches same color as vegetation.
> *In the good weather there was always an artist with his easel. Artists liked the way the palms grew and the bright colors of the hotels facing the garden and the sea.* Culture and nature happily fused. Image of euphoria.
> *Italians came from a long way off to look up at the war monument.* Euphoria qualified. War monument attracts the living but commemorates the dead. Looking associated with absence (of the dead). 'Italian opposed to 'American'.
> *It was made of bronze and glinted in the rain.* Inert mineral (bronze) opposed to organic vegetable (palm). Rain opposed to good weather. Euphoria recedes.
> *It was raining. Rain dripped from the palm trees.* Euphoria recedes further. Garden uninviting.
> *Water stood in pools on the gravel paths.* Image of stagnation.
> *The sea broke in a long line in the rain and slipped back down the beach to come up and break again in a long line in the rain.* Excess of wetness. Monotony. Ennui.
> *The motor cars were gone from the square by the war monument. Across the square in the doorway of the café a waiter stood looking out at the square.* Images of absence, loss, ennui.

The first paragraph, then, without containing a single narrative nucleus, establishes the thematic core of the story through oppositions between nature and culture, joy and ennui. Joy is associated with a harmonious union of culture and nature. The wife, looking out of the window at a scene made joyless by the rain, sees a cat with whose discomfort she emotionally identifies. Her husband, though offering to fetch it, implies his indifference to her emotional needs by not actually moving. The husband is reading, a 'cultural' use of the eyes. The wife is looking, a 'natural' use of the eyes.

Her looking, through the window, expresses a need for communion. His reading of a book is a substitute for communion, and a classic remedy for ennui. It is worth noticing that he is reading on the bed – a place made for sleeping and making love; and the perversity of this behaviour is symbolized by the fact that he is lying on the bed the wrong way round. As the story continues, the contrast between looking and reading, both activities expressing the loss or failure of love, becomes more insistent. Denied the kitty, a 'natural' object (opposed to book) which she could have petted as a substitute for being petted, the wife looks in the mirror, pining for a more natural feminine self. Then she looks out of the window again, while her husband, who has not shifted his position (his immobility opposed to the padrone's punctilious bowing) reads on and impatiently recommends her to 'get something to read'. One could summarize this story in the style of Greimas, as follows: loving is to quarrelling as stroking a cat is to reading a book, a narrative transformation of the opposition between joy and ennui, thus:

> Loving (Joy): Quarrelling (Ennui): stroking a cat (Non-joy, a giving but not receiving of pleasure): reading a book (Non-ennui).

Such a summary has this to recommend it: that it brings together the overt action of the story (the quest for the cat) with its implicit subject (the relationship between husband and wife). Whether it, and the preceding comments, enhance our understanding and appreciation of Hemingway's story, I leave others to judge.

Notes

1 Paper presented at *Synopsis* 2: 'Narrative Theory and Poetics of Fiction', an international symposium held at The Porter Institute for Poetics and Semiotics, Tel Aviv University, and the Van Leer Jerusalem Foundation, 16–22 June 1979. For the text of the story, see Appendix.

2 I do not mean to imply that theory can only be justified on such grounds. Theoretical research may have a purpose and value quite independent of its application to particular problems. I merely wish to consider whether exponents of 'practical', or descriptive and interpretative, criticism have anything useful to learn from recent developments in the theory of narrative and poetics of fiction.

3 For example, Northrop Frye, *Anatomy of Criticism* (Princeton, NJ, Princeton University Press, 1957) and Frank Kermode, *The Sense of an Ending* (New York and London, Oxford University Press, 1966).

4 A.J. Greimas, Sémantique structurale (Paris, Larousse, 1966); *Du Sens* (Paris, Seuil, 1970); *Maupassant. La Sémiologie due texte: exercises practiques* (Paris, Seuil, 1976).

5 Roland Barthes, *S/Z* tr. Richard Miller (London, Cape, 1975 [1970]); 'Introduction to the Structural Analysis of Narratives', in *Image – Music – Text* ed. and tr. Stephen Heath (London, Fontana, 1977 [1966]).

6 Kermode, The Sense of an Ending, p. 18.

7 Jonathan Culler, 'Defining Narrative Units', in Roger Fowler ed., *Style and*

Structure in Literature (Oxford, Basil Blackwell, 1975), p. 139.

8 Gérard Genette, 'Discours du récit', in *Figures III* (Paris, Seuil, 1972).

9 Seymour Chatman, *Story and Discourse: Narrative Structure in Fiction and Film* (Ithaca, NY, Cornell University Press, 1978).

10 Dorrit Cohn, *Transparent Minds: Narrative Modes for Presenting Consciousness* (Princeton, NJ, Princeton University Press, 1978).

11 Mark Schorer, 'Technique as Discovery', *Hudson Review* I (1948), pp. 67–86; 'Fiction and the Analogical Matrix', *Kenyon Review* XI (1949), pp. 539–60.

12 David Lodge, *Language of Fiction* (London, Routledge & Kegan Paul, 1966).

13 Roman Jakobson, 'Closing Statement: Linguistics and Poetics', in Thomas A. Sebeok, ed., *Style and Language* (Cambridge, Mass., MIT, 1960), p. 358.

14 Joseph Frank, 'Spatial Form in Modern Literature', in Mark Schorer, Josephine Miles and Gordon McKenzie, eds, *Criticism* (New York, Harcourt Brace, 1948 [1945]).

15 David Lodge, *The Modes of Modern Writing* (London, Arnold, and Ithaca, NY. Cornell University Press, 1977).

16 Roman Jakobson, 'Two Aspects of Language and Two Types of Linguistic Disturbances', in Jakobson and Morris Halle, *Fundamentals of Language* (The Hague, Mouton, 1956).

17 Christine Brooke-Rose, 'The Squirm of the True', *PTL* 1 (1976), pp. 265–94, 513–46; 2 (1977), pp. 517–61.

18 Ernest Hemingway, 'Cat in the Rain', in *In Our Time* (New York, Scribner, 1958 [1925]).

19 Carlos Baker, *Hemingway: The Writer as Artist* (Princeton, NJ, Princeton University Press, 1963 [1952]), pp. 135–6.

20 John V. Hagopian, 'Symmetry in "Cat in the Rain" ' in Jackson J. Benson, ed., *The Short Stories of Ernest Hemingway: Critical Essays* (Durham, NC, Duke University Press, 1975 [1962]), p. 231.

21 Chatman, *Story and Discourse: Narrative Structure in Fiction and Film*, p. 140.

22 Hagopian, 'Symmetry in "Cat in the Rain" ', p. 232.

23 Ibid.

24 My own effort was as follows: 'Bored young American staying with husband at Italian hotel fails to rescue a cat seen sheltering from the rain but is provided with a cat by the attentive manager.'

25 On further reflection I am inclined to think that there is another 'hidden' narrative nucleus in the story, related to the 'marital rift' theme, though it is to be inferred only from George's body language as reported in lines 74–5, and his appreciative speech at line 76: namely, the possibility that he will put aside his book and make love to his wife. This possibility is closed, negatively, at line 86.

26 Chatman, *Story and Discourse: Narrative Structure in Fiction and Film*, p. 48.

27 Perhaps this is overconfident, since it is rarely possible to disprove interpretations. Among the more far-fetched interpretations of 'Cat in the Rain' are Horst Kruse's argument that the man in the rubber cape is an allusion to the mysterious man in the mackintosh in the 'Hades' episode of Joyce's *Ulysses*, and therefore a symbol of death ('The appearance of a man in a raincoat in both *Ulysses* and 'Cat in the Rain' seems clear indication of the dependence of Hemingway's short story on the work of the Irish writer' (Horst Kruse, 'Hemingway's "Cat in the Rain" and Joyce's *Ulysses*', *Literatur in Wisssenschaft und Unterricht* III (1970), p. 28); and Ramesh Srivastava's suggestion that 'the cat

exists only in the imagination of the wife' (Ramesh Srivastava, 'Hemingway's "Cat in the Rain": an interpretation', Literary Criterion IX (1970), p. 83), which presumably entails reading the second sentence in paragraph 2 as free indirect speech.

28 Hagopian, 'Symmetry in "Cat in the Rain" ', p. 230.
29 Ibid., p. 231.
30 Carlos Baker, Ernest Hemingway (Harmondsworth, Penguin Books, 1972 [1969]), pp. 159, 161.
31 Ibid., p. 165.

APPENDIX

CAT IN THE RAIN*

There were only two Americans stopping at the hotel. They did not know any of the people they passed on the stairs on their way to and from their room. Their room was on the second floor facing the sea. It also faced the public garden and the war monument. There were big palms and green benches in the public garden. In the good weather there was always an artist with his easel. Artists liked the way the palms grew and the bright colors of the hotels facing the gardens and the sea. Italians came from a long way off to look up at the war monument. It was made of bronze and glistened in the rain. It was raining. The rain dripped from the palm trees. Water stood in pools on the gravel paths. The
10 sea broke in a long line in the rain and slipped back down the beach to come up and break again in a long line in the rain. The motor cars were gone from the square by the war monument. Across the square in the doorway of the café a waiter stood looking out at the empty square.

The American wife stood at the window looking out. Outside right under their
15 window a cat was crouched under one of the dripping green tables. The cat was trying to make herself so compact that she would not be dripped on.

'I'm going down and get that kitty,' the American wife said.

'I'll do it,' her husband offered from the bed.

'No, I'll get it. The poor kitty out trying to keep dry under a table.'
20 The husband went on reading, lying propped up with the two pillows at the foot of the bed.

'Don't get wet,' he said.

The wife went downstairs and the hotel owner stood up and bowed to her as she passed the office. His desk was at the far end of the office. He was an old
25 man and very tall.

'Il piove,' the wife said. She liked the hotel-keeper.

'Si, si, Signora, brutto tempo. It is very bad weather.'

He stood behind his desk in the far end of the dim room. The wife liked him. She liked the deadly serious way he received any complaints. She liked his
30 dignity. She liked the way he wanted to serve her. She liked the way he felt about being a hotelkeeper. She liked his old, heavy face and big hands.

Liking him she opened the door and looked out. It was raining harder. A man in a rubber cape was crossing the empty square to the café. The cat would be around to the right. Perhaps she could go along under the eaves. As she stood

35 in the doorway an umbrella opened behind her. It was the maid who looked after
their room.   ·

'You must not get wet,' she smiled, speaking Italian. Of course, the hotel-
keeper had sent her.

With the maid holding the umbrella over her, she walked along the gravel path
40 until she was under their window. The table was there, washed bright green in
the rain, but the cat was gone. She was suddenly disappointed. The maid looked
up at her.

'Ha perduto qualque cosa, Signora?'

'There was a cat,' said the American girl.

45 'A cat?'

'Si, il gatto.'

'A cat?' the maid laughed. 'A cat in the rain?'

'Yes,' she said, 'under the table.' Then, 'Oh, I wanted it so much. I wanted a
kitty.'

50 When she talked English the maid's face tightened.

'Come, Signora,' she said. 'We must get back inside. You will be wet.'

'I suppose so,' said the American girl.

They went back along the gravel path and passed in the door. The maid stayed
outside to close the umbrella. As the American girl passed the office, the padrone
55 bowed from his desk. Something felt very small and tight inside the girl. The
padrone made her feel very small and at the same time really important. She had
a momentary feeling of being of supreme importance. She went on up the stairs.
She opened the door of the room. George was on the bed, reading.

'Did you get the cat?' he asked, putting the book down.

60 'It was gone.'

'Wonder where it went to,' he said, resting his eyes from reading. She sat down
on the bed.

'I wanted it so much,' she said. 'I don't know why I wanted it so much. I
wanted that poor kitty. It isn't any fun to be a poor kitty out in the rain.'

65 George was reading again.

She went over and sat in front of the mirror of the dressing table looking at
herself with the hand glass. She studied her profile, first one side and then the
other. Then she studied the back of her head and her neck.

'Don't you think it would be a good idea if I let my hair grow out?' she asked,
70 looking at her profile again.

George looked up and saw the back of her neck, clipped close like a boy's.

'I like it the way it is.'

'I get so tired of it,' she said. 'I get so tired of looking like a boy.'

George shifted his position in the bed. He hadn't looked away from her since
75 she started to speak.

'You look pretty darn nice,' he said.

She laid the mirror down on the dresser and went over to the window and
looked out. It was getting dark.

'I want to pull my hair back tight and smooth and make a big knot at the back
80 that I can feel,' she said. 'I want to have a kitty to sit on my lap and purr when
I stroke her.'

'Yeah?' George said from the bed.

'And I want to eat at a table with my own silver and I want candles. And I

want it to be spring and I want to brush my hair out in front of a mirror and I
85 want a kitty and I want some new clothes.

'Oh, shut up and get something to read,' George said. He was reading again.

His wife was looking out of the window. It was quite dark now and still raining
in the palm trees.

'Anyway, I want a cat,' she said, 'I want a cat. I want a cat now. If I can't have
90 long hair or any fun, I can have a cat.'

George was not listening. He was reading his book. His wife looked out of the
window where the light had come on in the square.

Someone knocked at the door.

'Avanti,' George said. He looked up from his book.
95 In the doorway stood the maid. She held a big tortoise-shell cat pressed tight
against her and swung down against her body.

'Excuse me,' she said, 'the padrone asked me to bring this for the Signora.'

*'Cat in the Rain' by Ernest Hemingway from *In Our Time* is reprinted by
permission of Charles Scribner's Sons. Copyright 1925 Charles Scribner's
Sons; renewal copyright 1953 Ernest L Hemingway.

---

4 Roland Barthes,

'To Write: An Intransitive Verb?', in R. Macksey and E. Donate, ed.
The Structuralist Controversy (1966), pp. 134–45

To Write: An Intransitive Verb?[1]

For centuries Western culture conceived of literature not as we do today,
through a study of works, authors, and schools, but through a genuine
theory of language. This theory, whose name, *rhetoric*, came to it from
antiquity, reigned in the Western world from Gorgias to the Renaissance –
for nearly two thousand years. Threatened as early as the sixteenth century
by the advent of modern rationalism, rhetoric was completely ruined when
rationalism was transformed into positivism at the end of the nineteenth
century. At that point there was no longer any common ground of thought
between literature and language: literature no longer regarded itself as
language except in the works of a few pioneers such as Mallarmé, and
linguistics claimed very few rights over literature, these being [limited to]
a secondary philological discipline of uncertain status – stylistics.

As we know, this situation is changing, and it seems to me that it is in
part to take cognizance of this change that we are assembled here: literature
and language are in the process of finding each other again. The factors of
this *rapprochement* are diverse and complex; I shall cite the most obvious.
On one hand, certain writers since Mallarmé, such as Proust and Joyce, have
undertaken a radical exploration of writing, making of their work a search

for the total Book. On the other hand, linguistics itself, principally following the impetus of Roman Jakobson, has developed to include within its scope the poetic, or the order of effects linked to the message and not to its referent. Therefore, in my view, we have today a new perspective of consideration which, I would like to emphasize, is common to literature and linguistics, to the creator and the critic, whose tasks until now completely self-contained, are beginning to inter-relate, perhaps even to merge. This is at least true for certain writers whose work is becoming more and more a critique of language. It is in this perspective that I would like to place the following observations (of a prospective and not of a conclusive nature) indicating how the activity of writing can be expressed [énoncée] today with the help of certain linguistic categories.

This new union of literature and linguistics, of which I have just spoken, could be called, provisionally and for lack of a better name, *semio-criticism*, since it implies that writing is a system of signs. Semio-criticism is not to be identified with stylistics, even in a new form; it is much more than stylistics. It has a much broader perspective; its object is constituted not by simple accidents of form, but by the very relationships between the writer [*scripteur, not écrivain*] and language. This perspective does not imply a lack of interest in language but, on the contrary, a continual return to the 'truths' – provisional though they may be – of linguistic anthropology. I will recall certain of these truths because they still have a power of challenge in respect to a certain current idea of literature.

One of the teachings of contemporary linguistics is that there is no archaic language, or at the very least that there is no connection between simplicity and the age of a language: ancient languages can be just as complete and as complex as recent languages; there is no progressive history of languages. Therefore, when we try to find certain fundamental categories of language in modern writing, we are not claiming to reveal a certain archaism of the 'psyche'; we are not saying that the writer is returning to the origin of language, but that language is the origin for him.

A second principle, particularly important in regard to literature, is that language cannot be considered as a simple instrument, whether utilitarian or decorative, of thought. Man does not exist prior to language, either as a species or as an individual. We never find a state where man is separated from language, which he then creates in order to 'express' what is taking place within him: it is language which teaches the definition of man, not the reverse.

Moreover, from a methodological point of view, linguistics accustoms us to a new type of objectivity. The objectivity that has been required in the human sciences up until now is an objectivity of the given, a total acceptance of the given. Linguistics suggests, on the one hand, that we distinguish levels of analysis and that we describe the distinctive elements of each of these levels; in short, that we establish the distinctness of the fact and not the fact itself. On the other hand, linguistics asks us to recognize that unlike physical and biological facts, cultural facts are always double, that they refer us to something else. As Benveniste remarked, the discovery of the 'duplicity' of language gives Saussure's reflection all its value.[2]

These few preliminaries are contained in one final proposition which justifies all semio-critical research. We see culture more and more as a general system of symbols, governed by the same operations. There is unity in this symbolic field: culture, in all its aspects, is a language. Therefore it is possible today to anticipate the creation of a single, unified science of culture, which will depend on diverse disciplines, all devoted to analyzing, on different levels of description, culture as language. Of course semio-criticism will be only a part of this science, or rather of this discourse on culture. I feel authorized by this unity of the human symbolic field to work on a postulate, which I shall call a postulate of *homology*: the structure of the sentence, the object of linguistics, is found again, homologically, in the structure of works. Discourse is not simply an adding together of sentences: it is, itself, one great sentence. In terms of this hypothesis I would like to confront certain categories of language with the situation of the writer in relation to his writing.

The first of these categories is *temporality*. I think we can all agree that there is a linguistic temporality. This specific time of language is equally different from physical time and from what Benveniste calls 'chronicle time' [*temps chronique*], that is, calendar time.[3] Linguistic time finds quite different expression and *découpages* in various languages. For example, since we are going to be interested in the analysis of myths, many languages have a particular past tense of the verb to indicate the past time of myth. Once thing is sure: linguistic time always has its primary center [*centre générateur*] in the present of the statement [*énonciation*]. This leads us to ask whether there is, homological to linguistic time, a specific time of discourse. On this point we may take Benveniste's explanation that many languages, especially in the Indo-European group, have a double system of time. The first temporal system is that of the discourse itself, which is adapted to the temporality of the speaker [*énonciateur*] and for which the *énonciation* is always the point of origin [*moment générateur*]. The second is the system of history or of narrative, which is adapted to the recounting of past events without any intervention by the speaker and which is consequently deprived of present and future (except periphrastically). The specific tense of this second system is the aorist or its equivalent, such as our *passé simple* or the preterit. This tense (the aorist) is precisely the only one missing from the temporal system of discourse. Naturally the existence of this a-personal system does not contradict the essentially logocentric nature of linguistic time that I have just affirmed. The second system simply lacks the characteristics of the first.

Understood thus as the opposition of two radically different systems, temporality does not have the morphological mark of verbs for its only sign; it is marked by all the signs, often very indirect, which refer either to the a-personal tense of the event or to the personal tense of the locutor. The opposition in its fullness permits us first to account for some pure, or we might say classic, cases: a popular story and the history of France retold in our manuals are purely aoristic narratives; on the contrary, Camus' *L'Etranger*, written in the compound past, is not only a perfect form of autobiography (that of the narrator, and not of the author) but, what is more valuable, it permits us to understand better the apparently anomalous cases.[4] Being a historian, Michelet made all historical time pivot around a point of discourse with which he identified himself – the Revolution. His history is a narrative without the aorist, even if the simple past abounds in it; inversely, the preterit can very well serve to signify not the objective *récit*, but the depersonalisation of the discourse – a phenomenon which is the object of the most lively research in today's literature.

What I would like to add to this linguistic analysis, which comes from Benveniste, is that the distinction between the temporal system of discourse and the temporal system of history is not at all the same distinction as is traditionally made between objective discourse and subjective discourse. For the relationship between the speaker [*énonciateur*] and the referent on the one hand and that between the speaker and his utterance [*énonciation*] on the other hand are not to be confused, and it is only the second relationship which determines the temporal system of discourse.

It seems to me that these facts of language were not readily perceptible so long as literature pretended to be a transparent expression of either objective calendar time or of psychological subjectivity, that is to say, as long as literature maintained a totalitarian ideology of the referent, or more commonly speaking, as long as literature was realistic. Today, however, the literature of which I speak is discovering fundamental subtleties relative to temporality. In reading certain writers who are engaged in this type of exploration we sense that what is recounted in the aorist doesn't seem at all immersed in the past, in what has taken place, but simply in the impersonal [*la non-personne*], which is neither history, nor discursive information [*la science*], and even less the one of anonymous writing. (The *one* is dominated by the indefinite and not by the absence of person. I would even say that the pronoun *one* is marked in relation to person, while, paradoxically, *he* is not.) At the other extreme of the experience of discourse, the present-day writer can no longer content himself with expressing his own present, according to a lyrical plan for example. He must learn to distinguish between the present of the speaker, which is grounded on a psychological fullness, and the present of what is spoken [*la locution*] which is mobile and in which the event and the writing become absolutely coincidental. Thus literature, at least in some of its pursuits, seems to me to be following the same path as linguistics when, along with Gustave Guillaume (a linguist not presently in fashion but who may become so again), it concerns itself with operative time and the time proper to the utterance [*énonciation*] itself.[5]

A second grammatical category which is equally important in linguistics and in literature is that of *person*. Taking linguists and especially Benveniste as my basis once more, I would like to recall that person (in the grammatical sense of the term) certainly seems to be a universal of language, linked to the anthropology of language. Every language, as Benveniste has shown, organizes person into two broad pairs of opposites: a correlation of personality which opposes person (*I or thou*) to non-person, which is *il* (*he or it*), the sign of absence; and, within this first opposing pair, a correlation of subjectivity (once again in the grammatical sense) which opposes two persons, the *I* and the *non-I* (the *thou*). For our purposes we must, along with Benveniste, make three observations. First, the polarity of persons, a fundamental condition of language, is nevertheless peculiar and enigmatic, for this polarity involves neither equality nor symmetry: *I* always has a position of transcendence with respect to *thou*, I being interior to the *énoncé* and *thou* remaining exterior to it; however, *I* and *thou* are reversible – *I* can always become *thou* and vice versa. This is not true of the non-person (*he or it*) which can never reverse itself into person or vice versa. The second observation is that the linguistic *I* can and must be defined in a strictly a-psychological way: *I* is nothing other than 'la personne qui énonce la présente instance de discours contenant l'instance linguistique *je*' (Benveniste ['the person who utters the present instance of discourse containing the linguistic instance *I*']).[6] The last remark is that the *he* or the non-person never reflects the instance of discourse; *he* is situated outside of it. We must give its full weight to Benveniste's recommendation not to represent the *he* as a more or less diminished or removed person: *he* is absolutely non-person, marked by the absence of what specifically constitutes, linguistically, the *I* and the *thou*.

The linguistic explanation provides several suggestions for an analysis of literary discourse. First, whatever varied and clever forms person may take in passing from the level of the sentence to that of discourse, the discourse of the literary work is rigorously submitted to a double system of person and non-person. This fact may be obscured because classical discourse (in a broad sense) to which we are habituated is a mixed discourse which alternates – very quickly, sometimes within the same sentence – personal and a-personal *énonciation*, through a complex play of pronouns and descriptive verbs. In this type of classical or bourgeois story the mixture of person and non-person produces a sort of ambiguous consciousness which succeeds in keeping the personal quality of what is stated while, however, continuously breaking the participation of the *énonciateur* in the *énoncé*.

Many novelistic utterances, written with *he* (in the third person), are nevertheless discourses of the *person* each time that the contents of the statement depend on its subject. If in a novel we read '*the tinkling of the ice against the glass seemed to give Bond a sudden inspiration*', it is certain that the subject of the statement cannot be Bond himself – not because the sentence is written in the third person, since Bond could very well express himself through a *he*, but because of the verb *seem* which becomes a mark of the absence of person. Nevertheless, in spite of the diversity and often even the ruse of the narrative signs of the person, there is never but one sole and great opposition in the discourse, that of the person and the non-person; every narrative or fragment of a narrative is obliged to join one or the other of these extremes. How can we determine this division? In 're-writing' the discourse. If we can translate the *he* into *I* without changing anything else in the utterance, the discourse is in fact personal. In the sentence which we have cited, this transformation is impossible; we cannot say '*the tinkling of the ice seemed to give me a sudden inspiration*'. The sentence is impersonal. Starting from there, we catch a glimpse of how the discourse of the traditional novel is made; on the one hand it alternates the personal and the impersonal very rapidly, often even in the course of the same sentence, so as to produce, if we can speak thus, a proprietary consciousness which retains the mastery of what it states without participating in it; and on the other hand, in this type of novel, or rather, according to our perspective, in this type of discourse, when the narrator is explicitly an *I* (which has happened many times) there is confusion between the subject of the discourse and the subject of the reported action, as if – and this is a common belief – he who is speaking today were the same as he who acted yesterday. It is as if there were a continuity of the referent and the utterance through the person, as if the declaring were only a docile servant of the referent.

Now if we return to the linguistic definition of the first person (the one who says 'I' in the present instance of discourse), we may better understand the effort of certain contemporary writers (in France I think of Philippe Sollers's latest novel *Drame*) when they try to distinguish, at the level of the story, psychological person and the author of the writing. When a narrator recounts what has happened to him, the *I* who recounts is no longer the same *I* as the one that is recounted. In other words – and it seems to me that this is seen more and more clearly – the *I* of discourse can no longer be a place where a previously stored-up person is innocently restored. Absolute recourse to the instance of discourse to determine person is termed *nyn-egocentrism* by Damourette and Pichon (*nyn* from the Greek *nun*, 'now').[7] Robbe-Grillet's novel *Dans le labyrinthe* begins with an admirable declaration of nyn-egocentrism: 'Je suis seul ici maintenant.' [I am alone here now.][8] This recourse, imperfectly as it may still be practiced, seems to be a weapon against the general 'bad faith' of discourse which would make literary form simply the expression of an inferiority constituted previous to and outside of language.

To end this discussion of person, I would like to recall that in the process of communication the course of the *I* is not homogenous. For example, when I use [*libére*] the sign, *I*, I refer to myself inasmuch as I am talking: here there is an act which is always new, even if it is repeated, an act whose sense is always new. However, arriving at its destination, this sign is received by my interlocutor as a stable sign, product of a complete code whose contents are recurrent. In other words, the *I* of the one who writes *I* is not the same as the *I* which is read by *thou*. This fundamental dissymmetry of language, linguistically explained by Jespersen and then by Jakobson under the name of 'shifter' [*embrayeur*] or an overlapping of message and code, seems to be finally beginning to trouble literature in showing it that intersubjectivity, or rather interlocution, cannot be accomplished simply by wishing, but only by a deep, patient, and often circuitous descent into the labyrinths of meaning.[9]

There remains one last grammatical notion which can, in my opinion, further elucidate the activity of writing at its center, since it concerns the verb *to write* itself. It would be interesting to know at what point the verb *to write* began to be used in an apparently intransitive manner, the writer being no longer one who writes *something*, but one who writes, absolutely. (How often now we hear in conversations, at least in more or less intellectual circles: 'What is he doing?' – 'He's writing.') This passage from the verb *to write*, transitive, to the verb *to write*, apparently intransitive, is certainly the sign of an important change in mentality. But is it really a question of intransitivity? No writer, whatever age he belongs to, can fail to realise that he always writes *something*: one might even say that it was paradoxically at the moment when the verb *to write* appeared to become intransitive that its object, the book or the text, took on a particular importance. It is not, therefore, in spite of the appearances, on the side of intransitivity that we must look for the definition of the modern verb *to write*. Another linguistic notion will perhaps give us the key: that of *diathesis*, or, as it is called in classical grammars, *voice* (active, passive, middle). Diathesis designates the way in which the subject of the verb is affected by the action [*procès*]; this is obvious for the passive (if I say 'I am beaten', it is quite obvious that I am profoundly affected by the action of the verb *to beat*). And yet linguists tell us that, at least in Indo-European, the diathetical opposition is actually not between the active and the passive, but between the active and the middle. According to the classic example, given by Meillet and Benveniste, the verb *to sacrifice* (ritually) is active if the priest sacrifices the victim in my place for me, and it is middle voice if, taking the knife from the priest's hands, I make the sacrifice for myself.[10] In the case of the active, the action is accomplished outside the subject, because, although the priest makes the sacrifice, he is not affected by it. In the case of the middle voice, on the contrary, the subject affects himself in acting; he always remains inside the action, even if an object is involved. The middle voice does not, therefore, exclude transitivity. Thus defined, the middle voice corresponds exactly to the state of the verb *to write*: today to write is to make oneself the center of the action of speech [*parole*]; it is to effect writing in being affected oneself; it is to leave the writer [*scripteur*] inside the writing, not as a psychological subject (the Indo-European priest could very well overflow with subjectivity in actively sacrificing for his client), but as the agent of the action.

I think the diathetical analysis of the modern verb *to write*, which I have just tried to show a verb of middle voice, can be carried even further. You know that in French – for I am obliged to refer to strictly French examples – certain verbs have an active meaning in the simple form, for example, *aller, arriver, rentrer, sortir* [to go, to arrive, to return, to go out], but, curiously, these active verbs take the passive auxiliary, the verb *être* [to be] in the forms of *the passé composé*. Instead of saying *j'ai allé*, we say *je suis allé, je suis sorti, je suis arrivé, je suis rentré*, etc. To explain this bifurcation peculiar to the middle voice, Guillaume distinguishes between two *passés composés*. The first, which he calls *diriment*, 'separated,' is a *passé composé* with the auxiliary *avoir* [to have]; this tense supposes an interruption of the action due to the initiative of the speaker. Take for example the verb *marcher* [to walk], an entirely commonplace active verb: *'je marche; je m'arrête de marcher; j'ai marché* [I walk; I stop walking (by my own initiative); I have walked] - this is the *passé composé diriment*. The other *passé composé* that he calls *intégrant* is constructed with the verb *étre* [to be]; it designates a sort of semantic entity which cannot be delivered by the simple initiative of the subject. *'Je suis sorti'* or *'il est mort'* ['I went out' or 'he died'] (for I can't say 'I am dead') never refer to an interruption that would be at all like the *diriment* of the going out or the dying. I believe that this is an important opposition, for we see very well that the verb *to write* was traditionally an active verb and that its past tense is still today, formally a *diriment* past: *'jécris un livre; je le termine; je l'ai écrit.'* [I write a book; I end it; I have written it.] But in our literature, it seems to me, the verb is changing status, if not form, and the verb *to write* is becoming a middle verb with an *intégrant* past. This is true inasmuch as the modern verb *to write* is becoming a sort of indivisible semantic entity. So that if language followed literature – which, for once perhaps, has the lead – I would say that we should no longer say today *'j'ai écrit'* but, rather, *'je suis écrit'*, just as we say *'je suis né, il est mort, elle est éclose.'* There is no passive idea in these expressions, in spite of the verb *to be*, for it is impossible to transform *'je suis écrit'* (without forcing things, and supposing that I dare to use this expression at all) into *'on m'a écrit'* ['I have been written' or 'somebody wrote me']. It is my opinion that in the middle verb *to write* the distance between the writer and the language diminishes asymptotically. We could even say that it is subjective writings, like romantic writing, which are active, because in them the agent is not interior but *anterior* to the process of writing. The one who writes here does not write for himself, but, as if by proxy, for a person who is exterior and antecedent (even if they both have the same name). In the modern verb of middle voice *to write*, however, the subject is immediately contemporary with the writing, being effected and affected by it. The case of the Proustian narrator is exemplary: he exists only in writing.

These remarks suggest that the central problem of modern writing exactly coincides with what we could call the problematic of the verb in linguistics; just as temporality, person, and diathesis define the positional field of the subject, so modern literature is trying, through various experiments, to establish a new status in writing for the agent of writing. The meaning or the goal of this effort is to substitute the instance of discourse for the instance of reality (or of the referent),which has been, and still is, a mythical 'alibi' dominating the idea of literature. The field of the writer is nothing but writing itself, not as the pure 'form' conceived by an aesthetic of art for art's sake, but, much more radically, as the only area [*espace*] for the one who writes.

It seems to me to be necessary to remind those who might be tempted to accuse this kind of inquiry of solipsism, formalism, or, inversely, of scientism, that in returning to the fundamental categories of language, such as person, tense, and voice, we place ourselves at the very heart of a problematic of *inter*locution. For these categories are precisely those in which we may examine the relationships between the *je* and that which is deprived of the mark of *je*. Inasmuch as person, tense, and voice imply those remarkable linguistic beings – the 'shifters' – they oblige us to conceive language and discourse no longer in terms of an instrumental and reified nomenclature but in the very exercise of language [*parole*]. The pronoun, for example, which is without doubt the most staggering of the 'shifters', belongs structurally to speech [*parole*]. That is its scandal, if you like, and it is on this scandal that we must work today, in linguistics and literature. We are all trying, with different methods, styles, perhaps even prejudices, to get to the core of this linguistic pact [*pacte de parole*] which unites the writer and the other, so that – and this is a contradiction which will never be sufficiently pondered – each moment of discourse is both absolutely new and absolutely understood. I think that, with a certain amount of temerity, we could even give a historical dimension to this research. We know that the medieval *septenium*, in its grandiose classification of the universe, prescribed two great areas of exploration: on the one hand, the secrets of nature (the *quadrivium*) and, on the other, the secrets of language [*parole*] (the *trivium: grammatica, rhetorics, dialectica*). From the end of the Middle Ages to the present day, this opposition was lost, language being considered only as an instrument in the service of either reason or the heart. Today, however, something of this ancient opposition lives again: once again the exploration of language, conducted by linguistics, psychoanalysis, and literature, corresponds to the exploration of the cosmos. For literature is itself a science, or at least knowledge, no longer of the 'human heart' but of human language [*parole*]. Its investigation is not, however, addressed to the secondary forms and figures that were the object of rhetoric, but to the fundamental categories of language. Just as in Western culture grammar was not born until long after rhetoric, so it is only after having made its way for centuries through *le beau littéraire* that literature can begin to ponder the fundamental problems of language, without which it would not exist.

Notes

1 'Ecrire: Verbe intransitif?' The translation which follows is a composite of the communication which M. Barthes distributed in advance to the Symposium participants and the actual transcription of his address. The notes have been supplied by the translator.

2 Emile Benveniste, *Problèmes de la linguistique générale* (Paris, 1966), p 40. 'Qu'est-ce donc que cet object, que Saussure érige sur une table rase de toutes les notions reçues? Nous touchons ici à ce qu'il y a de primordial dans la doctrine saussurienne, à un principe qui présume une intuition totale du language, totale à la fois parce qu'elle embrasse la totalité de son objet. Ce principe est que *le langage*, sous quelque point de vue qu'on l'étudie, *est toujours un objet double*, formé de deux parties dont l'une ne vaut que par l'autre.'

3 Cf. Benveniste, 'Les Relations de temps dans le verbe français', ibid., pp. 237–50.

4 Cf. Jean-Paul Sartre, 'Explication de *L'Etranger*', *Situations* I (Paris, 1947), pp. 99–121.

5 Gustave Guillaume, *L'Architectonique du temps dans les langues classiques* (Copenhagen 1945). The work of Guillaume (who died in 1960) toward a 'psycho-systématique' has been continued in the contributions of Roch Valin (*Petite introduction à la psychomécanique du langage* [Québec, 1954]). For a statement by Guillaume about his relation to the tradition of Saussure. see *La langue est-elle ou n'est-elle pas un système? Cahiers de linguistique structurale de l'Université de Québec*, I (1952), p. 4.

6 Benveniste, *Problèmes de la linguistique générale*, p. 252.

7 J. Damourette and E. Pichon, *Des mots à la pensée: Essai de grammaire de la langue française* (Paris, 1911–36), V, #1604 and Vll, #2958. 'Le langage est naturellement centré sur le moi-ici-maintenant, c'est-à-dire sur la personne qui parle s'envisageant au moment même où elle parle; c'est ce qu'on peut appeler le *nynégocentrisme* naturel du langage' [#1604].

8 *Dans le labyrinthe* (Paris: Editions de Minuit, 1959). For essays by Roland Barthes bearing on the fictional method and theory of Robbe-Grillet, see *Essais critiques* (Paris, 1964), pp. 29–40, 63–70, 198–205.

9 Cf. Jakobson, *Shifters, Verbal Categories, and the Russian Verb* (Cambridge, Mass., 1957). [Translated into French by Nicolas Ruwet in *Essais de linguistique générale* (Paris, 1963), pp. 176–96.] For the origin of the term 'shifter,' see Otto Jespersen, *Language, its Nature, Development and Origin* (London, 1922), p. 123, and ibid., *The Philosophy of Grammar* (London, 1923), pp. 83–4.

10 Benveniste, 'Actif et moyen dans le verbe', *Problèmes de la linguistique générale*, pp. 168–75. Cf. the distinction initiated by Pānini (fl. 350 BC): *parasmaipada*, 'word for another', i.e., active, and *āmanepada*, word for self', middle. Thus *yajati* ('he sacrifices' [for another, *qua* priest]) vs. *yajate* ('he sacrifices' [for himself, *qua* offering]). Cf. Berthold Delbrück, *Vergleichende Syntax der Indogermanischen Sprachen* (Strassburg, 1893).

SECTION FOUR
MARXISM

Broadly speaking, as an approach to literature, Marxism attempts to draw conclusions about the relations between the literary and the social. Recent Marxist literary theory has been heavily influenced by the work of the French philosopher Louis Althusser and the literary critic, Pierre Macherey. Whilst these figures claim not to be Structuralists, and have explicitly criticised Structuralism, their theories exhibit striking similarities to aspects of Structuralist thought.[1] Indeed Raman Selden, in his account of contemporary literary theory,[2] considers them under the heading of 'Structuralist Marxism', and critics who have drawn upon Althusser's work are likely also to draw upon Structuralist/semiotic theories.

The initial influence of Structuralist Marxism on literary theory centred mainly around the concept of ideology, though Althusser's notion of 'Ideological State Apparatus' and of the construction ('interpellation') of the human subject has been taken up in some post-structuralist work. The extract reprinted here comes from Althusser's seminal essay 'Ideology and the State'[3] and whilst a full account of his work is not possible some contextualizing remarks seem necessary. We can start by saying that 'ideology' reproduces 'subjects' who are willing workers in the capitalist system. Capitalism requires not only the hands of labour, but also the willingness of workers to subject themselves to the system – to accept the 'status quo' – and it is in this area that ideology works. The central feature of Althusser's Marxism and one of the key areas of differences between his and previous Marxisms, is the way in which he conceived ideology.

For Althusser, ideology is not a matter of conscious beliefs, attitudes and values, nor is it a matter of 'false consciousness' – sets of false ideas imposed on individuals to persuade them that there is no real contradiction between capital and labour or, more crudely, between the interests of the working class and ruling class. It is, rather, a matter of the representation of imaginary versions of the real social relations that people live. These imaginary versions of the real relations are necessary for the perpetuation of the capitalist system. Ideology imposes itself not simply through consciousness nor through disembodied ideas but through systems and structures; ideology is inscribed in the representations (the signs) and the practices (the rituals) of everyday life. Most importantly, though, it is through ideology that individuals are constituted as 'subjects' – (mis)recognizing themselves as free and autonomous beings with unique subjectivities.

The main agencies for the reproduction of ideology and the subject are what Althusser calls the 'Ideological State Apparatuses' (ISAs), which include the church, the family, the media, and the cultural ISAs (literature, the arts, sports, etc.). The extract reprinted here begins with a consideration of Ideological State Apparatuses.

Balibar and Macherey take up Althusser's notion of ISAs. They examine the way that literature functions in the reproduction of ideology within the ISAs of the French education system. Literature, in their article, is seen in terms of the acquisition and distribution of what the French sociologist of culture, Pierre Bourdieu, has called 'cultural capital'. However, a residue of Macherey's previous work in *A Theory of Literary Production*[4] can be seen in the discussion of the relation between the literary text and social reality. *A Theory of Literary Production* had been an influential book offering a model of textual analysis based on Althusser's notion of 'symptomatic' reading. This model involved uncovering the significant absences of the texts, the ideological presuppositions on which the text was at once founded but of which it could not speak. It is a difficult model to grasp but a good account can be found in Jefferson and Robey[5] and an interesting adaptation of the model appears in Belsey.[6]

Terry Eagleton, in *Criticism and Ideology*,[7] draws on the work of Althusser and Macherey to provide a general framework for understanding the relation between the literary text and the social world, and for a model of textual analysis which will reveal the 'ideology of the text'. Literary works are scrutinized for the symptoms of the ideology that form the raw material of their production. Such a critical enterprise is now frequently undertaken, often in conjunction with a version of semiotics which looks at the 'representations' inscribed in texts. This mode of analysis owes a debt also to Roland Barthes, who had woven a notion of ideology into the semiotic model in *Mythologies*.[8]

Aspects of both Althusser's and Macherey's work would seem to be more in line with material represented in Part Two of this book – Althusser's notion of the interpellation of the subject, and his radical attack on humanism; Macherey's concern with 'absences' and with the practices of the institution of literary studies. However, their belief in a scientific procedure which would yield knowledge and explanation, their placing of literature between the realms of ideology and science, and their reification of structure, all connect them, if not wholly satisfactorily, to the material of Part One. Additionally, their initial influence on literary theory produced a critical practice that, in its endeavour to analyse and understand texts, belongs to the less radical break with the critical orthodoxy.

Notes

1 B. Harland, *Superstructuralism* (London, Methuen, 1987).
2 R. Selden, *A Reader's Guide to Contemporary Literary Theory* (Brighton, Sussex, Harvester Press).
3 L. Althusser, *Lenin and Philosophy and Other Essays*, tr. B. Brewster (London, New Left Books, 1977).
4 P. Macherey, *A Theory of Literary Production*, tr. G. Wall (London, Routledge & Kegan Paul, 1978).
5 A. Jefferson and D. Robey, eds. *Modern Literary Theory: A Comparative Introduction* (London, Batsford Academic and Educational Ltd, 1982).
6 C. Belsey, *Critical Practice* (London, Methuen, 1980).
7 T. Eagleton, *Criticism and Ideology* (London, New Left Books, 1976).
8 R. Barthes, *Mythologies*, tr. A. Lavers (London, Jonathan Cape, 1972).

5   Louis Althusser,

From 'Ideology and the State', in B. Brewster, tr. *Lenin and Philosophy and Other Essays* (1969), pp. 136–8; 152–3; 154–5; 155–6; 160–2; 162–4; 168–9

What are the ideological State apparatuses (ISAs)?

They must not be confused with the (repressive) State apparatus. Remember that in Marxist theory, the State Apparatus (SA) contains: the Government, the Administration, the Army, the Police, the Courts, the Prisons, etc., which constitute what I shall in future call the Repressive State Apparatus. Repressive suggests that the State Apparatus in question 'functions by violence' – at least ultimately (since repression, e.g. administrative repression, may take non-physical forms).

I shall call Ideological State Apparatuses a certain number of realities which present themselves to the immediate observer in the form of distinct and specialized institutions. I propose an empirical list of these which obviously have to be examined in detail, tested, corrected and reorganized. With all the reservations implied by this requirement, we can for the moment regard the following in situations as Ideological State Apparatuses (the order in which I have listed them has no particular significance):

- the religious ISA (the system of the different Churches),
- the educational ISA (the system of the different public and private 'Schools'),
- the family ISA,[1]
- the legal ISA,[2]
- the political ISA (the political system, including the different Parties),
- the trade-union ISA,

- the communications ISA (press, radio and television, etc.),
- the cultural ISA (Literature, the Arts, sports, etc.).

I have said that the ISAs must not be confused with the (Repressive) state Apparatus. What constitutes the difference?

As a first moment, it is clear that while there is *one* (Repressive) State apparatus, there is a *plurality* of Ideological State Apparatuses. Even presupposing that it exists, the unity that constitutes this plurality of ISAs as a body is not immediately visible.

As a second moment, it is clear that whereas the – unified – (Repressive) State Apparatus belongs entirely to the *public* domain, much the larger part of the Ideological State Apparatuses (in their apparent dispersion) are part, on the contrary, of the *private* domain. Churches, Parties, Trade Unions, families, some schools, most newspapers, cultural ventures, etc., etc., are private.

We can ignore the first observation for the moment. But someone is bound to question the second, asking me by what right I regard as Idealogical *State* Apparatuses, institutions which for the most part do not possess public status, but are quite simply *private* institutions. As a conscious Marxist, Gramsci already forestalled this objection in one sentence. The distinction between the public and the private is a distinction internal to bourgeois law, and valid in the (subordinate) domains in which bourgeois law exercises its 'authority'. The domain of the State escapes it because the latter is 'above the law': the State, which is the State of the ruling class, is neither public nor private; on the contrary, it is the precondition for any distinction between public and private. The same thing can be said from the starting-point of our State Ideological Apparatuses. It is unimportant whether the institutions in which they are realized are 'public' or 'private'. What matters is how they function. Private institutions can perfectly well 'function' as Ideological State Apparatuses. A reasonably thorough analysis of any one of the ISAs proves it.

But now for what is essential. What distinguishes the ISAs from the (Repressive) State Apparatus is the following basic difference: the Repressive State Apparatus functions 'by violence', whereas the Ideological State Apparatuses *function 'by ideology'*.

I can clarify matters by correcting this distinction. I shall say rather that every State Apparatus, whether Repressive or Ideological, 'functions' both by violence and by ideology, but with one very important distinction which makes it imperative not to confuse the Ideological State Apparatuses with the (Repressive) State Apparatus.

This is the fact that the (Repressive) State Apparatus functions massively and predominantly *by repression* (including physical repression), while functioning secondarily by ideology. (There is no such thing as a purely repressive apparatus.) For example, the Army and the Police also function by ideology both to ensure their own cohesion and reproduction, and in the 'values' they propound externally.

In the same way, but inversely, it is essential to say that for their part the Ideological State Apparatuses function massively and predominantly by *ideology*, but they also function secondarily by repression, even if ultimately, but only ultimately, this is very attentuated and concealed, even symbolic. (There is no such thing as purely ideological apparatus.) Thus Schools and Churches use suitable methods of punishment, expulsion, selection, etc., to 'discipline' not only their shepherds, but also their flocks. The same is true of the Family. . . . The same is true of the cultural IS Apparatus (censorship, among other things), etc.

. . . .

Ideology is a 'Representation' of the Imaginary Relationship of Individuals to their Real Conditions of Existence

In order to approach my central thesis on the structure and functioning of ideology, I shall first present two theses, one negative, the other positive. The first concerns the object which is 'represented' in the imaginary form of ideology, the second concerns the materiality of ideology.

THESIS I   Ideology represents the imaginary relationship of individuals to their real conditions of existence.

We commonly call religious ideology, ethical ideology, legal ideology, political ideology, etc., so many 'world outlooks'. Of course, assuming that we do not live one of these ideologies as the truth (e.g. 'believe' in God, Duty, Justice, etc. . . .), we admit that the ideology we are discussing from a critical point of view, examining it as the ethnologist examines the myths of a 'primitive society', that these 'world outlooks' are largely imaginary, i.e. do not 'correspond to reality'.

However, while admitting that they do not correspond to reality, i.e. that they constitute an illusion, we admit that they do make allusion to reality, and that they need only be 'interpreted' to discover the reality of the world behind their imaginary representation of that world (ideology = *illusion/ allusion*).

. . . .

Now I can return to a thesis which I have already advanced: it is not their real conditions of existence, their real world, that 'men' 'represent to themselves' in ideology, but above all it is their relation to those conditions of existence which is represented to them there. It is this relation which is at the centre of every ideological, i.e. imaginary, representation of the real world. It is this relation that contains the 'cause' which has to explain the imaginary distortion of the ideological representation of the real world. Or rather, to leave aside the language of causality it is necessary to advance the thesis that it is the *imaginary nature of this relation* which underlies all the imaginary distortion that we can observe (if we do not live in its truth) in all ideology.

To speak in a Marxist language, if it is true that the representation of the real conditions of existence of the individuals occupying the posts of agents of production, exploitation, repression, ideologization and scientific practices, does in the last analysis arise from the relations of production, and from relations deriving from the relations of production, we can say the following: all ideology represents in its necessarily imaginary distortion not the existing relations of production (and the other relations that derive from them), but above all the (imaginary) relationship of individuals to the relations of production and the relations that derive from them. What is represented in ideology is therefore not the system of the real relations which govern the existence of individuals, but the imaginary relation of those individuals to the real relations in which they live.

. . . .

THESIS II   Ideology has a material existence.
I have already touched on this thesis by saying that the 'ideas' or 'representations', etc., which seem to make up ideology do not have an ideal (*idéale and idéelle*) or spiritual existence, but a material existence. I even suggested that the ideal (*idéale, idéelle*) and spiritual existence of 'ideas' arises exclusively in an ideology of the 'idea' and of ideology, and let me add, in an ideology of what seems to have 'founded' this conception since the emergence of the sciences, i.e. what the practicians of the sciences represent to themselves in their spontaneous ideology as 'ideas', true or false. Of course, presented in affirmative form, this thesis is unproven. I simply ask that the reader be favourably disposed towards it, say, in the name of materialism. A long series of arguments would be necessary to prove it.

This hypothetical thesis of the not spiritual but material existence of 'ideas' or other 'representations' is indeed necessary if we are to advance in our analysis of the nature of ideology. Or rather, it is merely useful to us in order the better to reveal what every at all serious analysis of any ideology will immediately and empirically show to every observer, however critical.

While discussing the ideological State apparatuses and their practices, I said that each of them was the realization of an ideology (the unity of these different regional ideologies – religious, ethical, legal, political, aesthetic, etc. – being assured by their subjection to the ruling ideology). I now return to this thesis: an ideology always exists in an apparatus, and its practice, or practices. This existence is material.

Of course, the material existence of the ideology in an apparatus and its practices does not have the same modality as the material existence of a paving-stone or a rifle. But, at the risk of being taken for a Neo-Aristotelian

(NB Marx had a very high regard for Aristotle), I shall say that 'matter is discussed in many senses', or rather that it exists in different modalities, all rooted in the last instance in 'physical' matter.

. . . .

Ideology Interpellates Individuals as Subjects

This thesis is simply a matter of making my last proposition explicit: there is no ideology except by the subject and for subjects. Meaning, there is no ideology except for concrete subjects, and this destination for ideology is only made possible by the subject: meaning, *by the category of the subject* and its functioning.

By this I mean that, even if it only appears under this name (the subject) with the rise of bourgeois ideology, above all with the rise of legal ideology,[3] the category of the subject (which may function under other names: e.g., as the soul in Plato, as God, etc.) is the constitutive category of all ideology, whatever its determination (regional or class) and whatever its historical date – since ideology has no history.

I say: the category of the subject is constitutive of all ideology, but at the same time and immediately I add that *the category of the subject is only constitutive of all ideology insofar as all ideology has the function (which defines it) of 'constituting' concrete individuals as subjects*. In the interaction of this double constitution exists the functioning of all ideology, ideology being nothing but its functioning in the material forms of existence of that functioning.

In order to grasp what follows, it is essential to realize that both he who is writing these lines and the reader who reads them are themselves subjects, and therefore ideological subjects (a tautological proposition), i.e. that the author and the reader of these lines both live 'spontaneously' or 'naturally' in ideology in the sense in which I have said that 'man is an ideological animal by nature'.

That the author, insofar as he writes the lines of a discourse which claims to be scientific, is completely absent as a 'subject' from 'his' scientific discourse (for all scientific discourse is by definition a subject-less discourse, there is no 'Subject of science' except in an ideology of Science) is a different question which I shall leave on one side for the moment.

As St Paul admirably put it, it is in the 'Logos', meaning in ideology, that we 'live, move and have our being'. It follows that, for you and for me, the category of the subject is a primary 'obviousness' (obviousnesses are always primary): it is clear that you and I are subjects (free, ethical, etc. . . .). Like all obviousnesses, including those that make a word 'name a thing' or 'have a meaning' (therefore including the obviousness of the 'transparency' of language), the 'obviousness' that you and I are subjects – and that that does not cause any problems – is an ideological effect, the elementary ideological effect.[4] It is indeed a peculiarity of ideology that it imposes (without appearing to do so, since these are 'obviousnesses') obviousnesses as obviousnesses, which we cannot *fail to recognize* and before which we have the inevitable and natural reaction of crying out (aloud or in the 'still, small voice of conscience'): 'That's obvious! That's right! That's true!'

At work in this reaction is the ideological *recognition* function which is one of the two functions of ideology as such (its inverse being the function of *misrecognition – méconnaissance*).

To take a highly 'concrete' example, we all have friends who, when they knock on our door and we ask, through the door, the question 'Who's there?', answer (since 'it's obvious') It's me'. And we recognize (that 'it is him', or 'her'. We open the door, and 'it's true, it really was she who was there'. To take another example, when we recognize somebody of our (previous) acquaintance (*(re)-connaissance*) in the street, we show him that we have recognized him (and have recognized that he has recognized us) by saying to him 'Hello, my friend', and shaking his hand (a material ritual practice of ideological recognition in everyday life – in France, at least; elsewhere, there are other rituals).

In this preliminary remark and these concrete illustrations, I only wish to point out that you and I are *always already* subjects, and as such constantly practice the rituals of ideological recognition, which guarantee for us that we are indeed concrete, individual, distinguishable and (naturally) irreplaceable subjects. The writing I am currently executing and the reading you are currently[5] performing are also in this respect rituals of ideological recognition, including the 'obviousness' with which the 'truth' or 'error' of my reflections may impose itself on you.

. . . .

As a first formulation I shall say: *all ideology hails or interpellates concrete individuals as concrete subjects*, by the functioning of the category of the subject.

This is a proposition which entails that we distinguish for the moment between concrete individuals on the one hand and concrete subjects on the other, although at this level concrete subjects only exist insofar as they are supported by a concrete individual.

I shall then suggest that ideology 'acts' or 'functions' in such a way that it 'recruits' subjects among the individuals (it recruits them all), or 'transforms' the individuals into subjects (it transforms them all) by that very precise operation which I have called *interpellation* or hailing, and which can be imagined along the lines of the commonplace everyday police (or other) hailing: 'Hey, you there!'[6]

Assuming that the theoretical scene I have imagined takes place in the street, the hailed individual will turn round. By this mere one-hundred-and-eighty-degree physical conversion, he becomes a *subject*. Why? Because he has recognized that the hail was 'really' addressed to him, and that 'it was *really him* who was hailed' (and not someone else). Experience shows that the practical telecommunication of hailings is such that they hardly ever miss their man: verbal call or whistle, the one hailed always recognizes that it is really him who is being hailed. And yet it is a strange phenomenon, and one which cannot be explained solely by 'guilt feelings', despite the large numbers who 'have something on their consciences'.

Naturally for the convenience and clarity of my little theoretical theatre I have had to present things in the form of a sequence, with a before and an after, and thus in the form of a temporal succession. There are individuals walking along. Somewhere (usually behind them) the hail rings out: 'Hey, you there!' One individual (nine times out of ten it is the right one) turns round, believing/suspecting/knowing that it is for him, i.e. recognizing that 'it really is he' who is meant by the hailing. But in reality these things happen without any succession. The existence of ideology and the hailing or interpellation of individuals as subjects are one and the same thing.

I might add: what thus seems to take place outside ideology (to be precise, in the street), in reality takes place in ideology. What really takes place in ideology seems therefore to take place outside it. That is why those who are in ideology believe themselves by definition outside ideology: one of the effects of ideology is the practical *denegation* of the ideological character of ideology by ideology: ideology never says, 'I am ideological'. It is necessary to be outside ideology, i.e. in scientific knowledge, to be able to say: I am in ideology (a quite exceptional case) or (the general case): I was in ideology. As is well known, the accusation of being in ideology only applies to others, never to oneself (unless one is really a Spinozist or a Marxist, which, in this matter, is to be exactly the same thing). Which amounts to saying that ideology *has no outside* (for itself), but at the same time *that it is nothing but outside* (for science and reality).

. . . .

Let me summarise what we have discovered about ideology in general. The duplicate mirror-structure of ideology ensures simultaneously:

1 the interpellation of 'individuals' as subjects;
2 their subjection to the Subject;
3 the mutual recognition of subjects and Subject, the subjects' recognition of each other, and finally the subject's recognition of himself;[7]
4 the absolute guarantee that everything really is so, and that on condition that the subjects recognize what they are and behave accordingly, everything will be all right: Amen – 'So be it'.

Result: caught in this quadruple system of interpellation as subjects, of subjection to the Subject, of universal recognition and of absolute guarantee, the subjects 'work', they 'work by themselves' in the vast majority of cases, with the exception of the 'bad subjects' who on occasion provoke the intervention of one of the detachments of the (repressive) State apparatus. But the vast majority of (good) subjects work all right 'all by themselves', i.e. by ideology (whose concrete forms are realized in the Ideological State Apparatuses). They are inserted into practices governed by the rituals of the ISAs. They 'recognize' the existing state of affairs (*das Bestehende*), that 'it really is true that it is so and not otherwise', and that they must be obedient to God, to their conscience, to the priest, to de Gaulle, to the boss, to the engineer, that thou shalt 'love thy neighbour as thyself', etc. Their concrete, material behaviour is simply the inscription in life of the admirable words of the prayer: *'Amen – So be it'*.

Yes, the subjects 'work by themselves'. The whole mystery of this effect lies in the first two moments of the quadruple system I have just discussed, or, if you prefer, in the ambiguity of the term *subject*. In the ordinary use of the term, subject in fact means: (1) a free subjectivity, a centre of initiatives, author of and responsible for its actions; (2) a subjected being, who submits to a higher authority, and is therefore stripped of all freedom except that of freely accepting his submission. This last note gives us the meaning of this ambiguity, which is merely a reflection of the effect which produces it: the individual *is interpellated as a (free) subject in order that he shall submit freely to the commandments of the Subject, i.e. in order that he shall (freely) accept his subjection,* i.e. in order that he shall make the gestures and actions of his subjection 'all by himself'. *There are no subjects except by and for their subjection.* That is why they 'work all by themselves'.

Notes

1 The family obviously has other 'functions' than that of an ISA. It intervenes in the reproduction of labour power. In different modes of production it is the unit of production and/or the unit of consumption.

2 The 'Law' belongs both to the (Repressive) State Apparatus and to the system of the ISAs.

3 Which borrowed the legal category of 'subject in law' to make an ideological notion: man is by nature a subject.

4 Linguists and those who appeal to linguistics for various purposes often run up against difficulties which arise because they ignore the action of the ideological effects in all discourses – including even scientific discourses.

5 NB: this double 'currently' is one more proof of the fact that ideology is 'eternal', since these 'two 'currentlys' are separated by an indefinite interval; I am writing these lines on 6 April 1969, you may read them at any subsequent time.

6 Hailing as an everyday practice subject to a precise ritual takes a quite 'special' form in the policeman's practice of 'hailing' which concerns the hailing of 'suspects'.

7 Hegel is (unknowingly) an admirable 'theoretician' of ideology insofar as he is a

'theoretician' of Universal Recognition who unfortunately ends up in the ideology of Absolute Knowledge. Feuerbach is an astonishing 'theoretician' of the mirror connexion, who unfortunately ends up in the ideology of the Human Essence. To find the material with which to construct a theory of the guarantee, we must turn to Spinoza.

6 E. Balibar and P. Macherey,

From 'Literature as an Ideological Form', *Oxford Literary Review*, Vol. 3:1 (1978) pp. 6; 8; 11–12

Literature as an Ideological Form

It is important to 'locate' the production of literary effects historically as part of the ensemble of social practices. For this to be seen dialectically rather than mechanically, it is important to understand that the relationship of 'history' to 'literature' is not like the relationship or 'correspondence' of *two 'branches'*, but concerns the developing forms of an internal *contradiction*. Literature and history are not each set up externally to each other (not even as the history *of* literature, social and political history), but are in an intricate and connected relationship, the historical conditions of existence of anything like a literature. Very generally, this internal relationship is what constitutes the definition of literature as an ideological form.

But this definition is significant only in so far as its implications are then developed. Ideological forms, to be sure, are not straightforward systems of 'ideas' and 'discourses', but are manifested through the workings and history of determinate *practices* in determinate social relations, what Althusser calls the *Ideological State Apparatus* (ISA). The objectivity of literary production therefore is inseparable from given social practices in a given ISA. More precisely, we shall see that it is inseparable from a given *linguistic practice* (there is a 'French' literature because there is a linguistic practice 'French', i.e., a contradictory ensemble making a national tongue), in itself inseparable from an *academic or schooling practice* which defines both the conditions for the consumption of literature and the very conditions of its production also. By connecting the objective existence of literature to this ensemble of practices, one can define the material anchoring points which *make* literature an historic and social reality.

First, then, literature is historically constituted *in the bourgeois epoch* as an ensemble of language – or rather of specific linguistic practices – inserted in a general schooling process so as to provide appropriate fictional effects, thereby reproducing bourgeois ideology as the dominant ideology. Literature submits to a threefold determination: 'linguistic', 'pedagogic', and 'fictive' [*imaginaire*] (we must return to this point, for it involves the question of a recourse to psycho-analysis for an explanation of literary effects). There is a linguistic determination because the work of literary production depends on the existence of a common language codifying linguistic exchange, both for its material and for its aims – insomuch as literature *contributes* directly to the *maintenance* of a '*common* language'. That it has this starting point is proved by the fact that divergences from the common language are not arbitrary but determined. In our introduction to the work of R. Balibar and D. Laporte,[1] we sketched out an explanation of the historical process by which this 'common language' is set up. Following their thought, we stressed that the common language, i.e. the *national language*, is bound to the political form of 'bourgeois democracy' and is the historical outcome of particular class struggles. Like bourgeois *right*, its parallel, the common national language is needed to unify a new class domination thereby universalising it and providing it with progressive forms throughout its epoch. It refers therefore to a social *contradiction* perpetually reproduced via the process which surmounts it. What is the basis of this contradiction?

It is the effect of the historic conditions under which the bourgeois class established its political, economic and ideological dominance. To achieve hegemony, it had not only to transform the base, the relations of production, but also radically to transform the superstructure the ideological formations. This transformation could be called the bourgeois 'cultural revolution' since it involves not only the formation of a new ideology, but its realisation as the dominant ideology, through new ISAs and the remoulding of the relationships between the different ISAs. This revolutionary transformation, which took more than a century but which was preparing itself for far longer, is characterised by making the school apparatus the means of forcing submission to the dominant ideology – individual submission, but also, and more importantly, the submission of the very ideology of the dominated classes. Therefore in the last analysis, all the ideological contradictions rest on the contradictions of the school apparatus, and become contradictions subordinated to the form of schooling, within the form of schooling itself.

. . . .

The Specific Complexity of Literary Formations–
Ideological Contradictions and Linguistic Conflicts

The first principle of a materialist analysis would be: literary productions must not be studied from the standpoint of their *unity* which is illusory and false, but from their material *disparity*. One must not look for unifying effects but for signs of the contradictions (historically determined) which produced them and which appear as unevenly resolved conflicts in the text.

So, in searching out the determinant contradictions, the materialist analysis of literature rejects on principle the notion of 'the word' – i.e., the illusory presentation of the unity of a text, its totality, self-sufficiency and perfection (in both senses of the word: success and completion). More precisely, it recognises the notion of 'the work' (and its correlative, 'the author') only in order to identify both as necessary illusions written into the *ideology of literature*, the accompaniment of all literary production. The text is produced under conditions which represent it as a finished work providing a requisite order, expressing either a subjective theme or the spirit of the age, according to whether the reading is a naive or a sophisticated one. Yet in itself the text is none of these things: on the contrary, it is materially incomplete, disparate and diffuse from being the outcome of the conflicting contradictory effect of superimposing real processes which cannot be abolished in it except in an imaginary way.[2]

To be more explicit: literature is produced finally through the effect of one or more ideological contradictions precisely because these contradictions cannot be solved within the ideology, i.e., in the last analysis through the effect of contradictory class positions within the ideology, as such irreconcilable. Obviously these contradictory ideological positions are not in themselves 'literary' – that would lead us back into the closed circle of 'literature'. They are ideological positions within theory and practice, covering the whole field of the ideological class struggle, i.e. religious, judicial, and political, and they correspond to the conjunctures of the class struggle itself. But it would be pointless to look in the texts for the 'original' bare discourse of these ideological positions, as they were 'before' their 'literary' realisation, *for these ideological positions can only be formed in the materiality of the literary text.* That is, they can only appear in a form which provides their *imaginary solution*, or better still, which displaces them by substituting imaginary contradictions soluble within the ideological practice of religion, politics, morality, aesthetics and psychology.

Let us approach this phenomenon more closely. We shall say that literature 'begins' with the imaginary solution of implacable ideological contradictions, with the representation of that solution: not in the sense of representating i.e. 'figuring' (by images, allegories, symbols or arguments) a solution which is really there (to repeat, literature is produced because such a solution is impossible) but in the sense of providing a 'mise en scene', a *presentation as solution* of the very terms of an insurmountable contradiction, by means of various displacements and substitutions. For there to be a literature, it must be the very terms of the contradiction (and hence of the contradictory ideological elements) that are enunciated in a special language, a language of 'compromise' realising in advance the fiction of a forthcoming conciliation. Or better still, it finds a language of 'compromise' which presents the conciliation as 'natural' and so both necessary and inevitable.

. . . .

Fiction and realism: the mechanism of identification in literature

Here we must pause, even if over-schematically, to consider a characteristic literary effect which has already been briefly mentioned: the identification effect. Brecht was the first marxist theoretician to focus on this by showing how the ideological effects of literature (and of the theatre, with the specific transformations that implies) *materialise* via an identification process between the reader or the audience and the hero or anti-hero, the simultaneous mutual constitution of the fictive 'consciousness' of the character with the ideological 'consciousness' of the reader.

But it is obvious that any process of identification is dependent on the constitution and recognition of the individual as 'subject' – to use a very common ideological notion lifted by philosophy from the juridical and turning up under various forms in all other levels of bourgeois ideology. Now, all ideology, as Althusser shows in his essay 'Ideology and Ideological State Apparatuses',[3] must in a practical way 'hail or interpellate individuals as subjects': so that they perceive themselves as such, with rights and duties, the obligatory accompaniments. Each ideology has its specific mode: each gives to the 'subject' – and therefore to other real or imaginary subjects who confront the individual and present him with his ideological identification in a personal form – one or more appropriate names. In the ideology of literature the nomenclature is: Authors (i.e. signatures), Works (i.e. titles), Readers, and Characters (with their social background, real or imaginary). But in literature, the process of constituting subjects and setting up their relationships of mutual recognition necessarily takes a detour via the fictional world and its values, because that process (i.e. of constitution and setting-up) embraces within its circle the 'concrete' or 'abstract' 'persons' which the text stages. We now reach a classic general problem: what is specifically 'fictional' about literature?

. . . .

Literature is not fiction, a fictive image of the real, because it cannot define itself simply as a figuration, an appearance of reality. By a complex process, literature is the production of a certain reality, not indeed (one cannot over-emphasise this) an autonomous reality, but a material reality, and of a certain social effect (we shall conclude with this). Literature is not therefore fiction, but *the production of fictions*: or better still, the production of fiction-effects (and in the first place the provider of the material means for the production of fiction-effects).

Similarly, as the 'reflection of the life of a given society', historically given (Mao), literature is still not providing a 'realist' reproduction of it, even and least of all when it proclaims itself to be such, because even then it cannot be reduced to a straight mirroring. But it is true that the text does produce a *reality-effect*. More precisely it produces simultaneously a reality-effect and a fiction-effect, emphasising first one and then the other, interpreting each by each in turn but always *on the basis of their dualism.*

So, it comes to this once more: fiction and realism are not *the concepts for* the production of literature but on the contrary the notions produced by literature. But this leads to remarkable consequences for it means that the *model,* the real referent 'outside' the discourse which both fiction and realism presuppose, has no function here as a non-literary non-discursive anchoring point predating the text. (We know by now that this anchorage, the primacy of the real, is different from and more complex than a 'representation'.) But it does function as an effect of the discourse. *So, the literary discourse itself institutes and projects the presence of the 'real' in the manner of an hallucination.*

How is this materially possible? How can the text so control what it says, what it describes, what it sets up (or 'those' it sets up) with its sign of hallucinatory reality, or contrastingly, its fictive sign, diverging, infinitesimally perhaps, from the 'real'? On this point too, in parts of their deep analysis, the works we have used supply the material for an answer. Once more they refer us to the effects and forms of the fundamental linguistic conflict.

In a study of 'modern' French literary texts, carefully dated in each case according to their place in the history of the common language and of the educational system, R. Balibar refers to the production of 'imaginary French' [*français fictif*]. What does this mean? Clearly not pseudo-French, elements of a pseudo-language, seeing that these literary instances do also appear in certain contexts chosen by particular individuals, e.g. by compilers of dictionaries who illustrate their rubrics only with literary quotations. Nor is it simply a case of the language being produced *in* fiction (with its own usages, syntax and vocabulary), i.e. that of the characters in a narrative making an imaginary discourse in an imaginary language. Instead, it is a case of expressions which *always* diverge in one or more salient details from those used in practice outside the literary discourse, even when both are grammatically 'correct'. These are linguistic 'compromise formations', compromising between usages which are socially contradictory in practice and hence mutually exclude each other. In these compromise formations there is an essential place, more or less disguised but *recognisable,* for the reproduction of 'simple' language, 'ordinary' language, French 'just like that', i.e. the language which is taught in elementary school as the 'pure and simple' expression of 'reality'. In R. Balibar's book there are numerous examples which 'speak' to everyone, reawakening or reviving memories which are usually repressed (it is their presence, their reproduction – the reason for a character or his words and for what the 'author' makes himself responsible for without naming himself – which produces the effect of 'naturalness' and 'reality', even if it is only by a single phrase uttered as if in passing). In comparison, all other expressions seem 'arguable', 'reflected' in a subjectivity. It is necessary that first of all there should be expressions which seem *objective*: these are the ones which in the text itself produce the imaginary referent of an elusive 'reality'.

Finally, to go back to our starting point: the ideological effect of identification produced by literature or rather by literary texts, which Brecht, thanks to his position as a revolutionary and materialist dramatist, was the first to theorise. But there is only ever identification of *one subject with another* (potentially with 'oneself': 'Madame Bovary, c'est moi', familiar example, signed Gustave Flaubert). And there are only ever subjects through the interpellation of the individual into a subject by a Subject who names him, as Althusser shows: 'tu es Un tel, et c'est à toi que je m'adresse': 'Hypocrite lecteur, mon semblable, mon frère', another familiar example, signed Charles Baudelaire. Through the endless functioning of its texts, literature unceasingly 'produces' *subjects*, on display for everyone. So paradoxically using the same schema we can say: literature endlessly transforms (concrete) individuals into subjects and endows them with a quasi-real hallucinatory individuality. According to the fundamental mechanism of the whole of bourgeois ideology, to produce subjects ('persons' and 'characters') *one must oppose them to objects*, i.e. to *things*, by placing them *in* and *against* a world of 'real' things, outside it but always *in relation* to it. The realistic effect is the basis of this interpellation which makes characters or merely discourse 'live' and which makes readers take up an attitude towards imaginary struggles as they would towards real ones, though undangerously. They flourish here, the subjects we have already named: the Author and his Readers, but also the Author and his Characters, and the Reader and his Characters via the mediator, the Author – the Author identified with his Characters, or 'on the contrary' with one of their Judges, and likewise for the Reader. And from there, the Author, the Reader, the Characters opposite their universal abstract subjects: God, History, the People, Art. The list is neither final nor finishable: the work of literature is by definition to prolong and expand it indefinitely.

. . . .

The Aesthetic Effect of Literature as Ideological Domination-effect

Here is the index of the structure of the process of reproduction in which the literary effect is inserted. What is in fact 'the primary material' of the literary text? (But a raw material which always seems to have been already transformed by it.) It is the ideological contradictions which are *not* specifically literary but political, religious, etc.; in the last analysis, contradictory ideological realisations of determinate class positions in the class struggle. And what is the 'effect' of the literary text? (*At least* on those readers who recognise it as such, those of the *dominant* cultured class.) Its effect is to provoke other ideological discourses which can sometimes be recognised as literary ones but which are usually merely aesthetic, moral, political, religious discourses in which the dominant ideology is realised.

We can now say that the literary text is the *agent* for the *reproduction* of ideology in its ensemble. In other words, it induces by the literary effect the production of 'new' discourses which always reproduce (under constantly varied forms) the *same* ideology (with its contradictions). It enables individuals to *appropriate* ideology and make themselves its 'free' *bearers* and even its 'free' *creators*. The literary text is a privileged operator in the concrete relations between the individual and ideology in bourgeois society and ensures its reproduction. To the extent that it induces the ideological discourse to leave its subject matter which has always already been invested as the aesthetic effect, in the form of the work of art, it does not seem a mechanical imposition, forced, revealed like a religious dogma, on individuals who must repeat it faithfully. Instead it appears as if offered for interpretations, a free choice, for the subjective private use of individuals. It is the privileged agent of ideological subjection, in the democratic and 'critical' form of 'freedom of thought'.[4]

Under these conditions, the aesthetic effect is also inevitably an effect of *domination*: the subjection of individuals to the dominant ideology, the dominance of the ideology of the ruling class.

It is inevitably therefore an *uneven* effect which does not operate uniformly on individuals and particularly does not operate in the same way on different and antagonistic social classes. 'Subjection' must be felt by the dominant class as by the dominant but in two different ways. Formally, literature as an ideological formation realised in the common language, is provided and destined for all and makes no distinctions between readers but for their own differing tastes and sensibilities, natural or acquired. But concretely, subjection means one thing for the members of the educated dominant class: 'freedom' to think within ideology, a submission which is experienced and practised as if it were a mastery, another for those who belong to the exploited classes: manual workers or even skilled workers, employees, those who according to official statistics never 'read' or rarely. These find in reading nothing but the confirmation of their inferiority: subjection means domination and repression by the literary discourse of a discourse deemed 'inarticulate' and 'faulty' and inadequate for the expression of complex ideas and feelings.

This point is vital to an analysis. It shows that the difference is not set up *after the event* as a straightforward inequality of reading power and assimilation, conditioned by other social inequalities. It is implicit in the very production of the literary effect and materially inscribed in the constitution of the text.

But one might say, how is it clear that what is implicit in the structure of the text is not just the discourse of those who practice literature but also, *most significantly*, the discourse of those who do not know the text and whom it does not know; i.e. the discourse of those who 'write' (books) and 'read' them, and the discourse of those who do not know how to do it although quite simply they 'know how to read and write' – a play of words and a profoundly revealing double usage. One can understand this only by reconstituting and analysing the linguistic conflict in its determinant place as that which produced the literary text and which opposes two antagonistic usages, equal but inseparable of the common language: on one side, 'literary' French which is studied in higher education (l'enseignement secondaire et supérieur) and on the other 'basic', 'ordinary' French which, far from being natural, is also taught at the other level (à l'école primaire). It is 'basic' only by reason of its *unequal relation* to the other, which is 'literary' by the same reason. This is proved by a comparative and historical analysis of their lexical and syntactical forms – which R. Balibar is one of the first to undertake systematically.

So, if in the way things are, literature can and must be used in secondary education both to fabricate and simultaneously dominate, isolate and repress the 'basic' language' of the dominated classes, it is only on condition that that same basic language should be present in literature, as one of the terms of its constitutive contradiction – disguised and masked, but also necessarily given away and exhibited in the fictive reconstructions. And ultimately this is because literary French embodied in literary texts is both tendentially *distinguished from* (and opposed to) the common language and *placed with* its constitution and historic development so long as this process characterises general education because of its material importance to the development of bourgeois society. That is why it is possible to assert that the use of literature in schools and its place in education is only the converse of the *place of education in literature* and that therefore the basis of the production of literary effects is the very structure and historical role of the currently dominant ideological state apparatus. And that too is why it is possible to denounce as a den of their own real practice the claims of the writer and his cultured readers to rise above simple classroom exercises, and evade them.

The effect of domination realised by literary production presupposes the presence of the dominated ideology within the dominant ideology itself. It implies the constant 'activation' of the contradiction and its attendant ideological risk – it thrives on this very risk which is the source of its power. That is why, dialectically, in bourgeois democratic society, the agent of the reproduction of ideology moves tendentially via the effects of literary 'style' and linguistic forms of compromise. Class struggle is not abolished in the literary text and the literary effects which it produces. They bring about the reproduction, as dominant, of the ideology of the dominant class.

Notes

1 R. Balibar and D. Laporte, Le Français National: *constitution de la langue nationale commune a l'époque de la revolution démocratique bourgeoisie*, introduction by E. Balibar and P. Macherey (Paris, Éditions Hachette, 1974), in *Analyses*.

2 Rejecting the mythical unity and completeness of a work of art does not mean adopting a reverse position, i.e. the work of art as anti-nature, a violation of order (cf. *Tel Quel*). Such reversals are characteristic of conservative ideology: 'For oft a fine disorder stems from art' (Boileau)!

3 In *La Pensée* no. 151. June 1970; *Lenin and Philosophy*, tr. B. Brewster (London, New Left Books, 1971).

4 One could say that there is no proper *religious literature*; at least that there was not before the bourgeois epoch, by which time religion has been instituted as a form (subordinant and contradictory) of the bourgeois ideology itself. Rather, literature itself and the aesthetic ideology played a decisive part in the struggle against religion, the ideology of the dominant feudal class.

---

7 Terry Eagleton,

From *Criticism and Ideology* (1976), pp. 157–61

D.H. Lawrence

Of all the writers discussed in this essay, D.H. Lawrence, the only one of proletarian origin, is also the most full-bloodedly 'organicist' in both his social and aesthetic assumptions. As a direct twentieth-century inheritor of the 'Culture and Society' Romantic humanist tradition, Lawrence's fiction represents one of the century's most powerful literary critiques of industrial capitalism, launched from a deep-seated commitment to an organic order variously located in Italy, New Mexico, pre-industrial England and, metaphorically, in the novel-form itself. The novel for Lawrence is a delicate, labile organism whose elements are vitally interrelated; it spurns dogma and metaphysical absolutes, tracing instead the sensuous flux of its unified life-forms.[1] Yet Lawrence is also a dogmatic, metaphysically absolutist, radically dualistic thinker, fascinated by mechanism and disintegration; and it is in this contradiction that much of his historical significance lies.

What Lawrence's work dramatises, in fact, is a contradiction within the Romantic humanist tradition itself, between its corporate and individualist components. An extreme form of individualism is structural to Romantic humanist ideology – an application, indeed, of organicism to the individual self, which becomes thereby wholly autotelic, spontaneously evolving into 'wholeness' by its own uniquely determining laws. This ideological component – at once an idealised version of commonplace bourgeois individualism and a 'revolutionary' protest against the 'reified' society it produces – is strongly marked in Lawrence's writing, and enters into conflict with the opposing imperatives of impersonality and organic order. His social organicism decisively rejects the atomistic, mechanistic ideologies of industrial capitalism, yet at the same time subsumes the values of the bourgeois liberal tradition: sympathy, intimacy, compassion, the centrality of the 'personal'. These contradictions come to a crisis in Lawrence with the First World War, the most traumatic event of his life. The war signifies the definitive collapse of the liberal humanist heritage, with its benevolistic idealism and 'personal' values, clearing the way for the 'dark gods' of discipline, action, hierarchy, individual separateness, mystical impersonality – in short, for a social order which rejects the 'female' principle of compassion and sexual intimacy for the 'male' principle of power. 'The reign of love is passing, and the reign of power is coming again.'[2]

In this sense Lawrence was a major precursor of fascism, which is to say that he himself unqualifiedly accepted fascist ideology. He unequivocally condemned Mussolini, and correctly identified fascism as spuriously 'radical' response to the crisis of capitalism.[3] Lawrence was unable to embrace fascism because, while it signified a form of Romantic organistic reaction to bourgeois liberalism, it also negated the individualism which was for him a crucial part of the same Romantic heritage. This is the contradiction from which he was unable to escape, in his perpetual oscillation between a proud celebration of individual autonomy and a hunger for social integration; he wants men to be drilled soldiers but *individual* soldiers, desires to 'rule' over them but not 'bully' them.[4] To 'resolve' this contradiction, Lawrence had recourse to a metaphysic which dichotomised reality into 'male' and 'female' principles and attempted to hold them in dialectical tension. The male principle is that of power, consciousness, spirit, activism, individuation; the female principle that of flesh, sensuality, permanence, passivity. The male principle draws sustenance from the female, but must avoid collapsing inertly into it. Yet Lawrence's dualist metaphysic is ridden with internal contradictions, for a significant biographical reason: his mother, symbol of primordial sensual unity, was in fact petty-bourgeois, and so also represented individuation, aspiring consciousness and active idealism in contrast to the mute, sensuous passivity of his working-class father. This partial inversion of his parents' sexual roles, as defined by Lawrence, contorts and intensifies the contradictions which his metaphysic tries to resolve.[6] The mother, as symbol of the nurturing yet cloying flesh, is subconsciously resented for inhibiting true masculinity (as is the father's passivity), yet valued as an image of love, tenderness and personal intimacy. Conversely, her active, aspiring consciousness disrupts the mindless unity of sensual life symbolised by the father, but is preferred to his brutal impersonality. *Sons and Lovers* takes these conflicts as its subject-matter, on the whole rejecting the father and defending the mother; yet as Lawrence's fiction progresses, moving through and beyond the First World War, that priority is partly reversed. *Women in Love* struggles to complement a potentially claustrophobic sexual intimacy with the 'liberating' effect of a purely 'male' relationship; and the hysterical male chauvinism of the post-war novels (*Aaron's Rod, Kangaroo, The Plumed Serpent*) represents a strident rejection of sexual love for the male cult of power and impersonality. Lawrence's deepening hatred of women is a reaction both against bourgeois liberal values and the snare of a sensuality which violates individual autonomy; yet his commitment to sensual being as the source of social renewal contradictorily persists. In *Lady Chatterley's Lover*, the image of the father is finally rehabilitated in the figure of Mellors; yet Mellors combines impersonal male power with 'female' tenderness, working-class roughness with petty-bourgeois awareness, achieving a mythical resolution of the contradictions which beset Lawrence's work.

Lawrence's particular mode of relation to the dominant ideology, then, was in the first place a contradictory combination of proletarian and petty-bourgeois elements – a combination marked by a severe conflict between alternative ideological discourses which becomes encoded in his metaphysic. Yet this fact is of more than merely 'biographical' interest: for the ideological contradictions which the young Lawrence lives out – between power and love, community and autonomy, sensuality and consciousness, order and individualism – are a specific overdetermination of a deep-seated ideological crisis within the dominant formation as a whole. Lawrence's relation to that crisis is then doubly overdetermined by his expatriatism, which combines an assertive, deracinated individualism with a hunger for the historically mislaid 'totality'. The forms of Lawrence's fiction produce this ideological conjuncture in a variety of ways. The 'symptomatic' repressions and absences of the realist *Sons and Lovers* may be recuperated in the ultra-realist forms of *The Rainbow* – a text which 'explodes' realism in its letter, even as it preserves it in the 'totalising' organicism of its evolving generational structure. After the war, Lawrence's near-total ideological collapse, articulated with the crisis of aesthetic signification, presents itself in a radical rupturing and diffusion of literary form: novels like *Aaron's Rod* and *Kangaroo* are signally incapable of evolving a narrative, ripped between fragmentary plot, spiritual autobiography and febrile didacticism. But between these texts and *The Rainbow* occurs the unique moment of *Women in Love*. That work's break to synchronic form, away from the diachronic rhythms of *The Rainbow*, produces an 'ideology of the text' marked by stasis and disillusionment; yet it is precisely in its fissuring of organic form, in its 'montage' techniques of symbolic juxtaposition, that the novel enforces a 'progressive' discontinuity with a realist lineage already put into profound question by *Jude the Obscure*.

Conclusion

That the fissuring of organic form is a progressive act has not been a received position within a Marxist aesthetic tradition heavily dominated by the work of George Lukács. Yet to review a selection of English literary production from George Eliot to D.H. Lawrence in the light of the internal relations between ideology and literary form is to reactivate the crucially significant debate conducted in the 1930s between Lukács and Bertolt

Brecht.[7] Brecht's rejection of Lukác's nostalgic organicism, his traditionalist preference for closed, symmetrical totalities, is made in the name of an allegiance to open, multiple forms which bear in their torsions the very imprint of the contradictions they lay bare. In English literary culture of the past century, the ideological basis of organic form is peculiarly visible, as a progressively impoverished bourgeois liberalism attempts to integrate more ambitious and affective ideological modes. In doing so, that ideology enters into grievous conflicts which its aesthetic forms betray in the very act of attempted resolution. The destruction of corporate and organicist ideologies in the political sphere has always been a central task for revolutionaries; the destruction of such ideologies in the aesthetic region is essential not only for a scientific knowledge of the literary past, but for laying the foundation on which the materialist aesthetic and artistic practices of the future can be built.

Notes

1 See 'The Novel', *Phoenix II* (London, 1968).
2 'Blessed are the Powerful', *Phoenix II*.
3 See his comment in *St. Mawr*: 'Try fascism. Fascism would keep the surface of life intact, and carry on the undermining business all the better.' Lawrence was not a fascist rather perhaps in the sense that he was not a homosexual. He thought both fascism and homosexuality immoral, but was subconsciously fascinated by both.
4 *Fantasia of the Unconscious* (London, 1961), p. 84.
5 This duality is imaged in Lawrence's work in a whole gamut of antinomies love/law, light/dark, lion/unicorn, sun/moon, Son/Father, spirit/soul, sky/earth, and so on.
6 A contortion evident in the *reversibility* of some of Lawrence's symbolic antinomies: the Father, symbol of sensual phallic consciousness, is identifiable with the *female*; the lion may signify both active power and sensuality; the sun is sometimes male intellect and sometimes sensuous female warmth, while the moon may suggest female passivity or the cold abstract consciousness of the male.
7 See 'Brecht Against Lukács', *New Left Review* 84, March/April, 1974.

SECTION FIVE
READER THEORY

In contemporary literary theory the role of the reader has become increasingly prominent. An orientation toward the text/reader nexus has been taken up in Structuralist, Post-Structuralist, Formalist, Feminist, and psychoanalytic criticism. However there has also been a body of work produced that specifically concentrates upon the reader and whose primary orientation is toward the process of reading.

Basically, two linked trajectories can be noted. The first, often called the 'Aesthetics of Reception', develops out of phenomenological philosophy and concerns itself with the reading process in relation to the reader's consciousness. The second, 'reader response theory', is largely American in origin, comes in a variety of forms, and often lacks a fully coherent and cogent theoretical exposition. Reader-response theory includes the work of such figures as Norman Holland and David Bleich, working within a psychologistic frame, Michael Riffaterre working within semiotics, and Stanley Fish.[1] Fish's initial theoretical position, 'affective stylistics', concentrated on reading as a temporal, experiential process but was later reworked in the light of the realisation that the process he was describing could not be extrapolated out as *the* reading process, only as *a* reading process. In his reworking, he develops the more interesting notion of 'interpretive communities' – communities of readers with shared practices and competences. For Fish, it is the interpretive community that determines interpretations rather than the textual features of the work itself.

The essays chosen here to represent reader theory are first of all by two of the prominent critics from the Aesthetics of Reception: Wolfgang Iser and Hans Robert Jauss. Iser draws extensively on the work of the phenomenologist aesthetician Roman Ingarden, sharing his view of the text as a potential structure which is 'concretized' by the reader. For Iser this is a process which takes place in relation to the extra-literary norms and values through which the reader makes sense of experience. Iser's writings reveal a considerable degree of ambiguity about the extent of the reader's freedom to fill in the blanks in the text's 'schemata' according to his/her own experiential norms, and the extent to which the text controls or determines the way it will be read. What is clear, however, is Iser's commitment to a phenomenological view of the reading experience; the reader realizes the text as an aesthetic object according to his/her own experience but the norms which structure that experience will inevitably be modified and shifted by the reading experience itself. As we read we continually perceive and evaluate events with regard to our expectations of what will happen in the text, and against the background of what has already happened. Unexpected textual occurrences, however, will force us to reformulate our expectations and to reinterpret the significance which we have attributed to what has gone before. Iser sees the reader as someone who, above all, seeks coherence as the basis of sense-making and who will reconnect the different schemata of the text according to continual revisions which guarantee an overall meaning.

While Iser's theory presents us with a de-historicized reader confronting a de-contextualized text, Jauss's reception theory attempts a more historically situated understanding of the concretization process, positing an 'horizon of expectations' which lays down the criteria in each historical period according to which people read and evaluate literary works. The horizon of expectations at the original historical moment of production can only tell us something of how the work was understood and received at that time; it does not establish its absolute or universal meaning. Jauss draws extensively on the hermeneutic theory of Hans Gadamer, viewing the text as situated in an endless dialogue between past and present in which the present position of the interpreter will always influence how the past is understood and received. In attempting to make sense of the past we can only know it in the light of the present cultural horizon and thus Jauss argues for a 'fusion of horizons' which unite past and present. For Jauss the text's meaning and value is ultimately inseparable from the history of its reception.

The problem at the heart of this theory remains that of extrapolating from one's own concretization processes to a general reading and reception process, though Jauss circumscribes this to some extent through the historicizing notion of 'horizon of expectations'.

The third piece in this section is a transcript of an interview conducted in 1981 with the philosopher-critic Paul Ricoeur, whose work also emerges from engagement with the same phenomenological tradition as that of Iser and Jauss. Ricoeur's work since the 1970s has largely focused on the problem of interpretation. He insists that the act of interpretation must be regarded more dynamically as a dialectic between what he refers to as the 'distantiation' of the text, its formal and semantic autonomy, and its necessary 'appropriation' as the text is made part of the reader's own semantic world. The underlying assumption here is that the impulse to understand is always motivated by a need to make the world over into terms which are meaningful to the individual self. Like Hans-Georg Gadamer, Ricoeur regards his theory of interpretation as an act of resistance to scientific method as a search for fixed meaning: there can be no errorless, reliable origin. Gadamer's *Truth and Method*[2] was an important influence on this thesis – as indicated here in the discussion of 'prejudice' towards the end of the interview. What Ricoeur and Gadamer emphasize, however, is that an abandonment of the goal of absolute meaning need not entail collapse into purely subjective intuition. Interpretation is always a process of redescription, a productive engagement between reader and text situated in different moments of history. The readerly encounter with the 'otherness' of the text serves to challenge presuppositions and existing hermeneutic frameworks and therefore allows for the expansion of self-knowledge and awareness.

The final piece in this section is taken from Harold Bloom's *The Anxiety of Influence*[3] – a work almost impossible to categorize and one which draws on psychoanalytic ideas and deconstructive methods to offer a theory of poetic writing as creative misreading. Bloom takes up the idea advanced in T.S. Eliot's 'Tradition and the Individual Talent'[4] that no poet stands alone, every poet has his meaning in relation to the now dead ancestors who came before him. The quest of the poetic ephebe must be to evade the power of the precursor and to discover self-identity through the annihilation of the impulse to repeat by strong and creative misrepresentation. The strength of any poem is the poem it has managed to exclude; of any self, those other selves which have been evaded. Bloom's theory of writing is essentially a theory of mis-reading, individual talent always emerging as a creative misprision or 'swerve' from the tradition which precedes and makes possible the agonistic constitution of poem and self. The thesis is underpinned by the Freudian concepts of transference and Oedipal rivalry, both of which emphasize the notion of a repetition which undoes and affirms simultaneously: 'the strong imagination comes to its painful birth through savagery and misrepresentation'. Bloom's theory makes a straightforward equation between the defense mechanisms which protect the psyche in everyday life and the revisionary ratios which operate in poets: displacements serve to protect the psyche; creativity is a consequence of error; blindness gives birth to insight. To read a poem is necessarily to read the 'family romance' of the poet. Criticism, he tells us, 'is the art of knowing the hidden roads that go from poem to poem'.

Notes

1 See R.C. Holub, *Reception Theory: A Critical Introduction* (London, Methuen, 1984).
2 H.-G. Gadamer, *Truth and Method*, trans. G. Barden and W.G. Doerpl (New York, Seabury Press, 1975).
3 H. Bloom, *The Anxiety of Influence* (New York, Oxford University Press, 1973).
4 T.S. Eliot, 'Tradition and the Individual Talent', repr. in The Sacred Wood (London, Methuen, 1920), pp. 47–59.

8   Wolfgang Iser,

From 'The Reading Process', R.Cohen, ed., *New Directions in Literary, History* (1974), pp. 274–5; 276–7; 279–80; 281–2; 283–4; 285; 287–8; 290; 293–4; 294

The Reading Process: A Phenomenological Approach

The phenomenological theory of art lays full stress on the idea that, in considering a literary work, one must take into account not only the actual text but also, and in equal measure, the actions involved in responding to that text. Thus Roman Ingarden confronts the structure of the literary text with the ways in which it can be *konkretisiert* (realized)[1.] The text as such offers different 'schematised views' – through which the subject matter of the work can come to light, but the actual bringing to light is an action of *Konkretisation*. If this is so, then the literary work has two poles, which we might call the artistic and the esthetic: the artistic refers to the text created by the author, and the esthetic to the realization accomplished by the reader. From this polarity it follows that the literary work cannot be completely identical with the text, or with the realization of the text, but in fact must lie half-way between the two. The work is more than the text, for the text only takes on life when it is realized, and furthermore the realization is by no means independent of the individual disposition of the reader – though this in turn is acted upon by the different patterns of the text. The convergence of text and reader brings the literary work into existence, and this convergence can never be precisely pinpointed, but must always remain virtual, as it is not to be identified either with the reality of the text or with the individual disposition of the reader.

It is the virtuality of the work that gives rise to its dynamic nature, and this in turn is the precondition for the effects that the work calls forth. As the reader uses the various perspectives offered him by the text in order to relate the patterns and the 'schematized views' to one another, he sets the work in motion, and this very process results ultimately in the awakening of responses within himself. Thus, reading causes the literary work to unfold its inherently dynamic character.

. . . .

As a starting point for a phenomenological analysis we might examine the way in which sequent sentences act upon one another. This is of especial importance in literary texts in view of the fact that they do not correspond to any objective reality outside themselves. The world presented by literary texts is constructed out of what Ingarden has called *intentionale Satzkorrelate* (intentional sentence correlatives):

Sentences link up in different ways to form more complex units of meaning that reveal a very varied structure giving rise to such entities as a short story, a novel, a dialogue, a drama, a scientific theory. . . . In the final analysis, there arises a particular world, with component parts determined in this way or that, and with all the variations that may occur within these parts – all this as a purely intentional correlative of a complex of sentences. If this complex finally forms a literary work, I call the whole sum of sequent intentional sentence correlatives the 'world presented' in the work.[3]

This world, however, does not pass before the reader's eyes like a film. The sentences are 'components parts' insofar as they make statements, claims, or observations, or convey information, and so establish various perspectives in the text. But they remain only 'component parts' – they are not the sum total of the text itself. For the intentional correlatives disclose subtle connections which individually are less concrete than the statements, claims, and observations, even though these only take on their real meaningfulness through the interaction of their correlatives.

How is one to conceive the connection between the correlatives? It marks those points at which the reader is able to 'climb aboard' the text. He has to accept certain given perspectives, but in doing so he inevitably causes them to interact. When Ingarden speaks of intentional sentence correlatives in literature, the statements made or information conveyed in the sentence are already in a certain sense qualified: the sentence does not consist solely of a statement – which, after all, would be absurd, as one can only make statements about things that exist – but aims at Something beyond what it actually says. This is true of all sentences in literary works, and it is through the interaction of these sentences that their common aim is fulfilled. This is what gives them their own special quality in literary texts. In their capacity as statements, observations, purveyors of information, etc., they are always indications of something that is to come, the structure of which is foreshadowed by their specific content.

They set in motion a process out of which emerges the actual content of the text itself.

. . . .

As we have seen, the activity of reading can be characterised as a sort of kaleidoscope of perspectives, preintentions, recollections. Every sentence contains a preview of the next and forms a kind of viewfinder for what is to come; and this is turn changes the 'preview' and so becomes a 'viewfinder' for what has been read. This whole process represents the fulfillment of the potential, unexpressed reality of the text, but it is be seen only as a framework for a great variety of means by which the virtual dimension may be brought into being. The process of anticipation and retrospection itself does not by any means develop in a smooth flow. Ingarden has already drawn attention to this fact and ascribes a quite remarkable significance to it:

Once we are immersed in the flow of *Satzdenken* (sentence-thought), we are ready, after completing the thought of one sentence, to think out the 'continuation', also in the form of a sentence – and that is, in the form of a sentence that connects up with the sentence we have just thought through. In this way the process of reading goes effortlessly forward. But if by chance the following sentence has no tangible connection whatever with the sentence we have just thought through, there then comes a blockage in the stream of thought. This hiatus is linked with a more or less active surprise, or with indignation. This blockage must be overcome if the reading is to flow once more.[4]

The hiatus that blocks the flow of sentences is, in Ingarden's eyes, the product of chance, and is to be regarded as a flaw; this is typical of his adherence to the classical idea of art. If one regards the sentence sequence as a continual flow, this implies that the anticipation aroused by one sentence will generally be realized by the next, and the frustration of one's expectations will arouse feelings of exasperation. And yet literary texts are full of unexpected twists and turns, and frustration of expectations. Even in the simplest story there is bound to be some kind of blockage, if only because no tale can ever be told in its entirety. Indeed, it is only through inevitable omissions that a story gains its dynamism. Thus whenever the flow is interrupted and we are led off in unexpected directions, the opportunity is given to us to bring into play our own faculty for establishing connections – for filling in the gaps left by the text itself.[5]

These gaps have a different effect on the process of anticipation and retrospection, and thus on the 'gestalt' of the virtual dimension, for they may be filled in different ways. For this reason, one text is potentially capable of several different realizations, and no reading can ever exhaust the full potential, for each individual reader will fill in the gaps in his own way, thereby excluding the various other possibilities; as he reads, he will make his own decision as to how the gap is to be filled. In this very act the dynamics of reading are revealed. By making his decision he implicitly acknowledges the inexhaustibility of the text; at the same time it is this very inexhaustibility that forces him to make his decision. With 'traditional' texts this process was more or less unconscious, but modern texts frequently exploit it quite deliberately. They are often so fragmentary that one's attention is almost exclusively occupied with the search for connections between the fragments; the object of this is not to complicate the 'spectrum' of connections, so much as to make us aware of the nature of our own capacity for providing links. In such cases, the text refers back directly to our own preconceptions – which are revealed by the act of interpretation that is a basic element of the reading process. With all literary texts, then, we may say that the reading process is selective, and the potential text is infinitely richer than any of its individual realizations. This is borne out by the fact that a second reading of a piece of literature often produces a different impression from the first. The reasons for this may lie in the reader's own change of circumstances, still, the text must be such as to allow this variation. On a second reading familiar occurrences now tend to appear in a new light and seem to be at times corrected, at times enriched.

. . . .

The manner in which the reader experiences the text will reflect his own disposition, and in this respect the literary text acts as a kind of mirror; but at the same time, the reality which this process helps to create is one that will be *different* from his own (since, normally, we tend to be bored by texts that present us with things we already know perfectly well ourselves). Thus we have the apparently paradoxical situation in which the reader is forced to reveal aspects of himself in order to experience a reality which is different from his own. The impact this reality makes on him will depend largely on the extent to which he himself actively provides the unwritten part of the text, and yet in supplying all the missing links, he must think in terms of experiences different from his own; indeed, it is only by leaving behind the familiar world of his own experience that the reader can truly participate in the adventure the literary text offers him.

. . . .

The 'picturing' that is done by our imagination is only one of the activities through which we form the 'gestalt' of a literary text. We have already discussed the process of anticipation and retrospection, and to this we must add the process of grouping together all the different aspects of a text to form the consistency that the reader will always be in search of. While expectations may be continually modified, and images continually expanded, the reader will still strive, even if unconsciously, to fit everything together in a consistent pattern. 'In the reading of images, as in the hearing of speech, it is always hard to distinguish what is given to us from what we supplement in the process of projection which is triggered off by recognition . . . it is the guess of the beholder that tests the medley of forms and colours for coherent meaning, crystallizing it into shape when a consistent interpretation has been found.' By grouping together the written parts of the text, we enable them to interact, we observe the direction in which they are leading us, and we project onto them the consistency which we, as readers, require. This 'gestalt' must inevitably be colored by our own characteristic selection process. For it is not given by the text itself; it arises from the meeting between the written text and the individual mind of the reader with its own particular history of experience, its own consciousness, its own outlook. The 'gestalt' is not the true meaning of the text; at best it is a nonfigurative meaning; '. . . comprehension is an individual act of seeing-things-together, and only that.'[7] With a literary text such comprehension is inseparable from the reader's expectations, and where we have expectations, there too we have one of the most potent weapons in the writer's armory – illusion.

. . . .

The process is virtually hermeneutic. The text provokes certain expectations which in turn we project onto the text in such a way that we reduce the polysemantic possibilities to a single interpretation in keeping with the expectations aroused, thus extracting an individual, configurative meaning. The polysemantic nature of the text and the illusion-making of the reader are opposed factors. If the illusion were complete, the polysemantic nature could vanish; if the polysemantic nature were all-powerful, the illusion would be totally destroyed. Both extremes are conceivable, but in the individual literary text we always find some form of balance between the two conflicting tendencies. The formation of illusions, therefore, can never be total, but it is this very incompleteness that in fact gives it its productive value.

. . . .

As we work out a consistent pattern in the text, we will find our 'interpretation' threatened, as it were, by the presence of other possibilities of 'interpretation', and so there arise new areas of indeterminacy (though we may only be dimly aware of them, if at all, as we are continually making 'decisions' which will exclude them). In the course of the novel for instance, we sometimes find that characters, events, and backgrounds seem to change their significance; what really happens is that the other 'possibilities' begin to emerge more strongly, so that we become more directly aware of them. Indeed, it is this very shifting of perspectives that makes us feel that a novel is much more 'true-to-life'. Since it is we ourselves who establish the levels of interpretation and switch from one to another as we conduct our balancing operation, we ourselves impart to the text the dynamic lifelikeness which, in turn, enables us to absorb an unfamiliar experience into our personal world.

   As we read, we oscillate to a greater or lesser degree between the building and the breaking of illusions. In a process of trial and error, we organize and reorganize the various data offered us by the text. These are the given factors, the fixed points on which we base our 'interpretation', trying to fit them together in the way we think the author meant them to be fitted.

. . . .

The efficacy of a literary text is brought about by the apparent evocation and subsequent negation of the familiar. What at first seemed to be an affirmation of our assumptions leads to our own rejection of them, thus tending to prepare us for a re-orientation. And it is only when we have outstripped our preconceptions and left the shelter of the familiar that we are in a position to gather new experiences. As the literary text involves the reader in the formation of illusion and the simultaneous formation of the means whereby the illusion is punctured, reading reflects the process by which we gain experience. Once the reader is entangled, his own preconceptions are continually overtaken, so that the text becomes his 'present' while his own ideas fade into the 'past'; as soon as this happens he is open to the immediate experience of the text, which was impossible so long as his preconceptions were his 'present'.

. . . .

Text and reader no longer confront each other as object and subject, but instead the 'division' takes place within the reader himself. In thinking the thoughts of another, his own individuality temporarily recedes into the background, since it is supplanted by these alien thoughts which now become the theme on which his attention is focused. As we read, there occurs an artificial division of our personality, because we take as a theme for ourselves something that we are not. Consequently when reading we operate on different levels. For although we may be thinking the thoughts of someone else, what we are will not disappear completely – it will merely remain a more or less powerful virtual force. Thus, in reading there are these two levels – the alien 'me' and the real, virtual 'me' – which are never completely cut off from each other. Indeed, we can only make someone else's thoughts into an absorbing theme for ourselves, provided the virtual background of our own personality can adapt to it. Every text we read draws a different boundary within our personality, so that the virtual background (the real 'me') will take on a different form, according to the theme of the text concerned. This is inevitable, if only for the fact that the relationship between alien theme and virtual background is what makes it possible for the unfamiliar to be understood.

. . . .

Herein lies the dialectical structure of reading. The need to decipher gives us the chance to formulate our own deciphering capacity – i.e., we bring to the fore an element of our being of which we are not directly conscious. The production of the meaning of literary texts – which we discussed in connection with forming the 'gestalt' of the text – does not merely entail the discovery of the unformulated, which can then be taken over by the active imagination of the reader; it also entails the possibility that we may formulate ourselves and so discover what has previously seemed to elude our consciousness. These are the ways in which reading literature gives us the chance to formulate the unformulated.

Notes

1 Cf. Roman Ingarden, *Vom Erkennen des literarischen Kunstwerks* (Tübingen, 1968), pp. 49ff.

2 For a detailed discussion of this term see Roman Ingarden, *Das literarische Kunstwerk* (Tübingen,[2]1960), pp. 270ff.

3 Ingarden, *Vom Erkenmen des literarischen Kunstwerks*, p. 29.

4 Ingarden. *Vom Erkenmen des literarischen Kunstwerks* p. 32.

5 For a more detailed discussion of the function of 'gaps' in literary texts see Wolfgang Iser, 'Indeterminacy and the Reader's Response in Prose Fiction', *Aspects of Narrative* (English Institute Essays), ed. J. Hillis Miller (New York, 1971), pp. 1–45.

6 E.H. Gombrich, Art *and Illusion* (London, 1962), p. 204.

7 Louis O. Mink, 'History and Fiction as Modes of Comprehension', *New Literary History I*, (1970), p. 553.

9   H.R. Jauss,

From 'Literary History as a Challenge to Literary Theory', *New Literary History*, 2, (1967), pp. 11–19

The analysis of the literary experience of the reader avoids the threatening pitfalls of psychology if it describes the response and the impact of a work within the definable frame of reference of the reader's expectations: this frame of reference for each work develops in the historical moment of its appearance from a previous understanding of the genre, from the form and themes of already familiar works, and from the contrast between poetic and practical language.

My thesis is opposed to a widespread skepticism that doubts that an analysis of the aesthetic impact can approach the meaning of a work of art or can produce at best more than a plain sociology of artistic taste. René Wellek directs such doubts against the literary theory of I.A. Richards. Wellek argues that neither the individual consciousness, since it is immediate and personal, nor a collective consciousness as J. Mukarovsky assumes the effect of an art work to be, can be determined by empirical means.[1] Roman Jakobson wanted to replace the 'collective consciousness' by a 'collective ideology'. This he thought of as a system of values which exists for each literary work as *langue* and which becomes *parole* for the respondent – although incompletely and never as a whole.[2] This theory, it is true, limits the subjectivity of the impact, but it leaves open the question of which data can be used to interpret the impact of a unique work on a certain public and to incorporate it into a system of values. In the meantime there are empirical means which had never been thought of before – literary data which give for each work a specific attitude of the audience (an attitude that precedes the psychological reaction as well as the subjective understanding of the individual reader). As in the case of every experience, the first literary experience of a previously unknown work demands a 'previous knowledge which is an element of experience itself and which makes it possible that anything new we come across may also be read, as it were, in some context of experience.

A literary work, even if it seems new, does not appear as something absolutely new in an informational vacuum, but predisposes its reader to a very definite type of reception by textual strategies, overt and covert signals, familiar characteristics or implicit allusions. It awakens memories of the familiar, stirs particular emotions in the reader and with its 'beginning' arouses expectations for the 'middle and end', which can then be continued intact, changed, re-oriented or even ironically fulfilled in the course of reading according to certain rules of the genre or type of text. The psychical process in the assimilation of a text on the primary horizon of aesthetic experience is by no means only a random succession of merely subjective impressions, but the carrying out of certain directions in a process of directed perception which can be comprehended, from the motivations which constitute it and the signals which set it off and which can be described linguistically. If, along with W.D. Stempel one considers the previous horizon of expectations of a text as paradigmatic isotopy, which is transferred to an immanent syntactical horizon of expectations to the degree to which the message grows, the process of reception becomes describable in the expansion of a semiological procedure which arises between the development and the correction of the system.[4] A corresponding process of continuous horizon setting and horizon changing also determines the relation of the individual text to the succession of texts which form the genre. The new text evokes for the reader (listener) the horizon of expectations and rules familiar from earlier texts, which are then varied, corrected, changed or just reproduced. Variation and correction determine the scope, alteration and reproduction of the borders and structure of the genre.[5] The interpretative reception of a text always presupposes the context of experience of aesthetic perception. The question of the subjectivity of the interpretation and the taste of different readers or levels of readers can be asked significantly only after it has been decided which transsubjective horizon of understanding determines the impact of the text.

The ideal cases of the objective capability of such literary frames of reference are works which, using the artistic standards of the reader, have been formed by conventions of genre, style, or form. These purposely evoke responses so that they can frustrate them. This can serve not only a critical purpose but can even have a poetic effect. Thus Cervantes in *Don Quixote* fosters the expectations of the old tales of knighthood which the adventures of his last knight then parody seriously.[6] Thus Diderot in the beginning to *Jacques le Fataliste* evokes the expectations of the popular journey novel along with the (Aristotelian) convention of the romanesque fable and the providence peculiar to it, so that he can then confront the promised journey and love novel with a completely unromanesque 'verité de l'histoire': the bizarre reality and moral casuistry of the inserted stories in which the truth of life continually denies the lies of poetic fiction.[7] Thus Nerval in *Chimères* cites, combines, and mixes a quintessence of well-known romantic and occult motives to produce the expectation of a mythical metamorphosis of the world only in order to show his renunciation of romantic poetry. The mythical identification and relationships which are familiar to the reader dissolve in the unknown to the same degree as the attempted private myth of the lyrical 'I' fails; the law of sufficient information is broken and the darkness which has become expressive gains a poetic function.[8] There is also the possibility of objectifying the expectations in works which are historically less sharply delineated. For the specific reception which the author anticipates from the reader of a particular work can be achieved, even if the explicit signals are missing, by three generally acceptable means: first, by the familiar standards or the inherent poetry of the genre; second, by the implicit relationships to familiar works of the literary-historical context; and third, by the contrast between fiction and reality, between the poetic and the practical function of language, which the reflective reader can always realize while he is reading. The third factor includes the possibility that the reader of a new work has to perceive it not only within the narrow horizon of his literary expectations but also within the wider horizon of his experience of life.

. . . .

If the horizon of expectations of a work is reconstructed in this way, it is possible to determine its artistic nature by the nature and degree of its effect on a given audience. If the 'aesthetic distance' is considered as the distance between the given horizon of expectations and the appearance of a new work, whose reception results in a 'horizon change' because it negates familiar experience or articulates an experience for the first time, this aesthetic distance can be measured historically in the spectrum of the reaction of the audience and the judgment of criticism (spontaneous success, rejection or shock, scattered approval, gradual or later understanding).

The way in which a literary work satisfies, surpasses, disappoints, or disproves the expectations of its first readers in the historical moment of its appearance obviously gives a criterion for the determination of its aesthetic value. The distance between the horizon of expectations and the work, between the familiarity of previous aesthetic experiences and the 'horizon change'[9] demanded by the response to new works, determines the artistic nature of a literary work along the lines of the aesthetics of reception: the smaller this distance, which means that no demands are made upon the receiving consciousness to make a change on the horizon of unknown experience, the closer the work comes to the realm of 'culinary' or light reading. This last phrase can be characterised from the point of view of the aesthetics of reception in this way: it demands no horizon change but actually fulfills expectations, which are prescribed by a predominant taste, by satisfying the demand for the reproduction of familiar beauty, confirming familiar sentiments, encouraging dreams, making unusual experiences palatable as 'sensations' or even raising moral problems, but only to be able to 'solve' them in an edifying manner when the solution is already obvious.[10] On the other hand, if the artistic character of a work is to be measured by the aesthetic distance with which it confronts the expectations of its first readers, it follows that this distance, which at first is experienced as a happy or distasteful new perspective, can disappear for later readers to the same degree to which the original negativity of the work has become self-evident and, as henceforth familiar expectation, has even become part of the horizon of future aesthetic experience. Especially the classic nature of so-called masterworks belongs to this second horizon change; their self-evident beauty and their seemingly unquestionable 'eternal significance' bring them, from the point of view of the aesthetics of reception, into dangerous proximity with the irresistable convincing and enjoyable 'culinary' art, and special effort is needed to read them 'against the grain' of accustomed experience so that their artistic nature becomes evident again.[11]

The relationship between literature and the public encompasses more than the fact that every work has its specific, historically and sociologically determined audience, that every writer is dependent upon the milieu, views and ideology of his readers and that literary success requires a book 'which expresses what the group expects, a book which presents the group with its own portrait. . . '.[12] The objectivist determination of literary success based on the congruence of the intent of a work and the expectation of a social group always puts literary sociology in an embarrassing position whenever it must explain later or continuing effects. This is why R. Escarpit wants to presuppose a 'collective basis in space or time' for the 'illusion of continuity' of a writer, which leads to an astonishing prognosis in the case of Molière: he 'is still young for the Frenchman of the 20th century because his world is still alive and ties of culture, point of view and language still bind us to him . . . but the ties are becoming ever weaker and Molière will age and die when the things which our culture has in common with the France of Molière die' (p. 117). As if Molière had only reflected the manners of his time and had only remained successful because of this apparent intention! Where the congruence between work and social group does not exist or no longer exists, as for example in the reception of a work by a group which speaks a foreign language, Escarpit is able to help himself by resorting to a 'myth': 'myths which are invented by a later period which has become estranged from the reality which they represent' (p. 111). As if all reception of a work beyond the first socially determined readers were only 'distorted echoes', only a consequence of 'subjective myths' (p. 111) and did not have its objective *a priori* in the received work which sets boundaries and opens possibilities for later understanding! The sociology of literature does not view its object dialectically enough when it determines the circle of writers, work and readers so one-sidedly.[13] The determination is reversible: there are works which at the moment of their publication are not directed at any specific audience, but which break through the familiar horizon of literary expectations so completely that an audience can only gradually develop for them.[14] Then when the new horizon of expectations has achieved more general acceptance, the authority of the changed aesthetic norm can become apparent from the fact that readers will consider previously successful works as obsolete and reject them. It is only in view of such a horizon change that the analysis of literary effect achieves the dimension of a literary history of readers[15] and provides the statistical curves of the historical recognition of the bestseller.

A literary sensation from the year 1857 may serve as an example of this. In this year two novels were published: Flaubert's *Madame Bovary*, which has since achieved world-wide fame, and *Fanny* by his friend Feydeau, which is forgotten today. Although Flaubert's novel brought with it a trial for obscenity, *Madame Bovary* was at first overshadowed by Feydeau's novel: *Fanny* had thirteen editions in one year and success the likes of which Paris had not seen since Chateaubriand's *Atala*. As far as theme is concerned, both novels fulfilled the expectations of the new audience, which – according to Baudelaire's analysis – had rejected anything romantic and scorned grand as well as naive passion.[16] They treated a trivial subject – adultery – the one in a bourgeois and the other in a provincial milieu. Both authors understood how to give a sensational twist to the conventional, rigid triangle which in the erotic scenes surpassed the customary details. They presented the worn-out theme of jealousy in a new light by reversing the expected relationship of the three classic roles. Feydeau has the youthful lover of the 'femme de trente ans' becoming jealous of his lover's husband, although he has already reached the goal of his desires, and is perishing over this tormenting situation; Flaubert provides the adulteries of the doctor's wife in the provinces, which Baudelaire presents as a sublime form of 'dandysme', with a surprising ending, so that the ridiculous figure of the deceived Charles Bovary takes on noble traits at the end. In official criticism of the time there are voices which reject *Fanny* as well as *Madame Bovary* as a product of the new school of 'réalisme', which they accuse of denying all ideals and attacking the ideas on which the order of the society in the Second Empire was based.[17] The horizon of expectations of the public of 1857, here only sketched in, which did not expect anything great in the way of novels after the death of Balzac,[18] explains the differing success of the two novels only when these question of the effect of their narrative form is posed. Flaubert's innovation in form, his principle of 'impersonal telling' (*impassibilité*, which Barbey d'Aurevilly attacked with this comparison: if a story-telling machine could be made of English steel, it would function the same as Monsieur Flaubert[19]), must have shocked the same audience which was offered the exciting contents of *Fanny* in the personable tone of a confessional novel. It could also have found in Feydeau's descriptions[20] popular ideals and frustrations of the level of society which sets the style, and it could delight unrestrainedly in the lascivious main scene in which Fanny (without knowing that her lover is watching from the balcony) seduces her husband – for their moral indignation was forestalled by the reaction of the unfortunate witness. However, as *Madame Bovary*, which was understood at first only by a small circle of knowledgeable readers and called a turning point in the history of the novel, became a world-wide success, the group of readers who were formed by this book sanctioned the new canon of expectations, which made the weaknesses of Feydeau – his flowery style, his modish effects, his lyrical confessional clichés – unbearable and relegated *Fanny* to the class of bestsellers of yesterday.

. . . .

The reconstruction of the horizon of expectations, on the basis of which a work in the past was created and received, enables us to find the questions to which the text originally answered and thereby to discover how the reader of that day viewed and understood the work. This approach corrects the usually unrecognised values of a classical concept of art or of an interpretation that seeks to modernize, and it avoids the recourse to a general spirit of the age, which involves circular reasoning. It brings out the hermeneutic difference between past and present ways of understanding a work, points up the history of its reception – providing both approaches – and thereby challenges as platonizing dogma the apparently self-evident dictum of philological metaphysics that literature is timelessly present and that it has objective meaning, determined once and for all and directly open to the interpreter at any time.

Notes

1 R. Wellek, 'The Theory of Literary History', *Études dédiées au quatrième Congrès de linguistes*, Travaux du Cercle Linguistique de Prague (Prague, 1936), p. 179.

2 In *Slovo a slovenost*, I, 192, cited by Wellek, 'The Theory of Literary History', pp. 179ff.

3 G. Buck, *Lernen und Erfahrung* (Stuttgart, 1967), p. 56, who refers here to Husserl (*Erfahrung und Urteil*, esp. §8) but goes farther than Husserl in a lucid description of negativity in the process of experience, which is of importance for the horizon structure of aesthetic experience.

4 W.D. Stempel, *Pour une description des genres littéraires*, in: *Actes du XIIe congrès internat. de linguistique Romane* (Bucharest, 1968), also in *Beiträge zur Texlinguistik*, ed. by W.D. Stempel (Munich, 1970).

5 See also my treatment of this in '*Littérature médiévale et théorie des genres*', in *Poétique*, I (1970), pp. 79–101, which will also shortly appear in expanded form in volume I of *Grundriss der romanischen Literaturen des Mittelalters* (Heidelberg, 1970).

6 According to the interpretation of H.J. Neuschäfer, *Der Sinn der Parodie im Don Quijote*, Studia Romanica, V (Heidelberg, 1963).

7 According to the interpretation of R. Warning, *Allusion und Wirklichkeit in Tristram Shandy und Jacques le Fataliste*, Theorie und Geschichte der Literatur und der schönen Kunste, IV (Munich 1965), esp. pp. 80ff.

8 According to the interpretation of K. H. Stierle, *Dunkelheit und Form in Gérard de Nervals 'Chimères,'* Theorie und Geschichte der Literatur und der schönen Künste, V (Munich, 1967), esp. pp. 55 and 91.

9 See Buck, *Lernen und Erfahrung*, pp. 64 ff., about this idea of Husserl.

10 Here I am incorporating the results of the discussion of 'Kitsch', as a fringe manifestation of aesthetics, which took place during the third colloquium of the 'Forschungsgruppe Poetik und Hermeneutik' in the volume, *Die nicht mehr schönen Küste – Grenzphänomene des Asthetischen*, ed. H.R. Jauss (Munich, 1968). For the 'culinary' approach which presupposes mere light reading, the same thing holds true as for 'Kitsch', namely, that the 'demands of the consumers are *a priori* satisfied' (P. Beylin), that 'the fulfilled expectation becomes the standard for the product' (W. Iser) or that 'a work appears to be solving a problem when in reality it neither has nor solves a problem (M. Imdahl), pp. 651–67.

11 As also 'Epigonentum' (Decadence), for this see B. Tomasevskij (in: *Théorie de la littérature. Texts des formalistes russes*, ed. by T. Todorov [Paris, 1965], p. 306): 'L'apparition d'un génie équivaut toujours à une révolution littéraire qui détrône le canon dominant et donne le pouvoir aux procédés jusqu'alors subordonnés. [. . .] Les épigones répètent une combinaison usée des procédés, et d'originale et révolutionnaire qu'elle était, cette combinaison devient stéréotypée et traditionelle. Ainsi les épigones tuent parfois pour longtemps l'aptitude des contemporains à sentir la force esthétique des exemples qu'ils imitent: ils discréditent leurs maîtres.'

12 R. Escarpit, *Das Buch und der Leser: Entwurf einer Literatursoziologie* (Cologne and Opladen, 1961; first German expanded edition of *Sociologie de la littérature* [Paris, 1958]), p. 116.

13 K. H. Bender, *König und Vasall: Untersuchungen zur Chanson de Geste des XII. Jahrhunderts*, Studia Romanica, XIII (Heidelberg, 1967), shows which step is necessary in order to escape from this one-sided determination. In this history of the early French epic the apparent congruence of feudal society and epic ideality is represented as a process which is maintained through a continually changing discrepancy between 'reality' and 'ideology', that is between the historical constellations of feudal conflict and the poetic answers of the epic.

14 The much more sophisticated sociology of literature by Erich Auerbach brought to light this aspect in the variety of epoch-making disruptions of the relationship between author and reader. See also the evaluation of F. Schalk in his edition of E. Auerbach's *Gesämmelte Aufsätze zur romanischen Philologie* (Bern and Munich, 1967), pp. 11ff.

15 See H. Weinrich, 'Für eine Literaturgeschichte des Lesers', *Merkur*, XXI (November, 1967). Just as the linguistics of the speaker, which was earlier customary, has been replaced by the linguistics of the listener, Weinrich pleads for a methodical consideration for the perspective of the reader in literary history and thereby supports my aims. Weinrich shows especially how the empirical methods of literary sociology can be supplemented by the linguistic and literary interpretation of the role of the reader, which is implicit in the work.

16 In '*Madame Bovary* par Gustave Flaubert, Baudelaire, *Oeuvres complètes*, Pléiade ed. (Paris, 1951), p. 998: 'The last years of Louis-Philippe witnessed the last

explosions of a spirit still excitable by the play of the imagination; but the new novelist found himself faced with a completely worn-out society – worse than worn-out – stupified and gluttonous, with a horror only of fiction and love only for possession.'

17 Cf. *ibid.*, p. 999, as well as the accusation, speech for the defence, and verdict of the *Bovary* trial in Flaubert, *Oeuvres*, Pléiade edition (Paris, 1951), 1, pp. 649–717, esp. 717; also about *Fanny*, E. Montegut, 'Le roman intime de la littérature réaliste', *Revue des deux mondes*, XVIII (1858), pp. 196–213, esp. 201 and 209ff.

18 As Baudelaire testifies ('*Madame Bovary* par Gustave Flaubertt,' p. 996): 'for since the disappearance of Balzac . . . all curiosity relative to the novel has been stilled and slumbers.'

19 For these and other contemporary verdicts see H. R. Jauss, 'Die beiden Fassungen van Flauberts "Education sentimental"', *Heidelberger Jahrbücher*, 11 (1958), pp. 96–116, esp. 97.

20 See the excellent analysis by the contemporary critic E. Montegut ('Le roman intime de la littérature réaliste'), who explains in detail why the dreams and the figures in Feydeau's novel are typical for the readers in the section between the *Bourse* and the boulevard Montmartre (p. 209): they need an 'alcool poétique', enjoy seeing 'their vulgar adventures of yesterday and their vulgar projects of tomorrow poeticized' (p. 210) and have an 'idolatry of the material' by which term Montegut understands the ingredients of the 'dream factory' of 1959 – 'a sort of sanctimonious admiration, almost devout, for furniture, wallpaper, dress, escapes, like a perfume of patchouli, from each of its pages' (p. 201).

---

10 Paul Ricoeur,

'Phenomenology and Theory of Literature: An Interview with Paul Ricoeur', *Modern Language Notes*, 96:5 (December 1981), pp. 1084–90

Erik Nakjavani (Q): Professor Ricoeur, I have followed with increasing interest your lectures on the application of the phenomenological method to the concept of action in sociology and political science. You have opened up new perspectives in these disciplines, and have brought to them an intense light of a certain specific quality. It is the particular nature of this light which seems to be of an enormous interdisciplinary significance.

By profession and by inclination, I find myself in another field, that of literature. For us, as René Wellek has so perceptively pointed out, the most urgent need appears to be a cohesive theory of literature, an organon of methods which could satisfactorily deal with such fundamental problems as the nature of the literary creative process, the mode of existence of a work of literature, and its classification, explanation, and evaluation.

The remarkable efforts of Freudian and Marxist literary theorists have provided us with some powerful extrinsic or egocentric approaches to the study of literature. Unfortunately, they remain approaches from without and seem to have failed to offer us an adequate theory of literature capable of grasping the complexities of a work of literature from within and as an independent, autonomous phenomenon.

It would be invaluable to us if you would care to discuss the possibility of an intrinsic or egocentric phenomenological approach to the theory of literature, and its potentials and limitations.

Paul Ricoeur: The first task of a phenomenological approach to the problem of literature would be to define the boundaries of the idea of text. What is a text? It is a question which includes several questions. First, what are the absolutely fundamental characteristics of discourse? By discourse, I don't mean at all language, which the linguist might mean, but the messages which we produce freely on the foundation and the structure of language. So, there is already a specific feature of discourse, in comparison to language, which constitutes the first boundary of the literary object. First, among the traits of discourse, I would put it that discourse opens up a world. In short, it is a way of revealing a dimension of reality in relationship to dialogue with another person, the listener. Therefore, there is a triangular relationship among one who speaks, one who listens and answers, and, then, the world of things which one talks about. This triangular relationship is the very basis of the problem of literary criticism, because what is to be understood in a discourse is the quality of the world, the dimension of the world, isn't it?, which is opened up by communication. That would be the first level of an approach to the problem of the text.

The second level would be a reflection on what writing adds to this triangular relationship among one who speaks, one who listens, and the discovered reality which is made manifest by the dialogue. Primarily, through writing, the discourse slips away from the speaker, since writing has the power to preserve the discourse after the destruction and disappearance of the speaker. So, there is an autonomy of text in relationship to the occurrence of the discourse, which is at its origin and enables the text to have a destiny distinct from that of its author. The writer dies, but the text pursues its career, continues and produces its effects from time to time, which is vaster than the time of a human life. Therefore, if we go back to this triangular relationship, in regard to the author of the discourse, the text frees itself from the boundary of the history of its production and survives the occurrence of speech.

On the other hand, from the point of view of the listener, writing opens up a relationship which is much more comprehensive than the relationship of dialogue which remains locked up in the *I-thou* communication. A text opens up an audience, which is unlimited, while the relationship of dialogue is a closed relationship. The text is open to whoever knows how to read, and whose potential reader is everyone. There is, therefore, an opening in comparison to the closure of dialogue, which accounts, finally, for the literary work being an open work, an unlimited number of readings which are, for me, each a sort of new occurrence of speech taking possession of the text in order to give it a new actuality.

Third, the world which is opened up in this manner by writing is itself also a world which has an infinite horizon, while dialogue in spoken word is bound to the listener. Literature creates a world of fiction, of possibility, and, consequently, opens up a horizon of reality, too. Our sense of reality is multiplied by this world of fiction and possibility.

I think that that is the second approach to our problem of the nature of the text: What is a text?

I see, perhaps, a third problem which would be interesting: that would be to apply the category of work to utterance and discourse. In fact, we are constantly talking about a work of art. We talk about a piece of work. In English, the word work is very striking. Therefore, discourse may be the object of a work, and, as a result, one may apply the category of work to it.

If we define work as an activity through which we give form to matter, there is a literature because language is treated as matter which receives a form. The theory of forms is a part of literary criticism for this reason, because there are different genres of forms, whether they be the novel, poetry, or theatre. First of all, it is a paradox that one may think that work is contrary to speech; there is a literature because there is work done through speech and on speech, which is precisely to make a piece of work of it. That is particularly manifest in the case of poetry in which it is a veritable work done on language, because it is a work which consists in binding together, in an absolutely indissoluble manner, the sound and meaning, in such a way that the poem constitutes a sort of perfect object, closed on itself like a piece of sculpture.

If one adds these three categories: first, the category of discourse; second, the category of writing; third, the category of work, one discovers that the text is something to be interpreted, because it is open to an unlimited number of possible readings which will convert writing into living speech. Reading is a human act of considerable importance, which has rules distinct from listening to a dialogue. In short, it is something else to read a text than to listen to a spoken discourse. It is precisely because the text is mute and does not answer that it must be given life. There is a way of reanimating speech which is invested in the text. I would think that would be the function of hermeneutics to develop the theory of the act of reading which corresponds to this investment of discourse in writing and in literary work. The theory of hermeneutics, in my opinion, would consist of developing the parallel theory of genesis of text and of reading, and to show the flow of one to the other. This undertaking itself requires a very different operation, because the act of reading is, after all, a summing-up of numerous activities, going from the simple interpretation of sentences in their syntactic and semantic constitution to the comprehension of the work of an author in its living totality. Semantics does not go beyond the level of the isolated sentence, but hermeneutics begins with the work taken as a signifying totality, which is not simply a sum of sentences placed end-to-end but a relationship of all parts which has its own laws.

So, since the text has an autonomy in relation to the writer, and also in relation to the reader, one may certainly treat it primarily as a thing which is completely independent, both of the writer and the reader, and one may treat it as an absolute object. This is the tendency of French structuralism to treat a text as a structure which has its own laws and that one may study objectively, not in the least mixing it with the expectations, preferences, prejudices, or the hopes and affinities of the reader. This undertaking is perfectly legitimate, because it is justified by the very nature of the text as a kind of reality which has made itself autonomous in relation to the initial situation in which it was produced; therefore, it has become independent in relation to dialogue. Only, I would think that for me, this objective and absolutely disinterested study, in the right meaning of the word, therefore, without any relationship to our interest, is merely an abstract and preparatory phase for an appreciation of the text from which we make our own flesh and blood through a sort of appropriation which makes from what was strange something appropriate and familiar. I don't believe that these two attitudes, one much more objective, which triumphs in structuralism, the other much more subjective, which triumphs in what I have just called appropriation, contradict each other, because they mutually bring each other forth. A completely objective study kills the text, because one operates on a cadaver. But, inversely, reading which would be perfectly naive and would not have passed through all the mediations of an objective and structural approach would be only the projection of the subjectivity of the reader on the text. Consequently, it is necessary that subjectivity be held in some way at a distance and that the appropriation be in some way mediated by all the objectifying activities. I believe that phenomenology here is very enlightening, because it shows that all modes of relationship that one may have to another – and, after all, writing is a communicative relationship – pass through the mediation of the theory of objectifying acts, which Husserl develops in connection with an entirely different question, either the theory of perception or the theory of consciousness. This phase of objectification may be found everywhere in the lectures which I am giving at the moment on social and political theory, and plays a fundamental role. One sees that all social relationships pass through the intermediaries of institutions, of codes, of rules, which are very often anonymous and impenetrable. Well, literature is one of these mediations. But, contrary to the opaque mediations of politics, literature is a transparent mediation in which the institution becomes exactly a text. While the institutions are in great part indecipherable because the history which has produced them escapes us, the characteristic of literature is to create among us a transparent mediation, because it is entirely sustained by speech.

Q: You have talked about the phenomenology of the text. Now I would like to ask you what you think of the possibility of a phenomenology of the critic, because it seems to me that it would be useful to explore the relationship of the critic with the text.

Ricoeur: This is a very difficult question, for which I am not prepared, because I suspect that we lack here a wholly indispensable tool that comes from another discipline rather than from phenomenology. I am thinking about the critique of ideologies, in the fashion of the School of Frankfurt, which is a certain heritage of Marxism. But why introduce here the critique of ideologies, because the critic himself is always in a certain historical situation. He is tied to a certain culture and, consequently, he isn't this absolute, disinterested subject, a sort of non-involved ego. He is himself caught in the movement of the culture. So he doesn't have this kind of flight position or a view from above. He himself has a lateral vision of literary works. Consequently, he is exactly in the situation of a perceiving subject who always has only a side view; therefore, there is a sort of self-criticism of the critic, which is certainly an important part of the theory of literature.

You did very well to ask this question, because up to the present time we have chiefly had a theory of the literary object, and the activities on the literary object. But, what are the activities on the subject of the critic? There we have two extreme positions, which, it seems to me, would both be unacceptable. One would make of the critic a militant, who would be a person with a cause, and who, consequently, would like to show by means of literature that a certain morality, that a certain religion, that a certain politics is true. Then, at that moment, the criticism becomes apologetics. And then, at the other extreme, there would be the position which would claim that criticism has no set purpose, that criticism is neutral.

Between partisan criticism, which is an act of violence done to the text and, perhaps, to the reader, and this hypocritical claim that the critic belongs nowhere, there is this kind of self-criticism by the critic who knows that it is always from the basis of a prejudice that one understands something. In other words, it is necessary to understand that all comprehension implies a pre-comprehension; that is to say, a certain affinity with the object and, therefore, also a whole cultural equipment. It is from the depth of a certain culture that I approach a new object of the culture. As a result pre-comprehension and prejudice are necessarily a part of comprehension. There cannot be any self-criticism by a neutral critic. And, inversely, a critic cannot be partisan. So, there is an extremely delicate point of balance there between, on the one hand, the conviction that pre-comprehension and prejudgment are a vital part of comprehension of every object and, on the other hand and at the same time, the critique of the illusions of the subject which one may make with the aid of either Marxism or psychoanalysis.

But I myself don't believe that a single critique of ideologies suffices, because there is a truth in pre-comprehension. The question would then be posed again to the critic of ideologies: where does he stand himself and who will do the critique of the critic? Anyway, there is a pre-comprehension, because there is no comprehension without pre-comprehension. But pre-comprehension is at the same time prejudice. German is, however, very interesting from that point of view, because there is one word, *Vorurteil*, which means *préjugement* and *préjugé*, prejudgment and prejudice in English. Phenomenology of the critic is based upon the dialectic between prejudice and prejudgment.

Q: Mikel Dufrenne, in *Aesthetics and Philosophy*, talks about the triple function of the critic: to clarify, to explain, and to judge. I would like you to talk about his formulation, if you would, because I find it to be a sort of theorem of the critic's function.

Ricoeur: I believe that phenomenology only concerns, it seems to me, the first two, to clarify and to explain, because to clarify a work of literature, in the language which I was trying to develop in the beginning, is to understand the internal structure of it, to see how the different codes, the different subjacent structures, hold the message of the work; then, to explain is to put it in connection with its author, its public, its world in the triangular relationship which I have already explained, and which begins with discourse. I have an impression, that judging comes from another discipline which would be aesthetics, properly speaking, and which would be passing judgment on what Kant has called the judgment of taste. I wouldn't like to make of phenomenology an almighty science. Not everything is phenomenological. I believe that phenomenology stops at the threshold of judgment. After that comes the function of aesthetics, which is a kind of decision, isn't it? It seems to me that in phenomenology there is an inclination to stop short of judgments – beautiful, ugly, successful, unsuccessful – in short, an appreciation which is after all a value judgment. Perhaps after that, there will be a phenomenology of this appreciative activity in terms of what I was trying to say about the phenomenology of the critic. But I think it is always the function of the critic to help the public to judge by proposing a judgment to them, it is an absolutely fundamental educative function, for the reason that, mainly, we have learned to discern great works from lesser works because, after all, the critics have already judged them. One could say that what we call tradition is a sort of continued critical judgment. The tradition has ratified somehow that Greek tragedy, for example, is a thing of grandeur. There is, briefly, a recognition of grandeur, which is not merely the work of the individual critic but a sort of continued criticism from one century to another. It is also true that there are works which are judged great in a certain period, then, later, fall into oblivion and disdain. There is also the history of this critical judgment, which is a completely specific history and which has its own rules.

Q: Thank you very much, Professor Ricoeur, for having talked to us.

11 Harold Bloom,

From *The Anxiety of Influence* (1973), pp. 87–92

To the study of revisionary ratios that characterize intra-poetic relationships, I now add a third: *kenosis* or 'emptying', at once an 'undoing' and an 'isolating' movement of the imagination. I take *kenosis* from St. Paul's account of Christ 'humbling' himself from God to man. In strong poets, the *kenosis* is a revisionary act in which an 'emptying', or 'ebbing' takes place *in relation to the precursor*. This 'emptying' is a liberating discontinuity, and makes possible a kind of poem that a simple repetition of the precursor's afflatus or godhood could not allow. 'Undoing' the precursor's strength *in oneself* serves also to 'isolate' the self from the precursor's stance, and saves the latecomer-poet from becoming taboo in and to himself. Freud emphasizes the relation of defense mechanisms to the entire area of the taboo, and we note the relevance to the *kenosis* of the context of touching and washing taboos.

Why is influence, which might be a health, more generally an anxiety where strong poets are concerned? Do strong poets gain or lose more, *as poets*, in their wrestling with their ghostly fathers? Do *clinamen, tessera, kenosis*, and all other revisionary ratios that misinterpret or metamorphose precursors help poets to individuate themselves, truly to be themselves, or do they distort the poetic sons quite as much as they do the fathers? I am predicating that these revisionary ratios have the same function in intra-poetic relations that defense mechanisms have in our psychic life. Do the mechanisms of defence, in our daily lives, damage us more than the repetition compulsions from which they seek to defend us?

Freud, highly dialectical here, is clearest I think in the powerful late essay, 'Analysis Terminable and Interminable' (1937). If for his 'ego' we substitute the ephebe, and for his 'id' the precursor, then he gives us a formula for the ephebe's dilemma:

> For quite a long time flight and an avoidance of a dangerous situation serve as expedients in the face of external danger, until the individual is finally strong enough to remove the menace by actively modifying reality. But one cannot flee from oneself and no flight avails against danger from within; hence the ego's defensive mechanisms are condemned to falsify the inner perception, *so that it transmits to us only an imperfect and travestied picture of our id. In its relations with the id the ego is paralysed by its restrictions or blinded by its errors,* and the result in the sphere of psychical events may be compared to the progress of a poor walker in a country which he does not know.
>
> The purpose of the defensive mechanisms is to avert dangers. It cannot be disputed that they are successful; it is doubtful whether the ego can altogether do without them during its development, but it is also certain that they rhemselves may become dangerous. Nor infrequently it turns out that the ego

has paid too high a price for the services which these mechanisms render. [my italics; not Freud's]

This melancholy vision ends with the adult ego, at its strongest, defending itself against vanished dangers and even seeking substitutes for the vanished originals. In the *agon* of the strong poet, the achieved substitutes tend to be earlier versions of the ephebe himself, who in some sense laments a glory he never had. Without as yet abandoning the Freudian model, let us examine more closely the crucial mechanisms of 'undoing' and 'isolating,' before returning to the darkness I have called *kenosis* or 'emptying.'

Fenichel relates 'undoing' to expiation, a washing-clean that still obeys the taboo of washing, and which therefore intends to do the opposite of the compulsive act yet paradoxically performs the same act with an opposite unconscious meaning. Artistic sublimation, on this view, is connected to attitudes that intend an undoing of imaginative destructions. 'Isolating' keeps apart what belongs together, preserving traumata but abandoning their emotional meanings, while obeying the taboo against touching. Spatial and temporal distortions frequently abound in such phenomena of isolation, as we might expect from the connection here to the primordial taboo on touching.

Kenosis is a more ambivalent movement than *clinamen* or *tessera*, and necessarily brings poems more deeply into the realms of antithetical meanings. For, in *kenosis*, the artist's battle against art has been lost, and the poet falls or ebbs into a space and time that confine him, even as he undoes the precursor's pattern by a deliberate, willed loss in continuity. His stance *appears* to be that of his precursor (as Keats's stance appears to be Milton's in the first *Hyperion*), but the meaning of the stance is undone; the stance is *emptied* of its priority, which is a kind of godhood, and the poet holding it becomes more isolated, not only from his fellows, but from the continuity of his own self.

What is the use of this notion of poetic *kenosis*, to the reader attempting to describe any poem he feels compelled to describe? The ratios *clinamen* and *tessera* may be useful in aligning (and disaligning) elements in disparate poems, but this third ratio seems more applicable to poets than to poems. Since, as readers, we need to tell the dancer from the dance, the singer from his song, how are we aided in our difficult enterprise by this idea of a self-emptying that seeks to defend against the father, yet radically undoes the son? Is the *kenosis* of Shelley in his *Ode to the West Wind* an undoing, an isolating of Wordsworth or of Shelley? Who is emptied more fearfully in Whitman's *As I Ebb'd with the Ocean of Life*, Emerson or Whitman? When Stevens confronts the terrible auroras, is it his autumn or Keats's that is emptied of its humanizing solace? Ammons, walking the dunes of Corsons Inlet, empties himself of an Overall, now acknowledged to be beyond him, but does not the poem's meaning turn upon its conviction that Emerson's Overall was beyond even that sage? The palinode seems to be inevitable in the later phases of any Romantic poet's progress, but is it his own song he must sing over again in reversal? Dante, Chaucer, even Spenser can make their own recantation into poetry, but Milton, Goethe, Hugo recant their precursors' errors rather more than their own. With more ambivalent modern poets, even poets as strong as Blake, Wordsworth, Baudelaire, Rilke, Yeats, Stevens, every *kenosis* voids a precursor's powers, as though a magical undoing-isolating sought to save the Egotistical Sublime at a father's expense. *Kenosis*, in this poetic and revisionary sense, appears to be an act of self-abnegation, yet tends to make the fathers pay for their own sins, and perhaps for those of the sons also.

I arrive therefore at the pragmatic formula: 'Where the precursor was, there the ephebe shall be, but by the discontinuous mode of emptying the precursor of *his* divinity, while appearing to empty himself of his own.' However plangent or even despairing the poem of *kenosis*, the ephebe takes care to fall soft, while the precursor falls hard.

We need to stop thinking of any poet as an autonomous ego, however solipsistic the strongest of poets may be. Every poet is a being caught up in a dialectical relationship (transference, repetition, error, communication) with another poet or poets. In the archetypal *kenosis*, St. Paul found a pattern that no poet whatever could bear to emulate, as poet:

> Let nothing be done through strife or vainglory; but in lowliness of mind let each esteem others better than themselves.
>
> Look not every man on his own things, but every man also on the things of others.
>
> Let this mind be in you, which was also in Christ Jesus:
>
> Who, being in the form of God, thought it not robbery to be equal with God:
>
> But made himself of no reputation, and took upon him the form of a servant, and was made in the likeness of men: And being found in fashion as a man, he humbled himself, and became obedient unto death. . . .

Against this *kenosis*, we can set a characteristic *daemonic* parody of it which is the poetic *kenosis* proper, not so much a humbling of self as of all precursors, and necessarily a defiance unto death. Blake cries out to Tirzah:

> Whate'er is Born of Mortal Birth,
> Must be consumed with the Earth
> To rise from Generation free;
> Then what have I to do with thee?

SECTION SIX
FEMINISM

Perhaps more than any other mode of criticism, Feminist theory has cut across and drawn on multiple and contradictory traditions whilst presenting what is arguably one of the most fundamental challenges to critical orthodoxies: its revaluation of subjectivity and the category of 'experience'.

Early Feminist criticism drew extensively on Simone de Beauvoir's *The Second Sex*,[1] a work which had initiated the process of analysing the social construction of gender and of distinguishing between sex and gender; and on Kate Millett's *Sexual Politics*[2] which analysed the system of sex-role stereotyping and the oppression of women under patriarchial social organisation. Much of the criticism which drew on these texts and flourished, particulary in America, in the 1970s, concentrated its analysis on the 'images' of women represented in, or constructed through, cultural forms such as literature.[3] Rarely did this writing seek explicitly to question the category of 'literature' itself or the dominant expressive-mimetic aesthetics. It has thus been viewed by later Feminists[4] as often failing to offer an adequate analysis of the relationship between ideology and representation, and thus as inadvertently affirming the universalism and subjectivism of traditional liberal-humanist criticism.

In the article reprinted here, by the British Marxist-Feminist Collective, there is instead an attempt to study the literary text through an analysis of the *specific* articulations of patriarchy within capitalist society. Such an approach emphasises the need to situate the text in relation to an analysis, for example, of the economic position of women as a consequence of the division of labour and the organization of the family; the effects of this on female authorship and reading habits; the control and organization of reproduction and sexuality; the role of cultural forms such as literature in this process, and the specific organization of the institution of literature according to masculine discourses and valuations.

By the mid-70s there was increasing attention from both broadly 'liberal' or broadly 'socialist' or 'radical' Feminists to texts by women as opposed to the study of the representation of women in texts by male authors. This approach was explicitly advocated, in particular' by Elaine Showalter as the basis of 'Gynocriticism', and her A *Literature of Their Own*[5] attempted to construct an alternative tradition of women's writing, focusing specifically on female writing and experience. Although her work challenged the sexist bias of the liberal tradition, it failed to challenge its fundamental conception of the subject and of the literary text. Subjectivity was still conceived of in essential and unitary terms; tradition remained a continuous and seamless process and the text itself remained embedded in an expressive-mimetic aesthetic. In many ways, therefore, Showalter's work reaffirms the orthodox humanist belief in literature as the expression of a universal unity encompassing men *and* women and known as 'human nature'. The category is simply enlarged rather than undermined or deconstructed. Later Feminists were to challenge this conception of the literary process, drawing on the insights of Structuralist Marxism, psychoanalysis and deconstruction.

Notes

1 S. de Beauvoir, *The Second Sex*, tr. H.M. Parshley (Harmondsworth, Penguin, 1974).
2 K. Millett, *Sexual Politics* (London, Virago, 1977).
3 J. Donovan, *Feminist Literary Criticism: Explorations in Theory* (Kentucky, 1975); M. Ellman, ed., *Thinking about Women* (London, Virago, 1979).
4 C. Kaplan, *Sea Changes: Essays on Culture and Feminism* (London, Verso, 1986); T. Moi, *Sexual/Textual Criticism: Feminist Literary Theory* (London, Methuen, 1985).
5 E. Showalter, *A Literature of Their Own* (Princeton, NJ, Princeton University Press, 1977; London, Virago, 1978).

---

12 Elaine Showalter,

'Towards a Feminist Poetics', in M. Jacobus, ed. *Women Writing About Women* (1979), pp. 25–33; 34–6

Feminist criticism can be divided into two distinct varieties. The first type is concerned with *woman as reader* – with woman as the consumer of male-produced literature, and with the way in which the hypothesis of a female reader changes our apprehension of a given text, awakening us to the significance of its sexual codes. I shall call this kind of analysis the *feminist critique*, and like other kinds of critique it is a historically grounded inquiry which probes the ideological assumptions of literary phenomena. Its subjects include the images and stereotypes of women in literature, the omissions and misconceptions about women in criticism, and the fissures in male-constructed literary history. It is also concerned with the exploitation and manipulation of the female audience, especially in popular culture and film; and with the analysis of woman-as-sign in semiotic systems. The second type of feminist criticism is concerned with *woman as writer* – with woman as the producer of textual meaning, with the history, themes, genres and structures of literature by women. Its subjects include the psychodynamics of female creativity, linguistics and the problem of a female language; the trajectory of the individual or collective female literary career; literary history; and, of course, studies of particular writers and works. No term exists in English for such a specialised discourse, and so I have adapted the French term *la gynocritique*: 'gynocritics' (although the significance of the male pseudonym in the history of women's writing also suggested the term 'georgics').

The feminist critique is essentially political and polemical, with theoretical affiliations to Marxist sociology and aesthetics; gynocritics is more self-contained and experimental, with connections to other modes of new feminist research. In a dialogue between these two positions, Carolyn Heilbrun, the writer, and Catherine Stimpson, editor of the American journal *Signs: Women in Culture and Society*, compare the feminist critique to the Old Testament, 'looking for the sins and errors of the past', and gynocritics to the New Testament, seeking 'the grace of imagination'. Both kinds are necessary, they explain, for only the Jeremiahs of the feminist critique can lead us out of the 'Egypt of female servitude' to the promised land of the feminist vision. That the discussion makes use of these Biblical metaphors points to the connections between feminist consciousness and conversion narratives which often appear in women's literature; Carolyn Heilbrun comments on her own text, 'when I talk about feminist criticism, I am amazed at how high a moral tone I take'.[1]

The Feminist Critique: Hardy

Let us take briefly as an example of the way a feminist critique might proceed, Thomas Hardy's *The Mayor of Casterbridge*, which begins with the famous scene of the drunken Michael Henchard selling his wife and infant daughter for five guineas at a country fair. In his study of Hardy, Irving Howe has praised the brilliance and power of this opening scene:

> To shake loose from one's wife; to discard the drooping rag of a woman, with her mute complaints and maddening passivity; to escape not by a slinking abandonment but through the public sale of her body to a stranger, as horses are sold at a fair; and thus to wrest, through sheer amoral wilfulness, a second chance out of life – it is with this stroke, so insidiously attractive to male fantasy, that *The Mayor of Casterbridge* begins.[2]

It is obvious that a woman, unless she has been indoctrinated into being very deeply identified indeed with male culture, will have a different experience of this scene. I quote Howe first to indicate how the fantasies of the male critic distort the text; for Hardy tells us very little about the relationship of Michael and Susan Henchard, and what we see in the early scenes does not suggest that she is drooping, complaining or passive. Her role, however, is a passive one; severely constrained by her womanhood, and further burdened by her child, there is no way that *she* can wrest a second chance out of life. She cannot master events, but only accommodate herself to them.

What Howe, like other male critics of Hardy, conveniently overlooks about the novel is that Henchard sells not only his wife but his child, a child who can only be female. Patriarchal societies do not readily sell their sons, but their daughters are all for sale sooner or later. Hardy wished to make the sale of the daughter emphatic and central; in early drafts of the novel Henchard has two daughters and sells only one, but Hardy revised to make it clearer that Henchard is symbolically selling his entire share in the world of women. Having severed his bonds with this female community of love and loyalty, Henchard has chosen to live in the male community, to define his human relationships by the male code of paternity, money and legal contract. His tragedy lies in realising the inadequacy of this system, and in his inability to repossess the loving bonds he comes desperately to need.

The emotional centre of *The Mayor of Casterbridge* is neither Henchard's relationship to his wife, nor his superficial romance with Lucetta Templeman, but his slow appreciation of the strength and dignity of his wife's daughter, Elizabeth-Jane. Like the other women in the book, she is governed by her own heart – man-made laws are not important to her until she is taught by Henchard himself to value legality, paternity, external definitions, and thus in the end to reject him. A self-proclaimed 'woman-hater', a man who has felt at best a 'supercilious pity' for womankind, Henchard is humbled and 'unmanned' by the collapse of his own virile facade, the loss of his mayor's chain, his master's authority, his father's rights. But in Henchard's alleged weakness and 'womanishness', breaking through in moments of tenderness, Hardy is really showing us the man at his best. Thus Hardy's female characters in *The Mayor of Casterbridge*, as in his other novels, are somewhat idealised and melancholy projections of a repressed male self.

As we see in this analysis, one of the problems of the feminist critique is that it is male-oriented. If we study stereotypes of women, the sexism of male critics, and the limited roles women play in literary history, we are not learning what women have felt and experienced, but what men have thought women should be. In some fields of specialisation, this may require a long apprenticeship to the male theoretician, whether he be Althusser, Barthes, Macherey or Lacan; and then an application of the theory of signs or myths or the unconscious to male texts or films. The temporal and intellectual investment one makes in such a process increases resistance to questioning it, and to seeing its historical and ideological boundaries. The critique also has a tendency to naturalise women's victimisation, by making it the inevitable and obsessive topic of discussion. One sees, moreover, in works like Elizabeth Hardwick's *Seduction and Betrayal*, the bittersweet moral distinctions the critic makes between women merely betrayed by men, like Hetty in *Adam Bede*, and the heroines who make careers out of betrayal, like Hester Prynne in *The Scarlet Letter*. This comes dangerously close to a celebration of the opportunities of victimisation, the seduction *of* betrayal.[3]

Gynocritics and Female Culture

In contrast to this angry or loving fixation on male literature, the programme of gynocritics is to construct a female framework for the analysis of women's literature, to develop new models based on the study of female experience, rather than to adapt male models and theories. Gynocritics begins at the point when we free ourselves from the linear absolutes of male literary history, stop trying to fit women between the lines of the male tradition, and focus instead on the newly visible world of female culture. This is comparable to the ethnographer's effort to render the experience of the 'muted' female half of a society, Welch is described in Shirley Ardener's collection, *Perceiving Women*.[4] Gynocritics is related to feminist research in history, anthropology, psychology and sociology, all of which have developed hypotheses of a female subculture including not only the ascribed status, and the internalised constructs of femininity, but also the occupations, interactions and consciousness of women. Anthropologists study the female subculture in the relationships between women, as mothers, daughters, sisters and friends; in sexuality, reproduction and ideas about the body; and in rites of initiation and passage, purification ceremonies, myths and taboos. Michelle Rosaldo writes in *Woman, Culture, and Society*,

> the very symbolic and social conceptions that appear to set women apart and to circumscribe their activities may be used by the women as a basis for female solidarity and worth. When men live apart from women, they in fact cannot control them, and unwittingly they may provide them with the symbols and social resources on which to build a society of their own.[5]

Thus in some women's literature, feminine values penetrate and undermine the masculine systems which contain them; and women have imaginatively engaged the myths of the Amazons, and the fantasies of a separate female society, in genres from Victorian poetry to contemporary science fiction.

In the past two years, pioneering work by four young American feminist scholars has given us some new ways to interpret the culture of nineteenth-century American women, and the literature which was its primary expressive form. Carroll Smith-Rosenberg's essay 'The Female World of Love and Ritual' examines several archives of letters between women, and outlines the homosocial emotional world of the nineteenth century. Nancy Cott's *The Bonds of Womanhood: Woman's Sphere in New England 1780-1835* explores the paradox of a cultural bondage, a legacy of pain and submission, which none the less generates a sisterly solidarity, a bond of shared experience, loyalty and compassion. Ann Douglas's ambitious book, *The Feminization of American Culture*, boldly locates the genesis of American mass culture in the sentimental literature of women and clergymen, two allied and 'disestablished' post-industrial groups. These three are social historians; but Nina Auerbach's *Communities of Women: An idea in Fiction* seeks the bonds of womanhood in women's literature, ranging from the matriarchal households of Louisa May Alcott and Mrs Gaskell to the women's schools and colleges of Dorothy Sayers, Sylvia Plath and Muriel Spark. Historical and literary studies like these, based on English women, are badly needed; and the manuscript and archival sources for them are both abundant and untouched.[6]

Gynocritics: Elizabeth Barrett Browning and Muriel Spark

Gynocritics must also take into account the different velocities and curves of political, social and personal histories in determining women's literary choices and careers. 'In dealing with women as writers,' Virginia Woolf wrote in her 1929 essay, 'Women and Fiction', 'as much elasticity as possible is desirable; it is necessary to leave oneself room to deal with other things besides their work, so much has that work been influenced by conditions that have nothing whatever to do with art.'[7] We might illustrate the need for this completeness by looking at Elizabeth Barrett Browning, whose verse-novel *Aurora Leigh* (1856) has recently been handsomely reprinted by the Women's Press. In her excellent introduction Cora Kaplan defines Barrett Browning's feminism as romantic and bourgeois, placing its faith in the transforming powers of love, art and Christian charity. Kaplan reviews Barrett Browning's dialogue with the artists and radicals of her time; with Tennyson and Clough, who had also written poems on the 'woman question'; with the Christian Socialism of Fourier, Owen, Kingsley and Maurice; and with such female predecessors as Madame de Staël and George Sand. But in this exploration of Barrett Browning's intellectual milieu, Kaplan omits discussion of the male poet whose influence on her work in the 1850s would have been most pervasive: Robert Browning. When we understand how susceptible women writers have always been to the aesthetic standards and values of the male tradition, and to male approval and validation, we can appreciate the complexity of a marriage between artists. Such a union has almost invariably meant internal conflicts, self-effacement, and finally obliteration for the women, except in the rare cases – Eliot and Lewes, the Woolfs – where the husband accepted a managerial rather than a competitive role. We can see in Barrett Browning's letters of the 1850s the painful, halting, familiar struggle between her womanly love and ambition for her husband and her conflicting commitment to her own work. There is a sense in which she *wants* him to be the better artist. At the beginning of the decade she was more famous than he; then she notes with pride a review in France which praises him more; his work on *Men and Women* goes well; her work on *Aurora Leigh* goes badly (she had a young

child and was recovering from the most serious of her four miscarriages).
In 1854 she writes to a woman friend,

> I am behind hand with my poem . . . Robert swears he shall have his book ready
> in spite of everything for print when we shall be in London for the purpose, but,
> as for mine, it must wait for the next spring I begin to see clearly. Also it may
> be better not to bring out the two works together.

And she adds wryly; 'If mine were ready I might not say so perhaps.'[8]

Without an understanding of the framework of the female subculture, we
can miss or misinterpret the themes and structures of women's literature,
fail to make necessary connections within a tradition. In 1852, in an eloquent
passage from her autobiographical essay 'Cassandra', Florence Nightingale
identified the pain of feminist awakening as its essence, as the guarantee of
progress and free will. Protesting against the protected unconscious lives of
middle-class Victorian women, Nightingale demanded the restoration of
their suffering:

> Give us back our suffering, we cry to Heaven in our hearts – suffering rather
> than indifferentism – for out of suffering may come the cure. Better to have pain
> than paralysis: A hundred struggle and drown in the breakers. One discovers a
> new world.[9]

It is fascinating to see how Nightingale's metaphors anticipate not only her
own medical career, but also the fate of the heroines of women's novels in
the nineteenth and twentieth centuries. To waken from the drugged pleasant
sleep of Victorian womanhood was agonising; in fiction it is much more
likely to end in drowning than in discovery. It is usually associated with
what George Eliot in *Middlemarch* calls 'the chill hours of a morning
twilight', and the sudden appalled confrontation with the contingencies of
adulthood. Eliot's Maggie Tulliver, Edith Wharton's Lily Barth, Olive
Schreiner's Lyndall, Kate Chopin's Edna Pontellier wake to worlds which
offer no places for the women they wish to become; and rather than
struggling they die. Female suffering thus becomes a kind of literary
commodity which both men and women consume. Even in these important
women's novels – *The Mill on the Floss, Story of an African Farm, The House
of Mirth* – the fulfilment of the plot is a visit to the heroine's grave by a
male mourner.

According to Dame Rebecca West, unhappiness is still the keynote of
contemporary fiction by English women.[10] Certainly the literary landscape
is strewn with dead female bodies. In Fay Weldon's *Down Among the Women*
and *Female Friends*, suicide has come to be a kind of domestic
accomplishment, carried out after the shopping and the washing-up. When
Weldon's heroine turns on the gas, 'she feels that she has been half-dead
for so long that the difference in state will not be very great'. In Muriel
Spark's stunning short novel of 1970, *The Driver's Seat*, another half-dead
and desperate heroine gathers all her force to hunt down a woman-hating

psychopath, and persuade him to murder her. Garishly dressed in a purposely bought outfit of clashing purple, green and white – the colours of the suffragettes (and the colours of the school uniform in *The Prime of Miss Jean Brodie*) – Lise goes in search of her killer, lures him to a park, gives him the knife. But in Lise's careful selection of her death-dress, her patient pursuit of her assassin, Spark has given us the devastated postulates of feminine wisdom: that a woman creates her identity by choosing her clothes, that she creates her history by choosing her man. That, in the 1970s, Mr Right turns out to be Mr Goodbar, is not the sudden product of urban violence, but a latent truth which fiction exposes. Spark asks whether men or women are in the driver's seat, and whether the power to choose one's destroyer is women's only form of self-assertion. To label the violence or self-destructiveness of these painful novels as neurotic expressions of a personal pathology, as many reviewers have done, is to ignore, Annette Kolodny suggests.

the possibility that the worlds they inhabit may in fact be real, or true, and for them the only worlds available, and further, to deny the possibility that their apparently 'odd' or unusual responses, may in fact be justifiable or even necessary.[11]

But women's literature must go beyond these scenarios of compromise, madness and death. Although the reclamation of suffering is the beginning, its purpose is to discover the new world. Happily, some recent women's literature, especially in the United States where novelists and poets have become vigorously involved in the women's liberation movement, has gone beyond reclaiming suffering to its re-investment. This newer writing relates the pain of transformation to history. 'If I'm lonely,' writes Adrienne Rich in 'Song',

it must be the loneliness
of waking first, of breathing
dawn's first cold breath on the city
of being the one awake
in a house wrapped in sleep[12]

Rich is one of the spokeswomen for a new women's writing which explores the will to change. In her recent book, *Of Woman Born: Motherhood as Experience and Institution*, Rich challenges the alienation from and rejection of the mother that daughters have learned under patriarchy. Much women's literature in the past has dealt with 'matrophobia' or the fear of becoming one's mother.[13] In Sylvia Plath's *The Bell Jar*, for example, the heroine's mother is the target for the novel's most punishing contempt. When Esther announces to her therapist that she hates her mother, she is on the road to recovery. Hating one's mother was the feminist enlightenment of the fifties and sixties; but it is only a metaphor for hating oneself. Female literature of the 1970s goes beyond matrophobia to a courageously sustained quest for the mother, in such books at Margaret Atwood's *Surfacing*, and Lisa Alther's recent *Kinflicks*. As the death of the father has always been an archetypal rite of passage for the Western hero, now the death of the mother as witnessed and transcended by the daughter has become one of the most profound occasions of female literature. In analysing these purposeful awakenings, these reinvigorated mythologies of female culture, feminist criticism finds its most challenging, inspiriting and appropriate task.

. . . .

In *A Room of One's Own*, Virginia Woolf argued that economic independence was the essential precondition of an autonomous women's art. Like George Eliot before her, Woolf also believed that women's literature held the promise of a 'precious speciality', a distinctly female vision.

Feminine, Feminist, Female

All of these themes have been important to feminist literary criticism in the 1960s and 1970s but we have approached them with more historical awareness. Before we can even begin to ask how the literature of women would be different and special, we need to reconstruct its past, to rediscover the scores of women novelists, poets and dramatists whose work has been obscured by time, and to establish the continuity of the female tradition from decade to decade, rather than from Great Woman to Great Woman. As we recreate the chain of writers in this tradition, the patterns of influence and response from one generation to the next, we can also begin to challenge the periodicity of orthodox literary history, and its enshrined canons of achievement. It is because we have studied women writers in isolation that we have never grasped the connections between them. When we go beyond Austen, the Brontës and Eliot, say, to look at a hundred and fifty or more of their sister novelists, we can see patterns and phases in the evolution of a female tradition which correspond to the developmental phases of any subcultural art. In my book on English women writers, *A Literature of Their Own*, I have called these the Feminine, Feminist and Female stages.[14] During the Feminine phase, dating from about 1840 to 1880, women wrote in an effort to equal the intellectual achievements of the male culture, and internalised its assumptions about female nature. The distinguishing sign of this period is the male pseudonym, introduced in England in the 1840s, and a national characteristic of English women writers. In addition to the famous names we all know – George Eliot, Currer, Ellis and Acton Bell - dozens of other women chose male pseudonyms as a way of coping with a double literary standard. This masculine disguise goes well beyond the title page; it exerts an irregular pressure on the narrative, affecting tone, diction, structure and characterisation. In contrast to the English male pseudonym, which signals such clear self-awareness of the liabilities of female authorship, American women during the same period adopted super-feminine, little-me pseudonyms (Fanny Fern, Grace Greenwood, Fanny Forester), disguising behind these nominal bouquets their boundless energy, powerful economic motives and keen professional skills. It is pleasing to discover the occasional Englishwoman who combines both these techniques, and creates the illusion of male authorship with a name that contains the encoded domestic message of femininity – such as Harriet Parr, who wrote under the pen name 'Holme Lee'. The feminist content of feminine art is typically oblique, displaced, ironic and subversive; one has to read it between the lines, in the missed possibilities of the text.

In the Feminist phase, from about 1880 to 1920, or the winning of the vote, women are historically enabled to reject the accommodating postures of femininity and to use literature to dramatise the ordeals of wronged womanhood. The personal sense of injustice which feminine novelists such as Elizabeth Gaskell and Frances Trollope expressed in their novels of class struggle and factory life become increasingly and explicitly feminist in the 1880s, when a generation of New Women redefined the woman artist's role in terms of responsibility to suffering sisters. The purest examples of this phase are the Amazon Utopias of the 1890s, fantasies of perfect female societies set in an England or an America of the future, which were also protests against male government, male laws and male medicine. One author of Amazon Utopias, the American Charlotte Perkins Gilman, also analysed the preoccupations of masculine literature with sex and war, and the alternative possibilities of an emancipated feminist literature. Gilman's Utopian feminism carried George Eliot's idea of the 'precious speciality' to its matriarchal extremes. Comparing her view of sisterly collectivity to the beehive, she writes that

> the bee's fiction would be rich and broad, full of the complex tasks of comb-building and filling, the care and feeding of the young . . . It would treat of the vast fecundity of motherhood, the educative and selective processes of the group-mothers, and the passion of loyalty, of social service, which holds the hives together.[15]

This is Feminist Socialist Realism with a vengeance, but women novelists of the period – even Gilman, in her short stories – could not be limited to such didactic formulas, or such maternal topics.

In the Female phase, ongoing since 1920, women reject both imitation and protest – two forms of dependency – and turn instead to female experience as the source of an autonomous art, extending the feminist analysis of culture to the forms and techniques of literature. Representatives of the formal Female Aesthetic, such as Dorothy Richardson and Virginia Woolf, begin to think in terms of male and female sentences, and divide their work into 'masculine' journalism and 'feminine' fictions, redefining and sexualising external and internal experience. Their experiments were both enriching and imprisoning retreats into the celebration of consciousness;

even in Woolf's famous definition of life: 'a luminous halo, a semi-transparent envelope surrounding us from the beginning of consciousness to the end',[16] there is a submerged metaphor of uterine withdrawal and containment. In this sense, the Room of One's Own becomes a kind of Amazon Utopia, population 1.

Notes

I wish to thank Nina Auerbach, Kate Ellis, Mary Jacobus, Wendy Martin, Adrienne Rich, Helen Taylor, Martha Vicinus, Margaret Walters and Ruth Yeazell for sharing with me their ideas on feminist criticism.

1   'Theories of Feminist Criticism' in Josephine Donovan, ed., *Feminist Literary Criticism: Explorations in Theory* (Lexington, 1976), pp. 64, 68, 72.
2   Irving Howe, *Thomas Hardy* (London, 1968), p. 84. For a more detailed discussion of this problem, see my essay 'The Unmanning of the Mayor of Casterbridge' in Dale Kramer, ed., *Critical Approaches to Hardy* (London, 1979).
3   Elizabeth Hardwick, *Seduction and Betrayal* (New York, 1974).
4   Shirley Ardener, ed., *Perceiving Women* (London, 1975).
5   'Women, Culture, and Society: A Theoretical Overview' in Louise Lamphere and Michelle Rosaldo, eds., *Women, Culture and Society* (Stanford, 1974), p. 39.
6   Carroll Smith-Rosenberg, 'The Female World of Love and Ritual: Relations Between Women in Nineteenth-Century America', *Signs: Journal of Women in Culture and Society*, vol. i (Autumn 1975), pp. 1–30; Nancy Cott, *The Bonds of Womanhood* (New Haven, 1977); Ann Douglas, *The Feminization of American Culture* (New York, 1977); Nina Auerbach, *Communities of Women* (Cambridge, Mass., 1978).
7   'Women and Fiction' in Virginia Woolf, *Collected Essays*, vol. ii (London, 1967), p. 141.
8   Peter N. Heydon and Philip Kelley, eds, *Elizabeth Barrett Browning's Letters to Mrs. David Ogilvy* (London, 1974), p. 115.
9   'Cassandra' in Ray Strachey, ed., *The Cause* (London, 1928), p. 398.
10 Rebecca West, 'And They All Lived Unhappily Ever After', *TLS* (26 July 1974), p. 779.
11 Annette Kolodny, 'Some Notes on Defining a "Feminist Literary Criticism"', *Critical Inquiry*, vol. ii (1975), p. 84. For an illuminating discussion of *The Driver's Seat*, see Auerbach, *Communities of Women*, p. 181.
12 Adrienne Rich, *Diving into the Wreck* (New York, 1973), p. 20.
13 The term 'matrophobia' has been coined by Lynn Sukenick; see Rich, *Of Woman Born*, pp. 235 ff.
14 Elaine Showalter, *A Literature of Their Own: British Women Novelists from Brontë to Lessing* (Princeton, NJ, 1977).
15 Charlotte Perkins Gilman, *The Man-made World* (London, 1911), pp. 101–2.
16 Woolf, 'Modern Fiction', *Collected Essays*, vol. ii, p. 106.

13   The Marxist-Feminist Collective,

From 'Women Writing: Jane Eyre, Shirley, Villette, Aurora Leigh',
Ideology and Consciousness, 3, Spring (1978), pp. 30–5

In 1859, Charlotte Brontë made a final, impatient plea to Lewes:

> I wish you did not think me a woman. I wish all reviewers believed 'Currer Bell'
> to be a man; they would be more just to him. . . . I cannot, when I write, think
> always of myself and what you consider elegant and charming in femininity. . . .[1]

Criticism of women writers is in general divided between the extremes of
gender-disavowal and gender-obsession. The second tendency, which Brontë
struggles against in Lewes, patronises women writers as outsiders to literary
history, without justifying this apartheid. The Brontës are considered
important 'women novelists', not simply novelists. This kind of 'gender
criticism' subsumes the text into the sexually-defined personality of its author,
and thereby obliterates its literarity. To pass over the ideology of gender, on
the other hand, ignores the fact that the conditions of literary production and
consumption are articulated, in the Victorian period, in crucially different
ways for women and men. Any rigorous Machereyan analysis must account
for the ideology of gender as it is written into or out of texts by either sex.
Women writers, moreover, in response to their cultural exclusion, have
developed a relatively autonomous, clandestine tradition of their own.

Gender and genre come from the same root, and their connection in
literary history is almost as intimate as their etymology. The tradition into
which the woman novelist entered in the mid-19th century could be
polarised as at once that of Mary Wollstonecraft and of Jane Austen, with
the attendant polarisation of politics – between revolutionary feminism and
conservatism – and of genre – between romanticism and social realism.
Wollstonecraft and Austen between them pose the central question of access
to male education and discourse on the one hand, on the other the annexing
of women's writing to a special sphere, domestic and emotional.

Austen's refusal to write about anything she didn't know is as
undermining to the patriarchal hegemony as Wollstonecraft's demand for a
widening of women's choices: the very 'narrowness' of her novels gave
them a subversive dimension of which she herself was unaware, and which
has been registered in critics' bewilderment at what status to accord them.

Bourgeois criticism should be read symptomatically: most of its so-called
'evaluation' is a reinforcement of ideological barriers. Wollstonecraft's, and
later Brontë's, ambivalent relation to Romanticism, usually described as
clumsy Gothicism, is bound up with their feminism. Romanticism becomes
a problem for women writers because of its assumptions about the 'nature
of femininity'. The tidal rhythms of menstruation, the outrageous visibility

of pregnancy, lead, by a non-sequitur common to all sexual analogy, to the notion that women exist in a state of unreflective bias, the victims of instincts, intuitions, and the mysterious pulsations of the natural world. Intuition is held to be a pre-lapsarian form of knowledge, associated especially with angels, children, idiots, 'rustics' and women. These excluded, or fabulous, groups act for the patriarchy as a mirror onto which it nostalgically projects the exclusions of its discourse. As a glorified, but pre-linguistic communion with nature, intuition lowers women's status while appearing to raise it.

While Wollstonecraft and Brontë are attracted to Romanticism because reluctant to sacrifice, as women writers, their privileged access to feeling, both are aware that full participation in society requires suppression of this attraction. The drive to female emancipation, while fuelled by the revolutionary energy at the origins of Romanticism, has an ultimately conservative aim – successful integration into existing social structures.

Romanticism, after the disappointments of the French Revolution, was gradually depoliticised, and it is only in the mid-nineteenth century, in a period of renewed revolutionary conflict, that it once again becomes a nexus of ideological tension where gender, genre, politics and feminism converge.

Jane Eyre: Her Hand in Marriage

Charlotte Brontë's second preface to *Jane Eyre* states her authorial project as to 'scrutinise and expose' what she calls 'narrow human doctrines' of religion and morality.[2] Our reading of *Jane Eyre* identifies Charlotte Brontë's interrogation of the dominant ideology of love and marriage; but also suggests the Machereyan 'not-said' of the novel – what it is not possible for her to 'scrutinise and expose', woman as a desiring subject, a sexual subject seeking personal fulfilment within the existing structures of class and kinship, i.e. in a patriarchal capitalist society. *Jane Eyre* is *about* kinship, *about* the fact that the social position of a woman, whether rich or poor, pretty or plain, is mediated through the family – to which she may or may not belong.

The text of *Jane Eyre* speaks that desire in the interstices of the debate on woman's social role, between the romance/realism divide, the conflict between Reason and Imagination in her heroine's consciousness. It speaks of women's sexuality in Victorian England, opening the locked room of a tabooed subject – just as that part of the text which concerns Bertha Mason/Rochester disrupts the realistic narrative of Jane's search for an adequate kinship system, i.e. an opening into the family structure from which she is excluded. Charlotte Brontë's general fictional strategy is to place her heroines in varying degrees of marginality to the normative kinship patterns. Frances Henri, Crimsworth (a female surrogate), Jane, Shirley, Caroline Helstone and Lucy Snowe, all have a deviant socialisation, all confront the problem of a marriage not negotiated by a *pater familias*.

Why? By excluding them from a conventional family situation in which their socialisation and their exchange in marriage cannot follow the practice of Victorian middle-class women, Charlotte Bronte's fiction explores the constraints of the dominant ideology as they bear on female sexual and social identity.

At the centre of Charlotte Brontë's novels is a figure who either lacks or deliberately cuts the bonds of kinship.[3] But Eagleton, although stressing this structural characteristic, discusses it primarily in terms of class-mobility. This treatment of Jane Eyre herself as an asexual representative of the upwardly mobile bourgeoisie leads to a reductionist reading of the text. It neglects gender as a determinant, by subsuming gender under class. The meritocratic vision of 'individual self-reliance', as Eagleton puts its, *cannot* be enacted by a woman character in the same way as it can be by a male. For a woman to become a member of the 'master-class' depends on her taking a sexual master whereby her submission brings her access to the dominant culture.

The social and judicial legitimacy of this relationship – its encoding within the law – is of primary importance; hence Jane's rejection of the role of Rochester's mistress. She would not merely *not* acquire access – she would forfeit the possibility of ever doing so. The structure of the novel, Jane's development through childhood and adolescence into womanhood does not simply represent an economic and social progression from penniless orphan to member of the landed gentry class; it represents a woman's struggle for access to her own sexual and reproductive potential – in other words, her attempts to install herself as a full subject within a male-dominated culture.

For example, the structure of the five locales of the novel is customarily seen as the articulation of the heroine's progress – a progress described in liberal criticism as the moral growth of the individual, in vulgar sociological terms as 'upward social mobility'. To foreground kinship provides a radically different reading.

Jane's progress is from a dependent orphan to the acquisition of the family necessary for her full integration into mid-nineteenth century culture as a woman. Her cousins, the Rivers, and the Madeira uncle who intervenes twice – once via his agent, Bertha's brother, to save her from becoming a 'fallen woman' as Rochester's bigamous wife, and again at the end of the novel with a legacy which is in effect a dowry – provide Jane with the necessary basis for her exchange into marriage.

Each of the five houses through which the heroine passes traces the variety and instability of a kinship structure at a transitional historical period, and the ideological space this offers to women.

At Gateshead, as the excluded intruder into the Reed family and at Thornfield as the sexually tabooed and socially ambiguous governess, Jane's lack of familial status renders her particularly vulnerable to oppression and exploitation. At Lowood, she acquires a surrogate sister and mother in Helen Burns and Miss Temple – only to lose them through death and marriage. The instability of kinship relations is imaged in the patterns of gain and loss, acceptance and denial, enacted at each 'home' – most dramatically in the loss of a lawful wedded husband, spiritually and sexually akin but socially tabooed. The subsequent flight from Thornfield reduces her to a homeless vagrant lacking both past and identity. Throughout the text, the symmetrical arrangement of Reed and Rivers cousins, the Reed and Eyre uncles, the patterns of metaphors about kinship, affinity and identification articulate the proposition that a woman's social identity is constituted within familial relationships. Without the kinship reading, the Rivers' transformation into long-lost, bona-fide blood-relations at Moor End appears a gross and unmotivated coincidence. This apparently absurd plot manipulation is in fact dictated by the logic of the not-said.

Like such violations of probability, the Gothic elements in the novel are neither clumsy interventions to resolve the narrative problems nor simply the residues of the author's earlier modes of discourse, the childhood fantasies of Angria. Their main function is to evade the censorship of female sexuality within the signifying practice of mid-Victorian realism. For the rights and wrongs of women in social and political terms, there existed a rationalist language, a political rhetoric, inherited from Mary Wollstonecraft. But for the 'unspeakable' sexual desires of women, Charlotte Brontë returned on the one hand to Gothic and Romantic modes, on the other to a metonymic discourse of the human body – hands and eyes for penises, 'vitals' or 'vital organs' for women's genitalia – often to comic effect:

> I am substantial enough – touch me.' . . . .
> He held out his hand, laughing. 'Is that a dream?' said he, placing it close to my eyes. He had a rounded, muscular, and vigorous hand, as well as a long, strong arm.[4]

The tale told of women's sexual possibilities is a halting, fragmented and ambivalent one. The libidinal fire of Jane Eyre's 'vital organs' is not denied, not totally repressed, as the refusal of St John Rivers suggests:

> At his side, always and always restrained, always checked – forced to keep the fire of my nature continually low, to compel it to burn inwardly, and never utter a cry, though the imprisoned flame consume vital after vital.

The marriage proposed here, significantly, is an inter-familial one which denies the heroine's sexuality. If women's sexuality is to be integrated, reconciled with male patriarchal Law, a compromise must be achieved with the individual Law-bearer, in this case through a return to Edward Rochester.

The alternative to either repression or integration is examined through that part of the text concerned with Bertha Mason/Rochester. Her initial intervention, the uncanny laughter after Jane surveys from the battlements of Thornfield the wider world denied her as a woman, signifies the return of the repressed, the anarchic and unacted desires of women. Bertha's appearances constitute a punctuating device or notation of the not-said – the Pandora's box of unleashed female libido. Bertha's tearing of the veil on the eve of Jane's wedding, for example, is a triumphant trope for the projected loss of Jane's virginity unsanctioned by legitimate marriage. Thus while other spectres were haunting Europe, the spectre haunting Jane Eyre, if not Victorian England, was the insurgence of women's sexuality into the signifying practice of literature.

The myth of unbridled male sexuality is treated through Rochester, 'whose name evokes that of the predatory Restoration rake, here modified by Byronic sensibility. In the vocabulary of Lacanian psychoanalysis, his maiming by the author is not so much a punitive castration, but represents his successful passage through the castration complex. Like all human subjects he must enter the symbolic order through a necessary acceptance of the loss of an early incestuous love object, a process he initially tries to circumvent through bigamy. His decision to make Jane his bigamous wife attempts to implicate the arch-patriarch, God himself ('I know my maker sanctions what I do'). The supernatural lightning which this presumption provokes is less a re-establishing of bourgeois morality than an expression of disapproval by the transcendental phallic signifier of Rochester's Oedipal rivalry. It is God at the end of the novel who refuses to sanction Jane's marriage to St John Rivers when invoked in its support, and who sends Rochester's supernatural cry to call Jane to him; and it is God's judgement which Rochester, in his maimed condition, finally accepts with filial meekness.

By accepting the Law, he accepts his place in the signifying chain and enters the Symbolic order, as bearer rather than maker of the Law. Sexuality in a reduced and regulated form is integrated – legitimised – within the dominant kinship structure of patriarchy and within the marriage which he (by Bertha's death-by-fire), and Jane (by her acquisition of a family) is now in a position to contract. Jane Eyre does not attempt to rupture the dominant kinship structures. The ending of the novel ('Reader, I married him') affirms those very structures. The feminism of the text resides in its 'not-said', its attempt to inscribe women as sexual subjects within this system.

Notes

1 T.J. Wise and J.A. Symington, eds, The Brontës: Their Lives, Friendships and Correspondence, 4 Vols (Shakespeare Head, London, 1932), Vol. iii, p. 31.
2 Currer Bell, Preface to the Second Edition of Jane Eyre (London, Smith, Elder & Co., 1847).
3 T. Eagleton, Myths of Power.
4 Jane Eyre (Harmondsworth, Penguin, 1966), pp. 306–7.
5 Ibid, p. 433.

PART TWO

INTRODUCTION

The term 'Post-Structuralism' does not refer to a body of work that represents a coherent school or movement. Indeed there is an extensive debate about what constitutes Post-Structuralism and about its relation to Structuralism. For some it is a matter of a more radical reading of Saussure, for others it is the moment at which Structuralism becomes self-reflective. It is sometimes taken as a critique of Structuralism, sometimes a development of it. In some instances it has almost become synonymous with the name of Derrida and the mode of analysis he inaugurates – 'deconstruction'. However, it is usually used to refer to Derrida and the later Barthes, less certainly to Foucault and Lacan as the principal theorists in the field, and to work which develops out of the writings of these key figures. Our use of the term is related to the body of work that presupposes Structuralism, but that distances itself from certain of its features, and that presents a more radical attack on critical orthodoxies (Structuralism among them). In other words, while retaining a 'Post-Saussurean' definition[1] we have made the category as broad as possible, certainly not restricting it to the Derridean strand.

There are a number of problems with any attempt to classify work as either Structuralist or Post-Structuralist. The material is not naturally self-categorizing, rather, it forms a network: a web of interconnections and antitheses around which it is difficult to draw simple boundaries. Some of the work covered in Part One of this anthology relates more closely at times to the trajectories typical of the work represented in Part Two, and, by the same token, work covered in Part Two often slips back into the kind of mastery of explanation and use of metalanguage characteristic of Part One.

The problem is further complicated by the moments of appearance of Structuralism and Post-Structuralism. If one wanted to date the appearance of Post-Structuralism then 1966/7 would be a reasonable point to start. At the international symposium, 'The Languages of Criticism and the Sciences of Man', in 1966, a significant Post-structuralist impetus emerged.[2] Derrida published three books in 1967, among them *Of Grammatology* and *Writing and Difference*. Barthes's work was undergoing a transition from the Structuralism of *Elements of Semiology* (1964) to a Post-Structuralist position that can be traced in essays written between then and the publication of *S/Z* in 1972. Foucault's *Order of Things* and Lacan's *Ecrits* were published in 1966, and though these latter two might not be fully-fledged works of Post-Structuralism, they differ significantly from the Structuralism represented in Part One of this book.

But if there was a visible Post-structuralist impetus it became entangled (in Anglo-American theory at any rate) with Structuralism, for the latter was itself only taking significant hold in the mid-70s. Indeed the books cited above were not published in English translation until the mid/late-70s, while Culler's *Structuralist Poetics* and Hawkes's *Structuralism and Semiotics* had only appeared in the mid-70s. The moment of Structuralism and the moment of Post-Structuralism almost coincide in terms of their appearance and adoption in Anglo-American literary theory.

Roland Barthes's *S/Z* serves as a good illustration of the convergence and varying appropriations by Anglo-American criticism of Structuralist and Post-Structuralist work. The five codes Barthes had used in his implosive analysis of a short story by Balzac were taken by many critics to be the codes out of which the text was structured and which could therefore be used in textual criticism to reveal an absolute textual structure and meaning. However, a more radical reading of *S/Z* saw it not as providing the structural grid of the text but as *processing* the textual web in an act of structuration. The difference can be captured in the distinction between a 'product' orientation, where criticism sets out to reveal the construction of the product, and a 'process' orientation, where the act of criticism is acknowledged to be a processing act – an act of structuration which is itself an active part of that construction. Here the text is not revealed and explained but worked upon.

While there is a difficulty in simply ascribing certain writings to either a Structuralist or a Post-Structuralist position certain features of Post-Structuralism do distinguish it from Structuralism. Though language remains a central area of interest, Post-Structuralism takes up a more radical reading and/or critique of Saussurean theory. As we have seen, Saussure argued that 'language is a system of difference, with no positive terms'. Identities do not refer to essences and are not discrete but are articulated in difference; identities are events in language. Structuralism had tended to acknowledge this, but only to a limited degree; it did not extend such reasoning to the foundations of the literary discourse. In Post-Structuralism everything can be subjected to this formulation. All of the categories which literary studies assumes, and which form the basis of the critical act, are open to the re-evaluation and radical scepticism of a Post-Structuralist perspective, including the category 'Literature' itself. And if the categories of literature and literary study do not refer to things-in-themselves, but are constructed in difference then the act of criticism which articulates that difference cannot be viewed as subordinate. Rather, it is of equal importance to the literature it studies, for it is the very act that brings the 'literary' into being; it is the necessary supplement that endows 'literature' with its special and specific existence. In a Derridean inversion, the supplement becomes, paradoxically, the more important term, for without criticism 'literature' would have no meaning. It is not only the category of literature that can be subjected to such reasoning, but also that of the author and the literary text itself. Post-Structuralism effectively undermines all the categories that had previously been taken for granted as having an independent existence.

If this were all that Post-Structuralism amounted to then it would not be altogether radical. Though identities might be arbitrary, once they had been fixed in language then they would be defined and stable; however, Post-Structuralism goes further. In the system of difference proposed by Saussure the sign, made up of the signifier and the signified, is arbitrary, fixed by social contract. Once formed, the sign becomes a totality; signifier and signified are inseparable and the sign's form and meaning are self-identical. In other words, Saussure had argued that the continuum of the phenomenal world was 'cut up' by language; but once this process was complete, then the relationship between the arbitrary signifier and the arbitrary signified was fixed and they achieved a stable one-to-one correspondence. Post-Structuralism questions this assumption, arguing that signifiers do not carry with them well-defined signifieds; meanings are never as graspable or as 'present' as this suggests. Any attempt to define the meaning of a word illustrates the point for it inevitably ends up in a circularity of signifiers, with the signifiers sliding over the continuum of the field of the signified. For example, in the *Concise Oxford Dictionary* the meaning of the word 'meaning' is given as 'what is meant; significance . . .'; 'meant' in turn refers us to 'mean', 'mean' to 'signify'; meanwhile, 'significance' refers us to 'significant' which is defined as 'having a meaning'. The meaning of 'meaning' does not become present to us, it simply slips beneath a circularity of signifiers. And, of course, these signifiers are open to multiple meaning areas; 'mean' also refers us to 'inferior, poor'; 'not generous'; 'the mathematical mean', etc. Post-Structuralism argues, then, that the sign is not stable, that there is an indeterminacy or undecidability about meaning and that it is subject to 'slippage' from signifier to signifier. So, if literature, the author and the text no longer have an identity outside of difference, neither do they have a single, fixed and determinate meaning; they are relativized and unstable.

Post-Structuralism, whilst continuing the attack on humanist ideology and the Anglo-American critical tradition, also applies its perspectives to Structuralism. It argues that, in its claim to explain by unveiling an underlying structure, Structuralism is in the grip of another form of essentialism in that it presupposes a latent centre or core which gives rise to surface, manifest forms. Structuralism's appeal to a metalanguage of explanation cannot avoid the problems of interpretation and meaning. The signs of that metalanguage are themselves subject to slippage and indeterminacy; they can no more offer a full and final presence of meaning than the signs of an object language. And the metalanguage itself is always open, in its turn, to the gaze of an alternative metalanguage. Indeed, the distinction between an object language and a metalanguage breaks down in Post-Structuralism. From this position, the claim of Structuralism to effect a mastery and explanation of the world through the scientific investigation of sign systems is undermined and compromised.

The radical de-centring of identities and an emphasis on the signfier over the signified, form two central characteristics of Post-Structuralism. However, these characteristics are not evenly distributed throughout the work we have classified under the Post-Structuralism heading. Neither are they all that Post-Structuralism concerns itself with. Section Four represents critical developments which have arisen out of the Post-Structuralist critique of 'difference' and which tend either to draw on the political implications of this critique (Post-Colonialism) or its epistemological considerations (Postmodernism). In the final section is a later essay by Derrida in which he considers the impact of literary theory on the disciplinary formations of the academy.

Unlike the material represented in Part One, the work covered in Part Two cannot be seen in terms of schools or movements. However, certain key figures are significant and demand attention. To a large extent our introductions to each section revolve around these figures, since they provide landmarks on the map; they are used to locate areas of Post-Structuralist work and should be treated in this light rather than as the authoritative subjects of original theories. The first three sections can be seen to be informed principally by the work of Lacan, Derrida, and Foucault respectively but, as Young has pointed out, these '... are the names of problems, not "authors" of doctrines',[3] It is also important to recognize that, although we have grouped work under section headings, that work should not be seen as 'belonging' in any simple sense to particular classifications. Post-Structuralism is a network of interconnected notions and concepts, and work we have categorised in one section is often pertinent to another. Our categorisations should be seen, therefore, as convenient ways to locate work and as convenient ways of introducing themes.

However, we would contend that two distinct trajectories have developed in which both the object of enquiry and the way it is conceptualized, fundamentally differ. These trajectories we have called 'language' and 'discourse'. The former is concerned with the figures of language in abstraction, the latter situates language in the context of its use by (and use of) speaking and listening subjects. The language trajectory is concerned primarily with deconstructing the principles of ordering and the 'metaphysics of presence' (see section two) that are inescapably built into our language. It views all language as a web of signifiers bound up in an endless play of textuality (textuality being the condition of existence of signifiers where they refer endlessly to other textual occurrences, rather than to a pre-text). The discourse trajectory considers language as a practical activity intimately connected with the context in which it appears. Though the sign is unstable in both trajectories, here it is constantly being fixed and unfixed, or refixed, by different users and communities of users of the language. In this trajectory the actual mode of existence of language is central; it is seen to relate immediately to the socio-cultural formation in which it appears, and to the exercise of power.

Few critics or theorists would subscribe to one or other of these trajectories in any simple way. They represent the two poles of the Post-structural enterprise rather than either/or positions to be adopted. However, it is clear that where Derrida tends toward language, Foucault tends toward discourse. It is also clear that some of the 'deconstructionist' work that owes most to Derrida is firmly located at the language-end of the continuum.

We have chosen Roland Barthes's essay, 'The Death of the Author' to introduce our survey because it provides a short and useful introduction to some of the significant themes developed in Post-Structuralism. It is an essay which has achieved notoriety for its polemical stance in displacing the author from the centre of the critical act.

Notes

1 C. Belsey, *Critical Practice* (London, Methuen, 1980).
2 R. Macksey and E. Donato, eds, *The Structuralist Controversy: The Languages of Criticism and the Sciences of Man* (Baltimore, MD, Johns Hopkins University Press, 1972).
3 R. Young, ed., *Untying the Text: a Post-Structuralist Reader* (Boston, Mass., and London, Routledge & Kegan Paul, 1981).

---

14   Roland Barthes,
'The Death of the Author', S. Heath, tr. and ed. *Image, Music, Text* (1968), pp. 142–8

In his story *Sarrasine* Balzac, describing a castrato disguised as a woman writes the following sentence: '*This was woman, herself, with her sudden fears, her irrational whims, her instinctive worries, her impetuous boldness, her fussings, and her delicious sensibility.*' Who is speaking thus? Is it the hero of the story bent on remaining ignorant of the castrato hidden beneath the woman? Is it Balzac the individual, furnished by his personal experience with a philosophy of Woman? Is it Balzac the author professing 'literary' ideas on femininity? Is it universal wisdom? Romantic psychology? We shall never know, for the good reason that writing is the destruction of every voice, of every point of origin. Writing is that neutral, composite, oblique space where our subject slips away, the negative where all identity is lost, starting with the very identity of the body writing.

No doubt it has always been that way. As soon as a fact is *narrated* no longer with a view to acting directly on reality but intransitively, that is to say, finally outside of any function other than that of the very practice of the symbol itself, this disconnection occurs, the voice loses its origin, the author enters into his own death, writing begins. The sense of this phenomenon, however, has varied; in ethnographic societies the responsibility for a narrative is never assumed by a person but by a mediator, shaman or relator whose 'performance' – the mastery of the narrative code – may possibly be admired but never his 'genius'. The author is a modern figure, a product of our society insofar as, emerging from the Middle Ages and English empiricism, French rationalism and the personal faith of the Reformation, it discovered the prestige of the individual, of, as it is more nobly put, the 'human person'. It is thus logical that in literature it should be this positivism, the epitome and culmination of capitalist ideology, which has attached the greatest importance to the 'person' of the author. The *author* still reigns in histories of literature, biographies of writers, interviews, magazines, as in the very consciousness of men of letters anxious to unite their person and their work through diaries and memoirs. The image of literature to be found in ordinary culture is tyrannically centred on the author, his person, his life, his tastes, his passions, while criticism still consists for the most part in saying that Baudelaire's work is the failure of Baudelaire the man, Van Gogh's his madness, Tchaikovsky's his vice. The *explanation* of a work is always sought in the man or woman who produced it, as if it were always in the end, through the more or less transparent allegory of the fiction, the voice of a single person, the *author* 'confiding' in us.

Though the sway of the Author remains powerful (the new criticism has often done no more than consolidate it), it goes without saying that certain writers have long since attempted to loosen it. In France, Mallarmé was doubtless the first to see and to foresee in its full extent the necessity to substitute language itself for the person who until then has been supposed to be its owner. For him, for us too, it is language which speaks, not the author; to write, is, through a prerequisite impersonality (not at all to be confused with the castrating objectivity of the realist novelist), to reach that point, where only language acts, 'performs' and not 'me'. Mallarmé's entire poetics consists in suppressing the author in the interests of writing (which is, as will be seen, to restore the place of the reader). Valéry, encumbered by a psychology of the Ego, considerably diluted Mallarmé's theory but, his taste for classicism leading him to turn to the lessons of rhetoric, he never stopped calling into question and deriding the Author; he stressed the linguistic and, as it were, 'hazardous' nature of his activity, and throughout his prose works he militated in favour of the essentially verbal condition of literature, in the face of which all recourse to the writer's inferiority seemed to him pure superstition. Proust himself, despite the apparently psychological character of what are called his *analyses*, was visibly concerned with the task of inexorably blurring, by an extreme subtilisation, the relation between the writer and his characters; by making of the narrator not he who has seen and felt nor even he who is writing, but he who *is going to write* (the young man in the novel – but, in fact, how old is he and who is he? – wants to write but cannot; the novel ends when writing at last becomes possible), Proust gave modern writing its epic. By a radical reversal, instead of putting his life into his novel, as is so often maintained, he made of his very life a work for which his own book was the model; so that it is clear to us that Charlus does not imitate Montesquiou but that Montesquiou – in his anecdotal, historical reality – is no more than a secondary fragment, derived from Charlus. Lastly, to go no further than this prehistory of modernity, Surrealism, though unable to accord language a supreme place (language being system and the aim of the movement being, romantically, a direct subversion of codes – itself moreover illusory: a code cannot be destroyed, only 'played off'), contributed to the desacrilization of the image of the Author by ceaselessly recommending the abrupt disappointment of expectations of meaning (the famous surrealist 'jolt'), by entrusting the hand with the task of writing as quickly as possible what the head itself is unaware of (automatic writing), by accepting the principle and the experience of several people writing together. Leaving aside literature itself (such distinctions really becoming invalid), linguistics has recently provided the destruction of the Author with a valuable analytical tool by showing that the whole of the enunciation is an empty process, functioning perfectly without there being any need for it to be filled with the person of the interlocutors. Linguistically, the author is never more than the instance writing, just as *I* is nothing other than the instance saying *I*: language knows a 'subject', not a 'person', and this subject, empty outside of the very enunciation which defines it, suffices to make language 'hold together', suffices, that is to say, to exhaust it.

The removal of the Author (one could talk here with Brecht of a veritable 'distancing', the Author diminishing like a figurine at the far end of the literary stage) is not merely an historical fact or an act of writing; it utterly transforms the modern text (or – which is the same thing – the text is henceforth made and read in such a way that at all its levels the author is absent). The temporality is different. The Author, when believed in, is always conceived of as the past of his own book: book and author stand automatically on a single line divided into a *before* and an *after*. The Author is thought to *nourish* the book, which is to say that he exists before it, thinks, suffers, lives for it, is in the same relation of antecedence to his work as a father to his child. In complete contrast, the modern scriptor is born simultaneously with the text, is in no way equipped with a being preceding or exceeding the writing, is not the subject with the book as predicate; there is no other time than that of the enunciation and every text is eternally written *here and now*. The fact is (or, it follows) that *writing* can no longer designate an operation of recording, notation, representation, 'depiction' (as the Classics would say); rather, it designates exactly what linguists, referring to Oxford philosophy, call a performative, a rare verbal form (exclusively given in the first person and in the present tense) in which the enunciation has no other content (contains no other proposition) than the act by which it is uttered – something like the *I declare* of kings or the *I sing* of very ancient poets. Having buried the Author, the modern scriptor can thus no longer believe, as according to the pathetic view of his predecessors, that this hand is too slow for his thought or passion and that consequently, making a law of necessity, he must emphasize this delay and indefinitely 'polish' his form. For him, on the contrary, the hand, cut off from any voice, borne by a pure gesture of inscription (and not of expression), traces a field without origin – or which, at least, has no other origin than language itself, language which ceaselessly calls into question all origins.

We know now that a text is not a line of words releasing a single 'theological' meaning (the 'message' of the Author-God) but a multi-dimensional space in which a variety of writings, none of them original, blend and clash. The text is a tissue of quotations drawn from the innumerable centres of culture. Similar to Bouvard and Pécuchet, those eternal copyists, at once sublime and comic and whose profound ridiculousness indicates precisely the truth of writing, the writer can only imitate a gesture that is always anterior, never original. His only power is to mix writings, to counter the ones with the others, in such a way as never to rest on any one of them. Did he wish to *express himself*, he ought at least to know that the inner 'thing' he thinks to 'translate' is itself only a ready-formed dictionary, its words only explainable through other words, and so on indefinitely; something experienced in exemplary fashion by the young Thomas de Quincey, he who was so good at Greek that in order to translate absolutely modern ideas and images into that dead language, he had, so Baudelaire tells us (in *Paradis Artificiels*), 'created for himself an unfailing dictionary, vastly more extensive and complex than those resulting from the ordinary patience of purely literary themes'. Succeeding the Author, the scriptor no longer bears within him passions, humours, feelings, impressions, but rather this immense dictionary from which he draws a writing that can know no halt: life never does more than imitate the book, and the book itself is only a tissue of signs, an imitation that is lost, infinitely deferred.

Once the Author is removed, the claim to decipher a text becomes quite futile. To give a text an Author is to impose a limit on that text, to furnish it with a final signified, to close the writing. Such a conception suits criticism very well, the latter then allotting itself the important task of discovering the Author (or its hypostases: society, history, psyche, liberty) beneath the work: when the Author has been found, the text is 'explained' – victory to the critic. Hence there is no surprise in the fact that, historically, the reign of the Author has also been that of the Critic, nor again in the fact that criticism (be it new) is today undermined along with the Author. In the multiplicity of writing, everything is to be *disentangled*, nothing *deciphered*;

the structure can be followed, 'run' (like the thread of a stocking) at every point and at every level, but there is nothing beneath: the space of writing is to be ranged over, not pierced; writing ceaselessly posits meaning ceaselessly to evaporate it, carrying out a systematic exemption of meaning. In precisely this way literature (it would be better from now on to say *writing*), by refusing to assign a 'secret', an ultimate meaning, to the text (and to the world as text), liberates what may be called an anti-theological activity, an activity that is truly revolutionary since to refuse to fix meaning is, in the end, to refuse God and his hypostases – reason, science, law.

Let us come back to the Balzac sentence. No one, no 'person', says it: its source, its voice, is not the true place of the writing, which is reading. Another – very precise – example will help to make this clear: recent research (J.-P. Vernant[1]) has demonstrated the constitutively ambiguous nature of Greek tragedy, its texts being woven from words with double meanings that each character understands unilaterally (this perpetual misunderstanding is exactly the 'tragic'); there is, however, someone who understands each word in its duplicity and who, in addition, hears the very deafness of the characters speaking in front of him – this someone being precisely the reader (or here, the listener). Thus is revealed the total existence of writing: a text is made of multiple writings, drawn from many cultures and entering into mutual relations of dialogue, parody, contestation, but there is one place where this multiplicity is focused and that place is the reader, not, as was hitherto said, the author. The reader is the space on which all the quotations that make up a writing are inscribed without any of them being lost; a text's unity lies not in its origin but in its destination. Yet this destination cannot any longer be personal: the reader is without history, biography, psychology; he is simply that someone who holds together in a single field all the traces by which the written text is constituted. Which is why it is derisory to condemn the new writing in the name of a humanism hypocritically turned champion of the reader's rights. Classic criticism has never paid any attention to the reader; for it, the writer is the only person in literature. We are now beginning to let ourselves be fooled no longer by the arrogant antiphrastical recriminations of good society in favour of the very thing it sets aside, ignores, smothers, or destroys; we know that to give writing its future, it is necessary to overthrow the myth: the birth of the reader must be at the cost of the death of the Author.

Note

1 [Cf. Jean-Pierre Vernant (with Pierre Vidal-Naquet). *Mythe et tragédie en Grèce ancienne* (Paris, 1972), esp. pp. 19–40, 99–131.]

SECTION ONE
THE SUBJECT

The notion of the 'subject' has proved crucial to the Post-Structuralist enterprise; the concept can be traced in most varieties of Post-Structuralism and acts as a focal point for the critique of humanist ideology. Post-Structuralism uses the term 'subject' rather than 'self' or 'individual' in an attempt to avoid the presupposition that the human being is in some way 'given' and fully-formed prior to its entrance into the symbolic order of language or discourse. The term plays ambiguously between, on the one hand, *subject* as in the opposition subject/object, or subject as in grammar; and on the other hand, *subject* as in subject of the state, or subject to the law – that is, *subject* is both central and at the same time de-centred.

Humanist ideology depends upon a fundamental assumption about the primacy of the autonomous and unified individual. For humanism, 'man' is at the centre of meaning and action; the world is oriented around the individual. Each individual is different, each possesses a unique subjectivity; yet also, paradoxically, each shares a common human nature. The combination of unique individuality and common human essence coheres around the idea of a sovereign self, whose essential core of being transcends the outward signs of environmental and social conditioning. Post-Structuralism has sought to disrupt this man-centred view of the world, arguing that the subject, and that sense of unique subjectivity itself, is constructed in language and discourse; and rather than being fixed and unified, the subject is split, unstable or fragmented.

Of the Post-Structuralists to have written on the notion of the subject it is arguably the French psychoanalyst, Jacques Lacan, who has produced the most influential theory. His work is complex and the brief account given here concentrates on language. For fuller details see Coward and Ellis, Wright, Moi.[1] Lacan's theory of the subject owes much to Freud; however, he rereads Freud in the light of post-Saussurean linguistics and it is the latter which gives the work its Post-Structuralist inflection. Language is a crucial element in the theory for it is only in the moment of entry into the symbolic order of language that full subjectivity comes into being.

Before it enters the symbolic through the acquisition of language, the infant goes through the mirror stage, entering the realm of the imaginary (which the subject never entirely leaves). In the mirror stage, Lacan argues, the infant begins to recognise a distinction between its own body and the outside world. This is illustrated in the child's relation to its own image in the mirror; the infant lacks control of its limbs and its experience is a jumbled mass but its image in the mirror appears unified and in control. The child recognises its image and merges with it in a process of identification, creating an illusory experience of control of the self and the world – an imaginary correspondence of self and image. The two are perceived as self-identical. However, to achieve full distinction of the self, the subject has to enter the symbolic, where identity depends on difference rather than self-identicality. Language, the system of difference which articulates identities, constructs positions for the subject notably the subject position 'I' – which allows differentiation from others, and identity for the self. However, in the necessary acceptance of the subject-positions offered by language, the individual experiences a loss or lack because it is *subject to* the positions that are predefined for it and beyond its control. The sense of a full and unified subject is contradicted by a sense of being defined by the law of human culture. At this point, desire and the unconscious are also created. The unconscious is, as it were, the repository of that which has to be repressed when the subject takes on the pre-defined positions available in language. Subject-positions, meaning and consciousness, made available through the symbolic order, depend on language as a system of difference and hence they entail a loss of the full presence that seemed to characterize the imaginary realm. The individual desires to control meaning but this is not possible because of the nature of language. Language, Lacan argued, is not a matter of a one-to-one correspondence between signifier and signified. the signifiers of language cannot fix the arbitrary field of the signified; signifiers slide across the continuum and hence the desire for mastery of meaning is unsatisfiable. The unified and stable subject of humanism is contradicted and de-stabilized by this primacy of the signifier and loss of apparent one-to-one correspondence between signifier and signified.

Lacan's work has been criticized for its universalising and a-historical view of the construction of the subject – in other words, for a residual essentialism. This might seem to put his work into the first part of this book, however, it has provided a starting point for a set of concerns that have become a part of the Post-Structuralist enterprise and his view of language coincides with the post-structuralist view. Although Lacan's work had been available for some considerable time (indeed the essay reprinted dates from 1949), and had influenced Althusser's notion of interpellation, the attempt to use his psychoanalytic work in literary theory belongs more to the Post-Structuralist moment and impetus.

Lacan has also been taken to task, particularly by Feminist theorists, for the phallocentric (male-centred) orientation of his theory. However, his work has proved fertile ground for a number of feminist theorists. One of the foremost of these is Julia Kristeva, whose work encompasses and combines linguistics, literature and psychoanalysis. The interview reprinted here provides a brief illustration of one of the ways in which feminist writers have appropriated Lacanian theory to enable what Toril Moi has called a 'sexual/textual politics'. The essay by Hélène Cixous is more sceptical about the possibility of appropriating Freudian or post-Freudian psychoanalytic ideas for a theory of feminine subjectivity. Cixous argues that Freudianism represents another example of patriarchal voyeurism: when everything is reduced to the issue of having or not having the phallus, then woman is also and inevitably either reduced to passivity or to non-existence. Woman's libidinal economy has not yet been represented because it is outside the reference of the masculine economy. She argues instead for a utopian feminine plurality which abandons altogether the logocentric divide of masculinity/femininity. The essay is written in annunciatory mode: the time has come to exhume the buried feminine and 'invent the other history'.

Judith Butler's essay is written as a retrospective piece which revisits the milestones of contemporary Feminist theory from the 1970s and 1980s and in particular the pivotal concept of the distinction between sex and gender. She argues that it has never made sense to talk of an originary body which is somehow acculturated into gender, because gender is itself an originating activity 'incessantly taking place'. The sex/gender distinction was a product of Cartesian thinking which assumes an absolute split between mind and body, but where body effectively exists always in the mode of denial. Butler's anti-idealism leads her to be equally critical of the liberatory essentialism of some French feminisms and she insists on the importance to Feminism of recognizing the force of Foucault's critique of the countercultural and utopian discourses of the 1960s. Butler suggests that those Post-Structuralist Feminists who seek to locate an essential 'femininity' in the unexplored space of the pre-oedipal, effectively risk, once again, the conflation of biology with destiny.

The final piece in this section is taken from Jonathan Dollimore's book *Radical Tragedy*, and is offered as a very useful summary of the debate on the subject as it had progressed by the mid-1980s. As early as 1984, Dollimore could confidently assert that no issue is more central to English studies. Certainly the focus of his argument – the need to deconstruct the Enlightenment concept of autonomy in the name of a liberatory 'difference' – has become even more central to the practice of literary criticism in the 1990s (see the sections on 'History and Discourse'; 'Postmodernism and Postcolonialism').

Note

1 R. Coward and J. Ellis, *Language and Materialism: Developments in Semiology and the Theory of the Subject* (London, Routledge & Kegan Paul, 1977); E. Wright, *Psychoanalytic Criticism: Theory and Practice* (London, Methuen, 1984); T. Moi, *Sexual/Textual Criticism: Feminist Literary Theory* (London, Methuen, 1985).

15   Jacques Lacan,

'The Mirror Stage as Formative of the Function of the I as revealed in Psychoanalytic Experience', Alan Sheridan, tr. *Ecrits, A Selection* (1949), pp. 1–7

The conception of the mirror stage that I introduced at our last congress, thirteen years ago, has since become more or less established in the practice of the French group. However, I think it worthwhile to bring it again to your attention, especially today, for the light it sheds on the formation of the *I* as we experience it in psychoanalysis. It is an experience that leads us to oppose any philosophy directly issuing from the *Cogito*.

Some of you may recall that this conception originated in a feature of human behaviour illuminated by a fact of comparative psychology. The child, at an age when he is for a time, however short, outdone by the chimpanzee in instrumental intelligence, can nevertheless already recognize as such his own image in a mirror. This recognition is indicated in the illuminative mimicry of the *Aha-Erlebnis*, which Köhler sees as the expression of situational apperception, an essential stage of the act of intelligence.

This act, far from exhausting itself, as in the case of the monkey, once the image has been mastered and found empty, immediately rebounds in the case of the child in a series of gestures in which he experiences in play the relation between the movements assumed in the image and the reflected environment, and between this virtual complex and the reality it reduplicates – the child's own body, and the persons and things, around him.

This event can take place, as we have known since Baldwin, from the age of six months, and its repetition has often made me reflect upon the startling spectacle of the infant in front of the mirror. Unable as yet to walk, or even to stand up, and held tightly as he is by some support human or artificial (what, in France, we call a *'trotte-bébé'*), he nevertheless overcomes, in a flutter of jubilant activity, the obstructions of his support and, fixing his attitude in a slightly leaning-forward position, in order to hold it in his gaze, brings back an instantaneous aspect of the image.

For me, this activity retains the meaning I have given it up to the age of eighteen months. This meaning discloses a libidinal dynamism, which has hitherto remained problematic, as well as an ontological structure of the human world that accords with my reflections on paranoiac knowledge.

We have only to understand the mirror stage *as an identification*, in the full sense that analysis gives to the term: namely, the transformation that takes place in the subject when he assumes an image – whose predestination to this phase-effect is sufficiently indicated by the use, in analytic theory, of the ancient term *imago*.

This jubilant assumption of his specular image by the child at the *infans* stage, still sunk in his motor incapacity and nursling dependence, would seem to exhibit in an exemplary situation the symbolic matrix in which the *I* is precipitated in a primordial form, before it is objectified in the dialectic of identification with the other, and before language restores to it, in the universal, its function as subject.

This form would have to be called the Ideal-I,[1] if we wished to incorporate it into our usual register, in the sense that it will also be the source of secondary identifications, under which term I would place the functions of libidinal normalization. But the important point is that this form situates the agency of the ego, before its social determination, in a fictional direction, which will always remain irreducible for the individual alone, or rather, which will only rejoin the coming-into-being (*le devenir*) of the subject asymptotically, whatever the success of the dialectical syntheses by which he must resolve as *I* his discordance with his own reality.

The fact is that the total form of the body by which the subject anticipates in a mirage the maturation of his power is given to him only as *Gestalt*, that is to say, in an exteriority in which this form is certainly more constituent than constitute, but in which it appears to him above all in a contrasting size (*un relief de stature*) that fixes it and in a symmetry that inverts it, in contrast with the turbulent movements that the subject feels are animating him. Thus, this *Gestalt* – whose pregnancy should be regarded as bound up with the species, though its motor style remains scarcely recognizable – by these two aspects of its appearance, symbolizes the mental permanence of the *I*, at the same time as it prefigures its alienating destination; it is still pregnant with the correspondences that unite the *I* with the statue in which man projects himself, with the phantoms that dominate him, or with the automaton in which, in an ambiguous relation, the world of his own making tends to find completion.

Indeed, for the *imagos* – whose veiled faces it is our privilege to see in outline our daily experience and in the penumbra of symbolic efficacity[2] – the mirror-image would seem to be the threshold of the visible world, if we go by the mirror disposition that the *imago of one's own body* presents in hallucinations or dreams, whether it concerns its individual features, or even its infirmities, or its object-projections; or if we observe the role of the mirror apparatus in the appearance of the double, in which psychical realities, however heterogeneous, are manifested

That a *Gestalt* should be capable of formative effects in the organism is attested by a piece of biological experimentation that is itself so alien to the idea of psychical causality that it cannot bring itself to formulate its results in these terms. It nevertheless recognizes that it is a necessary condition for the maturation of the gonad of the female pigeon that it should see another member of its species, of either sex; so sufficient in itself is this condition that the desired effect may be obtained merely by placing the individual within reach of the field of reflection of a mirror. Similarly, in the case of the migratory locust, the transition within a generation from the solitary to the gregarious form can be obtained by exposing the individual, at a certain stage, to the exclusively visual action of a similar image, provided it is animated by movements of a style sufficiently close to that characteristic of the species. Such facts are inscribed in an order of homeomorphic identification that would itself fall within the larger question of the meaning of beauty as both formative and erogenic.

But the facts of mimicry are no less instructive when conceived as cases of heteromorphic identification, in as much as they raise the problem of the signification of space for the living organism – psychological concepts hardly seem less appropriate for shedding light on these matters than ridiculous attempts to reduce them to the supposedly supreme law of adaptation. We have only to recall how Roger Caillois (who was then very young, and still fresh from his breach with the sociological school in which he was trained) illuminated the subject by using the term 'legendary psychasthenia' to classify morphological mimicry as an obsession with space in its derealizing effect.

I have myself shown in the social dialectic that structures human knowledge as paranoiac[3] why human knowledge has greater autonomy than animal knowledge in relation to the field of force of desire, but also why human knowledge is determined in that 'little reality' (ce peu de réalité), which the Surrealists, in their restless way, saw as its limitation. These reflections lead me to recognize in the spatial captation manifested in the mirror-stage, even before the social dialectic, the effect in man of an organic insufficiency in his natural reality – in so far as any meaning can be given to the word 'nature'.

I am led, therefore, to regard the function of the mirror-stage as a particular case of the function of the imago, which is to establish a relation between the organism and its reality – or, as they say, between the Innenwelt and the Umwelt.

In man, however, this relation to nature is altered by a certain dehiscence at the heart of the organism, a primordial Discord betrayed by the signs of uneasiness and motor unco-ordination of the neo-natal months. The objective notion of the anatomical incompleteness of the pyramidal system and likewise the presence of certain humoral residues of the maternal organism confirm the view I have formulated as the fact of a real specific prematurity of birth in man.

It is worth noting, incidentally, that this is a fact recognized as such by embryologists, by the term foetalization, which determines the prevalence of the so-called superior apparatus of the neurax, and especially of the cortex, which psycho-surgical operations lead us to regard as the intra-organic mirror.

This development is experienced as a temporal dialectic that decisively projects the formation of the individual into history. The mirror stage is a drama whose internal thrust is precipitated from insufficiency to anticipation – and which manufactures for the subject, caught up in the lure of spatial identification, the succession of phantasies that extends from a fragmented body-image to a form of its totality that I shall call orthopaedic – and, lastly, to the assumption of the armour of an alienating identity, which will mark with its rigid structure the subject's entire mental development. Thus, to break out of the circle of the *Innenwelt* into the *Umwelt* generates the inexhaustible quadrature of the ego's verifications.

This fragmented body – which term I have also introduced into our system of theoretical references – usually manifests itself in dreams when the movement of the analysis encounters a certain level of aggressive disintegration in the individual. It then appears in the form of disjointed limbs, or of those organs represented in exoscopy, growing wings and taking up arms for intestinal persecutions – the very same that the visionary Hieronymus Bosch has fixed, for all time, in painting, in their ascent from the fifteenth century to the imaginary zenith of modern man. But this form is even tangibly revealed at the organic level, in the lines of 'fragilization' that define the anatomy of phantasy, as exhibited in the schizoid and spasmodic symptoms of hysteria.

Correlatively, the formation of the *I* is symbolized in dreams by a fortress, or a stadium – its inner arena and enclosure surrounded by marshes and rubbish-tips, dividing it into two opposed fields of contest where the subject flounders in quest of the lofty, remote inner castle whose form (sometimes juxtaposed in the same scenario) symbolizes the id in a quite startling way. Similarly, on the mental plane, we find realized the structures of fortified works, the metaphor of which arises spontaneously, as if issuing from the symptoms themselves, to designate the mechanisms of obsessional neurosis – inversion, isolation, reduplication, cancellation and displacement.

But if we were to build on these subjective givens alone – however little we free them from the condition of experience that makes us see them as partaking of the nature of a linguistic technique – our theoretical attempts would remain exposed to the charge of projecting themselves into the unthinkable of an absolute subject. This is why I have sought in the present hypothesis, grounded in a conjunction of objective data, the guiding grid for a *method of symbolic reduction*.

It establishes in the *defences of the ego* a genetic order, in accordance with the wish formulated by Miss Anna Freud, in the first part of her great work, and situates (as against a frequently expressed prejudice) hysterical repression and its return at a more archaic stage than obsessional inversion and its isolating processes, and the latter in turn as preliminary to paranoic alienation, which dates from the deflection of the specular *I* into the social *I*.

This moment in which the mirror-stage comes to an end inaugurates, by the identification with the *imago* of the counterpart and the drama of primordial jealousy (so well brought out by the school of Charlotte Bühler in the phenomenon of infantile *transitivism*), the dialectic that will henceforth link the *I* to socially elaborated situations.

It is this moment that decisively tips the whole of human knowledge into mediatization through the desire of the other, constitutes its objects in an abstract equivalence by the co-operation of others, and turns the I into that apparatus for which every instinctual thrust constitutes a danger, even though it should correspond to a natural maturation – the very normalization of this maturation being henceforth dependent, in man, on a cultural mediation as exemplified, in the case of the sexual object, by the Oedipus complex.

In the light of this conception, the term primary narcissism, by which analytic doctrine designates the libidinal investment characteristic of that moment, reveals in those who invented it the most profound awareness of semantic latencies. But it also throws light on the dynamic opposition between this libido and the sexual libido, which the first analysts tried to define when they invoked destructive and, indeed, death instincts, in order to explain the evident connection between the narcissistic libido and the alienating function of the I, the aggressivity it releases in any relation to the other, even in a relation involving the most Samaritan of aid.

In fact, they were encountering that existential negativity whose reality is so vigorously proclaimed by the contemporary philosophy of being and nothingness.

But unfortunately that philosophy grasps negativity only within the limits of a self-sufficiency of consciousness, which as one of its premises, links to the *méconnaissances* that constitute the ego, the illusion of autonomy to which it entrusts itself. This flight of fancy, for all that it draws, to an unusual extent, on borrowings from psychoanalytic experience, culminates in the pretension of providing an existential psychoanalysis.

At the culmination of the historical effort of a society to refuse to recognize that it has any function other than the utilitarian one, and in the anxiety of the individual confronting the 'concentrational'[4] form of the social bond that seems to arise to crown this effort, existentialism must be judged by the explanations it gives of the subjective impasses that have indeed resulted from it; a freedom that is never more authentic than when it is within the walls of a prison; a demand for commitment, expressing the impotence of a pure consciousness to master any situation; a voyeuristic-sadistic idealization of the sexual relation; a personality that realizes itself only in suicide; a consciousness of the other that can be satisfied only by Hegelian murder.

These propositions are opposed by all our experience, in so far as it teaches us not to regard the ego as centred on the *perception-consciousness system*, or as organized by the 'reality principle' – a principle that is the expression of a scientific prejudice most hostile to the dialectic of knowledge. Our experience shows that we should start instead from the *function of méconnaissance* that characterizes the ego in all its structures so markedly articulated by Miss Anna Freud. For, if the *Verneinung* represents the patent form of that function, its effects will, for the most part, remain latent, so long as they are not illuminated by some light reflected on to the level of fatality, which is where the id manifests itself.

We can thus understand the inertia characteristic of the formation of the *I*, and find there the most extensive definition of neurosis – just as the captation of the subject by the situation gives us the most general formula for madness, not only the madness that lies behind the walls of asylums, but also the madness that deafens the world with its sound and fury.

The sufferings of neurosis and psychosis are for us a schooling in the passions of the soul, just as the beam of the psychoanalytic scales, when we calculate the tilt of its threat to entire communities, provides us with an indication of the deadening of the passions in society.

At this junction of nature and culture, so persistently examined by modern anthropology, psychoanalysis alone recognises this knot of imaginary servitude that love must always undo again, or sever.

For such a task, we place no trust in altruistic feeling, we who lay bare the aggressivity that underlies the activity of the philanthropist, the idealist, the pedagogue, and even the reformer.

In the recourse of subject to subject that we preserve, psychoanalysis may accompany the patient to the ecstatic limit of the *'Thou art that'*, in which is revealed to him the cipher of his mortal destiny, but it is not in our mere power as practitioners to bring him to that point where the real journey begins.

Notes

1 Throughout this article I leave in its peculiarity the translation I have adopted for Freud's *Ideal-Ich* [i.e., 'je-idéal'], without further comment, other than to say that I have not maintained it since.
2 Cf. Claude Lévi-Strauss, *Structural Anthropology*, Chapter X.
3 Cf. 'Aggressivity in Psychoanalysis', p. 8 and *Écrits*, p. 180.
4 *'Concentrationnaire'*, an adjective coined after World War 11 (this article was written in 1949) to describe the life of the concentration-camp. In the hands of certain writers it became, by extension, applicable to many aspects of 'modern' life [Tr.]

---

16 Julia Kristeva,

'A Question of Subjectivity – an Interview', *Women's Review*, no. 12 (1986), pp. 19–21

Susan Sellers: As a professor of linguistics, and with publications on subjects ranging from philosophy to literary criticism, what led you also to train as a psychoanalyst?

Julia Kristeva: I don't believe one commits oneself to psychoanalysis without certain secret motivations ... difficulties living, a suffering which is unable to express itself. I talked to my psychoanalyst about this aspect of things and so today can speak about these motives for my work.

I wanted to examine the states at the limits of language; the moments where language breaks up in psychosis for example, or the moments where language doesn't yet exist such as during a child's apprenticeship to language. It seemed to me to be impossible to content oneself with a description which held itself to be objective and neutral in these two cases, because already the selection of examples presupposes a particular type of contact with the people who talk to you.

Also the interpretation of people's speech presupposes that you apply yourself to the meaning of what they say. I saw that there was no neutral objectivity possible in descriptions of language at its limits and that we are constantly in what psychoanalysis calls a 'transfer'. It seemed to me dishonest to apply this transfer without having myself undergone the experience of psychoanalysis.

Susan Sellers: An important part of your psychoanalytic research has been the process by which the individual acquires language. What does this 'process' entail?

Julia Kristeva I used the term 'process' whilst I was working on the texts of Antonin Artaud. Artaud is an extremely disturbing writer in modern French literature, partly because he underwent a dramatic experience of madness and partly because he thought carefully about the music in language. Anyone who reads Artaud's texts will realize that all identities are unstable: the identity of linguistic signs, the identity of meaning and, as a result, the identity of the speaker. And in order to take account of this destablization of meaning and of the subject I thought the term 'subject in process' would be appropriate. 'Process' in the sense of process but also in the sense of a legal proceeding where the subject is committed to trial, because our identities in life are constantly called into question, brought to trial, over-ruled.

I wanted to examine the language which manifests these states of instability because in ordinary communication – which is organized, civilized – we repress these states of incandescence. Creativity as well as suffering comprises these moments of instability, where language, or the signs of language, or subjectivity itself are put into 'process'. And one can extrapolate this notion and use it not just for the texts of Artaud but for every 'proceeding' in which we move outside the norms.

Susan Sellers: Writing about this process, one of the distinctions you have drawn in order to chart the development from non-differentiated infant to speaking subject is the distinction between 'the semiotic' and 'the symbolic'. Can you explain this distinction?

Julian Kristeva: In order to research this state of instability – the fact that meaning is not simply a structure or process, or that the subject is not simply a unity but is constantly called into question – I proposed to take into account two modalities or conditions of meaning which I called 'the semiotic' and 'the symbolic'. What I call 'the semiotic' takes us back to the pre-linguistic states of childhood where the child babbles the sounds s/he hears, or where s/he articulates rhythms, alliterations, or stresses, trying to imitate her/his surroundings. In this state the child doesn't yet possess the necessary linguistic signs and thus there is no meaning in the strict sense of the term. It is only after the mirror phase or the experience of castration in the Oedipus complex that the individual becomes subjectively capable of taking on the signs of language, of articulation as it has been prescribed – and I call that 'the symbolic'.

Susan Sellers: What actually happens during the mirror phase and the Oedipus complex?

Julia Kristeva: Identification takes place. What I call 'the semiotic' is a state of disintegration in which patterns appear but which do not have any stable identity: they are blurred and fluctuating. The processes which are at work here are those which Freud calls 'primary': processes of transfer. We have an example of this if we refer once again to the melodies and babblings of infants which are a sound image of their bodily instability. Babies and children's bodies are made up of erotogenic zones which are extremely excitable, or, on the contrary, indifferent, in a state of constant change, of excitation, or extinction, without there being any fixed identity.

A 'fixed identity': it's perhaps a fiction, an illusion – who amongst us has a 'fixed' identity? It's a phantasm; we do nevertheless arrive at a certain type of stability. There are several steps which lead to this stability and one step which has been accentuated by the French psychoanalyst Jacques Lacan is the specular identification which he calls 'the mirror phase'. In this phase one recognizes one's image in a mirror as one's self-image. It is a first identification of the chaotic, fragmented body; and is both violent and jubilatory. The identification comes about under the domination of the maternal image, which is the one nearest to the child and which allows the child both to remain close and to distance itself.

I see a face. A first differentiation takes place, and thus a first self-identity. This identity is still unstable because sometimes I take myself to be me, sometimes I confuse myself with my mother. This narcissistic instability, this doubt persists and makes me ask 'who am I?', 'is it me or is it the other?' The confusion with the maternal image as first other remains.

In order for us to be able to get out of this confusion, the classical pattern of development leads us to a confrontation inside the Oedipal triangle between our desire for the mother and the process of loss which is the result of paternal authority. In the ideal case, this finishes by stabilizing the subject, rendering her/him capable both of pronouncing sentences which conform to the rules, to the law, and of telling her/his own story – of giving her/his account.

These are symbolic acquisitions that are pre-conditioned by a certain psychic experience which is the stabilization of the self in relation to the other.

Susan Sellers: One of the images you have used to clarify this semiotic relationship to the maternal is that of the 'chora'. Could you explain this image?

Julia Kristeva: I believe that this archaic semiotic modality that I have referred to as infantile babblings, in order to give it clearer definition, is a modality which bears the most archaic memories of our link with the maternal body – Of the dependence that all of us have vis-à-vis the maternal body, and where a sort of self-eroticism is indissociable from the experience of the (m)other. We repress the vocal or gestural inscription of this experience under our subsequent acquisitions and this is an important condition for autonomy.

Nevertheless there may be different ways of repressing this experience. There may be a dramatic repression, after which we are building on sand because the foundation has been destroyed, suppressed. Or there may be an attempt to transpose this continent, this receptacle beyond the symbolic. In other words after the mirror phase, and Oedipal castration. (The word 'chora' means receptacle in Greek, which refers us to Winnicott's idea of 'holding': mother and child are in a permanent stricture in which one holds the other, there's a double entrance, the child is held but so is the mother.)

At that point we witness the possibility of creation, of sublimation. I think that every type of creation, even if it's scientific, is due to this possibility of opening the norms, towards pleasure, which refers to an archaic experience with a maternal pre-object.

Susan Sellers: What are the implications of this for literary creation? Do women, with their own real or potential experience of maternity, have a privileged relationship to the semiotic?

Julia Kristeva: What is obvious is that this experience of the semiotic chora in language produces poetry. It can be considered as the source of all stylistic effort, the modifying of banal, logical order by linguistic distortions such as metaphor, metonymy, musicality.

As far as women are concerned the question is rather complex. On the one hand many women – no matter what their particular case structure is: depressive, hysteric, or obsessional – complain that they experience language as something secondary, cold, foreign to their lives. To their passion. To their suffering. To their desire. As if language were a foreign body. And when they say this we are often given the impression that what they question is language as a logical exercise. This complaint can be heard two ways. There may be a refusal to submit to communication, which demands a sacrifice from everyone – from men as well as women. This refusal has often been interpreted by a certain type of romantic feminism as revolutionary, but this is not always the case. It can quite simply be an attempt to escape society and communication and to take refuge in a sort of mystical state which can be extremely regressive and narcissistic. I refuse logical communication; logical communication is a stranger to me and so I withdraw into my archaic experience where I seek the delights of the maternal body. And I give this out as a revolutionary challenge.

On the other hand I think we do have to listen to the truth of a certain suffering which these complaints translate. This consists in noting that often in the social code, in social communication, the basis for our identities which the semiotic forms within language is repressed, thrown into confusion, and the fact of not hearing it, of not giving it room (thus in a way of killing the maternal and the primordial link every subject has with the maternal), exposes us to depression, to a feeling of strangeness. Many women and men experience this. As an analyst up against this depression I am often looking for two things. On the one hand I am looking to release the hatred which has not been able to express itself, to manifest itself (depression is often the result of hatred which has not been exhausted).

At the same time I am searching for the inscriptions in language of the archaic contact with the maternal body which has been forgotten. Where are these inscriptions to be found? Often not in the meaning of what the patients say, because the meaning of their speech is frequently banal and clichéd, without real investment or relevance. They are to be found in the tempo of the voice, in the rapidity of the delivery, or in its monotony, or in certain musicalities. Or in certain alliterations, which mean that like *Alice in Wonderland* one has to cut the phrases up in order to look for the 'portmanteau words', the real meaning of the wounded desire in which this archaic relation to the mother takes refuge. This is necessary in order to be able to rehabilitate them, to create for each individual, and for women in particular, a new point of departure.

Susan Sellers: Is is possible to distinguish a language or writing which is specific to women?

Julia Kristeva: I am very uncertain on this point because what asserts itself today as 'women's writing' distinguishes itself from 'men's writing' mainly by the choice of themes. For example we would talk about the care of children or maternity in a way men would not be able to because we don't have the same historical, social or family experiences.

As far as style is concerned – the actual dynamics of language, this recourse to the semiotic, the inscription of the archaic relation to the mother in language – it isn't the monopoly of women. Men writers such as Joyce, Mallarmé or Artaud are proof of this. It's a question of subjectivity. It's possible that in aesthetic creation we occupy several positions. Any creator necessarily moves through an identification with the maternal, which is why the resurgence of this semiotic dynamic is important in every act of creation.

The question is: do men and women identify in the same way with the archaic mother? Formally, I don't really see a difference. Psychologically, I would say it's more difficult for women, because a woman is confronted by something not differentiable; she is confronted by the same. Because we are two women. Whereas for a man she's an other. For men this identification with the maternal involves a perverse pleasure, whilst for women there are psychotic risks attached. I might lose myself, lose my identity.

This explains perhaps why it's more difficult for women to get out of hell, this descent: Orpheus manages it but Eurydice doesn't.

Susan Sellers: Does this explain why so much of your work in literature has tended to concentrate on male writers?

Julia Kristeva: I am currently working on melancholia and I am using the texts of Marguerite Duras as an example of modern writing about suffering. In Duras' texts there is a thematization of suffering – a thematic description of suffering rather than any stylistic or linguistic research. Where stylistic innovation does occur it's mainly in the form of imperfection, awkwardness. It's through being imperfect that Duras' sentences translate suffering rather than in the fireworks of musical and vocal pleasure we find in Joyce. For Duras, the expression of pain is painful.

Susan Sellers: Your most recent work has explored the relationship between melancholy or depression and creativity. How did this particular area of your research come into being?

Julia Kristeva: It starts from the psychoanalytic observation that depression is virtually a sickness of our time. There are more and more people complaining about depression, and in psychoanalysis we note that many people who otherwise present themselves as hysteric, obsessional, etc. have an underlying depression. Various important because it's a problem situated at the cross-over point between biological and psychological research.

A few years ago psychoanalysis was confronted by the science of language, now there is a new challenge: neuro-biology. There are many anti-depressants, and these anti-depressants have a certain effectiveness. But as a psychoanalyst I think that the work of relieving the anguish and clearing the depression is not done by these pills. The root of the problem remains.

As far as literary-aesthetic creation is concerned (which is what interests me), I would say that the creative act is released by an experience of depression without which we would not call into question the stability of meaning or the banality of expression. A writer must at one time or another have been in a situation of loss – of ties, of meaning – in order to write.

There is nevertheless something paradoxical about a writer, who experiences depression in its most acute and dramatic form, but who also has the possibility of lifting her/himself out of it. For example, the writer is able to describe her/his depression to us, and this is already a triumph over depression. The texts of Marguerite Duras are about suffering, the experience of sadness, death, suicide. As are the texts of Dostoyevsky. The texts of Nerval, with all their references to the cultural tradition, show us to what extent sadness and suffering can be themes.

Yet even when it's a question of celebratory writing, it very often transpires when one knows the biography of the writer that there is a contra-investment: it's the bright side of the black sun of melancholy. There is a possibility of getting out of depression by inverting the negative contents, through transposing them in a positive way. Like the clown whose laugh translates a profound sadness. It's in this optic that I examine the imaginary as essentially melancholic and as a combat against melancholy.

Imaginary creations are a powerful anti-depressant. Provided we are able to create them . . .   *Susan Sellers*

---

17   Hélène Cixous,

'Sorties', *New French Feminisms*, Elaine Marks and Isabelle de Courtivoron, eds (1975), pp. 366–71

Where is she?

Activity/passivity,
Sun/Moon,
Culture/Nature,
Day/Night,

Father/Mother,
Head/heart,
Intelligible/sensitive,
Logos/Pathos.

Form, convex, step, advance, seed,
progress.
Matter, concave, ground – which supports
the step, receptacle.

Man
―――――――
Woman

Always the same metaphor: we follow it, it transports us, in all of its forms, wherever a discourse is organized. The same thread, or double tress leads us, whether we are reading or speaking, through literature, philosophy, criticism, centuries of representation, of reflection.

Thought has always worked by
opposition,
Speech/Writing
High/Low

By dual, *hierarchized*[1] oppositions, Superior/Inferior. Myths, legends, books, Philosophical systems. Wherever an ordering intervenes, a law organizes the thinkable by (dual, irreconcilable; or mitigable, dialectical) oppositions. And all the couples of oppositions are *couples*. Does this mean something? Is the fact that logocentrism subjects thought – all of the concepts, the codes, the values – to a two-term system, related to 'the' couple man/woman?

Nature/History,
Nature/Art,
Nature, Mind,
Passion/Action.

Theory of culture, theory of society, the ensemble of symbolic systems – art, religion, family, language, – everything elaborates the same systems. And the movement by which each opposition is set up to produce meaning is the movement by which the couple is destroyed. A universal battlefield. Each time a war breaks out. Death is always at work.

Father/son	Relationships of authority, of privilege, of force.
Logos/writing	Relationships: opposition, conflict, relief, reversion.
Master/slave	Violence. Repression.

And we perceive that the 'victory' always amounts to the same thing: it is hierarchized. The hierarchization subjects the entire conceptual organization to man. A male privilege, which can be seen in the opposition by which it sustains itself, between *activity* and *passivity*. Traditionally, the question of sexual difference is coupled with the same opposition: activity/passivity.

That goes a long way. If we examine the history of philosophy – in so far as philosophical discourse orders and reproduces all thought – we perceive[2] that: it is marked by an absolute constant, the orchestrator of values, which is precisely the opposition activity/passivity.

In philosophy, woman is always on the side of passivity. Every time the question comes up; when we examine kinship structures; whenever a family model is brought into play; in fact as soon as the ontological question is raised; as soon as you ask yourself what is meant by the question 'What is it?'; as soon as there is a will to say something. A will: desire, authority, you examine that, and you are led right back – to the father. You can even fail to notice that there's no place at all for women in the operation! In the extreme the world of 'being' can function to the exclusion of the mother. No need for mother – provided that there is something of the maternal: and it is the father then who acts as – is – the mother. Either the woman is passive; or she doesn't exist. What is left is unthinkable, unthought of. She does not enter into the oppositions, she is not coupled with the father (who is coupled with the son).

There is Mallarmé's[3] tragic dream, a father lamenting the mystery of paternity, which mourning tears out of the poet, the mourning of mournings, the death of the beloved son: this dream of a union between the father and the son – and no mother then. Man's dream is the face of death. Which always threatens him differently than it threatens woman.

'an alliance	
a union, superb	And dream of
	masculine
– and the life	filiation, dream of
	God the father
remaining in me	emerging from
	himself
I shall use it	in his son, – and
to –	no mother then
so no mother then?'	

She does not exist, she may be nonexistent; but there must be something of her. Of woman, upon whom he no longer depends, he retains only this space, always virginal, matter subjected to the desire that he wishes to imprint.

And if you examine literary history, it's the same story. It all refers back to man to his torment, his desire to be (at) the origin. Back to the father. There is in intrinsic bond between the philosophical and the literary (to the extent that it signifies, literature is commanded by the philosophical) and phallocentrism. The philosophical constructs itself starting with the abasement of woman. Subordination of the feminine to the masculine order which appears to be the condition for the functioning of the machine.

The challenging of this solidarity of logocentrism and phallocentrism has today become insistent enough – the bringing to light of the fate which has been imposed upon woman, of her burial – to threaten the stability of the masculine edifice which passed itself off as eternal-natural; by bringing forth from the world of femininity reflections, hypotheses which are necessarily ruinous for the bastion which still holds the authority. What would become of logocentrism, of the great philosophical systems, of world order in general if the rock upon which they founded their church were to crumble?

If it were to come out in a new day that the logocentric project had always been, undeniably, to found (fund)[4] phallocentrism, to insure for masculine order a rationale equal to history itself?

Then all the stories would have to be told differently, the future would be incalculable, the historical forces would, will, change hands, bodies; another thinking as yet not thinkable will transform the functioning of all society. Well, we are living through this very period when the conceptual foundation of a millenial culture is in process of being undermined by millions of a species of mole as yet not recognized.

When they awaken from among the dead, from among the words, from among the laws. . . .

What does one give?
The specific difference that has determined the movement of history as a movement of property is articulated between two economies that define themselves in relation to the problematics of giving.

The (political) economy of the masculine and of the feminine is organized by different requirements and constraints, which, when socialized and metaphorized, produce signs, relationships of power, relationships of production and of reproduction, an entire immense system of cultural inscription readable as masculine or feminine.

I am careful here to use the *qualifiers* of sexual difference, in order to avoid the confusion man/masculine, woman/feminine: for there are men who do not repress their femininity, women who more or less forcefully inscribe their masculinity. The difference is not, of course, distributed according to socially determined 'sexes'. Furthermore, when I speak of political economy and of libidinal economy, in putting the two together, I am not bringing into play the false question of origin, that tall tale sustained by male privilege. We must guard against falling complacently or blindly into the essentialist ideological interpretation, as, for example, Freud and Jones, in different ways, ventured to do; in their quarrel over the subject of feminine sexuality, both of them, starting from opposite points of view, came to support the awesome thesis of a 'natural', anatomical determination of sexual difference-opposition. And from there on, both implicitly support phallocentrism's position of power.

Let us review the main points of the opposing positions: [Ernest] Jones (in *Early Feminine Sexuality*), using an ambiguous approach, attacks the Freudian theses that make of woman an imperfect man.

For Freud:

1. The 'fatality' of the feminine situation is a result of an anatomical 'defectiveness'.
2. There is only one libido, and its essence is male; the inscription of sexual difference begins only with a phallic phase which both boys and girls go through. Until then, the girl has been a sort of little boy: the genital organization of the infantile libido is articulated by the equivalence activity/masculinity; the vagina has not as yet been 'discovered'.

3. The first love object being, for both sexes, the mother, it is only for the
   boy that love of the opposite sex is 'natural'.

For Jones: Femininity is an autonomous 'essence'
From the outset (starting from the age of six months) the girl has a *feminine*
desire for her father; an analysis of the little girl's earliest fantasms would
in fact show that, in place of the breast which is perceived as disappointing,
it is the penis that is desired, or an object of the same form (by an analogical
displacement). It follows, since we are already into the chain of
substitutions, that in the series of partial objects in place of the penis, would
come the child – for in order to counter Freud, Jones docilely returns to the
Freudian terrain. And then some. From the equation breast-penis-child, he
concludes that the little girl experiences with regard to the father a primary
desire. (And this would include the desire to have a child by the father as
well.) And, of course, the girl also has a primary love for the opposite sex.
She too, then, has a right to her Oedipal complex as a primary formation,
and to the threat of mutilation by the mother. At last she is a woman,
anatomically, without defect: her clitoris is not a minipenis. Clitoral
masturbation is not, as Freud claims, a masculine practice. And it would
seem in light of precocious fantasms that the vagina is discovered very early.

   In fact, in affirming that there is a specific femininity (while in other
respects preserving the theses of an orthodoxy) it is still phallocentrism that
Jones reinforces, on the pretext of taking the part of femininity (and of God,
who he recalls created them male and female – !). And bisexuality vanishes
into the unbridged abyss that separates the opponents here.

   As for Freud, if we subscribe to what he sets forth when he identifies
with Napoleon in his article of 1933 on *The Disappearance of the Oedipus
Complex*: 'anatomy is destiny', then we participate in the sentencing to death
of woman. And in the completion of all History.

   That the difference between the sexes may have psychic consequences is
undeniable. But they are surely not reducible to those designated by a
Freudian analysis. Starting with the relationship of the two sexes to the
Oedipal complex, the boy and the girl are oriented toward a division of
social roles so that women 'inescapably' have a lesser productivity, because
they 'sublimate' less than men and because symbolic activity, hence the
production of culture, is men's doing.[5]

   Freud moreover starts from what he calls the *anatomical* difference
between the sexes. And we know how that is pictured in his eyes: as the
difference between having/not having the phallus. With reference to these
precious parts. Starting from what will be specified, by Lacan, as the
transcendental signifier.

   But *sexual difference* is not determined by the fantasized relationship to
anatomy, which is based, to a great extent, upon the point of view, therefore
upon a strange importance accorded [by Freud and Lacan] to exteriority and
to the specular in the elaboration of sexuality. A voyeur's theory, of course.

No, it is at the level of sexual pleasure [*jouissance*] in my opinion that the difference makes itself most clearly apparent in as far as woman's libidinal economy is neither identifiable by a man nor referable to the masculine economy.

For me, the question 'What does she want?' that they ask of woman, a question that in fact woman asks herself because they ask it of her, because precisely there is so little place in society for her desire that she ends up by dint of not knowing what to do with it, no longer knowing where to put it, or if she has any, conceals the most immediate and the most urgent question: 'How do I experience sexual pleasure?' What is feminine *sexual pleasure*, where does it take place, how is it inscribed at the level of her body, of her unconscious? And then how is it put into writing?

We can go on at length about a hypothetical prehistory and about a matriarchal era. Or we can, as did Bachofen,[6] attempt to reconstitute a gynecocratic society, and to deduce from it poetic and mythical effects that have a powerfully subversive import with regard to the family and to male power.

All the other ways of depicting the history of power, property, masculine domination, the constitution of the State, the ideological apparatus have their effectiveness. But the change taking place has nothing to do with question of 'origin'. Phallocentrism *is*. History has never produced, recorded anything but that. Which does not mean that this form is inevitable or natural. Phallocentrism is the enemy. Of *everyone*. Men stand to lose by it, differently but as seriously as women. And it is time to transform. To invent the other history.

There is no such thing as 'destiny', 'nature', or essence, but living structures, caught up, sometimes frozen within historicocultural limits which intermingle with the historical scene to such a degree that it has long been impossible and is still difficult to think or even to imagine something else. At present, we are living through a transitional period – where the classical structure appears as if it might crack.

To predict what will happen to sexual difference – in another time (in two or three hundred years?) is impossible. But there should be no misunderstanding: men and women are caught up in a network of millenial cultural determinations of a complexity that is practically unanalyzable: we can no more talk about 'woman' than about 'man' without getting caught up in an ideological theater where the multiplication of representations, images, reflections, myths, identifications constantly transforms, deforms, alters each person's imaginary order and in advance, renders all conceptualization null and void.

There is no reason to exclude the possibility of radical transformations of behavior, mentalities, roles, and political economy. The effects of these transformations on the libidinal economy are unthinkable today. Let us imagine simultaneously a *general* change in all of the structures of formation, education, framework, hence of reproduction, of ideological effects, and let us imagine a real liberation of sexuality, that is, a transformation of our relationship to our body – and to another body), an approximation of the immense material organic sensual universe that we are, this not being possible, of course, without equally radical political transformations (imagine!). Then 'femininity', 'masculinity', would inscribe their effects of difference, their economy, their relationships to expenditure, to deficit, to giving, quite differently. That which appears as 'feminine' or 'masculine' today would no longer amount to the same thing. The general logic of difference would no longer fit into the opposition that still dominates. The difference would be a crowning display of new differences.

But we are still floundering about – with certain exceptions – in the Old order.

The masculine future:
There are exceptions. There always have been those uncertain, poetic beings, who have not let themselves be reduced to the state of coded mannequins by relentless repression of the homosexual component. Men or women, complex, mobile, open beings. Admitting the component of the other sex makes them at once much richer, plural, strong, and to the extent of this mobility, very fragile. We invent only on this condition: thinkers, artists, creators of new values, 'philosophers' of the mad Nietzchean sort, inventors and destroyers of concepts, of forms, inventors and destroyers of concepts, of forms, the changers of life cannot but be agitated by singularities – complementary or contradictory. This does not mean that in order to create you must be homosexual. But there is no *invention* possible, whether it be philosophical or poetic, without the presence in the inventing subject of an abundance of the other, of the diverse: persons-detached, persons-thought, peoples born of the unconscious, and in each desert, suddenly animated, a springing forth of self that we did not know about – our women, our monsters, our jackals, our Arabs, our fellow-creatures, our fears.[7] But there is no invention of other I's, no poetry, no fiction without a certain homosexuality (interplay therefore of bisexuality) making in me a crystallized work of my ultrasubjectivities. I is this matter, personal, exuberant, lively masculine, feminine or other in which I delights me and distresses me. And in the concert of personalizations called I, at the same time that you repress a certain homosexuality, symbolically, substitutively, it comes out through various signs – traits, comportments, manners, gestures – and it is seen still more clearly in writing.

Thus, under the name of Jean Genet,[8] what is inscribed in the movement of a text which divides itself, breaks itself into bits, regroups itself, is an abundant, maternal, pederastic femininity. A phantasmatical mingling of men, of males, of messieurs, of monarchs, princes, orphans, flowers, mothers, breasts, gravitates around a marvelous 'sun of energy' love, which bombards and disintegrates these ephemeral amorous singularities so that they may recompose themselves in other bodies for new passions. . . .

Notes

1 The translation is faithful to Hélène Cixous's many neologisms. – Translator.
2 This is what all of Derrida's work traversing – investigating the history of philosophy – seeks to make apparent. In Plato, Hegel, Nietzsche, the same process goes on, repression, exclusion, distancing of woman. Murder which intermingles with history as a manifestation and representation of masculine power.
3 *Pour un tombeau d'Anatole* (Paris, Editions du Seuil, 1961, p. 138) tomb in which Mallarmé preserves his son, guards him, he himself the mother, from death.
4 *Fonder* in French means both 'to found' and 'to fund'. – translator.
5 Freud's thesis is the following: when the Oedipal complex disappears the superego becomes its heir. At the moment when the boy begins to feel the threat of castration, he begins to overcome the Oedipus complex, with the help of a very severe superego. The Oedipus complex for the boy is a primary process: his first love object, as for the girl, is the mother. But the girl's development is inevitably controlled by the pressure of a less severe superego: the discovery of her castration results in a less vigorous superego. She never completely overcomes the Oedipus complex. The feminine Oedipus complex is not a primary process: the pre-Oedipal attachment to the mother entails for the girl a difficulty from which, says Freud, she never recovers: the necessity of changing objects (to love the father), in mid-stream is a painful conversion, which is accompanied by an additional renunciation: the passage from pre-Oedipal sexuality to 'normal' sexuality implies the abandonment of the clitoris in order to move on to the vagina. When this 'destiny' is fulfilled, women have a reduced symbolic activity: they have nothing to lose, to gain, to defend.
6 J.-J. Bachofen (1815–1887) Swiss historian of 'gynecocracy', 'historian' of a nonhistory. His project is to demonstrate that the nations (Greek, Roman, Hebrew) went through an age of 'gynecocracy', the reign of the Mother, before arriving at a patriarchy. This epoch can only be deduced, as it has no history. Bachofen advances that this state of affairs, humiliating for men, must have been repressed, covered over by historical forgetfulness. And he attempts to create (in *Das Mutterrecht* in particular, 1861) an archaeology of the matriarchal system, of great beauty, starting with a reading of the first historical texts, at the level of the symptom, of their unsaid. Gynecocracy, he says, is well-ordered materialism.
7 The French here, *nos semblables, nos frayeurs*, plays on and with the last line of Baudelaire's famous poem 'Au lecteur' [To the reader]: 'Hypocrite lecteur, – mon semblable, – mon frère.' – Translator.
8 Jean Genet, French novelist and playwright, to whose writing Hélène Cixous refers when she gives examples of the inscription of pederastic femininity. – Translator.

18 Judith Butler,

'Variations on Sex and Gender: Beauvoir, Wittig and Foucault',
Seyla Benhabib and Drucilla Cornell, eds *Feminism as Critique*
(1987), pp. 128–42

'One is not born, but rather becomes, a woman' – Beauvoir's now-famous formulation asserts the noncoincidence of natural and gendered identity. Because what we become is not what we already are, gender is dislodged from sex; the cultural interpretation of sexual attributes is distinguished from the facticity or simple existence of these attributes. The verb 'become' contains, however, a consequential ambiguity. Not only are we culturally constructed, but in some sense we construct ourselves. For Beauvoir, to *become* a women is a purposive and appropriative set of acts, the gradual acquisition of a skill, a 'project' in Sartrian terms, to assume a culturally established corporeal style and significance. When 'become' is taken to mean purposefully assume or embody', Beauvoir's declaration seems to shoulder the burden of Sartrian choice. If genders are in some sense chosen, then what happens to the definition of gender as a cultural interpretation of sex, that is, what happens to the ways in which we are, as it were, already culturally interpreted? How can gender be both a matter of choice and cultural construction?

Beauvoir does not claim to be describing a theory of gender identity or gender acquisition in *The Second Sex*, and yet her formulation of gender as a *project* seems to invite speculation on just such a theory. Monique Wittig, a French feminist who wrote an influential article 'One is Not Born a Woman' (1978), extends Beauvoir's theory on the ambiguous nature of gender identity, i.e. this cultural self that we become but which we seem to have been all along. The positions of Beauvoir and Wittig, though different in crucial respects, commonly suggest a theory of gender that tries to make cultural sense of the existential doctrine of choice. Gender becomes the corporeal locus of cultural meanings both received and innovated. And 'choice' in this context comes to signify a corporeal process of interpretation within a network of deeply entrenched cultural norms.

When the body is conceived as a cultural locus of gender meanings, it becomes unclear what aspects of this body are natural or free of cultural imprint. Indeed, how are we to find the body that preexists its cultural interpretation? If gender is the corporealization of choice, and the acculturation of the corporeal, then what is left of nature, and what has become of sex? If gender is determined in the dialectic between culture and choice, then what role does 'sex' serve, and ought we to conclude that the very distinction between sex and gender is anachronistic? Has Beauvoir refuted the original meaning of her famous formulation, or was that declaration more nuanced than we originally guessed? To answer, we must reconstruct Beauvoir's distinction between sex and gender, and consider her theory's present life in the work of Monique Wittig who, in fact, considers the distinction anachronistic. We will then turn to Michel Foucault's rejection of the category of 'natural sex', compare it with Wittig's position, and attempt a reformulation of gender as a cultural project.

Satrian Bodies and Cartesian Ghosts

The notion that we somehow choose our genders poses an ontological puzzle. It might at first seem impossible that we can occupy a position outside of gender in order to stand back and choose our genders. If we are always already gendered, immersed in gender, what sense does it make to say that we choose what we already are? Not only does the thesis appear tautological, but in so far as it postulates a choosing self prior to its own chosen gender, it seems to adopt a Cartesian view of the self, an egological structure that lives and thrives prior to language and cultural life. This view of the self runs counter to contemporary findings on the linguistic construction of personal agency and, as is the problem with Cartesian egos everywhere, their ontological distance from language and cultural life precludes the possibility of their eventual verification. If Beauvoir's claim is to have cogency, if it is true that we 'become' our genders through some kind of volitional and appropriative set of acts, then she must mean something other than an unsituated Cartesian act. That personal agency is a logical prerequisite for *taking on* a gender does not presuppose that this agency is itself disembodied; indeed, it is our genders that we become, and not our bodies. If Beauvoir's theory is to be understood as freed of the Cartesian ghost, we must first establish her view of embodied identity, and consider her musings on the possibilities of disembodied souls.

Whether consciousness has any discrete ontological status apart from the body is a question that Sartre answers inconsistently throughout *Being and Nothingness*.[2] This ambivalence toward a Cartesian mind/body dualism reemerges, although less seriously, in Beauvoir's *The Second Sex*. In fact, in *The Second Sex* we can see an effort to radicalize the one implication of Sartre's theory concerned with establishing an embodied notion of freedom. The chapter on 'The Body' in *Being and Nothingness* contains the echoes of Cartesianism which haunt his thinking, but also gives evidence of his own efforts to expel the Cartesian ghost. Although Sartre argues that the body is coextensive with personal identity (it is a 'perspective' that one lives), he also suggests that consciousness is in some sense beyond the body ('My body is a *point of departure* which I *am* and which at the same time I surpass.'). Instead of refuting Cartesianism, Sartre's theory assimilates the Cartesian moment as an immanent and partial feature of consciousness; Sartre's theory seeks to conceptualize the disembodied or transcendent feature of personal identity as paradoxically, yet essentially, related to consciousness as embodied. The duality of consciousness as both embodied and transcendent is intrinsic to personal identity; and the effort to locate personal identity exclusively in one or the other is, according to Sartre, a project in bad faith.

Although Sartre's references to 'surpassing' the body may be read as presupposing a mind/body dualism, we need to understand this self-transcendence as itself a corporeal movement, and thus rethink both our usual ideas of 'transcendence' and of the mind/body dualism itself. For Sartre, one may surpass the body, but this does not mean that one definitively gets beyond the body; the subversive paradox consists in the fact that the body itself is a surpassing. The body is not a static or self-identical phenomenon, but a mode of intentionality, a directional force and mode of desire. As a condition of access to the world, the body is a being comported beyond itself, referring to the world and thereby revealing its own ontological status as a referential reality. For Sartre, the body is lived and experienced as the context and medium for all human strivings.[3] Because for Sartre all human beings strive after possibilities not yet realized, human beings are to that extent 'beyond' themselves. This *ek-static* condition is itself a corporeal experience; the body is thus experienced as a mode of becoming. Indeed, for Sartre the natural body only exists in the mode of being surpassed: 'We can never apprehend this contingency as such in so far as our body is *for us*; for we are a choice, and for us to be is to choose ourselves . . . this inapprehensible body is precisely the necessity that *there be a choice*, that I do not exist *all at once*.'[4]

Beauvoir does not so much refute Sartre as take him at his non-Cartesian best.[5] Sartre writes in *Being and Nothingness* that 'it would be best to say, using 'exist' as a transitive verb, that consciousness *exists* its body.'[6] the transitive form of 'exist' is not far removed from Beauvoir's disarming use of 'become', and Beauvoir's concept of becoming a gender seems both a radicalization and concretization of the Sartrian formulation. In transposing the identification of corporeal existence and 'becoming' onto the scene of sex and gender, Beauvoir appropriates the ontological necessity of the paradox, but the tension in her theory does not reside between being 'in' and 'beyond' the body, but in the move from the natural to the acculturated body. That one is not born, but rather becomes, a woman does not imply that this 'becoming' traverses a path from disembodied freedom to cultural embodiment. Indeed, one is one's body from the start, and only thereafter becomes one's gender. The movement from sex to gender is internal to embodied life, a sculpting of the original body into a cultural form. To mix Sartrian phraseology with Beauvoir's, we might say that to 'exist' one's body in culturally concrete terms means, at least partially, to become one's gender.

Although we 'become' our genders in Beauvoir's view, the temporal movement of this becoming does not follow a linear progression. The origin of gender is not temporally discrete precisely because gender is not suddenly originated at some point in time after which it is fixed in form.

In an important sense, gender is not traceable to a definable origin because it itself is an originating activity incessantly taking place. No longer understood as a product of cultural and psychic relations long past, gender is a contemporary way of organizing past and future cultural norms, a way of situating oneself in and through those norms, an active style of living one's body in the world.

Gender as Choice

One chooses one's gender, but one does not choose it from a distance, which signals an ontological juncture between the choosing agent and the chosen gender. The Cartesian space of the deliberate 'chooser' is fictional, but if the distanced deliberations of the spectator are not the choices whereof Beauvoir speaks, then how are we to understand the choice at the origin of gender? Beauvoir's view of gender as an incessant project, a daily act of reconstruction and interpretation, draws upon Sartre's doctrine of prereflective choice and gives that abstract epistemological structure a concrete cultural meaning. Prereflective choice is a tacit and spontaneous act which Sartre terms 'quasi-knowledge'. Not wholly conscious, but nevertheless accessible to consciousness, it is the kind of choice we make and only later realize that we have made. Beauvoir seems to rely on this notion of choice in referring to the kind of volitional act through which gender is assumed. Taking on a gender is not possible at a moment's notice, but is a subtle and strategic project, laborious and for the most part covert. Becoming a gender is an impulsive yet mindful process of interpreting a cultural reality laden with sanctions, taboos and prescriptions. The choice to assume a certain kind of body, to live or wear one's body a certain way, implies a world of already established corporeal styles. To choose a gender is to interpret received gender norms in a way that reproduces and organizes them anew. Less a radical act of creation, gender is a tacit project to renew a cultural history in one's own corporeal terms. This is not a prescriptive task we must endeavor to do, but one in which we have been endeavoring all along.

By scrutinizing the mechanism of agency and appropriation, Beauvoir is attempting, in my mind, to infuse the analysis of women's oppression with emancipatory potential. Oppression is not a self-contained system that either confronts individuals as a theoretical object or generates them as its cultural pawns. It is a dialectical force that requires individual participation on a large scale in order to maintain its malignant life.

Beauvoir does not address directly the burden of freedom that gender presents, but we can extrapolate from her position how constraining gender norms work to subdue the exercise of gender freedom. The social constraints upon gender compliance and deviation are so great that most people feel deeply wounded if they are told that they exercise their manhood or womanhood improperly. In so far as social existence requires an unambiguous gender affinity, it is not possible to exist in a socially meaningful sense outside of established gender norms. The fall from established gender boundaries initiates a sense of radical dislocation which can assume a metaphysical significance. If human existence is always gendered existence, then to stray outside of established gender is in some sense to put one's very existence into question. In these moments of gender dislocation in which we realize that it is hardly necessary that we be the genders we have become, we confront the burden of choice intrinsic to living as a man or a woman or some other gender identity, a freedom made burdensome through social constraint.

The anguish and terror of leaving a prescribed gender or of trespassing upon another gender territory testifies to the social constraints upon gender interpretation as well as to the necessity *that there be* an interpretation, i.e., to the essential freedom at the origin of gender. Similarly, the widespread difficulty in accepting motherhood, for example, as an institutional rather than an instinctual reality expresses this same interplay of constraint and freedom. The effort to interpret maternal feelings as organic necessities discloses a desire to disguise motherhood as an optional practice. If motherhood becomes a choice, then what else is possible? This kind of questioning often engenders vertigo and terror over the possibility of losing social sanctions, of leaving a solid social station and place. That this terror is so well known gives the most credence to the notion that gender identity rests on the unstable bedrock of human invention.

Embodiment and Autonomy

Beauvoir's analysis of the body takes its bearings within the cultural situation in which men have traditionally been associated with the disembodied or transcendent feature of human existence and women with the bodily and immanent feature of human existence. Her own view of an embodied identity that 'incorporates' transcendence subscribes to neither position. Although she occasionally seems to embrace a view of authority modeled on the disembodied transcendence of consciousness, her criticism of this disembodied perspective suggests that another version of autonomy is implicitly at work in her theory.

Women are 'Other' according to Beauvoir in so far as they are defined by a masculine perspective that seeks to safeguard its own disembodied status through identifying women generally with the bodily sphere. Masculine disembodiment is only possible on the condition that women occupy their bodies as their essential and enslaving identities. If women *are* their bodies (to be distinguished from 'existing' their bodies, which implies living their bodies as projects or bearers of created meanings), if women are only their bodies, if their consciousness and freedom are only so many disguised permutations of bodily need and necessity, then women have, in effect,   exclusively monopolized the bodily sphere of life.

By defining women as 'Other', men are able through the shortcut of definition to dispose of their bodies, to make themselves other than their bodies – a symbol potentially of human decay and transience, of limitation generally – and to make their bodies other than themselves. From this belief that the body is Other, it is not a far leap to the conclusion that others *are* their bodies, while the masculine 'I' is a noncorporeal soul. The body rendered as Other – the body repressed or denied and, then, projected – reemerges for this 'I' as the view of others as essentially body. Hence, women become the Other; they come to embody corporeality itself. This redundancy becomes their essence, and existence as a woman becomes what Hegel termed 'a motionless tautology'.

Beauvoir's dialectic of self and Other argues the limits of a Cartesian version of disembodied freedom, and criticizes implicitly the model of autonomy upheld by these masculine gender norms. The pursuit of disembodiment is necessarily deceived because the body can never really be denied; its denial becomes the condition of its emergence in alien form. Disembodiment becomes a way of existing one's body in the mode of denial. And the denial of the body – as in Hegel's dialectic of master and slave – reveals itself as nothing other than the embodiment of denial.

The Body as Situation

Beauvoir suggests an alternative to the gender polarity of masculine disembodiment and feminine enslavement to the body in her notion of the body as a 'situation'. The body as situation has at least a twofold meaning. As a locus of cultural interpretations, the body is a material reality that has already been located and defined within a social context. The body is also the situation of having to take up and interpret that set of received interpretations. As a field of interpretive possibilities, the body is a locus of the dialectical process of interpreting anew a historical set of interpretations which have already informed corporeal style. The body becomes a peculiar nexus of culture and choice, and 'existing' one's body becomes a personal way of taking up and reinterpreting received gender norms. To the extent that gender norms function under the aegis of social constraints, the reinterpretation of those norms through the proliferation and variation of corporeal styles becomes a very concrete and accessible way of politicizing personal life.

If we accept the body as a cultural situation, then the notion of a natural body and, indeed, a natural 'sex' seem increasingly suspect. The limits to gender, the range of possibilities for a lived interpretation of a sexually differentiated anatomy, seem less restricted by anatomy than by the weight of the cultural institutions that have conventionally interpreted anatomy. Indeed, it becomes unclear when we take Beauvoir's formulation to its unstated consequences, whether gender need to be in any way linked with sex, or whether this linkage is itself cultural convention. If gender is a way of existing one's body, and one's body is a situation, a field of cultural possibilities both received and reinterpreted, then both gender and sex seem to be thoroughly cultural affairs. Gender seems less a function of anatomy than one of its possible uses: 'the body of woman is one of the essential elements in her situation in the world. But that body is not enough to define her as woman; there is no true living reality except as manifested by the conscious individual through activities and in the bosom of society.'[7]

The Body Politic

If the natural body – and natural 'sex' – is a fiction, Beauvoir's theory seems implicitly to ask whether sex was not gender all along. Monique Wittig formulates this challenge to natural 'sex' explicitly. Although Wittig and Beauvoir occupy very different sides of the feminist political spectrum in contemporary France, they are nevertheless joined theoretically in their refusal of essentialist doctrines of femininity. Wittig's article, 'One is Not Born a Woman', takes its title from Beauvoir's stated formulation, and was initially presented at the Simone de Beauvoir conference in New York City in 1979. Although that piece does not mention Beauvoir after the first few paragraphs, we can nevertheless read it as an effort to make explicit Beauvoir's tacit theory of gender acquisition.

For Wittig, the very discrimination of 'sex' takes place within a political and linguistic network that presupposes, and hence requires, that sex remain dyadic. The demarcation of sexual difference does not *precede* the interpretation of that difference, but this demarcation is itself an interpretive act laden with normative assumptions about a binary gender system. Discrimination is always 'discrimination', binary opposition always serves the purposes of hierarchy. Wittig realizes that her position is counterintuitive, but it is precisely the political education of intuition that she wants to expose. For Wittig, when we name sexual difference, we create it; we restrict our understanding of relevant sexual parts to those that aid in the process of reproduction, and thereby render heterosexuality an ontological necessity. What distinguishes the sexes are those anatomical features, which either bear on reproduction directly, or are construed to aid in its eventual success. Hence, Wittig argues that erogeneity, the body's sexual responsiveness, is restricted through the institutionalization of binary sexual difference; her question: why don't we name as sexual features our mouths, hands, and backs? Her answer: we only name sexual – read, feel sexual – those features functional in reproductive activity.

Her claim is counterintuitive because we see sexual difference constantly, and it seems to us an immediate given of experience. She argues:

Sex ... is taken as an 'immediate given', a sensible given, 'physical features', belonging to a natural order. But what we believe to be a physical and direct perception is only a sophisticated and mythic construction, an 'imaginary formation', which reinterprets physical features (in themselves as neutral as others but marked by a social system) through the network of relationships in which they are perceived.[8]

Like Beauvoir, Wittig understands gender as a proscription and a task; in effect, gender is a norm that we struggle to embody. In Wittig's words, 'We have been compelled in our bodies and our minds to correspond, feature by feature, with the *idea* of nature that has been established for us.'[9] That we experience ourselves or others as 'men' and 'women' are political categories and not natural facts.'[10]

Wittig's theory is alarming for a number of reasons, foremost among them the intimation that discourse about sex creates the misnomer of anatomy. If this were Wittig's point, it would seem that sexual difference has no necessary material foundation, and that seeing differences among bodies, which turn out to be binary, is a deep delusion indulged in by cultures in an almost universal fashion. Luckily, I do not think this is Wittig's claim. Surely, differences do exist which are binary, material and distinct, and we are not in the grips of political ideology when we assent to that fact. Wittig contests the social practice of valorizing certain anatomical features as being definitive not only of anatomical sex but of sexual identity. She points out that there are other kinds of differences among people, differences in shape and size, in earlobe formation and the lengths of noses, but we do not ask when a child enters the world what species of earlobe it has. We immediately ask about certain sexually differentiated anatomical traits because we assume that those traits will in some sense determine that child's social destiny, and that destiny, whatever else it is, is structured by a gender system predicated upon the alleged naturalness of binary oppositions and, consequently, heterosexuality. Hence, in differentiating infants in the ways that we do, we recapitulate heterosexuality as a precondition for human identity, and posit this constraining norm in the guise of a natural fact.

Wittig thus does not dispute the existence or facticity of sexual distinction, but questions the isolation and valorization of certain kinds of distinctions over others. Wittig's *Lesbian Body* is the literary portrayal of an erotic struggle to rewrite the relevant distinctions constitutive of sexual identity. Different features of the female body are detached from their usual places, and remembered, quite literally. The reclamation of diverse bodily parts as sources of erotic pleasure is, for Wittig, the undoing or rewriting of binary restriction imposed at birth. Erogeneity is restored to the entire body through a process of sometimes violent struggle. The female body is no longer recognizable as such; it no longer appears as an 'immediate given of experience'; it is disfigured, reconstructed and reconceived. The emancipation of this consists in the dissolution of the binary framework, in the emergence of essential chaos, polymorphousness, the precultural innocence of 'sex'.

It might well seem that Wittig has entered into a utopian ground that leaves the rest of us situated souls waiting impatiently this side of her liberating imaginary space. After all, the *Lesbian Body* is a fantasy, and it is not clear whether we readers are supposed to recognize a potential course of action in that text, or simply be dislocated from our usual assumptions about bodies and pleasure. Has Wittig decided that heterosexual norms are cultural norms while lesbian norms are somehow natural? Is the lesbian body that she posits as somehow being prior to and exceeding binary restrictions really a body at all? Has the lesbian preempted the place of the psychoanalytic polymorph in Wittig's particular sexual cosmogony?

Rather than argue for the superiority of a nonheterosexual culture, Wittig envisions a sexless society, and argues that sex, like class, is a construct that must inevitably be deposed. Indeed, Wittig's program seems profoundly humanistic in its call for an eradication of sex. She argues that

> a new personal and subjective definition for all humankind can be found beyond the categories of sex (man and woman) and that the advent of individual subjects demands first destroying the category of sex, ending the use of them, and rejecting all sciences which still use these categories as their fundamentals (practically all social sciences).[11]

On the one hand, Wittig calls for a transcendence of sex altogether, but her theory might equally well lead to an inverse conclusion, to the dissolution of binary restrictions through the *proliferation* of genders.

Because the category of 'sex' only makes sense in terms of a binary discourse on sex in which 'men' and 'women' exhaust the possibilities of sex, and relate to each other as complementary opposites, the category of 'sex' is always subsumed under the discourse of heterosexuality. Hence, Wittig argues that a lesbian is not a woman, because to be a woman means to be set in a binary relation with a man. Wittig does not argue that the lesbian is another sex or gender, but claims that the lesbian 'is the only concept I know which is beyond the category of sex'.[12] But even as Wittig describes the lesbian in relation to this binary opposition of 'man' and 'woman', she underscores the fact that this being beyond opposition is still a way of being related to that opposition, indeed a binary relation at that. In order that the lesbian avoid being caught up in another binary opposition, i.e., the opposition to heterosexuality itself, 'being lesbian' must itself become a multiple cultural phenomenon, a gender with no univocal essence. If binary oppositions imply hierarchies, then postulating a sexual identity 'beyond' culture promises to set up yet another pair of oppositions that, in turn, suggest another hierarchical arrangement; hegemonic heterosexual culture will stand as the 'Other' to that postcultural subject, and a new hierarchy may well replace the old – at least on a theoretical level. Moreover, to define culture as necessarily preoccupied with the reproduction of binary oppositions is to support a structuralist assumption that seems neither valid nor politically beneficial. After all, if binary restrictions are to be overcome in experience, they must meet their dissolution in the creation of new cultural forms. As Beauvoir says, and Wittig should know, there is no meaningful reference to a 'human reality' outside the terms of culture. The political program for overcoming binary restrictions ought to be concerned, then, with cultural innovation rather than myths of transcendence.

Wittig's theory finds support in Foucault's first volume of *The History of Sexuality* which holds improbable but significant consequences for feminist theory. In that Foucault seeks to subvert the binary configuration of power, the juridical model of oppressor and oppressed he offers some strategies for the subversion of gender hierarchy. For Foucault, the binary organization of power, including that based on strict gender polarities, is effected through a multiplication of productive and strategic forms of power. Hence, Foucault is interested no longer in the Marcusean dream of a sexuality without power, but is concerned with subverting and dissipating the existing terms of juridical power. In this sense, Wittig is paradoxically closer to Marcuse's theory of sexual emancipation as she does imagine a sexual identity and a sexuality freed of relations of domination. In effect, Foucault writes in the disillusioned aftermath of Marcuse's *Eros and Civilization*, rejecting a progressive model of history based on the gradual release of an intrinsically liberating *eros*. For Foucault, the *eros* which is liberated is always already structured culturally, saturated with power dynamics, thus implicitly raising the same political dilemmas as the repressive culture it was meant to liberate. Like Wittig, however, Foucault does reject 'natural sex' as a primary given, and attempts to understand how 'the deployment of sexuality . . . was what established this notion of "sex".' The category of sex belongs to a juridical model of power that assumes a binary opposition between the 'sexes'. The subversion of binary opposites does not result in their transcendence for Foucault, but in their proliferation to a point where binary oppositions become meaningless in a context where multiple differences, not restricted to binary differences, abound. Foucault seems to suggest 'proliferation' and 'assimilation' as strategies to diffuse the age-old power game of oppressor and oppressed. His tactic, if that it can be called, is not to transcend power relations, but to multiply their various configurations, so that the juridical model of power as oppression and regulation is no longer hegemonic. When oppressors themselves are oppressed, and the oppressed develop alternative forms of power, we are in the presence of postmodern relations of power. For Foucault, this interaction results in yet new and more complicated valences of power, and the power of binary opposition is diffused through the force of internal ambiguity.

For Foucault, the notion of natural sex is neither primary nor univocal. One's 'sex', i.e., one's anatomically differentiated sexual self, is intimately linked to 'sex' as an activity and a drive. The word compromises a variety of meanings that have been clustered under a single name to further certain strategic ends of hegemonic culture:

The notion of 'sex; made if possible to group together, in an artificial unity, anatomic elements, biological functions, conducts, sensations, and pleasures, and it enabled one to make use of this fictitious unity as a causal principle, an omnipresent meaning, a secret to be discovered everywhere: sex was thus able to function as a unique signifier and as a universal signified.[14]

Foucault no more wants to dispute the material reality of anatomically discrete bodies than does Wittig, but asks instead how the materiality of the body comes to signify culturally specific ideas. Hence, he imagines at the close of vol. I of *The History of Sexuality* 'a history of bodies [which shows] the manner in which what is most material and most vital in them has been invested'.[15]

Foucault conducts a phenomenology of such an 'investment' in publishing the journals of Herculine Barbin, a nineteenth-century hermaphrodite whose anatomical ambiguity culminates in an eventual 'confession' and suicide[16] In his introduction Foucault insists upon the irrelevance of established gender categories for Alexina's (Herculine's) sexual life:

One has the impression, at least if one gives credence to Alexina's story, that everything took place in a world of feelings – enthusiasm, pleasure, sorrow, warmth, sweetness, bitterness – where the identity of the partners and above all the enigmatic character around whom everything centered, had no importance. It was a world in which grins hung about without the cat.[17]

Herculine seems to have escaped univocal sex, and hence the binary system governing sex, and represents for Foucault the literalization of an ambiguity in sex and sexual identity which is the suppressed potential of every proper and univocal sex or gender. Herculine Barbin, our hermaphrodite, is neither here nor there, but neither is she in some discrete third place. She is an amalgamation of binary opposites, a particular configuration and conflation of male and female. Because of her uncanny intrusion into the male domain, she is punished and banished by the Church authorities, designed univocally as a male. Herculine does not transcend sex as much as she confuses it, and while we can see her fate as to a certain extent anatomical, it is clear that the legal and medical documents that address her anatomical transgression reveal an urgent social need to keep sex down to just the usual two. Hence, it is not her anatomy, but the ways in which that anatomy is 'invested', that causes problems. Her plight reveals in graphic terms the societal urge and strategy to discover and define anatomy within binary terms. Exploding the binary assumption is one of the ways of depriving male hegemony and compulsory heterosexuality of their most treasured of primary premises. When, on the other hand, binary sexual difference is made a function of ontology, then the options for sexual identity are restricted to traditional heterosexual terms; indeed, heterosexuality is itself reduced to a mythical version of itself, disguising its own potential multiplicity beneath a univocal presentation of itself.

Conclusion: Embodying Dissonance

In conclusion, it seems important to note that the challenge to a dyadic gender system that Beauvoir's theory permits and that Wittig and Foucault help to formulate, is also implicitly a challenge to those feminist positions that maintain sexual difference as irreducible, and which seek to give expression to the distinctively feminine side of that binary opposition. If natural sex is a fiction, then the distinctively feminine is a purely historical moment in the development of the category of sex, what Foucault calls, 'the most speculative, most ideal, and most internal element in a deployment of sexuality organized by power in its grip on bodies and their materiality'.[18]

The schematic outline of a theory of gender invention that I have been sketching here does not overcome the existential pitfalls of Sartrianism by the mere fact of its cultural application. Indeed, with Foucauldian proliferation at hand, we seem to have moved full circle back to a notion of radical invention, albeit one that employs and deploys culturally existent and culturally imaginable conventions. The problem with this theory seems twofold, and in many senses the objections that will surely be raised against these visions are ones that have, in altered form, been raised against the existential thesis from both Marxist and psychoanalytic perspectives. The Marxist problem may be understood as that of the social constitution of personal identity and, by implication, gender identity. I not only choose my gender, and not only choose it within culturally available terms, but on the street and in the world I am always constantly constituted by others, so that my self-styled gender may well find itself in comic or even tragic opposition to the gender that others see me through or with. Hence, even the Foucauldian prescription of radical invention presupposes an agency which, à la Descartes, definitionally eludes the gaze of the Other.

The psychoanalytic objection is perhaps the most trenchant, for psychoanalytic theories of gender identity and gender acquisition tend to insist that what we become is always in some sense what we have always been, although the process of becoming is of oedipal necessity a process of restricting our sexual ambiguity in accord with identity-founding incest taboos. Ambiguity, whether described in the discourse of bisexuality or polymorphousness, is always to be presupposed, and established gender identity both contains and conceals this repressed ambiguity. The proliferation of gender beyond binary oppositions would thus always constitute a return to a pre-oedipal ambiguity which, I suppose, would take us outside of culture as we know it. According to the psychoanalytic perspective, the normative ideal of multiplicitous genders would always be a peculiar mix of memory and fantasy to be understood in the context of an oedipally, conditioned subject in an affective quarrel with the incest taboo. This is the stuff of great literature, perhaps, but not necessarily practicable in the cultural struggle to renovate gender relations as we know them. In effect, speaking within this point of view, what I have provided here is a pre-oedipal fantasy that only makes sense in terms of a subject who can never realize this fantasy. In this sense, both the hypothetical Marxist and the psychoanalytic objection would charge that the theory I have presented lacks a reality principle. But, of course, such a charge is tricky, because it is unclear whether the principle governing this reality is a necessary one, or whether other principles of reality might well be 'invented', as it were, and whether such counterintuitive principles as these are part of the cultural fantasies that ultimately do come to constitute new organizations of reality. It is not clear to me that reality is something settled once and for all, and we might do well to urge speculation on the dynamic relation between fantasy and the realization of new social realities.

A good deal of French feminist scholarship has been concerned with specifying the nature of the feminine to settle the question of what women want, how that specific pleasure makes itself known, or represents itself obliquely in the rupture of logocentric language. This principle of femininity is sought in the female body, sometimes understood as the pre-oedipal mother and other times understood naturalistically as a pantheistic principle that requires its own kind of language for expression. In these cases, gender is not constituted, but is considered an essential aspect of bodily life, and we come very near the equation of biology and destiny, that conflation of fact and value, which Beauvoir spent her life trying to refute. In an article entitled 'Women can never be defined'. Julia Kristeva remarks that 'the belief that "one is a woman" is almost as absurd and obscurantist as the belief that "one is a man".'[19] Kristeva says 'almost as absurd' because there are practical, strategical reasons for maintaining the notion of women as a class regardless of its descriptive emptiness as a term. Indeed, accepting Wittig's argument that 'women' is a political category, Kristeva goes on to consider whether it might not be a *useful* political category at that. This brings us back to the Marxist objection proffered above, and yet Kristeva is prepared to forfeit the term altogether when its political efficacy is exhausted. Hence, she concludes, 'we must use "we are women" as an advertisement or slogan for our demands. On a deeper level, however, a woman cannot "be"; it is something which does not even belong in the order of *being*.'[20] Women is thus a false substantive and univocal signifier that disguises and precludes a gender experience internally varied and contradictory. And if women are, to return to Beauvoir, such a mode of becoming that is arrested prematurely, as it were, through the reductive imposition of a substantializing nomenclature, then the release of women's internally complex experience, an experience that would make of the very name 'women's experience', an empty signification, might well become released and or precipitated. And here the task is not simply to change language, but to examine language for its ontological assumptions, and to criticize those assumptions for their political consequences. In effect, to understand woman to exist on the metaphysical order of *being* is to understand her as that which is already accomplished, self-identical, static, but to conceive her on the metaphysical order of *becoming*, is to invent possibility into her experience, including the possibility of never becoming a substantive, self-identical 'woman'. Indeed, such substantives will remain empty descriptions, and other forms of active descriptions may well become desirable.

It is not surprising that Beauvoir derives her philosophical framework from existential philosophy, and that Wittig seems more indebted to Beauvoir than to those French feminists who write either for or against Lacan. Nor is it surprising that Foucault's theory of sexuality and his history of bodies is written against the background of Nietzsche's *Will to Power* and the *Genealogy of Morals* whose method of existential critique regularly revealed how values that appear natural can be reduced to their contingent cultural origins.

The psychoanalytic challenge does well to remind us of the deep-rootedness of sexual and gender identity and the Marxist qualification reinforces the notion that how we are constituted is not always our own affair. It may well be that Wittig and Foucault offer (a) new identity/ies which, despite all their qualification, remain utopian. But it is useful to remember Gayle Rubin's reading of psychoanalysis as the reconstruction of kinship structures in the form of modern gender identities.[21] If she is right to understand gender identity as the 'trace' of kinship, and to point out that gender has become increasingly free of the vestiges of kinship, then we seem justified in concluding that the history of gender may well reveal the gradual release of gender from its binary restrictions. Moreover, any theoretical effort to discover, maintain, or articulate an essential femininity must confront the following moral and empirical problem: What happens when individual women do not recognize themselves in the theories that explain their unsurpassable essences to them? When the essential feminine is finally articulated, and what we have been calling 'women' cannot see themselves in its terms, what then are we to conclude? We can argue that women have a more inclusive essence, or we can return to that promising suggestion of Simone de Beauvoir, namely, that women have no essence at all, and hence, no natural necessity, and that, indeed, what we call an essence or a material fact is simply an enforced cultural option which has disguised itself as natural truth.

Notes

1 Simone de Beauvoir, *The Second Sex* (New York, Vintage Press, 1973), p. 301. Parts of the discussion of Simone de Beauvoir's *The Second Sex* are taken from the author's article 'Sex and Gender in Beauvoir's *Second Sex*'. *Yale French Studies*.

2 Monique Wittig, 'One is Not Born a Woman', *Feminist Issues*, 1, 2 see also 'The Category of Sex', *Feminist Issues*, 2, 2.

3 See Thomas W. Busch, 'Beyond the Cogito: The Question of the Continuity of Sartre's Thought', *The Modern Schoolman*, LX (March 1983).

4 Jean-Paul Sartre, *Being and Nothingness: An Essay in Phenomenological Ontology*, tr. Hazel E. Barnes (New York, Philosophical Library, 1947), p. 329.
5 Beauvoir's defense of the non-Cartesian character of Sartre's account of the body can be found in 'Merleau-Ponty et le Pseudo-Sartrisme.' *Les Temps Modernes*, 10, (1955).
6 Sartre, *Being and Nothingness*, p. 329.
7 Beauvoir, *The Second Sex*, p. 41.
8 Wittig, 'One is Not Born a Woman', p. 48.
9 Ibid., p. 47.
10 Ibid.
11 Wittig, 'The Category of Sex', p. 22.
12 Wittig, 'One is Not Born a Woman', p. 53.
13 Michel Foucault, *The History of Sexuality* (New York, Random House, 1980), vol. I: *An Introduction*, tr. Robert Hurley, p. 154.
14 Ibid.
15 Ibid., p 152.
16 Michel Foucault, ed., *Herculine Barbin, Being the Recently Discovered Memoirs of a Nineteenth Century Hermaphrodite*, tr. Richard McDougall (New York, Pantheon, 1980).
17 Foucault, *Herculine Barbin*, p. xiii.
18 Foucault, *The History of Sexuality*, vol. I, p. 155.
19 Julia Kristeva, 'Women can Never be Defined', in Elaine Marks and Isabel de Courtrivon, eds, *New French Feminisms* (Brighton, Harvester, 1980), p. 137.
20 Ibid.
21 See Gayle Rubin, 'The Traffic in Women: The Political Economy of Sex', in Rayna R. Reiter, *Toward an Anthropology of Women* (New York, Monthly Review Press, 1975), pp. 178–92.

19   Jonathan Dollimore,

From *Radical Tragedy* (1984), pp 249–58; 267–71

Beyond Essentialist Humanism

Anti-humanism and its declared objective – the decentring of man – is probably the most controversial aspect of Marxist, structuralist and post-structuralist theory. An adequate account of the controversy and the issues it raises – essentialism, humanism, materialism, the subject/society relationship and more – would need a book in its own right and it is perhaps reckless to embark upon such a discussion in the space of a concluding chapter. I do so for three reasons at least.

First, it is a perspective important for the book as a whole since I have argued for the emergence in the Renaissance of a conception of subjectivity legitimately identified in terms of a materialist perspective rather than one of essentialist humanism. Second, for better or worse no issue is more central to English studies as it has been historically constituted than this question of subjectivity. Third, to reject the view that literature and criticism meet on some transhistorical plateau of value and meaning, leads inevitably to a discussion of the differences between incompatible critical perspectives; in this instance we are probably concerned with the most incompatible of all, namely the materialist as opposed to the idealist. But since what follows may seem far removed from the literary criticism familiar in English studies generally and of the Renaissance in particular, perhaps I should acknowledge that in a sense it is, and that its relevance lies in just this fact: the materialist conception of subjectivity (like historical materialism generally) aims not only to challenge all those forms of literary criticism premised on the residual categories of essentialist humanism and idealist culture but, even more importantly, invites a positive and explicit engagement with the historical, social and political realities of which both literature and criticism are inextricably a part.

Origins of the Transcendent Subject

Anti-humanism, like materialist criticism more generally, challenges the idea that 'man' possesses some given, unalterable essence which is what makes 'him' human, which is the source and *essential* determinant of 'his' culture and its priority over conditions of existence.

As I have already argued, it is the Enlightenment rather than the Renaissance which marks the emergence of essentialist humanism as we now know it; at that time concern shifts from the metaphysically derivative soul to what Robert Paul Wolff has termed 'individual centres of consciousness'[1] which are said to be self-determining, free and rational by nature. Those forms of individualism (e.g. 'abstract individualism')[2] premised on essentialism tend, obviously, to distinguish the individual from society and give absolute priority to the former. In effect the individual is understood in terms of a pre-social essence, nature, or identity and on that basis s/he is invested with a quasi-spiritual autonomy. The individual becomes the origin and focus of meaning – an individuated essence which precedes and – in idealist philosophy – transcends history and society.

Reflecting here its religious antecedents, idealist philosophy marks off the domain of the spiritual as superior to, and the ultimate counter-image of, actual, historical, social, existence. It is not only that (as Nietzsche contended) the entire counterfeit of transcendence and of the hereafter has grown up on the basis of an impoverished life, but that transcendence comes to constitute an ideological mystification of the conditions of impoverishment from which it grew: impoverishment shifts from being its cause to its necessary condition, that required to pressure one's true (spiritual) identity into its true transcendent realisation. As Robbe-Grillet puts it, in the humanist tragic sense of life 'interiority always leads to transcendence ... The pseudo-necessity of tragedy to a metaphysical beyond'; but at the same time it 'closes the door to any realist future' since the corollary of that beyond is a static, paralysed present.[3] The truth that people do not live by bread alone may then be appropriated ideologically to become the 'truth' that spiritual nourishment is an adequate substitute for bread and possibly even preferable to it.[4] But most importantly, the *revolutionary force of the ideal, which in its very unreality keeps alive the best desires of men amidst a bad reality*[5] is lost, displaced by ideals of renunciation and acquiescence. Rebellious desire is either abdicated entirely or tamed in service to the cultural reification of 'man', the human condition, the human spirit and so on.

Marcuse, writing in 1936, was trying to explain the transition from liberalism to authoritarianism which Europe was witnessing. We may be unable to accept some of Marcuse's conclusions but the task he set himself then seems as urgent as ever. In one thing he was surely right: the essentialism of western philosophy, especially that of the idealist tradition, could be used to sanction that process whereby 'the soul was able to become a useful factor in the technique of mass domination when, in the epoch of authoritarian states, all available forces had to be mobilised against a real transformation of social existence'.[6] The attacks upon idealist culture by Brecht, Walter Benjamin and Theodore Adorno were made from similar positions.[7] In their very different ways these three writers engage with the materialist conception of subjectivity, one which, in so far as it retains the concept of essence, construes it not as that which is eternally fixed but as social potential materialising within limiting historical conditions. Conditions will themselves change – in part under the pressure of actualised potential – thus enabling new potentialities to unfold.

Arguably, to accept with Marx that Feuerbach was wrong 'to resolve the essence of religion into the essence of *man*', since 'the real nature of man is the totality of social relations,[8] should be to dispense altogether with 'essence', 'nature' and 'man' as concepts implicated irredeemably in the metaphysic of determining origin. Such at least is the implication of cultural materialism and that most famous of its formulations by Marx: 'The mode of production of material life conditions the social, political and intellectual life process in general'.[9] Consequently it is social being that determines consciousness, not the reverse.[10]

In recent years the critique of essentialism has become even more searching partly in an attempt to explain its extraordinary recuperative power. Thus for Althusser humanism is characterised by two complementary and indissociable postulates: '(i) that there is a universal essence of man; (ii) that this essence is the attribute of "*each single individual*" who is its real subject'.[11] Humanism gives rise to the concept of 'man' which, says Althusser, must be abolished: 'It is impossible to *know* anything about men except on the absolute precondition that the philosophical (theoretical) myth of man is reduced to ashes'.[12] Against humanism, Althusser contends that 'The human subject is decentred, constituted by a structure which has no "centre" either, except in the imaginary misrecognition of the "ego", that is to say in the ideological formations where it finds recognition'[13]

Before continuing, two general points are worth remarking. First, Althusser is here drawing on psychoanalytic theory whereas I shall not. What follows involves cultural materialist, Marxist and post-structuralist analysis of a different kind.[14] Second, the controversy surrounding not just Althusser but the anti-humanism of Marxism, structuralism and post-structuralism generally has in part been due to a confusion of terms, and it has a long history. Thus Colin Wilson could declare in the fifties that he was an anti-humanist, yet his existentialist idealism is completely alien to the respective positions of, say, Althusser and Foucault. Indeed, according to those positions Wilson's own philosophy would be ineradicably humanist in virtue of its reliance on transcendent subjectivity.[15] Wilson acknowledges quite explicitly that his is an idealism struggling to get back to its religious roots: 'Religion *must* be the answer'.[16] And his definition of humanism includes, among other things, 'the values of the mass', 'scientific materialism' and 'progress'[17] – all of which materialist anti-humanism might endorse, though not uncritically. Anti-humanism would also utterly dissociate itself from Wilson's absurd contention that humanism (thus defined) has engendered 'nothing but mass-boredom and frustration, and periodic outbreaks of war'.[18] Wilson is not an anti-humanist in either Althusser's or Foucault's sense; he is, rather, anti-humanitarian and anti-democratic and in this resembles his precursors – T. E. Hulme, Eliot and others. Probably it is pointless to try and rescue the term anti-humanism, especially since the important issues can better be focussed by addressing a more fundamental division – of which the humanist/anti-humanist controversy is only a manifestation – namely, that between idealist and materialist conceptions of subjectivity.

Derrida has insisted that metaphysics is so deeply rooted in our discourses that there is no getting beyond it;[19] perhaps in this he is too fatalistic. Nevertheless his assertion is strikingly apt for the history of the essentialist humanism which has pervaded English studies and carried within it a residual metaphysic, one which makes for the ideological effacement of socio-cultural difference and historical context. It thereby denies or at least seeks to minimise the importance of material conditions of human existence for the forms which that existence takes. I cannot provide here a detailed history of essentialist humanism in all its post-Enlightenment complexity, but propose instead to indicate, through some important textual landmarks, its centrality for the development of English studies, especially in so far as it informs the critical perspectives argued against in previous chapters.

Essence and Universal; Enlightenment Transitions

Put very schematically, western metaphysics has typically had recourse to three indissociable categories: the universal (or absolute), essence, and teleology. If universals and essences designate, respectively, what ultimately and essentially exists, then teleology designates metaphysical destiny – for the universe as a whole and its essences in particular.

In Descartes we can see a crucial stage in the history of metaphysics, one whereby essence takes on a new importance in the schema: the metaphysically derivative soul gives way to the autonomous, individuated essence, the self-affirming consciousness. (But just as the individuated essence typically presupposed its counterpart and origin, the universal form, so the subject of essentialist humanism comes to presuppose a universal human nature/condition.) For Descartes the self was a pure, non-physical substance whose 'whole essence or nature . . . is to think'; he also equated mind, soul, understanding and reason.[20] Therefore he clearly retained an *a priori* and thoroughly metaphysical account of consciousness, one which was in important respects challenged, in others assimilated, by empiricists like Locke. But by elucidating in terms of empiricist epistemology a conception of the person which, however modified, contained an irreducibly metaphysical component, these empiricists were embarking upon a philosophical programme inherently problematic.

The trouble with Locke's definition of a person is that it still makes it a contingent rather than a necessary truth that people are of human form: 'It being the same consciousness that makes a man be himself to himself, personal identity depends on that only'.[21] But if Locke is here still working with Cartesian assumptions, his empiricist epistemology nevertheless leads him to the radical supposition that the mind is 'as we say, white Paper, void of all Characters, without any *ideas*'. He then asks 'how comes it to be furnished?. . . Whence has it all the *materials* of Reason and Knowledge? To this I answer, in one word, from *experience*. In that, all our Knowledge is founded'.[22] Elsewhere Locke asserts that of all men 'nine parts of ten are what they are, good or evil, useful or not, by their education'.[23]

Hume for his part conducts a devastating critique of essentialism, getting rid of *substance* (an age-old metaphysical category which in this context was the supposed basis of the self) and arguing instead that 'mankind . . . are nothing but a bundle or collection of different perceptions which succeed each other with an inconceivable rapidity and are in perpetual flux and movement'. There is not, he adds, 'any single power of the soul which remains unalterably the same', and regarding 'the mind . . . There is properly no *simplicity* in it at one time nor *identity* in different'.[24] And yet, contrary to what the foregoing might lead us to expect, Hume gives one of the most explicit statements of what Robert Solomon calls the 'transcendental pretence':[25] 'human nature remains still the same in its principles and operations . . . Mankind are so much the same, in all times and places, that history informs us of nothing new or strange in this particular. Its chief use is only to discover the constant and universal principles of human nature by showing men in all varieties of circumstances and situations'.[26] In effect, and crucially, 'man' as a universal remains, notwithstanding a radical transition from being given *a priori* to being given contingently, in 'nature'.[27]

There is yet another inconsistency, more important than any so far noted: Hume's 'universal principles of human nature' are not, even in his terms, universal after all, for he suspects 'negroes ... to be *naturally* inferior to whites. There never was a civilised nation of any other complexion than white'. And the reason? Nature ... made an original distinction betwixt these breeds [i.e. black and white]. Not to mention our colonies, there are NEGROE slaves dispersed all over EUROPE of which none ever discovered any symptom of ingenuity'.[28]

In the period between Locke and Hume we witness the emergence of a conception of man which rejected explicitly metaphysical categories only to re-import mutations of them in the guise of 'nature. *Pace* Hume, 'history informs us' that nature has been as powerful a metaphysical entity as any, God included.

In contrast to the emerging British empiricism, the tradition of philosophical idealism recast essentialism in an explicitly metaphysical form. Immanuel Kant said of Rousseau that he was 'the first to discover beneath the varying forms human nature assumes the deeply concealed essence of man'.[29] Rousseau's essence was, of course, an innate goodness or potentiality existing in contradistinction to the corruption of society. But Kant legitimated essentialism in the context of transcendental idealism, a revolutionary philosophy which posited the phenomenal world as determined by the structure of the human mind itself, by the formal categories of consciousness: 'Hitherto it has been assumed that all our knowledge must conform to objects' says Kant, only then to present the truth as precisely the reverse of this: 'objects must conform to our knowledge'.[30] Man as a rational being is part of the noumenal world possessed of an autonomous will serving its own law; he is an end in himself just as objects in the noumenal world are things in themselves. The enormous differences between the two philosophical traditions represented by Hume and Kant respectively could hardly be exaggerated yet on two things at least they agree: first (like Descartes) they begin with the individual taken in abstraction from any socio-political context; second, Kant concurs with Hume on the (human) condition of blacks: Mr Hume challenges anyone to cite a simple example in which a negro has shown talents ... So fundamental is the difference between these two races of men [black and white] and it appears to be as great in regard to mental capacities as in colour'.[31] This second point on which Hume and Kant agree is in part consequence of the first; the abstraction in abstract individualism (i.e. its metaphysics) is the means whereby the historically specific has been universalised as the naturally given.

Discrimination and Subjectivity

The example of racism is included here not as a gratuitous slur but rather as a reminder that the issues involved have not been, and still are not, limited to the realm of contemplative philosophy. As Popkin points out, the Enlightenment was the watershed of modern racial theories.[32] Essentialist theories of human nature, though not intrinsically racist, have contributed powerfully to the ideological conditions which made racism possible. Similarly, when an ideological legitimation of slavery proved necessary (because of growing opposition to it) such theories helped provide that too.[33]

The following is an instance of essentialist legitimation from our own country:

> History has shown, and daily shows anew, that man can be trained to be nothing that he is not genuinely, and from the beginning, in the depths of his being; against this law, neither precept, warning, punishment nor any other environmental influence avails. Realism in the study of man does not lie in attributing evil tendencies to him, but in recognising that all that man can do emerges in the last resort from himself, from his innate qualities.

Here essence and teleology are explicitly affirmed while 'history' becomes the surrogate absolute. If we are used to finding this kind of utterance in our own cultural history it comes as something of a shock to realise that these were the words of Alfred Bäumler, a leading Nazi 'philosopher' writing on race.[34] In part (that is, taking into account the historical context) they substantiate the claim of Marcuse that since Descartes essentialism has 'followed a course leading from autonomy to heteronomy, from the proclamations of the free, rational individual to his surrender to the powers of the authoritarian state.[35] This in turn underscores the importance of Derrida's contention that the critique of ethnocentrism, together with the emergence of ethnology and the corresponding decentring of European culture, are 'historically contemporaneous with destruction of the history of metaphysics'.[36] Metaphysics can be finally displaced only when the twin concepts of centred structure and determining origin are abandoned.[37]

Derrida writes also of the importance of passing beyond 'Man and humanism, the name of man being the name of that being who, throughout the history of metaphysics or of ontotheology – in other words throughout his entire history – has dreamed of full presence, the reassuring foundation, the origin and the end of play'.[38] If this echoes Levi-Strauss' pronouncement that 'the ultimate goal of the human sciences' is 'not to constitute, but to dissolve man',[39] or Foucault's equally notorious 'man is an invention of recent date', one likely soon to 'be erased, like a face drawn in sand at the edge of the sea'[40] – pronouncements upon which some in the humanist tradition have become fixated in horror – then it is worth interjecting that the anti-humanism of Foucault's variety at least does not involve the elimination of individuality, only of 'man'. In fact, it is those discourses centred around 'man' and human nature which, historically, have regulated and repressed *actual* diversity and *actual* human difference. To speak of the uniqueness of an individual may mean either that s/he is contingently unlike anyone else actually known *or* that s/he approximates more closely to a normative paradigm, spiritual or natural, than anyone else who has ever, or will, or can, exist. The materialist view of the subject would at least render the former possible by rejecting the premises of the latter; in that sense, far from eliminating individuality, it realises it.

In a sense Barthes is right to attack the petit-bourgeois for being 'unable to imagine the Other . . . because the Other is a scandal which threatens his essence',[41] but we should remember that the experience of this kind of threat has by no means been limited to the petit-bourgois, and the forms of discrimination which it has invited have operated in terms of several basic categories of identity, including race, sexuality and class.

The crucial point is surely this: essentialism, rooted as it is in the concept of centred structure and determining origin, constitutes a residual metaphysic within secularist thought which, though it has not entailed has certainly made possible the classic ideological effect: a specific cultural identity is universalised or naturalised; more specifically, in reaction to social change this residual metaphysic is activated in defence of one cultural formation, one conception of what it is to be truly human, to the corresponding exclusion of others.[42]

. . . .

Terry Eagleton is surely correct in remarking that since the demise of *Scrutiny* virtually no literary theory of major importance has appeared in Britain.[43] With the significant exception of the cultural materialism of Raymond Williams, it is to America and Europe that we have to look for developments in the post-war period. Yet for all its resourcefulness, American literary theory, as Frank Lentricchia has recently shown, co....nued the process whereby idealist strategies succeeded one another to keep occluded the historical and material conditions of human existence generally and literary practice specifically. So, for example, Northrop Frye's neo-Kantian reaction to Romantic subjectivism succeeded in recuperating an idealist view of human nature as answering to or evoking the structure of literature, while other critics, influenced now by existentialism, identified the subject in terms of an anguished consciousness situated in virtue of its capacity to create coherent fictions, in part-transcendence of a chaotic universe. According to Lentricchia, both Frye and the existentialists imply 'a last ditch' humanism in which human desire, conscious of itself as "lack", to cite Sartre's term, and conscious of the ontological nothingness of its images, confronts a grim reality which at every point denies us our needs . . . Our "environment" is alien, but . . . its very alien quality beckons forth our creative impulses to make substitutive fictive worlds'.[44]

The political fatalism among the post-war British intelligentsia has been attributed in part to a form of the same spiritual quietism, one prefigured, argues Edward Thompson, in Auden's verse. If that verse reveals 'a mind in recoil from experiences too difficult and painful to admit of easy solutions', the poet's revision of it indicates a regression to just such a solution, one arguably always latently there in the verse and according to which the traumas of Europe are to be understood not historically but in terms of an underlying human nature and the evil therein.[45] William Golding (to take just one other notorious example) has described his novel *Lord of the Flies* as an attempt to trace the defects of society back to the defects of human nature.[46] When existing political conditions are thus thought to be as unalterable as the fixed human condition of which they are, allegedly, only a reflection, then salvation comes, typically, to be located in the pseudo-religious absolute of Personal Integrity.[47] Across the years there echoes and re-echoes the disillusion of the radical intelligentsia after the French revolution: 'from the impulse of a just disdain,/Once more did I retire into myself'.[48] Dressed in existentialist guise it became Colin Wilson's return to religion via the Outsider, a reaffirmation of religion's 'Absolute essential framework', namely that its truth is 'determinable *subjectively* ... "Truth is subjectivity" (Kierkegaard)'.[49]

Such manifestations of essentialism allowed the implications of that uniquely uncompromising exploration of modernist alienation, Conrad's *Nostromo*, to be circumvented. In *Nostromo* we encounter the familiar alienated human condition but in this instance it is devoid even of the attenuated post-Romantic forms of transcendent subjectivity: 'Decoud caught himself entertaining a doubt of his own individuality. It had merged into the world of cloud and water, of natural forces and forms of nature.' Adrift in 'the solitude of the Placid Gulf', and beholding the universe only as 'a succession of incomprehensible images', Decoud shoots himself. The sea into which he falls 'remained untroubled by the fall of his body'; he disappears 'without a trace, swallowed up in the immense indifference of things.'[50] Such is the logic of an essentialism finally severed from its absolute counterpart. The absence of that absolute – Coleridge's inanimate cold world, here the immense indifference of things – finally engulfs and dissolves even the petrified subject.

The Decentred Subject

When Lawrence elaborates his philosophy of individualism he reminds us of the derivation of 'individual': that which is not divided, not divisible.[51] Materialist analysis tends to avoid the term for just those reasons which led Lawrence to embrace it, preferring instead 'subject'. Because informed by contradictory social and ideological processes, the subject is never an indivisible unity, never an autonomous, self-determining centre of consciousness.

The main historical antecedents of this process of decentring have often been cited: Copernicus displaced man and his planet from their privileged place at the centre of the universe; Darwin showed that the human species is not the *telos* or goal of that universe; Marx displaced man from the centre of history while Freud displaced consciousness as the source of individual autonomy. Foucault adds the decentring effected by the Nietzschean genealogy (an addition which would appropriately challenge the suspiciously sequential coherence of the foregoing 'history' of decentring!): 'What is found at the historical beginning of things is not the inviolable identity of their origin; it is the dissension of other things. It is disparity.'[52]

Foucault identifies an 'epistemological mutation' of history not yet complete because of the deep resistance to it, a resistance, that is, to 'conceiving of difference, to describing separations and dispersions, to dissociating the reassuring form of the identical'.[53] He summarises his own task as one of freeing thought from its subjection to transcendence and analysing it 'in the discontinuity that no teleology would reduce in advance; to map it in a dispersion that no pre-established horizon would embrace; to allow it to be deployed in an anonymity on which no transcendental constitution would impose the form of the subject; to open it up to a temporality that would not promise the return of any dawn. My aim was to cleanse it of all transcendental narcissism'.[54] Transcendental narcissism validates itself in terms of teleology, the subject, the pre-established horizon; against this Foucault's history charts discontinuity, anonymity, dispersion.

Barthes offers a similar emphasis. To speak positively of the decentred subject is never just to acknowledge his or her contradictions: 'It is a diffraction which is intended, a dispersion of energy in which there remains neither a central core nor a structure of meaning: I am not contradictory, I am dispersed'; 'today the subject apprehends himself *elsewhere*'.[55] This entails not only a non-centred conception of identity but, correspondingly, a non-centred form of political awareness: 'According to Freud . . . one touch of difference leads to racism. But a great deal of difference leads away from it, irremediably. To equalize, democratize, homogenize – all such efforts will never manage to expel "the tiniest difference", seed of racial intolerance. For that one must pluralise, refine, continuously'.[56] Sexual transgression is affirmed while recognising that it tends to carry within itself a limiting inversion of the normative regime being transgressed.[57] The more radical alternative to sexual liberation through transgression is a release of sexuality from meaning. Then there would be for example not homosexuality but *'homosexualities'* 'whose plural will baffle any constituted, centred discourse'.[58]

This dimension of post-structuralist theory arouses justifiable suspicion for seeming to advance subjective decentring simply in terms of the *idea* of an anarchic refusal adequate unto itself, thereby recuperating anti-humanism in terms of the idealism it rejects and rendering the subject so completely dispersed as to be incapable of acting as any agent, least of all an agent of change. Equally though, this criticism itself runs the risk of disallowing the positive sense of the ideal cited earlier – that which in virtue of its present unreality affirms known potentialities from within existing, stultifying, social realities. Ideologically ratified, those 'realities' become not merely an obstacle to the realisation of potential, to the possibility of social change, but work to make both potential and change literally unthinkable. This is why, quite simply, a vision of decentred subjectivity, like any other vision of liberation, cannot be divorced from a critique of existing social realities and their forms of ideological legitimation. It is here that we might, finally, invoke an earlier emphasis in Barthes' work. In *Mythologies* he reminded us that the myth of the human condition 'consists in placing Nature at the bottom of History'; to thus eternalise the nature of man is to render the destiny of people apparently unalterable. Hence the necessity to reverse the terms, to find history behind nature and thereby reveal nature itself as an ideologicial construct preempting change.[59]

Perhaps this remains the most important objective in the decentring of man, one which helps make possible an alternative conception of the relations between history, society and subjectivity, and invites that *'affirmation which then determines the noncentre otherwise than as loss of the centre'*.[60] It is a radical alternative which, in the context of materialist analysis, helps vindicate certain objectives: not essence but potential, not the human condition but cultural difference, not destiny but collectively identified goals.

Notes

1 Robert Paul Wolff, *The Poverty of Liberalism* (Boston, Beacon Press, 1968), p. 142.
2 For an excellent discussion of this and other forms of individualism, see Steven Lukes, *Individualism* (Oxford, Blackwell, 1973).
3 Alain Robbe-Grillet, 'Nature, Humanism and Tragedy', in *Snapshots and Towards a New Novel*, trans. Barbara Wright (London, Calder & Boyars, 1965), pp. 81, 84.
4 Herbert Marcuse, *Negations: Essays in Critical Theory*, trans. J. Shapiro (London, Allen Lane, the Penguin Press, 1968), pp. 109–22.
5 Ibid., p. 102.
6 Ibid., p. 114.
7 For Brecht and Benjamin see Terry Eagleton, *Walter Benjamin, or Towards a Revolutionary Criticism* (London, Verso, 1981) and Susan Buck-Morss, 'Walter Benjamin – Revolutionary Writer', *New Left Review* 128 (1981), 50–75; 129 (1981), 77–95. In *The Jargon of Authenticity* (trans. K. Tarnowski and Frederic Will, London, Routledge, 1973), Theodore Adorno offers a powerful critique of German existentialism in which, he argues, 'Man is the ideology of dehumanisation' (p. 59; see also pp. 60–76).
8 Karl Marx, *Selected Writings in Sociology and Social Philosophy*, ed. T. B. Bottomore and Maximilien Rubel (Harmondsworth, Penguin, 1963), p. 83.
9 Karl Marx, *Selected Works* (one volume, London, Lawrence & Wishart, 1968), p. 182.
10 This perspective does not entail determinism – as Roy Bhaskar's recent theory shows. His argument can best be summarised in terms of three of its conclusions

about society: (i) it 'stands to individuals ... as something that they never make, but that exists only in virtue of their activity'; (ii) it is 'a necessary condition for any intentional human act at all'; (iii) it is 'both the ever-present *condition* (material cause) and the continually reproduced *outcome of* human agency'. Consequently: 'people, in their conscious activity, for the most part unconsciously reproduce (and occasionally transform) the structures governing their substantive activities of production. Thus people do not marry to reproduce the nuclear family or work to sustain the capitalist economy. Yet it is nevertheless the unintended consequence (and inexorable result) of, as it is also a necessary condition for, their activity' (*the Possibility of Naturalism: A Philosophical Critique of the Contemporary Human Sciences* (Brighton, Harvester Press, 1979), pp. 42–4). Bhaskar's argument deserves more attention than I can give it here. But its importance lies in the fact that it shows how purposiveness, intentionality and self-consciousness characterise human actions but not necessarily transformations in the social structure; it also sustains 'a genuine concept of *change* and hence of *history*; (p. 47). As Bhaskar observes (p. 93), his theory is close to Marx's own contention that people make their own history but not in conditions of their choosing; to be historically positioned is not necessarily to be helplessly determined. Like Bhaskar, but from a different position, Anthony Giddens rejects determinism, insisting on the importance for social practice and human agency of what he calls *duality of structure*. It entails a view of reason and intention as constituted only within the reflexive monitoring of action which in turn presupposes, but also reconstitutes, the institutional organisation of society (*Central Problems in Social Theory* (London, Macmillan, 1979) chapters 2 and 3; see also Raymond Williams, *Marxism and Literature* (Oxford University Press, 1977), pp. 75–83.

11 Louis Althusser, *For Marx* (London, New Left Books, 1977), p. 228; the italicized phrase is a direct reference to Marx's sixth thesis on Feuerbach.

12 Ibid., p. 229.

13 Louis Althusser, *Lenin and Philosophy and Other Essays* London, New Left Books, 1977), p. 201.

14 On some important similarities and differences between cultural materialism, structuralism and post-structuralism as they affect English studies, see Raymond Williams, 'Crisis in English Studies', *New Left Review* 129 (1981), 51–66. To the extent that psychoanalytic theory still invokes universal categories of psychosexual development it is incompatible with the materialist perspective outlined here' on this, see Stuart Hall, 'Theories of Language and Ideology', in Stuart Hall et al., *Culture, Media, Language: Working Papers in Cultural Studies 1972–9* (London, Hutchinson, 1980), especially p. 160.

15 Best exemplified in Wilson's article 'Beyond the Outsider', in *Declaration*, ed. Tom Maschler (London, MacGibbon & Kee, 1957), pp. 38–40.

16 Ibid., p. 46; cf. pp. 37 and 40.

17 Ibid., pp. 36, 37, 41.

18 Ibid., p. 41.

19 Jacques Derrida, *Positions*, trans. Alan Bass (London, Athlone, 1981), p. 21.

20 Rene Descartes, *the Philosophical Works*, trans. Elizabeth S. Haldane and G. R. T. Ross, 2 vols. (Cambridge University Press, 1931), I. 102 and 152.

21 John Locke, *An Essay Concerning Human Understanding*, ed. Peter H. Nidditch (Oxford, Clarendon, 1975), II.27.10.

22 Ibid., 2.i.2.
23 John Locke, *Some Thoughts Concerning Education, in Educational Writings*, ed. James L. Axtell (Cambridge University Press, 1968), p. 114.
24 David Hume, *A Treatise of Human Nature*, ed. L. A. Selby-Bigge, 2nd edn (Oxford, Clarendon, 1962), I.iv.6.
25 The transcendental pretence is defined by Solomon as the ideological conviction that 'the white middle classes of European descent were the representatives of all humanity, and as human nature is one, so its history must be as well. This transcendental pretence was – and still is – the premise of our thinking about history, "humanity" and human nature'. Robert Solomon, *History and Human Nature* (Brighton, Harvester, 1980), p. xii.
26 David Hume, *An Enquiry Concerning Human Understanding*, L. A. Selby-Bigge, 2nd edn (Oxford, Clarendon, 1962), section VIII, part I.
27 Compare Macpherson on Locke: 'A market society generates class differentiation in effective rights and rationality, yet requires for its justification a postulate of equal natural rights and rationality. Locke recognised the differentiation in his own society, and read it back into natural society. At the same time he maintained the postulate of equal natural rights and rationality. Most of Locke's theoretical confusions, and most of his practical appeal, can be traced to this ambiguous position'. C. B. Macpherson, *the Political Theory of Possessive Individualism: Hobbes to Locke* (Oxford University Press, 1964), p. 269. See also Peter Gay, *The Enlightenment: An Interpretation*, 2 vols. (London, Weidenfeld & Nicolson, 1967–70), II. 167–74.
28 David Hume, *Essays, Moral, Political and Literary*, ed. T. H. Green and T. H. Grose, 2 vols. (London, Longmans, Green, 1875), I. 252.
29 Solomon, *History and Human Nature*, p. 54.
30 Immanuel Kant, *Critique of Pure Reason*, trans. Norman Kemp-Smith (London, Macmillan, 1968), p. 22.
31 Immanuel Kant, *Observations on the Feeling of the Beautiful and Sublime*, pp. 110–11; quoted in Richard Popkin, *The High Road to Pyrrhonism* (San Diego, Austin Hill, 1980), pp. 259–60.
32 Popkin, *The High Road to Pyrrhonism*, especially chapters 4 and 14.
33 Ashley Montagu, *Man's Most Dangerous Myth: The Fallacy of Race*, 5th edn (Oxford University Press, 1974), pp. 21 ff.
34 'Race: A Basic Concept in Education', quoted from p. 14 of Montagu, *Man's Most Dangerous Myth*.
35 Marcuse, *Negations*, pp. 44–5, see also p. 63: 'The intuition of essence helps set up "essential" hierarchies in which the material and vital values of human life occupy the lowest rank, while the types of the saint, the genius and the hero take first place'.
36 Jacques Derrida, *Writing and Difference*, trans. Alan Bass (London, Routledge, 1978), p. 282.
37 Ibid., pp. 278–9.
38 Ibid., p. 292.
39 Claude Lévi-Strauss, *The Savage Mind* (London, Weidenfeld & Nicolson, 1966), p. 247.
40 Michel Foucault, *The Order of Things: An Archaeology of the Human Sciences* (London, Tavistock, 1970), p. 387.
41 Roland Barthes, *Mythologies*, trans. A. Lavers (St Albans, Paladin, 1973), p. 151.

42 Although Hume's belief in universal man represents an important strand in his (Enlightenment) thinking, it coexists with a strong sense of actual human difference albeit, often, on a superior/inferior model (see D. Forbes, *Hume's Philosophical Politics* (Cambridge University Press, 1975), chapter 4). Hume here exemplifies (rather than being responsible for) something which has persisted in western culture: the ideology of 'man' incorporates both a universalist view of human nature as constant, and the view of human nature expressed in terms of cultural difference and diversity: the second has legitimated a superior/inferior classification, the first (in the name of basic sameness) cultural imperialism. A similar point is made, in relation to the history of anthropology, by Edmund Leach in *Social Anthropology* (Glasgow, Fontana, 1982), chapter 2. The racism which this often entails has, of course, found its way into certain strands of modernist literature.
43 Terry Eagleton, 'The Idealism of American Criticism', *New Left Review* 127 (1981), 53–65, at p. 59.
44 Frank Lentricchia, *After the New Criticism* (London, Athlone, 1980), pp. 33–4; cf. Frank Kermode: 'It is not that we are connoisseurs of chaos, but that we are surrounded by it, and equipped for coexistence with it only by our fictive powers', *the Sense of an Ending* (London, Oxford University Press, 1966), p. 64.
45 E. P. Thompson, *the Poverty of Theory* (London, Merlin, 1978), pp. 1–33.
46 William Golding, 'Fable', in *the Hot Gates and Other Occasional Pieces* (London, Faber, 1965).
47 Thompson, *the Poverty of Theory*, p. 28.
48 Wordsworth, quoted p. 4 of Thompson.
49 Colin Wilson, *The Outsider*, pp. 284–5.
50 Joseph Conrad, *Nostromo* (Harmondsworth, Penguin, 1963), pp. 409, 411–12.
51 D. H. Lawrence, *Selected Essays*, introduction by Richard Adlington (Harmondsworth, Penguin, 1950), p. 86.
52 Michel Foucault, *Language, Counter-Memory, Practice* (Ithaca and New York, Cornell University Press, 1977), p. 142.
53 Michel Foucault, *The Archaeology of Knowledge*, trans. A. M. Sheridan Smith (London, Tavistock, 1974), pp. 11–12.
54 Ibid., p. 203.
55 Roland Barthes, *Roland Barthes*, trans. Richard Howard (London, Macmillan, 1977), pp. 143, 168.
56 Ibid., p. 69.
57 Ibid., p. 64–5, 133.
58 Ibid., p. 69.
59 Barthes, *Mythologies*, p. 101.
60 Jacques Derrida, *Writing and Difference*, trans. Alan Bass (London, Routledge, 1978), p. 292, his italics.

SECTION TWO
LANGUAGE AND TEXTUALITY

The work represented in this trajectory of Post-Structuralist criticism tends to concentrate on abstract philosophical argument and speculation around language and textuality. For this trajectory, the text is taken not as referring to a pre-text but as inscribed within a web of textuality and difference. Its characteristic mode of operation is a spectacular play of language game around the texts it interrogates; its most formidable exponent is the French philosopher Jacques Derrida.

Derrida has been seen as almost synonymous with the post-structuralist enterprise. He has consistently critiqued and extended structuralism, rigorously following through the most radical implications of the Saussurean theory of language. Though Derrida is perhaps best known for inaugurating 'deconstruction', the various forms of textual analysis that claim to be 'deconstructing the text' often have only tenuous links with his consistent concern to undo the 'logocentric' impulse in texts. 'Lococentrism' is the term Derrida uses to cover that form of rationalism that presupposes a 'presence' behind language and text – a 'presence' such as an idea, an intention, a truth, a meaning or a reference for which language acts as a subservient and convenient vehicle of expression. But at the same time as language and text exhibit logocentric impulses, *writing*, as textuality, undoes that logocentrism through its rhetorical and troping figures; while the text attempts to suppress textuality, textuality inevitably imposes itself on the scene of writing.

Logocentrism, the mark of a 'metaphysics of presence' is, for Derrida, the very foundation of Western thought; it is undermined by Saussure's theory of language in which identities result only from difference. But, as Derrida shows, Saussure himself falls into a logocentrism. In *Of Grammatology* Derrida criticizes Saussure on the grounds that he privileges speech over writing. Speech becomes the authentic moment of language where meaning is identical to the speaker's intention and it thus bears the sign of presence, whereas writing is seen as a secondary and inferior form of speech. Typically, Derrida reverses the privileged term of the binary opposition, to show how speech can be seen as a form of writing (rather than *vice versa*), and how both exist in a mutually reciprocal dependence marked by *différance*.

Derrida reads Saussure radically, transposing difference to différance – where meaning is a matter of both difference and deferring. Meaning is never self-present in the sign, for if it were then the signifier would simply be the reference for the signified, the signifier 'standing-in' for the absent 'presence' of the concept that lies behind it. Meaning is a result of difference, but it is also deferred, there is always an element of 'undecidability' or 'play' in the unstable sign. This leads to an emphasis on the signifier and on textuality rather than the signified and meaning, since there is no point at which the slippage of signifiers can be stopped, no final resting point where the signifier yields up the truth of the signified, for that signified is just another signifier in a moment in différance.

Deconstruction is a twofold strategy of, on the one hand, uncovering and undoing logocentric rationality and on the other, drawing attention to the language of the text, to its figurative and rhetorical gestures and pointing up the text's existence in a web of textuality, in a network of signifiers where no final and transcendental signified can be fixed. If it is to sustain such a strategy then it must constantly refuse to set itself up as a systematic analysis independent of the text, a system that explains and masters, since to do so would be to fix the meaning of the text. Deconstruction appears, therefore, not as a rigid method or explanatory metalanguage, but more as a process and a performance closely tied to the texts it deconstructs. However, as Derrida notes, such strategies cannot ultimately escape logocentrism, they can only push at its limits; deconstructionist texts are themselves not beyond deconstruction, as Barbara Johnson has illustrated.[1]

For literary criticism the implications of deconstruction, and of Derrida's work in general, are profound. Literary studies has traditionally been concerned with the interpretation of texts, with revealing the 'meaning' behind the text (be that meaning the author's intention or the 'truth' of the human condition). Deconstructionist logic disrupts that interpretive mode. If the meaning of the text is unstable, undecidable, then the project of literary interpretation is compromised; interpretation is doomed to endlessly repeat the interpretive act, never able to reach that final explanation and understanding of the text – it is haunted by the continual play of différance. What is left to criticism is either a celebration of that play, or a rigorous argumentation around the logocentric versus textuality paradox. Both of these modes of criticism have been taken up directly by the American deconstructionists of the Yale School (Paul De Man, J. Hillis Miller, Geoffrey Hartman).[2]

Though Derrida's work has had a formative and direct influence on the American deconstructionists, it has also been highly influential in the development of post-structuralism in general. Indeed, it would be tempting to say that his 'presence' is pervasive in post-structuralist thought – but that would be wilfully logocentric. The essay by Derrida reprinted here interrogates the structuralist project and in particular the work of Lévi-Strauss, taking it to task over the notion of structure; for in structure, structuralism proposes a centre beyond the play of language. This essay is one of Derrida's most widely known pieces, one of the first to be translated into English.

Barthes's essay, 'From Work to Text'[3] was first published in 1971, one year after his seminal work of criticism, *S/Z*. As in *S/Z*, Barthes works on the notion of the 'plurality' of meaning and text. However, there is some hesitation about whether the text itself is the site of plurality or whether reading and interpreting, necessarily a process of structuration, governs this plurality. Barthes seems here, as he does in *the Pleasure of the Text* (1976) to imply that some texts are better than others because they actively engage in the 'moving-play of signifiers' rather than attempting to constrain and repress plurality (as in realism). His elusiveness over this point reinforces that sense of Barthes as post-structuralist, not prepared to produce the definitive meaning, but quite prepared to play undecidably between two.

Paul de Man was a leading figure in the so-called 'Yale School of deconstruction' and established his reputation with two books in particular, *Blindness and Insight* (1971) and *Allegories of Reading* (1979),[4] which continued the deconstructive project of demonstrating how rhetoric inevitably subverts logic. For de Man, literature avoids the bad faith of assuming otherwise because it is necessarily self-conscious about its own rhetorical status. Theory is important because, though it shares with philosophy a commitment to 'method', it also shares with literature a recognition of the limitations of systematic 'method': ultimately texts must acknowledge their own rhetorical performativity, their own linguistic self-referentiality. If no conceptual scheme can 'explain' a text, then in theory too, logic must succumb to rhetoric and a 'subversive element of unpredictability' will inevitably weaken any gesture towards explanatory systematization. Objections to theory, de Man suggests, may thus be regarded as displaced symptoms of a resistance which is inherent in the theoretical enterprise itself though inconceivable in the natural sciences and even 'unmentionable' in the social sciences.

The final essay in this section, by Barbara Johnson, represents one of the few female voices to be associated with the Yale School. The piece (published in 1985) is a polemic against the gender-bias of much deconstructive practice, and the main thrust of its argument can be summed up in the phrase 'the Yale School has always been a male school'. The subtlety of the essay, however, lies in Johnson's persuasive feminist re-reading of critical essays by Bloom, Hartman and de Man and her demonstration of the sleights of hand which effectively efface the female altogether in their readings. As she points out, what is not know is not seen as not known; accordingly she ends by subjecting her own earlier deconstructive readings to the same kind of feminist analysis. Simply because the Yale School included female critics is no reason at all to assume that it was anything other than a 'Male School'.

Notes

1 R. Young, ed., *Untying the Text: a Post-Structuralist Reader* (Boston, Mass., and London, Routledge & Kegan Paul, 1981).
2 C. Norris, *Deconstruction: Theory and Practice* (London, Methuen, 1982).
3 Repr. in *Image–Music–Text*, trans. Stephen Heath (London, Fontana, 1977).
4 Paul de Man, *Blindness and Insight: Essays in the Rhetoric of Contemporary Criticism* (New York, Oxford University Press, 1971); *Allegories of Reading: Figural Language in Rousseau, Nietzsche, Rilke and Proust* (New Haven, Yale University Press, 1979).

---

20   Jacques Derrida,

'Structure, Sign and Play in the Discourse of the Human Sciences', Alan Bass, tr. *Writing and Difference* (1966), pp. 278–95

> We need to interpret interpretations more than to interpret things.
>
> (Montaigne)

Perhaps something has occurred in the history of the concept of structure that could be called an 'event', if this loaded word did not entail a meaning which it is precisely the function of structural – or structuralist – thought to reduce or to suspect. Let us speak of an 'event' nevertheless, and let us use quotation marks to serve as a precaution. What would this event be then? Its exterior form would be that of a *rupture* and a *redoubling*.

It would be easy enough to show that the concept of structure and even the word 'structure' itself are as old as the *epistēmē* – that is to say, as old as Western science and Western philosophy – and that their roots thrust deep into the soil of ordinary language, into whose deepest recesses the *epistēmē* plunges in order to gather them up and to make them part of itself in a metaphorical displacement. Nevertheless, up to the event which I wish to mark out and define, structure – or rather the structurality of structure – although it has always been at work, has always been neutralized or reduced, and this by a process of giving it a center or of referring it to a point of presence, a fixed origin. The function of this center was not only to orient, balance, and organize the structure – one cannot in fact conceive of an unorganized structure – but above all to make sure that the organizing principle of the structure would limit what we might call the *play* of the structure. By orienting and organizing the coherence of the system, the centre of a structure permits the play of its elements inside the total form. And even today the notion of a structure lacking any center represents the unthinkable itself.

Nevertheless, the center also closes off the play which it opens up and makes possible. As center, it is the point at which the substitution of contents, elements, or terms is no longer possible. At the center, the permutation or the transformation of elements (which may of course be structures enclosed within a structure) is forbidden. At least this permutation has always remained *interdicted* (and I am using this word deliberately). Thus it has always been thought that the center, which is by definition unique, constituted that very thing within a structure which while governing the structure, escapes structurality. This is why classical thought concerning structure could say that the center is, paradoxically, *within* the structure and *outside* it. The center is at the center of the totality, and yet, since the center does not belong to the totality (is not part of the totality), the totality *has its center elsewhere*. The center is not the center. The concept of centered structure – although it represents coherence itself, the condition of the *epistēmē* as philosophy or science – is contradictorily coherent. And as always, coherence in contradiction expresses the force of a desire.[1] The concept of centered structure is in fact the concept of a play based on a fundamental ground, a play constituted on the basis of a fundamental immobility and a reassuring certitude, which itself is beyond the reach of play. And on the basis of this certitude anxiety can be mastered, for anxiety is invariably the result of a certain mode of being implicated in the game, of being caught by the game, of being as it were at stake in the game from the outset. And again on the basis of what we call the center (and which, because it can be either inside or outside, can also indifferently be called the origin or end, *archē* or *telos*), repetitions, substitutions, transformations, and permutations are always *taken* from a history of meaning [*sens*] – that is, in a word, a history – whose origin may always be reawakened or whose end may always be anticipated in the form of presence. This is why one perhaps could say that the movement of any archaeology, like that of any eschatology, is an accomplice of this reduction of the structurality of structure and always attempts to conceive of structure on the basis of a full presence which is beyond play.

If this is so, the entire history of the concept of structure, before the rupture of which we are speaking, must be thought of as a series of substitutions of center for center, as a linked chain of determinations of the center. Successively, and in a regulated fashion, the center receives different forms or names. The history of metaphysics, like the history of the West, is the history of these metaphors and metonymies. Its matrix – if you will pardon me for demonstrating so little and for being so elliptical in order to come more quickly to my principal theme – is the determination of Being as *presence* in all senses of this word. It could be shown that all the names related to fundamentals, to principles, or to the center have always designated an invariable presence – *eidos, archē, telos, energeia, ousia* (essence, existence, substance, subject) *alētheia*, transcendentality, consciousness, God, man, and so forth.

The event I called a rupture, the disruption I alluded to at the beginning of this paper, presumably would have come about when the structurality of structure had to begin to be thought, that is to say, repeated, and this is why I said that this disruption was repetition in every sense of the word. Henceforth, it became necessary to think both the law which somehow governed the desire for a center in the constitution of structure, and the process of signification which orders the displacements and substitutions for this law of central presence – but a central presence which has never been itself, has always already been exiled from itself into its own substitute. The substitute does not substitute itself for anything which has somehow existed before it. Henceforth, it was necessary to begin thinking that there was no center, that the center could not be thought in the form of a present-being, that the center had no natural site, that it was not a fixed locus but a function, a sort of nonlocus in which an infinite number of sign-substitutions came into play. This was the moment when language invaded the universal problematic, the moment when, in the absence of a center or origin, everything became discourse – provided we can agree on this word – that is to say, a system in which the central signified, the original or transcendental signified, is never absolutely present outside a system of differences. The absence of the transcendental signified extends the domain and the play of signification infinitely.

Where and how does this decentering, this thinking the structurality of structure, occur? It would be somewhat naïve to refer to an event, a doctrine, or an author in order to designate this occurrence. It is no doubt part of the totality of an era, our own, but still it has always already begun to proclaim itself and begun to *work*. Nevertheless, if we wished to choose several 'names', as indications only, and to recall those authors in whose discourse this occurrence has kept most closely to its most radical formulation, we doubtless would have to cite the Nietzschean critique of metaphysics, the critique of the concepts of Being and truth, for which were substituted the concepts of play, interpretation, and sign (sign without present truth); the Freudian critique of self-presence, that is, the critique of consciousness, of the subject, of self-identity and of self-proximity or self-possession; and, more radically, the Heideggerean destruction of metaphysics, of onto-theology, of the determination of Being as presence. But all these destructive discourses and all their analogues are trapped in a kind of circle. This circle is unique. It describes the form of the relation between the history of metaphysics and the destruction of the history of metaphysics. There is no sense in doing without the concepts of metaphysics in order to shake metaphysics. We have no language – no syntax and no lexicon – which is foreign to this history; we can pronounce not a single destructive proposition which has not already had to slip into the form, the logic, and the implicit postulations of precisely what it seeks to contest. To take one example from many: the metaphysics of presence is shaken with the help of the concept of *sign*. But, as I suggest a moment ago, as soon as one seeks to demonstrate in this way that there is no transcendental or privileged signified and that the domain or play of signification henceforth has no limit, one must reject even the concept and word 'sign' itself – which is precisely what cannot be done. For the signification 'sign' has always been understood and determined, in its meaning, as sign-of, a signifier referring to a signified, a signifier different from its signified. If one erases the radical difference between signifier and signified, it is the word 'signifier' itself which must be abandoned as a metaphysical concept. When Lévi-Strauss says in the preface to *The Raw and the Cooked* that he has 'sought to transcend the opposition between the sensible and the intelligible by operating from the outset at the level of signs,'[2] the necessity, force, and legitimacy of his act cannot make us forget that the concept of the sign cannot in itself surpass this opposition between the sensible and the intelligible. The concept of the sign, in each of its aspects, has been determined by this opposition throughout the totality of its history. It has lived only on this opposition and its system. But we cannot do without the concept of the sign, for we cannot give up this metaphysical complicity without also giving up the critique we are directing against this complicity, or without the risk of erasing difference in the self-identity of a signified reducing its signifier into itself or, amounting to the same thing, simply expelling its signifier outside itself. For there are two heterogenous ways of erasing the difference between the signifier and the signified: one, the classic way, consists in reducing or deriving the signifier, that is to say, ultimately in *submitting* the sign to thought; the other, the one we are using here against the first one, consists in putting into question the system in which the preceding reduction functioned: first and foremost, the opposition between the sensible and the intelligible. For the *paradox* is that the metaphysical reduction of the sign needed the opposition it was reducing. The opposition is systematic with the reduction. And what we are saying here about the sign can be extended to all the concepts and all the sentences of metaphysics, in particular to the discourse on 'structure'. But there are several ways of being caught in this circle. They are all more or less naïve, more or less empirical, more or less systematic, more or less close to the formulation – that is, to the formalization – of this circle. It is these differences which explain the multiplicity of destructive discourses and the disagreement between those who elaborate them. Nietzsche, Freud, and Heidegger, for example, worked within the inherited concepts of metaphysics. Since these concepts are not elements or atoms, and since they are taken from a syntax and a system, every particular borrowing brings along with it the whole of metaphysics. This is what allows these destroyers to destroy each other reciprocally – for example, Heidegger regarding Nietzsche, with as much lucidity and rigor as bad faith and misconstruction, as the last metaphysician, the last 'Platonist'. One could do the same for Heidegger himself, for Freud, or for a number of others. And today no exercise is more widespread.

What is the relevance of this formal schema when we turn to what are called the 'human sciences'? One of them perhaps occupies a privileged place –

ethnology. In fact one can assume that ethnology could have been born as a science only at the moment when a decentering had come about: at the moment when European culture – and, in consequence, the history of metaphysics and of its concepts – has been *dislocated*, driven from its locus, and forced to stop considering itself as the culture of reference. This moment is not first and foremost a moment of philosophical or scientific discourse. It is also a moment which is political, economic, technical, and so forth. One can say with total security that there is nothing fortuitous about the fact that the critique of ethnocentrism – the very condition for ethnology – should be systematically and historically contemporaneous with the destruction of the history of metaphysics. Both belong to one and the same era. Now, ethnology – like any science – comes about within the element of discourse. And it is primarily a European science employing traditional concepts, however much it may struggle against them. Consequently, whether he wants to or not – and this does not depend on a decision on his part – the ethnologist accepts into his discourse the premises of ethnocentrism at the very moment when he denounces them. This necessity is irreducible; it is not a historical contingency. We ought to consider all its implications very carefully. But if no one can escape this necessity, and if no one is therefore responsible for giving into it, however little he may do so, this does not mean that all the ways of giving in to it are of equal pertinence. The quality and fecundity of a discourse are perhaps measured by the critical rigor with which this relation to the history of metaphysics and to inherited concepts is thought. Here is a question both of a critical relation to the language of the social sciences and a critical responsibility of the discourse itself. It is a question of explicitly and systematically posing the problem of the status of a discourse which borrows from a heritage the resources necessary for the deconstruction of that heritage itself. A problem of *economy* and *strategy*.

If we consider, as an example, the texts of Claude Lévi-Strauss, it is not only because of the privilege accorded to ethnology among the social sciences, nor even because the thought of Lévi-Strauss weighs heavily on the contemporary theoretical situation. It is above all because a certain choice has been declared in the work of Lévi-Strauss and because a certain doctrine has been elaborated there, and precisely, in a *more or less explicit manner*, as concerns both this critique of language and this critical language in the social sciences.

In order to follow this movement in the text of Lévi-Strauss, let us choose as one guiding thread among others the opposition between nature and culture. Despite all its rejuvenations and disguises, this opposition is congenital to philosophy. It is even older than Plato. It is at least as old as the Sophists. Since the statement of the opposition *physis/nomos*, *physis/technē*, it has been relayed to us by means of a whole historical chain which opposes 'nature' to law, to education, to art, to technics – but also to liberty, to the arbitrary, to history, to society, to the mind, and so on. Now, from the outset of his researches, and from his first book (*The Elementary Structures of Kinship*) on, Lévi-Strauss simultaneously has experienced the necessity of utilizing this opposition and the impossibility of accepting it. In the *Elementary Structures*, he begins from this axiom or definition: that which is *universal* and spontaneous, and not dependent on any particular culture or on any determinate norm, belongs to nature. Inversely, that which depends upon a system of *norms* regulating society and therefore is capable of *varying* from one social structure to another, belongs to culture. These two definitions are of the traditional type. But in the very first pages of the *Elementary Structures* Lévi-Strauss, who has begun by giving credence to these concepts, encounters what he calls a *scandal*, that is to say, something which no longer tolerates the nature/culture opposition he has accepted, something which *simultaneously* seems to require the predicates of nature and of culture. This scandal is the *incest prohibition*. The incest prohibition is universal; in this sense one could call it natural. But it is also a prohibition, a system of norms and interdicts; in this sense one could call it cultural:

> Let us suppose then that everything universal in man relates to the natural order, and is characterized by spontaneity, and that everything subject to a norm is cultural and is both relative and particular. We are then confronted with a fact, or rather, a group of facts, which, in the light of previous definitions, are not far removed from a scandal: we refer to that complex group of beliefs, customs, conditions and institutions described succinctly as the prohibition of incest, which presents, without the slightest ambiguity, and inseparably combines, the two characteristics in which we recognize the conflicting features of two mutually exclusive orders. It constitutes a rule, but a rule which, alone among all the social rules, possesses at the same time a universal character.[3]

Obviously there is no scandal except within a system of concepts which accredits the difference between nature and culture. By commencing his work with the *factum* of the incest prohibition. Lévi-Strauss thus places himself at the point at which this difference, which has always been assumed to be self-evident, finds itself erased or questioned. For from the moment when the incest prohibition can no longer be conceived within the nature/culture opposition, it can no longer be said to be a scandalous fact, a nucleus of opacity within a network of transparent significations. The incest prohibition is no longer a scandal one meets with or comes up against in the domain of traditional concepts; it is something which escapes these concepts and certainly precedes them – probably as the condition of their possibility. It could perhaps be said that the whole of philosophical conceptualization, which is systematic with the nature/culture opposition, is designed to leave in the domain of the unthinkable the very thing that makes this conceptualization possible: the origin of the prohibition of incest.

This example, too cursorily examined, is only one among many others, but nevertheless it already shows that language bears within itself the necessity of its own critique. Now this critique may be undertaken along two paths, in two 'manners'. Once the limit of the nature/culture opposition makes itself felt, one might want to question systematically and rigorously the history of these concepts. This is a first action. Such a systematic and historic questioning would be neither a philological nor a philosophical action in the classic sense of these words. To concern oneself with the founding concepts of the entire history of philosophy, to deconstitute them, is not to undertake the work of the philologist or of the classic historian of philosophy. Despite appearances, it is probably the most daring way of making the beginnings of a step outside of philosophy. The step 'outside philosophy' is much more difficult to conceive than is generally imagined by those who think they made it long ago with cavalier ease, and who in general are swallowed up in metaphysics by the entire body of discourse which they claim to have disengaged from it.

The other choice (which I believe corresponds more closely to Lévi-Strauss's manner), in order to avoid the possibly sterilizing effects of the first one, consists in conserving all these old concepts within the domain of empirical discovery while here and there denouncing their limits, treating them as tools which can still be used. No longer is any truth value attributed to them; there is a readiness to abandon them, if necessary, should other instruments appear more useful. In the meantime, their relative efficacy is exploited, and they are employed to destroy the old machinery to which they belong and of which they themselves are pieces. This is how the language of the social sciences criticizes *itself*. Lévi-Strauss thinks that in this way he can separate *method* from *truth*, the instruments of the method and the objective significations envisaged by it. One could almost say that this is the primary affirmation of Lévi-Strauss; in any event, the first words of the *Elementary Structures* are: 'Above all, it is beginning to emerge that this distinction between nature and society ('nature' and 'culture' seem preferable to us today), while of no acceptable historical significance, does contain a logic, fully justifying its use by modern sociology as a methodological tool.'⁴

Lévi-Strauss will always remain faithful to this double intention: to preserve as an instrument something whose truth value he criticizes.

On the one hand, he will continue, in effect, to contest the value of the nature/culture opposition. More than thirteen years after the *Elementary Structures*, *The Savage Mind* faithfully echoes the text I have quoted: 'The opposition between nature and culture to which I attached much importance at one time . . . now seems to be of primarily methodological importance.' And this methodological value is not affected by its 'ontological' nonvalue (as might be said, if this notion were not suspect here): 'However, it would not be enough to reabsorb particular humanities into a general one. This first enterprise opens the way for others which . . . are incumbent on the exact natural sciences: the reintegration of culture in nature and finally of life within the whole of its physio-chemical conditions.'⁵

On the other hand, still in *The Savage Mind,* he presents as what he calls *bricolage* what might be called the discourse of this method. The *bricoleur,* says Lévi-Strauss, is someone who uses 'the means at hand', that is, the instruments he finds at his disposition around him, those which are already there, which had not been especially conceived with an eye to the operation for which they are to be used and to which one tries by trial and error to adapt them, not hesitating to change them whenever it appears necessary, or to try several of them at once, even if their form and their origin are heterogenous – and so forth. There is therefore a critique of language in the form of *bricolage,* and it has even been said that *bricolage* is critical language itself. I am thinking in particular of the article of G. Genette, 'Structuralisme et critique littéraire', published in homage to Lévi-Strauss in a special issue of L 'Arc (no. 26, 1965), where it is stated that the analysis of *bricolage* could 'be applied almost word for word' to criticism, and especially to 'literary criticism'.

If one calls *bricolage* the necessity of borrowing one's concepts from the text of a heritage which is more or less coherent or ruined, it must be said that every discourse is *bricoleur.* The engineer, whom Lévi-Strauss opposes to the *bricoleur,* should be the one to construct the totality of his language, syntax, and lexicon. In this sense the engineer is a myth. A subject who supposedly would be the absolute origin of his own discourse and supposedly would construct it 'out of nothing', 'out of whole cloth', would be the creator of the verb, the verb itself. The notion of the engineer who supposedly breaks with all forms of *bricolage* is therefore a theological idea; and since Lévi-Strauss tells us elsewhere that *bricolage* is mythopoetic, the odds are that the engineer is a myth produced by the *bricoleur.* As soon as we cease to believe in such an engineer and in a discourse which breaks with the received historical discourse, and as soon as we admit that every finite discourse is bound by a certain *bricolage* and that the engineer and the scientist are also species of *bricoleurs,* then the very idea of *bricolage* is menaced and the difference in which it took on its meaning breaks down.

This brings us to the second thread which might guide us in what is being contrived here.

Lévi-Strauss describes *bricolage* not only as an intellectual activity but also as a mythopoetical activity. One reads in *The Savage Mind,* 'Like *bricolage* on the technical plane, mythical reflection can reach brilliant unforeseen results on the intellectual plane. Conversely, attention has often been drawn to the mythopoetical nature of *bricolage.'*[6]

But Lévi-Strauss's remarkable endeavor does not simply consist in proposing, notably in his most recent investigations, a structural science of myths and of mythological activity. His endeavour also appears – I would say almost from the outset – to have the status which he accords to his own discourse on myths, to what he calls his 'mythologicals'. It is here that his discourse on the myth reflects on itself and criticises itself. And this moment, this critical period, is evidently of concern to all the languages which share the field of the human sciences. What does Lévi-Strauss say of his 'mythologicals'? It is here that we rediscover the mythopoetical virtue of *bricolage*. In effect, what appears most fascinating in this critical search for a new status of discourse is the stated abandonment of all reference to a *center*, to a *subject*, to a privileged *reference*, to an origin, or to an absolute *archia*. The theme of this decentering could be followed throughout the 'Overture' to his last book, *The Raw and the Cooked*. I shall simply remark on a few key points.

1 From the very start, Lévi-Strauss recognizes that the Bororo myth which he employs in the book as the 'reference myth' does not merit this name and this treatment. The name is specious and the use of the myth improper. This myth deserves no more than any other its referential privilege: 'In fact, the Bororo myth, which I shall refer to from now as the key myth, is, as I shall try to show, simply a transformation, to a greater or lesser extent, of other myths originating either in the same society or in neighboring or remote societies. I could, therefore, have legitimately taken as my starting point any one representative myth of the group. From this point of view, the key myth is interesting not because typical, but rather because of its irregular position within the group.'[7]

2 There is no unity or absolute source of the myth. The focus or the source of the myth are always shadows and virtualities which are elusive, unactualizable, and nonexistent in the first place. Everything begins with structure, configuration, or relationship. The discourse on the acentric structure that myth itself is, cannot itself have an absolute subject or an absolute center. It must avoid the violence that consists in centering a language which describes an acentric structure if it is not to shortchange the form and movement of myth. Therefore it is necessary to forego scientific or philosophical discourse, to renounce the epistēmē which absolutely requires, which is the absolute requirement that we go back to the source, to the center, to the founding basis, to the principle, and so on. In opposition to *epistemic* discourse, structural discourse on myths – *mythological* discourse – must itself be *mythomorphic*. It must have the form of that of which it speaks. This is what Lévi-Strauss says in *The Raw and the Cooked*, from which I would now like to quote a long and remarkable passage:

> The study of myths raises a methodological problem, in that it cannot be carried out according to the Cartesian principle of breaking down the difficulty into as many parts as may be necessary for finding the solution. There is no real end to methodological analysis, no hidden unity to be grasped once the breaking-down process has been completed. Themes can be split up *ad infinitum*. Just when you think you have disentangled and separated them, you realize that they are knitting together again in response to the operation of unexpected affinities. Consequently the unity of the myth is never more than tendential and projective and cannot reflect a state or a particular moment of myth. It is a phenomenon of

the imagination, resulting from the attempt at interpretation; and its function is to endow the myth with synthetic form and to prevent its disintegration into a confusion of opposites. The science of myths might therefore be termed 'anaclastic', if we take this old term in the broader etymological sense which includes the study of both reflected rays and broken rays. But unlike philosophical reflection, which aims to go back to its own source, the reflections we are dealing with here concern rays whose only source is hypothetical . . . And in seeking to imitate the spontaneous movement of mythological thought, this essay, which is also both too brief and too long, has had to conform to the requirements of that thought and to respect its rhythm. It follows that this book on myths is itself a kind of myth.[8]

This statement is repeated a little further on: 'As the myths themselves are based on secondary codes (the primary codes being those that provide the substance of language), the present work is put forward as a tentative draft of a tertiary code, which is intended to ensure the reciprocal translatability of several myths. This is why it would not be wrong to consider this book itself as a myth: it is, as it were, the myth of mythology.'[9] The absence of a centre is here the absence of a subject and the absence of an author. 'Thus the myth and the musical work are like conductors of an orchestra, whose audience becomes the silent performers. If it is now asked where the real center of the work is to be found, the answer is that this is impossible to determine. Music and mythology bring man face to face with potential objects of which only the shadows are actualized. . . . Myths are anonymous.'[10] The musical model chosen by Lévi-Strauss for the composition of his book is apparently justified by this absence of any real and fixed center of the mythical or mythological discourse.

Thus it is at this point that ethnographic *bricolage* deliberately assumes its mythopoetic function. But by the same token, this function makes the philosophical or epistemological requirement of a center appear as mythological, that is to say, as a historical illusion.

Nevertheless, even if one yields to the necessity of what Lévi-Strauss has done, one cannot ignore its risks. If the mythological is mythomorphic, are all discourses on myths equivalent? Shall we have to abandon any epistemological requirement which permits us to distinguish between several qualities of discourse on the myth? A classic, but inevitable question. It cannot be answered – and I believe that Lévi-Strauss does not answer it – for as long as the problem of the relations between the philosopheme or the theorem, on the one hand, and the mytheme or the mythopoem, on the other, has not been posed explicitly, which is no small problem. For lack of explicitly posing this problem, we condemn ourselves to transforming the alleged transgression of philosophy into an unnoticed fault within the philosophical realm. Empiricism would be the genus of which these faults would always be the species. Transphilosophical concepts would be transformed into philosophical naïvetés. Many examples could be given to demonstrate this risk: the concepts of sign, history, truth, and so forth. What

I want to emphasize is simply that the passage beyond philosophy does not consist in turning the page of philosophy (which usually amounts to philosophizing badly), but in continuing to read philosophers *in a certain way*. The risk I am speaking of is always assumed by Lévi-Strauss, and it is the very price of this endeavor. I have said that empiricism is the matrix of all faults menacing a discourse which continues, as with Lévi-Strauss in particular, to consider itself scientific. If we wanted to pose the problem of empiricism and *bricolage* in depth, we would probably end up very quickly with a number of absolutely contradictory propositions concerning the status of discourse in structural ethnology. On the one hand, structuralism justifiably claims to be the critique of empiricism. But at the same time there is not a single book or study by Lévi-Strauss which is not proposed as an empirical essay which can always be completed or invalidated by new information. The structural schemata are always proposed as hypotheses resulting from a finite quantity of information and which are subjected to the proof of experience. Numerous texts could be used to demonstrate this double postulation. Let us turn once again to the 'Overture' of *The Raw and the Cooked*, where it seems clear that if this postulation is double, it is because it is a question here of a language on language:

> If critics reproach me with not having carried out an exhaustive inventory of South American myths before analysing them, they are making a grave mistake about the nature and function of these documents. The total body of myth belonging to a given community is comparable to its speech. Unless the population dies out physically or morally, this totality is never complete. You might as well criticise a linguist for compiling the grammar of a language without having complete records of the words pronounced since the language came into being, and without knowing what will be said in it during the future part of its existence. Experience proves that a linguist can work out the grammar of a given language from a remarkably small number of sentences. . . . And even a partial grammar or an outline grammar is a precious acquisition when we are dealing with unknown languages. Syntax does not become evident only after a (theoretically limitless) series of events has been recorded and examined, because it is itself the body of rules governing their production. What I have tried to give is an outline of the syntax of South American mythology. Should fresh data come to hand, they will be used to check or modify the formulation of certain grammatical laws, so that some are abandoned and replaced by new ones. But in no instance would I feel constrained to accept the arbitrary demand for a total mythological pattern, since, as has been shown, such a requirement has no meaning.[11]

Totalization, therefore, is sometimes defined as *useless*, and sometimes as *impossible*. This is no doubt due to the fact that there are two ways of conceiving the limit of totalization. And I assert once more that these two determinations coexist implicitly in Lévi-Strauss's discourse. Totalization can be judged impossible in the classical style: one then refers to the empirical endeavor of either a subject or a finite richness which it can never master. There is too much, more than one can say. But nontotalization can also be determined in another way: no longer from the standpoint of a concept of finitude as relegation to the empirical, but from the standpoint of the concept of *play*. If totalization no longer has any meaning, it is not because the infiniteness of a field cannot be covered by a finite glance or a finite discourse, but because the nature of the field – that is, language and a finite language – excludes totalization. This field is in effect that of *play*, that is to say, a field of infinite substitutions only because it is finite, that is to say, because instead of being an inexhaustible field, as in the classical hypothesis, instead of being too large, there is something missing from it: a center which arrests and grounds the play of substitutions. One could say – rigorously using that word whose scandalous signification is always obliterated in French – that this movement of play, permitted by the lack or absence of a center or origin, is the movement of *supplementarity*. One cannot determine the center and exhaust totalization because the sign which replaces the center, which supplements it, taking the center's place in its absence – this sign is added, occurs as a surplus, as a *supplement*.[12] 'The movement of signification adds something, which results in the fact that there is always more, but this addition is a floating one because it comes to perform a vicarious function, to supplement a lack on the part of the signified. Although Lévi-Strauss in his use of the word 'supplementary' never emphasizes, as I do here, the two directions of meaning which are so strangely compounded within it, it is not by chance that he uses this word twice in his 'Introduction to the Work of Marcel Mauss', at one point where he is speaking of the 'overabundance of signifier, in relation to the signifieds to which this overabundance can refer':

> In this endeavor to understand the world, man therefore always has at his disposal a surplus of signification (which he shares out amongst things according to the laws of symbolic thought – which is the task of ethnologists and linguists to study). This distribution of a *supplementary* allowance [*ration supplémentaire*] – if it is permissible to put it that way – is absolutely necessary in order that on the whole the available signifier and the signified it aims at may remain in the relationship of complementarity which is the very condition of the use of symbolic thought.[13]

(It could no doubt be demonstrated that this *ration supplémentaire* of signification is the origin of the *ratio* itself.) The word reappears a little further on, after Lévi-Strauss has mentioned 'this floating signifier, which is the servitude of all finite thought':

> In other words – and taking as our guide Mauss's precept that all social phenomena can be assimilated to language – we see in *mana, Wakau, oranda* and other notions of the same type, the conscious expression of a semantic function, whose role it is to permit symbolic thought to operate in spite of the contradiction which is proper to it. In this way are explained the apparently insoluble antinomies attached to this notion . . . . At one and the same time force and action, quality and state, noun and verb; abstract and concrete, omnipresent and localized – *mana* is in effect all these things. But is it not precisely because it is

none of these things that *mana* is a simple form, or more exactly, a symbol in the pure state, and therefore capable of becoming charged with any sort of symbolic content whatever? In the system of symbols constituted by all cosmologies, *mana* would simply be a zero symbolic value, that is to say, a sign marking the necessity of a symbolic content *supplementary* [my italics] to that with which the signified is already loaded, but which can take on any value required, provided only that this value still remains part of the available reserve and is not, as phonologists put it, a group-term.

Lévi-Strauss adds the note:

> Linguists have already been led to formulate hypotheses of this type. For example: 'A zero phoneme is opposed to all other phonemes in French in that it entails no differential characters and no constant phonetic value. On the contrary, the proper function of the zero phoneme is to be opposed to phoneme absence.' (R. Jakobson and J. Lutz, 'Notes on the French Phonemic Pattern', *Word* 5, no. 2 [August 1949]: 155.) Similarly, if we schematise the conception I am proposing here, it could almost be said that the function of notions like *mana* is to be opposed to the absence of signfication, without entailing by itself any particular signification.[14]

The *overabundance* of the signifier, its *supplementary* character, is thus the result of a finitude, that is to say, the result of a lack which must be *supplemented*.

It can now be understood why the concept of play is important in Lévi-Strauss. His references to all sorts of games, notably to roulette, are very frequent, especially in his *Conversations*,[15] in *Race and History*,[16] and in *The Savage Mind*. Further, the reference to play is always caught up in tension.

Tension with history, first of all. This is a classical problem, objections to which are now well worn. I shall simply indicate what seems to me the formality of the problem: by reducing history, Lévi-Strauss has treated as it deserves a concept which has always been in complicity with a teleological and eschatological metaphysics, in other words, paradoxically, in complicity with that philosophy of presence to which it was believed history could be opposed. The thematic of historicity, although it seems to be a somewhat late arrival in philosophy, has always been required by the determination of Being as presence. With or without etymology, and despite the classic antagonism which opposes these significations throughout all of classical thought, it could be shown that the concept of *epistēmē* has always called forth that of *historia*, if history is always the unity of a becoming, as the tradition of truth or the development of science of knowledge oriented toward the appropriation of truth in presence and self-presence, toward knowledge in consciousness-of-self. History has always been conceived as the movement of a resumption of history, as a detour between two presences. But if it is legitimate to suspect this concept of history, there is a risk, if it is reduced without an explicit statement of the problem I am indicating here, of falling back into an ahistoricism of a classical type, that is to say, into a determined moment of the history of metaphysics. Such is the algebraic formality of the problem as

I see it. More concretely, in the work of Lévi-Strauss it must be recognized that the respect for structurality, for the internal originality of the structure, compels a neutralisation of time and history. For example, the appearance of a new structure, of an original system, always comes about – and this is the very condition of its structural specificity – by a rupture with its past, its origin, and its cause. Therefore one can describe what is peculiar of the structural organization only by not taking into account, in the very moment of this description, its past conditions: by omitting to posit the problem of the transition from one structure to another, by putting history between brackets. In this 'structuralist' moment, the concepts of chance and discontinuity are indispensable. And Lévi-Strauss does in fact often appeal to them, for example, as concerns that structure of structures, language, of which he says in the 'Introduction to the Work of Marcel Mauss' that it 'could only have been born in one fell swoop':

> Whatever may have been the moment and the circumstances of its appearance on the scale of animal life, language could only have been born in one fell swoop. Things could not have set about acquiring signification progressively. Following a transformation the study of which is not the concern of the social sciences, but rather of biology and psychology, a transition came about from a stage where nothing had a meaning to another where everything possessed it.[17]

This standpoint does not prevent Lévi-Strauss from recognizing the slowness, the process of maturing, the continuous toil of factual transformations, history (for example, in *Race and History*). But, in accordance with a gesture which was also Rousseau's and Husserl's, he must 'set aside all the facts' at the moment when he wishes to recapture the specificity of a structure. Like Rousseau, he must always conceive of the origin of a new structure on the model of catastrophe – an overturning of nature in nature, a natural interruption of the natural sequence, a setting aside *of* nature.

Besides the tension between play and history, there is also the tension between play and presence. Play is the disruption of presence. The presence of an element is always a signifying and substitutive reference inscribed in a system of differences and the movement of a chain. Play is always play of absence and presence, but if it is to be thought radically, play must be conceived of before the alternative of presence and absence. Being must be conceived as presence or absence on the basis of the possibility of play and not the other way around. If Lévi-Strauss, better than any other, has brought to light the play of repetition and the repetition of play, one no less perceives in his work a sort of ethic of presence, an ethic of nostalgia for origins, an ethic of archaic and natural innocence, of a purity of presence and self-presence in speech – an ethic, nostalgia, and even remorse, which he often presents as the motivation of the ethnological project when he moves toward the archaic societies which are exemplary societies in his eyes. These texts are well known.[18]

Turned towards the lost or impossible presence of the absent origin, this structuralist thematic of broken immediacy is therefore the saddened, *negative*, nostalgic, guilty, Rousseauistic side of the thinking of play whose other side would be the Nietzschean *affirmation*, that is the joyous affirmation of the play of the world and of the innocence of becoming, the affirmation of a world of signs without fault, without truth, and without origin which is offered to an active interpretation. *This affirmation then determines the noncenter otherwise than as loss of the center.* And it plays without security. For there is a sure play: that which is limited to the *substitution* of *given* and *existing*, *present*, pieces. In absolute chance, affirmation also surrenders itself to *genetic* indetermination, to the *seminal* adventure of the trace.

There are thus two interpretations of interpretation; of structure, of sign, of play. The one seeks to decipher, dreams of deciphering a truth or an origin which escapes play and the order of the sign, and which lives the necessity of interpretation as an exile. The other, which is no longer turned toward the origin, affirms play and tries to pass beyond man and humanism, the name of man being the name of that being who, throughout the history of metaphysics or of ontotheology – in other words, throughout his entire history – has dreamed of full presence, the reassuring foundation, the origin and the end of play. The second interpretation of interpretation, to which Nietzsche pointed the way, does not seek in ethnography, as Lévi-Strauss does, the 'inspiration of a new humanism' (again citing the 'Introduction to the Work of Marcel Mauss').

There are more than enough indications today to suggest we might perceive that these two interpretations of interpretation – which are absolutely irreconcilable even if we live them simultaneously and reconcile them in an obscure economy – together share the field which we call, in such a problematic fashion, the social sciences.

For my part, although these two interpretations must acknowledge and accentuate their difference and define their irreducibility, I do not believe that today there is any question of *choosing* – in the first place because here we are in a region (let us say, provisionally, a region of historicity) where the category of choice seems particularly trivial; and in the second, because we must first try to conceive of the common ground, and the *différance* of this irreducible difference. Here there is a kind of question, let us still call it historical, whose *conception, formation, gestation*, and *labor* we are only catching a glimpse of today. I employ these words, I admit, with a glance toward the operations of childbearing – but also with a glance toward those who, in a society from which I do not exclude myself, turn their eyes away when faced by the as yet unnamable which is proclaiming itself and which can do so, as is necessary whenever a birth is in the offing, only under the species of the nonspecies, in the formless, mute, infant, and terrifying form of monstrosity.

Notes

1 TN. The reference, in a restricted sense, is to the Freudian theory of neurotic symptoms and of dream interpretation in which a given symbol is understood contradictorily as both the desire to fulfill an impulse and the desire to suppress the impulse. In a general sense the reference is to Derrida's thesis that logic and coherence themselves can only be understood contradictorily, since they presuppose the suppression of *différance*, 'writing' in the sense of the general economy. Cf. 'La pharmacie de Platon', in *La dissemination*, pp. 125–6, where Derrida uses the Freudian model of dream interpretation in order to clarify the contractions embedded in philosophical coherence.

2 *The Raw and the Cooked*, trn. John and Doreen Wightman (New York, Harper & Row, 1969), p. 14. [Translation somewhat modified.]

3 *The Elementary Structures of Kinship*, trn. James Bell, John von Sturmer, and Rodney Needham (Boston, Mass., Beacon Press, 1969), p. 8.

4 Ibid., p. 3.

5 *The Savage Mind* (London, George Weidenfeld & Nicolson; Chicago, The University of Chicago Press, 1966), p. 247.

6 Ibid., p. 17.

7 *The Raw and the Cooked*, p. 2.

8 Ibid., pp. 5–6.

9 Ibid., p. 12.

10 Ibid., pp. 17–18.

11 Ibid., pp. 7–8.

12 TN. This double sense of supplement – to supply something which is missing, or to supply something additional – is at the center of Derrida's deconstruction of traditional linguistics in *De la grammatologie*. In a chapter entitled 'The Violence of the Letter: From Lévi-Strauss to Rousseau' (pp. 149ff.), Derrida expands the analysis of Lévi-Strauss begun in this essay in order further to clarify the ways in which the contradictions of traditional logic 'program' the most modern conceptual apparatuses of linguistics and the social sciences.

13 'Introduction à l'oeuvre de Marcel Mauss', in Marcel Mauss, *Sociologie et anthropologie* (Paris, P.U.F., 1950), p. xlix.

14 Ibid., pp. xlix–l.

15 George Charbonnier, *Entretiens avec Claude Lévi-Strauss* (Paris, Plon, 1961).

16 *Race and History* (Paris, Unesco Publications, 1958).

17 'Introduction à l'oeuvre de Marcel Mauss', p. xlvi.

18 TN. The reference is to *Tristes tropiques*, trn. John Russel (London, Hutchinson & Co., 1961).

---

21 Roland Barthes,

'From Work to Text', S. Heath, ed. *Image, Music, Text* (1971) p. 155–64

It is a fact that over the last few years a certain change has taken place (or is taking place) in our conception of language and, consequently, of the literary work which owes at least its phenomenal existence to this same language. The change is clearly connected with the current development of (amongst other disciplines) linguistics, anthropology, Marxism and psychoanalysis (the term 'connection' is used here in a deliberately neutral way: one does not decide a determination, be it multiple and dialectical). What is new and which affects the idea of the work comes not necessarily from the internal recasting of each of these disciplines, but rather from their encounter in relation to an object which traditionally is the province of none of them. It is indeed as though the *interdisciplinarity* which is today held up as a prime value in research cannot be accomplished by the simple confrontation of specialist branches of knowledge. Interdisciplinarity is not the calm of an easy security; it begins *effectively* (as opposed to the mere expression of a pious wish) when the solidarity of the old disciplines breaks down – perhaps even violently, via the jolts of fashion – in the interests of a new object and a new language neither of which has a place in the field of the sciences that were to be brought peacefully together, this unease in classification being precisely the point from which it is possible to diagnose a certain mutation. The mutation in which the idea of the work seems to be gripped must not, however, be over-estimated: it is more in the nature of an epistemological slide than of a real break. The break, as is frequently stressed, is seen to have taken place in the last century with the appearance of Marxism and Freudianism; since then there has been no further break, so that in a way it can be said that for the last hundred years we have been living in repetition. What History, our History, allows us today is merely to slide, to vary, to exceed, to repudiate. Just as Einsteinian science demands that the relativity of the frames of reference be included in the object studied, so the combined action of Marxism, Freudianism and structuralism demands, in literature, the relativization of the relations of writer, reader and observer (critic). Over against the traditional notion of the *work*, for long – and still – conceived of in a, so to speak, Newtonian way, there is now the requirement of a new object, obtained by the sliding or overturning of former categories. That object is the *Text*. I know the word is fashionable (I am myself often led to use it) and therefore regarded by some with suspicion, but that is exactly why I should like to remind myself of the principal propositions at the intersection of which I see the Text as standing. The word 'proposition' is to be understood more in a grammatical than in a logical sense: the following are not argumentations but enunciations, 'touches', approaches that consent to remain metaphorical. Here then are these propositions; they concern method, genres, signs, plurality, filiation, reading and pleasure.

1 The Text is not to be thought of as an object that can be computed. It would be futile to try to separate out materially works from texts. In particular, the tendency must be avoided to say that the work is classic, the text avant-garde; it is not a question of drawing up a crude honours list in the name of modernity and declaring certain literary productions 'in' and

others 'out' by virtue of their chronological situation: there may be 'text' in a very ancient work, while many products of contemporary literature are in no way texts. The difference is this: the work is a fragment of substance, occupying a part of the space of books (in a library for example), the Text is a methodological field. The opposition may recall (without at all reproducing term for term) Lacan's distinction between 'reality' and 'the real': the one is displayed, the other demonstrated; likewise, the work can be seen (in bookshops, in catalogues, in exam syllabuses), the text is a process of demonstration, speaks according to certain rules (or against certain rules); the work can be held in the hand, the text is held in language, only exists in the movement of a discourse (or rather, it is Text for the very reason that it knows itself as text); the Text is not the decomposition of the work, it is the work that is the imaginary tail of the Text; or again, *the Text is experienced only in an activity of production*. It follows that the Text cannot stop (for example on a library shelf); its constitutive movement is that of cutting across (in particular, it can cut across the work, several works).

2 In the same way, the Text does not stop at (good) Literature; it cannot be contained in a hierarchy, even in a simple division of genres. What constitutes the Text is, on the contrary (or precisely), its subversive force in respect of the old classifications. How do you classify a writer like Georges Bataille? Novelist, poet, essayist, economist, philosopher, mystic? The answer is so difficult that the literary manuals generally prefer to forget about Bataille who, in fact, wrote texts, perhaps continuously one single text. If the Text poses problems of classification (which is furthermore one of its 'social' functions), this is because it always involves a certain experience of limits (to take up an expression from Philippe Sollers). Thibaudet used already to talk – but in a very restricted sense – of limit-works (such as Chateaubriand's *Vie de Rancé*, which does indeed come through to us today as a 'text'); the Text is that which goes to the limit of the rules of enunciation (rationality, readability, etc.). Nor is this a rhetorical idea, resorted to for some 'heroic' effect: the Text tries to place itself very exactly *behind* the limit of the *doxa* (is not general opinion – constitutive of our democratic societies and powerfully aided by mass communications – defined by its limits, the energy with which it excludes, its *censorship*?). Taking the word literally, it may be said that the Text is always *paradoxical*.

3 The Text can be approached, experienced, in reaction to the sign. The work closes on a signified. There are two modes of signification which can be attributed to this signified: either it is claimed to be evident and the work is then the object of a literal science, of philology, or else it is considered to be secret, ultimate, something to be sought out, and the work then falls under the scope of a hermeneutics, of an interpretation (Marxist, psychoanalytic, thematic, etc.); in short, the work itself functions as a general sign and it is normal that it should represent an institutional category of the civilisation of the Sign. The Text, on the contrary, practices the infinite deferment of the signified, is dilatory; its field is that of the

signifier and the signifier must not be conceived of as 'the first stage of meaning', its material vestibule, but, in complete opposition to this, as its *deferred action*. Similarly, the *infinity* of the signifier refers not to some idea of the ineffable (the unnameable signified) but to that of a *playing*; the generation of the perpetual signifier (after the fashion of a perpetual calender) in the field of the text (better, of which the text is the field) is realized not according to an organic progress of maturation or a hermeneutic course of deepening investigation, but, rather, according to a serial movement of disconnections, overlappings, variations. The logic regulating the Text is not comprehensive (define 'what the work means') but metonymic; the activity of associations, contiguities, carryings-over coincides with a liberation of symbolic energy (lacking it, man would die); the work – in the best of cases – is *moderately* symbolic (its symbolic runs out, comes to a halt); the Text is *radically* symbolic: *a work conceived, perceived and received in its integrally symbolic nature is a text*. Thus is the Text restored to language; like language, it is structured but off-centred, without closure (note, in reply to the contemptuous suspicion of the 'fashionable' sometimes directed at structuralism, that the epistemological privilege currently accorded to language stems precisely from the discovery there of a paradoxical idea of structure: a system with neither close nor centre).

4 The Text is plural. Which is not simply to say that it has several meanings, but that it accomplishes the very plurality of meaning: an *irreducible* (and not merely an acceptable) plural. The Text is not a co-existence of meanings but a passage, an overcrossing; thus it answers not to an interpretation, even a liberal one, but to an explosion, a dissemination. The plural of the Text depends, that is, not on the ambiguity of its contents but on what might be called the *stereographic plurality* of its weave of signifiers (etymologically, the text is a tissue, a woven fabric). The reader of the Text may be compared to someone at a loose end (someone slackened off from any imaginary); this passably empty subject strolls – it is what happened to the author of these lines, then it was that he had a vivid idea of the Text – on the side of a valley, a *oued* flowing down below (*oued* is there to bear witness to a certain feeling of unfamiliarity); what he perceives is multiple, irreducible, coming from a disconnected, heterogeneous variety of substances and perspectives: lights, colours, vegetation, heat, air, slender explosions of noises, scant cries of birds, children's voices from over on the other side, passages, gestures, clothes of inhabitants near or far away. All these *incidents* are half identifiable: they come from codes which are known but their combination is unique, founding the stroll in a difference repeatable only as difference. So the Text: it can be only in its difference (which does not mean its individuality), its reading is semelfactive (this rendering illusory any inductive-deductive science of texts – no 'grammar' of the text) and nevertheless woven entirely with citations, references, echoes, cultural languages (what language is not?), antecedent or contemporary, which cut across it through and through in a vast

stereophony. The intertextual in which every text is held, it itself being the text-between of another text, is not to be confused with some origin of the text: to try to find the 'sources', the 'influences' of a work, is to fall in with the myth of filiation; the citations which go to make up a text are anonymous, untraceable, and yet *already read*: they are quotations without inverted commas. The work has nothing disturbing for any monistic philosophy (we know that there are opposing examples of these); for such a philosophy, plural is the Evil. Against the work, therefore, the text could well take as its motto the words of the man possessed by demons (*Mark* 5:9): 'My name is Legion: for we are many.' The plural of demoniacal texture which opposes text to work can bring with it fundamental changes in reading, and precisely in areas where monologism appears to be the Law: certain of the 'texts' of Holy Scripture traditionally recuperated by theological monism (historical or anagogical) will perhaps offer themselves to a diffraction of meanings (finally, that is to say, to a materialist reading), while the Marxist interpretation of works, so far resolutely monistic, will be able to materialise itself more by pluralising itself (if, however, the Marxist 'institutions' allow it).

5 'The work is caught up in a process of filiation. Three things are postulated: a *determination* of the work by the world (by race, then by History), a *consecution* of works amongst themselves, and a *conformity* of the work to the author. The author is reputed the father and the owner of his work: literary science therefore teaches respect for the manuscript and the author's declared intentions, while society asserts the legality of the relation of author to work (the *'droit d'auteur'* or 'copyright', in fact of recent date since it was only really legalized at the time of the French Revolution). As for the Text, it reads without the inscription of the Father. Here again, the metaphor of the Text separates from that of the work: the latter refers to the image of an *organism* which grows by vital expansion, by 'development' (a word which is significantly ambiguous, at once biological and rhetorical); the metaphor of the Text is that of the *network*; if the Text extends itself, it is as a result of a combinatory systematic (an image, moreover, close to current biological conceptions of the living being). Hence no vital 'respect' is due to the Text: it can be *broken* (which is just what the Middle Ages did with two nevertheless authoritative texts – Holy Scripture and Aristotle); it can be read without the guarantee of its father, the restitution of the inter-text paradoxically abolishing any legacy. It is not that the Author may not 'come back' in the Text, in his text, but he then does so as a 'guest'. If he is a novelist, he is inscribed in the novel like one of his characters, figured in the carpet; no longer privileged, paternal, aletheological, his inscription is ludic. He becomes, as it were, a paper-author: his life is no longer the origin of his fictions but a fiction contributing to his work; there is a reversion of the work on to the life (and no longer the contrary); it is the work of Proust, of Genet which allows their lives to be read as a text. The word 'bio-graphy' re-acquires a strong, etymological sense, at the same time as the sincerity

of the enunciation – a veritable 'cross' borne by literary morality – becomes a false problem: the *I* which writes the text, it too, is never more than a paper-*I*.

6 The work is normally the object of consumption; no demagogy is intended here in referring to the so-called consumer culture but it has to be recognized that today it is the 'quality' of the work (which supposes finally an appreciation of 'taste') and not the operation of reading itself which can differentiate between books: structurally, there is no difference between 'cultured' reading and casual reading in trains. The Text (if only by its frequent 'unreadability') decants the work (the work permitting) from its consumption and gathers it up as play, activity, production, practice. This means that the Text requires that one try to abolish (or at the very least to diminish) the distance between writing and reading, in no way by intensifying the projection of the reader into the work but by joining them in a single signifying practice. The distance separating reading from writing is historical. In the times of the greatest social division (before the setting up of democratic cultures), reading and writing were equally privileges of class. Rhetoric, the great literary code of those times, taught one to *write* (even if what was then normally produced were speeches, not texts). Significantly, the coming of democracy reversed the word of command: what the (secondary) School prides itself on is teaching to *read* (well) and no longer to write (consciousness of the deficiency is becoming fashionable again today: the teacher is called upon to teach pupils to 'express themselves', which is a little like replacing a form of repression by a misconception). In fact, *reading*, in the sense of consuming, is far from *playing* with the text. 'Playing' must be understood here in all its polysemy: the text itself *plays* (like a door like a machine with 'play') and the reader plays twice over, playing the Text as one plays a game, looking for a practice which re-produces it, but, in order that that practice not be reduced to a passive, inner *mimesis* (the Text is precisely that which resists such a reduction), also playing the Text in the musical sense of the term. The history of music (as a practice, not as an 'art') does indeed parallel that of the Text fairly closely: there was a period when practising amateurs were numerous (at least within the confines of a certain class) and 'playing' and 'listening' formed a scarcely differentiated activity; then two roles appeared in sucession, first that of the performer, the interpreter to whom the bourgeois public (though still itself able to play a little – the whole history of the piano) delegated its playing, then that of the (passive) amateur, who listens to music without being able to play (the gramophone record takes the place of the piano). We know that today post-serial music has radically altered the role of the 'interpreter', who is called on to be in some sort the co-author of the score, completing it rather than giving it 'expression'. The Text is very much a score of this new kind: it asks of the reader a practical collaboration. Which is an important change, for who executes the work? (Mallarmé posed the question, wanting the audience to *produce* the book). Nowadays only the

critic executes the work (accepting the play on words). The reduction of reading to a consumption is clearly responsible for the 'boredom' experienced by many in the face of the modern ('unreadable') text, the avant-garde film or painting: to be bored means that one cannot produce the text, open it out, *set it going*.

7 This leads us to pose (to propose) a final approach to the Text, that of pleasure. I do not know whether there has ever been a hedonistic aesthetics (eudaemonist philosophies are themselves rare). Certainly there exists a pleasure of the work (of certain works); I can delight in reading and re-reading Proust, Flaubert, Balzac, even – why not? – Alexandre Dumas. But this pleasure, no matter how keen and even when free from all prejudice, remains in part (unless by some exceptional critical effort) a pleasure of consumption; for if I can read these authors, I also know that I cannot *re-write* them (that it is impossible today to write 'like that') and this knowledge, depressing enough, suffices to cut me off from the production of these works, in the very moment their remoteness establishes my modernity (is not to be modern to know clearly what cannot be started over again?). As for the Text, it is bound to *jouissance*, that is to a pleasure without separation. Order of the signifier, the Text participates in its own way in a social utopia; before History (supposing the latter does not opt for barbarism), the Text achieves, if not the transparency of social relations, that at least of language relations: the Text is that space where no language has a hold over any other, where languages circulate (keeping the circular sense of the term).

These few propositions, inevitably, do not constitute the articulations of a Theory of the Text and this is not simply the result of the failings of the person here presenting them (who in many respects has anyway done no more than pick up what is being developed round about him). It stems from the fact that a Theory of the Text cannot be satisfied by a meta-linguistic exposition: the destruction of meta-language, or at least (since it may be necessary provisionally to resort to meta-language) its calling into doubt, is part of the theory itself: the discourse on the Text should itself be nothing other than text, research, textual activity, since the Text is that *social* space which leaves no language safe, outside, nor any subject of the enunciation in position as judge, master, analyst, confessor, decoder. The theory of the Text can coincide only with a practice of writing.

22   Paul de Man,

'The Resistance to Theory', *Yale French Studies*, 63, (1982)
p. 355–71

This essay was not originally intended to address the question of teaching directly, although it was supposed to have a didactic and an educational function – which it failed to achieve. It was written at the request of the Committee on the Research Activities of the Modern Language Association as a contribution to a collective volume entitled *Introduction to Scholarship in Modern Languages and Literatures*. I was asked to write the section on literary theory. Such essays are expected to follow a clearly determined program: they are supposed to provide the reader with a select but comprehensive list of the main trends and publications in the field, to synthesize and classify the main problematic areas and to lay out a critical and programmatic projection of the solutions which can be expected in the foreseeable future. All this with a keen awareness that, ten years later, someone will be asked to repeat the same exercise.

I found it difficult to live up, in minimal good faith, to the requirements of this program and could only try to explain, as concisely as possible, why the main theoretical interest of literary theory consists in the impossibility of its definition. The Committee rightly judged that this was an inauspicious way to achieve the pedagogical objectives of the volume and commissioned another article. I thought their decision altogether justified, as well as interesting in its implications for the teaching of literature.

I tell this for two reasons. First, to explain the traces in the article of the original assignment which account for the awkwardness of trying to be more retrospective and more general than one can legitimately hope to be. But secondly, because the predicament also reveals a question of general interest: that of the relationship between the scholarship (the key word in the title of the MLA volume), the theory, and the teaching of literature.

Overfacile opinion notwithstanding, teaching is not primarily an intersubjective relationship between people but a cognitive process in which self and other are only tangentially and contiguously involved. The only teaching worthy of the name is scholarly, not personal; analogies between teaching and various aspects of show business or guidance counselling are more often than not excuses for having abdicated the task. Scholarship has, in principle, to be eminently teachable. In the case of literature, such scholarship involves at least two complementary areas: historical and philological facts as the preparatory condition for understanding, and methods of reading or interpretation. The latter is admittedly an open discipline, which can, however, hope to evolve by rational means, despite internal crises, controversies and polemics. As a controlled reflection on the formation of method, theory rightly proves to be entirely compatible with teaching, and one can think of numerous important theoreticians who are or were also prominent scholars. A question arises only if a tension develops between methods and the knowledge which those methods allow one to reach. If there is indeed something about literature, as such, which allows for a discrepancy between truth and method, between *Wahrheit* and *Methode*, then scholarship and theory are no longer necessarily compatible; as a first casualty of this complication, the notion of 'literature as such' as well as the clear distinction between history and interpretation can no longer be taken for granted. For a method that cannot be made to suit the 'truth' of its object can only teach delusion. Various developments, not only in the contemporary scene but in the long and complicated history of literary and linguistic instruction, reveal symptoms that suggest that such a difficulty is an inherent focus of the discourse about literature. These uncertainties are manifest in the hostility directed at theory in the name of ethical and aesthetic values, as well as in the recuperative attempts of theoreticians to reassert their own subservience to these values. The most effective of these attacks will denounce theory as an obstacle to scholarship and, consequently, to teaching. It is worth examining whether, and why, this is the case. For if this is indeed so, then it is better to fail in teaching what should not be taught than to succeed in teaching what is not true.

A general statement about literary theory should not, in theory, start from pragmatic considerations. It should address such questions as the definition of literature (what is literature?) and discuss the distinction between literary and non-literary uses of language, as well as between literary and non-verbal forms of art. It should then proceed to the descriptive taxonomy of the various aspects and species of the literary genus and to the normative rules that are bound to follow from such a classification. Or, if one rejects a scholastic for a phenomenological model, one should attempt a phenomenology of the literary activity as writing, reading or both, or of the literary work as the product, the correlate of such an activity. Whatever the approach taken (and several other theoretically justifiable starting-points can be imagined) it is certain that considerable difficulties will arise at once, difficulties that cut so deep that even the most elementary task of scholar-ship, the delimitation of the corpus and the *état présent* of the question, is bound to end in confusion, not necessarily because the bibliography is so large but because it is impossible to fix its borderlines. Such predictable difficulties have not prevented many writers on literature from proceeding along theoretical rather than pragmatic lines, often with considerable success. It can be shown however that, in all cases, this success depends on the power of a system (philosophical, religious or ideological) that may well remain implicit but that determines an *a priori* conception of what is 'literary' by starting out from the premises of the system rather than from the literary thing itself – if such a 'thing' indeed exists. This last qualification is of course a real question which in fact accounts for the predictability of the difficulties just alluded to: if the condition of existence of an entity is itself particularly critical, then the theory of this entity is bound to fall back into the pragmatic. The difficult and inconclusive history of literary theory indicates that this is indeed the case for literature in an even more manifest manner than for other verbalized occurrences such as jokes, for example, or even dreams. The attempt to treat literature theoretically may as well resign itself to the fact that it has to start out from empirical considerations.

Pragmatically speaking, then, we know that there has been, over the last fifteen to twenty years, a strong interest in something called literary theory and that, in the United States, this interest has at times coincided with the importation and reception of foreign, mostly but not always continental influences. We also know that this wave of interest now seems to be receding as some satiation or disappointment sets in after the initial enthusiasm. Such an ebb and flow is natural enough, but it remains interesting, in this case, because it makes the depth of the resistance to literary theory so manifest. It is a recurrent strategy of any anxiety to defuse what it considers threatening by magnification or minimization, by attributing to it claims to power of which it is bound to fall short. If a cat is called a tiger it can easily be dismissed as a paper tiger; the question remains however why one was so scared of the cat in the first place. The same tactic works in reverse: calling the cat a mouse and then deriding it for its pretence to be mighty. Rather than being drawn into this polemical whirlpool, it might be better to try to call the cat a cat and to document, however briefly, the contemporary version of the resistance to theory in this country.

The predominant trends in North American literary criticism, before the 1960s, were certainly not averse to theory, if by theory one understands the rooting of literary exegesis and of critical evaluation in a system of some conceptual generality. Even the most intuitive, empirical and theoretically low-key writers on literature made use of a minimal set of concepts (tone, organic form, allusion, tradition, historical situation, etc.) of at least some general import. In several other cases, the interest in theory was publicly asserted and practised. A broadly shared methodology, more or less overtly proclaimed, links together such influential text books of the era as *Understanding Poetry* (Brooks and Warren), *Theory of Literature* (Wellek and Warren) and *The Fields of Light* (Reuben Brower) or such theoretically oriented works as *The Mirror and the Lamp*, *Language as Gesture*, and *The Verbal Icon*.

Yet, with the possible exception of Kenneth Burke and, in some respects, Northrop Frye, none of these authors would have considered themselves theoreticians in the post-1960 sense of the term, nor did their work provoke as strong reactions, positive or negative, as that of later theoreticians. There were polemics, no doubt, and differences in approach that cover a wide spectrum of divergencies, yet the fundamental curriculum of literary studies as well as the talent and training expected for them were not being seriously challenged. New Critical approaches experienced no difficulty fitting into the academic establishments without their practitioners having to betray their literary sensibilities in any way; several of its representatives pursued successful parallel careers as poets or novelists next to their academic functions. Nor did they experience difficulties with regard to a national tradition which, though certainly less tyrannical than its European counterparts, is nevertheless far from powerless. The perfect embodiment of the New Criticism remains, in many respects, the personality and the ideology of T. S. Eliot, a combination of original talent, traditional learning, verbal wit and moral earnestness, an Anglo-American blend of intellectual gentility not so repressed as not to afford tantalising glimpses of darker psychic and political depths, but without breaking the surface of an ambivalent decorum that has its own complacencies and seductions. The normative principles of such a literary ambiance are cultural and ideological rather than theoretical, oriented towards the integrity of a social and historical self rather than towards the impersonal consistency that theory requires. Culture allows for, indeed advocates, a degree of cosmopolitanism, and the literary spirit of the American Academy of the fifties was anything but provincial. It had no difficulty appreciating and assimilating outstanding products of a kindred spirit that originated in Europe: Curtius, Auerbach, Croce, Spitzer, Alonso, Valéry and also, with the exception of some of his works, J. P. Sartre. The inclusion of Sartre in this list is important, for it indicates that the dominant cultural code we are trying to evoke cannot simply be assimilated to a political polarity of the left and the right, of the academic and the non-academic, of Greenwich Village and Gambier, Ohio. Politically oriented and predominantly non-academic journals, of which the *Partisan Review* of the fifties remains the best example, did not (after due allowance is made for all proper reservations and distinctions) stand in any genuine opposition to the New Critical approaches. The broad, though negative, consensus that brings these extremely diverse trends and individuals together is their shared resistance to theory. This diagnosis is borne out by the arguments and complicities that have since come to light in a more articulate opposition to the common opponent.

The interest of these considerations would be at most anecdotal (the historical impact of twentieth-century literary discussion being so slight) if it were not for the theoretical implications of the resistance to theory. The local manifestations of this resistance are themselves systematic enough to warrant one's interest.

What is it that is being threatened by the approaches to literature that developed during the sixties and that now, under a variety of designations, make up the ill-defined and somewhat chaotic field of literary theory? These approaches cannot be simply equated with any particular method or country. Structuralism was not the only trend to dominate the stage, not even in France, and structuralism as well as semiology are inseparable from prior tendencies in the Slavic domain. In Germany, the main impulses have come from other directions, from the Frankfurt school and more orthodox Marxists, from post-Husserlian phenomenology and post-Heideggerian hermeneutics, with only minor inroads made by structural analysis. All these trends have had their share of influence in the United States, in more or less productive combinations with nationally rooted concerns. Only a nationally or personally competitive view of history would wish to hierarchize such hard-to-label movements. The possibility of doing literary theory, which is by no means to be taken for granted, has itself become a consciously reflected-upon question and those who have progressed furthest in this question are the most controversial but also the best sources of information. This certainly includes several of the names loosely connected with structuralism, broadly enough defined to include Saussure, Jakobson and Barthes as well as Greimas and Althusser, that is to say, so broadly defined as to be no longer of use as a meaningful historical term.

Literary theory can be said to come into being when the approach to literary texts is no longer based on non-linguistic, that is to say historical and aesthetic, considerations or, to put it somewhat less crudely, when the object of discussion is no longer the meaning or the value but the modalities of production and of reception of meaning and of value prior to their establishment – the implication being that this establishment is problematic enough to require an autonomous discipline of critical investigation to consider its possibility and its status. Literary history, even when considered at furthest remove from the platitudes of positivistic historicism, is still the history of an understanding of which the possibility is taken for granted. The question of the relationship between aesthetics and meaning is more complex, since aesthetics apparently has to do with the *effect* of meaning rather than with its content *per se*. But aesthetics is in fact, ever since its development just before and with Kant, a phenomenalism of a process of meaning and understanding, and it may be naive in that it postulates (as its name indicates) a phenomenology of art and of literature which may well be what is at issue. Aesthetics is part of a universal system of philosophy rather than a specific theory. In the nineteenth-century philosophical tradition, Nietzsche's challenge of the system erected by Kant, Hegel and their successors, is a version of the general question of philosophy. Nietzsche's critique of metaphysics includes, or starts out from, the aesthetic, and the same could be argued for Heidegger. The invocation of prestigious philosophical names does not intimate that the present-day development of literary theory is a by-product of larger philosophical speculations. In some rare cases, a direct link may exist between philosophy and literary theory. More frequently, however, contemporary literary theory is a relatively autonomous version of questions that also surface, in a different context, in philosophy, though not necessarily in a clearer and more rigorous form. Philosophy, in England as well as on the Continent, is less freed from traditional patterns than it sometimes pretends to believe and the prominent, though never dominant, place of aesthetics among the main components of the system is a constitutive part of this system. It is therefore not surprising that contemporary literary theory came into being from outside philosophy and sometimes in conscious rebellion against the weight of its tradition. Literary theory may now well have become a legitimate concern of philosophy but it cannot be assimilated to it, either factually or theoretically. It contains a necessarily pragmatic moment that certainly weakens it as theory but that adds a subversive element of unpredictability and makes it something of a wild card in the serious game of the theoretical disciplines.

The advent of theory, the break that is now so often being deplored and that sets it aside from literary history and from literary criticism, occurs with the introduction of linguistic terminology in the metalanguage about literature. By linguistic terminology is meant a terminology that designates reference prior to designating the referent and takes into account, in the consideration of the world, the referential function of language or, to be somewhat more specific, that considers reference as a function of language and not necessarily as an intuition. Intuition implies perception, consciousness, experience, and leads at once into the world of logic and of understanding with all its correlatives, among which aesthetics occupies a prominent place. The assumption that there can be a science of language which is not necessarily a logic leads to the development of a terminology which is not necessarily aesthetic. Contemporary literary theory comes into its own in such events as the application of Saussurian linguistics to literary texts.

The affinity between structural linguistics and literary texts is not as obvious as, with the hindsight of history, it now may seem. Peirce, Saussure, Sapir and Bloomfield were not originally concerned with literature at all but with the scientific foundations of linguistics. But the interest of philologists such as Roman Jakobson or literary critics such as Roland Barthes in semiology reveals the natural attraction of literature to a theory of linguistic signs. By considering language as a system of signs and of signification rather than as an established pattern of meanings, one displaces or even suspends the traditional barriers between literary and presumably non-literary uses of language and liberates the corpus from the secular weight of textual canonization. The results of the encounter between semiology and literature went considerably further than those of many other theoretical models – philological, psychological or classically epistemological – which writers on literature in quest of such models had tried out before. The responsiveness of literary texts to semiotic analysis is visible in that, whereas other approaches were unable to reach beyond observations that could be paraphrased or translated in terms of common knowledge, these analyses revealed patterns that could only be described in terms of their own, specifically linguistic, aspects. The linguistics of semiology and of literature apparently have something in common that only their shared perspective can detect and that pertains distinctively to them. The definition of this something, often referred to as literariness, has become the object of literary theory.

Literariness, however, is often misunderstood in a way that has provoked much of the confusion which dominates today's polemics. It is frequently assumed, for instance, that literariness is another word for, or another mode of, aesthetic response. The use, in conjunction with literariness, of such terms as style and stylistics, form or even 'poetry' (as in 'the poetry of grammar'), all of which carry strong aesthetic connotations, helps to foster this confusion, even among those who first put the term in circulation. Roland Barthes, for example, in an essay properly and revealingly dedicated to Roman Jakobson, speaks eloquently of the writer's quest for a perfect coincidence of the phonic properties of a word with its signifying function.

> We would also wish to insist on the Cratylism of the name (and of the sign) in Proust... Proust sees the relationship between signifier and signified as motivated, the one copying the other and representing in its material form the signified essence of the thing (and not the thing itself)... This realism (in the scholastic sense of the word), which conceives of names as the 'copy' of the ideas, has taken, in Proust, a radical form. But one may well ask whether it is not more or less consciously present in all writing and whether it is possible to be a writer without some sort of belief in the natural relationship between names and essences. The poetic function, in the widest sense of the word, would thus be defined by a Cratylian awareness of the sign, and the writer would be the conveyor of this secular myth which wants language to imitate the idea and which, contrary to the teachings of linguistic science, thinks of signs as motivated signs.[1]

To the extent that Cratylism assumes a convergence of the phenomenal aspects of language, as sound, with its signifying function as referent, it is an aesthetically oriented conception; one could, in fact, without distortion, consider aesthetic theory, including its most systematic formulation in Hegel, as the complete unfolding of the model of which the Cratylian conception of language is a version. Hegel's somewhat cryptic reference to Plato, in the *Aesthetics*, may well be interpreted in this sense. Barthes and Jakobson often seem to invite a purely aesthetic reading, yet there is a part of their statement that moves in the opposite direction. For the convergence of sound and meaning celebrated by Barthes in Proust and, as Gérard Genette has decisively shown,[2] later dismantled by Proust himself as a seductive temptation to mystified minds, is also considered here to be a mere *effect* which language can perfectly well achieve, but which bears no substantial relationship, by analogy or by ontologically grounded imitation, to anything beyond that particular effect. It is a rhetorical rather than an aesthetic function of language, an identifiable trope (paranomasis) that operates on the level of the signifier and contains no responsible pronouncement on the nature of the world – despite its powerful potential to create the opposite illusion. The phenomenality of the signifier, as sound, is unquestionably involved in the correspondence between the name and the thing named, but the link, the relationship between word and thing is not phenomenal but conventional.

This gives the language considerable freedom from referential restraint, but it makes it epistemologically highly suspect and volatile, since its use can no longer be said to be determined by considerations of truth and falsehood, good and evil, beauty and ugliness, or pleasure and pain. Whenever this autonomous potential of language can be revealed by analysis, we are dealing with literariness and, in fact, with literature as the place where this negative knowledge about reliability of linguistic utterance is made available. The ensuing foregrounding of material, phenomenal aspects of the signifier creates a strong illusion of aesthetic seduction at the very moment when the actual aesthetic function has been, at the very least, suspended. It is inevitable that semiology or similarly oriented methods be considered formalistic, in the sense of being aesthetically rather than semantically valorized, but the inevitability of such an interpretation does not make it less aberrant. Literature involves the voiding, rather than the affirmation, of aesthetic categories. One of the consequences of this is that, whereas we have traditionally been accustomed to reading literature by analogy with the plastic arts and with music, we now have to recognise the necessity of a non-perceptual, linguistic moment in painting and in music, and learn to *read* pictures rather than to *imagine* meaning.

If literariness is not an aesthetic quality, it is also not primarily mimetic. Mimesis becomes one trope among others, language choosing to imitate a non-verbal entity just as paranomasis 'imitates' a sound without any claim to identity (or reflection on difference) between the verbal and non-verbal elements. The most misleading representation of literariness, and also the most recurrent objection to contemporary literary theory, considers it as pure verbalism, as a denial of the reality principle in the name of absolute fictions, and for reasons that are said to be ethically and politically shameful. The attack reflects the anxiety of the aggressors rather than the guilt of the accused. By allowing for the necessity of a non-phenomenal linguistics, one frees the discourse on literature from naive oppositions between fiction and reality, which are themselves an offspring of an uncritically mimetic conception of art. In a genuine semiology as well as in other linguistically oriented theories, the referential function of language is not being denied – far from it; what is in question is its authority as a model for natural or phenomenal cognition. Literature is fiction not because it somehow refuses to acknowledge 'reality', but because it is not *a priori* certain that language functions according to principles which are those, or which are *like* those, of the phenomenal world. It is therefore not *a priori* certain that literature is a reliable source of information about anything but its own language.

It would be unfortunate, for example, to confuse the materiality of the signifier with the materiality of what it signifies. This may seem obvious enough on the level of light and sound, but it is less so with regard to the more general phenomenality of space, time or especially of the self: no one in his right mind will try to grow grapes by the luminosity of the word 'day', but it is very difficult not to conceive the pattern of one's past and future existence as in accordance with temporal and spatial schemes that belong to fictional narratives and not to the world. This does not mean that fictional narratives are not part of the world and of reality; their impact upon the world may well be all too strong for comfort. What we call ideology is precisely the confusion of linguistic with natural reality, of reference with phenomenalism. It follows that, more than any other mode of inquiry, including economics, the linguistics of literariness is a powerful and indispensable tool in the unmasking of ideological aberrations, as well as a determining factor in accounting for their occurrence. Those who reproach literary theory for being oblivious to social and historical (that is to say ideological) reality are merely stating their fear at having their own ideological mystifications exposed by the tool they are trying to discredit. They are, in short, very poor readers of Marx's *German Ideology*.

In these all too summary evocations of arguments that have been much more extensively and convincingly made by others, we begin to perceive some of the answers to the initial question: what is it about literary theory that is so threatening that it provokes such strong resistances and attacks? It upsets rooted ideologies by revealing the mechanics of their workings; it goes against a powerful philosophical tradition of which aesthetics is a prominent part; it upsets the established canon of literary works and blurs the borderlines between literary and non-literary discourse. By implication, it may also reveal the links between ideologies and philosophy. All this is ample enough reason for suspicion, but not a satisfying answer to the question. For it makes the tension between contemporary literary theory and the tradition of literary studies appear as a mere historical conflict between two modes of thought that happen to hold the stage at the same time. If the conflict is merely historical, in the literal sense, it is of limited theoretical interest, a passing squall in the intellectual weather of the world. As a matter of fact, the arguments in favor of the legitimacy of literary theory are so compelling that it seems useless to concern oneself with the conflict at all. Certainly, none of the objections to theory, presented again and again, always misinformed or based on crude misunderstandings of such terms as mimesis, fiction, reality, ideology, reference and, for that matter, relevance, can be said to be of genuine rhetorical interest.

It may well be, however, that the development of literary theory is itself over-determined by complications inherent in its very project and unsettling with regard to its status as a scientific discipline. Resistance may be a built-in constituent of its discourse, in a manner that would be inconceivable in the natural sciences and unmentionable in the social sciences. It may well be, in other words, that the polemical opposition, the systematic non-understanding and misrepresentation, the unsubstantial but eternally recurrent objections, are the displaced symptoms of a resistance inherent in the theoretical enterprise itself. To claim that this would be a sufficient reason not to envisage doing literary theory would be like rejecting anatomy because it has failed to cure mortality. The real debate of literary theory is not with its polemical opponents but rather with its own methodological assumptions and possibilities. Rather than asking why literary theory is threatening, we should perhaps ask why it has such difficulty going about its business and why it lapses so readily either into the language of self-justification and self-defence or else into the overcompensation of a programmatically euphoric utopianism. Such insecurity about its own project calls for self-analysis, if one is to understand the frustrations that attend upon its practitioners, even when they seem to dwell in serene methodological self-assurance. And if these difficulties are indeed an integral part of the problem, then they will have to be, to some extent, a-historical in the temporal sense of the term. The way in which they are encountered on the present local literary scene as a resistance to the introduction of linguistic terminology in aesthetic and historical discourse about literature is only one particular version of a question that cannot be reduced to a specific historical situation and called modern, post-modern, post-classical or romantic (not even in Hegel's sense of the term), although its compulsive way of forcing itself upon us in the guise of a system of historical periodization is certainly part of its problematic nature. Such difficulties can be read in the text of literary theory at all times, at whatever historical moment one wishes to select. One of the main achievements of the present theoretical trends is to have restored some awareness of this fact. Classical, medieval and Renaissance literary theory is now often being read in a way that knows enough about what it is doing not to wish to call itself 'modern.'

We return, then, to the original question in an attempt to broaden the discussion enough to inscribe the polemics inside the question rather than having them determine it. The resistance to theory is a resistance to the use of language about language. It is therefore a resistance to language itself or to the possibility that language contains factors or functions that cannot be reduced to intuition. But we seem to assume all too readily that, when we refer to something called 'language', we know what it is we are talking about, although there is probably no word to be found in the language that is as overdetermined, self-evasive, disfigured and disfiguring as 'language'. Even if we choose to consider it at a safe remove from any theoretical model, in the pragmatic history of 'language', not as a concept, but as a didactic assignment that no human being can bypass, we soon find ourselves confronted by theoretical enigmas. The most familiar and general of all linguistic models, the classical *trivium*, which considers the sciences of language as consisting of grammar, rhetoric and logic (or dialectics), is in fact a set of unresolved tensions powerful enough to have generated an infinitely prolonged discourse of endless frustration of which contemporary literary theory, even at its most self-assured, is one more chapter. The difficulties extend to the internal articulations between the constituent parts as well as to the articulation of the field of language with the knowledge of the world in general, the link between the trivium and the *quadrivium*, which covers the non-verbal sciences of number (arithmetic), of space (geometry), of motion (astronomy) and of time (music). In the history of philosophy, this link is traditionally, as well as substantially, accomplished by way of logic, the area where the rigor of the linguistic discourse about itself matches up with the rigor of the mathematical discourse about the world. Seventeenth-century epistemology, for instance, at the moment when the relationship between philosophy and mathematics is particularly close, holds up the language of what it calls geometry (*mos geometricus*), and which in fact includes the homogeneous concatenation between space, time and number, as the sole model of coherence and economy. Reasoning *more geometrico* is said to be 'almost the only mode of reasoning that is infallible, because it is the only one to adhere to the true method, whereas all other ones are by natural necessity in a degree of confusion of which only geometrical minds can be aware.[3] This is a clear instance of the interconnection between a science of the phenomenal world and a science of language conceived as definitional logic, the pre-condition for a correct axiomatic-deductive, synthetic reasoning. The possibility of thus circulating freely between logic and mathematics has its own complex and problematic history as well as its contemporary equivalences with a different logic and a different mathematics. What matters for our present argument is that this articulation of the sciences of language with the mathematical sciences represents a particularly compelling version of a continuity between a theory of language, as logic, and the knowledge of the phenomenal world to which mathematics give access. In such a system, the place of aesthetics is preordained and by no means alien, provided the priority of logic, in the model of the *trivium*, is not being questioned. For even if one assumes, for the sake of argument and against a great deal of historical evidence, that the link between logic and the natural sciences is secure, this leaves open the question, within the confines of the *trivium* itself, of the relationship between grammar, rhetoric and logic. And this is the point at which literariness, the use of language that foregrounds the rhetorical over the grammatical and the logical function, intervenes as a decisive but unsettling element which, in a variety of modes and aspects, disrupts the inner balance of the model and, consequently, its outward extension to the non-verbal world as well.

Logic and grammar seem to have a natural enough affinity for each other and, in the tradition of Cartesian linguistics, the grammarians of Port-Royal experienced little difficulty at being logicians as well. The same claim persists today in very different methods and terminologies that nevertheless maintain the same orientation toward the universality that logic shares with science. Replying to those who oppose the singularity of specific texts to the scientific generality of the semiotic project, A.J. Greimas disputes the right to use the dignity of 'grammar' to describe a reading that would not be committed to universality. Those who have doubts about the semiotic method, he writes, 'postulate the necessity of constructing a grammar for each particular text. But the essence (*le propre*) of a grammar is its ability to account for a large number of texts, and the metaphorical use of the term ... fails to hide the fact that one has, in fact, given up on the semiotic project.[14] There is no doubt that what is here prudently called 'a large number' implies the hope at least of a future model that would in fact be applicable to the generation of all texts. Again, it is not our present purpose to discuss the validity of this methodological optimism, but merely to offer it as an instance of the persistent symbiosis between grammar and logic. It is clear that, for Greimas as for the entire tradition to which he belongs, the grammatical and the logical function of language are co-extensive. Grammar is an isotope of logic.

It follows that, as long as it remains grounded in grammar, any theory of language, including a literary one, does not threaten what we hold to be the underlying principle of all cognitive and aesthetic linguistic systems. Grammar stands in the service of logic which, in turn, allows for the passage to the knowledge of the world. The study of grammar, the first of the *artes liberales*, is the necessary pre-condition for scientific and humanistic knowledge. As long as it leaves this principle intact, there is nothing threatening about literary theory. The continuity between theory and phenomenalism is asserted and preserved by the system itself. Difficulties occur only when it is no longer possible to ignore the epistemological thrust of the rhetorical dimension of discourse, that is, when it is no longer possible to keep it in its place as a mere adjunct, a mere ornament within the semantic function.

The uncertain relationship between grammar and rhetoric (as opposed to that between grammar and logic) is apparent, in the history of the *trivium*, in the uncertain status of figures of speech or tropes, a component of language that straddles the disputed borderlines between the two areas. Tropes used to be part of the study of grammar but were also considered to be the semantic agent of the specific function (or effect) that rhetoric performs as persuasion as well as meaning. Tropes, unlike grammar, pertain primordially to language. They are text-producing functions that are not necessarily patterned on a non-verbal entity, whereas grammar is by definition capable of extra-linguistic generalization. The latent tension between rhetoric and grammar precipitates out in the problem of reading, the process that necessarily partakes of both. It turns out that the resistance to theory is in fact a resistance to reading, a resistance that is perhaps at its more effective, in contemporary studies, in the methodologies that call themselves theories of reading but nevertheless avoid the function they claim as their object.

What is meant when we assert that the study of literary texts is necessarily dependent on an act of reading, or when we claim that this act is being systematically avoided? Certainly more than the tautology that one has to have read at least some parts, however small, of a text (or read some part, however small, of a text about this text) in order to be able to make a statement about it. Common as it may be, criticism by hearsay is only rarely held up as exemplary. To stress the by no means self-evident necessity of reading implies at least two things. First of all, it implies that literature is not a transparent message in which it can be taken for granted that the distinction between the message and the means of communication is clearly established. Second, and more problematically, it implies that the grammatical decoding of a text leaves a residue of indetermination that has to be, but cannot be, resolved by grammatical means, however extensively conceived. The extension of grammar to include para-figural dimensions is in fact the most remarkable and debatable strategy of contemporary semiology, especially in the study of syntagmatic and narrative structures. The codification of contextual elements well beyond the syntactical limits of the sentence leads to the systematic study of metaphrastic dimensions and has considerably refined and expanded the knowledge of textual codes. It Is equally clear, however, that this extension is always strategically directed towards the replacement of rhetorical figures by grammatical codes. The tendency to replace a rhetorical by a grammatical terminology (to speak of hypotaxis, for instance, to designate anamorphic or metonymic tropes) is part of an explicit program, a program that is entirely admirable in its intent since it tends towards the mastering and the clarification of meaning. The replacement of a hermeneutic by a semiotic model, of interpretation by decoding, would represent, in view of the baffling historical instability of textual meanings (including, of course, those of canonical texts) a considerable progress. Much of the hesitation associated with 'reading' could thus be dispelled.

The argument can be made, however, that no grammatical decoding, however refined, could claim to reach the determining figural dimensions of a text. There are elements in all texts that are by no means ungrammatical, but whose semantic function is not grammatically definable, neither in themselves nor in context. Do we have to interpret the genitive in the title of Keats' unfinished epic *The Fall of Hyperion* as meaning 'Hyperion's fall', the case story of the defeat of an older by a newer power, the very recognizable story from which Keats indeed started out but from which he increasingly strayed away, or as 'Hyperion falling', the much less specific but more disquieting evocation of an actual process of falling, regardless of its beginning, its end or the identity of the entity to whom it befalls to be falling. This story is indeed told in the later fragment entitled *The Fall of Hyperion*, but it is told about a character who resembles Apollo rather than Hyperion, the same Apollo who, in the first version (called *Hyperion*), should definitely be triumphantly standing rather than falling if Keats had not been compelled to interrupt, for no apparent reason, the story of

Apollo's triumph. Does the title tell us that Hyperion is fallen and that Apollo stands, or does it tell us that Hyperion and Apollo (and Keats, whom it is hard to distinguish, at times, from Apollo) are interchangeable in that all of them are necessarily and constantly falling? Both readings are grammatically correct, but it is impossible to decide from the context (the ensuring narrative) which version is the right one. The narrative context suits neither and both at the same time, and one is tempted to suggest that the fact that Keats was unable to complete either version manifests the impossibility, for him as for us, of reading his own title. One could then read the word 'Hyperion' in the title *The Fall of Hyperion* figurally, or, if one wishes, intertextually, as referring not to the historical or mythological character but as referring to the title of Keats' own earlier text (*Hyperion*). But are we then telling the story of the failure of the first text as the success of the second, the Fall of *Hyperion* as the Triumph of *The Fall of Hyperion*? Manifestly yes, but not quite, since the second text also fails to be concluded. Or are we telling the story of why all texts, as texts, can always be said to be falling? Manifestly yes, but not quite, either, since the story of the fall of the first version, as told in the second, applies to the first version only and could not legitimately be read as meaning also the fall of *The Fall of Hyperion*. The undecidability involves the figural or literal status of the proper name Hyperion as well as of the verb falling, and is, thus a matter of figuration and not of grammar. In 'Hyperion's Fall', the word 'fall' is plainly figural, the representation of a figural fall, and we, as readers, read this fall standing up. But in 'Hyperion falling', this is not so clearly the case, for if Hyperion can be Apollo and Apollo can be Keats, then he can also be us and his figural (or symbolic) fall becomes his and our literal falling as well. The difference between the two readings is itself structured as a trope. And it matters a great deal how we read the title, as an exercise not only in semantics, but in what the text actually does to us. Faced with the ineluctable necessity to come to a decision, no grammatical or logical analysis can help us out. Just as Keats had to break off his narrative, the reader has to break off his understanding at the very moment when he is most directly engaged and summoned by the text. One could hardly expect to find solace in this 'fearful symmetry' between the author's and the reader's plight since, at this point, the symmetry is no longer a formal but an actual trap, and the question no longer 'merely' theoretical.

This undoing of theory, this disturbance of the stable cognitive field that extends from grammar to logic to a general science of man and of the phenomenal world, can in its turn be made into a theoretical project of rhetorical analysis that will reveal the inadequacy of grammatical models of non-reading. Rhetoric, by its actively negative relationship to grammar and to logic, certainly undoes the claims of the trivium (and by extension, of language) to be an epistemologically stable construct. The resistance to theory is a resistance to the rhetorical or tropological dimension of language, a dimension which is perhaps more explicitly in the foreground in literature (broadly conceived) than in other verbal manifestations or – to be somewhat less vague – which can be revealed in any verbal event when it is read textually. Since grammar as well as figuration is an integral part of reading, it follows that reading will be a negative process in which the grammatical cognition is undone, at all times, by its rhetorical displacement. The model of the *trivium* contains within itself the pseudo-dialectic of its own undoing and its history tells the story of this dialectic.

This conclusion allows for a somewhat more systematic description of the contemporary theoretical scene. This scene is dominated by an increased stress on reading as a theoretical problem or, as it is sometimes erroneously phrased, by an increased stress on the reception rather than on the production of texts. It is in this area that the most fruitful exchanges have come about between writers and journals of various countries and that the most interesting dialogue has developed between literary theory and other disciplines, in the arts as well as in linguistics, philosophy and the social sciences. A straightforward *report* on the present state of literary theory in the United States would have to stress the emphasis on reading, a direction which is already present, moreover, in the New Critical tradition of the forties and the fifties. The methods are now more technical, but the contemporary interest in a poetics of literature is clearly linked, traditionally enough, to the problems of reading. And since the models that are being used certainly are no longer *simply* intentional and centered on an identifiable self, nor *simply* hermeneutic in the postulation of a single originary, pre-figural and absolute text, it would appear that this concentration on reading would lead to the rediscovery of the theoretical difficulties associated with rhetoric. This is indeed the case, to some extent; but not quite. Perhaps the most instructive aspect of contemporary theory is the refinement of the techniques by which the threat inherent in rhetorical analysis is being avoided at the very moment when the efficacy of these techniques has progressed so far that the rhetorical obstacles to understanding can no longer be mistranslated in thematic and phenomenal commonplaces. The resistance to theory which, as we saw, is a resistance to reading, appears in its most rigorous and theoretically elaborated form among the theoreticians of reading who dominate the contemporary theoretical scene.

It would be a relatively easy, though lengthy, process to show that this is so for theoreticians of reading who, like Greimas or, on a more refined level, Riffaterre or, in a very different mode, H. R. Jauss or Wolfgang Iser – all of whom have a definite, though sometimes occult, influence on literary theory in this country – are committed to the use of grammatical models or, in the case of *Rezeptionsaesthetik*, to traditional hermeneutic models that do not allow for the problematization of the phenomenalism of reading and therefore remain uncritically confined within a theory of literature rooted in aesthetics. Such an argument would be easy to make because, once a reader has become aware of the rhetorical dimensions of a text, he will not be amiss in finding textual instances that are irreduceable to grammar or to historically determined meaning, provided only he is willing to acknowledge what he is bound to notice. The problem quickly becomes the more baffling one of having to account for the shared reluctance to acknowledge the obvious. But the argument would be lengthy because it has to involve a textual analysis that cannot avoid being somewhat elaborate; one can succinctly suggest the grammatical indetermination of a title such as *The Fall of Hyperion*, but to confront such an undecidable enigma with the critical reception and reading of Keat's text requires some space.

The demonstration is less easy (though perhaps less ponderous) in the case of theoreticians of reading whose avoidance of rhetoric takes another turn. We have witnessed, in recent years, a strong interest in certain elements in language whose function is not only not dependent on any form of phenomenalism but on any form of cognition as well, and which thus excludes, or postpones, the consideration of tropes, ideologies, etc., from a reading that would be primarily performative. In some cases, a link is reintroduced between performance, grammar, logic, and stable referential meaning, and the resulting theories (as in the case of Ohmann) are not in essence distinct from those of avowed grammarians or semioticians. But the most astute practitioners of a speech act theory of reading avoid this relapse and rightly insist on the necessity to keep the actual performance of speech acts, which is conventional rather than cognitive, separate from its causes and effects – to keep, in their terminology, the illocutionary force separate from its perlocutionary function. Rhetoric, understood as persuasion, is forcefully banished (like Coriolanus) from the performative moment and exiled in the affective area of perlocution. Stanley Fish, in a masterful essay, convincingly makes this point.[5] What awakens one's suspicion about this conclusion is that it relegates persuasion, which is indeed inseparable from rhetoric, to a purely affective and intentional realm and makes no allowance for modes of persuasion which are no less rhetorical and no less at work in literary texts, but which are of the order of persuasion by *proof* rather than persuasion by seduction. Thus to empty rhetoric of its epistemological impact is possible only because its tropological, figural functions are being bypassed. It is as if, to return for a moment to the model of the *trivium*, *rhetoric* could be isolated from the generality that grammar and logic have in common and considered as a mere correlative of an illocutionary power. The equation of rhetoric with psychology rather than with epistemology opens up dreary prospects of pragmatic banality, all the drearier if compared to the brilliance of the performative analysis. Speech act theories of reading in fact repeat, in a much more effective way, the grammatization of the *trivium* at the expense of rhetoric. For the characterization of the performative as sheer convention reduces it in effect to a grammatical code among others. The relationship between trope and performance is actually closer but more disruptive than what is here being proposed. Nor is this relationship properly captured by reference to a supposedly 'creative' aspect of performance, a notion with which Fish rightly takes issue. The performative power of language can be called positional, which differs considerably from conventional as well as from 'creatively' (or, in the technical sense, intentionally) constitutive. Speech act oriented theories of reading read only to the extent that they prepare the way for the rhetorical reading they avoid.

But the same is still true even if a 'truly' rhetorical reading that would stay clear of any undue phenomenalization or of any undue grammatical or performative codification of the text could be conceived – something which is not necessarily impossible and for which the aims and methods of literary theory should certainly strive. Such a reading would indeed appear as the methodical undoing of the grammatical construct and, in its systematic disarticulation of the *trivium*, will be theoretically sound as well as effective. Technically correct rhetorical readings may be boring, monotonous, predictable and unpleasant, but they are irrefutable. They are also totalizing (and potentially totalitarian) for since the structures and functions they expose do not lead to the knowledge of an entity (such as language) but are an unreliable process of knowledge production that prevents all entities, including linguistic entities, from coming into discourse as such, they are indeed universals, consistently defective models of language's impossibility to be a model language. They are, always in theory, the most elastic theoretical and dialectical model to end all models and they can rightly claim to contain within their own defective selves all the other defective models of reading-avoidance, referential, semiological, grammatical, performative, logical, or whatever. They are theory and not theory at the same time, the universal theory of the impossibility of theory. To the extent however that they are theory, that is to say teachable, generalizable and highly responsive to systematization, readings, like the other kinds, still avoid and resist the reading they advocate. Nothing can overcome the resistance to theory since theory is itself this resistance. The loftier the aims and the better the methods of literary theory, the less possible it becomes. Yet literary theory is not in danger of going under; it cannot help but flourish, and the more it is resisted, the more it flourishes, since the language it speaks is the language of self-resistance. What remains impossible to decide is whether this flourishing is a triumph or a fall.

Notes

1 Roland Barthes, 'Proust et les noms' in *To honor Roman Jakobson* (The Hague, 1967) part I, pp. 157ff.
2 'Proust et le langage indirect' in *Figures II* (Paris, 1969).
3 Pascal, 'De l'esprit géométrique et de l'art de persuader', in *Oeuvres complètes* presented by L. Lafuma (Paris, Editions du Seuil, 1963), pp. 349ff.
4 A.J. Greimas, *Du Sens* (Paris, Editions du Seuil, 1970), p. 13.
5 Stanley Fish, 'How to do things with Austin and Searle: Speech Act Theory and Literary Criticism', in *MLN* 91 (1976), pp. 983–1025. See especially p. 1008.

23   Barbara Johnson,

'Gender Theory and The Yale School', Robert Con Davis and
Ronald Schiefer, eds *Rhetoric and Form* (1985), pp. 45–55

As Harold Bloom puts it in the opening essay of the Yale School's non-
manifesto, *Deconstruction and Criticism*: 'Reading well is not necessarily a
polite process. . . . Only the capacity to wound gives a healing capacity the
chance to endure, and so to be heard.'[1] I hope, therefore, that my hosts
will understand the spirit in which I will use them as the starting point for
the depiction of a much larger configuration, and that by the end of this
paper I will not have bitten off more of the hand that feeds me than I can
chew.

In January of this year, shortly after the death of Paul de Man, I received
a call from Robert Con Davis inviting me to attempt the painful and
obviously impossible task of replacing de Man in a conference in which
Geoffrey Hartman, Hillis Miller, and Paul de Man had been asked to
speak about genre theory in relation to their own work. I was invited
to speak, however, not about *my* own work but about de Man's. The
reasons for this are certainly understandable. I could easily sympathize
with the conference organizers' impulse: there is nothing I could wish
more than that de Man had not died. But the invitation to appear as de
Man's *supplément* – supplemented in turn by a panel of my own choosing
– gave me pause. For it falls all too neatly into patterns of female effacement already well established by the phenomenon of the critical 'school'
as such. Like others of its type, the Yale School has always been a Male
School.

Would it have been possible for there to have been a female presence in
the Yale School? Interestingly, in Jonathan Culler's bibliography to *On
Deconstruction* Shoshana Felman's book *La Folie et la chose littéraire* is
described as 'a wide-ranging collection of essays by a member of the "école
de Yale".'[2] Felman, in other words, *was* a member of the Yale School, but
only in French. This question of the foreignness of the female language will
return, but for now, suffice it to say that there was no reason other than
gender why Felman's work – certainly closer to de Man's and Derrida's
than the work of Harold Bloom – should not have been seen as an integral
part of the Yale School.

At the time of the publication of *Deconstruction and Criticism*, several of
us – Shoshana Felman, Gayatri Spivak, Margaret Ferguson, and I –
discussed the possibility of writing a companion volume inscribing female
deconstructive protest and affirmation centering not on Shelley's 'The
Triumph of Life' (as the existing volume was originally slated to do) but on
Mary Shelley's *Frankenstein*. That book might truly have illustrated the

Girardian progression 'from mimetic desire to the monstrous double'. Unfortunately, this *Bride of Deconstruction and Criticism* never quite got off the ground, but it is surely no accident that the project was centered around monstrosity. As Derrida puts it in 'The Law of Genre' – which is also, of course, a law of gender – 'As soon as genre announces itself, one must respect a norm, one must not cross a line of demarcation, one must not risk impurity, anomaly, or monstrosity.[3] After all, Aristotle, the founder of the law of gender as well as of the law of genre, considered the female as the first distortion of the genus 'man' en route to becoming a monster. But perhaps it was not *Frankenstein* but rather *The Last Man*, Mary Shelley's grim depiction of the gradual extinction of humanity altogether, that would have made a fit counterpart to 'The Triumph of Life'. Shelley is entombed in both, along with a certain male fantasy of Romantic universality. The only universality that remains in Mary Shelley's last novel is the plague.

It would be easy to accuse the male Yale School theorists of having avoided the issue of gender entirely. What I intend to do, however, is to demonstrate that they have had quite a lot to say about the issue, often without knowing it. Before moving on to a female version of the Yale School, therefore, I will begin by attempting to extract from the essays in *Deconstruction and Criticism* and related texts an implicit theory of the relations between gender and criticism. For the purposes of this paper, I will focus on the four members of the Yale School who actually teach full time at Yale. Since Derrida, the fifth participant in *Deconstruction and Criticism*, has in contrast consistently and explicitly foregrounded the question of gender, his work would demand far more extensive treatment than is possible here. I will confine myself to the more implicit treatments of the subject detectable in the writings of Bloom, Hartman, Miller, and de Man.

Geoffrey Hartman, ever the master of the throwaway line, has not failed to make some memorable remarks about the genderedness of the reading process. 'Much reading', he writes in *The Fate of Reading*, 'is indeed, like girl-watching, a simple expense of spirit.'[4] And in *Beyond Formalism*, he claims: 'Interpretation is like a football game. You spot a hole and you go through. But first you may have to induce that opening.'[5]

In his essay in *Deconstruction and Criticism*, Hartman examines a poem in which Wordsworth, suddenly waylaid by a quotation, addresses his daughter Dora with a line from Milton's Samson that harks back to the figure of blind Oedipus being led by his daughter Antigone:

> A Little onward lend the guiding hand
> To these dark steps, a little further on! (*DC*, p. 215)

This is certainly a promising start for an investigation of gender relations. Yet Wordsworth and Hartman combine to curb the step of this budding Delilah and to subsume the daughter under the Wordsworthian category of 'child' who, as everyone knows, is *Father* of the man. While the poem works out a power reversal between blind father and guiding daughter, restoring the father to this role of natural leader, the commentary works out its patterns of reversibility between Wordsworth and Milton. 'Let me, thy happy guide, now point thy way/And how precede thee....' When Wordsworth leads his daughter to the edge of the abyss, it is the abyss of intertextuality.

While brooding on the abyss in *The Fate of Reading*, Hartman looks back at his own precursor self and says:

> In *The Unmediated Vision* the tyranny of sight in the domain of sensory organization is acknowledged, and symbol making is understood as a kind of 'therapeutic alliance' between the eye and other senses through the medium of art. I remember how easy it was to put a woman in the landscape, into every eyescape rather; and it struck me that in works of art there were similar centers, depicted or inferred.

Yet the woman in Wordsworth's poemscape is precisely what Hartman does not see. And this may be just what Wordsworth intended. In the short paragraph in which Hartman acknowledges that there may be something Oedipal about this Oedipus figure, he describes the daughter as *barred* by the incest prohibition. The poem would then transmit a disguised desire for the daughter, repressed and deflected into literary structures. Yet might it not also be that Wordsworth so often used incest figures in his poetry as a way, precisely, of barring the reality of the woman as other, a way of keeping the woman in and *only* in the eyescape, making a nun out of a nymph? For the danger here is that the daughter will neither follow nor lead, but simply leave:

> the birds salute
> The cheerful dawn, brightening for me the east;
> For me, thy natural leader, once again
> Impatient to conduct thee, not as erst
> A tottering infant, with compliant stoop
> From flower to flower supported; but to curb
> Thy nymph-like step swift-bounding o'er the lawn,
> Along the loose rocks, or the slippery verge
> Of foaming torrents. . . .

The family romance takes a slightly different form in Hillis Miller's essay, 'The Critic as Host'. In that essay, Miller discusses Booth's and Abrams's image of deconstructive criticism as 'parasitical' on the 'obvious or univocal reading' of a text. Miller writes:

> 'Parasitical' – the word suggests the image of 'the obvious or univocal reading' as the mighty oak, rooted in the solid ground, endangered by the insidious twining around it of deconstructive ivy. That ivy is somehow feminine, secondary, defective, or dependent. It is a clinging vine, able to live in no other way but by drawing the life sap of its host, cutting off its light and air. I think of Hardy's *The Ivy-Wife*. . . .

Such sad love stories of a domestic affection which introduces the parasitical into the closed economy of the home no doubt describe well enough the way some people feel about the relation of a 'deconstructive' interpretation to 'the obvious or univocal reading'. The parasite is destroying the host. The alien has invaded the house, perhaps to kill the father of the family in an act which does not look like parricide, but is. Is the 'obvious' reading, though, so 'obvious' or even so 'univocal'? May it not itself be the uncanny alien which is so close that it cannot be seen as strange? (*DC*, p. 218)

It is interesting to note how effortlessly the vegetal metaphor is sexualized in Miller's elaboration of it. If the parasite is the feminine, then the feminine must be recognized as that uncanny alien always already in the house – and in the host. What turns out, in Miller's etymological analysis, to be uncanny about the relation between host and parasite – and by extension between male and female – is that each is already inhabited by the other as a difference from itself. Miller then goes on to describe the parasite as invading virus in the following terms:

The genetic pattern of the virus is so coded that it can enter a host cell and violently reprogram all the genetic material in that cell, turning the cell into a little factory for manufacturing copies of itself, so destroying it. This is *The Ivy-Wife* with a vengeance. (*DC*, p. 222)

Miller then goes on to ask, 'Is this an allegory, and if so, of what?' Perhaps of the gender codes of literature, or of criticism. But this image of cancerous femininity may be less a fear of takeover by women than an extreme version of the desire to deny difference. There is perhaps something reassuring about total annihilation as opposed to precarious survival. The desire to deny difference is in fact, in a euphoric rather than a nightmarish spirit, the central desire dramatized by the Shelley poems Miller analyzes. The obsessive cry for oneness, for sameness, always, however, meets the same fate: it cannot subsume and erase the trace of its own elaboration. The story told, again and again, by Shelley is the story of the failure of the attempt to abolish difference. As Miller points out, difference is rediscovered in the linguistic traces of that failure. But a failed erasure of difference is not the same as a recognition of difference. Unless, as Miller's analysis suggests, difference can only be recognized in the failure of its erasure.

If the parasite is both feminine and parricidal, then the parasite can only be a daughter. Miller does not follow up on the implications of a parricidal daughter, but Harold Bloom, whose critical system is itself a garden of parricidal delights, gives us a clue to what would be at stake for him in such an idea. In *the Map of Misreading* he writes:

Nor are there Muses, nymphs who *know*, still available to tell us the secrets of continuity, for the nymphs certainly are now departing. I prophesy though that the first true break with literary continuity will be brought about in generations to come, if the burgeoning religion of Liberated Woman spreads from it clusters of enthusiasts to dominate the West. Homer will cease to be the inevitable precursor, and the rhetoric and forms of our literature then may break at last from tradition.[6]

In Bloom's prophetic vision of the breaking of tradition through the liberation of woman, it is as though the Yale School were in danger of becoming a Jael School.[7]

The dependence of Bloom's revisionary ratios upon a linear patriarchal filiation has been pointed out often enough – particularly in the groundbreaking work of Sandra Gilbert and Susan Gubar – that there is no need to belabor it here. I will therefore, instead, analyze the opening lines of Bloom's essay 'The Breaking of Form' as a strong misreading of the question of sexual difference. The essay begins:

> The word *meaning* goes back to a root that signifies 'opinion' or 'intention', and is closely related to the word *moaning*. A poem's meaning is a poem's complaint, its version of Keats' Belle Dame, who looked *as if* she loved, and made sweet moan. Poems instruct us in how they break form to bring about meaning, so as to utter a complaint, a moaning intended to be all their own. (*DC*, p. 1)

If the relation between the reader and the poem is analogous to the relation between the knight-at-arms and the Belle Dame, things are considerably more complicated than they appear. For the encounter between male and female in Keats's poem is a perfectly ambiguous disaster:

LA BELLE DAME SANS MERCI
A Ballad

I

O what can ail thee, knight-at-arms,
Alone and palely loitering?
The sedge has withered from the lake,
And no birds sing.

II

O what can ail thee, knight-at-arms,
So haggard and so woebegone?
The squirrel's granary is full,
And the harvest's done.

III

I see a lily on thy brow,
With anguish moist and fever dew,
And on thy cheeks a fading rose
Fast withereth too.

IV

I met a lady in the meads,
Full beautiful – a fairy's child,
Her hair was long, her foot was light,
And her eyes were wild.

V

I made a garland for her head,
And bracelets too, and fragrant zone;
She looked at me as she did love,
And made sweet moan.

VI

I set her on my pacing steed,
And nothing else saw all day long,
For sidelong would she bend, and sing
A fairy's song.

VII

She found me roots of relish sweet,
And honey wild, and manna dew,
And sure in language strange she said –
'I love thee true.'

VIII

She took me to her elfin grot,
And there she wept, and sighed full sore,
And there I shut her wild wild eyes
With kisses four.

IX

And there she lullèd me asleep,
And there I dreamed – Ah! woe betide!
The latest dream I ever dreamed
On the cold hillside.

X

I saw pale kings and princes too,
Pale warriors, death-pale were they all;
They cried – 'La Belle Dame sans Merci
Hath thee in thrall!'

XI

I saw their starved lips in the gloam,
With horrid warning gapèd wide,
And I awoke and found me here,
On the cold hill's side.

XII

And this is why I sojourn here,
Alone and palely loitering,
Though the sedge has withered from the lake,
And no birds sing.

Rather than a clear 'as if', Keats writes: 'She looked at me *as* she did love,/And made sweet moan.' Suspicion of the woman is not planted quite so clearly, nor quite so early. In changing 'as' to 'as if', Bloom has removed from the poem the possibility of reading this first mention of the woman's feelings as straight description. 'As she did love' would still be the knight's own interpretations, but it would be an interpretation that does not recognize itself as such. Perhaps Bloom is here demonstrating what he says elsewhere about the study of poetry being 'the study of what Stevens called "the intricate evasions of as".' By the end of the poem, it becomes impossible to know whether one has read a story of a knight enthralled by a witch or of a woman seduced and abandoned by a male hysteric. And the fine balance of that undecidability depends on the 'as'.

If the poem, like the woman, 'makes sweet moan', then there is considerable doubt about the reader's capacity to read it. This becomes all the more explicit in the knight's second interpretive assessment of the woman's feelings. 'And sure in language strange she said – "I love thee true." ' The problem of understanding the woman is here a problem of translation. Even her name can only be expressed in another tongue. The sexes stand in relation to each other not as two distinct entities but as two foreign languages. The drama of male hysteria is a drama of premature assurance of understanding followed by premature panic at the intimation of otherness. Is she mine, asks the knight, or am I hers? If these are the only two possibilities, the foreignness of the languages cannot be respected. What Bloom demonstrates, perhaps without knowing it, is that if reading is the gendered activity he paints it as, the reading process is less a love story than a story of failed translation.

That the question of gender is a question of language becomes even more explicit in an essay by Paul de Man entitled 'The Epistemology of Metaphor.'[8] Translation is at issue in that essay as well, in the very derivation of the word 'metaphor'. 'It is no mere play of words', writes de Man, 'that "translate" is translated in German as "übersetzen" which itself translates the Greek "*meta phorein*" or metaphor.' (p. 17) In all three words, what is described is a motion from one place to another. As we shall see, the question of the relation between gender and figure will have a great deal to do with this notion of *place*.

De Man's essay begins as follows:

Metaphors, tropes, and figural language in general have been a perennial problem and, at times, a recognized source of embarrassment for philosophical discourse and, by extension, for all discursive uses of language including historiography and literary analysis. It appears that philosophy either has to give up its own constitutive claim to rigor in order to come to terms with the figurality of its language or that it has to free itself from figuration altogether. And if the latter is considered impossible, philosophy could at least learn to control figuration by keeping it, so to speak, in its place, by delimiting the boundaries of its influence and thus restricting the epistemological damage that it may cause. (p. 13)

This opening paragraph echoes, in its own rhetoric, a passage which occurs later in the essay in which de Man is commenting on a long quotation from Locke. Locke concludes his discussion of the perils of figuration as follows:

Eloquence, like the fair sex, has too prevailing beauties in it to suffer itself ever to be spoken against. And it is in vain to find fault with those arts of deceiving wherein men find pleasure to be deceived. (p. 15)

De Man glosses the Locke passage as follows:

Nothing could be more eloquent than this denunciation of eloquence. It is clear that rhetoric is something one can decorously indulge in as long as one knows where it belongs. Like a woman, which it resembles ('like the fair sex'), it is a fine thing as long as it is kept in its proper place. Out of place, among the serious affairs of men ('if we would speak of things as they are'), it is a disruptive scandal – like the appearance of a real woman in a gentleman's club where it would only be tolerated as a picture, preferably naked (like the image of Truth), framed and hung on the wall. (pp. 15–16)

Following this succinct tongue-in-cheek description of the philosophical tradition as a men's club, de Man goes on to claim that there is 'little epistemological risk in a flowery, witty passage about wit like this one', that things only begin to get serious when the plumber must be called in, but the epistemological damage may already have been done. For the question of language in Locke quickly comes to be centered on the question, 'What essence is the property of man?' This is no idle question, in fact, because what is at stake in the answer is what sort of monstrous births it is permissible to kill. Even in the discussion of Condillac and Kant, the question of sexual difference lurks, as when de Man describes Condillac's discussion of abstractions as bearing a close resemblance to a novel by Ann Radcliffe or Mary Shelley, or when Kant is said to think that rhetoric can be rehabilitated by some 'tidy critical housekeeping'. De Man's conclusion can be read as applying to the epistemological damage caused as much by gender as by figure:

In each case, it turns out to be impossible to maintain a clear line of distinction between rhetoric, abstraction, symbol, and all other forms of language. In each case, the resulting undecidability is due to the asymmetry of the binary model that opposes the figural to the proper meaning of the figure. (p. 28)

The philosopher's place is always within, not outside, the asymmetrical structures of language and of gender, but that place can never, in the final analysis, be proper. It may be impossible to know whether it is the gender question that is determined by rhetoric or rhetoric by gender difference, but it does seem as though these are the terms in which it might be fruitful to pursue the question.

In order to end with a meditation on a possible female version of the Yale School, I would like now to turn to the work of a Yale daughter. For this purpose I have chosen to focus on *The Critical Difference* by Barbara Johnson.[9] What happens when one raises Mary Jacobus's question – 'Is there a woman in this text?' The answer is rather surprising. For no book produced by the Yale School seems to have excluded women as effectively as *The Critical Difference*. No women authors are studied. Almost no women critics are cited. And, what is even more surprising, there are almost no female characters in any of the stories analyzed. *Billy Budd*, however triangulated, is a tale of three *men* in a boat. Balzac's *Sarrasine* is the story of a woman who turns out to be a castrated man. And in Johnson's analysis of 'The Purloined Letter', the story of Oedipal triangularity is transformed into an endlessly repeated chain of fraternal rivalries. In a book that announces itself as a study of difference, the place of the woman is constantly being erased.

This does not mean, however, that the question of sexual difference does not haunt the book from the beginning. In place of a dedication, *The Critical Difference* opens with a quotation from Paul de Man in which difference is dramatized as a scene of exasperated instruction between Archie Bunker and his wife:

> Asked by his wife whether he wants to have his bowling shoes laced over or laced under, Archie Bunker answers with a question: 'What's the difference?' Being a reader of sublime simplicity, his wife replies by patiently explaining the difference between lacing over and lacing under, whatever this may be, but provokes only ire. 'What's the difference?' did not ask for difference but means instead 'I don't give a damn what the difference is.' The same grammatical pattern engenders two meanings that are mutually exclusive: the literal meaning asks for the concept (difference) whose existence is denied by the figurative meaning. As long as we are talking about bowling shoes, the consequences are relatively trivial; Archie Bunker, who is a great believer in the authority of origins (as long, of course, as they are the right origins) muddles along in a world where literal and figurative meanings get in each other's way, though not without discomforts. But suppose that it is a *de*-bunker rather than a 'Bunker', and a de-bunker of the arche (or origin), an archie Debunker such as Nietzsche or Jacques Derrida, for instance, who asks the question "What is the Difference?' – and we cannot even tell from his grammar whether he 'really' wants to know 'what' difference is or is just telling us that we shouldn't even try to find out. Confronted with the question of the difference between grammar and rhetoric, grammar allows us to ask the question, but the sentence by means of which we ask it may deny the very possibility of asking. For what is the use of asking, I ask, when we cannot even authoritatively decide whether a question asks or doesn't ask?

Whatever the rhetorical twists of this magnificent passage, the fact that it is framed as an intersexual dialogue is not irrelevant.

Another essay in *The Critical Difference*, a study of Mallarmé's prose poem 'The White Waterlily', offers an even more promising depiction of the rhetoric of sexual difference. The essay begins:

> If human beings were not divided into two biological sexes, there would probably be no need for literature. And if literature could truly say what the relations between the sexes are, we would doubtless not need much of it then, either. Somehow, however, it is not simply a question of literature's ability to say or not to say the truth of sexuality. For from the moment literature begins to try to set things straight on that score, literature itself becomes inextricable from the sexuality it seeks to comprehend. It is not the life of sexuality that literature cannot capture; it is literature that inhabits the very heart of what makes sexuality problematic for us speaking animals. Literature is not only a thwarted investigator but also an incorrigible perpetrator of the problem of sexuality. (p. 13)

But the prose poem in question ends up dramatizing an inability to know whether the woman one is expecting to encounter has ever truly been present or not. It is as though *The Critical Difference* could describe only the escape of the difference it attempts to analyze. This is even more true of the essay subtitled 'What the Gypsy Knew'. With such a title, one would expect to encounter at last something about female knowledge. But the point of the analysis is precisely that the poem does not tell us what the gypsy knew. Her prophecy is lost in the ambiguities of Apollinaire's syntax.

There may, however, be something accurate about this repeated dramatization of woman as simulacrum, erasure, or silence. For it would not be easy to assert that the existence and knowledge of the female subject could simply be produced, without difficulty or epistemological damage, within the existing patterns of culture and language. *The Critical Difference* may here be unwittingly pointing to 'woman' as one of the things 'we do not know we do not know'. Johnson concludes her preface with some remarks about ignorance that apply ironically well to her book's own demonstration of an ignorance that pervades Western discourse as a whole:

> What literature often seems to tell us is the consequences of the way in which what is not known is not *seen* as unknown. It is not, in the final analysis, what you don't know that can or cannot hurt you. It is what you don't *know* you don't know that spins out and entangles 'that perpetual error we call life'. (p. xii)

It is not enough to be a woman writing in order to resist the naturalness of female effacement in the subtly male pseudo-genderlessness of language. It would be no easy task, however, to undertake the effort of re-inflection or translation required to retrieve the lost knowledge of the gypsy, or to learn to listen with re-trained ears to Edith Bunker's patient elaboration of an answer to the question, 'What is the difference?'

Notes

1 'The Breaking of Form', in Harold Bloom, eds., *Deconstruction and Criticism* (New

York, The Seabury Press, 1979), pp. 6, 5. Further references to this and other essays in the volume will be indicated in the text by the abbreviation *DC* followed by a page number.

2 Jonathan Culler, *On Deconstruction* (Ithaca, NY, Cornell University Press, 1982), p. 289.

3 Jacques Derrida, 'The Law of Genre', *Glyph*, 7 (Baltimore, MD, The Johns Hopkins University Press, 1980), pp. 203–4.

4 Geoffrey Hartman, *The Fate of Reading* (Chicago, University of Chicago Press, 1975), p. 248.

5 Geoffrey Hartman, *Beyond Formalism* (New Haven, Yale University Press, 1970), p. 351.

6 Harold Bloom, *A Map of Misreading* (New York, Oxford University Press, 1975), p. 33. I would like to thank Susan Suleiman for calling my attention to this quotation.

7 The story of Jael is found in Judges 4. Jael invites Sisera, the commander of the Canaanite army, into her tent, gives him a drink of milk, and then, when he has fallen asleep, drives a tent peg through his head and kills him. (I would like to thank Sima Godfrey for this pun.)

8 Paul de Man, 'The Epistemology of Metaphor', *Critical Inquiry*, 5 (1978).

9 Barbara Johnson, *The Critical Difference* (Baltimore, MD, The Johns Hopkins University Press, 1980).

SECTION THREE
HISTORY AND DISCOURSE

Broadly speaking the earliest formative writings in this trajectory can be seen as, on the one hand, Michel Foucault's work on discourse and power, and, on the other, Volosinov/Bakhtin's work on discourse as concrete, socio-ideological communication. These form key points on the conceptual map of this aspect of Post-Structuralism. In common with the deconstructive tendency, and in contradistinction to Structuralism, this trajectory acknowledges that meaning is not fixed and stable, and that there can be no single, final and true interpretation. However, unlike deconstruction, Volosinov/Bakhtin sees, in the social conditions of language use, a variety of temporal, provisional and contested fixings of meaning, while Foucault sees, in the configuration of discourse, power and knowledge the production and surveillance of the social itself. In this model the relations between language and socio-cultural practice often seem to emphasize discourse as control and repression, but this function is frequently set against a fascination for forms and writings which escape or transgress social/official rationality.

The work of Volosinov/Bakhtin first emerged alongside Russian Formalism in the 1920s and though Volosinov's concern was primarily with linguistics and Bakhtin's with literature, their work exhibits a number of common features which, along with other evidence, suggest that they were one and the same person, forced by circumstance in Stalin's Russia to publish under two names. In recent years the work undertaken by Volosinov/Bakhtin has proved fertile ground for literary theorists for though aspects of the work mark it as 'of its time', it also contains some remarkably Post-Structuralist themes.

In *Marxism and the Philosophy of Language* (1929) Volosinov undertakes a powerful critique of the 'abstract objectivism' of Saussure's theory of language. The basis of his critique is the recognition that language is a social *process*; language is utterance, emerging from concrete social communication not from any abstract, objective system of langue. When viewed in its social contexts language appears not as a closed system of 'self-identical forms' (that is, the one-to-one correspondence of a signifier to a signified) but as a generative and continuous process, as utterances which respond to and anticipate other utterances. These utterances, existing in and as social interchange, form the arena of struggle between different social groups who inflect the same sign-forms with different 'evaluative accepts' to produce different 'ideological themes' or meanings for their utterances. So, whilst acknowledging that the sign is not stable or fixed, Volosinov adds that 'multiplicity of meaning' has to be seen in relation to what he calls 'multi-accentuality' – that is, its openness to different evaluative orientations.

Bakhtin develops this view, seeing language not as singular and monolithic, but as plural and multiple; languages inscribed with various evaluative accents become socio-ideological languages intimately bound up with material and social conditions and with the contexts of their production – i.e. their 'heteroglossia'. Bakhtin applies this to the novel, the form which is exemplary in its ability to represent a dialogic interanimation of socio-ideological languages. The dialogic nature of the novel can be either open or closed; the author can either let the interplay of languages speak for itself or can impose a privileged authorial metalanguage. In Bakhtin the dialogic is closely linked to his notion of carnivalization – to popular forms that disrupt and relativize meaning in opposition to the 'official' discourse and its attempt to close down the polysemy of language.[1]

Bakhtin's theory of the text can be seen as oriented towards literary production in that the novel is emphasized as a form which juxtaposes the various meaning-systems of socio-ideological languages. In the essay by Bennett, reprinted here, the inter-animation of discourses and discursive practices – different meaning systems – is used to develop a model that is oriented toward consumption/reading, one that acknowledges the indeterminacy of the text but places it more firmly in social practice and discursive context.

For Michel Foucault the 'social' is produced in the network of discourses and discursive practices through which we seem to acquire knowledge about the world. Broadly, Foucault's argument is that it is the modalities of discourses and discursive practices that actually produce both that knowledge and the social itself, and the modalities function differently in different historical 'epistemes'. (An episteme is an historical period that is unified by the rules and procedures – the modalities – for producing knowledge.) The history of epistemes is not a matter of progression or continuity, but of discontinuity. In his earlier work Foucault attempts to uncover the concealed modalities of discourse which govern and produce various 'knowledges'. In *Birth of the Clinic* (1963) and *The Order of Things* (1966)[2] he investigated the 'discursive formations' of medicine and the human sciences, noting how these 'discourses' delimited a field of objects, defined legitimate practices and positions for 'subjects' to adopt, and fixed the norms for producing concepts and theories.

Foucault's work has been concerned primarily with the configuration of discourse, knowledge and power, and it is through these three key notions that he elaborates a complex theory. In his earlier work, he emphasizes discourse; in his later work the emphasis shifts to power. 'The Order of

Discourse' is balanced between this shift in emphasis. Where, in earlier work, he had sought to delineate the principles of regularity by which knowledge was produced, here he outlines the forces and technologies of power by which the production of discourse and knowledge is surveyed and controlled; however, if power here appears to be simply repressive, account should be taken of his later writings where he is careful to point out that power is productive – power *produces* discourse, as well as setting its boundaries. This insight, more than any other, was the starting point for that constellation of critical practices which is now referred to as the New Historicism.

According to one of its leading proponents, Stephen Greenblatt, New Historicism is not so much a theory or doctrine of literary criticism as a textual practice. It is, however, a method of reading informed by and arising out of the theoretical ferment of the 1970s, so that its concern to examine the textual traces of the past is premised on the notion that the past is available to us only in the form of a textuality which is also embedded in that of the present. Old 'historicism', with its Hegelian idealist sense of history as a developing totality or its evolutionary notion of teleology, had produced such classic literary critical accounts of history as Tillyard's *The Elizabethan World Picture* (1943). For New Historicists, however, there can be no such seamless, overarching unity, but only the shifting and contradictory representations of numerous 'histories'. History can only be a narrative construction involving a dialectical relationship of past and present concerns. Thus the critic is neither a transcendent commentator nor an objective chronicler because he/she is always implicated in the discourses which help to construct the object of knowledge. Hypothetical grand narratives such as the 'Elizabethan World Picture' are ideological projections based on the exclusivity of sameness. The New Historicist is more concerned to focus attention on the multiple and contradictory material practices which embed each historical event or expressive act as contexts of production and reception.

These material practices do not, however, constitute historical 'givens'. Eroding the distinction between text and context, the new historicist views social contexts in themselves as narrative constructions produced through the discursive management of relations of power. There is no 'background' and no absolute and autonomous literary text: literariness as well as cultural value are terms opened to contestation and reconstruction.

The practice of New Historicism is mainly associated with two groups of critics, one arising within studies of Romanticism (Marilyn Butler, Marjorie Levinson, Jerome McGann and David Simpson) and the other within Renaissance Studies (Jonathan Goldberg, Stephen Greenblatt and Louis Montrose). The first have been concerned to offer a critique of Romanticism's own self-presentation as aesthetic transcendence, egotistical sublime or poetic autonomy. The second group have used colonialism and theatricality both as political concepts and as looser metaphors to examine strategies of subversion and containment in Renaissance texts.

Stephen Greenblatt named the New Historicism in 1988, but the practice had been developing throughout the eighties, particularly in the pages of the journal *Representations*. In 1987 Marilyn Butler had called for a New Historicist practice in her Cambridge lecture 'Repossessing the Past: The Case for an Open Literary History'. In this, she called also for the study of actual literary communities as they function within larger communities in time and in particular places. Butler and Greenblatt emphasize that political and social needs shape literary production and reception and argue that criticism must therefore examine the ways in which traces of social circulation are effaced to produce the illusion of the 'autonomous' literary work: the Ideal Poem.

New Historicism follows a trajectory out of American formalist criticism with its close reading practices, through a hybrid mix of seventies theory, in order to return to history. Influences include Bakhtin, Althusser, Hayden White, Gadamer, Raymond Williams, Clifford Geertz and Foucault. Specific theoretical insights are derived from: Althusser's notion of ideology as contradictory and lived and his concept of the *relative* autonomy of the text and the interpellation of subjects in history; Gadamer's hermeneutic understanding of the past as ever constructed in relation to a present which is also a development out of that past; Hayden White's view of history as narrative construction or 'stories' and Bakhtin's articulation of all human utterances (including literary texts) as social acts which are multiaccentual and available for divergent uses.

Probably the most pervasive influence on New Historicist practice, however, is the work of Foucault. His writings have consistently shown how so-called objective historical accounts are always products of a will to power enacted through formations of knowledge within specific institutions. His own 'histories' resist the allure of 'total theories 'which offer overarching narratives and instead focus attention on the 'other' excluded by and constructed through such accounts. His view of power as omniscient though not omnipotent has been taken up by Greenblatt, but also by British 'cultural materialists' such as Jonathan Dollimore who also draw on Raymond Williams's later work on ideology. Greenblatt remains pessimistic, however, about the possibilities of subversion, viewing resistance as ultimately always contained. Cultural materialists tend to be more politically optimistic, tracing the potential for radical appropriation of dominant cultural meanings and values.

Two essays have been chosen to represent the New Historicist turn. Jerome McGann's essay demonstrates the move away from formalist concerns or the pursuit of totally coherent theoretical paradigms and advocates a more historically oriented and particularized engagement with the text. McGann argues for the recognition of poetry as a social act and distinguishes between the text which is 'complete' and the poem which is ever open. His focus is on the circulation and reception of texts, arguing against the Kantian sense of the poem as Idea and viewing the critical failure to engage with the materiality of a text as necessarily leading to the blindness of literary critics to the time-bound nature of their own discourses. Greenblatt's essay pursues issues of the same kind, but with a performative panache which seeks to enact the New Historicism in a more theatrical rather than sociological mode. The essay appeared in the collection entitled *Learning to Curse* (1990) and is written with a characteristic stylistic blend of wit and lucidity, 'resonance and wonder', which makes Greenblatt perhaps the most entertaining, as well as perspicacious, of the New Historicists. Writing partly in response to those critics who have accused him of denying any agency to the human subject and of reading history as a narrative of containment, Greenblatt argues that the New Historicism should on the contrary, be regarded as a critical practice concerned to tread a new path between the demand for strict 'relevance' on the one hand and an ahistorical formalism on the other. Neither human subjects nor human artefacts exist outside of history, but to admit therefore that both are historically shaped is not to suggest that they have no power to intervene in the processes of history. He regards his own work as concerned with a process of negotiation and exchange which leaves space for an attitude of 'wonder' (rather than reverence) towards the artefacts of the past which is yet inseparable from a sense of their hermeneutic resonance in the present. The aim is to grasp, simultaneously, 'the historicity of texts and the textuality of history'.

Notes

1 M.M. Bakhtin, *The Dialogic Imagination: Four Essays*, trans. M. Holquist and C. Emerson (Austin, University of Texas Press, 1981); P. Stallybrass and A. White, *The Politics of Poetic Transgression* (London, Methuen, 1986).
2 M. Foucault, *The Birth of the Clinic*, trans. A.M. Sheridan-Smith (New York, Vintage and Random House, 1975); *The Order of Things* (London, Tavistock, 1970).

---

24   M.M. Bakhtin,

From 'Discourse in the Novel', M. Holquist, ed. *The Dialogic Imagination* (1934), pp. 269–73; 295–6; 301–5

The novel is an artistic genre. Novelistic discourse is poetic discourse, but one that does not fit within the frame provided by the concept of poetic discourse as it now exists. This concept has certain underlying presuppositions that limit it. The very concept – in the course of its historical formulation from Aristotle to the present day – has been oriented toward the specific 'official' genres and connected with specific historical tendencies in verbal ideological life. Thus a whole series of phenomena remained beyond its conceptual horizon.

Philosophy of language, linguistics and stylistics (i.e., such as they have come down to us) have all postulated a simple and unmediated relation of speaker to his unitary and singular 'own' language, and have postulated as well a simple realization of this language in the monologic utterance of the individual. Such disciplines actually know only two poles in the life of language, between which are located all the linguistic and stylistic phenomena they know: on the one hand, the system of a *unitary language*, and on the other the *individual* speaking in this language.

Various schools of thought in the philosophy of language, in linguistics and stylistics have, in different periods (and always in close connection with the diverse concrete poetic and ideological styles of a given epoch), introduced into such concepts as 'system of language', 'monologic utterance', 'the speaking *individuum*', various differing nuances of meaning, but their basic content remains unchanged. This basic content is conditioned by the specific sociohistorical destinies of European languages and by the destinies of ideological discourse, and by those particular historical tasks that ideological discourse has fulfilled in specific social spheres and at specific stages in its own historical development.

These tasks and destinies of discourse conditioned specific verbal-ideological movements, as well as various specific genres of ideological discourse, and ultimately the specific philosophical concept of discourse itself – in particular, the concept of poetic discourse, which has been at the heart of all concepts of style.

The strength and at the same time the limitations of such basic stylistic categories become apparent when such categories are seen as conditioned by specific historical destinies and by the task that an ideological discourse assumes. These categories arose from and were shaped by the historically *aktuell* forces at work in the verbal-ideological evolution of specific social groups; they comprised the theoretical expression of actualising forces that were in the process of creating a life for language.

These forces are the *forces that serve to unify and centralize the verbal-ideological world*.

Unitary language constitutes the theoretical expression of the historical processes of linguistic unification and centralization, an expressions of the centripetal forces of language. A unitary language is not something given [*dan*] but is always in essence posited [*zadan*] – and at every moment of its linguistic life it is opposed to the realities of heteroglossia. But at the same time it makes its real presence felt as a force for overcoming this heteroglossia, imposing specific limits to it, guaranteeing a certain maximum of mutual understanding and crystalizing into a real, although still relative, unity – the unity of the reigning conversational (everyday) and literary language, 'correct language'.

A common unitary language is a system of linguistic norms. But these norms do not constitute an abstract imperative; they are rather the generative forces of linguistic life, forces that struggle to overcome the heteroglossia of language, forces that unite and centralize verbal-ideological thought, creating within a heteroglot national language the firm, stable linguistic nucleus of an officially recognized literary language, or else defending an already formed language from the pressure of growing heteroglossia.

What we have in mind here is not an abstract linguistic minimum of a common language, in the sense of a system of elementary forms (linguistic symbols) guaranteeing a *minimum* level of comprehension in practical communication. We are taking language not as a system of abstract grammatical categories, but rather language conceived as ideologically saturated, language as a world view, even as a concrete opinion, insuring a *maximum* of mutual understanding in all spheres of ideological life. Thus a unitary language gives expression to forces working toward concrete verbal and ideological unification and centralization, which develop in vital connection with the processes of sociopolitical and cultural centralization.

Aristotelian poetics, the poetics of Augustine, the poetics of the medieval church, of 'the one language of truth', the Cartesian poetics of neoclassicism, the abstract grammatical universalism of Leibniz (the idea of a 'universal grammar'), Humboldt's insistence on the concrete – all these, whatever their differences in nuance, give expression to the same centripetal forces in socio-linguistic and ideological life; they serve one and the same project of centralizing and unifying the European languages. The victory of one reigning language (dialect) over the others, the supplanting of languages, their enslavement, the process of illuminating them with the True Word, the incorporation of Barbarians and lower social strata into a unitary language of culture and truth, the canonization of ideological systems, philology with its methods of studying and teaching dead languages, languages that were by that very fact 'unities', Indo-European linguistics with its focus of attention, directed away from language plurality to a single proto-language – all this determined the content and power of the category of 'unitary language' in linguistic and stylistic thought, and determined its creative, style-shaping role in the majority of the poetic genres that coalesced in the channel formed by those same centripetal forces of verbal-ideological life.

But the centripetal forces of the life of language, embodied in a 'unitary language', operate in the midst of heteroglossia. At any given moment of its evolution, language is stratified not only into linguistic dialects in the strict sense of the word (according to formal linguistic markers, especially phonetic), but also – and for us this is the essential point – into languages that are socio-ideological: languages of social groups, 'professional' and 'generic' languages, languages of generations and so forth. From this point of view, literary language itself is only one of these heteroglot languages – and in its turn is also stratified into languages (generic, period-bound and others). And this stratification and heteroglossia, once realized, is not only a static invariant of linguistic life, but also what insures its dynamics: stratification and heteroglossia widen and deepen as long as language is alive and developing. Alongside the centripetal forces, the centrifugal forces of language carry on their uninterrupted work; alongside verbal-ideological centralization and unification, the uninterrupted processes of decentralization and disunification go forward.

Every concrete utterance of a speaking subject serves as a point where centrifugal as well as centripetal forces are brought to bear. The processes of centralization and decentralization, of unification and disunification, intersect in the utterance; the utterance not only answers the requirements of its own language as an individualized embodiment of a speech act, but it answers the requirements of heteroglossia as well; it is in fact an active participant in such speech diversity. And this active participation of every utterance in living heteroglossia determines the linguistic profile and style of the utterance to no less a degree than its inclusion in any normative-centralizing system of a unitary language.

Every utterance participates in the 'unitary language' (in its centripetal forces and tendencies) and at the same time partakes of social and historical heteroglossia (the centrifugal, stratifying forces).

Such is the fleeting language of a day, of an epoch, a social group, a genre, a school and so forth. It is possible to give a concrete and detailed analysis of any utterance, once having exposed it as a contradiction-ridden, tension-filled unity of two embattled tendencies in the life of language.

The authentic environment of an utterance, the environment in which it lives and takes shape, is dialogized heteroglossia, anonymous and social as language, but simultaneously concrete, filled with specific content and accented as an individual utterance.

At the time when major divisions of the poetic genres were developing under the influence of the unifying centralizing, centripetal forces of verbal-ideological life, the novel – and those artistic-prose genres that gravitate toward it – was being historically shaped by the current of decentralizing, centrifugal forces. At the time when poetry was accomplishing the task of cultural, national and political centralization of the verbal-ideological world in the higher official socio-ideological levels, on the lower levels, on the stages of local fairs and at buffoon spectacles, the heteroglossia of the clown sounded forth, ridiculing all 'languages' and dialects; there developed the literature of the *fabliaux* and *Schwänke* of street songs, folksayings, anecdotes, where there was no language-center at all, where there was to be found a lively play with the 'languages' of poets, scholars, monks, knights and others, where all 'languages' were masks and where no language could claim to be an authentic, incontestable face.

Heteroglossia, as organized in these low genres, was not merely heteroglossia vis-à-vis the accepted literary language (in all its various generic expressions), that is, vis-à-vis the linguistic center of the verbal-ideological life of the nation and the epoch, but was a heteroglossia consciously opposed to this literary language. It was parodic, and aimed sharply and polemically against the official languages of its given time. It was heteroglossia that had been dialogized.

. . . .

Concrete socio-ideological language consciousness, as it becomes creative – that is, as it becomes active as literature – discovers itself already surrounded by heteroglossia and not at all a single, unitary language, inviolable and indisputable. The actively literary linguistic consciousness at all times and everywhere (that is, in all epochs of literature historically available to us) comes upon 'languages' and not language. Consciousness finds itself inevitably facing the necessity of *having to choose a language*. With each literary-verbal performance, consciousness must actively orient itself amidst heteroglossia, it must move in and occupy a position for itself within it, it chooses, in other words, a 'language'. Only by remaining in a closed environment, one without writing or thought, completely off the maps of socio-ideological becoming, could a man fail to sense this activity of selecting a language and rest assured in the inviolability of his own language, the conviction that his language is predetermined.

Even such a man, however, deals not in fact with a single language, but with languages – except that the place occupied by each of these languages is fixed and indisputable, the movement from one to the other is predetermined and not a thought process; it is as if these languages were in different chambers. They do not collide with each other in his consciousness, there is no attempt to coordinate them, to look at one of these languages through the eyes of another language.

Thus an illiterate peasant, miles away from any urban center, naively immersed in an unmoving and for him unshakable everyday world, nevertheless lived in several language systems: he prayed to God in one language (Church Slavonic), sang songs in another, spoke to his family in a third and, when he began to dictate petitions to the local authorities through a scribe, he tried speaking yet a fourth language (the official-literate language, 'paper' language). All these are *different languages*, even from the point of view of abstract socio-dialectological markers. But these languages were not dialogically coordinated in the linguistic consciousness of the peasant; he passed from one to the other without thinking, automatically: each was indisputably in its own place, and the place of each was indisputable. He was not yet able to regard one language (and the verbal world corresponding to it) through the eyes of another language (that is, the language of everyday life and the everyday world with the language of prayer or song, or vice versa).[1]

As soon as a critical interanimation of languages began to occur in the consciousness of our peasant, as soon as it became clear that these were not only various different languages but even internally variegated languages, that the ideological systems and approaches to the world that were indissolubly connected with these languages contradicted each other and in no way could live in peace and quiet with one another – then the inviolability and predetermined quality of these languages came to an end, and the necessity of actively choosing one's orientation among them began.

The language and world of prayer, the language and world of song, the language and world of labor and everyday life, the specific language and world of local authorities, the new language and world of the workers freshly immigrated to the city – all these languages and worlds sooner or later emerged from a state of peaceful and moribund equilibrium and revealed the speech diversity in each.

Of course the actively literary linguistic consciousness comes upon an even more varied and profound heteroglossia within literary language itself, as well as outside it. Any fundamental study of the stylistic life of the word must begin with this basic fact. The nature of the heteroglossia encountered and the means by which one orients oneself in it determine the concrete stylistic life that the word will lead.

. . . .

The compositional forms for appropriating and organizing heteroglossia in the novel, worked out during the long course of the genre's historical development, are extremely heterogeneous in their variety of genetic types. Each such compositional form is connected with particular stylistic possibilities, and demands particular forms for the artistic treatment of the heteroglot 'languages' introduced into it. We will pause here only on the most basic forms that are typical for the majority of novel types.

The so-called comic novel makes available a form for appropriating and organising heteroglossia that is both externally very vivid and at the same time historically profound; its classic representatives in England were Fielding, Smollett, Sterne, Dickens, Thackeray and others, and in Germany Hippel and Jean Paul.

In the English comic novel we find a comic-parodic re-processing of almost all the levels of literary language, both conversational and written, that were current at the time. Almost every novel we mentioned above as being a classic representative of this generic type is an encyclopedia of all strata and forms of literary language: depending on the subject being represented, the story-line parodically reproduces first the forms of parliamentary eloquence, then the eloquence of the court, or particular forms of parliamentary protocol, or court protocol, or forms used by reporters in newspaper articles, or the dry business language of the City, or the dealings of speculators, or the pedantic speech of scholars, or the high epic style, or Biblical style, or the style of the hypocritical moral sermon or finally the way one or another concrete and socially determined personality, the subject of the story, happens to speak.

This usually parodic stylization of generic, professional and other strata of language is sometimes interrupted by the direct authorial word (usually as an expression of pathos, of Sentimental or idyllic sensibility), which directly embodies (without any refracting) semantic and axiological intentions of the author. But the primary source of language usage in the comic novel is a highly specific treatment of 'common language'. This 'common language' – usually the average norm of spoken and written language for a given social group – is taken by the author precisely as the *common view*, as the verbal approach to people and things normal for a given sphere of society, as the *going point of view* and the going *value*. To one degree or another, the author distances himself from this common language, he steps back and objectifies it, forcing his own intentions to refract and diffuse themselves through the medium of this common view that has become embodied in language (a view that is always superficial and frequently hypocritical).

The relationship of the author to a language conceived as the common view is not static – it is always found in a state of movement and oscillation that is more or less alive (this sometimes is a rhythmic oscillation): the author exaggerates, now strongly, now weakly, one or another aspect of the 'common language', sometimes abruptly exposing its inadequacy to its object and sometimes, on the contrary, becoming one with it, maintaining an almost imperceptible distance, sometimes even directly forcing it to reverberate with his own 'truth', which occurs when the author completely merges his own voice with the common view. As a consequence of such a merger, the aspects of common language, which in the given situation had been parodically exaggerated or had been treated as mere things, undergo change. The comic style demands of the author a lively to-and-fro movement in his relation to language, it demands a continual shifting of the distance between author and language, so that first some, then other aspects of language are thrown into relief. If such were not the case, the style would be monotonous or would require a greater individualization of the narrator – would, in any case, require a quite different means for introducing and organizing heteroglossia.

Against this same backdrop of the 'common language', of the impersonal, going opinion, one can also isolate in the comic novel those parodic stylizations of generic, professional and other languages we have mentioned, as well as compact masses of direct authorial discourse – pathos-filled, moral-didactic, sentimental-elegiac or idyllic. In the comic novel the direct authorial word is thus realized in direct, unqualified stylizations of poetic genres (idyllic, elegiac, etc.) or stylizations of rhetorical genres (the pathetic, the moral-didactic). Shifts from common language to parodying of generic and other languages and shifts to the direct authorial word may be gradual, or may be on the contrary quite abrupt. Thus does the system of language work in the comic novel.

We will pause for analysis on several examples from Dickens, from his novel *Little Dorrit*.

1. The conference was held at four or five o'clock in the afternoon, when all the region of Harley Street, Cavendish Square, was resonant of carriages-wheels and double-knocks. It had reached this point when Mr. Merdle came home from *his daily occupation of causing the British name to be more and more respected in all parts of the civilized globe capable of appreciation of wholewide commercial enterprise and gigantic combinations of skill and capital.* For, though nobody knew with the last precision what Mr. Merdle's business was, except that it was to coin money, these were the terms in which everybody defined it on all ceremonious occasions, and which it was the last new polite reading of the parable of the camel and the needle's eye to accept without inquiry. (Book I, ch. 33)

The italicized portion represents a parodic stylization of the language of ceremonial speeches (in parliaments and at banquets). The shift into this style is prepared for by the sentence's construction, which from the very beginning is kept within bounds by a somewhat ceremonious epic tone. Further on – and already in the language of the author (and consenquently in a different style) – the parodic meaning of the ceremoniousness of Merdle's labors becomes apparent: such a characterization turns out to be 'another's speech', to be taken only in quotation marks ('these were the terms in which everybody defined it on all ceremonious occasions').

Thus the speech of another is introduced into the author's discourse (the story) in *concealed form*, that is, without any of the *formal* markers usually accompanying such speech, whether direct or indirect. But this is not just another's speech in the same 'language' – it is another's utterance in a language that is itself 'other' to the author as well, in the archaicized language of oratorical genres associated with hypocritical official celebrations.

2. In a day or two it was announced to all the town, that Edmund Sparkler, Esquire, son-in-law of the eminent Mr. Merdle of worldwide renown, was made one of the Lords of the Circumlocution Office; and proclamation was issued, to all true believers, that this admirable *appointment was to be hailed as a graceful and gracious mark of homage, rendered by the graceful and gracious Decimus, to that commercial interest which must ever in a great commercial country – and all the rest of it, with blast of trumpet.* So, bolstered by this mark of Government homage, the *wonderful* Bank and all the other *wonderful* undertakings went on and went up; and gapers came to Harley Street, Cavendish Square, only to look at the house where the golden-wonder lived. (Book 2, ch. 12)

Here, in the italicized portion, another's speech in another's (official-ceremonial) language is openly introduced as indirect discourse. But it is surrounded by the hidden, diffused speech of another (in the same official-ceremonial language) that clears the way for the introduction of a form more easily perceived *as* another's speech and that can reverberate more fully as such. The clearing of the way comes with the word 'Esquire', characteristic of official speech, added to Sparkler's name; the final confirmation that this is another's speech comes with the epithet 'wonderful'. This epithet does not of course belong to the author but to that same 'general opinion' that had created the commotion around Merdle's inflated enterprises.

> 3. It was a dinner to provoke an appetite, though he had not had one. The rarest dishes, sumptuously cooked and sumptuously served; the choicest fruits, the most exquisite wines; marvels of workmanship in gold and silver, china and glass; innumerable things delicious to the senses of taste, smell, and sight, were insinuated into its composition. *O, what a wonderful man this Merdle, what a great man, what a master man, how blessedly and enviably endowed – in one word, what a rich man!* (Book 2, ch. 12)

The beginning is a parodic stylization of high epic style. What follows is an enthusiastic glorification of Merdle, a chorus of his admirers in the form of the concealed speech of another (the italicized portion). The whole point here is to expose the real basis for such glorification which is to unmask the chorus' hypocrisy: 'wonderful', 'great', 'master', 'endowed' can all be replaced by the single word 'rich'. This act of authorial unmasking, which is openly accomplished within the boundaries of a single simple sentence, merges with the unmasking of another's speech. The ceremonial emphasis on glorification is complicated by a second emphasis that is indignant, ironic, and this is the one that ultimately predominates in the final unmasking words of the sentence.

We have before us a typical double-accented, double-styled *hybrid construction*.

What we are calling a hybrid construction is an utterance that belongs, by its grammatical (syntactic) and compositional markers, to a single speaker, but that actually contains mixed within it two utterances, two speech manners, two styles, two 'languages', two semantic and axiological belief systems. We repeat, there is no formal – compositional and syntactic – boundary between these utterances, styles, languages, belief systems, the division of voices and languages takes place within the limits of a single syntactic whole, often within the limits of a simple sentence. It frequently happens that even one and the same word will belong simultaneously to two languages, two belief systems that intersect in a hyrid construction – and, consequently, the word has two contradictory meanings, two accents. As we shall see, hybrid constructions are of enormous significance in novel style.

> 4. But Mr. Tite Barnacle was a buttoned-up man, and *consequently* a weighty one. (Book 2, ch. 12)

The above sentence is an example of *pseudo-objective motivation*, one of the forms for concealing another's speech – in this example, the speech of 'current opinion'. If judged by the formal markers above, the logic motivating the sentence seems to belong to the author, i.e., he is formally at one with it; but in actual fact, the motivation lies within the subjective belief system of his characters, or of general opinion.

Pseudo-objective motivation is generally characteristic of novel style,[2] since it is one of the manifold forms for concealing another's speech in hybrid constructions. Subordinate conjunctions and link words ('thus', 'because', 'for the reason that', 'in spite of' and so forth), as well as words used to maintain a logical sequence ('therefore', 'consequently', etc.) lose their direct authorial intention, take on the flavour of someone else's language, become refracted or even completely reified.

Notes

1 We are of course deliberately simplifying: the real life peasant could and did do this to a certain extent.
2 Such a device is unthinkable in the epic.

25   Michel Foucault,

From 'The Order of Discourse', R. Young, ed. *Untying the Text* (1971), pp. 52–64

II

Here is the hypothesis which I would like to put forward tonight in order to fix the terrain – or perhaps the very provisional theatre – of the work I am doing: that in every society the production of discourse is at once controlled, selected, organised and redistributed by a certain number of procedures whose role is to ward off its powers and dangers, to gain mastery over its chance events, to evade its ponderous, formidable materiality.

In a society like ours, the procedures of exclusion are well known. The most obvious and familiar is the prohibition. We know quite well that we do not have the right to say everything, that we cannot speak of just anything in any circumstances whatever, and that not everyone has the right to speak of anything whatever. In the taboo on the object of speech, and the ritual of the circumstances of speech, and the privileged or exclusive right of the speaking subject, we have the play of three types of prohibition which intersect, reinforce or compensate for each other, forming a complex grid which changes constantly. I will merely note that at the present time the regions where the grid is tightest, where the black squares are most numerous, are those of sexuality and politics; as if discourse, far from being that transparent or neutral element in which sexuality is disarmed and politics pacified, is in fact one of the places where sexuality and politics exercise in a privileged way some of their most formidable powers. It does not matter that discourse appears to be of little account, because the prohibitions that surround it very soon reveal its link with desire and with power. There is nothing surprising about that, since, as psychoanalysis has shown, discourse is not simply that which manifests (or hides) desire – it is also the object of desire; and since, as history constantly teaches us, discourse is not simply that which translates struggles or systems of domination, but is the thing for which and by which there is struggle, discourse is the power which is to be seized.

There exists in our society another principle of exclusion, not another prohibition but a division and a rejection. I refer to the opposition between reason and madness. Since the depths of the Middle Ages, the madman has been the one whose discourse cannot have the same currency as others. His word may be considered null and void, having neither truth nor importance, worthless as evidence in law, inadmissible in the authentification of deeds or contracts, incapable even of bringing about the trans-substantiation of bread into body at Mass. On the other hand, strange powers not held by any other may be attributed to the madman's speech: the power of uttering a hidden truth, of telling the future, of seeing in all naivety what the others' wisdom cannot perceive. It is curious to note that for centuries in Europe the speech of the madman was either not heard at all or else taken for the word of truth. It either fell into the void, being rejected as soon as it was proffered, or else people deciphered in it a rationality, naive or crafty, which they regarded as more rational than that of the sane. In any event, whether excluded, or secretly invested with reason, the madman's speech, strictly, did not exist. It was through his words that his madness was recognised; they were the place where the division between reason and madness was exercised, but they were never recorded or listened to. No doctor before the end of the eighteenth century had ever thought of finding out what was said, or how and why it was said, in this speech which nonetheless determined the difference. This whole immense discourse of the madman was taken for mere noise, and he was only symbolically allowed to speak, in the theatre, where he would step forward, disarmed and reconciled, because there he played the role of truth in a mask.

You will tell me that all this is finished today or is coming to an end; that the madman's speech is no longer on the other side of the divide; that it is no longer null and void; and on the contrary, it puts us on the alert; that we now look for a meaning in it, for the outline or the ruins of some oeuvre; and that we have even gone so far as to come across this speech of madness in what we articulate ourselves, in that slight stumbling by which we lose track of what we are saying. But all this attention to the speech of madness does not prove that the old division is no longer operative. You have only to think of the whole framework of knowledge through which we decipher that speech, and of the whole network of institutions which permit someone – a doctor or a psychoanalyst – to listen to it, and which at the same time permit the patient to bring along his poor words or, in desperation, to withhold them. You have only to think of all this to become suspicious that the division, far from being effaced, is working differently, along other lines, through new institutions, and with effects that are not at all the same. And even if the doctor's role were only that of lending an ear to a speech that is free at last, he still does this listening in the context of the same division. He is listening to a discourse which is invested with desire, and which – for its greater exaltation or its greater anguish – thinks it is loaded with terrible powers. If the silence of reason is required for the curing of monsters, it is enough for that silence to be on the alert, and it is in this that the division remains.

It is perhaps risky to consider the opposition between true and false as a third system of exclusion, along with those just mentioned. How could one reasonably compare the constraint of truth with divisions like those, which are arbitrary to start with or which at least are organised around historical contingencies; which are not only modifiable but in perpetual displacement; which are supported by a whole system of institutions which impose them and renew them; and which act in a constraining and sometimes violent way?

Certainly, when viewed from the level of a proposition, on the inside of a discourse, the division between true and false is neither arbitrary nor modifiable nor institutional nor violent. But when we view things on a different scale, when we ask the question of what this will to truth has been and constantly is, across our discourses, this will to truth which has crossed so many centuries of our history; what is, in its very general form, the type of division which governs our will to know (notre volonté de savoir), then what we see taking shape is perhaps something like a system of exclusion, a historical, modifiable, and institutionally constraining system.

There is no doubt that this division is historically constituted. For the Greek poets of the sixth century BC, the true discourse (in the strong and valorised sense of the word), the discourse which inspired respect and terror, and to which one had to submit because it ruled, was the one pronounced by men who spoke as of right and according to the required ritual; the discourse which dispensed justice and gave everyone his share; the discourse which in prophesying the future not only announced what was going to happen but helped to make it happen, carrying men's minds along with it and thus weaving itself into the fabric of destiny. Yet already a century later the highest truth no longer resided in what discourse was or did, but in what it said: a day came when truth was displaced from the ritualised, efficacious and just act of enunciations, towards the utterance itself, its meaning, its form, its object, its relation to its reference. Between Hesiod and Plato a certain division was established, separating true discourse from false discourse: a new division because henceforth the true discourse is no longer precious and desirable, since it is no longer the one linked to the exercise of power. The sophist is banished.

This historical division probably gave our will to know its general form.

However, it has never stopped shifting: sometimes the great mutations in scientific thought can perhaps be read as the consequences of a discovery, but they can also be read as the appearance of new forms in the will to truth. There is doubtless a will to truth in the nineteenth century which differs from the will to know characteristic of Classical culture in the forms it deploys, in the domains of objects to which it addresses itself, and in the techniques on which it is based. To go back a little further: at the turn of the sixteenth century (and particularly in England), there appeared a will to know which, anticipating its actual contents, sketched out schemes of possible, observable, measurable, classifiable objects; a will to know which imposed on the knowing subject, and in some sense prior to all experience, a certain position, a certain gaze and a certain function (to see rather than to read, to verify rather than to make commentaries on); a will to know which was prescribed (but in a more general manner than by any specific instrument) by the technical level where knowledges had to be invested in order to be verifiable and useful. It was just as if, starting from the great Platonic division, the will to truth had its own history, which is not that of constraining truths: the history of the range of objects to be known, of the functions and positions of the knowing subject, of the material, technical, and instrumental investments of knowledge.

This will to truth, like the other systems of exclusion, rests on an institutional support: it is both reinforced and renewed by whole strata of practices, such as pedagogy, of course; and the system of books, publishing, libraries; learned societies in the past and laboratories now. But it is also renewed, no doubt more profoundly, by the way in which knowledge is put to work, valorised, distributed, and in a sense attributed, in a society. Let us recall at this point, and only symbolically, the old Greek principle: though arithmetic may well be the concern of democratic cities, because it teaches about the relations of equality, geometry alone must be taught in oligarchies, since it demonstrates the proportions within inequality.

Finally, I believe that this will to truth – leaning in this way on a support and an institutional distribution – tends to exert a sort of pressure and something like a power of constraint (I am still speaking of our own society) on other discourses. I am thinking of the way in which for centuries Western literature sought to ground itself on the natural, the 'vraisemblable', on sincerity, on science as well – in short, on 'true' discourse. I am thinking likewise of the manner in which economic practices, codified as precepts or recipes and ultimately as morality, have sought since the sixteenth century to ground themselves, rationalise themselves, and justify themselves in a theory of wealth and production. I am also thinking of the way in which a body as prescriptive as the penal system sought its bases or its justification, at first of course in a theory of justice, then, since the nineteenth century, in a sociological, psychological, medical, and psychiatric knowledge: it is as if even the word of the law could no longer be authorized, in our society, except by a discourse of truth.

Of the three great Systems of exclusion which forge discourse – the forbidden speech, the division of madness and the will to truth, I have spoken of the third at greatest length. The fact is that it is towards this third system that the other two have been drifting constantly for centuries. The third system increasingly attempts to assimilate the others, both in order to modify them and to provide them with a foundation. The first two are constantly becoming more fragile and more uncertain, to the extent that they are now invaded by the will to truth, which for its part constantly grows stronger, deeper, and more implacable.

And yet we speak of the will to truth no doubt least of all. It is as if, for us, the will to truth and its vicissitudes were masked by truth itself in its necessary unfolding. The reason is perhaps this: although since the Greeks 'true' discourse is no longer the discourse that answers to the demands of desire, or the discourse which exercises power, what is at stake in the will to truth, in the will to utter this 'true' discourse, if not desire and power? 'True' discourse, freed from desire and power by the necessity of its form, cannot recognise the will to truth which pervades it; and the will to truth, having imposed itself on us for a very long time, is such that the truth it wants cannot fail to mask it.

Thus all that appears to our eyes is a truth conceived as a richness, a fecundity, a gentle and insidiously universal force, and in contrast we are unaware of the will to truth, that prodigious machinery designed to exclude. All those who, from time to time in our history, have tried to dodge this will to truth and to put it into question against truth, at the very point where truth undertakes to justify the prohibition and to define madness, all of them, from Nietzsche to Artaud and Bataille, must now serve as the (no doubt lofty) signs for our daily work.

III

There are, of course, many other procedures for controlling and delimiting discourse. Those of which I have spoken up to now operate in a sense from the exterior. They function as systems of exclusion. They have to do with the part of discourse which puts power and desire at stake.

I believe we can isolate another group: internal procedures, since discourses themselves exercise their own control; procedures which function rather as principles of classification, of ordering, of distribution, as if this time another dimension of discourse had to be mastered: that of events and chance.

In the first place, commentary. I suppose – but without being very certain – that there is scarcely a society without its major narratives, which are recounted, repeated, and varied; formulae, texts, and ritualised sets of discourses which are recited in well-defined circumstances; things said once and preserved because it is suspected that behind them there is a secret or a treasure. In short, we may suspect that there is in all societies, with great consistency, a kind of gradation among discourses: those which are said in the ordinary course of days and exchanges, and which vanish as soon as they have been pronounced; and those which give rise to a certain number of new speech-acts which take them up, transform them or speak of them, in short, those discourses which, over and above their formulation, are said indefinitely, remain said, and are to be said again. We know them in our own cultural system: they are religious or juridical texts, but also those texts (curious ones, when we consider their status) which are called 'literary'; and to a certain extent, scientific texts.

This differentiation is certainly neither stable, nor constant, nor absolute. There is not, on the one side, the category of fundamental or creative discourses, given for all time, and on the other, the mass of discourses which repeat, gloss, and comment. Plenty of major texts become blurred and disappear, and sometimes commentaries move into the primary position. But though its points of application may change, the function remains; and the principle of a differentiation is continuously put back in play. The radical effacement of this gradation can only ever be play, utopia, or anguish. The Borges-style play of a commentary which is nothing but the solemn and expected reappearance word for word of the text that is commented on; or the play of a criticism that would speak forever of a work which does not exist. The lyrical dream of a discourse which is reborn absolutely new and innocent at every point, and which reappears constantly in all freshness, derived from things, feelings or thoughts. The anguish of that patient of Janet's for whom the least utterance was gospel truth, concealing inexhaustible treasures of meaning and worthy to be repeated, re-commenced, and commented on indefinitely: 'When I think,' he would say when reading or listening, 'when I think of this sentence which like the others will go off into eternity, and which I have perhaps not yet fully understood.'

But who can fail to see that this would be to annul one of the terms of the relation each time, and not to do away with the relation itself? It is a relation which is constantly changing with time; which takes multiple and divergent forms in a given epoch. The juridical exegesis is very different from the religious commentary (and this has been the case for a very long time). One and the same literary work can give rise simultaneously to very distinct types of discourse: the 'Odyssey' as a primary text is repeated, in the same period, in the translation by Bérard, and in the endless 'explications de texte', and in Joyce's 'Ulysses'.

For the moment I want to do no more than indicate that, in what is broadly called commentary, the hierarchy between primary and secondary text plays two roles which are in solidarity with each other. On the one hand it allows the (endless) construction of new discourses: the dominance of the primary text, its permanence, its status as a discourse which can always be re-actualised, the multiple or hidden meaning with which it is credited, the essential reticence and richness which is attributed to it, all this is the basis for an open possibility of speaking. But on the other hand the commentary's only role, whatever the techniques used, is to say at last what was silently articulated 'beyond', in the text. By a paradox which it always displaces but never escapes, the commentary must say for the first time what had, nonetheless, already been said, and must tirelessly repeat what had, however, never been said. The infinite rippling of commentaries is worked from the inside by the dream of a repetition in disguise: at its horizon there is perhaps nothing but what was at its point of departure – mere recitation. Commentary exorcises the chance element of discourse by giving it its due; it allows us to say something other than the text itself, but on condition that it is this text itself which is said, and in a sense completed. The open multiplicity, the element of chance, are transferred, by the principle of commentary, from what might risk being said, on to the number, the form, the mask, and the circumstances of the repetition. The new thing here lies not in what is said but in the event of its return.

I believe there exists another principle of rarefaction of a discourse, complementary to the first, to a certain extent: the author. Not, of course, in the sense of the speaking individual who pronounced or wrote a text, but in the sense of a principle of grouping of discourses, conceived as the unity and origin of their meanings, as the focus of their coherence. This principle is not everywhere at work, nor in a constant manner: there exist all around us plenty of discourses which circulate without deriving their meaning or their efficacity from an author to whom they could be attributed: everyday remarks, which are effaced immediately; decrees or contracts which require signatories but no author; technical instructions which are transmitted anonymously. But in the domains where it is the rule to attribute things to an author – literature, philosophy, science – it is quite evident that this attribution does not always play the same role. In the order of scientific discourse, it was indispensable during the Middle Ages, that a text should be attributed to an author, since this was an index of truthfulness. A proposition was considered as drawing even its scientific value from its author. Since the seventeenth century, this function has steadily been eroded in scientific discourse: it now functions only to give a name to a theorem, an effect, an example, a syndrome. On the other hand, in the order of literary discourse, starting from the same epoch, the function of the author has steadily grown stronger: all those tales, poems, dramas or comedies which were allowed to circulate in the Middle Ages in at least a relative anonymity are now asked (and obliged to say) where they come from, who wrote them. The author is asked to account for the unity of the texts which are placed under his name. He is asked to reveal or at least carry authentification of the hidden meaning which traverses them. He is asked to connect them to his lived experiences, to the real history which saw their birth. The author is what gives the disturbing language of fiction its unities, its nodes of coherence, its insertion in the real.

I know that I will be told: 'But you are speaking there of the author as he is reinvented after the event by criticism, after he is dead and there is nothing left except for a tangled mass of scribblings; in those circumstances a little order surely has to be introduced into all that, by imagining a project, a coherence, a thematic structure that is demanded of the consciousness or the life of an author who is indeed perhaps a trifle fictitious. But that does not mean he did not exist, this real author, who bursts into the midst of all these worn-out words, bringing to them his genius or his disorder.'

It would, of course, be absurd to deny the existence of the individual who writes and invents. But I believe that – at least since a certain epoch – the individual who sets out to write a text on the horizon of which a possible œuvre is prowling, takes upon himself the function of the author: what he writes and what does not write, what he sketches out, even by way of provisional drafts, as an outline of the oeuvre, and what he lets fall by way of commonplace remarks – this whole play of differences is prescribed by the author-function, as he receives it from his epoch, or as he modifies it in his turn. He may well overturn the traditional image of the author; nevertheless, it is from some new author-position that he will cut out, from everything he could say and from all that he does say every day at any moment, the still trembling outline of his œuvre.

The commentary-principle limits the chance-element in discourse by the play of an identity which would take the form of repetition and sameness. The author-principle limits this same element of chance by the play of an identity which has the form of individuality and the self.

We must also recognise another principle of limitation in what is called, not sciences but 'disciplines': a principle which is itself relative and mobile; which permits construction, but within narrow confines.

The organization of disciplines is just as much opposed to the principle of commentary as to that of the author. It is opposed to the principle of the author because a discipline is defined by a domain of objects, a set of methods, a corpus of propositions considered to be true, a play of rules and definitions, of techniques and instruments: all this constitutes a sort of anonymous system at the disposal of anyone who wants to or is able to use it, without their meaning or validity being linked to the one who happened to be their inventor. But the principle of a discipline is also opposed to that of commentary: in a discipline, unlike a commentary, what is supposed at the outset is not a meaning which has to be rediscovered, nor an identity which has to be repeated, but the requisites for the construction of new statements. For there to be a discipline, there must be a possibility of formulating new propositions, ad infinitum.

But there is more; there is more, no doubt, in order for there to be less: a discipline is not the sum of all that can be truthfully said about something; it is not even the set of all that can be accepted about the same data in virtue of some principle of coherence or systematicity. Medicine is not constituted by the total of what can be truthfully said about illness; botany cannot be defined by the sum of all the truths concerning plants. There are two reasons for this: first of all, botany and medicine are made up of errors as well as truths, like any other discipline – errors which are not residues or foreign bodies but which have positive functions, a historical efficacity, and a role that is often indissociable from that of the truths. And besides, for a proposition to belong to botany or pathology, it has to fulfil certain conditions, in a sense stricter and more complex than pure and simple truth: but in any case, other conditions. It must address itself to a determinate plane of objects: from the end of the seventeenth century, for example, for a proposition to be 'botanical' it had to deal with the visible structure of the plant, the system of its close and distant resemblances or the mechanism of its fluids; it could no longer retain its symbolic value, as was the case in the sixteenth century, nor the set of virtues and properties which were accorded to it in antiquity. But without belonging to a discipline, a proposition must use conceptual or technical instruments of a well-defined type; from the nineteenth century, a proposition was no longer medical – it fell 'outside medicine' and acquired the status of an individual phantasm or popular imagery – if it used notions that were at the same time metaphorical, qualitative, and substantial (like those of engorgement, of overheated liquids or of dried-out solids). In contrast it could and had to make use of notions that were equally metaphorical but based on another model, a functional and physiological one (that of the irritation, inflammation, or degeneration of the tissues). Still further: in order to be part of a discipline, a proposition has to be able to be inscribed on a certain type of theoretical horizon: suffice it to recall that the search for the primitive language, which was a perfectly acceptable theme up to the eighteenth century, was sufficient, in the second half of the nineteenth century, to make any discourse fall into – I hesitate to say error – chimera and reverie, into pure and simple linguistic monstrosity.

Within its own limits, each discipline recognises true and false propositions; but it pushes back a whole teratology of knowledge beyond its margins. The exterior of a science is both more and less populated than is often believed: there is of course immediate experience, the imaginary themes which endlessly carry and renew immemorial beliefs; but perhaps there are no errors in the strict sense, for error can only arise and be decided inside a definite practice; on the other hand, there are monsters on the prowl whose form changes with the history of knowledge. In short, a proposition must fulfil complex and heavy requirements to be able to belong to the grouping of a discipline; before it can be called true or false, it must be 'in the true', as Canguilhem would say.

People have often wondered how the botanists or biologists of the nineteenth century managed not to see that what Mendel was saying was true. But it was because Mendel was speaking of objects, applying methods, and placing himself on a theoretical horizon which were alien to the biology of his time. Naudin, before him, had of course posited the thesis that hereditary traits are discrete; yet, no matter how new or strange this principle was it was able to fit into the discourse of biology at least as an enigma. What Mendel did was to constitute the hereditary trait as an absolutely new biological object, thanks to a kind of filtering which had never been used before: he detached the trait from the species and from the sex which transmits it; the field in which he observed it being the infinitely open series of the generations, where it appears and disappears according to statistical regularities. This was a new object which called for new conceptual instruments and new theoretical foundations. Mendel spoke the truth, but he was not 'within the true, of the biological discourse of his time: it was not according to such rules that biological objects and concepts were formed. It needed a complete change of scale, the deployment of a whole new range of objects in biology for Mendel to enter into the true and for his propositions to appear (in large measure) correct. Mendel was a true monster, which meant that science could not speak of him; whereas about thirty years earlier, at the height of the nineteenth century, Scheiden, for example, who denied plant sexuality, but in accordance with the rules of biological discourse, was merely formulating a disciplined error.

It is always possible that one might speak the truth in the space of a wild exteriority, but one is 'in the true' only by obeying the rules of a discursive 'policing' which one has to reactivate in each of one's discourses.

The discipline is a principle of control over the production of discourse. The discipline fixes limits for discourse by the action of an identity which takes the form of a permanent re-actuation of the rules.

We are accustomed to see in an author's fecundity, in the multiplicity of the commentaries, and in the development of a discipline so many infinite resources for the creation of discourses. Perhaps so, but they are nonetheless principles of constraint; it is very likely impossible to account for their positive and multiplicatory role if we do not take into consideration their restrictive and constraining function.

IV

There is, I believe, a third group of procedures which permit the control of discourses. This time it is not a matter of mastering their powers or averting the unpredictability of their appearance, but of determining the condition of their application, of imposing a certain number of rules on the individuals who hold them, and thus of not permitting everyone to have access to them. There is a rarefaction, this time, of the speaking subjects; none shall enter the order of discourse if he does not satisfy certain requirements or if he is not, from the outset, qualified to do so. To be more precise: not all the regions of discourse are equally open and penetrable; some of them are largely forbidden (they are differentiated and differentiating), while others seems to be almost open to all winds and put at the disposal of every speaking subject, without prior restrictions.

In this regard I should like to recount an anecdote which is so beautiful that one trembles at the thought that it might be true. It gathers into a single figure all the constraints of discourse: those which limit its powers, those which master its aleatory appearances, those which carry out the selection among speaking subjects. At the beginning of the seventeenth century, the Shogun heard tell that the Europeans' superiority in matters of navigation, commerce, politics, and military skill was due to their knowledge of mathematics. He desired to get hold of so precious a knowledge. As he had been told of an English sailor who possessed the secret of these miraculous discourses, he summoned him to his palace and kept him there. Alone with him, he took lessons. He learned mathematics. He retained power, and lived to a great old age. It was not until the nineteenth century that there were Japanese mathematicians. But the anecdote does not stop there: it has its European side too. The story has it that this English sailor, Will Adams, was an autodidact, a carpenter who had learnt geometry in the course of working in a shipyard. Should we see this story as the expression of one of the great myths of European culture? The universal communication of knowledge and the infinite free exchange of discourses in Europe, against the monopolised and secret knowledge of Oriental tyranny?

This idea, of course, does not stand up to examination. Exchange and communication are positive figures working inside complex systems of restriction, and probably would not be able to function independently of them. The most superficial and visible of these systems of restriction is constituted by what can be gathered under the name of ritual. Ritual defines the qualification which must be possessed by individuals who speak (and who must occupy such-and-such a position and formulate such-and-such a type of statement, in the play of a dialogue, of interrogation or recitation); it defines the gestures, behaviour, circumstances, and the whole set of signs which must accompany discourse; finally, it fixes the supposed or imposed efficacity of the words, their effect on those to whom they are addressed, and the limits of their constraining value. Religious, judicial, therapeutic, and in large measure also political discourses can scarcely be dissociated from this deployment of a ritual which determines both the particular properties and the stipulated roles of the speaking subjects.

A somewhat different way of functioning is that of the 'societies of discourse', which function to preserve or produce discourses, but in order to make them circulate in a closed space, distributing them only according to strict rules, and without the holders being dispossessed by this distribution. An archaic model for this is provided by the groups of rhapsodists who possessed the knowledge of the poems to be recited or potentially to be varied and transformed. But though the object of this knowledge was after all a ritual recitation, the knowledge was protected, defended and preserved within a definite group by the often very complex exercises of memory which it implied. To pass an apprenticeship in it allowed one to enter both a group and a secret which the act of recitation showed but did not divulge; the roles of speaker and listener were not interchangeable.

There are hardly any such 'societies of discourse' now, with their ambiguous play of the secret and its divulgation. But this should not deceive us: even in the order of 'true' discourse, even in the order of discourse that is published and free from all ritual, there are still forms of appropriation of secrets, and non-interchangeable roles. It may well be that the act of writing as it is institutionalized today, in the book, the publishing-system and the person of the writer, takes place in a 'society of discourse', which though diffuse is certainly constraining. The difference between the writer and any other speaking or writing subject (a difference constantly stressed by the writer himself), the intransitive nature (according to him) of his discourse, the fundamental singularity which he has been ascribing for so long to 'writing', the dissymmetry that is asserted between 'creation' and any use of the linguistic system – all this shows the existence of a certain 'society of discourse', and tends moreover to bring back its play of practices. But there are many others still, functioning according to entirely different schemes of exclusivity and disclosure: e.g., technical or scientific secrets, or the forms of diffusion and circulation of medical discourse, or those who have appropriated the discourse of politics or economics.

At first glance, the 'doctrines' (religious, political, philosophical) seem to constitute the reverse of a 'society of discourse', in which the number of speaking individuals tended to be limited even if it was not fixed; between those individuals, the discourse could circulate and be transmitted. Doctrine, on the contrary, tends to be diffused, and it is by the holding in common of one and the same discursive ensemble that individuals (as many as one cares to imagine) define their reciprocal allegiance. In appearance, the only prerequisite is the recognition of the same truths and the acceptance of a certain rule of (more or less flexible) conformity with the validated discourses. If doctrines were nothing more than this, they would not be so very different from scientific disciplines, and the discursive control would apply only to the form or the content of the statement, not to the speaking subject. But doctrinal allegiance puts in question both the statement and the speaking subject, the one by the other. It puts the speaking subject in question through and on the basis of the statement, as is proved by the procedures of exclusion and the mechanisms of rejection which come into action when a speaking subject has formulated one or several unassimilable statements; heresy and orthodoxy do not derive from a fanatical exaggeration of the doctrinal mechanisms, but rather belong fundamentally to them. And conversely the doctrine puts the statements in question on the basis of the speaking subjects, to the extent that the doctrine always stands as the sign, manifestation and instrument of a prior adherence to a class, a social status, a race, a nationality, an interest, a revolt, a resistance or an acceptance. Doctrine binds individuals to certain types of enunciation and consequently forbids them all others; but it uses, in return, certain types of enunciation to bind individuals amongst themselves, and to differentiate them by that very fact from all others. Doctrine brings about a double subjection: of the speaking subjects to discourses, and of discourses to the (at least virtual) group of speaking individuals.

On a much broader scale, we are obliged to recognise large cleavages in what might be called the social appropriation of discourses. Although education may well be, by right, the instrument thanks to which any individual in a society like ours can have access to any kind of discourse whatever, this does not prevent it from following, as is well known, in its distribution, in what it allows and what it prevents, the lines marked out by social distances, oppositions and struggles. Any system of education is a political way of maintaining or modifying the appropriation of discourses, along with the knowledges and powers which they carry.

I am well aware that it is very abstract to separate speech-rituals, societies of discourse, doctrinal groups and social appropriations, as I have just done. Most of the time, they are linked to each other and constitute kinds of great edifices which ensure the distribution of speaking subjects into the different types of discourse and the appropriation of discourses to certain categories of subject. Let us say, in a word, that those are the major procedures of subjection used by discourse. What, after all, is an education system, other than a ritualisation of speech, a qualification and a fixing of the roles for speaking subjects, the constitution of a doctrinal group, however diffuse, a distribution and an appropriation of discourse with its powers and knowledges? What is 'écriture' (the writing of the 'writers') other than a similar system of subjection, which perhaps takes slightly different forms, but forms whose main rhythms are analogous? Does not the judicial system, does not the institutional system of medicine likewise constitute, in some of their aspects at least, similar systems of subjection of and by discourse?

26 Jerome J. McGann,
'The Text, the Poem, and the Problem of Historical Method', in *The Beauty of Inflections* (1985), pp. 111–32

I

At this point in academic time, the problem of historical method emerges most dramatically at the elementary levels of textual interpretation. The problem appears in two typical forms which are inversely related to each other. On the one hand, intrinsic critics cannot see that historical studies go to the heart of literary objects. Since the latter appear to address problems (and people) which are not historically limited, the 'problem' with historical studies is that they continue to be pursued at all. Why should works which transcend the originary moment require historical analysis and commentary?

On the other hand, historical method is also a problem for scholars and critics who work in any of the areas of extrinsic criticism: in bibliography and textual criticism, in philology, in biography and literary history, and so forth. In this case, the difficulty is that the scholar's work so often does seem irrelevant to the understanding and appreciation of poetry. What is most disturbing about this situation is that so few scholars even acknowledge that their methods require a theoretical grounding in hermeneutics.

These brief remarks will come as news to no one. We are all aware of the situation. Before I try to suggest how we might try to deal with these issues, however, permit me another brief essay into familiar territory. For I believe that we can best come to grips with these problems of historical method if we see more clearly how they came to assume their present form.

It is well known that the most advanced literary studies in the nineteenth century were those which developed and modified the enormous advances in theory and method made in classical and biblical philology and textual criticism. Wolf and Eichhorn are only the most familiar names among that group of brilliant, predominantly German, critics of the late eighteenth century who made the initial breakthrough in transforming literary studies into a modern scientific discipline. These are the scholars who created both the Lower (or textual) Criticism and the Higher (or philological) Criticism. Historical philology in the nineteenth century brought analytic techniques to bear upon previously synthesized material in order to see more clearly the strokes of the tulip and the parts of the rainbow. The most advanced of such critics – in England, men like Coleridge and Arnold hoped to enlist these analytic techniques in the service of a new and higher synthesis: to adapt Coleridge's famous declaration, by dissolving, diffusing, and dissipating, 'to recreate . . . to idealize and to unify'.

In the twentieth century, however, the historical methods of the Lower and Higher Criticism gave way before the advance of several sorts of formal criticism and structural analysis. As we know, the principal impetus behind these critical movements came from language study and especially from linguistics. What Wolf, Lachmann, and Strauss were to nineteenth-century literary criticism, Saussure and Hjelmslev have been to the twentieth century. Hjelmslev's lucid *Prolegomena to a Theory of Language* (1943) accurately describes the shift which took place as a deliberate effort to break free of the descriptive, atomistic, and empirical approaches which flourished in the nineteenth century. 'The study of literature and the study of art', Hjelmslev says, had been carried out under 'historically descriptive rather than systematising disciplines', and his project, which explicitly follows Saussure, proposes a systematic rather than an empirical analytic of humanistic phenomena. *A priori* it would seem to be a generally valid thesis that for *every process* there is a corresponding *system*, by which the process can be analyzed and described by means of a limited number of premises. It must be assumed that any process can be analyzed into a limited number of elements recurring in various combinations.[1] In this passage Hjelmslev prepares the ground for a systematic linguistics, but his words clearly underwrite any number of other twentieth century programmes of a formal or structural sort (Bultmann in biblical criticism, Lévi-Strauss in anthropology, Propp, Greimas, and many others in literary studies). These new semiological methods can be applied in all humanistic disciplines, as Hjelmslev well knew.

The shift from an empirical to a structural analytic has deeply influenced twentieth-century approaches to literary works, with far-reaching consequences. Before I turn to them, however, and thus reconnect with my initial two-handed 'problem of historical method', let me point out an interesting peripheral remark in Hjelmslev's book. When he attacks the empirical methods of the nineteenth century, its anti-systematic bias, he also explains the particular aesthetic position which underlies that

> humanistic tradition which, in various dress, has till now predominated ... According to this view, humanistic, as opposed to natural, phenomena, are non-recurrent and for that very reason cannot, like natural phenomena, be subjected to exact and generalizing treatment. In the field of the humanities, consequently, there would have to be a different method – namely, mere description, which would be nearer to poetry than to exact science – or, at any event, a method that restricts itself to a discursive form of presentation, in which the phenomena pass by, one by one, without being interpreted through a system. (pp. 8–9)

As far as the appreciation of poetry is concerned, the nineteenth century's 'humanistic' methods sought to preserve and illuminate the uniqueness of the poetic object. We would do well to remember this fact about nineteenth-century philology, for in the modern period – as we survey those prelapsarian Germanic tomes of dryasdust scholarship – we do not always recall (indeed, their authors do not always recall) the aesthetic phenomena those critical procedures were designed to illuminate. Our preoccupation with the minute particularities of poetical works emerged from the philological traditions which gave us 'textual criticism'. The contemporary vulgarisation of this philological term eloquently demonstrates the position that modern literary studies takes in relation to its immediate forebears.

The structural and semiological approaches to language and, in particular, to literature provided modern critics with operational procedures for analysing literature in a Kantian mode. In the *Critique of Judgement*, Kant offered a novel philosophy of art grounded in the notion that aesthetic works were integral phenomena whose finality was exhausted in the individual's experience of the work. The modern concept of 'the poem itself' as a self-referential linguistic system is fundamentally Kantian, though twentieth-century developments in linguistics provided this Kantian approach with its basic procedural rules for an actual critical practice.

These procedural rules operated under one fundamental premise: that literary works are special sorts of linguistic 'texts', that every poem is coextensive with its linguistic structure. Twentieth-century literary criticism contains a rich variety of schools and methods- analytical, structural, rhetorical, stylistic – but for all their important differences, they tend to share the conviction that poems are self-subsistent linguistic systems. The function of criticism is to illuminate the operations of those linguistic structures which we now like to call 'texts'. According to the classic formulation of Roman Jakobson: 'Poetics deals with problems of verbal structure . . . Since linguistics is the global science of verbal structure, poetics may be regarded as an integral part of linguistics.'[2]

This idea of the poem as verbal object is so commonplace in modern criticism that we may seem perverse to question it. Still we must do so, for the 'problem of historical method' – whether we approach it from an 'intrinsic' or an 'extrinsic' point of view – will never be opened to solutions until we see one of the signal failures of modern criticism: its inability to distinguish clearly between a concept of the *poem* and a concept of the *text*. Indeed, when we recover this essential analytic distinction, we will begin to reacquire some other, equally crucial distinctions which have fallen into disuse: for example, the distinction between concepts of *poem* and of *poetical work*. For the present I will concentrate on the first of these distinctions, and my analysis will proceed through a series of illustrative examples.[3]

II

When Byron sent the manuscript of *Don Juan* Cantos I and II to his publisher John Murray late in 1818, the poet was not only, with Goethe, the most famous writer in the Western world, his works were the most saleable products on the English literary market. He was not an author Murray wanted to lose. But this new work set Murray back on his heels. He was filled with wonder at its genius and with loathing at its immorality – at its obscenity, its blasphemy, its libellous attacks upon the poet laureate, and its seditious attitude toward the English government's policies at home and abroad.[4]

In the struggle that ensued, Murray and his London circle (which included some of Byron's best and oldest friends) pressed the poet either to withdraw the poem altogether or to revise it drastically and remove its objectionable parts. Byron agreed to some revisions, but his final line of retreat still seemed a fearful one to his publisher. When Byron threatened to take his poem elsewhere, Murray agreed to publish; he did not, however, tell his celebrated author precisely *how* he would publish.

For Murray, the problem was how to issue this inflammatory work without provoking a legal action against himself either by the government directly or by the notorious Society for the Suppression of Vice. His plan of action was ingenious but, in the end, self-defeating. Murray decided to issue a short run (1,500 copies) of the poem in a sumptuous quarto edition and to print it without either Byron's name as author or even his own as publisher. The price – £1 11s. 6d. – was set high in order to ensure a circulation limited alike in numbers and in social class.

The immediate effect of this manoeuvre was successful, for *Don Juan* stole into the world without provoking any moral outcry. The earliest reviewers were generally quite favourable, even from entrenched conservative quarters like *The Literary Gazette*.

But Murray's plan for avoiding the censors failed, in the end, because it was, in the words of Hugh J. Luke, Jr., 'a contradictory one'.[5] Murray avoided prosecution for issuing *Don Juan*, but his method of publication ensured a widespread piratical printing of the poem in the radical press. Thousands of copies of *Don Juan* were issued in cheap pirated editions, and as the work received wider celebrity and distribution, so the moral outcry against it was raised, and spread.

The significance which this story holds for my present purposes – i.e. for my aim to elucidate the problematics of the 'text' – is neatly explained by an anonymous article (possibly by Southey) printed in the conservative *Quarterly Review* in April 1822. In its quarto form, the reviewer notes, *Don Juan*

> would have been confined by its price to a class of readers with whom its faults might have been somewhat compensated by its merits; with whom the ridicule, which it endeavors to throw upon virtue, might have been partially balanced by that with which it covers vice, particularly the vice to which the class of readers to whom we are alluding are most subject – that which pleads romantic sensibility, or ungovernable passion; to readers, in short, who would have turned with disgust from its indecencies, and remembered only its poetry and its wit.[6]

But the poem was issued in numerous cheap piracies and therein lay the mischief, 'some publishing it with obscene engravings, others in weekly numbers, and all in a shape that brought it within the reach of purchasers on whom its poison would operate without mitigation – who would search its pages for images to pamper a depraved imagination and for a sanction for the insensibility to the sufferings of others, which is often one of the most unhappy results of their own'. In short as the reviewer says so well: 'Don Juan in quarto and on hot-pressed paper would have been almost innocent – in a whity-brown duodecimo it was one of the worst of the mischievous publications that have made the press a snare'.

Several important conclusions follow from this eventful narrative. In this first place, the example illustrates how different texts, in the bibliographical sense, embody different poems (in the aesthetic sense) despite the fact that both are linguistically identical. In the second place, the example also suggests that the method of printing or publishing a literary work carries with it enormous cultural and aesthetic significance for the work itself.

Finally, we can begin to see, through this example, that the essential character of a work of art is not determined *sui generis* but is, rather, the result of a process involving the actions and interactions of a specific and socially integrated group of people.[7]

The contemporary fashion of calling literary works 'texts' carries at least one unhappy critical result: it suggests that poems and works of fiction possess their integrity *as poems and works of fiction* totally aside from the events and materials describable in their bibliographies. In this usage we are dealing with 'texts' which transcend their concrete and actual textualities. This usage of the word *text* does not mean anything written or printed in an actual physical state; rather, it means the opposite: it points to an *Ur*-poem or meta-work whose existence is the Idea that can be abstracted out of all concrete and written texts which have ever existed or which ever will exist.[8] All these different texts are what can be called – Ideally – 'The Text'.

This Ideal Text is the object of almost all the critical scrutiny produced in the New Critical and post-New Critical traditions, whether formal, stylistic, or structural.[9] To arrive at such a Text, however, the critic normally obligates himself to make certain that his physical text is 'correct', which is to say that it corresponds, linguistically, to the author's final intentions about what editors call his work's substantive and accidental features. By meeting this obligation the critic pays his dues to the philological traditions of the last three hundred years. At the same time, the critic places himself in a position from which he can treat the literary work as if it were a timeless object, unconnected with history. The Text is viewed *sub specie aeternitatis*, and modern criticism approaches it much as the pre-critical scholar of Sacred Scripture approached the Word of God.

But in fact not even a linguistic uniformity sanctioned by philology can deliver over to us a final, definitive Text which will be the timeless object of critical interpretation and analysis. The example from Byron suggests this, clearly, but that case is merely paradigmatic. No literary work is definable purely in linguistic terms, and the illustration from Byron could easily be replaced by examples from any writer one might choose. It would not be very difficult to show, from the works of William Blake, that linguistic uniformity will hardly serve to establish a definitive Text. Of course everyone knows that Blake's *words* do not comprehend Blake's 'poetical works', so that (Ideally) critics recognize the necessity of 'reading' Blake in facsimile editions; and, in fact, facsimile editions do deliver more of Blake's work to the reader. But a Blake text comprising both words and illustrative matter still falls short of delivering this artist's work to an audience today.

Since Blake's work operates in an integrated verbal and visual medium, we are forced to see that the 'linguistic level' of this work corresponds to the entire mixed medium and not merely to the verbal one. But that Blake's 'poetical works' are not finished and complete in some Ideal mixed-medium Text is apparent if we simply recall the character of Blake's original methods of 'publication'. He is probably the most private and individualistic artist ever to emerge from England, and each of his engraved works was a unique publication by itself. It was part of Blake's artistic project that each of his works *be* unique, and he in fact achieved his purpose – most notoriously, I suppose, in his masterwork *Jerusalem*. Fewer than ten original copies of this work survive, and each is quite distinct. To speak of the Text of *Jerusalem*, then, as if that term comprehended some particular concrete reality rather than a heuristic idea, is manifestly to talk nonsense. One might as well try to speak of the Text of Emily Dickinson's verse. In reality, there is no such Text; there are only texts, of various kinds, prepared by various people (some by the author), at various periods, for particular and various purposes.

Yet the example of Blake carries a moral which takes us beyond the insight that an artist's work is not equivalent to an Ideal Text, nor even to some particular text or edition (say, an especially meticulous one prepared by a skilled editor). For every work of art is the product of an interaction between the artist, on the one hand, and a variety of social determinants on the other. Even the simplest textual problem establishing a work's *linguistic* correctness – can involve other problems that are, quite literally, insoluble. Keats, we recall, wrote two distinct and finished versions of 'La Belle Dame Sans Merci'.[10] But even if one were to set aside these special problems and assume that we can establish 'the author's final intentions' toward the language or even the entire format of a work we would still have, as readers, merely one text of the work, or – as scholars – the means for producing a number of possible editions, or texts.

The fact is that the works of an artist are produced, at various times and places, and by many different sorts of people, in a variety of different textual constitutions (some better than others). Each of these texts is the locus of a process of artistic production and consumption involving the originary author, other people (his audience[s], his publisher, etc.), and certain social institutions. Blake's special way of creating his works emphasizes the presence of these impinging social factors precisely because Blake strove so resolutely, even so obsessively, to produce work that was wholly his own. Each original copy of *Jerusalem* is unique, and in them Blake has achieved an extraordinary degree of artistic freedom. Had his work been reproduced through the procedures maintained by the ordinary publishing institutions of his day, it would have been a very different product altogether (it would have been reviewed, for example, and it would have fallen into many people's hands).[11] Nor are these differences merely accidental, and unimportant for the 'meaning' of Blake's work. Certainly to Blake they seemed immensely consequential; indeed – and he was quite right – they seemed definitive of the difference between one sort of art (free, creative) and another (commonplace, generalized).

In his own day Blake insisted upon having his artistic freedom, and the proper measure of his success in this aim – ironic though it seems lies in his contemporary artistic anonymity. Yet the social life of an artist transcends his particular historical moment, and so Blake, lost to his own age, was 'discovered' by the Pre-Raphaelites, who initiated the process of full social integration which his work has since achieved. Blake's unique works, in consequence, would become mass-produced, and his fierce individuality would itself become deeply integrated into various ideologies and social institutions. We may well see an irony in this event. Even more, however, should we see how it illustrates a fundamental fact about all art: that it is a social product with various, and changing, social functions to perform.

The initial example from Byron and the general case of Blake illustrate very clearly, I think, that a work of art – a poem, in this case – is no more the isolate creation of an artist then 'the poem itself' is defined either by some particular text on the one hand, or by the Ideal Text on the other. Poems are artistic works produced, and maintained, under specific socialized conditions. It is the business of analytic criticism to isolate and categorize the various social factors which meet and interact in various works of art, and finally, to explain those interactions.

In attempting to show how different poetical works have acquired different textual constitutions, I have drawn attention to certain physical characteristics of some texts of *Don Juan* and *Jerusalem*. The physical differences between the several texts stand as signs of a productive process which is different in each case, and which, consequently, produces several different artistic works. The first two cantos of *Don Juan*, as issued by Murray, are not the same work as the first two cantos as issued by the pirates. The fact that Byron's *Don Juan* should have called out these two sorts of edition is one sign of its creative power, just as the poem's long and complex bibliographical history has testified to its trans-historical character and relevance.

Let there be no confusion in this matter, however: when we see that an author's work exists in many different textual constitutions, we do not mean to suggest that, for example, there are as many poems called *Jerusalem* as there are texts or editions. We must resist the modern fashion of referring to poems as 'texts' precisely because this vulgar usage confuses the fundamental difference between a poem's *text* – which is one thing – and a poem – which is quite another. Preserving this distinction is crucial for purposes of critical method, since the distinction facilitates a clear view of a poem's changing life in human society. Speaking of poems as 'texts' implicitly affirms an idea of literary works which involves two contradictory propositions: (1) that a poem is equivalent to its linguistic constitution and (2) that the textual differences in a poem's bibliographical history have no necessary relation to issues of literary criticism as such. The poem-as-text, then, is a critical idea which at once reduces poetry to a verbal construct and inflates it to the level of an immaterial, non-particular pure Idea (the poem as Ideal Text). This result seems paradoxical, but in fact it is the necessary consequence of a view of literary works which is founded on a contradiction.

The example of *Don Juan* must not be taken to suggest, however, that a poetical work is the product of a social engagement entered into, voluntarily or otherwise, by author, printer, and publisher alone. Rather, the local publishing relationship among these three persons is itself a sign needing critical analysis. The fact that Blake deliberately avoided any involvement in this, the normal publishing relationship of his day, is of immense critical significance for his work and especially for a late work like *Jerusalem*. To know the publishing options taken (and refused) by Chaucer, or Donne, or Pope, or Blake, or Byron enables the critic to explain the often less visible, but more fundamental, social engagements which meet in and generate the work in question.

The illustration from Byron is especially illuminating because it brings to our attention another crucial productive figure (anterior to the audience of consumers) who participates in the artistic process initiated by the artist. I mean, of course, the reviewer (or critic), who is the final mediating force between author and audience. It is the function of the (contemporary) reviewer and (subsequent) critic to make explicit the lines of interpretation which exist *in potentia* in their respective audiences. Critics and reviewers – to adapt a phrase from Shelley imagine what students and audiences already know about the works they are to read.

III

At this point in the analysis, though we have, I believe, established the generic functional usefulness of preserving distinctions among texts, poems, and poetical works, the specific value of such distinctions for literary criticism is still unclear. Are these the sort of distinctions which, in the end, make no difference?

In the example which follows I mean to illustrate two related points: first (on the negative side), that the failure to maintain these distinctions creates a procedural error which necessarily threatens any subsequent practical criticism with disaster; and second (on the positive side), that the pursuit and elucidation of such distinctions sharply increases our understanding of poetry and poems in both the theoretical and the practical spheres. This second aspect of the demonstration will return us to the 'problem of historical method' which was raised at the outset. By framing these historically self-conscious demonstrations along the traditional 'intrinsic' lines of formal and thematic analysis, I propose to show: (1) that poems are, by the nature of the case (or, as Kant might say, 'transcendentally'), time- and place-specific; (2) that historical analysis is, therefore, a necessary and essential function of any advanced practical criticism.

The case I propose to consider is Allen Tate's famous interpretation of

Emily Dickinson's poem 'Because I could not Stop for Death'.[12] His discussion raises, once again, the whole range of unresolved problems which lie in wait for any critical method which cannot make serious distinctions between texts and poems.

Tate begins by quoting the poem in full and declaring it to be 'one of the greatest in the English language' and 'one of the perfect poems in English'. His argument for these judgements rests upon T.S. Eliot's famous discussion of the 'dissociation of sensibility'. Dickinson's poem is 'perfect' because it displays a perfect 'fusion of sensibility and thought': 'The framework of the poem is, in fact, the two abstractions, mortality and eternity, which are made to associate in equality with images: she sees the ideas, and thinks the perceptions. She did, of course, nothing of the sort; but we must use the logical distinctions, even to the extent of paradox, if we are to form any notion of this rare quality of mind' (p. 161). Tate argues for this general position by instancing what he sees as the poem's precision and tight structure of rhythm, image, and theme. The poem has nothing to excess; it is marked throughout by 'a restraint that keeps the poet from carrying' her dramatic images too far. As for the poem's ideas, they are something altogether different from 'the feeble poetry of moral ideals that flourished in New England in the eighties':

> The terror of death is objectified through this figure of the genteel driver, who is made ironically to serve the end of Immortality. This is the heart of the poem: she has presented a typical Christian theme in its final irresolution, without making any final statements about it. There is no solution to the problem; there can be only a presentation of it in the full context of intellect and feeling. A construction of the human will, elaborated with all the abstracting powers of the mind, is put to the concrete test of experience: the idea of immortality is confronted with the fact of physical disintegration. We are not told what to think; we are told to look at the situation. (p. 161)

In evaluating this criticism we begin with the text quoted by Tate. When he calls the poem 'The Chariot', as he does at the beginning of his discussion, he tells us what his text shows: Tate is reading the work printed in 1890 by Todd and Higginson. But of course, 'The Chariot' is not what Dickinson wrote, at any time; rather, it is a text which her first editors produced when they carefully worked over the (untitled) text written by the author. Among other, less significant changes, an entire stanza was removed (the fourth) and several lines underwent major alteration.[13] Since Tate's argument for the greatness of the poem depends heavily upon his view of its linguistic perfection, we are faced with a rather awkward situation. Under the circumstances, one would not find it very difficult to embarrass Tate's reading by subjecting it to an ironical inquisition on the subject of textual criticism.

Of course, Tate had no access to the text Dickinson actually wrote. Nevertheless, his critical judgement ought to have been warned that textual problems existed since he did have available to him another – and, as it happens, more accurate – text of Dickinson's work. This text appeared in Martha Dickinson Bianchi's 1924 edition of *The Complete Poems*, and it is the one cited by Yvor Winters in the critique of Tate's essay first published by Winters in *Maule's Curse*.[14] But Tate's critical method could not prepare him to deal with problems in textual criticism. Indeed, he could not even see such problems, much less analyse their critical relevance. In this case, the impoverished historical sense of his general critical method appears as an inability to make critical judgements about poetic texts, to make distinctions between poems and their texts, and to relate those judgements and distinctions to the final business of literary criticism.

We have no call, nor any desire, to ridicule Tate's essay on this matter. Nevertheless, the issue must be faced squarely, for the problems raised by Tate's lack of textual scrupulousness appear at other points, and in other forms, in his discussion, and his example typifies the sorts of problem that remain widespread in Western modes of formal, stylistic, structural, and post-structural procedures. We may observe the congruence of his critical practice – the symmetry between his lack of interest in textual matters and his general interpretive approach – by examining his remarks on the poem's thematic concerns. We shall notice two matters here: first, a tendency to overread the poem at the linguistic level; and second, a reluctance to take seriously, or even notice, either the fact or the importance of the poem's ideological attitudes. In each case we are dealing with something fundamental to Tate's literary criticism and to twentieth-century interpretive approaches generally: their attempt to lift the poem out of its original historical context and to erase the distance between that original context and the immediate context of the critical act.

In this next phase of my analysis, then, I am proposing to extend the discussion from its specific interest in 'the problem of the text' to the more general issue which that problem localizes. Critics who do not or cannot distinguish between the different concrete texts which a poem assumes in its historical passage are equally disinclined to study the aesthetic significance of a poem's topical dimensions, or its didactic, ethical, or ideological materials. Poems that have no textual histories have, at the thematic level, only those meanings and references which 'transcend' the particulars of time and place. The poetry of poems, in this view, is a function not of specific ideology or topical matters but of 'universal' themes and references – and the *most* universal of these universals are a poem's formal, stylistic, or structural excellences. The ultimate consequence of such approaches is that the present critic loses altogether his awareness that his own criticism is historically limited and time-bound in very specific ways. Losing a critical sense of the past, the interpreter necessarily loses his ability to see his own work in a critical light.

Let me return to Tate's analysis and the Dickinson poem, however, where we can study these problems as they emerge in concrete forms. When Tate says, for example, that the poem presents 'the problems of immortality ... confronted with the fact of physical disintegration', we observe a critical move characteristic of twentieth-century criticism: that is, the habit of dealing with poetry's substantive concerns at the most abstract and generalized thematic levels. I will have more to say about this sort of critical abstraction in a moment. For now we want most to query Tate's interpretation of the thematic aspects of the Dickinson poem. When he argues, for example, that the poem does not treat 'moral ideas', and that it takes a non-committal ('unresolved') stance toward a serious intellectual problem, we are surely justified in demurring. The civil kindliness of Death is of course ironically presented, but the irony operates at the expense of those who foolishly, the poem implies – regard Death as a fearful thing and who give all their attention to their mortal affairs ('My labor, and my leisure too') either because of their fear or as a consequence of it. Like the poem's speaker before Death 'stopped' for her, the readers of the poem are assumed to be fearful of Death and too busy with the affairs of their lives to 'stop' for him.[15] The poem does indeed have 'a moral', and it appears in an unmistakable form in the final stanza:

> Since then – 'tis Centuries – and yet
> Feels shorter than the Day
> I first surmised the Horses Heads
> Were toward Eternity –

'We are not told what to think' by the poem, Tate asserts, but his position is only technically correct. Of course the poem does not *tell* us what to think, but its message about the benevolence of Death is plain enough. This message, however, like the poem which carries it, is no simple-minded pronouncement; the message is rich and affecting because it is delivered in human rather than abstract space. Dickinson's poem locates a set of relationships in which Dickinson, her fictive speaker, and her invited readers engage with each other in various emotional and intellectual ways.[16] The focus of these engagements is the poem's commonplace Christian theme: that people who are too busily involved with their worldly affairs give little serious thought to Death and the Afterlife. Criticizing such thoughtlessness, the poem encourages its readers to ponder Death and the Afterlife in a positive way. Its procedure for doing so involves the assumption of another thematic commonplace – that people fear to think about Death – and then undermining its force by a play of wit.

The wit appears most plainly in the rhetorical structure of the poem, which pretends to be spoken by a person already dead. Like some Christian Blessed Damozel from New England, Dickinson's speaker addresses this world from the other side, as it were, and lets us know that Death leads us not to oblivion but to 'Eternity' and 'Immortality'.[7] But the wit goes deeper, for Dickinson does not present her fiction as anything *but* fiction. The playfulness of the poem – which is especially evident in the final stanza, whose quiet good humour has been remarked upon frequently – is the work's most persuasive argument that Death can be contemplated not merely without fear but – more positively – with feelings of civilized affection. The kindliness and civility of the carriage driver are qualities we recognize in the *voice* of the poem's speaker and in the *wit* of its maker.

When we speak of the poem's wit, however, we should not lose ourselves in a hypnotic fascination with its verbal reality alone. The wit is at least as much a function of Dickinson's perspicuous observations of, and comments upon, social reality as it is of her facility with language. We may see this more clearly if we recall the standard critical idea that the figure of Death in this poem is – in the words of a recent critic – a 'gentlemanly suitor'.[18] Tate seems to have initiated this reading when he spoke of the driver as 'a gentleman taking a lady out for a drive', and when he proceeded to notice the 'erotic motive' associated with 'this figure of the genteel driver'. His commentary shows an acute awareness of one of the poem's subtlest and least explicit aspects, but it also displays a failure to see a more obvious but no less important fact about the driver.

This man is not a suitor but an undertaker, as we see quite clearly in the penultimate line's reference to 'Horses Heads'.[19] This small matter of fact has considerable importance for anyone wishing to develop an accurate critical account of the poem. It forces us to see, for example, that the journey being presented is not some unspecified drive in the country, but a funeral ride which is located quite specifically in relation to Emily Dickinson and her Amherst world. The hearse in the poem is on its way out from Pleasant Street, past Emily Dickinson's house, to the cemetery located at the northern edge of the town just beyond the Dickinson homestead.[20] Of course, these details are not verbalized into the Dickinson poem as explicit description. They are only present implicitly, as an originally evoked context which we – at our historical remove – can (and must) reconstitute if we wish to focus and explain the special emotional character of the work.

Consider once again, for example, the undertaker who appears in the poem. The behaviour of this man – his correctness, his rather stiff but kindly formality, his manner of driving the carriage – defines a character-type well-known in nineteenth-century culture, and a favourite one with contemporary caricaturists.[21] Behind the civility and kindly formal behaviour of Emily Dickinson's undertaker lies a tradition which saw in this man a figure of grotesque obsequiousness, as we know from Mark Twain's memorable scene in *Huckleberry Finn*. Indeed, I do not see how one could fully appreciate the finesse of what Tate calls the 'erotic motive' without also seeing just how the poem plays with it, and how Dickinson's poetic style both represents and quietly modifies the contemporary stereotype of this important social functionary so well known to the inhabitants of towns like Amherst. The poem's general ideology, as a work of Christian consolation, would be merely religious claptrap without these 'poetic'[22] elements; and such elements can only escape the critical method which does not seek to grasp the poem at a level more comprehensive than a merely linguistic one.

The power of the poem, then, rests in its ability to show us not merely the thoughts and feelings of Dickinson and her fictive speaker, but the attitudes of her implied readers as well. For all her notorious privacy, Emily Dickinson is, like every poet, a creator of those structures of social energy which we call poems. 'Because I could not Stop for Death' locates not merely an expressive lyrical act, but a significant relationship between the poet and her readers which we, as still later readers, are meant to recognize, enter into, and (finally) extend. Our sympathy with the poem may not be the same as that felt by a Christian reader, whether contemporary with the poem or not; nevertheless, it is *continuous* with the sympathy of such readers (who are consciously and explicitly assumed by the poem) because it takes those readers as seriously as it takes Emily Dickinson and her fictive speaker. Indeed, it must do this, for all are part of the poem in question. Later readers may not share the ideologies of the people represented by this poem, but they cannot read it without recognising and respecting those ideologies – without, in fact, perpetuating them in a critical human memory whose sympathetic powers are drawn from a historical consciousness.

Having discussed the 'ideological set' of this poem – its poetically rendered 'message' – let us return to Allen Tate's essay, where an absence of ideological commitments is imputed to Dickinson's work. We return to ask why Tate should insist upon 'misreading' the poem as he has done.

The reason emerges when we ponder carefully Tate's use of T.S. Eliot. Tate's interpretation shows that he shares Eliot's ideas about how moral concepts should appear in verse (not 'didactically' but dramatically); that he prizes Eliot's views on Metaphysical verse and its excellences; and that he is anxious to deliver his praise of Dickinson's poem in critical terms that will draw her into the company of those poets who illustrate Eliot's standards. In short, Tate reads Emily Dickinson in the same spirit that Eliot read Donne and the Metaphysicals. *Why* Tate, and Eliot before him, should have taken such a position toward the moral aspects of poetry – and especially of Christian poetry in its various forms – is beyond the scope of this analysis, though scholars recognize that the answer lies in the historical factors which generated modernism and its various ideologies.[23]

I have not dwelt upon Tate's discussion in order to debunk it, but rather in order to show the consonance between his interpretation of the Dickinson poem and his ignorance of its textual problems. Tate's eye is no more focused upon Dickinson's poem than it is on the 1890 text of 'The Chariot'. Rather, Tate has 'taken "The Chariot" for his text', as we might say of one who delivers a sermon or a moral lesson. 'The Chariot' is the occasion for his ideological polemic on behalf of certain aesthetic criteria.

One important lesson to be drawn from this investigation of Tate's essay is that literary criticism – and even the analysis of poems – is not fundamentally a study of verbal structure *per se*. The very existence of Tate's influential and justly admired essay demonstrates that fact. Literary criticism must study poetic texts – the 'verbal structures' of poems – but the analysis of these verbal structures does not comprehend a poetic analysis. This paradox of critical method emerges forcibly in Tate's essay, which dramatizes, in its very limitations, the distinction between text and poem – a distinction, indeed, which Tate's analysis is incapable of making. Yet the distinction must be made – and textual criticism, in the traditional sense, must be revived among literary critics – if our received works of literature are to regain their full human resources – that is to say, if the entire history of poetry and all the potential of specific poems are to be made known and available to each new generation. Poetry and poems are, in this sense, trans-historical, but they acquire this perpetuity by virtue of the particular historical adventures which their texts undergo from their first appearance before their author's eyes through all their subsequent constitutions.

The textual histories of poems, in other words, are paradigm instances of the historically specific character of all poetry. By clarifying the distinction between a poem and its various texts, the examples from Byron and Blake illustrate the need for a systematic theory and method of historical criticism. On the other hand, the example from Dickinson argues, at the level of practical criticism, the specific critical powers inherent in a historical method. These powers appear as a special capacity for elucidating, in a systematic way, whatever in a poem is most concrete, local, and particular to it. Criticism cannot analyse poems, or reveal their special characteristics and values, if it abstracts away from their so-called accidental features. Attending merely to the formal or linguistic phenomena of poems constitutes an initial and massive act of abstraction from what are some of the most crucial particulars of all poems.

Facing the poem and its texts, then, historical criticism tries to define what is most peculiar and distinctive in specific poetical works. Moreover, in specifying these unique features and sets of relationships, it transcends the concept of the-poem-as-verbal-object to reveal the poem as a special sort of communication event. This new understanding of poems takes place precisely because the critical act, occurring in a self-conscious present, can turn to look upon poems created in the past not as fixed objects but as the locus of certain past human experiences. Some of these are dramatized *in* the poems, while others are presented *through* the poetical works, which embody various human experiences *with* the poems, beginning with the author's own experiences. In this way does a historical criticism define poetry not as a formal structure or immediate event but as a continuing human process. That *act* of definition is the fundamental *fact* of literary criticism.

The new fact about *historical* criticism, however, is that it systematically opposes its own reification. Being first of all an *act* of definition rather than a *set* of definitions, historical criticism calls attention to the time-specific and heuristic character of its abstractions. Like the poetry it studies, criticism is always tendentious because it always seeks to define and preserve human values. One of the special values of historical criticism, to my view at any rate, lies in its eagerness to specify and examine its polemical positions. This self-critical aspect of an historical approach seems to be a direct function of its basic method, for in attempting to specify historical distinctions, we set a gulf between our past and our present. It is this gulf which enables us to judge and criticize the past, but it is equally this gulf which enables the past – so rich in its achievements – to judge and criticize us. Thus in our differences do we learn about, and create, a community.

(1980–1)

Notes

1 Louis Hjelmslev, *Prolegomena to a Theory of Language*, tr. Francis J. Whitfield (Madison, Wis., 1961), p. 9.

2 Roman Jakobson,'Linguistics and Poetics', in *Style in Language*, ed. T.A. Sebeok (Cambridge, Mass., 1960), p. 350. In the latest, post-structural phase of these traditions the models are more generically semiological than linguistic. The shift in emphasis – from specific 'text' to the process of 'textuality' – marks the increased self-consciousness in this tradition, but not a departure from its fundamental premises.

3 Literary criticism in general would benefit if certain clear distinctions were preserved when using words (and concepts) like *text, poem,* and *poetical work*. In the present essay, the word *text* is used as a purely bibliographical concept which means to deal with the material of poetry in a purely physical or impersonal frame of reference. The term deliberately abstracts away the critic's or the reader's immediate (social) point of view. Poetry is a social phenomenon, but the concept of *text* withholds from consideration all matters that relate to the involvement of reader or audience in the reproduction of the work. It does so, of course, for analytic purposes, and *only provisionally*. I propose that we use the term *text* when we deal with poems as they are part of a productive (or reproductive) process, but when we are withholding from consideration all matters that relate to the process of consumption. *Poem*, on the other hand, is the term I will use to refer to the work as it is the locus of a specific process of production (or reproduction) and consumption. *Poetical work* is my term for the global history of some particular work's process of production/reproduction and consumption. I use the term *poetry* to refer generically to imaginative literary works without respect to any specific social or historical factors. The terms *text* and *Ideal Text* also appear in this essay, and these refer to various (non-historical and non-sociological) twentieth-century critical concepts.

I hope it is clear that these distinctions mean to counter the semiological approach to the concepts of *text* and *textuality*. A paradigm example of the latter approach will be found in Roland Barthes's famous essay 'From Work to Text': see above, pp. 191–8.

4 See *Don Juan: A Variorum Edition*, ed. T.G. Steffan and W.W. Pratt (Austin, Tex.,) 1957), i. 11–32 and iv. 293–308.

5 'The Publishing of *Don Juan*', *PMLA* lxxx (June 1965), p. 200.

6 For the *Quarterly Review* quotations see ibid., p. 202.

7 Cf. Levin Schüking. *The Sociology of Literary Taste* (London, 1966).

8 Post-structural critiques of their own (formalist) tradition have been widespread during the past ten years and have contributed to the break-up of the academic consensus which developed between 1935 and 1965. See John Fekete, *The Critical Twilight* (London, 1978). The attacks upon the New Criticism have tended to accuse it of an arrogant and technocratic empiricism, with its insistence upon taking the poem as *sui generis*. These attacks – see Richard Palmer, *Hermeneutics* (Evanston, Ill., 1969), for example – charge the New Criticism with a crude theory of the poem as 'object' or 'thing'. This sort of attack is deeply misguided and misses entirely the fundamental Idealism of both the New Criticism in particular and its later formalist context in general. A revisionist commentator like Gerald Graff has been able to see the mistake in such critiques and to suggest what is in fact the case: that New Criticism and its academic inheritors (including many of its recent antagonists) are part of a single tradition (*Literature Against Itself*, Chicago, 1979, chap. 5). As Graff notes, New Criticism was marked throughout by contradictions along an Ideal/Empirical fault-line; nor could it have been otherwise with a fundamentally Idealist theory which was seeking to establish its authority in a scientific, rational, and technological world. Graff's views have been anticipated by a number of trenchant critiques put out from relatively orthodox Marxist writers: see, e.g. Robert Weimann, 'Past Significance and Present Meaning in Literary History', in *New Directions in Literary History*, ed. Ralph Cohen (Baltimore, 1974), esp. pp. 43–50.

9 That an Ideal Text is the object of contemporary 'textual' interpreters is patent; see also Tony Bennett, *Formalism and Marxism* (London, 1979, pp. 70–1).

10 For a more thorough discussion see chap. I of *Keats and the Historical Method in Literary Criticism*, pp. 15–67, by McGann in the same book *The Beauty of Inflections*.

11 As is well known, Blake purchased his artistic freedom at a fearful personal cost, for his conscious artistic policies ensured his contemporary isolation. Appealing to what Byron called 'the Avenger, Time, Blake's work had to wait for the justice of history. Cf. the discussion in J. W. Saunders, *The Profession of Letters* (London, 1964) pp. 146–73 *passim* and, on Blake particularly, pp. 164–6; see also Jerome J. McGann, *A Critique of Modern Textual Criticism* (Chicago, 1983, pp. 44–7).

12 This is poem no. 172 in *The Poems of Emily Dickinson*, ed. Thomas H. Johnson (Cambridge, Mass., 1955) ii. 546–7. For Tate's discussion, see his 'New England Culture and Emily Dickinson', in *The Recognition of Emily Dickinson*, ed. C.E. Blake and C.F. Wells (Ann Arbor, Mich., 1968), pp. 153–67, esp. pp. 160–2, from which the quotations below are taken.

13 See *Poems by Emily Dickinson*, ed. Mabel Loomis Todd and Thomas W. Higginson (Boston, Mass., 1890). Also see Johnson's edition, where the textual issues are succinctly presented.

14 Winters' essay is reprinted in Blake and Wells, eds, *The Recognition of Emily Dickinson*; see esp. pp. 192–3.

15 This motif is an ancient one in the tradition of Christian art and poetry. For its biblical sources see Matt. 24:43 and I Thess. 5:2–4. An excellent contemporary example is to be found in Alan Dugan's 'Tribute to Kafka for Someone Taken'.

16 See V.N. Volosinov (i.e. M.M. Bakhtin), 'Discourse in Life and Discourse in Art', in *Freudianism, A Marxist Critique*, tr. I.R. Titunik (New York, 1976), where Bakhtin distinguishes among the author, the reader, and the figure he calls 'the hero' or the 'third participant'.

17 In adopting this rhetorical model. Dickinson was following a literary practice

that had grown extremely popular in the nineteenth century. See Ann Douglas, 'Heaven Our Home: Consolation Literature in the Northern United States 1830–1880', in *Death in America*, ed. Daniel Stannard, (Philadelphia, 1974); see esp. pp. 58–9, 61–2. But the procedure is deeply traditional: see also Rosemary Woolf, *English Religious Lyric in the Middle Ages* (Oxford, 1963), chap. 9 *passim*.

18 Robert Weisbuch, *Emily Dickinson's Poetry* (Chicago, 1972), p. 114.

19 That is to say, a suitor's carriage would have had only one horse.

20 The hearse's journey to the Amherst cemetery – one of the new. so-called rural cemeteries – must have been appallingly familiar to Emily Dickinson. The mortality rate in Amherst was high, and Emily Dickinson's room overlooked the cemetery route. See Millicent Todd Bingham, *Emily Dickinson's Home* (New York, 1955), the map facing p. 62 and pp. 179–80; also Jay Leyda, *The Years and Hours of Emily Dickinson* (New Haven, 1969), ii. 2–3. Emily Dickinson's bedroom was the best vantage in the house for observing the stately procession of the funeral hearse as it moved out from Pleasant Street to the cemetery. The special location of the Dickinson house meant that the funeral hearse would always pass by, no matter where the deceased person had lived in town. One should also note that the poem's references to the 'School' and the 'Fields of Gazing Grain' are precise. In point of fact, 'Because I could not Stop for Death' narrates the imagined (non imaginary) journey of the hearse from somewhere in the central part of Amherst out along Pleasant Street, past the schoolhouse on the left, and out to the beginning of the 'Fields of Gazing Grain', at which point the undertaker would have turned to the right and driven past more fields to the gravesite. For a general discussion of the rural cemetery see Neil Harris, 'The Cemetery Beautiful', in *Passing: The Vision of Death in America*, ed. Charles O. Jackson (Westport, Conn., 1977), pp. 103–11.

21 See Alfred Scott Warthen,'The Period of Caricature' and 'The Modern Dance of Death', in *The Physician of the Dance of Death* (New York, 1934). Twain was fond of presenting the undertaker from a comic point of view. See *Huckleberry Finn*, chap. 27, and his essay 'The Undertaker's Chat'.

22 What makes them 'poetic' is their ability to dramatize the relationships which exist between specific social realities and a complex set of related – and often antagonistic – ideological attitudes and formations.

23 See Richard Ohmann. 'Studying Literature at the End of Ideology', in *The Politics of Literature*, ed. Louis Kampf and Paul Lauter (New York, 1973), esp. pp. 13–49; Renato Poggioli, *The Theory of the Avant-Garde*. tr. Gerald Fitzgerald (New York, 1971); and see nn. 3 and 8 above.

---

27   Stephen Greenblatt,

'Resonance and Wonder', *Bulletin of the American Academy of the Arts and Sciences*, 43, (1990), pp. 11–34

In a small glass case in the library of Christ Church, Oxford, there is a round, broad-brimmed cardinal's hat; a note card identifies it as having belonged to Cardinal Wolsey. It is altogether appropriate that this hat should have wound up at Christ Church, for the college owed its existence to Wolsey, who had decided at the height of his power to found in his own honor a magnificent new Oxford college. But the hat was not a direct bequest; historical forces, as we sometimes say – in this case, taking the ominous form of Henry VIII – intervened, and Christ Church, like Hampton Court Palace, was cut off from its original benefactor. Instead, as the note informs us, after it had passed through the hands of various owners – including Bishop Burnet, Burnet's son, Burnet's son's housekeeper, the Dowager Countess of Albemarle's butler, the countess herself, and Horace Walpole – the hat was acquired for Christ Church in the nineteenth century, purchased, we are told, for the sum of sixty-three pounds, from the daughter of the actor Charles Kean. Kean is said to have worn the hat when he played Wolsey in Shakespeare's *Henry VIII*. If this miniature history of an artifact is too slight to be of much consequence, it nonetheless evokes a vision of cultural production that I find compelling. The peregrinations of Wolsey's hat suggest that cultural artifacts do not stay still, that they exist in time, and that they are bound up with personal and institutional conflict, negotiations, and appropriations.

The term culture has, in the case of the hat, a convenient material referent – a bit of red cloth stitched together – but that referent is only a tiny element in a complex symbolic construction that originally marked the transformation of Wolsey from a butcher's son to a prince of the church. Wolsey's gentleman usher, George Cavendish, has left a remarkably circumstantial contemporary account of that construction, an account that enables us even to glimpse the hat in its place among all the other ceremonial regalia:

And after Mass he would return in his privy chamber again and, being advertised of the furniture of his chamber without with noblemen and gentlemen . . . , would issue out into them apparelled all in red in the habit of a Cardinal; which was either of fine scarlet or else of crimson satin, taffeta, damask, or caffa [a rich silk cloth], the best that he could get for money; and upon his head a round pillion with a neck of black velvet, set to the same in the inner side. . . . There was also borne before him first the Great Seal of England, and then his Cardinal's hat by a nobleman or some worthy gentleman right solemnly, bareheaded. And as soon as he was entered into his chamber of presence where was attending his coming to await upon him to Westminster Hall, as well noblemen and other worthy gentlemen as noblemen and gentlemen of his own family; thus passing forth with two great crosses of silver borne before him, with also two great pillars of silver, and his sergeant at arms with a great mace of silver gilt. Then his gentlemen ushers cried and said, 'On my lords and masters, make way for my lord's grace!'[1]

The extraordinary theatricality of this manifestation of clerical power did not escape the notice of the Protestant reformers who called the Catholic church 'the Pope's playhouse'. When the Reformation in England dismantled the histrionic apparatus of Catholicism, they sold some of its gorgeous properties to the professional players – not only a mark of thrift but a polemical gesture, signifying that the sanctified vestments were in reality mere trumpery whose proper place was a disreputable world of illusion-mongering. In exchange for this polemical service, the theatrical joint-stock companies received more than an attractive, cut-rate wardrobe; they acquired the tarnished but still potent charisma that clung to the old vestments, charisma that in paradoxical fashion the players at once emptied out and heightened. By the time Wolsey's hat reached the library at Christ Church, its charisma must have been largely exhausted, but the college could confer upon it the prestige of an historical curiosity, as a trophy of the distant founder. And in its glass case it still radiates a tiny quantum of cultural energy.

Tiny indeed – I may already have seemed to make much more of this trivial relic than it deserves. But I am fascinated by transmigrations of the kind I have just sketched here – from theatricalized rituals to the stage to the university library or museum – because they seem to reveal something critically important about the *textual* relics with which my profession is obsessed. They enable us to glimpse the social process through which objects, gestures, rituals, and phrases are fashioned and moved from one zone of display to another. The display cases with which I am most involved – books – characteristically conceal this process, so that we have a misleading impression of fixity and little sense of the historical transactions through which the great texts we study have been fashioned. Let me give a literary example, an appropriately tiny textual equivalent of Wolsey's hat. At the close of Shakespeare's *Midsummer Night's Dream*, the Fairy King Oberon declares that he and his attendants are going to bless the beds of the three couples who have just been married. This ritual of blessing will ensure the happiness of the newlyweds and ward off moles, harelips, and other prodigious marks that would disfigure their offspring. 'With this field-dew consecrate,' the Fairy King concludes,

> Every fairy take his gait,
> And each several chamber bless,
> Through this palace, with sweet peace,
> And the owner of it blest
> Ever shall in safety rest.
>
> (5.1.415–20)

Oberon himself, we are told, will conduct the blessing upon the 'best bride-bed', that of the ruler Theseus and his Amazon queen Hippolyta.

The ceremony – manifestly the sanctification of ownership and caste, as well as marriage – is a witty allusion to the traditional Catholic blessing of the bride-bed with holy water, a ceremony vehemently attacked as pagan superstition and banned by English Protestants. But the conventional critical term 'allusion' seems inadequate, for the term usually implies a bloodless, bodiless thing, while even the tiny, incidental detail of the field dew bears a more active charge. Here, as with Wolsey's hat, I want to ask what is at stake in the shift from one zone of social practice to another, from the old religion to public theater, from priests to fairies, from holy water to field dew, or rather to theatrical fairies and theatrical field dew on the London stage. When the Catholic ritual is made into theatrical representation, the transposition at once naturalises, denaturalises, mocks, and celebrates. It naturalises the ritual by transforming the specially sanctified water into ordinary dew; it denaturalises the ritual by removing it from human agents and attributing it to the fairies; it mocks Catholic practice by associating it with notorious superstition and then by enacting it on the stage where it is revealed as a histrionic illusion; and it celebrates such practice by reinvesting it with the charismatic magic of the theater.

Several years ago, intending to signal a turn away from the formal, decontextualized analysis that dominates new criticism, I used the term 'new historicism' to describe an interest in the kinds of issues I have been raising – in the embeddedness of cultural objects in the contingencies of history – and the term has achieved a certain currency. But like most labels, this one is misleading. The new historicism, like the Holy Roman Empire, constantly belies its own name. *The American Heritage Dictionary* gives three meanings for the term 'historicism':

1. The belief that processes are at work in history that man can do little to alter.
2. The theory that the historian must avoid all value judgments in his study of past periods or former cultures.
3. Veneration of the past or of tradition.

Most of the writing labelled new historicist, and certainly my own work, has set itself resolutely against each of these positions.

1.   *The belief that processes are at work in history that man can do little to alter.* This formulation rests upon a simultaneous abstraction and evacuation of human agency. The men and women who find themselves making concrete choices in given circumstances at particular times are transformed into something called 'man'. And this colorless, nameless collective being cannot significantly intervene in the 'processes . . . at work in history' processes that are thus mysteriously alienated from all of those who enact them.

New historicism, by contrast, eschews the use of the term 'man'; interest lies not in the abstract universal but in particular, contingent cases, the selves fashioned and acting according to the generative rules and conflicts of a given culture. And these selves, conditioned by the expectations of their class, gender, religion, race and national identity, are constantly effecting changes in the course of history. Indeed if there is any inevitability in the new historicism's vision of history it is this insistence on agency, for even inaction or extreme marginality is understood to possess meaning and therefore to imply intention. Every form of behavior, in this view, is a strategy: taking up arms or taking flight is a significant social action, but so is staying put, minding one's business, turning one's face to the wall. Agency is virtually inescapable.

Inescapable but not simple: new historicism, as I understand it, does not posit historical processes as unalterable and inexorable, but it does tend to discover limits or constraints upon individual intervention. Actions that appear to be single are disclosed as multiple; the apparently isolated power of the individual genius turns out to be bound up with collective, social energy; a gesture of dissent may be an element in a larger legitimation process, while an attempt to stabilise order of things may turn out to subvert it. And political valences may change, sometimes abruptly: there are no guarantees, no absolute, formal assurances that what seems progressive in one set of contingent circumstances will not come to seem reactionary in another.

The new historicism's insistence on the pervasiveness of agency has apparently led some of its critics to find in it a Nietzschean celebration of the ruthless will to power, while its ironic and skeptical reappraisal of the cult of heroic individualism has led others to find in it a pessimistic doctrine of human helplessness. Hence, for example, from a Marxist perspective one critic characterises the new historicism as a 'liberal disillusionment' that finds that 'any apparent site of resistance ultimately serves the interests of power' (33), while from a liberal humanist perspective, another critic proclaims that 'anyone who, like me, is reluctant to accept the will to power as the defining human essence will probably have trouble with the critical procedures of the new historicists and with their interpretive conclusion'.[2] But the very idea of 'defining human essence' is precisely what new historicists find vacuous and untenable, as I do the counter-claim that love rather than power makes the world go round. The Marxist critique is more plausible, but it rests upon an assertion that new historicism argues that '*any* apparent site of resistance' is ultimately coopted. Some are, some aren't.

I argued in an essay published some years ago that the sites of resistance in Shakespeare's second tetralogy are coopted in the plays' ironic, complex, but finally celebratory affirmation of charismatic kingship. That is, the formal structure and rhetorical strategy of the plays make it difficult for audiences to withhold their consent from the triumph of Prince Hal. Shakespeare shows that the triumph rests upon a claustrophobic narrowing of pleasure, a hypocritical manipulation of appearances, and a systematic betrayal of friendship, and yet these manifestations of bad faith only contrive to heighten the spectators' knowing pleasure and the ratification of applause. The subversive perceptions do not disappear, but insofar as they remain within the structure of the play, they are contained and indeed serve to heighten a power they would appear to question.

I did not propose that all manifestation of resistance in all literature (or

even in all plays by Shakespeare) were coopted – one can readily think of
plays where the forces of ideological containment break down. And yet
characterisations of this essay in particular, and new historicism in general,
repeatedly refer to a supposed argument that any resistance is impossible.[3]
A particularizing argument about the subject position projected by a set of
plays is at once simplified and turned into a universal principle from which
contingency and hence history itself is erased.

Moreover, even my argument about Shakespeare's second tetralogy is
misunderstood if it is thought to foreclose the possibility of dissent or
change or the radical alteration of the processes of history. The point is that
certain aesthetic and political structures work to contain the subversion
perceptions they generate, not that those perceptions simply wither away.
On the contrary, they may be pried loose from the order with which they
were bound up and may serve to fashion a new and radically different set
of structures. How else could change ever come about? No one is forced –
except perhaps in school – to take aesthetic or political wholes as sacrosanct.
The order of things is never simply a given: it takes labor to produce,
sustain, reproduce, and transmit the way things are, and this labor may be
withheld or transit formed. Structures may be broken in pieces, the pieces
altered, inverted, rearranged. Everything can be different than it is;
everything could have been different than it was. But it will not do to
imagine that this alteration is easy, automatic, without cost or obligation.
My objection was to the notion that the rich ironies in the history plays were
themselves inherently liberating, that to savor the tetralogy's skeptical
cunning was to participate in an act of political resistance. In general I find
dubious the assertion that certain rhetorical features in much-loved literary
works constitute authentic acts of political liberation; the fact that this
assertion is now heard from the left, where in my college days it was more
often heard from the right, does not make it in most instances any less
fatuous and presumptuous. I wished to show, at least in the case of
Shakespeare's histories and in several analogous discourses, how a set of
representational and political practices in the late sixteenth century could
produce and even batten upon what appeared to be their own subversion.

To show this is not to give up on the possibility of altering historical
processes – if this is historicism I want no part of it – but rather to eschew
an aestheticized and idealised politics of the imagination.

2.   *The theory that the historian must avoid all value judgments in his study
of past periods or former cultures.* Once again, if this is an essential tenet of
historicism, then the new historicism belies its name. My own critical
practice and that of many others associated with new historicism was
decisively shaped by the American 1960s and early 70s, and especially by
the opposition to the Viet Nam War. Writing that was not engaged, that
withheld judgments, that failed to connect the present with the past seemed
worthless. Such connection could be made either by analogy or causality;

that is, a particular set of historical circumstances could be represented in such a way as to bring out homologies with aspects of the present or, alternatively, those circumstances could be analyzed as the generative forces that led to the modern condition. In either mode, value judgments were implicated, because a neutral or indifferent relation to the present seemed impossible. Or rather it seemed overwhelmingly clear that neutrality was itself a political position, a decision to support the official policies in both the state and the academy.

To study the culture of sixteenth-century England did not present itself as an escape from the turmoil of the present; it seemed rather an intervention, a mode of relation. The fascination for me of the Renaissance was that it seemed to be powerfully linked to the present both analogically and causally. This doubled link at once called forth and qualified my value judgments: called them forth because my response to the past was inextricably bound up with my response to the present; qualified them because the analysis of the past revealed the complex, unsettling historical genealogy of the very judgments I was making. To study Renaissance culture then was simultaneously to feel more rooted and more estranged in my own values.[4]

Other critics associated with the new historicism have written directly and forcefully about their own subject position and have made more explicit than I the nature of this engagement.[5] If I have not done so to the same extent, it is not because I believe that my values are somehow suspended in my study of the past but because I believe they are pervasive: in the textual and visual traces I choose to analyze, in the stories I choose to tell, in the cultural conjunctions I attempt to make, in my syntax, adjectives, pronouns. 'The new historicism', someone has written in a lively critique, 'needs at every point to be more overtly self-conscious of its methods and its theoretical assumptions, since what one discovers about the historical place and function of literary texts is in large measure a function of the angle from which one looks and the assumptions that enable the investigation.'[6] I am certainly not opposed to methodological self-consciousness, but I am less inclined to see overtness – an explicit articulation of one's values and methods – as inherently necessary or virtuous. Nor, though I believe that my values are everywhere engaged in my work, do I think that there need be a perfect integration of those values and the objects I am studying. On the contrary, some of the most interesting and powerful ideas in cultural criticism occur precisely at moments of disjunction, disintegration, unevenness. A criticism that never encounters obstacles, that celebrates predictable heroines and rounds up the usual suspects, that finds confirmation of its values everywhere it turns, is quite simply boring.[7]

3.   *Veneration of the past or of tradition.* The third definition of historicism obviously sits in a strange relation to the second, but they are not simply

alternatives. The apparent eschewing of value judgments was often accompanied by a still more apparent admiration, however cloaked as objective description, of the past. One of the more irritating qualities of my own literary training had been its relentlessly celebratory character: literary criticism was and largely remains a kind of secular theodicy. Every decision made by a great artist could be shown to be a brilliant one; works that had seemed flawed and uneven to an earlier generation of critics bent on displaying discriminations in taste were now revealed to be organic masterpieces. A standard critical assignment in my student years was to show how a text that seemed to break in parts was really a complex whole: thousands of pages were dutifully churned out to prove that the bizarre subplot of The Changeling was cunningly integrated into the tragic mainplot or that every tedious bit of clowning in Doctor Faustus was richly significant. Behind these exercises was the assumption that great works of art were triumphs of resolution, that they were, in Bakhtin's term, monological – the mature expression of a single artistic intention. When this formalism was combined, as it often was, with both ego psychology and historicism, it posited aesthetic integration as the reflection of the artist's psychic integration and posited that psychic integration as the triumphant expression of a healthy, integrated community. Accounts of Shakespeare's relation to Elizabethan culture were particularly prone to this air of veneration, since the Romantic cult of poetic genius could be conjoined with the still older political cult that had been created around the figure of the Virgin Queen.

Here again new historicist critics have swerved in a different direction. They have been more interested in unresolved conflict and contradiction than in integration; they are as concerned with the margins as with the center; and they have turned from a celebration of achieved aesthetic order to an exploration of the ideological and material bases for the production of this order. Traditional formalism and historicism, twin legacies of early nineteenth-century Germany, shared a vision of high culture as a harmonising domain of reconciliation based upon an aesthetic labor that transcends specific economic or political determinants. What is missing is psychic, social, and material resistance, a stubborn, unassimilable otherness, a sense of distance and difference. New historicism has attempted to restore this distance, hence its characteristic concerns have seemed to some critics off-center or strange. 'New historicists', writes a Marxist observer, 'are likely to seize upon something out of the way, obscure, even bizarre: dreams, popular or aristocratic festivals, denunciations of witchcraft, sexual treatises, diaries and autobiographies, descriptions of clothing, reports on disease, birth and death records, accounts of insanity.'[8] What is fascinating to me is that concerns like these should have come to seem bizarre, especially to a critic who is committed to the historical understanding of culture. That they have done so indicates how narrow the boundaries of historical understanding had become, how much these boundaries needed to be broken.

For none of the cultural practices on this list (and one could extend it considerably) is or should be 'out of the way' in a study of Renaissance literature or art; on the contrary, each is directly in the way of coming to terms with the period's methods of regulating the body, its conscious and unconscious psychic strategies, its ways of defining and dealing with marginals and deviants, its mechanisms for the display of power and the expression of discontent, its treatment of women. If such concerns have been rendered 'obscure', it is because of a disabling idea of causality that confines the legitimate field of historical agency within absurdly restrictive boundaries. The world is parcelled out between a predictable group of stereotypical causes and a large, dimly lit mass of raw materials that the artist chooses to fashion.

The new historicist critics are interested in such cultural expressions as witchcraft accusations, medical manuals, or clothing not as raw materials but as 'cooked' – complex symbolic and material articulations of the imaginative and ideological structures of the society that produced them. Consequently, there is a tendency in at least some new historicist writings (certainly in my own) for the focus to be partially displaced from the work of art that is their formal occasion onto the related practices that had been adduced ostensibly in order to illuminate that work. It is difficult to keep those practices in the background if the very concept of historical background has been called into question.

I have tried to deal with the problem of focus by developing a notion of cultural negotiation and exchange, that is, by examining the points at which one cultural practice intersects with another, borrowing its forms and intensities or attempting to ward off unwelcome appropriations or moving texts and artifacts from one place to another. But it would be misleading to imagine that there is a complete homogenization of interest; my own concern remains centrally with imaginative literature, and not only because other cultural structures resonate powerfully within it. If I do not approach works of art in a spirit of veneration, I do approach them in a spirit that is best described as wonder. Wonder has not been alien to literary criticism, but it has been associated (if only implicitly) with formalism rather than historicism. I wish to extend this wonder beyond the formal boundaries of works of art, just as I wish to intensify resonance within those boundaries.

It will be easier to grasp the concepts of resonance and wonder if we think of the way in which our culture presents to itself not the textual traces of its past but the surviving visual traces, for the latter are put on display in galleries and museums specially designed for the purpose. By resonance I mean the power of the object displayed to reach out beyond its formal boundaries to a larger world, to evoke in the viewer the complex, dynamic cultural forces from which it has emerged and for which as metaphor or more simply as metonymy it may be taken by a viewer to stand. By wonder I mean the power of the object displayed to stop the viewer in his tracks, to convey an arresting sense of uniqueness, to evoke an exalted attention.

The new historicism obviously has distinct affinities with resonance; that is, its concern with literary texts has been to recover as far as possible the historical circumstances of their original production and consumption and to analyse the relationship between these circumstances and our own. New historicist critics have tried to understand the intersecting circumstances not as a stable, prefabricated background against which the literary texts can be placed, but as a dense network of evolving and often contradictory social forces. The idea is not to find outside the work of art some rock onto which literary interpretation can be securely chained but rather to situate the work in relation to other representational practices operative in the culture at a given moment in both its history and our own. In Louis Montrose's convenient formulation, the goal has been to grasp simultaneously the historicity of texts and the textuality of history.

Insofar as this approach, developed for literary interpretation, is at all applicable to visual traces, it would call for an attempt to reduce the isolation of individual 'masterpieces', to illuminate the conditions of their making, to disclose the history of their appropriation and the circumstances in which they come to be displayed, to restore the tangibility, the openness, the permeability of boundaries that enabled the objects to come into being in the first place. An actual restoration of tangibility is obviously in most cases impossible, and the frames that enclose pictures are only the ultimate formal confirmation of the closing of the borders that marks the finishing of a work of art. But we need not take that finishing so entirely for granted; museums can and on occasion do make it easier imaginatively to recreate the work in its moment of openness.

That openness is linked to a quality of artifacts that museums obviously dread, their precariousness. But though it is perfectly reasonable for museums to protect their objects – I would not wish it any other way – precariousness is a rich source of resonance. Thomas Greene, who has written a sensitive book on what he calls the 'vulnerable texts', suggests that the symbolic wounding to which literature is prone may confer upon it power and fecundity. 'The vulnerability of poetry', Greene argues, 'stems from four basic conditions of language: its historicity, its dialogic function, its referential function, and its dependence on figuration.'[9] Three of these conditions are different for the visual arts, in ways that would seem to reduce vulnerability: painting and sculpture may be detached more readily than language from both referentiality and figuration, and the pressures of contextual dialogue are diminished by the absence of an inherent *logos*, a constitutive word. But the fourth condition – historicity – is in the case of material artifacts vastly increased, indeed virtually literalized. Museums function, partly by design and partly in spite of themselves, as monuments to the fragility of cultures, to the fall of sustaining institutions and noble houses, the collapse of rituals, the evacuation of myths, the destructive effects of warfare, neglect, and corrosive doubt.

I am fascinated by the signs of alteration, tampering, even destructiveness which many museums try simply to efface: first and most obviously, the act of displacement that is essential for the collection of virtually all older artifacts and most modern ones – pulled out of chapels, peeled off church walls, removed from decaying houses, seized as spoils of war, stolen, 'purchased' more or less fairly by the economically ascendent from the economically naive, the poor, the hard-pressed heirs of fallen dynasties and impoverished religious orders. Then too there are the marks on the artifacts themselves: the attempt to scratch out or deface the image of the devil in numerous late-medieval and Renaissance paintings, the concealing of the genitals in sculptured and painted figures, the iconoclastic smashing of human or divine representations, the evidence of cutting or reshaping to fit a new frame or purpose, the cracks or scorch marks or broken-off noses that indifferently record the grand disasters of history and the random accidents of trivial incompetence. Even these accidents – the marks of a literal fragility – can have their resonance: the climax of an absurdly hagiographical Proust exhibition several years ago was a display case holding a small, patched, modest vase with a notice, 'This vase broken by Marcel Proust.'

As this comical example suggests, wounded artifacts may be compelling not only as witnesses to the violence of history but as signs of use, marks of the human touch, and hence links with the openness to touch that was the condition of their creation. The most familiar way to recreate the openness of aesthetic artifacts without simply renewing their vulnerability is through a skillful deployment of explanatory texts in the catalogue, on the walls of the exhibit, or on cassettes. The texts so deployed introduce and in effect stand in for the context that has been effaced in the process of moving the object into the museum. But insofar as that context is partially, often primarily, visual as well as verbal, textual contextualism has its limits. Hence the mute eloquence of the display of the palette, brushes, and other implements that an artist of a given period would have employed or of objects that are represented in the exhibited paintings or of materials and images that in some way parallel or intersect with the formal works of art.

Among the most resonant moments are those in which the supposedly contextual objects take on a life of their own, make a claim that rivals that of the object that is formally privileged. A table, a chair, a map, often seemingly placed only to provide a decorative setting for a grand work, become oddly expressive, significant not as 'background' but as compelling representational practices in themselves. These practices may in turn impinge upon the grand work, so that we begin to glimpse a kind of circulation: the cultural practice and social energy implicit in map-making drawn into the aesthetic orbit of a painting which has itself enabled us to register some of the representational significance of the map. Or again the threadbare fabric on the old chair or the gouges in the wood of a cabinet juxtapose the privileged painting or sculpture with marks not only of time but of use, the imprint of the human body on the artifact, and call attention to the deliberate removal of certain exalted aesthetic objects from the threat of that imprint.

For the effect of resonance does not necessarily depend upon a collapse of the distinction between art and non-art; it can be achieved by awakening in the viewer a sense of the cultural and historically contingent construction of art objects, the negotiations, exchanges, swerves, exclusions by which certain representational practices come to be set apart from other representational practices that they partially resemble. A resonant exhibition often pulls the viewer away from the celebration of isolated objects and toward a series of implied, only half-visible relationships and questions. How have the objects come to be displayed? What is at stake in categorizing them as of 'museum-quality'? How were they originally used? What cultural and material conditions made possible their production? What were the feelings of those who originally held these objects, cherished them, collected them, possessed them? What is the meaning of my relationship to these same objects now that they are displayed here, in this museum, on this day?

It is time to give a more sustained example. Perhaps the most purely resonant museum I have ever seen is the State Jewish Museum in Prague. This is housed not in a single building but in a cluster of old synagogues scattered through the city's former Jewish Town. The oldest of these – known as the Old-New Synagogue – is a twin-nave medieval structure dating to the last third of the 13th century; the others are mostly Renaissance and Baroque. In these synagogues are displayed Judaica from 153 Jewish communities throughout Bohemia and Moravia. In one there is a permanent exhibition of synagogue silverworks, in another there are synagogue textiles, in a third there are Torah scrolls, ritual objects, manuscripts and prints illustrative of Jewish beliefs, traditions, and customs. One of the synagogues shows the work of the physician and artist Karel Fleischmann, principally drawings done in the Terezin concentration camp during his months of imprisonment prior to his deportation to Auschwitz. Next door in the Ceremonial Hall of the Prague Burial Society there is a wrenching exhibition of children's drawings from Terezin. Finally, one synagogue, closed at the time of my visit to Prague, has simply a wall of names – thousands of them – to commemorate the Jewish victims of Nazi persecution in Czechoslovakia.

'The Museum's rich collections of synagogue art and the historic synagogue buildings of Prague's Jewish town', says the catalogue of the State Jewish Museum, 'form a memorial complex that has not been preserved to the same extent anywhere else in Europe.' 'A memorial complex' – this museum is not so much about artifacts as about memory, and the form the memory takes is a secularised kaddish, a commemorative prayer for the dead. The atmosphere has a peculiar effect on the act of viewing. It is mildly interesting to note the differences between the mordant Grosz-like lithographs of Karel Fleischmann in the pre-war years and the tormented style, at once detached and anguished, of the drawings in the camps, but aesthetic discriminations feel weird, out-of-place. And it seems wholly absurd, even indecent, to worry about the relative artistic merits of the drawings that survive by children who did not survive.

The discordance between viewing and remembering is greatly reduced with the older, less emotionally charged artifacts, but even here the ritual objects in their glass cases convey an odd and desolate impression. The oddity, I suppose, should be no greater than in seeing a Mayan god or, for that matter, a pyx or a ciborium, but we have become so familiarized to the display of such objects, so accustomed to considering them works of art, that even pious Catholics, as far as I know, do not necessarily feel disconcerted by their transformation from ritual function to aesthetic exhibition. And until very recently the voices of the tribal peoples who might have objected to the display of their religious artifacts have not been heard and certainly not attended to.

The Jewish objects are neither sufficiently distant to be absorbed into the detached ethos of anthropological display nor sufficiently familiar to be framed and encased alongside the altarpieces and reliquaries that fill Western museums. And moving as they are as mnemonic devices, most of the ritual objects in the State Jewish Museum are not, by contrast with Christian liturgical art, particularly remarkable either for their antiquity or their extraordinary beauty. They are the products of a people with a resistance to joining figural representation to religious observance, a strong anti-iconic bias. The objects have, as it were, little will to be observed; many of them are artifacts – ark curtains, Torah crowns, breastplates, pointers, and the like – whose purpose was to be drawn back or removed in order to make possible the act that mattered: not vision but reading.

But the inhibition of viewing in the Jewish Museum is paradoxically bound up with its resonance. This resonance depends not upon visual stimulation but upon a felt intensity of names, and behind the names, as the very term resonance suggests, of voices: the voices of those who chanted, studied, muttered their prayers, wept, and then were forever silenced. And mingled with these voices are others – of those Jews in 1389 who were murdered in the Old-New Synagogue where they were seeking refuge; of the great sixteenth-century Kabbalist, Jehuda ben Bezalel, known as Rabbi Loew, who is fabled to have created the Golem; of the twentieth-century's ironic Kabbalist, Franz Kafka.

It is Kafka who would be most likely to grasp imaginatively the State Jewish Museum's ultimate source of resonance: the fact that most of the objects are located in the museum – were displaced, preserved, and transformed categorically into works of art – because the Nazis stored the articles they confiscated in the Prague synagogues that they chose to preserve for this very purpose. In 1941 the Nazi Hochschule in Frankfurt had established an Institute for the Exploration of the Jewish Question which in turn had initiated a massive effort to confiscate Jewish libraries, archives, religious artifacts, and personal property. By the middle of 1942 Heydrich, as Hitler's chief officer within the so-called Protectorate of Bohemia and Moravia, had chosen Prague as the site of the Central Bureau for Dealing with the Jewish Question, and an SS officer, Untersturmführer Karl Rahm, had assumed control of the small existing Jewish museum, founded in 1912, which was renamed the Central Jewish Museum. The new charter of the museum announced that 'the numerous, hitherto scattered Jewish possessions of both historical and artistic value, on the territory of the entire Protectorate, must be collected and stored.'[10]

During the following months, tens of thousands of confiscated items arrived, the dates of the shipments closely coordinated with the 'donors' ' deportation to the concentration camps. The experts formally employed by the original Jewish museum were compelled to catalogue the items, and the Nazis compounded this immense task by also ordering the wretched, malnourished curators to prepare a collections guide and organize private exhibitions for SS staff. Between September 1942 and October 1943 four major exhibitions were mounted. Since these required far more space than the existing Jewish Museum's modest location, the great old Prague synagogues – made vacant by the Nazi prohibition of Jewish public worship – were partially refurbished for the occasion. Hence in March 1943, for example, in the seventeenth-century Klaus Synagogue there was an exhibition of Jewish festival and life-cycle observances; 'when Sturmbannführer Günther first toured the collection on April 6, he demanded various changes, including the translation of all Hebrew texts and the addition of an exhibit on kosher butchering' (Precious Legacy, p. 36). Plans were drawn up for other exhibitions, but the curators – who had given themselves to the task with a strange blend of selflessness, irony, helplessness, and heroism – were themselves at this point sent to concentration camps and murdered.

After the war, the few survivors of the Czech Jewish community apparently felt they could not sustain the ritual use of the synagogues or maintain the large collections. In 1949 the Jewish Community Council offered as a gift to the Czechoslovak government both the synagogues and their contents. These became the resonant, impure 'memorial complex' they are – a cultural machine that generates an uncontrollable oscillation between homage and desecration, longing and hopelessness, the voices of the dead and silence. For resonance, like nostalgia, is impure, a hybrid forged in the barely acknowledged gaps, the cesurae, between words like State, Jewish, and Museum.

I want to avoid the implication that resonance must be necessarily linked to destruction and absence; it can be found as well in unexpected survival. The key is the intimation of a larger community of voices and skills, an imagined ethnographic thickness. Here another example will serve: in the

Yucatan there is an extensive, largely unexcavated late-Classic Maya site called Coba, whose principal surviving feature is a high pyramid known as Nahoch Mull. After a day of tramping around the site, I was relaxing in the pool of the nearby Club Med Archaeological Villa in the company of a genial structural engineer from Little Rock. To make conversation, I asked my pool-mate what he as a structural engineer thought of Nahoch Mul. 'From an engineeer's point of view,' he replied, 'a pyramid is not very interesting – it's just an enormous gravity structure.' 'But', he added, 'did you notice that Coca-Cola stand on the way in? That's the most impressive example of contemporary Maya architecture I've ever seen.' I thought it quite possible that my leg was being pulled, but I went back the next day to check – I had, of course, completely blocked out the Coke stand on my first visit. Sure enough, some enterprising Mayan had built a remarkably elegant shelter with a soaring pyramidal roof constructed out of ingeniously intertwining sticks and branches. Places like Coba are thick with what Spenser called the Ruins of Time – with a nostalgia for a lost civilisation, in a state of collapse long before Cortés or Montejo cut their paths through the jungle. But, despite frequent colonial attempts to drive them or imagine them out of existence, the Maya have not in fact vanished, and a single entrepreneur's architectural improvisation suddenly had more resonance for me than the mounds of the 'lost' city.

My immediate thought was that the whole Coca-Cola stand could be shipped to New York and put on display in the Museum of Modern Art. And that impulse moves us away from resonance and toward wonder. For the MOMA is one of the great contemporary places not for the hearing of intertwining voices, not for historical memory, not for ethnographic thickness, but for intense, indeed enchanting looking. Looking may be called enchanted when the act of attention draws a circle around itself from which everything but the object is excluded, when intensity of regard blocks out all circumambient images, stills all murmuring voices. To be sure, the viewer may have purchased a catalogue, read an inscription on the wall, switched on a cassette, but in the moment of wonder all of this apparatus seems mere static.

The so-called boutique lighting that has become popular in recent years – a pool of light that has the surreal effect of seeming to emerge from within the object rather than to focus upon it from without – is an attempt to provoke or to heighten the experience of wonder, as if modern museum designers feared that wonder was increasingly difficult to arouse or perhaps that it risked displacement entirely onto the windows of designer dress shops and antique stores. The association of that lighting – along with transparent plastic rods and other devices to create the magical illusion of luminous, weightless suspension – with commerce would seem to suggest that wonder is bound up with acquisition and possession, yet the whole experience of most art museums is about *not* touching, *not* carrying home, *not* owning the marvelous objects. Modern museums in effect at once evoke the dream of possession and evacuate it.[11] (Alternatively, we could say that they displace that dream onto the museum gift shop, where the boutique lighting once again serves to heighten acquisition, now of reproductions that stand for the unattainable works of art.)

That evacuation or displacement is an historical rather than structural aspect of the museum's regulation of wonder: that is, collections of objects calculated to arouse wonder arose precisely in the spirit of personal acquisition and were only subsequently detached from it. In the Middle Ages and Renaissance we characteristically hear about wonders in the context of those who possessed them (or who gave them away). Hence, for example, in his *Life of Saint Louis*, Joinville writes that 'during the king's stay at Saida someone brought him a stone that split into flakes':

> It was the most marvelous stone in the world, for when you lifted one of the flakes you found the form of a sea-fish between the two pieces of stone. This fish was entirely of stone, but there was nothing lacking in its shape, eyes, bones, or colour to make it seem otherwise than if it had been alive. The king gave me one of these stones. I found a tench inside; it was brown in colour, and in every detail exactly as you would expect a tench to be.[12]

The wonder-cabinets of the Renaissance were at least as much about possession as display. The wonder derived not only from what could be seen but from the sense that the shelves and cases were filled with unseen wonders, all the prestigious property of the collector. In this sense, the cult of wonder originated in close conjunction with a certain type of resonance, a resonance bound up with the evocation not of an absent culture but of the great man's superfluity of rare and precious things. Those things were not necessarily admired for their beauty; the marvelous was bound up with the excessive, the surprising, the literally outlandish, the prodigious. They were not necessarily the manifestations of the artistic skill of human makers: technical virtuosity could indeed arouse admiration, but so could nautilus shells, ostrich eggs, uncannily large (or small) bones, stuffed crocodiles, fossils. And, most importantly, they were not necessarily objects set out for careful viewing.

The experience of wonder was not initially regarded as essentially or even primarily *visual*; reports of marvels had a force equal to the seeing of them. Seeing was important and desirable, of course, but precisely in order to make reports possible, reports which then circulated as virtual equivalents of the marvels themselves. The great medieval collections of marvels are almost entirely textual: Friar Jordanus's *Marvels of the East*, Marco Polo's *Book of Marvels*, Mandeville's *Travels*. Some of the manuscripts, to be sure, were illuminated but these illuminations were almost always ancillary to the textual record of wonders, just as emblem books were originally textual and only subsequently illustrated. Even in the sixteenth century, when the power of direct visual experience was increasingly valued, the marvelous was principally theorised as a textual phenomenon, as it had been in the antiquity. 'No one can be called a poet', writes the influential Italian critic Minturno in the 1550s, 'who does not excel in the power of arousing wonder.'[13] For Aristotle wonder was associated with pleasure as the end of poetry, and in the *Poetics* he examined the strategies by which tragedians and epic poets employ the marvelous to arouse wonder. For the Platonists too wonder was conceived as an essential element in literary art: in the sixteenth century, the Neo-Platonist Francesco Patrizi defined the poet as principal 'maker of the marvelous,' and the marvelous is found, as he put it, when men 'are astounded, ravished in ecstasy'. Patrizi goes so far as to posit marvelling as a special faculty of the mind, a faculty which in effect mediates between the capacity to think and the capacity to feel.'[14]

Modern art museums reflect a profound transformation of the experience: the collector – a Getty or a Mellon – may still be celebrated, and market value is even more intensely registered, but the heart of the mystery lies with the uniqueness, authenticity, and visual power of the masterpiece, ideally displayed in such a way as to heighten its charisma, to compel and reward the intensity of the viewer's gaze, to manifest artistic genius. Museums display works of art in such a way as to imply that no one, not even the nominal owner or donor, can penetrate the zone of light and actually possess the wonderful object. The object exists not principally to be owned but to be viewed. Even the *fantasy* of possession is no longer central to the museum-gaze, or rather it has been inverted, so that the object in its essence seems not to be a possession but rather to be itself the possessor of what is most valuable and enduring.[15] What the work possesses is the power to arouse wonder, and that power, in the dominant aesthetic ideology of the West, has been infused into it by the creative genius of the artist.

It is beyond the scope of this essay to account for the transformation of the experience of wonder from the spectacle of proprietorship to the mystique of the object – an exceedingly complex, overdetermined history centering on institutional and economic shifts – but I think it is important to say that at least in part this transformation was shaped by the collective project of Western artists and reflects their vision. Already in the early sixteenth century, when the marvelous was still principally associated with the prodigious, Dürer begins, in a famous journal entry describing Mexican objects sent to Charles V by Cortés, to reconceive it:

> I saw the things which have been brought to the King from the new golden land: a sun all of gold a whole fathom broad, and a moon all of silver of the same size, also two rooms full of the armour of the people there, and all manner of wondrous weapons of theirs, harness and darts, wonderful shields, strange clothing, bedspreads, and all kinds of wonderful objects of various uses, much more beautiful to behold than prodigies. These things were all so precious that they have been valued at one hundred thousand gold florins. All the days of my life I have seen nothing that has gladdened my heart so much as these things, for I saw amongst them wonderful works of art, and I marvelled at the subtle *ingenia* of men in foreign lands. Indeed, I cannot express all that I thought there.[16]

Dürer's description is full of the conventional marks of his period's sense of wonder: he finds it important that the artifacts have been brought as a kind of tribute to the king, that large quantities of precious metals have been used, that their market value has been reckoned; he notes the strangeness of them, even as he uncritically assimilates that strangeness to his own culture's repertory of objects (which include harness and bedspreads). But he also notes, in perceptions highly unusual for his own time, that these objects are 'much more beautiful to behold than prodigies', Dürer relocates the source of wonder from the outlandish to the aesthetic, and he understands the effect of beauty as a testimony to creative genius: 'I saw amongst them wonderful works of art, and I marvelled at the subtle *ingenia* of men in foreign lands.'

It would be misleading to strip away the relations of power and wealth that are encoded in the artist's response, but it would be still more misleading, I think, to interpret that response as an unmediated expression of those relations. For Dürer gives voice to an aesthetic understanding – a form of wondering and admiring and knowing – that is at least partly independent of the structures of politics and the marketplace.

This understanding – by no means autonomous and yet not reducible to the institutional and economic forces by which it is shaped – is centered on a certain kind of looking, a looking whose origins lie in the cult of the marvelous and hence in the art work's capacity to generate in the spectator surprise, delight, admiration, and intimations of genius. The knowledge that derives from this kind of looking may not be very useful in the attempt to understand another culture, but it vitally important in the attempt to understand our own. For it is one of the distinctive achievements of our culture to have fashioned this type of gaze, and one of the most intense pleasures that it has to offer. This pleasure does not have an inherent and necessary politics, either radical or imperialist, but Dürer's remarks suggest that it originates at least in respect and admiration for the *ingenia* of others. This respect is a response worth cherishing and enhancing. Hence, for all of my academic affiliations and interests, I am skeptical about the recent attempt to turn our museums from temples of wonder into temples of resonance.

Perhaps the most startling instance of this attempt is the transfer of the paintings in the Jeu de Paume and the Louvre to the new Musée d'Orsay. The Musée d'Orsay is at once a spectacular manifestation of French cultural *dépense* and a highly self-conscious, exceptionally stylish generator of resonance, including the literal resonance of voices in an enormous vaulted railway station. By moving the Impressionist and Post-Impressionist masterpieces into proximity with the work of far less well-known painters – Jean Béraud, Guillaume Dubuffe, Paul Sérusier, and so forth – and into proximity as well with the period's sculpture and decorative arts, the museum remakes a remarkable group of highly individuated geniuses into engaged participants in a vital, conflict-ridden, immensely productive period in French cultural history. The reimagining is guided by many well-designed informative boards – cue cards, in effect – along, of course, with the extraordinary building itself.

All of this is intelligently conceived and dazzlingly executed – on a cold winter day in Paris, the museum-goer may look down from one of the high balconies by the old railway clocks and savor the swirling pattern formed by the black and gray raincoats of the spectators below, as they pass through the openings in the massive black stone partitions of Gay Aulenti's interior. The pattern seems spontaneously to animate the period's style – if not Manet, then at least Caillebotte; it is as if a painted scene had recovered the power to move and to echo.

But what has been sacrificed on the altar of cultural resonance is visual wonder centered on the aesthetic masterpiece. Attention is dispersed among a wide range of lesser objects that collectively articulate the impressive creative achievement of French culture in the late nineteenth century, but the experience of the old Jeu de Paume – intense looking at Manet, Monet, Cézanne and so forth – has been radically reduced. The paintings are there, but they are mediated by the resonant contextualism of the building itself and its myriad objects and its descriptive and analytical plaques. Moreover, many of the greatest paintings have been demoted, as it were, to small spaces where it is difficult to view them adequately – as if the design of the museum were trying to assure the triumph of resonance over wonder.

But is a triumph of one over the other necessary? I have, for the purposes of this exposition, obviously exaggerated the extent to which these are alternative models for museums (or for the reading of texts): in fact, almost every exhibition worth the viewing has strong elements of both. I think that the impact of most exhibitions is likely to be greater if the initial appeal is wonder, a wonder that then leads to the desire for resonance, for it is easier to pass from wonder to resonance than from resonance to wonder. Why this should be so is suggested by a remarkable passage in his *Commentary on the Metaphysics of Aristotle* by Aquinas's teacher, Albert the Great:

> wonder is defined as a constriction and suspension of the heart caused by amazement at the sensible appearance of something so portentous, great, and unusual, that the heart suffers a systole. Hence wonder is something like fear in its effect on the heart. This effect of wonder, then, this constriction and systole of the heart, spring from an unfulfilled but felt desire to know the cause of that which appears portentous and unusual: so it was in the beginning when men, up to that time unskilled, began to philosophize. . . . Now the man who is puzzled and wonders apparently does not know. Hence wonder is the movement of the man who does not know on his way to finding out, to get at the bottom of that at which he wonders and to determine its cause. . . . Such is the origin of philosophy.[17]

Such too, from the perspective of the new historicism, is the origin of a meaningful desire for cultural resonance. But while philosophy would seek to supplant wonder with secure knowledge, it is the function of the new historicism continually to renew the marvelous at the heart of the resonant.

Notes

1 George Cavendish, *The Life and Death of Cardinal Wolsey*, in *Two Early Tudor Lives*, ed. Richard S. Sylvester and Davis P. Harding (New Haven and London, Yale University Press, 1962), pp. 24–5. We get another glimpse of the symbolism of hats later in the text, when Wolsey is beginning his precipitous fall from power: 'And talking with Master Norris upon his knees in the mire, he would have pulled off his under cap of velvet, but he could not undo the knot under his chin. Wherefore with violence he rent the laces and pulled it from his head and so kneeled bareheaded' (p. 106). I am grateful to Anne Barton for correcting my description of the hat in Christ Church and for transcribing the note card that details its provenance.

2 Walter Cohen, 'Political Criticism of Shakespeare', in *Shakespeare Reproduced: The Text in History and Ideology*, ed. Jean E. Howard and Marion F. O'Connor (New York and London, Methuen, 1987), p. 33; Edward Pechter, 'The New Historicism and Its Discontents'. in *PLMA* 102 (1987), p. 301.

3 'The new historicists and cultural materialists', one typical summary puts it, 'represent, and by representing, reproduce in their *new* history of ideas, a world which is hierarchical, authoritarian, hegemonic, unsubvertable. . . . In this world picture, Stephen Greenblatt has poignantly asserted, there can be no subversion – and certainly not for *us!*' Poignantly or otherwise, I asserted no such thing; I argued that the spectator of the history plays was continually tantalized by a resistance simultaneously powerful and deferred.

4 See my *Renaissance Self-Fashioning: from More to Shakespeare* (Chicago, University of Chicago Press, 1980), pp. 174–5: 'We are situated at the close of the cultural movement initiated in the Renaissance; the places in which our social and psychological world seems to be cracking apart are those structural joints visible when it was first constructed.'

5 Louis Adrian Montrose, 'Renaissance Literary Studies and the Subject of History', in *English Literary Renaissance* 16 (1986), pp. 5–12; Don Wayne, 'Power, Politics, and the Shakespearean Text: Recent Criticism in England and the United States', in *Shakespeare Reproduced*, ed. Howard and O'Connor, pp. 47–67; Catherine Gallagher, 'Marxism and the New Historicism', in *The New Historicism*, ed. Harold Veeser (New York and London, Routledge, 1989).

6 Jean E. Howard, 'The New Historicism in Renaissance Studies', in *Renaissance Historicism: Selections from 'English Literary Renaissance'*, ed. Arthur F. Kinney and Dan S. Collins (Amherts: University of Massachusetts Press, 1987), pp. 32–3.

7 If there is then no suspension of value judgments in the new historicism, there is at the same time a complication of those judgments, what I have called a sense of estrangement. This estrangement is bound up with the abandonment, the values of the present could no longer seem the necessary outcome of an irreversible teleological progression, whether of enlightenment or decline. An older historicism that proclaimed self-consciously that it had avoided all value judgments in its account of the past – that it had given us historical reality *wie es eigentlilch gewesen* – did not thereby avoid all value judgments; it simply

Modern Literary Theory

provided a misleading account of what it had actually done. In this sense the new historicism, for all its acknowedgment of engagement and partiality, may be slightly less likely than the older historicism to impose its values belligerently on the past, for those values seem historically contingent.

8 Cohen, in *Shakespeare Reproduced*, pp. 33–4.

9 Thomas Greene, *The Vulnerable Text: Essays on Renaissance Literature* (New York, Columbia University Press, 1986), p. 100.

10 Quoted in Linda A. Altshuler and Anna R. Cohn, 'The Precious Legacy', in David Altshuler, ed., *The Precious Legacy: Judaic Treasures from the Czechoslovak State Collections* (New York, Summit Books, 1983), p. 24. My sketch of the genesis of the State Jewish Museum is largely paraphrased from this chapter.

11 In effect that dream of possessing wonder is at once aroused and evacuated in commerce as well, since the minute the object – shoe or dress or soup tureen – is removed from its magical pool of light, it loses its wonder and returns to the status of an ordinary purchase.

12 Joinville, *Life of Saint Louis*, in *Chronicles of the Crusades*, tr. M.R.B. Shaw (Harmondsworth, Penguin, 1963), p. 315.

13 Quoted in J.V. Cunningham, *Woe or Wonder: The Emotional Effect of Shakespearean Tragedy* (Denver, Alan Swallow, 1960; orig. edn 1951), p. 82.

18 Hathaway, pp. 66–9. Hathaway's account of Patrizi is taken largely from Bernard Weinberg, *A History of Literary Criticism in the Italian Renaissance*, 2 vols. (Chicago, University of Chicago Press, 1961).

15 It is a mistake then to associate the gaze of the museum-goer with the appropriative male gaze about which so much has been written recently. But then I think that the discourse of the appropriative male gaze is itself in need of considerable qualification.

16 Quoted in Hugh Honour, *The New Golden Land: European Images of America from the Discoveries to the Present Time* (New York, Pantheon Books, 1975), p. 28.

17 Quoted in Cunningham, *Woe or Wonder*, pp. 77–8.

SECTION FOUR
POSTMODERNISM AND POSTCOLONIALISM

For the American novelist John Barth, commenting on the term in 1980, Postmodernism was essentially a continuation but modification of cultural modernism, a way of 'telling stories'. By 1990, although the term has spilled out of the boundaries of literary critical debate, it still carries with it this earlier sense, but the stories are now indistinguishable from what was once assumed to be knowledge: scientific truth, ethics, law, history. Somewhere in the 1980s, the term shifted from functioning primarily as a description of a range of aesthetic practices involving irony, parody, self-consciousness, fragmentation, playful self-reflexivity and parataxis, to a use encompassing a more general shift of thought and registering a pervasive loss of faith in the progressivist and rationalist discourses of Enlightened modernity. It is now used variously as a term to describe the cultural epoch through which we are living (often apocalyptically, sometimes as the logic of Late Capitalism); an aesthetic practice (viewed as co-extensive with the commodified surfaces of this culture or as a disruption of its assumptions from within through a 'micropolitics' or 'politics of desire') or as a critique of the foundationalist assumptions of Enlightened political and philosophical thought. Lyotard's *The Postmodern Condition* (1979),[1] marked the point where the specifically literary critical debate began to be dissolved into the larger theoretical and cultural one, though Post-Structuralists had already undermined the concept of grand- and metanarratives, the unity and autonomy of the subject and the ability of discourses to stabilize and contain cultural meanings.

Postmodernism is a 'mood' expressed theoretically across a diverse range of theoretical discourses and involving: a focus on the collapse of grand narratives into local incommensurable language games or 'little narratives'; a Foucauldian emphasis on the discontinuity and plurality of history as discursively produced and formulated, and a tendency to view the discourses of Enlightenment reason as complicit with the instrumental rationalization of modern life. The historian Arnold Toynbee first used the term in 1947 to describe the current, fourth and final, phase of Western history, dominated by anxiety and irrationalism. In the contemporary version, there is no longer a transcendent space from which to offer a critique of this culture: only disruption from within, micropolitics, language games, parody and fragmentation. Postmodernism wages war on totality. Postmodernists claim the exhaustion of all metanarratives which claim to legitimate foundations for truth, though some surreptitiously import new foundationalisms (the body, the aesthetic, desire). History becomes a plurality of islands of discourse arising out of the institutionally produced languages which we bring to bear on it. Or it is a network of agonistic language games where surface phenomena can no longer be 'explained' as the manifestations of deeper underlying truths. Absolute systems of knowledge give way to contingencies and ironies, aesthetic fictionality displaces philosophical certainty.

Whether influenced by post-Heideggerian hermeneutics, Nietzschean perspectivism or Wittgensteinian language games, Postmodernists such as Lyotard, Baudrillard and Rorty see knowledge of the world as indissociable from being-in-the-world: knowledge and experience are inextricably bound to each other and always culturally situated. There can be no transcendental 'view from nowhere', no position from outside culture from which to offer a criticism of it. Implication is all. We live in a pluralized culture surrounded by a multiplicity of styles, knowledges, stories that we tell ourselves about the world. To attempt to impose an overarching narrative on such experience is to perpetuate the violences of modernity with their exclusions and terrors. The relativization of styles which is postmodernism, throws into doubt the claims of any one discourse or story to be offering the 'truth' about the world or an authoritative version of the real. Issues of ethics, law, equality and authority become deeply problematic in such a context: how is one to legitimate knowledge and where to locate value?

Jameson's essay reprinted here locates the Postmodern as a condition arising out of the development in the sixties of a late, consumer phase of capitalism. It is characterized by the proliferation of depthless surface and the penetration of capital into all areas of social and cultural experience. Jameson seems to suggest our inevitable implication in the fragmentariness of the Postmodern, but he does underpin his argument with a 'totalizing' economic theory derived from Mandel's book *Late Capitalism* (1978).[2] The essay on Feminism and Postmodernism examines the implications for political movements such as Feminism of the postmodern dismantling of foundationalist arguments and of the concepts of universal justice, unity and liberation.

bell hooks's essay on 'Postmodern Blackness' provides a useful bridge between the consideration of Postmodernism and gender, on the one hand, and Postmodernism and race, on the other. She suggests that the postmodern concept of 'difference' is too often used as a vague umbrella term to refer to a Western sense of the exhaustion of high Modernism and a crisis of authority in the legacy of Enlightenment. In its unspecified and unsituated appropriation and as a gesture of radical chic, the term merely reproduces the blindnesses of Modernism, though in reverse and negative mode. Her argument is that the concepts of 'otherness' and 'difference' must be anchored more specifically to the politics of race and gender. Just as the black movement of the 1960s largely failed to connect with Feminist critiques of patriarchy, so Postmodernists have tended to ignore issues of race. A similar preoccupation with relations betwen power and knowledge in the construction of 'otherness' and, in particular, in the construction of the colonial subject, is the focus of the piece by Homi BhaBha. Together, hooks's essay and BhaBha's piece consider and enact a constellation of concerns and concepts which encompasses the shared discursive spaces of Postmodernism and Postcolonialism: the critique of essentialism; the deconstruction of Enlightenment models of the Subject; the crisis in Western rationalism and its discourses of authority; the analysis of the cultural nexus of power and knowledge.

The specific space of 'Postcolonialism', however, was first articulated in Edward Said's book *Orientalism*, published in 1978.[3] Like 'Postmodernism', the term has come to refer both to a condition (here postcoloniality) and to the discourses which theorize that condition. As a condition, however, Postcolonialism is hardly new. In the excerpt reprinted here from Said's later book, *Culture and Imperialism* (1993), the analysis of Conrad's *Heart of Darkness* reminds us that postcoloniality may refer as much to the Roman conquest of Britain and its aftermath as to the more recent historical recovery from the 'scramble for Africa' in the nineteenth century. 1947, however, saw the beginning of the formal dissolution of the European colonial empires and the granting of independence after world-wide campaigns of anti-colonial resistance. The contemporary postcolonial situation begins, therefore, in 1947, though Postcolonialism as a discursive and theoretical space is not named until 1978. In his earlier book, Said examined those forms of Western scholarship and cultural representation which codified knowledge about non-metropolitan cultures under colonial control. The book drew eclectically on Foucauldian Post-Structuralism and on the Gramscian concept of hegemony in order to demonstrate that Europe's construction of the Orient is a paradigm of all colonial and imperial structures. In each case, the mysterious and duplicitous 'other' which is the colonized culture functions as a means of stabilizing and affirming the identity of the imperialist power. Said's book emphasized the centrality of cultural representation in this process. If colonized peoples are to become subjects of history then 'Postcolonialism' must strengthen as well as analyse the discursive process of resistance to colonialist perspectives. In his own analysis of Conrad, Said shows how imperialism maintains power through the designation of a discursive space which makes silent and invisible all those perspectives which are excluded by and from its frame. He shows, through an analysis of Conrad's representation of Africa, how the construction of 'them' is necessary for the affirmation of 'us'.

Notes

1 J.-F. Lyotard, *The Postmodern Condition*, first pub. in English by Manchester University Press, 1985.
2 E. Mandel, *Late Capitalism* (London, 1978).
3 E. Said, *Orientalism* (London, Routledge & Kegan Paul, 1978).

---

28   Fredric Jameson,

'Periodizing the 60s', *The Sixties Without Apology* (1984)
pp. 178–218

Nostalgic commemoration of the glories of the 60s and abject public confession of the decade's many failures and missed opportunities are two errors that cannot be avoided by some middle path that threads its way in between. The following sketch starts from the position that History is Necessity, that the 60s had to happen the way it did, and that its opportunities and failures were inextricably intertwined, marked by the objective constraints and openings of a determinate historical situation, of which I thus wish to offer a tentative and provisional model.

To speak of the 'situation' of the 60s, however, is necessarily to think in terms of historical periods and to work with models of historical periodization, which are at the present moment theoretically unfashionable, to say the least. Leave aside the existential fact that the veterans of the decade, who have seen so many things change dramatically from year to year think more historically than their predecessors; the classification by generations has become as meaningful for us as it was for the Russians of the late nineteenth century, who sorted character types out with reference to specific decades. And intellectuals of a certain age now find it normal to justify their current positions by way of a historical narrative ('then the limits of Althusserianism began to be evident', etc.). Now, this is not the place for a theoretical justification of periodization in the writing of history, but to those who think that cultural periodization implies some massive kinship and homogeneity or identity within a given period, it may quickly be replied that it is surely only against a certain conception of what is historically dominant or hegemonic that the full value of the exceptional – what Raymond Williams calls the 'residual' or 'emergent' – can be assessed. Here, in any case, the period in question is understood not as some omnipresent and uniform shared style or way of thinking and acting, but rather as the sharing of an objective situation, to which a whole range of varied responses and creative innovations is then possible, but always within that situation's structural limits.

Yet a whole range of rather different theoretical objections will also bear on the selectiveness of such a historical narrative: if the critique of periodization questions the possibilities of diachrony, these involve the problems of synchrony and in particular of the relationship to be established between the various 'levels' of historical change singled out for attention. Indeed, the present narrative will claim to say something meaningful about the 60s by way of brief sketches of but four of those levels: the history of philosophy, revolutionary political theory and practice, cultural production, and economic cycles (and this in a context limited essentially to the United States, France, and the Third World). Such selectiveness seems not merely to give equal historical weight to base and superstructure indifferently, but also to raise the spectre of practice of homologies – the kind of analogical parallelism in which the poetic production of Wallace Stevens is somehow 'the same' as the political practice of Che Guevara – which have been thought abusive at least as far back as Spengler.

There is of course no reason why specialized and elite phenomena, such as the writing of poetry, cannot reveal historical trends and tendencies as vividly as 'real life' – or perhaps even more visibly, in their isolation and semi-autonomy which approximates a laboratory situation. In any case, there is a fundamental difference between the present narrative and those of an older organic history that sought 'expressive' unification through analogies and homologies between widely distinct levels of social life. Where the latter proposed identities between the forms on such various levels, what will be argued here is a series of significant homologies between the *breaks* in those forms and their development. What is at stake, then, is not some proposition about the organic unity of the 60s on all its levels, but rather a hypothesis about the rhythm and dynamics of the fundamental situation in which those very different levels develop according to their own internal laws.

At that point, what looked like a weakness in this historical or narrative procedure turns out to be an unexpected strength, particularly in allowing for some sort of 'verification' of the separate strands of the narrative. One sometimes believes – especially in the area of culture and cultural histories and critiques – that an infinite number of narrative interpretations of history are possible, limited only by the ingenuity of the practitioners whose claim to originality depends on the novelty of the new theory of history they bring to market. It is more reassuring, then, to find the regularities hypothetically proposed for one field of activity (e.g., the cognitive, or the aesthetic, or the revolutionary) dramatically and surprisingly 'confirmed' by the reappearance of just such regularities in a widely different and seemingly unrelated field, as will be the case with the economic in the present context.

At any rate, it will already have become clear that nothing like a history of the 60s in the traditional, narrative sense will be offered here. But historical representation is just as surely in crisis as its distant cousin, the linear novel, and for much the same reasons. The most intelligent 'solution' to such a crisis does not consist in abandoning historiography altogether, as an impossible aim and an ideological category all at once, but rather – as in the modernist aesthetic itself – in reorganising its traditional procedures on a different level. Althusser's proposal seems the wisest in this situation: as old-fashioned <u>narrative</u> or 'realistic' <u>historiography</u> became problematical, the historian should reformulate her vocation – not any longer to produce some vivid representation of History 'as it really happened', but rather to produce the *concept* of history. Such will at least be the gamble of the following pages.

1 Third World Beginnings

It does not seem particularly controversial to mark the beginnings of what will come to be called the 60s in the Third World with the great movement of decolonization in British and French Africa. It can be argued that the most characteristic expressions of a properly First World 60s are all later than this, whether they are understood in countercultural terms – drugs and rock – or in the political terms of a student New Left and a mass antiwar movement. Indeed, politically, a First World 60s owed much to Third-Worldism in terms of politicocultural models, as in a symbolic Maoism, and, moreover, found its mission in resistance to wars aimed precisely at stemming the new revolutionary forces in the Third World. Belden Fields has indeed suggested that the two First World nations in which the most powerful student mass movements emerged – the United States and France – became privileged political spaces precisely *because* these were two countries involved in colonial wars, although the French New Left appears after the resolution of the Algerian conflict. The one significant exception to all this is in many ways the most important First World political movement of all – the new black politics and the civil rights movement, which must be dated, not from the Supreme Court decision of 1954, but rather from the first sit-ins in Greensboro, North Carolina, in February of 19␣␣. Yet it might be argued that this was also a movement of decolonization, and in any case the constant exchange and mutual influences between the American black movements and the various African and Caribbean ones are continuous and incalculable throughout this period.

The independence of Ghana (1957), the agony of the Congo (Lumumba was murdered in January 1961), the independence of France's sub-Saharan colonies following the Gaullist referendum of 1959, finally the Algerian Revolution (which might plausibly mark our schema here with its internal high point, the Battle of Algiers, in January-March 1957, as with its diplomatic resolution in 1962) – all of these signal the convulsive birth of what will come in time to be known as the 60s:

> Not so very long ago, the earth numbered two thousand million inhabitants: five hundred million *men* and one thousand five hundred million *natives*. The former had the Word; the others merely had use of it.[1]

The 60s was, then, the period when all these 'natives' became human beings, and this internally as well as externally: those inner colonized of the First World – 'minorities', marginals, and women – fully as much as its external subjects and official 'natives'. The process can and has been described in a number of ways, each one of which implies a certain 'vision of History' and a certain uniquely thematized reading of the 60s proper: it can be seen as a decisive and global chapter in Croce's conception of history as the history of human freedom; as a more classically Hegelian process of the coming to self-consciousness of subject peoples; as some post-Lukácsean or more Marcusean, New Left conception of the emergence of new 'subjects of history' of a nonclass type (blacks, students, Third World peoples); or as some poststructuralist, Foucaultean notion (significantly anticipated by Sartre in the passage just quoted) of the conquest of the right to speak in a new collective voice, never before heard on the world stage – and of the concomitant dismissal of the intermediaries (liberals, First World intellectuals) who had hitherto claimed to talk in your name; not forgetting the more properly political rhetoric of self-determination or independence, or the more psychological and cultural rhetoric of new collective 'identities'.

It is, however, important to situate the emergence of these new collective 'identities' or 'subjects of history' in the historical situation which made that emergence possible, and in particular to relate the emergence of these new social and political categories (the colonised, race, marginality, gender, and the like) to something like a crisis in the more universal category that had hitherto seemed to subsume all the varieties of social resistance, namely the classical conception of social class. This is to be understood, however, not in some intellectual but rather in an institutional sense; it would be idealistic to suppose the deficiencies in the abstract idea of social class, and in particular in the Marxian conception of class struggle, can have been responsible for the emergence of what seem to be new nonclass forces. What can be noted, rather, is a crisis in the institutions through which a real class politics has however imperfectly been able to express itself. In this respect, the merge of the AFL and the CIO in 1955 can be seen as a fundamental 'condition of possibility' for the unleashing of the new social and political dynamics of the 60s: that merger, a triumph of McCarthyism, secured the expulsion of the Communists from the American labour movement, consolidated the new antipolitical 'social contract' between American business and the American labour unions, and created a situation in which the privileges of a white male labour force take precedence over the demands of black and women workers and other minorities. These last have therefore no place in the classical institutions of an older working-class politics. They will thus be 'liberated' from social class, in the charged and ambivalent sense that Marxism gives to that word (in the context of enclosure, for instance); they are separated from the older institutions and thus 'released' to find new modes of social and political expression.

The virtual disappearance of the American Communist Party as a small but significant political force in American society in 1956 suggests another dimension to this general situation: the crisis of the American party is 'overdetermined' by its repression under McCarthyism and by the 'revolution' in the Soviet bloc unleashed by Khrushchev's de-Stalinization campaign, which will have analogous but distinct and specific equivalents for the European Communist parties. In France, in particular, after the brief moment of a Communist 'humanism', developed essentially by philosophers in the eastern countries, and with the fall of Khrushchev himself and the definitive failure of his various experiments in 1964, an unparalleled situation emerges in which, virtually for the first time since the Congress of Tours in 1919, it becomes possible for radical intellectuals to conceive of revolutionary work outside and independent of the French Communist Party. The older attitudes – 'we know all about it, we don't like it much, but nothing is to be done politically without the CP' – are classically expressed in Sartre's own political journalism, in particular in *Les Communistes et la paix*. Now Trotskyism gets a new lease on life, and the new Maoist forms, followed by a whole explosion of extraparliamentary formations of all ideological complexions, the so-called groupuscules, offer the promise of a new kind of politics equally 'liberated' from the traditional class categories.

Two further key events need to be noted here before we go on. For many of us, indeed, the crucial detonator – a new Year I, the palpable demonstration that revolution was not merely a historical concept and a museum piece but real and achievable – was furnished by a people whose imperialist subjugation had developed among North Americans a sympathy and a sense of fraternity we could never have for other Third World peoples in their struggle, except in an abstract and intellectual way. Yet by January 1, 1959, the Cuban Revolution remained symbolically ambiguous. It could be read as a Third World revolution of a type different from either the classical Leninist one or the Maoist experience, for it had a revolutionary strategy entirely its own, the *foco* theory, which we will discuss later. This great event also announces the impending 60s as a period of unexpected political innovation rather than as the confirmation of older social and conceptual schemes.

Meanwhile, personal testimony seems to make it clear that for many white American students – in particular for many of those later active in the New Left – the assassination of President Kennedy played a significant role in delegitimizing the state itself and in discrediting the parliamentary process, seeming to mark the decisive end of the well-known passing of the torch to a younger generation of leadership, as well as the dramatic defeat of some new spirit of public or civic idealism. As for the reality of the appearance, it does not much matter that, in hindsight, such a view of the Kennedy presidency may be wholly erroneous, considering his conservatism and anticommunism, the gruesome gamble of the 'missile crisis', and his responsibility for the American engagement in Vietnam itself. More significant, the legacy of the Kennedy regime to the development of a 60s politics may well have been the rhetoric of youth and of the 'generation gap' which he exploited, but which outlived him and dialectically offered itself as an expressive form through which the political discontent of American students and young people could articulate itself.

Such were some of the preconditions or 'conditions of possibility' – both in traditional working-class political institutions and in the arena of the legitimation of state power – for the 'new' social forces of the 60s to develop as they did. Returning to these new forces, there is a way in which their ultimate fate marks the close of the 60s as well: the end of 'Third-Worldism' in the U.S. and Europe largely predates the Chinese Thermidor, and coincides with the awareness of increasing institutional corruption in many of the newly independent states of Africa and the almost complete militarisation of the Latin American regimes after the Chilean coup of 1973 (the later revolutionary truimphs in the former Portuguese colonies are henceforth felt to be 'Marxist' rather than 'Third-Worldist', whereas Vietnam vanishes from American consciousness as completely after the ultimate American withdrawal as did Algeria from French consciousness after the Evian accords of 1963). In the First World of the late 60s, there is certainly a return to a more internal politics, as the antiwar movement in the United States and May 68 in France testify. Yet the American movement remains organically linked to its Third World 'occasion' in the Vietnam War itself, as well as to the Maoist inspiration of the Progressive Labor-type groups which emerge from SDS, such that the movement as a whole will lose its momentum as the war winds down and the draft ceases. In France, the 'common program' of the left (1972) – in which the current Socialist government finds its origins – marks a new turn toward Gramscian models and a new kind of Eurocommunist spirit which owes very little to Third World antecedents of any kind. Finally, the black movement in the U.S. enters into a crisis at much the same time, as its dominant ideology – cultural nationalism, an ideology profoundly linked to Third World models – is exhausted. The women's movement also owed something to this kind of Third World inspiration, but it too, in the period 1972–74, will know an increasing articulation into relatively distinct ideological positions ('Bourgeois' feminism, lesbian separatism, socialist feminism).

For reasons enumerated above, and others, it seems plausible to mark the end of the 60s around 1972–74; the problem of this general 'break' will be returned to at the end of this sketch. For the moment we must complete our characterization of the overall dynamic of Third World history during this period, particularly if it is granted that this dynamic or 'narrative line' entertains some privileged relationship of influence on the unfolding of a First World 60s (through direct intervention – wars of national liberation – or through the prestige of exotic political models – most obviously, the Maoist one – or finally, owing to some global dynamic which both worlds share and respond to in relatively distinct ways).

This is, of course the moment to observe that the 'liberation' of new forces in the Third World is as ambiguous as this term frequently tends to be (freedom as separation from older systems); to put it more sharply, it is the moment to recall the obvious, that decolonisation historically went hand in hand with neocolonialism, and that the graceful, grudging, or violent end of an old-fashioned imperialism certainly meant the end of one kind of domination but evidently also the invention and construction of a new kind – symbolically, something like the replacement of the British Empire by the International Monetary Fund. This is, incidentally, why the currently fashionable rhetoric of power and domination (Foucault is the most influential of these rhetoricians, but the basic displacement from the economic to the political is already made by Max Weber) is ultimately unsatisfactory; it is of course politically important to 'contest' the various forms of power and domination, but the latter cannot be understood unless their functional relationships to economic exploitation are articulated – that is, until the political is once again subsumed beneath the economic. (On the other hand – particularly in the historicizing perspective of the present essay – it will obviously be a significant historical and social *symptom* that, in the mid-60s, people felt it necessary to express their sense of the situation and their projected praxis in a reified political language of power, domination, authority and antiauthoritarianism, and so forth: here, Second and Third World developments – with their conceptions of a 'primacy of the political' under socialism – offer an interesting and curious cross-lighting.) Meanwhile, something similar can be said of the conceptions of collective identity and in particular of the poststructuralist slogan of the conquest of speech, of the right to speak in your own voice, for yourself; but to articulate new demands, in your own voice, is not necessarily to satisfy them, and to speak is not necessarily to achieve a Hegelian recognition from the Other (or at least then only in the more sombre and baleful sense that the Other now has to take you into consideration in a new way and to invent new methods for dealing with that new presence you have achieved). In hindsight, the 'materialist kernel' of this characteristic rhetoric or ideological vision of the 60s may be found in a more fundamental reflection on the nature of cultural revolution itself (now independent of its local and now historical Chinese manifestation).

The paradoxical, or dialectical, combination of decolonization and neo-colonialism can perhaps best be grasped in economic terms by a reflection on the nature of another process whose beginning coincides with the general beginnings we have suggested for this period as a whole. This is a process generally described in the neutral but obviously ideological language of a technological 'revolution' in agriculture: the so-called Green Revolution, with its new applications of chemical procedures to fertilisation, its intensified strategies of mechanization, and its predictable celebration of progress and wonder-working technology, supposedly destined to free the world from hunger (the Green Revolution, incidentally, finds its Second World equivalent in Khrushchev's disastrous 'virgin lands' experiment). But these are far from neutral achievements; nor is their export – essentially pioneered by the Kennedys – a benevolent and altruistic activity. In the nineteenth and early twentieth centuries, capitalist penetration of the Third World did not necessarily mean a capitalist transformation of the latter's traditional modes of production. Rather, they were for the most part left intact, 'merely' exploited by a more political and military structure. The very enclave nature of these older agricultural modes – in combination with the violence of the occupier and that other violence, the introduction of money – established a sort of tributary relation that was beneficial to the imperialist metropolis for a considerable period. The Green Revolution carries this penetration and expansion of the 'logic of capital' into a new stage.

The older village structure and procapitalist forms of agriculture are now systematically destroyed, to be replaced by an industrial agriculture whose effects are fully as disastrous as, and analogous to, the moment of enclosure in the emergence of capital in what was to become the First World. The 'organic' social relations of village societies are now shattered, an enormous landless preproletariat produced, which migrates to the urban areas (as the tremendous growth of Mexico City can testify), while new, more proletarian, wage-working forms of agricultural labour replaced the older collective or traditional kinds. Such ambiguous 'liberation' needs to be described with all the dialectical ambivalence with which Marx and Engels celebrate the dynamism of capital itself in the *Manifesto* or the historical progress achieved by the British occupation of India.

The conception of the Third World 60s as a moment when all over the world chains and shackles of a classical imperialist kind were thrown off in a stirring wave of 'wars of national liberation' is an altogether mythical simplification. Such resistance is generated as much by the new penetration of the Green Revolution as it is by the ultimate impatience with the older imperialist structures, the latter itself overdetermined by the historical spectacle of the supremacy of another former Third World entity, namely Japan, in its sweeping initial victories over the old imperial powers in World War II. Eric Wolf's indispensable *Peasant Wars of the Twentieth Century* (1969) underscores the relationship between possibilities of resistance, the development of a revolutionary ethos, and a certain constitutive distance from the more absolutely demoralizing social and economic logic of capital.

The final ambiguity with which we leave this topic is the following: the 60s, often imagined as a period when capital and First World power are in retreat all over the globe, can just as easily be conceptualized as a period when capital is in full dynamic and innovative expansion, equipped with a whole armature of fresh production techniques and new 'means of production'. It now remains to be seen whether this ambiguity, and the far greater specificity of the agricultural developments in the Third World, have any equivalent in the dynamics with which the 60s unfold in the advanced countries themselves.

2 The Politics of Otherness

If the history of philosophy is understood not as some sequence of timeless yet somehow finite positions in the eternal, but rather as the history of attempts to conceptualize a historical and social substance itself in constant dialectical transformation, whose aporias and contradictions mark all of those successive philosophies as determinate failures, yet failures from which we can read off something of the nature of the object on which they themselves came to grief – then it does not seem quite so farfetched to scan the more limited trajectory of that now highly specialized discipline for symptoms of the deeper rhythms of the 'real' or 'concrete' 60s itself.

As far as the history of philosophy during that period is concerned, one of the more influential versions of its story is told as follows: the gradual supersession of a hegemonic Sartrean existentialism (with its essentially phenomenological perspectives) by what is often loosely called 'structuralism', namely, by a variety of new theoretical attempts which share at least a single fundamental 'experience' – the discovery of the primacy of Language or the Symbolic (an area in which phenomenology and Sartrean existentialism remain relatively conventional or traditional). The moment of high structuralism – whose most influential monuments are seemingly not philosophical at all, but can be characterized, alongside the new linguistics itself, as linguistic transformations of anthropology and psychoanalysis by Claude Lévi-Strauss and Jacques Lacan respectively – is, however, inherently unstable and has the vocation of becoming a new type of universal mathesis, under pain of vanishing as one more intellectual fad. The breakdown products of that moment of high structuralism can then be seen, on the one hand, as the reduction to a kind of scientism, to sheer method and analytical technique (in *semiotics*); and, on the other hand, as the transformation of structuralist approaches into active ideologies in which ethical, political, and historical consequences are drawn from the hitherto more epistemological 'structuralist' positions; this last is of course the moment of what is now generally known as *poststructuralism*, associated with familiar names like those of Foucault, Deleuze, Derrida, and so forth. That the paradigm, although obviously French in its references, is not merely local can be judged from an analogous mutation of the classical Frankfurt School via problems of communication, in the work of Habermas; or by the current revival of pragmatism in the work of Richard Rorty, which has a home-grown American 'poststructuralist' feeling to it (Pierce after all having largely preceded and outclassed Saussure).

The crisis of the philosophical institution and the gradual extinction of the philosopher's classic political vocation, of which Sartre was for our time the supreme embodiment, can in some ways be said to be about the so-called death of the subject: the individual ego or personality, but also the supreme philosophical Subject, the cogito but also the *auteur* of the great philosophical *system*. It is certainly possible to see Sartre as one of the last great system builders of traditional philosophy (but then at least one dimension of classical existentialism must also be seen as an ideology or a metaphysic: that of the heroic pathos of existential choice and freedom in the void, and that of the 'absurd', more particularly in Camus). Some of us also came to *Marxism* through dialectical elements in the early Sartre (he himself then turning to follow up this avenue in his own later, more Marxian work, such as the *Critique of Dialectical Reason* [1960]). But on balance the component of his work that underwent the richest practical elaboration at other people's hands as well as his own was his theory of interpersonal relations, his stunning rewrite of Hegel's Master/Slave chapter, his conception of the Look as the most concrete mode in which I relate to other subjects and struggle with them, the dimension of my alienation in my 'being-for-other-people', in which each of us vainly attempts, by looking at the other, to turn the tables and transform the baleful alienating gaze of the Other into an object for my equally alienating gaze. Sartre will go on, in the *Critique*, to try to erect a more positive and political theory of group dynamics on this seemingly sterile territory; the struggle between two people now becoming dialectically transformed into the struggle between groups themselves. The *Critique* was an anticipatory work, however, whose import and significance would not finally be recognised until May 68 and beyond, whose rich consequences indeed have not even fully been drawn to this day. Suffice it to say, in the present context, that the *Critique* fails to reach its appointed terminus, and to complete the projected highway that was to have led from the individual subject of existential experience all the way to fully constituted social classes. It breaks down at the point of the constitution of small groups and is ultimately usable principally for ideologies of small guerilla bands (in a later moment of the 60s) and of microgroups (at the period's end). The significance of this trajectory will soon be clear.

However, at the dawn of the 60s, the Sartrean paradigm of the Look and the struggle for recognition between individual subjects will also be appropriated dramatically for a very different model of political struggle, in Frantz Fanon's enormously influential vision (*The Wretched of the Earth* [1961]) of the struggle between Colonizer and Colonized, where the objectifying reversal of the Look is apocalyptically rewritten as the act of redemptive violence of Slave against Master, the moment when, in fear and the anxiety of death, the hierarchical positions of Self and Other, Centre and Margin, are forcibly reversed, and when the subservient consciousness of the Colonized achieves collective identity and self-affirmation in the face of coloniziers in abject fight.

What is at once significant is the way in which what had been a technical philosophical subject (the 'problem' of solipsism, the nature of relationships between individual subjects or 'cogitos') has fallen into the world and become an explosive and scandalous political ideology: a piece of the old-fashioned technical philosophical system of high existentialism breaking off and migrating outside philosophy departments altogether, into a more frightening landscape of praxis and terror. Fanon's great myth could be read at the time, by those it appalled equally well as by those it energized, as an irresponsible call to mindless violence. In retrospect, and in the light of Fanon's other, clinical work (he was a psychiatrist working with victims of colonization and of the torture and terror of the Algerian war), it can more appropriately be read as a significant contribution to a whole theory of cultural revolution as the collective reeducation (or even collective psychoanalysis) of oppressed peoples or unrevolutionary working classes. Cultural revolution as a strategy for breaking the immemorial habits of subalternity and obedience which have become internalized as a kind of second nature in all the laborious and exploited classes in human history – such is the vaster problematic to which, today, Gramsci and Wilhelm Reich, Fanon and Rudolf Bahro, can be seen as contributing as richly as the more official practices of Maoism.

3 Digression on Maoism

But with this new and fateful reference, an awkward but unavoidable parenthetical digression is in order: Maoism, richest of all the great new ideologies of the 60s, will be a shadowy but central presence throughout this essay, yet owing to its very polyvalence it cannot be neatly inserted at any point or exhaustively confronted on its own. One understands, of course, why Left militants here and abroad, fatigued by Maoist dogmatisms, must have heaved a collective sigh of relief when the Chinese turn consigned 'Maoism' itself to the ashcan of history. Theories, however, are often liberated on their own terms when they are thus radically disjoined from the practical interests of state power. Meanwhile, as I have suggested above, the symbolic terrain of the present debate is fully as much chosen and dictated by the Right as by Left survivors; and the current propaganda campaign, everywhere in the world, to Stalinize and discredit Maoism and the experience of the Chinese cultural revolution – now rewritten as yet another Gulag to the East – all of this, make no mistake about it, is part and parcel of the larger attempt to trash the 60s generally. It would not be prudent to abandon rapidly and without thoughtful reconsideration any of this terrain to the 'other side'.

As for the more ludicrous features of Western Third-Worldism generally – a kind of modern exotic or orientalist version of Marx's revolutionaries of 1848, who 'anxiously conjure up the spirits of the Great Revolution of 1789 to their service and borrow from them names, battle cries and costumes'[2] – these are now widely understood in a more cynical light, as in Regis Debray's remark: 'In France, the Columbuses of political modernity thought that following Godards's *La Chinoise* they were discovering China in Paris, when in fact they were landing in California.'[3]

Most paradoxical and fascinating of all, however, is the unexpected and unpredictable sequel to the Sino-Soviet split itself: the new Chinese rhetoric, intent on castigating the Soviet bureaucracy as revisionistic and 'bourgeois', will have the curious effect of evacuating the class content of these slogans. There is then an inevitable terminological slippage and displacement: the new binary opposite to the term 'bourgeois' will no longer be 'proletarian' but rather 'revolutionary', and the new qualifications for political judgments of this kind are no longer made in terms of class or party affiliation but rather in terms of personal life – your relationship to special privileges, to middle-class luxuries and dachas and managerial incomes and other perks – Mao Zedong's own monthly 'salary', we are told, was something in the neighbourhood of a hundred American dollars. As with all forms of anticommunism, this rhetoric can of course be appropriated by the anti-Marxist thematics of 'bureaucracy', of the end of ideology and social class, and so forth. But it is important to understand how for Western militants what began to emerge from this at first merely tactical and rhetorical shift was a whole new political space, a space which will come to be articulated by the slogan 'the personal is the political', and into which – in one of the most stunning and unforeseeable of historical turns – the women's movement will triumphantly move at the end of the decade, building a Yenan of a new and unpredictable kind which is still impregnable at the present moment.

4 The Withering Away of Philosophy

The limit as well as the strength of the stark Fanonian model of struggle was set by the relative simplicity of the colonial situation; this can be shown in two ways, first of all in the sequel to the 'war of national independence'. For with the Slave's symbolic and literal victory over the (now former) Master, the 'politics of otherness' touches its limit as well; the rhetoric of a conquest of collective identity has then nowhere else to go but into a kind of recessionary logic of which black cultural nationalism and (later on) lesbian separatism are the most dramatic examples (the dialectic of cultural and linguistic independence in Quebec province would be yet another instructive one). But this result is also contradictory, insofar as the newly constituted group (we here pick up Sartre's account in the *Critique*) needs outside enemies to survive as a group, to produce and perpetuate a sense of collective cohesion and identity. Ultimately, in the absence of the clear-cut Manichean situation of the older imperialist period, this hard-won collective self-definition of a first moment of resistance will break up into the smaller and more comfortable unities of face-to-face micro-groups (of which the official political sects are only one example).

The gradual waning of the Fanonian model can also be described from the perspective of what will shortly become its 'structuralist' critique. On this view, it is still a model based on a conception of individual subjects, albeit mythical and collective ones. It is thereby both anthropomorphic and transparent, in the sense in which nothing intervenes between the great collective adversaries, between the Master and the Slave, between the Colonizer and the Colonized. Yet even in Hegel, there was always a third term, namely matter itself, the raw materials on which the Slave is made to labour and to work out a long and anonymous salvation through the rest of history. The 'third term' of the 60s is, however, rather different from this. It was as though the protracted experiences of the earlier part of the decade gradually burned into the minds of the participants a specific lesson. In the United States, it was the experience of the interminable Vietnam War itself; in France, it was the astonishing and apparently invincible technocratic dynamism, and the seemingly unshakable inertia and resistance to de-Stalinization of the French Communist party; and everywhere, it was the tremendous expansion of the media apparatus and the culture of consumerism. This lesson might well be described as the discovery, within a hitherto antagonistic and 'transparent' political praxis, of the opacity of the Institution itself as the radically transindividual, with its own inner dynamic and laws, which are not those of individual human action or intention, something which Sartre theorised in the *Critique* as the 'pactico-inert', and which will take the definitive form, in competing structuralism, of 'structure' or 'synchronic system', a realm of impersonal logic in terms of which human consciousness is itself little more than an 'effect of structure'.

On this reading, then, the new philosophical turn will be interpreted less in the idealistic perspective of some discovery of a new scientific truth (the Symbolic) than as the symptom of an essentially protopolitical and social experience, the shock of some new, hard, unconceptualized, resistant object which the older conceptuality cannot process and which thus gradually generates a whole new problematic. The conceptualization of this new problematic in the coding of linguistics or information theory may then be attributed to the unexpected explosion of information and messages of all kinds in the media revolution, which will be discussed in more detail in the following section. Suffice it to remark at this point that there is some historical irony in the way in which this moment, essentially the Third Technological Revolution in the West (electronics, nuclear energy) – in other words, a whole new step in the conquest of nature by human praxis – is philosophically greeted and conceptually expressed in a kind of thought officially designated as 'antihumanist' and concerned to think what transcends or escapes human consciousness and intention. Similarly, the Second Technological Revolution of the late nineteenth century – an unparalleled quantum leap in human power over nature – was the moment of expression of a whole range of nihilisms associated with 'modernity' or with high modernism in culture.

In the present context, the Althusserian experiment of the mid- to late 60s is the most revealing and suggestive of the various 'structuralisms', since it was the only one to be explicitly political and indeed to have very wide-ranging political effects in Europe and Latin America. The story of Althusserianism can be told only schematically here: its initial thrust is twofold, against the unliquidated Stalinist tradition (strategically designated by the code words 'Hegel' and 'expressive causality' in Althusser's own texts), and against the 'transparence' of the Eastern attempts to reinvent a Marxist humanism on the basis of the theory of alienation in Marx's early manuscripts. That Althusserianism is essentially a meditation on the 'institutional' and on the opacity of the 'practico-inert' may be judged by the three successive formulations of this object by Althusser himself in the course of the 60s: that of a 'structure in dominance' or *structure à dominante* (in *For Marx*), that of 'structural causality' (in *Reading Capital*), and that of ideological state apparatuses (in the essay of that name). What is less often remembered, but what should be perfectly obvious from any rereading of *For Marx*, is the origin of this new problematic in Maoism itself, and particularly in Mao Zedong's essay 'On Contradiction', in which the notion of the complex, already-given *overdetermined* conjuncture of various kinds of antagonistic and nonantagonistic contradictions is mapped out.

The modification that will emerge from Althusser's 'process of theoretical production' as it works over its Maoist raw materials can be conveyed by the problem and slogan of the 'semi-autonomy' of the levels of social life (a problem already invoked in our opening pages). This formula will involve a struggle on two fronts: on the one hand, against the monism or 'expressive causality' of Stalinism, in which the 'levels' are identified, conflated, and brutally collapsed into one another (changes in economic production will be 'the same' as political and cultural changes), and, on the other, against bourgeois avant-garde philosophy, which finds just such a denunciation of organic concepts of totality most congenial, but draws from it the consequence of a post- or anti-Marxist celebration of Nietzschean heterogeneity. The notion of a semi-autonomy of the various levels or instances, most notably of the political instance and of the dynamics of state power, will have enormous resonance (outstandingly in the work of Nicos Poulantzas), since it seems to reflect, and to offer a way of theorizing, the enormous growth of the state bureaucracy since the war, the 'relative autonomy' of the state apparatus from any classical and reductive functionality in the service of big business, as well as the very active new terrain of political struggle presented by government or public sector workers. The theory could also be appealed to justify a semi-autonomy in the cultural sphere, as well, and especially a semi-autonomous cultural politics, of a variety that ranges from Godard's films and *situationisme* to the 'festival' of May 68 and the Yippie movement here (not excluding, perhaps, even those forms of so-called terrorism that aimed, not at any classical seizure of state power, but rather at essentially pedagogical or informational demonstrations, e.g., 'forcing the state to reveal its fundamentally fascist nature').

Nonetheless, the attempt to open up a semi-autonomy of the levels in one hand, while holding them altogether in the ultimate unity of some 'structural totality' (with its still classical Marxian ultimately determining instance of the economic), tends under its own momentum, in the centrifugal force of the critique of totality it had itself elaborated, to self-destruct (most dramatically so in the trajectory of Hindess and Hirst). What will emerge is not merely a heterogeneity of *levels* – henceforth, semi-autonomy will relax into autonomy *tout court*, and it will be conceivable that in the decentred and 'schizophrenic' world of late capitalism the various instances may really have no organic relationship to one another at all – but, more important, the idea will emerge that the struggles appropriate to each of these levels (purely political struggles, purely economic struggles, purely cultural struggles, purely 'theoretical' struggles) may have no necessary relationship to one another either. With this ultimate 'meltdown' of the Althusserian apparatus we are in the (still contemporary) world of microgroups and micropolitics – variously theorized as local or molecular politics, but clearly characterized, however different the various conceptions are, as a repudiation of old-fashioned class and party politics of a 'totalizing' kind, and most obviously epitomised by the challenge of the women's movement, whose unique new strategies and concerns cut across (or in some cases undermine and discredit altogether) many classical inherited forms of 'public' or 'official' political action, including the electoral kind. The repudiation of 'theory' itself as an essentially masculine enterprise of 'power through knowledge' in French feminism (see in particular the work of Luce Irigaray) may be taken as the final moment in this particular 'withering away of philosophy'.

Yet there is another way to read the density of Althusserianism, a way that will form the transition to our subsequent discussion of the transformation of the cultural sphere in the 60s; and this involves the significance of the slogan of 'theory' itself as it comes to replace the older term philosophy throughout this period. The 'discovery' of the Symbolic, the development of its linguistic-related thematics (as, e.g., in the notion of understanding as an essentially synchronic process, which influences the construction of relatively ahistorical 'structures', such as the Althusserian one described above), is now to be correlated with a modification of the practice of the symbolic, of language itself in the 'structuralist' texts, henceforth characterized as 'theory', rather than work in a particular traditional discipline. Two features of this evolution, or mutation, must be stressed. The first is a consequence of the crisis in, or the disappearance of, classical *canon* of philosophical writings which necessarily results from the contestation of philosophy as a discipline and an institution. Henceforth, the new 'philosophical' text will no longer draw its significance from an insertion into the issues and debates of the philosophical tradition, which means that its basic 'intertextual' references become random, an *ad hoc* constellation that forms and dissolves on the occasion of each new text. The new text must necessarily be a commentary on other texts (indeed, that dependence on a body of texts to be glossed, rewritten, interconnected in fresh ways will now intensify if anything), yet those texts, drawn from the most wildly distant disciplines (anthropology, psychiatry, literature, history of science), will be selected in a seemingly arbitrary fashion: Mumford side by side with Antonin Artaud, Kant with Sade, pre-Socratic philosophy, President Schreber, a novel of Maurice Blanchot, Owen Lattimore on Mongolia, and a host of obscure Latin medical treatises from the eighteenth century. The vocation of what was formerly 'philosophy' is thereby restructured and displaced: since there is no longer a tradition of philosophical problems in terms of which new positions and new statements can meaningfully be proposed, such works now tend toward what can be called metaphilosophy – the very different work of coordinating a series of pregiven, already constituted codes or systems of signifiers, of producing a discourse fashioned out of the already fashioned discourse of the constellation of *ad hoc* reference works. 'Philosophy' thereby becomes radically occasional; one would want to call it disposable theory, the production of a *metabook*, to be replaced by a different one next season, rather than the ambition to express a proposition, a position, or a system with greater 'truth' value. (The obvious analogy with the evolution of literary and cultural studies today, with the crisis and disappearance of the latter's own canon of great books – the last one having been augmented to include the once recalcitrant 'masterpieces' of high modernism – will be taken for granted in our next section.)

All of this can perhaps be grasped in a different way by tracing the effects of another significant feature of contemporary theory, namely its privileged theme in the so-called critique of representation. Traditional philosophy will now be grasped in those terms, as a practice of representation in which the philosophical text or system (misguidedly) attempts to express something other than itself, namely truth or meaning (which now stands as the 'signified' to the 'signifier' of the system). If, however, the whole aesthetic of representation is metaphysical and ideological, philosophical discourse can no longer entertain this vocation, and it must stand as the mere addition of another text to what is now conceived as an infinite chain of texts (not necessarily all verbal – daily life is a text, clothing is a text, state power is a text, that whole external world, about which 'meaning' or 'truth' were once asserted and which is now contemptuously characterized as the illusion of reference or the 'referent', is an indeterminate superposition of texts of all kinds). Whence the significance of the currently fashionable slogan of 'materialism', when sounded in the area of philosophy and theory: materialism here means the dissolution of any belief in 'meaning' or in the 'signified' conceived as ideas or concepts that are distinct from their linguistic expressions. However paradoxical a 'materialist' philosophy may be in this respect, a 'materialist theory of language' will clearly transform the very function and operation of 'theory', since it opens up a dynamic in which it is no longer ideas, but rather texts, material texts, which struggle with one another. Theory so defined (and it will have become clear that the term now greatly transcends what used to be called philosophy and its specialized content) conceives of its vocation, not as the discovery of truth and the repudiation of error, but rather as a struggle about purely linguistic formulations, as the attempt to formulate verbal propositions (material language) in such a way that they are unable to imply unwanted or ideological consequences. Since this aim is evidently impossible to achieve, what emerges from the practice of theory – and this was most dramatic and visible during the high point of Althusserianism itself in 1967–68 – is a violent and obsessive return to ideological critique in the new form of a perpetual guerrilla war among the material signifiers of textual formulations. With the transformation of philosophy into a material practice, however, we touch on a development that cannot fully be appreciated until it is replaced in the context of a general mutation of culture throughout this period, a context in which 'theory' will come to be grasped as a specific (or semi-autonomous) form of what must be called postmodernism generally.

5 The Adventures of the Sign

Postmodernism is one significant framework in which to describe what happened to culture in the 60s, but a full discussion of this hotly contested concept is not possible here. Such a discussion would want to cover, among other things, the following features: that well-known poststructuralist theme, the 'death' of the subject (including the creative subject, the *auteur* or the 'genius'); the nature and function of a *culture of the simulacrum* (an idea developed out of Plato by Deleuze and Baudrillard to convey some specificity of a reproducible object world, not of copies or reproductions marked as such, but of a proliferation of trompe-l'oeil copies *without originals*); the relation of this last to media culture of the 'society of the spectacle' (Debord), under two heads: (1) the peculiar new status of the image, the 'material' or what might better be called the 'literal', signifier: a materiality or literality from which the older sensory richness of the medium has been abstracted (just as on the other side of the dialectical relationship, the old individuality of the subject and his/her 'brushstrokes' have equally been effaced); and (2) the emergence, in the work's temporality, of an aesthetic of *textuality* or what is often described as schizophrenic time; the eclipse, finally, of all depth, especially *historicity* itself, with the subsequent appearance of pastiche and nostalgia art (what the French call *la mode rétro*), and including the supersession of the accompanying models of depth-interpretation in philosophy (the various forms of hermeneutics, as well as the Freudian conception of 'repression', of manifest and latent levels).

What is generally objected to in characterizations of this kind is the empirical observation that all these features can be abundantly located in this or that variety of high modernism; indeed, one of the difficulties in specifying postmodernism lies in its symbiotic or parasitical relationship to the latter. In effect, with the canonisation of a hitherto scandalous, ugly, disonant, amoral, antisocial, bohemian high modernism offensive to the middle classes, its promotion to the very figure of high culture generally, and perhaps most important, its enshrinement in the academic institution, postmodernism emerges as a way of making creative space for artists now oppressed by those henceforth hegemonic modernist categories of irony, complexity, ambiguity, dense temporality, and particularly, aesthetic and utopian monumentality. In some analogous way, it will be said, high modernism itself won its autonomy from the preceding hegemonic realism (the symbolic language or mode of representation of classical or market capitalism). But there is a difference in that realism itself underwent a significant mutation: it became *naturalism* and at once generated the representation forms of mass culture (the narrative apparatus of the contemporary best seller is an invention of naturalism and one of the most stunningly successful of French cultural exports). High modernism and mass culture then develop in dialectical opposition and interrelationship with one another. It is precisely the waning of their opposition, and some new conflation of the forms of high and mass culture, that characterizes postmodernism itself.

The historical specificity of postmodernism must therefore finally be argued in terms of the social functionality of culture itself. As stated above, high modernism, whatever its overt political content, was oppositional and marginal within a middle-class Victorian or Philistine or gilded-age culture. Although postmodernism is equally offensive in all the respects enumerated (think of punk rock or pornography), it is no longer at all oppositional in that sense; indeed, it constitutes the very dominant or hegemonic aesthetic of consumer society itself and significantly serves the latter's commodity production as a virtual laboratory of new forms and fashions. The argument for a conception of postmodernism as a periodizing category is thus based on the presupposition that, even if *all* the formal features enumerated above were already present in the older high modernism, the very significance of those features changes when they become a cultural *dominant*, with a precise socio-economic functionality.

At this point it may be well to shift the terms (or the 'code') of our description to the seemingly more traditional one of a cultural sphere, a conception developed by Herbert Marcuse in what is to my mind his single most important text, the great essay 'The Affirmative Character of Culture' (1937). (It should be added that the conception of a 'public sphere' generally is a very contemporary one in Germany in the works of Habermas and Negt and Kluge, where such a system of categories stands in interesting contrast to the code of 'levels' or 'instances' in French poststructuralism.) Marcuse there rehearses the paradoxical dialectic of the classical (German) aesthetic, which projects as play and 'purposefulness without purpose' a Utopian realm of beauty and culture beyond the fallen empirical world of money and business activity, thereby winning a powerful critical and negative value through its capacity to condemn, by its own very existence, the totality of *what is*, at the same time forfeiting all ability to social or political intervention in what is, by virtue of its constitutive disjunction or autonomy from society and history.

The account therefore begins to coincide in a suggestive way with the problematic of autonomous or semi-autonomous levels developed in the preceding section. To historicize Marcuse's dialectic, however, would demand that we take into account the possibility that in our time this very autonomy of the cultural sphere (or level or instance) may be in the process of modification; and that we develop the means to furnish a description of the process whereby such modification might take place, as well as of the prior process whereby culture became 'autonomous' or 'semi-autonomous' in the first place.

This requires recourse to yet another (unrelated) analytic code, one more generally familiar to us today, since it involves the now classical structural concept of the sign, with its two components, the signifier (the material vehicle or image – sound or printed word) and the signified (the mental image, meaning, or 'conceptual' content), and a third component – the external object of the sign, its reference or 'referent' – henceforth expelled from the unity and yet haunting it as a ghostly residual aftereffect (illusion or ideology). The scientific value of this conception of the sign will be bracketed here since we are concerned, on the one hand, to historicize it, to interpret it as a conceptual symptom of developments in the period, and, on the other, to 'set it in motion', to see whether changes in its inner structure can offer some adequate small-scale emblem or electrocardiogram of changes and permutation in the cultural sphere generally throughout this period.

Such changes are already suggested by the fate of the 'referent' in the 'conditions of possibility' of the new structural concept of the sign (a significant ambiguity must be noted, however: theorists of the sign notoriously glide from a conception of reference as designating a 'real' object outside the unity of signifier and signified to a position in which the signified itself – or meaning, or the idea or the concept of a thing – becomes somehow identified with the referent and stigmatised along with it; we will return to this below). Saussure, at the dawn of the semiotic revolution, liked to describe the relationship of signifier to signified as that of the two sides, the recto and verso of a sheet of paper. In what is then a logical sequel, and a text that naturally enough becomes equally canonical, Borges will push 'representation' to the point of imagining a map so rigorous and referential that it becomes coterminous with its object. The stage is then set for the structuralist emblem par excellence, the Moebius Strip, which succeeds in peeling itself off its referent altogether and thus achieves a free-floating closure in the void, a kind of absolute self-referentiality and autocirculatory from which all remaining traces of reference, or of any externality, have triumphantly been effaced.

To be even more eclectic about it, I will suggest that this process, seemingly internal to the sign itself, requires a supplementary explanatory code, that of the more universal process of reification and fragmentation at one with the logic of capital itself. Nonetheless, taken on its own terms, the inner convulsions of the sign is a useful initial figure of the process of transformation of culture generally, which must in some first moment (that described by Marcuse) separate itself from the 'referent' the existing social and historical world itself, only in a subsequent stage of the 60s, in what is here termed 'postmodernism', to develop further into some new and heightened, free-floating, self-referential 'autonomy'.

The problem now turns around this very term, 'autonomy', with its paradoxical Althusserian modification, the concept of 'semi-autonomy'. The paradox is that the sign, as an 'autonomous' unity in its own right as a realm divorced from the referent, can preserve that initial autonomy, and the unity and coherence demanded by it, only at the price of keeping a phantom of reference alive, as the ghostly reminder of its own outside or exterior, since this allows it closure, self-definition, and an essential boundary line. Marcuse's own tormented dialectic expresses this dramatically in the curious oscillation whereby his autonomous realm of beauty and culture returns upon some 'real world' to judge and negate it, at the same time separating itself so radically from that real world as to become a place of mere illusion and impotent 'ideals', the 'infinite' and so on.

The first moment in the adventures of the sign is perplexing enough as to demand more concrete, if schematic, illustration in the most characteristic cultural productions themselves. It might well be demonstrated in the classical French *nouveau roman* (in particular the novels of Robbe-Grillet him-self), which established its new language in the early 1960s, using systematic variations of narrative segments to 'undermine' representation, yet in some sense confirming this last by teasing and stimulating an appetite for it.

Because an American illustration seems more appropriate, however, something similar may be seen in connection with the final and canonical form of high modernism in American poetry, namely the work of Wallace Stevens, which becomes, in the years following the poet's death in 1956, institutionalised in the university as a purer and more quintessential fulfillment of poetic language than the still impure (read: ideological and political) works of an Eliot or a Pound, and can therefore be numbered among the literary 'events' of the early 60s. As Frank Lentricchia has shown, in *After the New Criticism*,[4] the serviceability of Stevens' poetic production for this normative and hegemonic role depends in large measure on the increasing conflation, in that work of poetic practice and poetic theory:

> This endlessly elaborating poem
> Displays the theory of poetry
> As the life of poetry. . .

'Stevens' is therefore a locus and fulfillment of aesthetics and aesthetic theory fully as much as the latter's exemplar and privileged exegetical object; the theory or aesthetic ideology in question is very much an affirmation of the 'autonomy' of the cultural sphere in the sense developed above, a valorization of the supreme power of the poetic imagination over the 'reality' it produces. Stevens' work, therefore, offers an extraordinary laboratory situation in which to observe the autonomization of culture as a process: a detailed examination of his development (something for which we have no space here) would show how some initial 'set toward' or 'attention to' a kind of poetic *pensée sauvage*, the operation of great preconscious *stereotypes*, opens up a vast inner world in which little by little the images of things and their ideas begin to be substituted for the things themselves. Yet what distinguishes this experience in Stevens is the sense of a vast systematicity in all this, the operation of a whole set of cosmic oppositions far too complex to be reduced to the schemata of 'structuralist' binary oppositions, yet akin to those in spirit, and somehow pregiven in the Symbolic Order of the mind, discoverable to the passive exploration of the 'poetic imagination', that is, of some heightened and impersonal power of free association in the realm of 'objective spirit' or 'objective culture'. The examination would further show the strategic limitation of this process to landscape, the reduction of the ideas and images of things to the names for things, and finally to those irreducibles that are place names, among which the exotic has a privileged function (Key West, Oklahoma, Yucatan, Java). Here the poetic 'totality' begins to trace a ghostly mimesis or *analogon* of the totality of the imperialist world system itself, with Third World materials in a similarly strategic, marginal, yet essential place (much as Adorno showed how Schoenberg's twelve-tone system unconsciously produced a formal imitation of the 'total system' of capital). This very unconscious replication of the 'real' totality of the world system in the mind is then what allows culture to separate itself as a closed and self-sufficient 'system' in its own right: reduplication, and at the same time, floating above the real. It is an impulse shared by most of the great high modernisms, as has been shown most dramatically in the recent critiques of architectural modernism, in particular of the international style, whose great monumental objects constitute themselves, by protecting a protopolitical and utopian spirit of transformation *against* a fallen city fabric all around them and, as Venturi has demonstrated, end up necessarily displaying and speaking of themselves alone. Now, this also accounts for what must puzzle any serious reader of Stevens' verse, namely the extraordinary combination of verbal richness and experimental hollowness or impoverishment in it (the latter being attributable as well to the impersonality of the poetic imagination in Stevens, and to the essentially contemplative and epistemological stance of the subject in it, over and against the static object world of his landscapes).

The essential point here, however, is that this characteristic movement of the high modernist impulse needs to justify itself by way of an ideology, an ideological supplement which can generally be described as that of 'existentialism' (the supreme fiction, the meaninglessness of a contingent object world unredeemed by the imagination, etc.). This is the most uninteresting and banal dimension of Stevens work, yet it betrays along with other existentialisms (e.g., Sartre's tree root in *Nausea*) that fatal seam or link that must be retained in order for the contingent, the 'outside world', the meaningless referent, to be just present enough dramatically to be overcome within the language. Nowhere is this ultimate point so clearly deduced, over and over again, as in Stevens, in the eye of the blackbird, the angels, or the Sun itself – that last residual vanishing point of reference as distant as a dwarf star upon the horizon, yet which cannot disappear altogether without the whole vocation of poetry and the poetic imagination being called back into question. Stevens thus exemplifies for us the fundamental paradox of the 'autonomy' of the cultural sphere: the sign can become autonomous only by remaining semi-autonomous, and the realm of culture can absolutize itself over against the real world only at the price of retaining a final tenuous sense of that exterior or external world of which it is the replication and the imaginary double.

All of this can also be demonstrated by showing what happens when, in a second moment, the perfectly logical conclusion is drawn that the referent is itself a myth and does not exist, a second moment hitherto described as postmodernism. Its trajectory can be seen as a movement from the older *Nouveau roman* to that of Sollers or of properly 'schizophrenic' writing, or from the primacy of Stevens to that of John Ashbery. This new moment is a radical break (which can be localized around 1967 for reasons to be given later), but it is important to grasp it as dialectical, that is, as a passage from quantity to quality in which the *same* force, reaching a certain threshold of excess, in its prolongation now produces qualitatively distinct effects and seems to generate a whole new system.

That force has been described as reification, but we can now also begin to make some connections with another figural language used earlier: in a first moment, reification 'liberated' the sign from its referent, but this is not a force to be released with impunity. Now, in a second moment, it continues its work of dissolution, penetrating the interior of the sign itself and liberating the signifier from the signified, or from meaning proper. This play, no longer of a realm of signs, but of pure or literal signifiers freed from the ballast of their signifieds, their former meanings, now generates a new kind of textuality in all the arts (and in philosophy as well, as we have seen above) and begins to project the mirage of some ultimate language of pure signifiers which is also frequently associated with schizophrenic discourse. (Indeed, the Lacanian theory of schizophrenia – a language disorder in which syntactical time breaks down and leaves a succession of empty signifiers, absolute moments of a perpetual present, behind itself – has offered one of the more influential explanations and ideological justifications for postmodernist textual practice.)

Such an account would have to be demonstrated in some detail by way of a concrete analysis of the postmodernist experience in all the arts today;

but the present argument can be concluded by drawing the consequences of this second moment – the aculture of the signifier or of the simulacrum – for the whole problematic of some 'autonomy' of the cultural sphere which has concerned us here. For that autonomous realm is not itself spared by the intensified process by which the classical sign is dissolved; if its autonomy depended paradoxically on its possibility of remaining 'semi-autonomous' (in an Althusserian sense) and of preserving the last tenuous link with some ultimate referent (or, in Althusserian language, of preserving the ultimate unity of a properly 'structural totality'), then evidently in the new cultural moment culture will have ceased to be autonomous, and the realm of an autonomous play of signs becomes impossible, when that ultimate final referent to which the balloon of the mind was moored is now definitively cut. The break-up of the sign in mid-air determines a fall back into a now absolutely fragmented and anarchic social reality; the broken pieces of language (the pure signifiers) now fall again into the world, as so many more pieces of material junk among all the other rusting and superannuated apparatuses and buildings that litter the commodity landscape and that strew the 'collage city', the 'delirious New York' of a postmodernist late capitalism in full crisis.

But, returning to a Marcusean terminology, all of this can also be said in a different way: with the eclipse of culture as an autonomous space or sphere, culture itself falls into the world, and the result is not its disappearance but its prodigious expansion, to the point where culture becomes coterminous with social life in general; now all the levels become 'acculturated', and in the society of the spectacle, the image, or the simulacrum, everything has at length become cultural, from the superstructures down into the mechanisms of the infrastructure itself. If this development then places acutely on the agenda the neo-Gramscian problem of a new cultural politics today – in a social system in which the very status of both culture and politics have been profoundly, functionally, and structurally modified – it also renders problematic any further discussion of what used to be called 'culture' proper, whose artifacts have become the random experiences of daily life itself.

6 In the Sierra Maestra

The preceding section will, however, have been little more than a lengthy excursion into a very specialized (or 'elite') area, unless it can be shown that the dynamic therein visible, with something of the artificial simplification of the laboratory situation, finds striking analogies or homologies in very different and distant areas of social practice. It is precisely this replication of a common diachronic rhythm or 'genetic code' which we will not observe in the very different realities of revolutionary practice and theory in the course of the 60s in the Third World.

From the beginning, the Cuban experience affirmed itself as an original one, as a new revolutionary model, to be radically distinguished from more traditional forms of revolutionary practice. *Foco* theory, indeed, as it was associated with Che Guevara and theorized in Regis Debray's influential handbook, *Revolution in the Revolution*? (1967), asserted itself (as the title of the book suggests) both against a more traditional Leninist conception of party practice and against the experience of the Chinese revolution in its first essential stage of the conquest of power (what will later come to be designated as 'Maoism', China's own very different 'revolution in the revolution', or Great Proletarian Cultural Revolution, will not become visible to the outside world until the moment when the fate of the Cuban strategy has been sealed).

A reading of Debray's text shows that *foco* strategy, the strategy of the mobile guerrilla base or revolutionary foyer, is conceived as yet a third term, as something distinct from *either* the traditional model of class struggle (an essentially *urban* proletariat rising against a bourgeoisie or ruling class) *or* the Chinese experience of a mass peasant movement in the countryside (and also has little in common with a Fanonian struggle for recognition between Colonizer and Colonized). The *foco*, or guerrilla operation, is conceptualized as being neither 'in' nor 'of' either country or city; geographically, of course, it is positioned in the countryside, yet that location is not the permanently 'liberated territory' of the Yenan region, well beyond the reach of the enemy forces of Chiang Kai-shek or of the Japanese occupier. It is not indeed located in the cultivated area of the peasant fields at all, but rather in that third or nonplace which is the wilderness of the Sierra Maestra, neither country nor city, but rather a whole new element in which the guerrilla band moves in perpetual displacement.

This peculiarity of the way in which the spatial coordinates of the Cuban strategy is conceived has, then, immediate consequences for the way in which the class elements of the revolutionary movement are theorized. Neither city nor country; by the same token, paradoxically, the guerrillas themselves are grasped as being neither workers nor peasants (still less, intellectuals), but rather something entirely new, for which the prerevolutionary class society has no categories: new revolutionary subjects, forged in the guerrilla struggle indifferently out of the social material of peasants, city workers, or intellectuals, yet now largely transcending those class categories (just as this moment of Cuban theory will claim largely to transcend the older revolutionary ideologies predicted on class categories, whether those of Trotskyist workerism, Maoist populism and peasant consciousness, or of Leninist vanguard intellectualism).

What becomes clear in a text like Debray's is that the guerrilla *foco* – so mobile as to be beyond geography in the static sense – is in and of itself a *figure* for the transformed, revolutionary society to come. Its revolutionary militants are not simply 'soldiers' to whose specialized role and function one would then have to 'add' supplementary roles in the revolutionary division of labour, such as political commissars and the political vanguard party itself, both explicitly rejected here. Rather, in them is abolished all such prerevolutionary divisions and categories. This conception of a newly emergent revolutionary 'space' – situated outside the 'real' political, social, and geographical world of country and city, and of the historical social classes, yet at one and the same time a figure or small-scale image and prefiguration of the revolutionary transformation of that real world – may be designated as a properly Utopian space, a Hegelian 'inverted world', an autonomous revolutionary sphere, in which the fallen real world over against it is itself set right and transformed into a new socialist society.

For all practical purposes, this powerful model is exhausted, even before Che's own tragic death in Bolivia in 1967, with the failure of the guerrilla movements in Peru and Venezuela in 1966; not uncoincidentally, that failure will be accompanied by something like a disinvestment of revolutionary libido and fascination on the part of a First World Left, the return (with some leavening of the newer Maoism) to its own current situation, in the American antiwar movement and May 68. In Latin America, however, the radical strategy that effectively replaces *foco* theory is that of the so-called urban guerrilla movement, pioneered in Uruguay by the Tupamaros; it will have become clear that this break-up of the utopian space of the older guerrilla *foco*, the fall of politics back into the world in the form of a very different style of political practice indeed – one that seeks to dramatize features of state power, rather than, as in traditional revolutionary movements, to build toward some ultimate encounter with it – will be interpreted here as something of a structural equivalent to the final stage of the sign as characterized above.

Several qualifications must be made, however. For one thing, it is clear that this new form of political activity will be endowed, by association, with something of the tragic prestige of the Palestinian liberation movement, which comes into being in its contemporary form as a result of the Israeli seizure of the West Bank and the Gaza Strip in 1967, and which will thereafter become one of the dominant worldwide symbols of revolutionary praxis in the late 60s. Equally clearly, however, the struggle of this desperate and victimized people cannot be made to bear responsibility for the excesses of this kind of strategy elsewhere in the world, whose universal results (whether in Latin America, or with Cointelpro in the United States, or, belatedly, in West Germany and Italy) have been to legitimize an intensification of the repressive apparatus of state power.

This objective coincidence between a misguided assessment of the social and political situation on the part of Left militants (for the most part students and intellectuals eager to force a revolutionary conjuncture by voluntaristic acts) and a willing exploitation by the state of precisely those provocations suggests that what is often loosely called 'terrorism' must be the object of complex and properly dialectical analysis. However rightly a responsible Left chooses to dissociate itself from such strategy (and the Marxian opposition to terrorism is an old and established tradition that goes back to the nineteenth century), it is important to remember that 'terrorism', as a 'concept', is also an ideologeme of the Right and must therefore be refused in that form. Along with the disaster films of the late 60s and early 70s, mass culture itself makes clear that 'terrorism' – the image of the 'terrorist' – is one of the privileged forms in which an ahistorical society imagines radical social change; meanwhile, an inspection of the content of the modern thriller or adventure story also makes it clear that the 'otherness' of so-called terrorism has begun to replace older images of criminal 'insanity' as an unexamined and seemingly 'natural' motivation in the construction of plots – yet another sign of the ideological nature of this particular pseudoconcept. Understood in this way, 'terrorism' is a collective obsession, a symptomatic fantasy of the American political unconscious, which demands decoding and analysis in its own right.

As for the thing itself, for all practical purposes it comes to an end with the Chilean coup in 1973 and the fall of virtually all the Latin American countries to various forms of military dictatorship. The belated reemergence of this kind of political activity in West Germany and in Italy must surely at least in part be attributed to the fascist past of these two countries, to their failure to liquidate that past after the war, and to a violent moral revulsion against it on the part of a segment of the youth and intellectuals who grew up in the 60s.

7 Return of the 'Ultimately Determining Instance'

The two breaks that have emerged in the preceding section – one in the general area around 1967, the other in the immediate neighbourhood of 1973 – will not serve as the framework for a more general hypothesis about the periodization of the 60s in general. Beginning with the second of these, a whole series of other, seemingly unrelated events in the general area of 1972–74 suggests that this moment is not merely a decisive one on the relatively specialized level of Third World or Latin American radical politics, but signals the definitive end of what is called the 60s in a far more global way. In the First World, for example, the end of the draft and the withdrawal of American forces from Vietnam (in 1973) spell the end of the mass politics of the antiwar movement (the crisis of the New Left itself – which can be largely dated from the break up of SDS in 1969 – would seem related to the other break mentioned, to which we will return below), while the signing of the Common Program between the Communist party and the new Socialist party in France (as well as the wider currency of slogans associated with 'Eurocommunism' at this time) would seem to mark a strategic turn away from the kinds of political activities associated with May 68 and its sequels. This is also the movement when as a result of the Yom Kippur war, the oil weapon emerges and administers a different kind of shock to the economies, the political strategies, and the daily life habits of the advanced countries. Concomitantly, on the more general cultural and ideological level, the intellectuals associated with the establishment itself (particularly in the

United States) begin to recover from the fright and defensive posture that was theirs during the decade now ending, and again find their voices in a series of attacks on 60s culture and 60s politics, which, as was noted at the beginning, are not even yet at an end. One of the more influential documents was Lionel Trilling's *Sincerity and Authenticity* (1972), an Arnoldian call to reverse the tide of 60s countercultural 'barbarism'. (This will, of course, be followed by the equally influential diagnosis of some 60s concept of 'authenticity' in terms of a 'culture of narcissism'.) Meanwhile, in July 1973, some rather different 'intellectuals', representing various concrete forms of political and economic power, will begin to rethink the failure in Vietnam in terms of a new global strategy for American and First World interests; their establishment of the Trilateral Commission will at least symbolically be a significant marker in the recovery of momentum by what must be called 'the ruling classes'. The emergence of a widely accepted new popular concept and term at this same time, the notion of the 'multinational corporation', is also another symptom, signifying, as the authors of *Global Reach* have suggested, the moment when private business finds itself obliged to emerge in public as a visible 'subject of history' and a visible actor on the world stage – think of the role of ITT in Chile – when the American government, having been badly burned by the failure of the Vietnam intervention, is generally reluctant to undertake further ventures of this kind.

For all these reasons it seems appropriate to mark the definitive end of the '60s' in the general area of 1972–74. But we have omitted until now the decisive element in any argument for a periodization or 'punctuation' of this kind, and this new kind of material will direct our attention to a 'level' or 'instance' which has hitherto significantly been absent from the present discussion, namely the economic itself. For 1973–74 is the moment of the onset of a worldwide economic crisis, whose dynamic is still with us today, and which put a decisive full stop to the economic expansion and prosperity characteristic of the postwar period generally and of the 60s in particular. When we add to this another key economic marker – the recession in West Germany in 1966 and that in the other advanced countries, in particular in the United States a year or so later – we may well thereby find ourselves in a better position more formally to conceptualize the sense of a secondary break around 1967–68 which has begun to surface on the philosophical, cultural, and political levels as they were analyzed or 'narrated' above.

Such confirmation by the economic 'level' itself of periodizing reading derived from other, sample levels or instances of social life during the 60s will now perhaps put us in a better position to answer the two theoretical issues raised at the beginning of this essay. The first had to do with the validity of Marxist analysis for a period whose active political categories no longer seemed to be those of social class, and in which in a more general way traditional forms of Marxist theory and practice seemed to have entered a 'crisis'. The second involved the problem of some 'unified field theory' in terms of which such seemingly distant realities as Third World peasant movements and First World mass culture (or indeed, more abstractly, intellectual or superstructural levels like philosophy and culture generally, and those of mass resistance and political practice) might conceptually be related in some coherent way.

A pathbreaking synthesis of Ernest Mandel, in his book *Late Capitalism*,[5] will suggest a hypothetical answer to both these questions at once. The book presents, among other things, an elaborate system of business cycles under capitalism, whose most familiar unit, the seven-to-ten-year alternation of boom, overproduction, recession, and economic recovery, adequately enough accounts for the midpoint break in the 60s suggested above.

Mandel's account of the worldwide crisis of 1974, however, draws on a far more controversial conception of vaster cycles of some thirty- to fifty-year periods each – cycles which are then obviously much more difficult to perceive experientially or 'phenomenologically' insofar as they transcend the rhythms and limits of the biological life of individuals. These 'Kondratiev waves' (named after the Soviet economist who hypothesized them) have, according to Mandel, been renewed four times since the eighteenth century, and are characterized by quantum leaps in the technology of production, which enable decisive increases in the rate of profit generally, until at length the advantages of the new production processes have been explored and exhausted and the cycle therewith comes to an end. The latest of these Kondratiev cycles is that marked by computer technology, nuclear energy, and the mechanization of agriculture (particularly in foodstuffs and also primary materials), which Mandel dates from 1940 in North America and the postwar period in the other imperialist countries; what is decisive in the present context is his notion that, with the worldwide recession of 1973–74, the dynamics of this latest 'long wave' are spent.

The hypothesis is attractive, however, not only because of its abstract usefulness in confirming our periodization schemes, but also because of the actual analysis of this latest wave of capitalist expansion, and of the properly Marxian version he gives of a whole range of developments that have generally been thought to demonstrate the end of the 'classical' capitalism theorized by Marx and to require this or that post-Marxist theory of social mutation (as in theories of consumer society, postindustrial society, and the like).

We have already described the way in which neocolonialism is characterized by the radically new technology (the so-called Green Revolution in agriculture: new machinery, new farming methods, and new types of chemical fertilizer and genetic experiments with hybrid plants and the like), with which capitalism transforms its relationship to its colonies from an old-fashioned imperialist control to market penetration, destroying the older village communities and creating a whole new wage-labour pool and lumpenproletariat. The militancy of the new social forces is at one and the same time a result of the 'liberation' of peasants from the older self-sustaining village communities, and a movement of self-defence, generally originating in the stabler yet more isolated areas of a given Third World country, against what is rightly perceived as a far more thoroughgoing form of penetration and colonization than the older colonial armies.

It is now in terms of this process of 'mechanization' that Mandel will make the link between the neocolonialist transformation of the Third World during the 60s and the emergence of that seemingly very different thing in the First World, variously termed consumer society, postindustrial society, media society, and the like:

> Far from representing a postindustrial society, late capitalism ... constitutes *generalised universal industrialization* for the first time in history. Mechanization, standardization, overspecialization and parcellization of labor, which in the past determined only the realm of commodity production in actual industry, now penetrate into all sectors of social life. It is characteristic of late capitalism that agriculture is step by step becoming just as industrialized as industry, the sphere of circulation [e.g., credit cards and the like] just as much as the sphere of production, and recreation just as much as the organization of work. (p. 387)

With this last, Mandel touches on what he elsewhere calls the mechanization of the superstructure, or, in other words, the penetration of culture itself by what the Frankfurt School called the culture industry, and of which the growth of the media is only a part. We may thus generalize his description as follows: late capitalism in general (and the 60s in particular) constitute a process in which the last surviving internal and external zones of precapitalism – the last vestiges of noncommodified or traditional space within and outside the advanced world – are now ultimately penetrated and colonized in their turn. Late capitalism can therefore be described as the moment when the last vestiges of Nature which survived on into classical capitalism are at length eliminated: namely the Third World and the unconscious. The 60s will then have been the momentous transformational period when this systemic restructuring takes place on a global scale.

With such an account, our 'unified field theory' of the 60s is given: the discovery of a single process at work in First and Third Worlds, in global economy, and in consciousness and culture, a properly *dialectical* process, in which 'liberation' and domination are inextricably combined. We may now therefore proceed to a final characterization of the period as a whole.

The simplest yet most universal formulation surely remains the widely shared feeling that in the 60s, for a time, everything was possible; that this period, in other words, was a moment of a universal liberation, a global unbinding of energies. Mao Zedong's figure for this process is in this respect most revealing: 'Our nation', he cried, 'is like an atom. . . . When this atom's nucleus is smashed, the thermal energy released will have really tremendous power!'[6] The image evokes the emergence of a genuine mass democracy from the breakup of the older feudal and village structures, and from the therapeutic dissolution of the habits of those structures in cultural revolutions. Yet the effects of fission, the release of molecular energies, the unbinding of 'material signifiers', can be a properly terrifying spectacle; and we now know that Mao Zedong himself drew back from the ultimate consequences of the process he had set in motion, when, at the supreme moment of the Cultural Revolution Commune, he called a halt to the dissolution of the party apparatus and effectively reversed the direction of this collective experiment as a whole (with consequences only too obvious at the present time). In the West, also, the great explosions of the 60s have led, in the worldwide economic crisis, to powerful restorations of the social order and a renewal of the repressive power of the various state apparatuses.

Yet the forces these must now confront, contain, and control are new ones, on which the older methods do not necessarily work. We have described the 60s as a moment when the enlargement of capitalism on a global scale simultaneously produced an immense freeing or unbinding of social energies, a prodigious release of untheorized new forces: the ethnic forces of black and 'minority', or Third World, movements everywhere, regionalisms, the development of new and militant bearers of 'surplus consciousness' in the student and women's movements, as well as in a host of struggles of other kinds. Such newly released forces do not only not seem to compute in the dichotomous class model of traditional Marxism; they also seem to offer a realm of freedom and voluntarist possibility beyond the classical constraints of the economic infrastructure. Yet this sense of freedom and possibility – which is for the course of the 60s a momentarily objective reality, as well as (from the hindsight of the 80s) a historical illusion – can perhaps best be explained in terms of the superstructural movement and play enabled by the transition from one infrastructural or systemic stage of capitalism to another. The 60s were in that sense an immense and inflationary issuing of superstructural credit; a universal abandonment of the referential gold standard; an extraordinary printing up of ever more devalued signifiers. With the end of the 60s, with the world economic crisis, all the old infrastructural bills then slowly come due once more; and the 80s will be characterized by an effort, on a world scale, to proletarianize all those unbound social forces that gave the 60s their energy, by an extension of class struggle, in other words, into the farthest reaches of the globe as well as the most minute configurations of local institutions (such as the university system). The unifying force here is the new vocation of a henceforth global capitalism, which may also be expected to unify the unequal, fragmented, or local resistances to the process. And this is finally also the solution to the so-called crisis of Marxism and to the widely noted inapplicability of its forms of class analysis to the new social realities with which the 60s confronted us: 'traditional' Marxism, if 'untrue' during this period of a proliferation of new subjects of history, must necessarily become true again when the dreary realities of exploitation, extraction of surplus value, proletarianization, and the resistance to it in the form of class struggle, all slowly reassert themselves on a new and expanded world scale, as they seem currently in the process of doing.

Notes

1 J.P. Sartre, Preface to Frantz Fanon, *The Wretched of the Earth*, tr. Constance Farrington (New York, 1965).
2 Karl Marx, *The Eighteenth Brumaire of Louis Bonaparte* (New York, 1969), p. 15.
3 Régis Debray, 'A Modest Contribution', *New Literary Review*, 115 (May–June 1979). p. 58
4 Frank Lentricchia. *After the New Criticism* (Chicago, 1980), esp. pp. 31–5.
5 Ernest Mandel, *Late Capitalism* (London, 1978).
6 Mao Zedong, *Chairman Mao Talks to the People*, ed. S. Schram (New York, 1974), pp. 92–43.

29   Patricia Waugh,

Stalemates?: Feminists, Postmodernists and Unfinished Issues in Modern Aesthetics

George Eliot's Mr. Brooke could not have known as he reflected upon the perils of reading Adam Smith that his reservations about the benefits of a little theory would become central to many of the aesthetic debates of the late twentieth century: 'The fact is, human reason may carry you a little too far – over the hedge in fact. It carried me a good way at one time; but I saw it would not do. I pulled up; I pulled up in time. But not too hard.' Gentle deceleration is preferred, as he goes on to explain, because 'we must have Thought, else we shall be landed back in the dark ages'.[1]

However, reading much of the aesthetic theory arising out of the so-called 'Postmodern debate', it is difficult to avoid feeling that not only are we landed back in the dark ages but that it is the rationalisms of Enlightenment thought that have marooned us there in the first place.

Modernity, we are told, is coming to an end, strangled by its own contradictory logic, born astride of the grave which has become its own abyss. Just as Greek civilization or the Feudal Age had come to an end and just as Nietzsche had announced the death of God a century earlier, so contemporary theorists like Foucault have announced the end of modern Western man, a face in the sand eroded by an ever encroaching sea. Yet while postmodernist thinkers (dare one say it – largely male) were proclaiming their own death (the end of humanism), feminists were in their most optimistic vein. For postmodernists, modernity might be exhausted, but for feminists it was clearly unfinished, needing to be renovated perhaps, but not abandoned.

Postmodernism was first used as a period term in the early fifties by Arnold Toynbee who announced that we were entering the fourth and final phase of Western history: one of irrationalism, anxiety and helplessness. If Modernism had tried to anchor in consciousness (that of the heroic, socially alienated artist) a centre which could no longer hold, Postmodernism had shown us an even darker side of modernity and the aporias of its aesthetic. It had shown that there is nothing for consciousness to be anchored to: no universal ground of truth, justice or reason, so that consciousness itself is thus 'decentred', no longer origin, author, location of intentional agency but a function through which impersonal forces pass and intersect – Dover beach displaced by an international airport lounge. In this context art seems to have no special role. In a world where truth is only the effect of power or rhetoric, where all interpretative models are provisional and contingent, neither the Romantic concept of poets as the unacknowledged legislators of mankind, nor the late Romantic (Freudian) concept of universal mind as a poeticizing instrument, seem to carry any validity. Both concepts seemed to have been turned back on themselves in a bleak parody: if everything is fictional or textual then there can be no 'outside', no real', no way of saying that one act or text is better than another; no ethics, no aesthetics because existence is itself aestheticized and no ideology because no 'truth': at best provisional consensus, pragmatism, interpretative communities.

Such is the generally Apocalyptic vision of much postmodern thought. But, as Kermode had reminded us in the late sixties, if we do not have a sense of an ending, we invent one: concordances are reassuring, they produce the illusion of retrospective significance. Endings confer meaning and for all human beings, 'the End they imagine will reflect their irreducibly intermediary preoccupations . . . we thrive on epochs'.[2] Could it be that Postmodernism is the Ending invented by its theorists searching for their own significance? Of what will that significance consist? Why have feminists on the whole, though registering the transitionality of the current epoch, not represented it through the same sense of an ending? Redemption through retrospective narrative significance is in itself, of course, also central to the modernist aesthetic. In that key text for Modernism, *Heart of Darkness*, when Marlow chooses to interpret Kurtz's acknowledgement of 'the horror' as an heroic act, one can see in Marlow's eloquence a mirror of Kurtz's own: it is the retrospective narrative rather than the experiential act which 'redeems'. But, despite the heroic adventure story quest form, redemption can, in the end, only be offered through the rhetorical structures of that same Enlightenment vocabulary which Conrad's text has exposed as corrupt and fraudulent. Nevertheless, to read this text is to feel that one remains in a state of hesitation about whether it is art or experience which redeems. Not so with Postmodernism. Here, the sense of an ending has *continuously* to be revised through the endless deferral of repeated narrative reconstruction. There can be no experience outside text. History is narratives. The End is the insight that there can be no ending, no beginning, no ground and no telos. Again, however, in this world of hyperinflated discourse,[3] one may begin to feel, indeed, that it is not the worst so long as we can say it is the worst, and thus to begin to question *whose* Apocalypse is being represented.

Which brings me to silence. And at last to feminism. Nietzsche's critique of Enlightenment modernity was basically that it had not been modern enough. He saw all its major institutions and categories of thought as redescriptions of Christianity: a slave mentality which could not confront the existence of the 'will to truth' as a form of the 'will to power'.[4] Postmodernism seems, in its renunciation of modernity, to have embraced an insistent secularism. It seems to me though that its rhetoric of Apocalypse is just as insistently religious as the modernist search for redemption through Art. Just as the narratives of Modernism search for their own self-grounded formal redemption, so too the narratives of postmodern theory seek a self-overcoming, though one outside the ultimately Aristotelian notion of form which underlies the modernist concept of formal autonomy. What alarms me as a feminist, however, is the pervasive redescription of this posibility of redemption, this space of the sacred beyond the linearity of Aristotelian form, as the space of the feminine. Kurtz's Intended continues to be used as the justification for that necessary Lie which seems to offer us a Paradise regained outside the logic of modernity. Before this tendency is examined more closely, however, I wish to look briefly and more generally at the history of the relations between feminism and Postmodernism.

Modernity, Postmodernism and Feminism

Feminism as a discourse clearly arises out of modernity and its models of reason, justice and subjectivity. Feminism, however, has also been one of the discourses which has with similar clarity revealed some of the most entrenched and disguised contradictions and limitations of Enlightenment thought. To this extent, it can be seen as intrinsically postmodern, if problematically so. Yet, until very recently, the debates within Postmodernism have tended to ignore those taking place within feminist discourse, and vice versa. Things have begun to change. Feminist theory has developed a self-conscious awareness of its own hermeneutic perspectivism based on the recognition of a central contradiction in its attempts to define an epistemology: that women seek equality and valorisation for a gendered identity which has been constructed through the very culture and ideology that feminism seeks to challenge. In fact, one can see such contradictions manifesting themselves as early as 1971 in Kristeva's essay 'Women's Time'. The concept of a 'women's identity' functions in terms both of affirmation and negation, even within feminism itself. There can be no simple legitimation for feminists in throwing off a 'false consciousness' and revealing a true 'female self'. To embrace 'difference' in essentialist terms is to come dangerously close to reproducing that very patriarchal construction of gender which feminists have set out to contest.

Feminism of late, therefore, has developed a self-reflexive mode: questioning its own legitimating procedures in a manner which seems to bring it close to a Postmodernism which has absorbed the lessons of post-structuralism and consists at the most general level of a crisis of legitimation across culture, politics and aesthetic theory and practice. The slogan 'Let us wage war on totality', however, could be Postmodernism's response to that earlier slogan of the feminist movement, 'The personal is the political.' But if the latter can be seen as a rallying cry, the former implies a hostile attitude towards its implicit ideals of collectivism and community. In fact the feminist cry situated its politics firmly within what Lyotard wishes to denounce and what Jürgen Habermas calls the 'project of modernity'.[5] It will be my argument that even if feminists have come to recognise in their discourses some of the epistemological doubt and perspectivism that afflicts Postmodernism, feminism must still continue to define itself as an emancipatory movement broadly within the terms of the aforementioned project. Is it possible for feminists to draw on the aesthetics of Postmodernism as strategies for narrative disruption without embracing its nihilistic pragmatism? Surely to assume otherwise is in itself to embrace a naively reflectionist aesthetic which sees representation necessarily reflective of prior structures or ideologies. Can feminists occupy a position of hermeneutic perspectivism which questions epistemology without, therefore, relinquishing ethics in an embrace of hermeneutic anarchism where no discourse is seen as more valid than any other, simply more useful at a particular time or place? Can feminism remain opposed to Postmodernism's circular tendency to project itself onto the contemporary world and thus, not surprisingly, to find in that world an affirmation of its own theoretical presuppositions? Can it in other words continue to resist the implicitly religious terminology of the Postmodern sense of an Ending while recognizing the force of its critique of epistemology?

One way of approaching these issues is to think about the implications of the various models of subjectivity with which feminists and postmodernists have worked. What the preceding discussion has suggested is that the epistemological and ethical contradictions now confronting both of them are fundamentally issues about identity and difference. Subjective transformation has been central to feminist agendas for political change. Similarly, over the last thirty years, the deconstruction of liberal individualism and the dissolution of traditional aesthetic conceptualisations of character have been central to postmodern art and theory. Like feminism, Postmodernism has been engaged in a re-examination of the Enlightenment concepts of subjectivity, truth and reason enshrined in the belief that human beings are collectively engaged in a progressive movement towards moral and intellectual self-realization through the application to their situation of a universal rational faculty.

Personal freedom or autonomy in these terms has been defined as freedom from the irrational forces within and the social forces without. Freud's work has been seen as axiomatic for the former and the work of Marx for the latter. The focus of much postmodern theory has been to dismantle the basic assumptions of their writing to lay bare an epistemology and methodology which, it is argued, is at one with an oppressive and authoritarian rationalism which has produced terror in place of emancipation and disguised its will to power as a disinterested 'scientific' desire for truth. The self-determining subject has had a similarly difficult time of it in postmodern fiction. Such fictions are often enactments of the frustration of attempting to find correspondences to their linguistic condition outside of language itself. In Robert Coover's 'Panel Game', he parodies the attempt to find an all-encompassing truth in language by showing the narrator caught up in a maze of the myriad possibilities of meaning, of *paroles* with no discoverable *langues*, while all the possible formal functions of language – emotive, referential, poetic, conative, phatic and finally, metalingual – whirl about him: 'So think. Stickleback. Freshwaterfish. Freshwaterfish: green seaman. Seaman: semen. Yes, but green: raw? spoiled? vigorous? Stickle: stubble. Or maybe scruple. Back: Bach: Bachus: Bachate: berry. Rawberry? Strawberry.'[6] Through the emphasis on the arbitrary associations of sound, rhyme and image, attention is drawn to the formal organization of language and away from its referential potential. The quotation could almost be an exercise in Jakobsonian linguistics as the internal operations of language produce that poetic equivalence which endlessly substitutes one arbitrary phoneme for another: Stickleback. Freshwaterfish (metonymic). Freshwaterfish: green seaman (metonymic/ metaphoric) seaman: semen (metaphoric).

In Donald Barthelme's fictions abstract nouns and passive constructions almost entirely replace personal assertion or human agency. The story 'Brain Damage'[7] begins: 'At the restaurant, sadness was expressed'; moods are reflexes of disembodied signifiers rather than of personal feeling. Endless lists, catalogues, insistent stylisation flaunt the materiality of writing as depthlessness, again seem to present a self-conscious articulation of the rules of selection and combination in grammar, an endless play of linguistic substitution for its own sake; metaphors proliferate, syntax continuously breaks down. The reader is offered sentences such as: 'The world is sagging, snagging, scaling, spalling, pulling, pinging, pitting, warping, checking, fading, chipping, cracking, yellowing, leaking, staling, shrinking and in dynamic unbalance'[8]. Certainly this sentence is, for as the material world shrinks, the linguistic one expands and it is the materiality of language again, what Jameson has characterized[9] as the schizophrenic present of Postmodernism, which is obsessively foregrounded.

Barthelme's sentence, of course, enacts entropy, another postmodern image of Apocalypse. I think Jameson is quite correct, however, in the essay mentioned above, to connect the 'schizophrenic' tendency in Postmodernism with a pervasive nostalgia. It is worth thinking about this in relation to feminism. It seems to me that postmodernist writing is pervaded by a nihilism produced through nostalgia (Nietzsche is one of several thinkers who have connected these impulses). Often in such texts the possibility of humanist affirmation is destroyed by an insistent and excessive but familiar enough Romantic desire to rediscover a transcendent metaphysical truth, an essence of Being, whose impossible realization produces the urge to render absurd or to destroy altogether what can be: the human subject as an ethical, affective and effective historical agent.

In Pynchon's *V*, for example, V functions as both goal and negation of Stencil's quest for transcendent meaning and is pictured thus:

> skin radiant with the bloom of some new plastic; both eyes glass but now containing some photoelectric cells, connected by silver electrodes to optic nerves of purest copper wire leading to a brain exquisitely wrought as a diode matrix ever could be. Soleroid relays would be her ganglia, serio-actuators move her flawless nylon limbs, hydraulic fluid be sent by a platinum heart-pump through buthyrane veins and arteries.[10]

For those who wish to equate 'totality' with totalitarianism (as Lyotard at times) or to conflate linguistic or textual with political subversion, then such postmodern strategies, which appear to dissolve humanist subjectivity into textual play, have been hailed as the only means of resisting the oppressive structures of global capitalism, of patriarchal surveillance and control of the pleasure principle. They are seen as part of the assault on the bondage of thought to regulative ideals such as 'truth' and 'goodness'. In response, one might point out some obvious difficulties here: why is V a woman, and surely it matters that Nietzsche insisted that such regulative ideals were tied to what he saw as phallic castration, an emasculation of the intellect he associated with all emancipatory movements, particularly feminism. The idea of truth as untruth has repeatedly been articulated through the image of the seductive woman, a Salome who is only her veils, whose adornments disguise a gaping absence. She continues to appear with monotonous frequency in the metaphorical femininity of postmodern writing. This grotesque version of the wearisome metaphor, for example, appears in Nietzsche's *My Sister and I*: 'Truth is still elusive. However, she is no longer a young girl but an old bitch with all her front teeth missing'.[11] Before examining in more depth what such rhetoric means for actual women, whether, indeed, Pynchon's V assaults the oppressive structures of Late Capitalism for women, in particular, we need first to look at the historical and philosophical foundations of postmodernist and feminist aesthetics and to see whether it is indeed possible to move beyond the position of stalemate.

Founding Assumptions: Feminism and Postmodernism

Fredric Jameson has suggested that Postmodernism's most radical insight may be seen as the view that the bourgeois individual subject is not only a thing of the past but also a myth. We have never possessed this sort of autonomy: 'Rather this construct is merely a philosophical and cultural mystification which sought to persuade people that they had individual subjects and possessed this unique personal identity'.[12] If the subject is a myth and if narrative as the reflection of the grand 'master plot' of history is a redundant illusion, why should I have the feeling, as I read much postmodernist writing, that its apocalyptic nihilism about the possibility of ethical and imaginative subjective existence is grounded in that very nostalgia of which I spoke earlier? A nostalgia for an ideal autonomous self. Nostalgia involves the projection of the self onto history through identification. It rewrites history in the terms of desire, for to see the past as past is to recognize one's own mortality and temporality, fundamentally to disturb one's sense of presence. Nostalgia is the desire to recover the past as Paradise, as a myth of origins. Identification, however, necessitates ideal images with which to identify. It seems to me that feminists are highly unlikely to bear this sort of relationship to history or to the ideal autonomous self central to the discourses of modernity. Those who have been excluded from the constitution of that so-called 'universal subject' – whether for reasons of gender, class, race, sexuality – are unlikely either to long nostalgically for what they have never experienced or possessed or to revel in the 'jouissance' of its disintegration. Never having experienced it as an ethical ideal which might be materially realised they are unlikely therefore to fall into nihilistic Apocalypticism at the recognition it may simply not be realizable at all in its pure or original form.

They will be more likely surely to want to occupy its position and to be able to offer a critique from both within and outside of it. In my view, the decentred and fragmented subject of much postmodernist writing is one whose existence is premised upon the disintegration of a pre-existing belief in the possibility of realizing the full autonomous subject of Enlightenment rhetoric, of German Idealist philosophy and Kantian aesthetics. It is present at least as a structure of feeling if not fully articulated. It is clear from recent feminist scholarship that most women are unlikely to have experienced history in this way. Thus the goals of agency, autonomy and self-determination are not ones which feminists have taken for granted or glibly seen as exhausted. They are ideals which feminism has helped to reformulate, modify and challenge. Feminism needs a subject and it seems to me it has found a means of articulating it which both avoids the fetishization of Pure Reason as the locus of subjecthood and the irrationalism born out of the perceived failure of this ideal.

Alternative Histories

As part of our current experience, of the impossibility ultimately of separating knowledge from experience (which both Postmodernism and feminism have taught us), it is difficult to talk about 'origins' in relation to either. Postmodernism is a notoriously unstable concept, whether used in the more narrow aesthetic sense or the philosophical or sociological one. It entered American criticism in the fifties in Charles Olson's attempt to define the existence of a new non-anthropocentric poetry whose Heideggerian anti-humanism was directed at seeing 'man' as in the world, an object among objects. A similar tendency can be detected at around the same time in the French New Novel and its theorization in the writings of Robbe-Grillet and in Susan Sontag's rejection of a hermeneutic depth/surface model of interpretation for a return to the sensual surface, an 'erotics' of literature. John Barth talked of abandoning the literature of exhaustion for the essentially parodic literature of replenishment, Leslie Fiedler of a new art which would bridge the gap between high and mass culture. For both Sontag and Ihab Hassan, in particular, Postmodernism, an art of the surface, was the contemporary period's answer to Adorno's 'negative aesthetics' of Modernism: an art which in making itself opaque and difficult would refuse consumption even as it partook of a culture of consumption. By the early eighties, however, the term shifts from one used to describe a range of aesthetic practices involving playful irony, parody, self-consciousness, fragmentation, to one which encompasses a more general shift in thought and seems to register a pervasive cynicism about the progressivist ideals of modernity and a sense of a new cultural epoch in which distinctions between critical and functional knowledge break down and in which capitalism in its last and most insidious phase invades everything, leaving no oppositional space outside itself. Just as many novels of the seventies had displayed the hidden processes of artistic production, so too post-structuralist thought now proceeded by exposing the concealed rhetorical mechanisms which both produce and subvert conceptual meaning. Both undermine classical conceptions of representation in which truth precedes or determines the representations which either communicate it directly or mediate it indirectly. Postmodernism had gradually become a phrase describing a whole new 'episteme' of Western culture.

None of this says or said much about gender or feminism. In fact, as I mentioned earlier, although postmodern theory increasingly draws on a highly idealized and generalized notion of femininity as 'other' in its search for a space outside of the disintegrating logic of modernity, it rarely talks about (or to, one suspects) actual women or about feminism as a political practice. Yet there are obvious historical points of contact: both attacked the Romantic-Modernist cultivation of the Aesthetic as an autonomous realm, both assault Enlightenment discourses which universalize white, Western, middle-class male experience. Both recognize the need for a new ethics. Fundamentally each has offered critiques of foundationalist thinking to produce the recognition that gender is not a consequence of anatomy just as social institutions do not so much reflect universal truths as construct historical and provisional ones. Postmodernism is 'grounded' in the epistemological problematization of grounding itself, of the idea of identity as absolute or truth as essential. In terms of aesthetic practice, writers like Barth or Borges foreground epistemological and ontological questions about the construction of the 'real' and the 'self' by playing metafictionally on the textual paradox of the book as artefact and the book as world. Others, such as Rushdie, foreground the paradox of history as both a series of events which happened and also the imposition of a retrospective, paradigmatic and provisional linguistic structure which is itself the product of its own historical situation conceived of as an interplay of textual paradigms . . . ad infinitum. Postmodern writing may, indeed, proceed from this critique of foundationalism to social or political critique. In Salman Rushdie's *Shame*, for example, the intervention of alternative narrative voices is used as part of a critique of regimes of 'truth' as effects of power. As a strategy for dismantling oppressive concepts of truth, such narrative perspectivism is highly effective, but in a text where all positions are seen to be effects of rhetoric, the possibility of an oppositional space is also dismantled.

Feminism has also, of course, provided its own critique of essentialist and foundationalist assumptions. Arguably, though, however it draws upon postmodern narrative strategies, it cannot repudiate entirely the framework of Enlightened modernity without perhaps fatally undermining itself as an emancipatory politics. In proceeding through the demands of political practice, feminism must posit some belief in the notion of effective human agency, the necessity for historical continuity in formulating identity and a belief in historical progress. Even if people are shaped by historical forces, they are not simply reflexive epiphenomena of impersonal deep structures or of a global agonistics of circulating and competing language games. Feminism must believe in the possibility of a community of address situated in an oppositional space which can allow for the connection of the 'small personal voice' (Doris Lessing's term) of one feminist to another and to other liberationist movements. One writer producing personal confessional novels about 'women's identity' can then be seen to connect with the activity of another woman rewriting the history of slavery or one camped on the mud of Greenham Common, even as they accept and recognize each other's differences.

Glancing through the various Postmodernisms, in fact, one can see how the range of conceptualizations of difference has entered feminist theory and aesthetic practice. An invigorating imaginative playfulness has appeared in recent feminist writing. Too often though political claims are made for avant-garde formal disruption which are difficult to justify. Ironically one can again see a reflectionist aesthetics at work here which sees one form of disruption simply reflecting another sort. Concepts are transferred unproblematically from the context of aesthetic to political practice with no analysis of the sort of problems mentioned above. Surely feminists should keep in mind the centrality to his work of Lyotard's assertion that emancipatory discourses are no longer possible because there can no longer be a belief in privileged metadiscourses which transcend local and contingent conditions in order to ground the 'truths' of all first order discourses.[13] According to this view, gender can only be seen as positional, shifting, and cannot be used cross-culturally to explain the practices of human societies. In one sense this is the state of affairs feminism is aiming for in the ideal society it imagines to be possible. It should not, however, mean that feminists should abandon their struggle against sexual oppression because 'gender' as a metanarrative is necessarily a repressive enactment of metaphysical authority. Lyotard unnecessarily conflates the concept of totality with that of totalitarianism. Feminists should remember that 'totalities', political unity, need not mean uniformity, that they can be enabling and liberating.

The postmodern concept of language games, dissensus and dispersal, developed by Lyotard's reading of Wittgenstein, has again often been naively appropriated by an avant-garde desire to conflate linguistic or textual disruption with political subversion and to claim a massive political significance for formally innovative writing, modernist and postmodernist. Feminists such as Kristeva have done as much as postmodernists like Lyotard to popularize this concept. It is here that the dangerous metaphor of 'femininity' as 'otherness' is most apparent in what seems to me to be the reproduction of a masculine space of the sacred which continues to be dependent upon concepts which deny the *material* existence of actual women. From Nietzsche through Hassan and Lacan, femininity has been used to signify an 'otherness' which has effectively been essentialized as the disruption of the legitimate (viewed as everything from the logic of the Law of the Father – the psychoanalytic version of God – to the Logocentric). This 'otherness' has itself been variously expressed as the repressed other, the hysterical body, the semiotic, the pre-oedipal, ecstatic, fluid, the maternal body. Women, however, have no privileged access to it, though several male avant-garde writers can speak it. In fact, as often as not this celebration of difference goes hand in hand with an amazing indifference to the material and psychological circumstances of actual women. The postmodern espousal of psychotextual 'decentring' as liberatory says little about women as beings in the world who continue to find themselves displaced and invisible even within a critique of epistemology which has supposedly, in deconstructing the centre, therefore done away with the margins. The idea of alterity as feminine can be seen as the attempt to name a space outside the rationalizing logic of modernity – a new space of the sacred. As in most religious discourses, it promises a non-linear space outside the sense of ending, a space of redemption beyond time, language, fixity. Within postmodern psychoanalytic theory it has been described as 'the body without organs' (the small boy's view of the mother?), 'becoming woman' (the male fantasy of plenitude) and the 'hysterical body' (the female object through which psychoanalysis first arrived at its definition of the implicitly masculine subject).[14] It seems that as postmodernists obsessively register their sense of the collapsing legitimacy of the frameworks of Western knowledge, they are also registering unconsciously and metaphorically a fear specifically of the loss of the legitimacy of Western *patriarchal* grand narratives: a new form of fear of women, in effect. As always, appropriation becomes one of the means of dealing with this. Is it a coincidence that at the very historical moment when (male) postmodernists intensify their interest in (and master through their own discourses) a (religious) space described as the 'feminine' and nothing to do with actual women, feminists are establishing an (Enlightened modern) sense of their coherent identity as women through the very categories and discourses which postmodernists claim to have dismantled and done away with in the name of this 'femininity'. Surely this has an ominously familiar ring to it? Could one see the oppressed (women) returning in the form of the repressed (femininity) in postmodern discourse only to be worked through and mastered yet again in the language of theory?

If femininity has become, once more, a metaphor for a state beyond metaphysics, feminists should be certain that its tenor is not simply the contemporary theoretical counterpart to the Victorian parlour. If they have any suspicions then they should continue to hammer through its boundaries, those between public and private, in an assertion of their continued belief in their own capacity for agency and historical reconstruction. If Barthes writes a pseudo-autobiography to articulate the idea that 'to write an essay on oneself may seem a pretentious idea, but it is a simple idea, simple as the idea of suicide',[15] feminists should remind themselves that the shelves of books by Barthes in libraries all over the world proclaim a confidence in his authorship even as he disclaims it. They should not be surprised then that so many women writers in the seventies articulated a desire to become 'authors of their own lives' at precisely the moment that Barthes was announcing the death of that concept. Whose death?

Jean Baudrillard's work, it seems to me, is even more problematic for feminism. For him postmodernity signifies the state of contemporary culture which exists as a simulacrum of signs where the information age has utterly dissolved identity through reflections to maskings, to complete absence. In this perspective all that literature can do is to play off 'alternative worlds' in a state of pluralistic anarchy where the subject is simply a simulating machine of commercial images, the mass a silent majority and the very idea of resistance, an absurdity. Simulation replaces imagination and human beings are left with no capacity to reshape their world even in their own heads. They act like the characters in Robert Coover's novel *Gerald's Party* (1986), as dense points of transmission for all the cop and thriller and porn movies which construct their desires and which churn out incessantly throughout this text in an orgy of hedonistic sensationalism. It may be that Coover is using the parodic mode of the postmodern to offer a critique of postmodernity from within its own codes, but again one is left with the claustrophobic sense that there can be no real opposition to it because there is no place outside. In most versions of the postmodern, in fact, any claim to a substantive reality outside representation, is discredited: if signs determine reality, there can be no opposition because no space which is not already reproduced.

One difficulty in discussing Postmodernism is that the apocalypticism of the theory may have unduly affected our response to the fictional artefacts (if I may be so old-fashioned as to hang onto such a distinction). It seems to me this is an important distinction to hang onto, because it is evident that many women writers are using postmodern aesthetic strategies of disruption to re-imagine the world in which we live, while resisting the nihilistic implications of the theory. Certainly one can see the writing of Angela Carter, Jeanette Winterson, Margaret Atwood, Maggie Gee, Fay Weldon, to name but a few, in this way. This is perhaps not so very surprising since women have always experienced themselves in a 'postmodern' fashion – decentred, lacking agency, defined through others. Which is why, it seems to me, they had to attempt to occupy the centre in the early seventies. It is why women began to seek a subjective sense of agency and collective identity within the terms of the discourses of modernity at precisely the moment when postmodernists were engaged in the repudiation of such discourses, proclaiming the 'death of the author' and the end of humanism. Much feminist fiction of this period, therefore, was either confessional or concerned with the idea of discovering an authentic identity. If its philosophical roots are clearly anywhere it is in existentialism rather than post-structuralism. It may now appear to be philosophically naive and formally unadventurous, espousing an uncontested aesthetics of expressive realism or a simple reversal of the romance quest plot which did little to problematize ideologies of romantic love or essential identity. I have argued that perhaps feminist writers needed to formulate a sense of identity, history and agency within these terms before they could begin to deconstruct them. However, feminist writers did not subsequently rush off to embrace the postmodern – indeed they have largely maintained a cautious distance, certainly from much of the theory. This is where I shall declare my own distance as a feminist in offering some 'grand and totalizing' narratives which allow us to think of subjectivity in ways which neither simply repeat the Enlightenment concept of modernity nor repudiate it in an embrace of anarchic dispersal.

Rethinking Subjectivity and Aesthetics: Alternative Feminist Positions

I want to suggest, somewhat tentatively, that despite differences in the theoretical construction of modernity and postmodernity, common to them both is the inheritance of a particular ideal of subjectivity defined in terms of transcendence and pure rationality. Postmodernism can be seen as a response to the perceived failure of this ideal. This notion of subjectivity, whether expressed through Descartes' rational 'I' and refined into Kant's categorical imperatives, or through Nietzsche's 'übermensch' or Lacan's phallogocentric symbolic order, has not only excluded women but has made their exclusion on the grounds of emotionality, failure of abstract intellect or whatever, the basis of its own identity. This position has been reproduced across philosophy, psychoanalysis and literature. In viewing this situation as fundamentally unchanged, I am, in effect, repudiating the postmodern notion that there are no longer any generally legitimated metanarratives. What I am saying is that patriarchal metanarratives function just as effectively within our so-called 'postmodern age' as in any other age and in its metaphorical play on notions of the feminine they continue insidiously to function powerfully within postmodern theory itself.

Jameson has diagnosed postmodernism as the schizophrenic condition of late capitalism, but I would argue that the autonomous transcendent self of German Idealism, Enlightenment humanism, European Romanticism and realist aesthetics and the impersonally fragmented self of Postmodernism are a product of the same cultural tradition. Schizophrenia is clinically defined as a splitting of thought and feeling: the 'schizophrenia' of Postmodernism can be seen as a fin-de-siècle parody or caricature of a dualism inherent in the Western tradition of thought where the self is defined as a transcendent rationality which necessitates splitting off what is considered to be the irrational, emotion, and projecting it as the 'feminine' onto actual women. It is to see T.S. Eliot's 'dissociation of sensibility' from a feminist rather than a High Tory position. Freud, of course, has taught us that reason and feeling are inextricably bound up with each other, but even he believed that ego could and should master id, that impersonal reason is the basis of personal autonomy. Increasingly in this century, such a contracted 'rational' self cannot make sense of the world: whether in the fictions of Kafka or Bellow, for example, or in the aetiolated dramas of Samuel Beckett. When transcendence fails however, the threat of disorder is seen to come from the split off (and therefore uncontrollable) aspects of the psyche, the non-rational projected onto and thus defining women, racial minorities, so-called 'sexual deviants' or even 'the masses'.

Postmodernism may seek to locate the possibility of disruption or 'jouissance' in this space, but in continuing to regard it as 'feminine', whether it speaks of actual women or not, then it simply continues the process of projection and does little to overcome the dualism and psychological defensiveness inherent in it. Often in postmodernist fiction, for example, traditional images of the castrating female, the unknown and therefore uncontrollable woman, are overlaid in a technological age with their representation as machines which have outstripped the controlled and rational dominance of the male (one thinks of V again). The 'emotionality' thus projected onto the feminine or onto women in order to retain rationality and autonomy as the core of masculine identity produces both images of woman as the 'other' of romantic desire and woman who, thus beyond control, threatens annihilation or incorporation. If feminists wish to argue a politics of femininity as avant-garde disruptive desire they should first think about some of the meanings of, for example, V or Nurse Ratched.

In fact, in both modernist and postmodernist writing, when order conceived of as a circumscribed rationality seems no longer to cohere in either the self or in history, then it is projected onto the impersonal structures of language or of history conceived of as myth, a static and synchronic space. Despite the new 'perspectivism' which enters literary history in the early part of the century, the potential for the re-evaluation of the relations between subjectivity and objectivity, so many of the aesthetic manifestoes of the time and later critical accounts of the period emphasise 'impersonality', 'autonomy', 'objectivity', 'universal 'significant form', 'spatial form', 'objective correlative' – even when many of the artefacts, such as *Ulysses*, clearly problematize such notions. The New Critical theorization of literature, in particular the modernist text, as an autonomous linguistic structure, reinforced this. Since then the increasing professionalization of literature has extended this: defamiliarization, systems of signs, the death of the author, the free play of the signifier, simulations . . .

One can see in much modernist literature both the attempted assertion and the failure of Enlightened modernity's ideal of autonomy. The belief in absolute self-determination, whether that of Stephen Dedalus or Mr. Ramsay, is always discovered to be dependent on the desires of others. Whereas a transcendent being could anchor desire as absolute, to express it in relation to others is always seen to produce delusion, deception, jealousy, a whole variety of epistemological crises which modernist texts explore. The possibility of Art itself as an absolute autonomous realm, however, often comes to take the place of the sacred here. Art, as religion, seems to offer precisely that illusion of utter self-determination and transcendence which relations with other mortals must always shatter. It is interesting how many of the male heroes of modernist literature achieve an apparent self-determination in aesthetic terms through a refusal of social relationship. Hence the figure of the alienated artist who affirms his own autonomy, his independence from the mediation of others at the price of the cessation of human relationship and desire: Marcel writing in his room, Ralph Touchett vicariously living through Isabel, Malone talking to himself, Mann's Leverkühn, Hesse's Steppenwolf. Art as the impersonal focus for desire displaces the possibility of human relationship because it involves no mediation through the desire of the other. Hovering behind these texts is Nietzsche's self-creating and self-affirming artist for whom to recognize the other would be to fall into a slave mentality.

In my view it is the identification of self with an impossible ideal of autonomy which can be seen to produce the failure of love and relationship in so many texts by male modernist and postmodernist writers. Can one rethink the self outside of this concept without abandoning subjectivity to dispersal and language games? Not only do I believe that one can, I also believe that many feminist writers have done so. This is the really 'grand

and totalizing' part of my argument. It seems to me that autonomy defined as transcendence, impersonality and absolute independence, whether an idealised goal or a nostalgic nihilism, whether informing the aesthetics of Modernism or those of Postmodernism, is not a mode with which most feminists, nor indeed, most women, can very easily identify. Feminist theory, though drawing on anti-humanist discourses to sharpen its understanding of social processes, has emphasised that 'impersonal' historical determinants are lived out through experience. This distance from anti-humanist discourse has allowed feminist academics to connect with grass roots activists outside the academy. Their own historical experience has tended to develop in women strongly 'humanist' qualifies in the broader sense of the term and feminism has always been rooted in women's subjective experience of the conflicting demands of home and work, family and domestic ties and the wider society.

Psychoanalysis, Gender and Aesthetics

Jürgen Habermas has recently suggested that modernity is not exhausted, simply unfinished. His view of this is not incompatible with some of the ideas I am trying to develop here. What he has argued is that instead of abandoning its ideals we need to modify them by redefining the model of Reason which underlies them. His work is part of a tradition of critical thinking which sees Enlightenment reason failing because defined too narrowly in the terms of an instrumental, purposive or utilitarian epistemology. He proposes instead a model of what he calls 'communicative reason', based on speech act theory and emphasizing not individual autonomy but intersubjectivity.[16] Like so many theorists within the postmodern debate, however, he seems singularly unaware of many of the developments in feminist thinking over the last twenty years. It seems to me that many feminists have been working for some time with models which are not fundamentally incompatible with Habermas's whether or not they have used them in specifically theoretical ways. I will now examine some of these ideas and suggest that through them it is possible to arrive not only at an alternative definition of the aesthetic but also of subjectivity itself.

According to most psychoanalytic theories and their popularly disseminated forms, subjecthood is understood as the achievement of separation. Maturity is seen to be reached when the dependent infant comes to regard its primary caretaker (nearly always a woman) as simply an object through which it defines its own identity and position in the world. This is then maintained through the defensive patrolling of boundaries. Implicit then in most theories of identity is the assumption that the 'otherness' analysed by feminists from de Beauvoir on, is the necessary condition of women – certainly as long as women mother. Separation and objectivity rather than relationship and connection become the markers of identity.

Freudian theory has been used to support this view. Both the liberal self and the postmodern 'decentred subject' can be articulated through Freud's notion of the unconscious, dominated by instinctual and universal drives seeking impossible gratification. In the liberal version, ego as rationality can master the drives either intrapsychically or with the help of the silent, impersonal and objective analyst who will be uncontaminated by countertransference. In the postmodern version, rationality breaks down and the anarchy of desire as impersonal and unconscious energy is unleashed either in the freeplay of the signifier of the avant-garde text or that of the marketplace of Late Capitalism. Freud's infant hovers behind both: an autoerotic isolate, inherently aggressive and competitive, its sexuality and identity oedipally resolved only by fear, seeking to discharge libidinal energy which is necessarily in conflict with 'rational' and 'enlightened' concern for others and for society as a whole.

Can we imagine alternative models of subjectivity? If knowledge is inextricably bound up with experience then it seems that we certainly can, for this is not a description of universal experience. In fact Freud himself hints at other possibilities in less familiar parts of his writings. In the paper 'On Narcissism', for example, he says: 'A strong egotism is a protection against falling ill, but in the last resort we must begin to love in order not to fall ill and we are bound to fall ill if in consequence of frustration, we are unable to love'.[17] In fact, in the development of selfhood, the ability to conceive of oneself as separate from and mutually independent with the parent develops with the ability to accept one's dependency and to feel secure enough to relax the boundaries between self and other without feeling one's identity to be threatened. Why, then, is autonomy always emphasized as the goal of maturity? Why not emphasize equally the importance of maintaining connection and intersubjectivity? As Joan Rivière has argued, 'There is no such thing as a single human being pure and simple, unmixed with other human beings ... we are members one of another'.[18] Parts of other people, the parts we have had relationships with, are parts of us, so the self is both constant and fluid, ever in exchange, ever redescribing itself through its encounters with others. It seems to be this recognition of mediation as that which renders total self-determination impossible which so many male modernist and postmodernist writers find unacceptable. Yet much women's, particularly feminist, writing has been different in that it has neither attempted to transcend relationship through the impersonal embrace of Art as formal autonomy or sacred space nor through rewriting its own Apocalyptic sense of an ending.

Returning to psychoanalysis, however, one can see some of the reasons why the definition of subjectivity as transcendence and autonomy has been so powerful and why it has come to be seen not as a description of the experience of most white, Western males, but of universal structures of subjectivity. In psychoanalytic terms, if subjectivity is defined as separateness, its acquisition will involve radical disidentification with women in a society where women are normally the exclusive caretakers of children. This will be true even for girls who, at the level of gender, will also seek to identify with the mother. Fathers are not perceived as threatening non-identity for in classical analysis they are seen as outside the pre-oedipal world of primary socialization with its intense ambivalences and powerful Imagos. They are from the start associated with the clear, rational world of work and secondary socialization. Object relations theorists like Nancy Chodorow,[19] however, have pointed out that the desire for radical disidentification with the mother will be more acute for boys for the perception of women as mothers will be bound up with pre-oedipal issues of mergence and potential loss of identity requiring a culturally reinforced masculine investment in denial and separation. The world of secondary socialization associated with the father comes to be seen as superior and as inherently male. Subjectivity thus comes to be seen as autonomy or as role-definition through work. Truth is defined as objectivity and transcendence. Science in the form of an instrumental technology will be overvalued and defined in terms of objectivity; philosophy comes to deal only with universal and metaphysical truths (whatever the theoretical challenges to these notions). Women (or the 'feminine') come to be identified in Cartesian or post-structuralist philosophy with all that cannot be rationally controlled and thus threatening dissolution or non-identity: mortality, the body, desire, emotionality, nature. Post-structuralist 'femininity' is simply another way of making actual femininity safe, of controlling through a process of naming which in post-structuralist fashion prises the term utterly away from the anatomical body of woman.

If the female sex thus represents, in Sartre's words 'the obscenity . . . of everything which gapes open',[20] then men seem to be justified in their instrumental attitude to women and to everything, including nature, which has been 'feminized' and which must therefore be distanced, controlled, aestheticized, subdued (one might call this the Gilbert Osmond syndrome). Women appear threatening in this way because they carry the culture's more widespread fear of the loss of boundaries, of the uncontrollable, more threatening because unconsciously split off in order to retain the purity of a subjectivity, a humanness defined as autonomy, pure reason and transcendence. Cartesian dualism thus persists along with strict empiricism in science and impersonality and formalism in literary theory and criticism.

If women's identity is broadly speaking, and allowing for a range of differences, experienced in terms which do not necessarily valorize separation at the expense of connection, one would expect some expression of this in fictional writing as well as in theory. Women's sense of ego is more likely, for psychological and cultural reasons, to consist of a more diffuse sense of the boundaries of self and their notion of identity understood in relational and intersubjective terms. Virginia Woolf has been so important for feminist literary criticism because both formally and thematically her work articulates a critique of patriarchal institutions through its exploration of the relatedness of subjects and of subjects and objects. Beyond this, however, she simultaneously offers a critique of the exclusive identification of women with relationality through an exploration of its negative effects in characters like Mrs. Dalloway and Mrs. Ramsay. For relationality as the basis of identity in a society where women are perceived as culturally inferior, has often functioned to reinforce their desire to please, to serve others and seek definition through them, internalizing masochistically any anger about this as a failure of (essential) femininity. We are back, therefore, to the contradiction at the heart of feminism expressed at the beginning of this essay: that women have sought recognition for a concept of identity which they simultaneously attempt to change, viewing it as a construction of patriarchy. The formal and thematic expression of identity as mutually defined, the centrality of primary affectional relationships need not, however, be experienced in pathological ways, and, indeed, as writers like Alice Walker, Doris Lessing and Toni Morrison have recently shown us, are essential for the survival of the human race. Freud emphasized that the development of the ego is the work of culture. If that culture's ideal of selfhood is that of an impersonal, contained rationality, then it seems to me that culture can only produce incomplete and divided human beings. Postmodern beings.

Much feminist writing has, over the last thirty years, explored modes of relational identity, often, indeed, also drawing on postmodern ideas about 'situatedness' or using its techniques of parody, irony, playfulness. Such a relational understanding of identity makes possible ethically and imaginatively, a new, negative capability which can transform both the Enlightened discourses of emancipation as well as those of subjectivity. A writer whose work is particularly important in this respect, for example, is Doris Lessing. In her novel *Memoirs of a Survivor* (1976), she explores how Utopian impulses fail because they are still tied to a model of human subjectivity based on autonomy, separateness and overvaluation of a particular definition of rationality. The narrator, struggling to preserve an order within her psyche which has disappeared from the world outside, finds herself drawn towards a perception of the fundamental inter-dependence of human beings, of the persistence in us of an elemental hunger, the need to be fed – the novel abounds with images of eating and orality – to give food and to receive it, which binds us physically and psychologically to one another. She reflects:

> As for our thoughts, our intellectual apparatus, our rationalisms and our deductions, our logics and so on, it can be said with absolute certainty that dogs and cats and monkeys cannot make a rocket or fly to the moon or weave artificial dress materials out of the by-products of petroleum, but as we sit in the ruins of this variety of intelligence it is hard to give it much value.[21]

340 Modern Literary Theory

The most frightening aspect of the 'now' of this novel is that its children of violence, the wild, anarchic, semi-humans born out of upheaval and brutality, out of the failures of over-rationalized logic and the denial of human relational need, can no longer recognise their own or other's needs, cannot nurture each other and have, literally, turned cannibal and are consuming each other. For Lessing, salvation can only come through a profound and full recognition of our relational being, which means trying to imagine a world not constructed as an extension of a model of self as isolated, competitive ego nor one where ethics is reduced to nihilistic performance. She may use the formal modes of postmodern art but to articulate an imaginative world which is very far from those which emerge in most postmodern theory. Lessing's novel is apocalyptic in the sense that it is set after a holocaust, but it does not proclaim either the end of modernity nor the end of hope. We can compare this with, for example, Kroker's vision of postmodernity as a 'dead space which will be marked by increasing and random outbursts of political violence, schizoid behaviour and the implosion of all signs of communication, as Western culture runs down toward the brilliant illumination of a final burn out'.[22] If Lessing's 'small personal voice' is heard only as a whisper, it seems to me it can, drawing on postmodern *aesthetic* forms, speak to more people, women and men, but in ways which resist Kroker et al.'s *theoretically* ubiquitous postmodern Bang.

Notes

1 G. Eliot, *Middlemarch* (Harmondsworth, 1972).
2 F. Kermode, *The Sense of an Ending* (Oxford, 1967).
3 C. Newman, *The Postmodern Aura* (Evanston, Ill., 1985).
4 F. Nietzsche, *The Will to Power* (New York, Random House, 1967).
5 J. Habermas, *The Philosophical Discourse of Modernity*, tr. F.G. Lawrence (Cambridge and Oxford, 1987).
6 R. Coover, *Pricksongs and Descants* (New York, 1969).
7 D. Barthelme, *City Life* (London, 1971).
8 D. Barthelme, *Guilty Pleasures* (New York, 1974).
9 F. Jameson, 'Postmodernism and Consumer Society', in H. Foster, ed., *Postmodern Culture* (London and Sydney, 1985).
10 T. Pynchon, *V* (Harmondsworth, 1979), p. 406.
11 Nietzsche, *My Sister and I*, p. 114.
12 Jameson, 'Postmodernism and Consumer Society', p. 115.
13 J.-F. Lyotard, *The Postmodern Condition: A Report on Knowledge*, tr. Bennington and Massumi (Minneapolis, 1984).
14 A.A. Jardine, *Gynesis: Configurations of Women and Modernity* (Ithaca, NY, and London, 1985).
15 R. Barthes, *Roland Barthes by Roland Barthes*, tr. Richard Howard (London, 1977).
16 Habermas, *The Philosophical Discourse of Modernity*.
17 S. Freud, 'On Narcissism: an Introduction', *Standard Edition* vol. 14, ed. James

Strachey (London, 1957).

18 J. Rivière, 'The Unconscious Phantasy of an Inner World Reflected on Examples from Literature', *New Directions in Psychoanalysis*, ed. Melanie Klein (London, 1977).

19 N. Chodorow, *The Reproduction of Mothering: Psychoanalysis and the Sociology of Gender* (Berkeley, Calif., and London, 1978).

20 J.-P. Sartre, *Being and Nothingness*, tr. H.E. Barnes (London, 1958).

21 D. Lessing, *Memoirs of a Survivor* (London, Pan/Picador, 1976), p. 74.

22 A. Kroker and D. Cook, *The Postmodern Scene: Excremental Culture and Hyper-Aesthetics* (London, 1988), p. xvii.

30 bell hooks,

'Postmodern Blackness', in *Yearning: Race, Gender, and Cultural Politics* (1991), pp. 23–31

Postmodernist discourses are often exclusionary even as they call attention to, appropriate even, the experience of 'difference' and 'Otherness' to provide oppositional political meaning, legitimacy and immediacy when they are accused of lacking concrete relevance. Very few African-American intellectuals have talked or written about postmodernism. At a dinner party I talked about trying to grapple with the significance of postmodernism for contemporary black experience. It was one of those social gatherings where only one other black person was present. The setting quickly became a field of contestation. I was told by the other black person that I was wasting my time, that 'this stuff does not relate in any way to what's happening with black people'. Speaking in the presence of a group of white onlookers, staring at us as though this encounter were staged for their benefit, we engaged in a passionate discussion about black experience. Apparently, no one sympathized with my insistence that racism is perpetuated when blackness is associated solely with concrete gut level experience conceived as either opposing or having no connection to abstract thinking and the production of critical theory. The idea that there is no meaningful connection between black experience and critical thinking about aesthetics or culture must be continually interrogated.

My defense of postmodernism and its relevance to black folks sounded good, but I worried that I lacked conviction, largely because I approach the subject cautiously and with suspicion.

Disturbed not so much by the 'sense' of postmodernism but by the conventional language used when it is written or talked about and by those who speak it, I find myself on the outside of the discourse looking in. As a discursive practice it is dominated primarily by the voices of white male intellectuals and/or academic elites who speak to and about one another with coded familiarity. Reading and studying their writing to understand postmodernism in its multiple manifestations, I appreciate it but feel little inclination to ally myself with the academic hierarchy and exclusivity pervasive in the movement today.

Critical of most writing on postmodernism, I perhaps am more conscious of the way in which the focus on 'Otherness and difference' that is often alluded to in these works seems to have little concrete impact as an analysis or standpoint that might change the nature and direction of postmodernist theory. Since much of this theory has been constructed in reaction to and against high modernism, there is seldom any mention of black experience or writings by black people in this work's specifically black women (though in more recent work one may see a reference to Cornel West, the black male scholar who has most engaged postmodernist discourse). Even if an aspect of black culture is the subject of postmodern critical writing, the works cited will usually be those of black men. A work that comes immediately to mind is Andrew Ross's chapter 'Hip, and the long front of color' in *No Respect: Intellectuals and popular culture*; while it is an interesting reading, it constructs black culture as though black women have had no role in black cultural production. At the end of Meaghan Morris' discussion of postmodernism in her collection of essays *The Pirate's Fiancé: Feminism and Postmodernism*, she provides a bibliography of works by women, identifying them as important contributions to a discourse on postmodernism that offer new insight as well as challenging male theoretical hegemony. Even though many of the works do not directly address postmodernism, they address similar concerns. There are no references to works by black women.

The failure to recognize a critical black presence in the culture and in most scholarship and writing on postmodernism compels a black reader, particularly a black female reader, to interrogate her interest in a subject where those who discuss and write about it seem not to know black women exist or even to consider the possibility that we might be somewhere writing or saying something that should be listened to, or producing art that should be seen, heard, approached with intellectual seriousness. This is especially the case with works that go on and on about the way in which postmodernist discourse has opened up a theoretical terrain where 'difference and Otherness' can be considered legitimate issues in the academy. Confronting both the absence of recognition of black female presence that much postmodernist theory re-inscribes and the resistance on the part of most black folks to hearing about real connection between postmodernism and black experience, I enter a discourse, a practice, where there may be no ready audience for my words, no clear listener, uncertain, then, that my voice can or will be heard.

During the sixties, the black power movement was influenced by perspectives that could easily be labeled modernist. Certainly many of the ways black folks addressed issues of identity conformed to a modernist universalizing agenda. There was little critique of patriarchy as a master narrative among black militants. Despite the fact that black power ideology reflected a modernist sensibility, these elements were soon rendered irrelevant as militant protest was stifled by a powerful, repressive postmodern state. The period directly after the black power movement was a time when major news magazines carried articles with cocky headlines like 'Whatever happened to Black America?' This response was an ironic reply to the aggressive, unmet demand by decentered, marginalized black subjects who had at least momentarily successfully demanded a hearing, who had made it possible for black liberation to be on the national political agenda. In the wake of the black power movement, after so many rebels were slaughtered and lost, many of these voices were silenced by a repressive state; others became inarticulate. It has become necessary to find new avenues to transmit the messages of black liberation struggle, new ways to talk about racism and other politics of domination. Radical postmodernist practice, most powerfully conceptualized as a 'politics of difference', should incorporate the voices of displaced, marginalized, exploited and oppressed black people. It is sadly ironic that the contemporary discourse which talks the most about heterogeneity, the decentered subject, declaring breakthroughs that allow recognition of otherness, still directs its critical voice primarily to a specialized audience that shares a common language rooted in the very master narratives it claims to challenge. If radical postmodernist thinking is to have a transformative impact, then a critical break with the notion of 'authority' as 'mastery over' must not simply be a rhetorical device. It must be reflected in habits of being, including styles of writing as well as chosen subject matter. Third world nationals, elites and white critics who passively absorb white supremacist thinking, and therefore never notice or look at black people on the streets or at their jobs, who render us invisible with their gaze in all areas of daily life, are not likely to produce liberatory theory that will challenge racist domination, or promote a breakdown in traditional ways of seeing and thinking about reality, ways of constructing aesthetic theory and practice. From a different standpoint, Robert Storr makes a similar critique in the global issue of *Art in America* when he asserts:

> To be sure, much postmodernist critical inquiry has centered precisely on the issues of 'difference' and 'Otherness'. On the purely theoretical plane the exploration of these concepts has produced some important results, but in the absence of any sustained research into what artists of color and others outside the mainstream might be up to, such discussions become rootless instead of radical. Endless second guessing about the latent imperialism of intruding upon other cultures only compounded matters, preventing or excusing these theorists from investigating what black, Hispanic, Asian and Native American artists were actually doing.

Without adequate concrete knowledge of and contact with the non-white 'Other', white theorists may move in discursive theoretical directions that are threatening and potentially disruptive of that critical practice which would support radical liberation struggle.

The postmodern critique of 'identity', though relevant for renewed black liberation struggle, is often posed in ways that are problematic. Given a pervasive politic of white supremacy which seeks to prevent the formation of radical black subjectivity, we cannot cavalierly dismiss a concern with identity politics. Any critic exploring the radical potential of postmodernism as it relates to racial difference and racial domination would need to consider the implications of a critique of identity for oppressed groups. Many of us are struggling to find new strategies of resistance. We must engage decolonization as a critical practice if we are to have meaningful chances of survival even as we must simultaneously cope with the loss of political grounding which made radical activism more possible. I am thinking here about the postmodernist critique of essentialism as it pertains to the construction of identity as one example.

Postmodern theory that is not seeking to simply appropriate the experience of 'Otherness' to enhance the discourse or to be radically chic should not separate the 'politics of difference' from the politics of racism. To take racism seriously one must consider the plight of underclass people of color, a vast majority of whom are black. For African-Americans our collective condition prior to the advent of postmodernism and perhaps more tragically expressed under current postmodern conditions has been and is characterized by continued displacement, profound alienation and despair. Writing about blacks and postmodernism, Cornel West describes our collective plight:

> There is increasing class division and differentiation, creating on the one hand a significant black middle-class, highly anxiety-ridden, insecure, willing to be co-opted and incorporated into the powers that be, concerned with racism to the degree that it poses constraints on upward social mobility; and, on the other, a vast and growing black underclass, an underclass that embodies a kind of walking nihilism of pervasive drug addiction, pervasive alcoholism, pervasive homicide, and an exponential rise in suicide. Now because of the deindustrialization, we also have a devastated black industrial working class. We are talking here about tremendous hopelessness.

This hopelessness creates longing for insight and strategies for change that can renew spirits and reconstruct grounds for collective black liberation struggle. The overall impact of postmodernism is that many other groups now share with black folks a sense of deep alienation, despair, uncertainty, loss of a sense of grounding even if it is not informed by shared circumstance. Radical postmodernism calls attention to those shared sensibilities which cross the boundaries of class, gender, race, etc., that could be fertile ground for the construction of empathy – ties that would promote recognition of common commitments, and serve as a base for solidarity and coalition.

Yearning is the word that best describes a common psychological state shared by many of us, cutting across boundaries of race, class, gender and sexual practice. Specifically, in relation to the postmodernist reconstruction of 'master' narratives, the yearning that wells in the hearts and minds of those whom such narratives have silenced is the longing for critical voice. It is no accident that 'rap' has usurped the primary position of rhythm and blues music among young black folks as the most desired sound or that it began as a form of 'testimony' for the underclass. It has enabled underclass black youth to develop a critical voice, as a group of young black men told me, a 'common literacy'. Rap projects a critical voice, explaining, demanding, urging. Working with this insight in his essay 'Putting the pop back into postmodernism', Lawrence Grossberg comments:

> The postmodern sensibility appropriates practices as boasts that announce their own – and consequently our own – existence, like a rap song boasting of the imaginary (or real – it makes no difference) accomplishments of the rapper. They offer forms of empowerment not only in the face of nihilism but precisely through the forms of nihilism itself: an empowering nihilism, a moment of positivity through the production and structuring of affective relations.

Considering that it is as subject one comes to voice, then the postmodernist focus on the critique of identity appears at first glance to threaten and close down the possibility that this discourse and practice will allow those who have suffered the crippling effects of colonization and domination to gain or regain a hearing. Even if this sense of threat and the fear it evokes are based on a misunderstanding of the postmodernist political project, they nevertheless shape responses. It never surprises me when black folks respond to the critique of essentialism, especially when it denies the validity of identity politics, by saying, 'Yeah, it's easy to give up identity, when you got one.' Should we not be suspicious of postmodern critiques of the 'subject' when they surface at a historical moment when many subjugated people feel themselves coming to voice for the first time. Though an apt and oftentimes appropriate comeback, it does not really intervene in the discourse in a way that alters and transforms.

Criticisms of directions in postmodern thinking should not obscure insights it may offer that open up our understanding of African-American experience. The critique of essentialism encouraged by postmodernist thought is useful for African-Americans concerned with reformulating outmoded notions of identity. We have too long had imposed upon us from both the outside and the inside a narrow, constricting notion of blackness. Postmodern critiques of essentialism which challenge notions of universality and static over-determined identity within mass culture and mass consciousness can open up new possibilities for the construction of self and the assertion of agency.

Employing a critique of essentialism allows African-Americans to acknowledge the way in which class mobility has altered collective black experience so that racism does not necessarily have the same impact on our lives. Such a critique allows us to affirm multiple black identities, varied black experience. It also challenges colonial imperialist paradigms of black identity which represent blackness one-dimensionally in ways that reinforce and sustain white supremacy. This discourse created the idea of the 'primitive' and promoted the notion of an 'authentic' experience, seeing as 'natural' those expressions of black life which conformed to a pre-existing pattern or stereotype. Abandoning essentialist notions would be a serious challenge to racism. Contemporary African-American resistance struggle must be rooted in a process of decolonization that continually opposes re-inscribing notions of 'authentic' black identity. This critique should not be made synonymous with a dismissal of the struggle of oppressed and exploited peoples to make ourselves subjects. Nor should it deny that in certain circumstances this experience affords us a privileged critical location from which to speak. This is not a re-inscription of modernist master narratives of authority which privilege some voices by denying voice to others. Part of our struggle for radical black subjectivity is the quest to find ways to construct self and identity that are oppositional and liberatory. The unwillingness to critique essentialism on the part of many African-Americans is rooted in the fear that it will cause folks to lose sight of the specific history and experience of African-Americans and the unique sensibilities and culture that arise from that experience. An adequate response to this concern is to critique essentialism while emphasizing the significance of 'the authority of experience'. There is a radical difference between a repudiation of the idea that there is a black 'essence' and recognition of the way black identity has been specifically constituted in the experience of exile and struggle.

When black folks critique essentialism, we are empowered to recognize multiple experiences of black identity that are the lived conditions which make diverse cultural productions possible. When this diversity is ignored, it is easy to see black folks as falling into two categories: nationalist or assimilationist, black-identified or white-identified. Coming to terms with the impact of postmodernism for black experience, particularly as it changes our sense of identity, means that we must and can rearticulate the basis for collective bonding. Given the various crises facing African-Americans (economic, spiritual, escalating racial violence, etc.), we are compelled by circumstance to reassess our relationship to popular culture and resistance struggle. Many of us are as reluctant to face this task as many non-black postmodern thinkers who focus theoretically on the issue of 'difference' are to confront the issue of race and racism.

Music is the cultural product created by African-Americans that has most attracted postmodern theorists. It is rarely acknowledged that there is far greater censorship and restriction of other forms of cultural production by black folks – literary, critical writing, etc. Attempts on the part of editors and publishing houses to control and manipulate the representation of black culture, as well as the desire to promote the creation of products that will attract the widest audience, limit in a crippling and stifling way the kind of work many black folks feel we can do and still receive recognition. Using myself as an example, that creative writing I do which I consider to be most reflective of a postmodern oppositional sensibility, work that is abstract, fragmented, non-linear narrative, is constantly rejected by editors and publishers. It does not conform to the type of writing they think black women should be doing or the type of writing they believe will sell. Certainly I do not think I am the only black person engaged in forms of cultural production, especially experimental ones, who is constrained by the lack of an audience for certain kinds of work. It is important for postmodern thinkers and theorists to constitute themselves as an audience for such work. To do this they must assert power and privilege within the space of critical writing to open up the field so that it will be more inclusive. To change the exclusionary practice of postmodern critical discourse is to enact a postmodernism of resistance. Part of this intervention entails black intellectual participation in the discourse.

In his essay 'Postmodernism and Black America', Cornel West suggests that black intellectuals 'are marginal – usually languishing at the interface of Black and white cultures or thoroughly ensconced in Euro-American settings'. He cannot see this group as potential producers of radical postmodernist thought. While I generally agree with this assessment, black intellectuals must proceed with the understanding that we are not condemned to the margins. The way we work and what we do can determine whether or not what we produce will be meaningful to a wider audience, one that includes all classes of black people. West suggests that black intellectuals lack 'any organic link with most of Black life' and that this 'diminishes their value to Black resistance'. This statement bears traces of essentialism. Perhaps we need to focus more on those black intellectuals, however rare our presence, who do not feel this lack and whose work is primarily directed towards the enhancement of black critical consciousness and the strengthening of our collective capacity to engage in meaningful resistance struggle. Theoretical ideas and critical thinking need not be transmitted solely in written work or solely in the academy. While I work in a predominantly white institution, I remain intimately and passionately engaged with black community. It's not like I'm going to talk about writing and thinking about postmodernism with other academics and/or intellectuals and not discuss these ideas with underclass non-academic black folks who are family, friends and comrades. Since I have not broken the ties that bind me to underclass poor black community, I have seen that knowledge, especially that which enhances daily life and strengthens our capacity to survive, can be shared. It means that critics, writers and academics have to give the same critical attention to nurturing and cultivating our ties to black community that we give to writing articles, teaching and lecturing. Here again I am really talking about cultivating habits of being that reinforce awareness that knowledge can be disseminated and shared on a number of fronts. The extent to which knowledge is made available, accessible, etc., depends on the nature of one's political commitments.

Postmodern culture with its decentered subject can be the space where ties are severed or it can provide the occasion for new and varied forms of bonding. To some extent, ruptures, surfaces, contextuality, and a host of other happenings create gaps that make space for oppositional practices which no longer require intellectuals to be confined by narrow separate spheres with no meaningful connection to the world of the everyday. Much postmodern engagement with culture emerges from the yearning to do intellectual work that connects with habits of being, forms of artistic expression and aesthetics that inform the daily life of writers and scholars as well as a mass population. On the terrain of culture, one can participate in critical dialogue with the uneducated poor, the black underclass who are thinking about aesthetics. One can talk about what we are seeing, thinking or listening to; a space is there for critical exchange. It's exciting to think, write, talk about and create art that reflects passionate engagement with popular culture, because this may very well be 'the' central future location of resistance struggle, a meeting place where new and radical happenings can occur.

31   Edward Said,

From *Culture and Imperialism* (1993), pp. 20–35

Two Visions in *Heart of Darkness*

Domination and inequities of power and wealth are perennial facts of human society. But in today's global setting they are also interpretable as having something to do with imperialism, its history, its new forms. The nations of contemporary Asia, Latin America, and Africa are politically independent but in many ways are as dominated and dependent as they were when ruled directly by European powers. On the one hand, this is the consequence of self-inflicted wounds, critics like V.S. Naipaul are wont to say: *they* (everyone knows that 'they' means coloureds, wogs, niggers) are to blame for what 'they' are, and it's no use droning on about the legacy of imperialism. On the other hand, blaming the Europeans sweepingly for the misfortunes of the present is not much of an alternative. What we need to do is to look at these matters as a network of interdependent histories that it would be inaccurate and senseless to repress, useful and interesting to understand.

The point here is not complicated. If while sitting in Oxford, Paris, or New York you tell Arabs or Africans that they belong to a basically sick or unregenerate culture, you are unlikely to convince them. Even if you prevail over them, they are not going to concede to you your essential superiority or your right to rule them despite your evident wealth and power. The history of this stand-off is manifest throughout colonies where white masters were once unchallenged but finally driven out. Conversely, the triumphant natives soon enough found that they needed the West and that the idea of *total* independence was a nationalist fiction designed mainly for what Fanon calls the 'rationalist bourgeoisie', who in turn often ran the new countries with a callous, exploitative tyranny reminiscent of the departed masters.

And so in the late twentieth century the imperial cycle of the last century in some way replicates itself, although today there are really no big empty spaces, no expanding frontiers, no exciting new settlements to establish. We live in one global environment with a huge number of ecological, economic, social, and political pressures tearing at its only dimly perceived, basically uninterpreted and uncomprehended fabric. Anyone with even a vague consciousness of this whole is alarmed at how such remorselessly selfish and narrow interests – patriotism, chauvinism, ethnic, religious, and racial hatreds – can in fact lead to mass destructiveness. The world simply cannot afford this many more times.

One should not pretend that models for a harmonious world order are ready at hand, and it would be equally disingenuous to suppose that ideas of peace and community have much of a chance when power is moved to action by aggressive perceptions of 'vital national interests' or unlimited sovereignty. The United States' clash with Iraq and Iraq's aggression against Kuwait concerning oil are obvious examples. The wonder of it is that the schooling for such relatively provincial thought and action is still prevalent unchecked, uncritically accepted, recurringly replicated in the education of generation after generation. We are all taught to venerate our nations and admire our traditions: we are taught to pursue their interests with toughness and in disregard for other societies. A new and in my opinion appalling tribalism is fracturing societies, separating peoples, promoting greed, bloody conflict, and uninteresting assertions of minor ethnic or group particularity. Little time is spent not so much in 'learning about other cultures' – the phrase has an inane vagueness to it – but in studying the map of interactions, the actual and often productive traffic occurring on a day-by-day, and even minute-by-minute basis among states, societies, groups, identities.

No one can hold this entire map in his or her head, which is why the geography of empire and the many-sided imperial experience that created its fundamental texture should be considered first in terms of a few salient configurations. Primarily, as we look back at the nineteenth century, we see that the drive toward empire in effect brought most of the earth under the domination of a handful of powers. To get hold of part of what this means, I propose to look at a specific set of rich cultural documents in which the interaction between Europe or America on the one hand and the imperialized world on the other is animated, informed, made explicit as an experience for both sides of the encounter. Yet before I do this, historically and systematically, it is a useful preparation to look at what still remains of imperialism in recent cultural discussion. This is the residuum of a dense, interesting history that is paradoxically global and local at the same time, and it is also a sign of how the imperial past lives on, arousing argument and counter-argument with surprising intensity. Because they are contemporary and easy at hand, these traces of the past in the present point the way to a study of the histories the plural is used advisedly – created by empire, not just the stories of the white man and woman but also those of the non-whites whose lands and very being were at issue, even as their claims were denied or ignored.

One significant contemporary debate about the residue of imperialism – the matter of how 'natives' are represented in the Western media – illustrates the persistence of such interdependence and overlapping, not only in the debate's content but in its form, not only in what is said but also in how it is said, by whom, where, and for whom. This bears looking into, although it requires a self-discipline not easily come by, so well-developed, tempting, and ready at hand are the confrontational strategies. In 1984, well before *The Satanic Verses* appeared, Salman Rushdie diagnosed the spate of films and articles about the British Raj, including the television series *The Jewel in the Crown* and David Lean's film of *A Passage to India*. Rushdie noted that the nostalgia pressed into service by these affectionate-recollections of British rule in India coincided with the Falklands War, and that 'the rise of Raj revisionism, exemplified by the huge success of these fictions, is the artistic counterpart to the rise of conservative ideologies in modern Britain'. Commentators responded to what they considered Rushdie's wailing and whining in public and seemed to disregard his principal point. Rushdie was trying to make a larger argument, which presumably should have appealed to intellectuals for whom George Orwell's well-known description of the intellectual's place in society as being inside and outside the whale no longer applied; modern reality in Rushdie's terms was actually 'whaleless, this world without quiet corners [in which] there can be no easy escapes from history, from hullabaloo, from terrible, unquiet fuss'.[1] But Rushdie's main point was *not* the point considered worth taking up and debating. Instead the main issue for contention was whether things in the Third World hadn't in fact declined after the colonies had been emancipated, and whether it might not be better on the whole to listen to the rare – luckily, I might add, extremely rare – Third World intellectuals who manfully ascribed most of their present barbarities, tyrannies, and degradations to their own native histories, histories that were pretty bad before colonialism and that reverted to that state after colonialism. Hence, ran *this* argument, better a ruthlessly honest V.S. Naipaul than an absurdly posturing Rushdie.

One could conclude from the emotions stirred up by Rushdie's own case, then and later, that many people in the West came to feel that enough was enough. After Vietnam and Iran – and note here that these labels are usually employed equally to evoke American domestic traumas (the student insurrections of the 1960s, the public anguish about the hostages in the 1970s) as much as international conflict and the 'loss' of Vietnam and Iran to radical nationalisms – after Vietnam and Iran, lines had to be defended. Western democracy had taken a beating, and even if the physical damage had been done abroad, there was a sense, as Jimmy Carter once rather oddly put it, of 'mutual destruction'. This feeling in turn led to Westerners rethinking the whole process of decolonization. Was it not true, ran their new evaluation, that 'we' had given 'them' progress and modernization? Hadn't we provided them with order and a kind of stability that they haven't been able since to provide for themselves? Wasn't it an atrocious misplaced trust to believe in their capacity for independence, for it had led to Bokassas and Amins, whose intellectual correlates were people like Rushdie? Shouldn't we have held on to the colonies, kept the subject or inferior races in check, remained true to our civilizational responsibilities?

I realize that what I have just reproduced is not entirely the thing itself, but perhaps a caricature. Nevertheless it bears an uncomfortable resemblance to what many people who imagined themselves speaking for the West said. There seemed little scepticism that a monolithic 'West' in fact existed, any more than an entire ex-colonial world described in one sweeping generalization after another. The leap to essences and generalizations was accompanied by appeals to an imagined history of Western endowments and free hand-outs, followed by a reprehensible sequence of ungrateful bitings of that grandly giving 'Western' hand. 'Why don't they appreciate us, after what we did for them?[2]

How easily so much could be compressed into that simple formula of unappreciated magnanimity! Dismissed or forgotten were the ravaged colonial peoples who for centuries endured summary justice, unending economic oppression, distortion of their social and intimate lives, and a recourseless submission that was the function of unchanging European superiority. Only to keep in mind the millions of Africans who were supplied to the slave trade is to acknowledge the unimaginable cost of maintaining that superiority. Yet dismissed most often are precisely the infinite number of traces in the immensely detailed, violent history of colonial intervention – minute by minute, hour by hour – in the lives of individuals and collectivities, on both sides of the colonial divide.

The thing to be noticed about this kind of contemporary discourse, which assumes the primacy and even the complete centrality of the West, is how totalizing is its form, how all-enveloping its attitudes and gestures, how much it shuts out even as it includes, compresses, and consolidates. We suddenly find ourselves transported backward in time to the late nineteenth century.

This imperial attitude is, I believe, beautifully captured in the complicated and rich narrative form of Conrad's great novella *Heart of Darkness*, written between 1898 and 1899. On the one hand, the narrator Marlow acknowledges the tragic predicament of all speech – that 'it is impossible to convey the life-sensation of any given epoch on one's existence – that which makes its truth, its meaning – its subtle and penetrating essence ... We live, as we dream – alone'[3] – yet still manages to convey the enormous power of Kurtz's African experience through his own overmastering narrative of his voyage into the African interior towards Kurtz. This narrative in turn is connected directly with the redemptive force, as well as the waste and horror, of Europe's mission in the dark world. Whatever is lost or elided or even simply made up in Marlow's immensely compelling recitation is compensated for in the narrative's sheer historical momentum, the temporal forward movement – with digressions, descriptions, exciting encounters, and all. Within the narrative of how he journeyed to Kurtz's Inner Station, whose source and authority he now becomes, Marlow moves backward and forward materially in small and large spirals, very much the way episodes in the course of his journey up-river are then incorporated by the principal forward trajectory into what he renders as 'the heart of Africa'.

Thus Marlow's encounter with the improbably white-suited clerk in the middle of the jungle furnishes him with several digressive paragraphs, as does his meeting later with the semi-crazed, harlequin-like Russian who has been so affected by Kurtz's gifts. Yet underlying Marlow's inconclusiveness, his evasions, his arabesque meditations on his feelings and ideas, is the unrelenting course of the journey itself, which, despite all the many obstacles, is sustained through the jungle, through time, through hardship, to the heart of it all, Kurtz's ivory-trading empire. Conrad wants us to see how Kurtz's great looting adventure, Marlow's journey up the river, and the narrative itself all share a common theme: Europeans performing acts of imperial mastery and will in (or about) Africa.

What makes Conrad different from the other colonial writers who were his contemporaries is that, for reasons having partly to do with the colonialism that turned him, a Polish expatriate, into an employee of the imperial system, he was so self-conscious about what he did. Like most of his other tales, therefore, *Heart of Darkness* cannot just be a straightforward recital of Marlow's adventures: it is also a dramatization of Marlow himself, the former wanderer in colonial regions, telling his story to a group of British listeners at a particular time and in a specific place. That this group of people is drawn largely from the business world is Conrad's way of emphasizing the fact that during the 1890s the business of empire, once an adventurous and often individualistic enterprise, had become the empire of business. (Coincidentally we should note that at about the same time Halford Mackinder, an explorer, geographer, and Liberal Imperialist, gave a series of lectures on imperialism at the London Institute of Bankers:[4] perhaps Conrad knew about this.) Although the almost oppressive force of Marlow's narrative leaves us with a quite accurate sense that there is no way out of the sovereign historical force of imperialism, and that it has the power of a system representing as well as speaking for everything within its dominion, Conrad shows us that what Marlow does is contingent, acted out for a set of like-minded British hearers, and limited to that situation.

Yet neither Conrad nor Marlow gives us a full view of what is *outside* the world-conquering attitudes embodied by Kurtz, Marlow, the circle of listeners on the deck of the *Nellie*, and Conrad. By that I mean that *Heart of Darkness* works so effectively because its politics and aesthetics are, so to speak, imperialist, which in the closing years of the nineteenth century seemed to be at the same time an aesthetic, politics, and even epistemology inevitable and unavoidable. For if we cannot truly understand someone else's experience and if we must therefore depend upon the assertive authority of the sort of power that Kurtz wields as a white man in the jungle or that Marlow, another white man, wields as narrator, there is no use looking for other, non-imperialist alternatives; the system has simply eliminated them and made them unthinkable. The circularity, the perfect closure of the whole thing is not only aesthetically but also mentally unassailable.

Conrad is so self-conscious about situating Marlow's tale in a narrative moment that he allows us simultaneously to realize after all that imperialism, far from swallowing up its own history, was taking place in and was circumscribed by a larger history, one just outside the tightly inclusive circle of Europeans on the deck of the *Nellie*. As yet, however, no one seemed to inhabit that region, and so Conrad left it empty.

Conrad could probably never have used Marlow to present anything other than an imperialist world-view, given what was available for either Conrad or Marlow to see of the non-European at the time. Independence was for whites and Europeans; the lesser or subject peoples were to be ruled; science, learning, history emanated from the West. True, Conrad scrupulously recorded the differences between the disgraces of Belgian and British colonial attitudes, but he could only imagine the world carved up into one or another Western sphere of dominion. But because Conrad also had an extraordinarily persistent residual sense of his own exilic marginality, he quite carefully (some would say maddeningly) qualified Marlow's narrative with the provisionality that came from standing at the very juncture of this world with another, unspecified but different. Conrad was certainly not a great imperialist entrepreneur like Cecil Rhodes or Frederick Lugard, even though he understood perfectly how for each of them, in Hannah Arendt's words, to enter 'the maelstrom of an unending process of expansion, he will, as it were, cease to be what he was and obey the laws of the process, identify himself with anonymous forces that he is supposed to serve in order to keep the whole process in motion, he will think of himself as mere function, and eventually consider such functionality, such an incarnation of the dynamic trend, his highest possible achievement'.[5] Conrad's realization is that if, like narrative, imperialism has monopolized the entire system of representation – which in the case of *Heart of Darkness* allowed it to speak for Africans as well as for Kurtz and the other adventurers, including Marlow and his audiences – your self-consciousness as an outsider can allow you actively to comprehend how the machine works, given that you and it are fundamentally not in perfect synchrony or correspondence. Never the wholly incorporated and fully acculturated Englishman, Conrad therefore preserved an ironic distance in each of his works.

The form of Conrad's narrative has thus made it possible to derive two possible arguments, two visions, in the post-colonial world that succeeded his. One argument allows the old imperial enterprise full scope to play itself out conventionally, to render the world as official European or Western imperialism saw it, and to consolidate itself after World War Two. Westerners may have physically led their old colonies in Africa and Asia, but they retained them not only as markets but as locales on the ideological map over which they continued to rule morally and intellectually. 'Show me the Zulu Tolstoy', as one American intellectual has recently put it. The assertive sovereign inclusiveness of this argument courses through the words of those who speak today for the West and for what the West did, as well as for what the rest of the world is, was, and may be. The assertions of this discourse exclude what has been represented as 'lost' by arguing that the colonial world was in some ways ontologically speaking lost to begin with, irredeemable, irrecusably inferior. Moreover, it focuses not on what was shared in the colonial experience, but on what must never be shared, namely the authority and rectitude that come with greater power and development. Rhetorically, its terms are the organization of political passions, to borrow from Julien Benda's critique of modern intellectuals, terms which, he was sensible enough to know, lead inevitably to mass slaughter, and if not to literal mass slaughter then certainly to rhetorical slaughter.

The second argument is considerably less objectionable. It sees itself as Conrad saw his own narratives, local to a time and place, neither unconditionally true nor unqualifiedly certain. As I have said, Conrad does not give us the sense that he could imagine a fully realized alternative to imperialism: the natives he wrote about in Africa, Asia, or America were incapable of independence, and because he seemed to imagine that European tutelage was a given, he could not foresee what would take place when it came to an end. But come to an end it would, if only because – like all human effort, like speech itself – it would have its moment, then it would have to pass. Since Conrad *dates* imperialism, shows its contingency, records its illusions and tremendous violence and waste (as in *Nostromo*), he permits his later readers to imagine something other than an Africa carved up into dozens of European colonies, even if, for his own part, he had little notion of what that Africa might be.

To return to the first line out of Conrad, the discourse of resurgent empire proves that the nineteenth-century imperial encounter continues today to draw lines and defend barriers. Strangely, it persists also in the enormously complex and quietly interesting interchange between former colonial partners, say between Britain and India, or between France and the Francophone countries of Africa. But these exchanges tend to be overshadowed by the loud antagonisms of the polarized debate of pro- and anti-imperialists, who speak stridently of national destiny, overseas interests, neo-imperialism, and the like, drawing like-minded people – aggressive Westerners and, ironically, those non-Westerners for whom the new nationalist and resurgent Ayatollahs speak – away from the other ongoing interchange. Inside each regrettably constricted camp stand the blameless, the just, the faithful, led by the omnicompetent, those who know the truth about themselves and others; outside stands a miscellaneous bunch of querulous intellectuals and wishy-washy sceptics who go on complaining about the past to little effect.

An important ideological shift occurred during the 1970s and 1980s, accompanying this contraction of horizons in what I have been calling the first of the two lines leading out of *Heart of Darkness*. One can locate it, for instance, in the dramatic change in emphasis and, quite literally, direction among thinkers noted for their radicalism. The later Jean-François Lyotard and Michel Foucault, eminent French philosophers who emerged during the 1960s as apostles of radicalism and intellectual insurgency, describe a striking new lack of faith in what Lyotard calls the great legitimizing narratives of emancipation and enlightenment. Our age, he said in the 1980s, is post-modernist, concerned only with local issues, not with history but with problems to be solved, not with a grand reality but with games.[6] Foucault also turned his attention away from the oppositional forces in modern society which he had studied for their undeterred resistance to exclusion and confinement – delinquents, poets, outcasts, and the like – and decided that since power was everywhere it was probably better to concentrate on the local micro-physics of power that surround the individual. The self was therefore to be studied, cultivated, and, if necessary, refashioned and constituted.[7] In both Lyotard and Foucault we find precisely the same trope employed to explain the disappointment in the politics of liberation: narrative, which posits an enabling beginning point and a vindicating goal, is no longer adequate for plotting the human trajectory in society. There is nothing to look forward to: we are stuck within our circle. And now the line is enclosed by a circle. After years of support for anti-colonial struggles in Algeria, Cuba, Vietnam, Palestine, Iran, which came to represent for many Western intellectuals their deepest engagement in the politics and philosophy of anti-imperialist decolonization, a moment of exhaustion and disappointment was reached.[8] One began to hear and read how futile it was to support revolutions, how barbaric were the new regimes that came to power, how – this is an extreme case – decolonization had benefited 'world communism'.

Enter now terrorism and barbarism. Enter also the ex-colonial experts whose well-publicized message was: these colonial peoples deserve only colonialism or, since 'we' were foolish to pull out of Aden, Algeria, India, Indochina, and everywhere else, it might be a good idea to reinvade their territories. Enter also various experts and theoreticians of the relationship between liberation movements, terrorism, and the KGB. There was a resurgence of sympathy for what Jeane Kirkpatrick called authoritarian (as opposed to totalitarian) regimes who were Western allies. With the onset of Reaganism, Thatcherism, and their correlates, a new phase of history began.

However else it might have been historically understandable, peremptorily withdrawing 'the West' from its own experiences in the 'peripheral world' certainly was and is not an attractive or edifying activity for an intellectual today. It shuts out the possibility of knowledge and of discovery of what it means to be outside the whale. Let us return to Rushdie for another insight:

> We see that it can be as false to create a politics-free fictional universe as to create one in which nobody needs to work or eat or hate or love or sleep. Outside the whale it becomes necessary, and even exhilarating, to grapple with the special problems created by the incorporation of political material, because politics is by turns farce and tragedy, and sometimes (e.g., Zia's Pakistan) both at once. Outside the whale the writer is obliged to accept that he (or she) is part of the crowd, part of the ocean, part of the storm, so that objectivity becomes a great dream, like perfection, an unattainable goal for which one must struggle in spite of the impossibility of success. Outside the whale is the world of Samuel Beckett's famous formula: *I can't go on, I'll go on.*

The terms of Rushdie's description, while they borrow from Orwell, seem to me to resonate even more interestingly with Conrad. For here is the second consequence, the second line leading out of Conrad's narrative form; in its explicit references to the outside, it points to a perspective outside the basically imperialist representations provided by Marlow and his listeners. It is a profoundly secular perspective, and it is beholden neither to notions about historical destiny and the essentialism that destiny always seems to entail, nor to historical indifference and resignation. Being on the inside shuts out the full experience of imperialism, edits it and subordinates it to the dominance of one Eurocentric and totalizing view; this other perspective suggests the presence of a field without special historical privileges for one party.

I don't want to overinterpret Rushdie, or put ideas in his prose that he may not have intended. In this controversy with the local British media (before *The Satanic Verses* sent him into hiding), he claimed that he could not recognize the truth of his own experience in the popular media representations of India. Now I myself would go further and say that it is one of the virtues of such conjunctures of politics with culture and aesthetics that they permit the disclosure of a common ground obscured by the controversy itself. Perhaps it is especially hard for the combatants directly involved to see this common ground when they are fighting back more than reflecting. I can perfectly understand the anger that fuelled Rushdie's argument because like him I feel outnumbered and outorganized by a prevailing Western consensus that has come to regard the Third World as an atrocious nuisance, a culturally and politically inferior place. Whereas we write and speak as members of a small minority of marginal voices, our journalistic and academic critics belong to a wealthy system of interlocking informational and academic resources with newspapers, television networks, journals of opinion, and institutes at its disposal. Most of them have now taken up a strident chorus of rightward-tending damnation, in which they separate what is non-white, non-Western, and non-Judeo-Christian from the acceptable and designated Western ethos, then herd it all together under various demeaning rubrics such as terrorist, marginal second-rate, or unimportant. To attack what is contained in these categories is to defend the Western spirit.

Let us return to Conrad and to what I have been referring to as the second, less imperialistically assertive possibility offered by *Heart of Darkness*. Recall once again that Conrad sets the story on the deck of a boat anchored in the Thames; as Marlow tells his story the sun sets, and by the end of the narrative the heart of darkness has reappeared in England; outside the group of Marlow's listeners lies an undefined and unclear world. Conrad sometimes seems to want to fold that world into the imperial metropolitan discourse represented by Marlow, but by virtue of his own dislocated subjectivity he resists the effort and succeeds in so doing, I have always believed, largely through formal devices. Conrad's self-consciously circular narrative forms draw attention to themselves as artificial constructions, encouraging us to sense the potential of a reality that seemed inaccessible to imperialism, just beyond its control, and that only well after Conrad's death in 1924 acquired a substantial presence.

This needs more explanation. Despite their European names and mannerisms, Conrad's narrators are not average unreflecting witnesses of European imperialism. They do not simply accept what goes on in the name of the imperial idea: they think about it a lot, they worry about it, they are actually quite anxious about whether they can make it seem like a routine thing. But it never is. Conrad's way of demonstrating this discrepancy between the orthodox and his own views of empire is to keep drawing attention to how ideas and values are constructed (and reconstructed) through dislocations in the narrator's language. In addition, the recitations are meticulously staged: the narrator is a speaker whose audience and the reason for their being together, the quality of whose voice, the effect of what he says – are all important and even insistent aspects of the story he tells. Marlow, for example, is never straightforward. He alternates between garrulity and stunning eloquence, and rarely resists making peculiar things seem more peculiar by surprisingly misstating them, or rendering them vague and contradictory. Thus, he says, a French warship fires 'into a continent'; Kurtz's eloquence is enlightening as well as fraudulent; and so on – his speech so full of these odd discrepancies (well discussed by Ian Watt as 'delayed decoding'[10]) that the net effect is to leave his immediate audience as well as the reader with the acute sense that what he is presenting is not quite as it should be or appears to be.

Yet the whole point of what Kurtz and Marlow talk about is in fact imperial mastery, white Europeans *over* black Africans and their ivory, civilization *over* the primitive dark continent. By accentuating the discrepancy between the official 'idea' of empire and the remarkably disorienting actuality of Africa, Marlow unsettles the reader's sense not only of the very idea of empire but of something more basic, reality itself. For if Conrad can show that all human activity depends on controlling a radically unstable reality to which words approximate only by will or convention, the same is true of empire, of venerating the idea, and so forth. With Conrad, then, we are in a world being made and unmade more or less all the time. What appears stable and secure – the policeman at the corner, for instance – is only slightly more secure than the white men in the jungle, and requires the same continuous (but precarious) triumph over an all-pervading darkness, which by the end of the tale is shown to be the same in London and in Africa.

Conrad's genius allowed him to realize that the ever-present darkness could be colonized or illuminated – *Heart of Darkness* is full of references to the *mission civilisatrice*, to benevolent as well as cruel schemes to bring light to the dark places and peoples of this world by acts of will and deployments of power – but that it also had to be acknowledged as independent. Kurtz and Marlow acknowledge the darkness, the former as he is dying, the latter as he reflects retrospectively on the meaning of Kurtz's final words. They (and of course Conrad) are ahead of their time in understanding that what they call 'the darkness' has an autonomy of its own, and can reinvade and reclaim what imperialism had taken for *its* own. But Marlow and Kurtz are also creatures of their time and cannot take the next step, which would be to recognise that what they saw, disablingly and disparagingly, as a non-European 'darkness' was in fact a non-European world *resisting* imperialism so as one day to regain sovereignty and independence, and not, as Conrad reductively says, to reestablish the darkness. Conrad's tragic limitation is that even though he could see clearly that on one level imperialism was essentially pure dominance and land-grabbing, he could not then conclude that imperialism had to end so that 'natives' could lead lives free from European domination. As a creature of his time, Conrad could not grant the natives their freedom, despite his severe critique of the imperialism that enslaved them.

The cultural and ideological evidence that Conrad was wrong in his Eurocentric way is both impressive and rich. A whole movement, literature, and theory of resistance and response to empire exists, and in greatly

disparate post-colonial regions one sees tremendously energetic effo...
engage with the metropolitan world in equal debate so as to testify to the
diversity and differences of the non-European world and to its own agendas,
priorities, and history. The purpose of this testimony is to inscribe, reinterpret,
and expand the areas of engagement as well as the terrain contested with
Europe. Some of this activity – for example, the work of two important and
active Iranian intellectuals, Ali Shariati and Jalal Ali i-Ahmed, who by means
of speeches, books, tapes, and pamphlets prepared the way for the Islamic
Revolutions – interprets colonialism by asserting the absolute opposition of
the native culture: the West is an enemy, a disease, an evil. In other instances,
novelists like the Kenyan Ngugi and the Sudanese Tayib Salih appropriate
for their fiction such great *topoi* of colonial culture as the quest and the voyage
into the unknown, claiming them for their own, post-colonial purposes.
Salih's hero in *Season of Migration to the North* does (and is) the reverse of
what Kurtz does (and is): the Black man journeys north into white territory.

Between classical nineteenth-century imperialism and what it gave rise
to in resistant native cultures, there is thus both a stubborn confrontation
and a crossing over in discussion, borrowing back and forth, debate. Many
of the most interesting post-colonial writers bear their past within them –
as scars of humiliating wounds, as instigation for different practices, as
potentially revised visions of the past tending towards a new future, as
urgently reinterpretable and redeployable experiences, in which the
formerly silent native speaks and acts on territory taken back from the
empire. One sees these aspects in Rushdie, Derek Walcott, Aimé Césaire,
Chinua Achebe, Pablo Neruda, and Brian Friel. And now these writers can
truly read the great colonial masterpieces, which not only misrepresented
them but assumed they were unable to read and respond directly to what
had been written about them, just as European ethnography presumed the
natives' incapacity to intervene in scientific discourse about them.

Notes

1 Salman Rushdie, 'Outside the Whale,' in *Imaginary Homelands: Essays and Criticism 1981–1991* (London, Viking/Granta, 1991), pp. 92, 101.
2 This is the message of Conor Cruise O'Brien's 'Why the Wailing Ought to Stop,' *The Observer*, June 3, 1984.
3 Joseph Conrad, 'Heart of Darkness,' in *Youth and Two Other Stories* (Garden City Doubleday, Page, 1925), p. 82.
4 For Mackinder, see Neil Smith, *Uneven Development: Nature, Capital and the Production of Space* (Oxford, Blackwell, 1984), pp. 102–3. Conrad and triumphalist geography are at the heart of Felix Driver, 'Geography's Empire: Histories of Geographical Knowledge,' *Society and Space*, 1991.
5 Hannah Arendt, *The Origins of Totalitarianism* (1951; new ed., New York, Harcourt Brace Jovanovich, 1973), p. 215 See also Fredric Jameson. *The Political Unconsious: Narrative as a Socially Symbolic Act* (Ithaca: Cornell University Press, 1981).
6 Jean-François Lyotard, *The Postmodern Condition: A Report on Knowledge*, trans,

on and Brian Massumi (Minneapolis, University of Minnesota
. 37.

y Foucault's late work, *The Care of the Self*, trans. Robert Hurley (New
eon, 1986). A bold new interpretation arguing that Foucault's entire
bout the self, and his in particular, is advanced in *The Passion of Michel*
by James Miller (New York, Simon & Schuster, 1993).

8 See, for example, Gérard Chaliand, *Revolution in the Third World* (Harmondsworth, Penguin, 1978).

9 Rushdie, 'Outside the Whale,' pp. 100–1.

10 Ian Watt, *Conrad in the Nineteenth Century* (Berkeley, University of California Press, 1979), pp. 175–9.

32 Homi BhaBha,

'Of Mimicry and Man: The Ambivalence of Colonial Discourse',
October, no. 28, Spring (1983)*, pp. 125–33

Mimicry reveals something in so far as it is distinct from what might
be called an itself that is behind. The effect of mimicry is camouflage.
... It is not a question of harmonizing with the background, but
against a mottled background, of becoming mottled – exactly like
the technique of camouflage practised in human warfare.

Jacques Lacan,
'The Line and Light', *Of the Gaze*

It is out of season to question at this time of day, the original policy
of conferring on every colony of the British Empire a mimic
representation of the British Constitution. But if the creature so
endowed has sometimes forgotten its real insignificance and under
the fancied importance of speakers and maces, and all the
paraphernalia and ceremonies of the imperial legislature, has dared
to defy the mother country, she has to thank herself for the folly of
conferring such privileges on a condition of society that has no
earthly claim to so exalted a position. A fundamental principle
appears to have been forgotten or overlooked in our system of
colonial policy – that of colonial dependence. To give to a colony the
forms of independence is a mockery; she would not be a colony for
a single hour if she could maintain an independent station.

Sir Edward Cust,
'Reflections on West African Affairs ... addressed to the Colonial
Office', Hatchard, London 1839

The discourse of post-Enlightenment English colonialism often speaks in a
tongue that is forked, not false. If colonialism takes power in the name of

history, it repeatedly exercises its authority through the figures of farce. For the epic intention of the civilizing mission, 'human and not wholly human' in the famous words of Lord Rosebery, 'writ by the finger of the Divine'[1] often produces a text rich in the traditions of *trompe l'oeil*, irony, mimicry, and repetition. In this comic turn from the high ideals of the colonial imagination to its low mimetic literary effects, mimicry emerges as one of the most elusive and effective strategies of colonial power and knowledge.

Within that conflictual economy of colonial discourse which Edward Said[2] describes as the tension between the synchronic panoptical vision of domination – the demand for identity, stasis – and the counter-pressure of the diachrony of history – change, difference – mimicry represents an *ironic* compromise. If I may adapt Samuel Weber's formulation of the marginalizing vision of castration,[3] then colonial mimicry is the desire for a reformed, recognizable Other, as *a subject of a difference that is almost the same, but not quite*. Which is to say, that the discourse of mimicry is constructed around an *ambivalence*; in order to be effective, mimicry must continually produce its slippage, its excess, its difference. The authority of that mode of colonial discourse that I have called mimicry is therefore stricken by an indeterminacy: mimicry emerges as the representation of a difference that is itself a process of disavowal. Mimicry is, thus, the sign of a double articulation; a complex strategy of reform, regulation, and discipline, which 'appropriates' the Other as it visualizes power. Mimicry is also the sign of the inappropriate, however, a difference of recalcitrance which coheres the dominant strategic function of colonial power, intensifies surveillance, and poses an immanent threat to both 'normalized' knowledges and disciplinary powers.

The effect of mimicry on the authority of colonial discourse is profound and disturbing. For in 'normalizing' the colonial state or subject, the dream of post-Enlightenment civility alienates its own language of liberty and produces another knowledge of its norms. The ambivalence which thus informs this strategy is discernible, for example, in Locke's Second Treatise which *splits* to reveal the limitations of liberty in his double use of the word 'slave': first simply, descriptively as the locus of a legitimate exercise of power. What is articulated in that distance between the two uses of the absolute, imagined difference between the 'Colonial' State of Carolina and the Original State of Nature.

It is for this area between mimicry and mockery, where the reforming, civilizing mission is threatened by the displacing gaze of its disciplinary double, that my instances of colonial imitation come. What they all share is a discursive process by which the excess or slippage produced by the *ambivalence* of mimicry (almost the same, *but not quite*) does not merely 'rupture' the discourse, but becomes transformed into an uncertainty which fixes the colonial subject as a 'partial' presence. By 'partial' I mean both 'incomplete' and 'virtual'. It is as if the very emergence of the 'colonial' is dependent for its representation upon some strategic limitation or prohi-

bition *within* the authoritative discourse itself. The success of colonial appropriation depends on a proliferation of inappropriate objects that ensure its
strategic failure, so that mimicry is at once resemblance and menace.

A classic text of such partiality is Charles Grant's 'Observations on the
State of Society among the Asiatic Subjects of Great Britain' (1792)[4] which
was only superseded by James Mills's *History of India* as the most influential
early nineteenth-century account of Indian manners and morals. Grant's
dream of an evangelical system of mission education conducted
uncompromisingly in English was partly a belief in political reform along
Christian lines and partly an awareness that the expansion of company rule
in India required a system of 'interpellation' – a reform of manners, as Grant
put it, that would provide the colonial with 'a sense of personal identity as
we know it.' Caught between the desire for religious reform and the fear
that the Indians might become turbulent for liberty, Grant implies that it is,
in fact the 'partial' diffusion of Christianity, and the 'partial' influence of
moral improvements which will construct a particularly appropriate form
of colonial subjectivity. What is suggested is a process of reform through
which Christian doctrines might collude with divisive caste practices to
prevent dangerous political alliances. Inadvertently, Grant produces a
knowledge of Christianity as a form of social control which conflicts with
the enunciatory assumptions which authorize his discourse. In suggesting,
finally, that 'partial reform' will produce an empty form of 'the *imitation* of
English manners which will induce them [the colonial subjects] to remain
under our protection',[5] Grant mocks his moral project and violates the
Evidences of Christianity – a central missionary tenet – which forbade any
tolerance of heathen faiths.

The absurd extravagance of Macaulay's *Infamous Minute* (1835) – deeply
influenced by Charles Grant's *Observations* – makes a mockery of Oriental
learning until faced with the challenge of conceiving of a 'reformed' colonial
subject. Then the great tradition of European humanism seems capable only
of ironizing itself. At the intersection of European learning and colonial
power, Macaulay can conceive of nothing other than 'a class of interpreters
between us and the millions whom we govern – a class of persons Indian
in blood and colour, but English in tastes, in opinions, in morals and in
intellect'[6] – in other words a mimic man raised 'through our English School',
as a missionary educationist wrote in 1819, 'to form a corps of translators
and be employed in different departments of Labour',[7] The line of descent
of the mimic man can be traced through the works of Kipling, Forster,
Orwell, Naipaul, and to his emergence, most recently, in Benedict
Anderson's excellent essay on nationalism, as the anomalous Bipin Chandra
Pal.[8] He is the effect of a flawed colonial mimesis, in which to be Anglicized,
is *emphatically* not to be English.

The figure of mimicry is locatable within what Anderson describes as 'the
inner incompatability of empire and nation.'[9] It problematizes the signs of
racial and cultural priority, so that the 'national' is no longer naturalizable.

What emerges between mimesis and mimicry is a *writing*, a mode of representation, that marginalizes the monumentality of history, quite simply mocks its power to be a model, that power which supposedly makes it imitable. Mimicry *repeats* rather than *re-presents* and in that diminishing perspective merges Decoud's displaced European vision of Sulaco as

> the endlessness of civil strife where folly seemed even harder to bear than its ignominy . . . the lawlessness of a populace of all colours and races, barbarism, irremediable tyranny. . . . America is ungovernable.[10]

Or Ralph Singh's apostasy in Naipaul's *The Mimic Men*:

> We pretended to be real, to be learning, to be preparing ourselves for life, we mimic men of the New World, one unknown corner of it, with all its reminders of the corruption that came so quickly to the new.[11]

Both Decoud and Singh, and in their different ways Grant and Macaulay, are the parodists of history. Despite their intentions and invocations they inscribe the colonial text erratically, eccentrically across a body politic that refuses to be repesentative, in a narrative that refuses to be representational. The desire to merge as 'authentic' through mimicry – through a process of writing and repetition – is the final irony of partial representation.

What I have called mimicry is not the familiar exercise of *dependent* colonial relations through narcissistic identification so that, as Fanon has observed,[12] the black man stops being an actional person for only the white man can represent his self-esteem. Mimicry conceals no presence or identity behind its mask: it is not what Césaire describes as 'colonization-thingification'[13] behind which there stands the essence of the *présence Africaine*. The *menace* of mimicry is its *double* vision which in disclosing the ambivalence of colonial discourse also disrupts its authority. And it is a double-vision that is a result of what I've described as the partial representation/recognition of the colonial object. Grant's colonial as partial imitator, Macaulay's translator, Naipaul's colonial politician as playactor, Decoud as the scene setter of the *opéra bouffe* of the New World, these are the appropriate objects of a colonialist chain of command, authorized versions of otherness. But they are also, as I have shown, the figures of a doubling, the part-objects of a metonymy of colonial desire which alienates the modality and normality of those dominant discourses in which they emerge as 'inappropriate' colonial subjects. A desire that, through the repetition of *partial presence*, which is the basis of mimicry, articulates those disturbances of cultural, racial, and historical difference that menace the narcissistic demand of colonial authority. It is a desire that reverses 'in part' the colonial appropriation by now producing a partial vision of the colonizer's presence. A gaze of otherness, that shares the acuity of the genealogical gaze which, as Foucault describes it, liberates marginal elements and shatters the unity of man's being through which he extends his sovereignty.[14]

I want to turn to this process by which the look of surveillance returns as the displacing gaze of the disciplined, where the observer becomes the observed and 'partial' representation rearticulates the whole notion of *identity* and alienates it from essence. But not before observing that even an exemplary history like Eric Stokes's *The English Utilitarians in India* acknowledges the anomalous gaze of otherness but finally disavows it in a contradictory utterance:

> Certainly India played *no* central part in fashioning the distinctive qualities of English civilisation. In many ways it acted as a disturbing force, a magnetic power placed at the periphery tending to distort the natural development of Britain's character. . . .[15]

What is the nature of the hidden threat of the partial gaze? How does mimicry emerge as the subject of the scopic drive and the object of colonial surveillance? How is desire disciplined, authority displaced?

If we turn to a Freudian figure to address these issues of colonial textuality, that form of difference that is mimicry – *almost the same but not quite* – will become clear. Writing of the partial nature of fantasy, caught *inappropriately*, between the unconscious and the preconscious, making problematic, like mimicry, the very notion of 'origins', Freud has this to say:

> Their mixed and split origin is what decides their fate. We may compare them with individuals of mixed race who taken all round resemble white men but who betray their coloured descent by some striking feature or other and on that account are excluded from society and enjoy none of the privileges.[16]

Almost the same but not white: the visibility of mimicry is always produced at the site of interdiction. It is a form of colonial discourse that is uttered *inter dicta*: a discourse at the crossroads of what is known and permissible and that which though known must be kept concealed; a discourse uttered between the lines and as such both against the rules and within them. The question of the representation of difference is therefore always also a problem of authority. The 'desire' of mimicry, which is Freud's *striking feature* that reveals so little but makes such a big difference, is not merely that impossibility of the Other which repeatedly resists signification. The desire of colonial mimicry – an interdictory desire – may not have an object, but it has strategic objectives which I shall call the *metonymy of presence*.

Those inappropriate signifiers of colonial discourse – the difference between being English and being Anglicized; the identity between stereotypes which, through repetition, also become different; the discriminatory identities constructed across traditional cultural norms and classifications, the Simian Black, the Lying Asiatic – all these are metonymies of presence. They are strategies of desire in discourse that make the anomalous representation of the colonized something other than a process of 'the return of the repressed', what Fanon unsatisfactorily characterized as collective catharsis.[17] These instances of metonymy are the nonrepressive productions of contradictory and multiple belief. They cross the boundaries of the culture of enunciation through a strategic confusion of the metaphoric and metonymic axes of the cultural production of meaning. For each of these instances of 'a difference that is almost the same but not quite' inadvertently creates a crisis for the cultural priority given to the *metaphoric* as the process of repression and substitution which negotiates the difference between paradigmatic systems and classifications. In mimicry, the representation of identity and meaning is rearticulated along the axis of metonymy. As Lacan reminds us, mimicry is like camouflage, not a harmonization or repression of difference, but a form of resemblance that differs/defends presence by displaying it in part, metonymically. Its threat, I would add, comes from the prodigious and strategic production of conflictual, fantastic, discriminatory 'identity effects' in the play of a power that is elusive because it hides no essence, no 'itself'. And that form of *resemblance* is the most terrifying thing to behold, as Edward Long testifies in his *History of Jamaica* (1774). At the end of a tortured, negrophobic passage, that shifts anxiously between piety, prevarication, and perversion, the text finally confronts its fear; nothing other than the repetition of its resemblance 'in part':

> (Negroes) are represented by all authors as the vilest of human kind, to which they have little more pretension of resemblance *than what arises from their exterior forms* (my italics).[18]

From such a colonial encounter between the white presence and its black semblance, there emerges the question of the ambivalence of mimicry as a problematic of colonial subjection. For if Sade's scandalous theatricalization of language repeatedly reminds us that discourse can claim 'no priority', then the work of Edward Said will not let us forget that the 'ethnocentric and erratic will to power from which texts can spring'[19] is itself a theater of war. Mimicry, as the metonymy of presence is, indeed, such an erratic, eccentric strategy of authority in colonial discourse. Mimicry does not merely destroy narcissistic authority through the repetitious slippage of difference and desire. It is the process of the *fixation* of the colonial as a form of cross-classificatory, discriminatory knowledge in the defiles of an interdictory discourse, and therefore necessarily raises the question of the *authorization* of colonial representations. A question of authority that goes beyond the subject's lack of priority (castration) to a historical crisis in the conceptuality of colonial man as an *object* of regulatory power, as the subject of racial, cultural, national representation.

'This culture . . . fixed in its colonial status', Fanon suggests, '(is) both present and mummified, it testified against its members. It defines them in fact without appeal.'[20] The ambivalence of mimicry – almost but not quite – suggests that the fetishized colonial culture is potentially and strategically an insurgent counter-appeal. What I have called its 'identify-effects', are always crucially *split*. Under cover of camouflage, mimicry, like the fetish, is a part-object that radically revalues the normative knowledges of the priority of race, writing, history. For the fetish mimes the forms of authority at the point at which it deauthorizes them. Similarly, mimicry rearticulates presence in terms of its 'otherness', that which it disavows. There is a crucial difference between this *colonial* articulation of man and his doubles and that which Foucault describes as 'thinking the unthought'[21] which, for nineteenth-century Europe, is the ending of man's alienation by reconciling him with his essence. The colonial discourse that articulates an *interdictory* 'otherness' is precisely the 'other scene' of this nineteenth-century European desire for an authentic historical consciousness.

The 'unthought' across which colonial man is articulated is that process of classificatory confusion that I have described as the metonymy of the substitutive chain of ethical and cultural discourse. This results in the *splitting* of colonial discourse so that two attitudes towards external reality persist; one takes reality into consideration while the other disavows it and replaces it by a product of desire that repeats, rearticulates 'reality' as mimicry.

So Edward Long can say with authority, quoting variously, Hume, Eastwick, and Bishop Warburton in his support, that:

> Ludicrous as the opinion may seem I do not think that an orangutang husband would be any dishonour to a Hottentot female.[22]

Such contradictory articulations of reality and desire – seen in racist stereotypes, statements, jokes, myths – are not caught in the doubtful circle of the return of the repressed. They are the effects of a disavowal that denies the differences of the other but produces in its stead forms of authority and multiple belief that alienate the assumptions of 'civil' discourse. If, for a while, the ruse of desire is calculable for the uses of discipline soon the repetition of guilt, justification, pseudoscientific theories, superstition, spurious authorities, and classifications can be seen as the desperate effort to 'normalize' *formally* the disturbance of a discourse of splitting that violates the rational, enlightened claims of its enunciatory modality. The ambivalence of colonial authority repeatedly turns from *mimicry* – a difference that is almost nothing but not quite – to *menace* – a difference that is almost total but not quite. And in that other scene of colonial power, where history turns to farce and presence to 'a part', can be seen the twin figures of narcissism and paranoia that repeat furiously, uncontrollably.

In the ambivalent world of the 'not quite/not white', on the margins of metropolitan desire, the *founding objects* of the Western world become the eratic, eccentric, accidental *objets trouvés* of the colonial discourse – the part-objects of presence. It is then that the body and the book loose their representational authority. Black skin splits under the racist gaze, displaced into signs of bestiality, genitalia, grostesquerie, which reveal the phobic myth of the undifferentiated whole white body. And the holiest of books – the Bible – bearing both the standard of the cross and the standard of empire finds itself strangely dismembered. In May 1817 a missionary wrote from Bengal:

Still everyone would gladly receive a Bible. And why? – that he may lay it up as a curiosity for a few pice; or use it for waste paper. Such it is well known has been the common fate of these copies of the Bible. . . . Some have been bartered in the markets, others have been thrown in snuff shops and used as wrapping paper.[23]

Notes

*This paper was first presented as a contribution to a panel of 'Colonialist and Post-Colonialist Discourse', organized by Gayatri Chakravorty Spivak for the Modern Language Association Convention in New York, December 1983. I would like to thank Professor Spivak for inviting me to participate on the panel and Dr. Stephen Feuchtwang for his advice in the preparation of the paper.

1 Cited in Eric Stokes, *The Political Ideas of English Imperialism* (Oxford, Oxford University Press, 1960), pp. 17–18.
2 Edward Said, *Orientalism* (New York, Pantheon Books, 1978), p. 240.
3 Samuel Weber: 'The Sideshow, Or: Remarks on a Canny Moment', *Modern Language Notes*, vol. 88, no. 6 (1973), p. 1112.
4 Charles Grant, 'Observations on the State of Society among the Asiatic Subjects of Great Britain', *Sessional Papers 1812–13*, X (282), East India Company.
5 Ibid., chap. 4, p. 104.
6 T.B. Macaulay, 'Minute on Education,' in *Sources of Indian Tradition*, vol. II, ed. William Theodore de Bary (New York, Columbia University Press, 1958), p. 49.
7 Mr Thomason's communication to the Church Missionary Society, September 5, 1819, in *The Missionary Register*, 1821, pp. 54–5.
8 Benedict Anderson, *Imagined Communities* (London, Verso, 1983), p. 88.
9 Ibid., pp. 88–9.
10 Joseph Conrad, *Nostromo* (London, Penguin, 1979), p. 161.
11 V.S. Naipaul, *The Mimic Men* (London, Penguin, 1967), p. 146.
12 Frantz Fanon, *Black Skin, White Masks* (London, Paladin, 1970), p. 109.
13 Aimé Césaire, *Discourse on Colonialism* (New York, Monthly Review Press, 1972), p. 21.
14 Michel Foucault, 'Nietzsche, Genealogy, History', in *Language, Counter-Memory, Practice,* tr. Donald F. Bouchard and Sherry Simon (Ithaca, NY, Cornell University Press), p. 153.
15 Eric Stokes, *The English Utilitarians and India,* (Oxford, Oxford University Press, 1959), p. xi.
16 Sigmund Freud, 'The Unconscious' (1915), *SE*, XIV, pp. 190–1.
17 Fanon, *Black Skin, White Masks*, p. 103.
18 Edward Long, *A History of Jamaica* (1774), vol. II, p. 353.
19 Edward Said, 'The Text, the World, the Critic', in *Textual Strategies*, ed. J.V. Harari (Ithaca, NY, Cornell University Press, 1979), p. 184.
20 Frantz Fanon, 'Racism and Culture', in *Toward the African Revolution* (London, Pelican, 1967), p. 44.
21 Michel Foucault, *The Order of Things* (New York, Pantheon, 1970), part II, chap. 9.
22 Long, *A History of Jamaica*, p. 364.
23 *The Missionary Register*, May 1817, p. 186.

SECTION FIVE

LOOKING BACK ON THE STATES OF THEORY

Derrida's essay is offered as a retrospective meditation on the significance of the so-called 'theoretical revolution'. He claims that the explosion of theory into literary studies has produced a new multidisciplinarity which is unique to the institution of literature. Theory makes no claim to be either science or philosophy but has been articulated in ways which have profoundly challenged and destabilized the foundations of both. Literary criticism emerges as a new model for knowledge – neither science nor art, but a writing practice which disturbs conventional distinctions between the two.

---

33 Jacques Derrida,

'Some Statements and Truisms About Neo-Logisms, Newisms, Postisms, Parasitisms, and Other Small Seismisms', David Carroll, ed. *The States of 'Theory'* (1990), pp. 81–94

What is this 'theory'?

First, it isn't what is called 'theory' in mathematics or physics. 'Theory' isn't a scientific theory; it isn't a theorization or a set of theorems. Scientists would shrug their shoulders if what is being done in the name of 'theory' in the American departments of literature was put forward as a scientific, indeed epistemologcal 'theory'. They would indeed be right if there was a claim to adjust this concept of 'theory' to their models of scientific theory. But since no such claim is being made, they would be wrong because they wouldn't have understood this concept of theory.

Second, this concept, which isn't scientific in the classical sense, isn't a philosophical concept of 'theory' either. No philosopher – *stricto sensu* – in no tradition and in no philosophical institution in the world, including this country, will recognize this concept of 'theoria' or of theoretics in what is done, said, published under the name of 'theory' in some American departments of literature. All the philosophers in the world would say: this isn't, strictly speaking, worthy of what, in philosophy, we call *theoretics*.

If this 'theory' is admissible neither from the point of view of science nor from that of philosophy, that is, from the point of view of the episteme, which, opposing the *doxa*, has always legitimated, valorized, and distinguished theoretics, what, then, constitutes, determines, legitimates what for the last twenty years has been called 'theory' in this country? What exactly is it? And why are there also so many people, and not only among scientists and philosophers, who are – quotation and quotation marks again – 'against "theory" '? The fact that what I will call from now on 'the states of theory' – instead of each time saying 'theory' in quotation marks – is neither scientific nor philosophical must not be interpreted negatively. The 'States' theory' isn't *a* theory but the opening of a space, the emergence of an element in which a certain number of phenomena usually associated with literature will call for trans-, inter-, and above all ultra-disciplinary approaches, which, up to now, met nowhere, in no department, in no area of any discipline. They will call for a multiplicity of problematics which are now often classified, serialised in a sometimes comical and irrational way in the programs of some universities and departments, in the blurbs of some books, and which Jonathan Culler mentioned in the article I quoted a moment ago. Forgive me for quoting a long passage, especially a long passage in which I am referred to, but I don't want to play here the purposeless game of academic politeness, and it wouldn't be fair not to quote, for this one reason, a text which seems to me important here if we want to start thinking what 'the States' theory', 'theory' with quotation marks, means here.

> The major critical development of the past twenty years in America has been the impact of various theoretical perspectives and discourses: linguistics, psychoanalysis, feminism structuralism, deconstruction. A corollary of this has been the expansion of the domain of literary studies to include many concerns previously remote from it. In most American universities today a course on Freud is more likely to be offered in the English or French Departments than in the Psychology Department; Nietzsche, Sartre, Gadamer, Heidegger, Derrida are more often discussed by teachers of literature than teachers of philosophy; Saussure is neglected by linguists and appreciated by students and teachers of literature. The writings of authors such as these fall into a miscellaneous genre whose most convenient designation is simply 'theory', which today has come to refer to works that succeed in challenging and reorienting thinking in fields other than those to which they ostensibly belong, because their analyses of language, or mind, or history, or culture offer novel and persuasive accounts of signification.[1]

The emergence of this new element (with the exportation of discourses outside of their field, with the taking into account of those transplants, of those multiplicities of languages and axiomatics, of the irreducibility of the literary and of language, of sexual difference, of the unconscious, etc.) is *positive*: it is a mutation which no area of the institutional discipline had been able to perform, neither in this country nor in any other. However, this mutation, as enriching and positive as it may be, remains dangerous and is felt to be so. For it remains to be explained why this 'States' theory' – in its irreducible emergence – cannot, does not, and must not want to claim the title of a science or a philosophy.

It is because it has been accompanied, carried on, provoked, penetrated (as you wish, I don't know which word is best and no classical schema of causality seems relevant here) by a form of questioning and of writing, of questioning writing but *not* only questioning, which destabilized the axiomatics, the founding and organizing schemes of science and philosophy themselves – and even the new categories in the history of ideas (such as episteme or paradigm) that allowed one to think this new configuration in the mode of self-consciousness.

Let us call this an effect of deconstruction. And with this word I refer neither to specific texts nor to specific authors, and above all not to this formation which disciplines the process and effect of deconstruction into *a* theory or *a* method called deconstructionism or deconstructionisms. This effect of deconstruction disorganized not only the axiomatics of philosophical and scientific discourses as such, of epistemological discourse, of the various methodologies of literary criticism (New Criticism, formalism, thematism, classical or Marxist historicism), but even the axiomatics of knowledge simultaneously at work in the 'States' theory' (I quote Culler again): 'linguistics, psychoanalysis, feminism [wherever, I want to add, 'feminism' formed itself into an institutional discipline and into a corpus of philosophical – hence phallogocentric – axioms], structuralism.' Hence an element of the series, that is, deconstruction, no longer simply belonged to the series, and introduced into it an element of perturbation, disorder, or irreducible turmoil – that is, a principle of dislocation. I'm now going to describe, in the most schematic way, a certain number of *typical* consequences – i.e., general and regularly occurring consequences. For convenience, I'll use again the word 'jetty', in which I distinguish, on the one hand, the force of the movement which throws something or throws itself (*jette* or *se jette*) forward and backwards at the same time, prior to any subject, object, or project, prior to any rejection or abjection, from, on the other hand, its institutional and protective consolidation, which can be compared to the jetty, the pier in a harbor meant to break the waves and maintain low tide for boats at anchor or for swimmers. Of course, these two functions of the *jetty* are ideally distinct, but in fact they are difficult to dissociate, if not indissociable. All the difficulties of analysis, all the confusions, all the ambiguities lie not only in the difficulty of an effective principial distinction of the two jetties, of the two phenomena of the jetty, but also in the strategic interests involved – for all sides and for various reasons – in confusing or creating a certain interdependence between the two.

For the convenience of terminology, and again in relation to the title of the colloquium, I will call the first jetty the destabilizing jetty or even more artificially the *devastating* jetty, and the other one the stabilizing, establishing, or simply *stating* jetty – in reference to the supplementary fact that at this moment of *stasis*, of stanza, the stabilizing jetty proceeds by predicative clauses, reassures with assertory statements, with assertions, with statements such as 'this is that': for example, deconstruction is this or that.

For instance, one assertion, one statement, a true one, would be, and I would subscribe to it: Deconstruction is neither a theory nor a philosophy. It is neither a school nor a method. It is not even a discourse, nor an act, nor a practice. It is what happens, what is happening today in what they call society, politics, diplomacy, economics, historical reality, and so on and so forth. Deconstruction is the case. I say this not only because I think it is true and because I could demonstrate it if we had time, but also to give an example of a *statement* in the static form of the jetty.

In its essential vagueness – which in my opinion is in no way negative – the concept of 'theory' that we are discussing at the moment had no counterpart, either in this country or anywhere else in any discipline, as I have already said, until the end of the 1960s. I quote here Paul de Man, who writes in *The Resistance to Theory* – the resistance to theory, a concept and a slogan which I will comment on in a moment – 'Yet with the possible exception of Kenneth Burke and, in some respects, Northrop Frye, none of these authors (Brooks, Wellek, Warren, Brower) would have considered themselves theoreticians in the post 1960 sense of the term, nor did their work provoke as strong reactions, positive or negative, as that of later theoreticians – there were polemics, no doubt, and differences in approach that cover a wide spectrum of divergences, yet the fundamental curriculum of literary studies as well as the talent and training expected for them were not being seriously challenged'.[2] Hence, it is all this, and especially the curriculum, which has changed, which has been challenged within the institution by the devastating or destabilizing jetty.

But the paradox, as far as the effects of the deconstructive jetty are concerned, is that it has simultaneously provoked in the last twenty years several absolutely heterogeneous types of 'resistance to theory'. In trying to classify their 'ideal types' I will try to conceptualize both what 'theory' means in that context and what is here the strange and disconcerting logic of resistance.

There is to begin with, I would say, the *destabilizing* and *devastating* jetty itself, and its effects of deconstruction – a jetty which is paradoxically, in itself, *a* 'resistance to theory'. It is a resistance which produces theory and theories. It resists theorization first because it functions in a place which the jetty questions, and destabilizes the conditions of the possibility of objectivity, the relationship to the *object*, everything that constitutes and institutes the assurance of *subjectivity* in the indubitable presence of the *cogito*, the certainty of self-consciousness, the original project, the relation to the other determined as ecological intersubjectivity, the principle of reason and the system of representation associated with it, and hence everything that supports a modern concept of theory as objectivity. Deconstruction resists theory then because it demonstrates the impossibility of closure, of the closure of an ensemble or totality on an organized network of theorems, laws, rules, methods. The coherence or the consistency of the deconstructive jetty is not a theoretical set, nor is it a system either, inasmuch as the system, in the strict sense of the term, is a very determined form of assembling, of being-together of a set of theoretical propositions. And it is not a *system* because the deconstructive jetty in itself is no more propositional than *positional*; it deconstructs precisely the *thesis*, both as philosophical thesis (and deconstruction is no more philosophical than scientific) and as *theme*. As a matter of fact, it has included as one of its essential paths in the literary field a deconstruction of thematic, or rather thematicist, reading.

Neither philosophical, nor scientific, nor critical (in the sense of literary criticism but also in the Kantian sense, inasmuch as criticism assumes propositional judgment and decidability), the deconstructive jetty isn't theoretical, it resists theory in another sense. From the start – and this has become more and more pronounced – it has never simply been concerned with discursive meaning or content, the thematics or the semantics of a discourse. The reason is because it isn't simply a reading or an interpretation, but also because the deconstruction of phallogocentrism placed itself in a place where insulating semantic content (on the one hand, the signified, and, on the other, the signifier, as we used to say twenty years ago) – that is, thematic and conceptual content – was impracticable in a rigorous way. Hence the necessity for deconstruction to deal with texts in a different way than as discursive contents, themes or theses, but always as institutional structures and, as is commonly said, as being political-juridical-sociohistorical – none of these last words being reliable enough to be used easily, hence their relative rare use in the most cautious texts called deconstructive. This in no way means a lack of interest or a withdrawal as regards those things – reality, history, society, law, politics – and moreover this is absolutely consistent with the concept of text which is based on the deconstruction of logocentrism and irreducible to discourse or the book or to what some still delimit as the textual by trying to distinguish it from or oppose it to reality, to the social, the historical, etc. This is the normal monstrosity I talked about a moment ago. Using an outdated language, one might thus say that the deconstructive jetty isn't essentially theoretical, thetic or thematic because it is also ethical-political. But of course, for the most obvious reasons, this assertion calls for the strictest vigilance and quotation marks. Finally, the deconstructive jetty affirmatively resists theory, particularly literary theory, because it isn't *regional* – it not only doesn't fix the text in a thematic or thetic station, a *stanza*, but it also first deconstructs – and this was my primary concern in *of Grammatology* – the hierarchizing structure, which, in philosophy, as a general metaphysics, a fundamental ontology, a transcendental critique or phenomenology, orders a multiplicity of regions, discourses, or beings under a fundamental or transcendental agency. The deconstructive jetty institutes itself neither as a regional theory (for example, of literature) nor as a theory of theories. It is in this way that it is a form of resistance. And in addition, it was articulated with a thinking of *resistance* (or rather of *restance*) which I cannot discuss here.

As I have said, this form of resistance to theory didn't consist in reactively opposing theorization but on the contrary in regularly deconstructing the philosophical assumptions of existing theories or the theories implicit in discourses denigrating philosophy or theory. What was at stake then was to exceed the theoretical rather than to hinder it and take positions 'against theory'. The result, both paradoxical and foreseeable, is that the very thing which exceeds at the same time the theoretical, the thematic, the thetic, the philosophical, and the scientific provokes, as gestures of reappropriation and suture, theoretical movements, productions of theorems, which, in the sort of hyperactivity, turmoil, turbulence which has characterised the past twenty years, are themselves so many forms of *resistance*, but this time in another sense, to the deconstructive jetty. This time the resistance institutes – it is indeed essentially instituting – the consolidating and *stabilizing* structure of the jetty. It constructs and fortifies theories, it offers thematics and theses, it organizes methods, disciplines, indeed schools. But there again this institutional and stabilizing jetty, in which the term 'resistance' could have the meaning it has in the French expression *résistance des matériaux* (strength of materials) – that which architects must carefully calculate in order to avoid collapses – (this jetty) constructs *fortifications* whose relation to the deconstructive jetty may be of two, or, depending on the case, three types. But in any case, the resistance concerns what threatens, exceeds, or destabilizes the *stanza* of a coherent theory, its standing or statement. This time, the resistance reconstitutes the stanza into a system, a method, a discipline, and in the worst case an institution with its legitimating orthodoxy.

The closest type, the stabilizing jetty which resembles the destabilizing jetty most, is what is called poststructuralism, alias deconstructionism. It's not bad, it isn't an evil, and even if it were one, it would be a necessary evil. It consists in formalizing certain strategic necessities of the deconstructive jetty and in putting forward – thanks to this formalization – a system of technical rules, teachable methodological procedures, a discipline, school phenomena, a kind of knowledge, principles, theorems, which are for the most part principles of interpretation and reading (rather than of writing). Deconstructionism isn't monolithic – among deconstructionisms and deconstructionists there are differences in style, orientation, and even serious conflicts – but I think one can say that there is *deconstructionism in general* each time that the destabilizing jetty closes and stabilizes itself in a teachable set of theorems, each time that there is self-presentation of *a*, or more problematically, of *the* theory. We know that deconstructionism mainly developed in the space of literary studies, concerned precisely with the difficulty, which remains total, of delimiting a field or an essence of literature. It wouldn't be correct to say that the elements in deconstructionism which may *sometimes* be stabilizing and normalizing with regard to the effects of the deconstructive jetty stem from the fact that deconstructionism mainly developed in the space of literary studies. For this would give in one way or another the impression that, as the crudest readers sometimes suggest, deconstruction gives into formalism or aestheticism, indeed to a textualism which would confuse text and discourse, page, book, and the world, society or history and the library. No, I think that the most advanced things happening in literary studies avoid these traps. And this is not fortuitous. It is undoubtedly due to literature. When Gasché, for example, in his latest book[3] and elsewhere, reproaches certain literary deconstructionists for not being radical enough because they fail to reexamine the premises of or even the kind of priority given to the deconstruction of philosophy, his gesture seems to me at the same time necessary and risky. Necessary, because to reconstitute the deconstructive jetty into theory, into a theory, into a deconstructionist jetty, runs the risk of losing the essential force and excess which consist in unsettling the entire philosophical foundation of which I have already spoken. It runs the risk of reconstituting an old concept of text, of confining oneself to one area (the literary one), etc. But conversely, the equivocal risk that Gasché's book runs – not necessarily in the texture and in the careful and cautious details of his analysis, which are subtle enough to avoid this risk, but in the global and massive effect to which books are unfortunately reduced once they have been closed and once they start being discussed – this risk would be to reconstitute the deconstructive jetty as a *philosophy of deconstruction*, with – I use Gasché's words, without keeping the 'quasi' and the quotation marks that attenuate and complicate them with its 'infrastructures', its sysᵗᵉmaticity, etc. One would then be faced with a deconstructionist philosophy or metaphilosophy, with a theory of theories, a deconstructionist supertheory. Once again it doesn't seem to me that it is Gasché or what he writes that runs this risk, but rather it is the global effect of this nevertheless necessary appeal to the philosophical scene of deconstruction. Besides, this appeal should be addressed more to philosophers than to literary critics.

It is in reaction against a certain deconstructionist post-structural*ism*, against the image of a certain stabilizing jetty, that the most recent and most interesting developments of Marxism and of what is called new historicism posit themselves. If deconstructionism were what it is accused of being, and *when* it is and *where* it is formalist, aestheticist, ignorant of reality, of history, enclosed in language, word play, books, literature, indifferent to politics – I would consider Marxism and new historicism absolutely legitimate, necessary, urgent. Moreover I believe in a certain necessity, sometimes in a certain novelty, if not of the theory at least of style of investigation, and thus of certain objects or areas of research, of what presents itself under the title of Marxism or new historicism. I very sincerely wish that they develop even more, and I would be very happy to contribute to this development. It doesn't seem to me that any rejection of these attempts is desirable or interesting. But as theories, this Marxism and this new historicism have at least one trait in common (for I don't want to confuse one with the other) in the present stage of their critique. It is that they institute themselves in reaction to a deconstructionist poststructuralism which is itself either nothing but a figure or a stabilizing reappropriation of deconstruction or else a caricatural myth projected by Marxists and new historicists out of self-interest or misunderstanding.

I will say a few concluding words, very rapidly and very dryly, about these misunderstandings. Marxism and new historicism are very different theoretical phenomena. The former is a theory, the latter sometimes associates itself with reactions 'against theory' (to quote the by now well-known title which won its fame more as a symptom of resistance than for its content). Nevertheless they have in common only that their most *significant* present traits come from *within* the space of the deconstructive jetty and consist *in* their marked opposition to stabilizing deconstruction*ism*. This is why they seem to me more interesting than any reaction which is directly conservative or simply and precisely 'reactive' and of which I won't say anything for lack of time, although it is much more widely represented and much stronger than what we say about it in a small circle concerned with more subtle differences. Of course, it sometimes happens that the different types contaminate each other.

I will disregard – for lack of time and because these mistakes are really too crude, even if they are long lasting – everything that consists in reducing the concept of text to that of written discourse, in forgetting that deconstruction is all the less confined to the prisonhouse of language because it *starts* by tackling logocentrism. I refer here to Dominick LaCapra's book *Rethinking Intellectual History: Text, Context, Language*,[4] which, in its reading of Jameson and Hayden White, discusses some of these misinterpretations and points out some essential complications.

Disregarding these misunderstandings, I'll nevertheless say a few words about history, although they could be transposed to 'reality', 'society', 'politics', and other similar big words. The criticism addressed by certain Marxists or new historicists concerning the treatment of history relies on a fundamental misunderstanding, which is sometimes shared by certain deconstructionist poststructualists. For deconstruction starts, so to speak, with a *double gesture*.

It starts, on the one hand, with a critique of *historicism*, which radicalizes the Husserlian critique of historicism, as it is developed in 'philosophy as a Rigorous Science' against Dilthey, the critique of the theory of 'world views', the empiricisms, relativisms, and scepticisms, which follow each other in their inability to account for something like a theorem or a philosopheme, for science, philosophy, or philosophy as science, and for any project of universal and true discourse. I have totally subscribed, and I still do, to this Husserlian argumentation, to this critical sequence of phenomenology, which seems to me to be indispensable for any deconstruction, even if it isn't enough and if it meets there its own limit. It is especially indispensable to free from historicist empiricism the original possibility of ideal objects – whether they be scientific theorems or cultural productions – for example, aesthetic or literary productions.

For, on the other hand, as you know, Husserl doesn't stop with this critique of empirical historicism. And he didn't present it in the name of an ahistorical Platonism. He only carries through the critique of empirical historicism in order to bring out, recognize, and describe the historical specificity of the theorems, of the ideal objects of science – for example, of mathematics – and indeed he does it in the name of a transcendental historicity. To pay attention to history, to history in general and to the original historicity of culture, language, and above all of theory, of the institutions which theorems are – since this is what we are here to talk about – all this assumes at least that one follow this sequence, which I call Husserlian, through to its end. It has been indispensable for me – since *The Origin of Geometry* – for what later developed under the title of deconstruction, even if it led to a deconstructive reading of Husserl and Heidegger. This is also the reason why the philosophical retreading of the relation of deconstruction to philosophy is so necessary, so constantly necessary.

Finally, for this very reason, the deconstructive jetty is, throughout, motivated, set into motion by a concern with history, even if it leads to destabilizing certain concepts of history, the absolutizing or hypo*stasing* concept of a neo-Hegelian or Marxist kind, the Husserlian concept of history, and even the Heideggerian concept of historical epochality. I refer here to Bennington's text 'Demanding History' in *Post-Structuralism and the Question of History*,[5] which offers a remarkable elaboration and which formalizes in the most rigorous and economical way – as always – the givens of this strange situation. As Young and Bennington remind us in the introduction to the same book: 'If post-structuralism reintroduces history into structuralism (or, more accurately, shows that effects of history have been reduced), it also poses questions to the concept of history as such'.[6] This is the very difference between *New Criticism* and *poststructuralism*, the analogies between which, given their careful approach to texts, have been underlined by certain critics. But poststructuralism – and deconstruction in general – also dislocates the borders, the framing of texts, everything which should preserve their immanence and make possible an internal reading, or merely reading in the classical sense of the term. And, by the way, I think that the problematic of the border and of framing – that is, of context – is seriously missing in new historicism; and I think that this is the question new historicists should address with the utmost urgency in some of the texts called deconstructionist. This would avoid the reconstitution of a new archivism or of a new documentalism.

I have taken up more than enough of your time and abused your patience. I won't conclude with a *statement*. Having thrown out (*jeté*) a few disordered aphorisms about the *jetty*, I want simply to make it clear, for the *chute* or the *envoi* that this word or concept of 'jetty' remains essentially equivocal, in the same manner as 'theory'. But the equivocation which I would like to clear up, at the moment of the chute, concerns precisely the *chute*, the fall. You may have had the impression that I was making a distinction between the destabilizing jetty (for example, deconstructions) and the stabilizing jetty (for example, the reappropriations and the reactions in the form of deconstructionism, Marxist or new historicist theories, or discourses 'against theory'), as a distinction between the movement which gives momentum, on the one hand, and, on the other hand, the inert fallout which, in a style that would remind us of Bergson, would take momentum and life back down, towards inert solidity. It would be a final and very serious misunderstanding. The destabilizing jetty doesn't go up. On the contrary, it is the stabilizing jetty that goes upwards. It stands; it is a standing, a station, or a stanza; it erects, institutes, and edifies. It is edifying, essentially edifying. The destabilizing jetty goes neither up nor down; it may not go anywhere. Since it is late and there would be too much to say about this topology, let's assume that the jetty – a jetty with or without a relation to its other – doesn't exist. It doesn't consist in anything, it doesn't have any *status*, it simply doesn't take place, doesn't have an exclusive place which could be attributed to it. Deconstruction, in that sense, doesn't have any status, any theoretical status. There is no manifesto for it, no manifestation as such. Those who set themselves against it know this very well. In Northern California, in this very state, I was told last week that Searle, once he had explained his views on literature, announced to his audience that for twenty years deconstruction hasn't existed, or, more precisely, that it has consisted of, and here I quote Searle, a 'mist' hiding everything. This is true, it has neither consistency nor existence, and besides, it wouldn't have lasted very long anyway if it had. Especially in the States. All I would have liked to say, if I had had time, is something concerning the 'jetty' (for example, through and beyond Heidegger's *Geworfenheit* and Artaud's *subjectile*). Can we, do we have the right to ask the question: What is this 'jetty' before and outside any object, subject (the 'subject in question', someone has said), project, or reject, before and outside any consistency, any existence, any stanza? What is this jetty whose *restance* defies all questions in the form of 'what is?' and of 'What does it mean?'

In short, I have tried to introduce here in a very preliminary way this quasi-concept of 'jetty' which has no status yet either in the state of theory or in the 'States' theory' today. And I have tried to explain the reasons why it would be very difficult to turn it into a theorem or a 'theoretical object'.

Notes

1 J. Culler, 'Criticism and Institutions: The American University', p. 87.
2 P. de Man, *The Resistance to Theory* (Minneapolis, University of Minnesota Press, 1986), p. 6.
3 Gasché, *The Tain of the Mirror: Derrida and the Philosophy of Reflection* (Cambridge, Mass., Harvard University Press, 1986).
4 D. LaCapra, *Rethinking Intellectual History: Text, Context, Language* (Ithaca, NY, Cornell University Press, 1983).

SELECT BIBLIOGRAPHY

General Works on Literary Theory

Douglas Atkins, G. and Morrow, Laura, eds, *Contemporary Literary Theory* (London, Macmillan, 1989).

Eagleton, T., *Literary Theory: An Introduction* (Oxford, Basil Blackwell, 1983).

— *The Ideology of the Aesthetic* (Oxford, Blackwell, 1990).

Hawthorn, J., *Unlocking the Text* (London, Edward Arnold 1987).

Jefferson, A. and Robey, D. ed., *Modern Literary Theory: A Comparative Introduction* (London, Batsford Academic and Educational Ltd, 1982).

Selden, R., *A Reader's Guide to Contemporary Literary Theory* (Brighton, Sussex, Harvester Press, 1985).

Russian Formalism

Bann, S. and Bowlt, J.E., eds, *Russian Formalism* (Edinburgh, Scottish Academic Press, 1973).

Bennett, T. *Formalism and Marxism* (London and New York, Methuen, 1979).

Erlich, V., *Russian Formalism: History-Doctrine* (3rd edn) (New Haven and London, Yale University Press, 1981).

Jameson, F., *The Prison-House of Language: A Critical Account of Structuralism and Russian Formalism* (Princeton and London: Princeton University Press, 1972).

Lemon, L.T. and Reis, M.J., *Russian Formalist Criticism: Four Essays* (Lincoln: University of Nebraska Press, 1965).

Matejka, L. and Pomorska, K. eds, *Readings in Russian Poetics: Formalist and Structuralist Views* (Cambridge, Mass., and London, MIT Press, 1971).

Medvedev, P.N. and Bakhtin, M.M., *The Formal Method in Literary Scholarship: An Introduction to Sociological Poetics* (Baltimore, MD, and London, Johns Hopkins University Press, 1978).

Saussure and Structuralism

Barthes, R., *Elements of Semiology*, tr. A. Lavers and C. Smith (London, Jonathan Cape, 1967).

— *Writing Degree Zero*, tr. A. Lavers and C. Smith (London, Jonathan Cape, 1967).

Culler, J., *Structuralist Poetics: Structuralism, Linguistics and the Study of Literature* (London, Routledge & Kegan Paul, 1975).

— *Saussure* (London, Fontana/Collins, 1976).
— *The Pursuit of Signs* (London: Routledge & Kegan Paul, 1981).
Eco, U., *A Theory of Semiotics* (Bloomington and London: Indiana University Press, 1977).
Genette, G., *Narrative Discourse* (Oxford, Blackwell, 1980).
Hawkes, T. *Structuralism and Semiotics* (London, Methuen, 1977).
Jackson, L., *The Poverty of Structuralism: Literature and Structuralist Theory* (London and New York, Longman, 1991).
Lodge, D., *The Modes of Modern Writing: Metaphor, Metonymy and the Typology of Modern Literature* (London, Edward Arnold, 1977).
— *Working with Structuralism* (London, Routledge and Kegan Paul, 1981).
Macksey, R. and Donato, E., eds, *The Structuralist Controversy: The Languages of Criticism and the Sciences of Man* (Baltimore, MD, Johns Hopkins University Press, 1972).
Rimmon-Kenan, S., *Narrative Fiction: Contemporary Poetics* (London, Methuen, 1983).
Robey, D., ed, *Structuralism: an Introduction* (Oxford: Clarendon Press, 1973).
Saussure, F. de, *Course in General Linguistics*, tr. W. Baskin (London, Fontana/Collins, 1974).
Scholes, R., *Structuralism in Literature: An Introduction* (New Haven and London, Yale University Press, 1974).
Todorov, T., *The Fantastic: a Structural Approach to a Literary Genre*, tr. R. Howard (Ithaca, NY, Cornell University Press, 1975).
— *The Poetics of Prose*, tr. R. Howard (Oxford, Blackwell, 1977).

Marxism

Althusser, L., *For Marx*, tr. B. Brewster (London, New Left Books, 1977).
— *Lenin and Philosophy and Other Essays*, tr. B. Brewster (London, New Left Books, 1977).
Bathes, R., *Mythologies*, tr. A. Lavers (London, Jonathan Cape, 1972).
Bennett, T., *Formalism and Marxism* (London and New York, Methuen, 1979).
Eagleton, T., *Marxism and Literary Criticism* (London, Methuen, 1976).
— *Criticism and Ideology* (London, New Left Books, 1976).
— *Ideology* (London and New York, Verso, 1991).
Frow, J., *Marxism and Literary History* (Oxford, Blackwell, 1986).
Jameson, F., *Marxism and Form* (Princeton, NJ, Princeton University Press, 1971).
Macherey, P., *A Theory of Literary Production*, tr. G. Wall (London, Routledge & Kegan Paul, 1978).
Williams, R., *Marxism and Literature* (Oxford, Oxford University Press, 1977).

Reader Theory

Eco, U., *The Role of the Reader: Explorations in the Semiotics of Texts* (Bloomington, Indiana University Press, 1979).
Fish, S., *Is There a Text in This Class?* (Cambridge, Mass., Harvard University Press, 1975).
Holub, R.C., *Reception Theory: A Critical Introduction* (London, Methuen, 1984).
Ingarden, R., *The Literary Work of Art*, tr. G.G. Grabowicz (Evanston, Ill.,

Northwestern University Press, 1973).

Iser, W., *The Act of Reading: A Theory of Aesthetic Response* (Baltimore, MD, and London, Johns Hopkins University Press, 1978).

Jauss, H.R., *Toward an Aesthetic of Reception*, tr. T. Bahti (Brighton, Sussex, Harvester Press, 1982).

Suleiman, S. and Crossman, I., eds, *The Reader in the Text: Essays on Audience and Interpretation* (Princeton, NJ, Princeton University Press 1980).

Tompkins, J.P., ed. *Reader Response Criticism: From Formalism to Post-Structuralism* (Baltimore, MD, Johns Hopkins University Press, 1980).

Feminism

Barrett, M., *Women's Oppression Today* (London, New Left Books, 1980).

Beauvoir, S. de, *The Second Sex*, tr. H.M. Parshley (Harmondsworth, Penguin, 1974).

Brunt, R. and Rowan, C., *Feminism, Culture and Politics* (London, Lawrence & Wishart, 1982).

Eisenstein, H., *Contemporary Feminist Thought* (London and Sydney, Unwin, 1984).

Ellman, M., ed., *Thinking about Women* (London, Virago, 1979).

Felski, R., *Beyond Feminist Aesthetics: Feminist Literature and Social Change* (London, Hutchinson, 1989).

Greene, G. and Kahn, C. *Making a Difference: Feminist Literary Criticism* (London and New York, Methuen, 1985).

Humm, M., *Feminist Criticism: Women as Contemporary Critics* (Brighton, Sussex, Harvester, 1986).

Kaplan, C., *Sea Changes: Essays on Culture and Feminism* (London, Verso, 1986).

Jacobus, M., ed., *Women Writing and Writing about Women* (London, Croom Helm, 1979).

Millett, K., *Sexual Politics* (London, Virago, 1977).

Moi, T., *Sexual/Textual Criticism: Feminist Literary Theory* (London, Methuen, 1985).

Showalter, E., *A Literature of Their Own* (Princeton, NJ, Princeton University Press, 1977; London, Virago, 1978).

— *The New Feminist Criticism* (London, Virago, 1986).

Warhol, R. and Herndl, D.P., *Feminisms: An Anthology of Literary Theory and Criticism* (New Brunswick and New Jersey, Rutgers University Press,

Waugh, P., *Feminine Fictions: Revisiting the Postmodern* (London and New York, Routledge, 1989).

Wolff, J., *Feminine Sentences: Essays on Women and Culture* (Cambridge, Polity, 1990).

Post-Structuralism

Barthes, R. *S/Z*, tr. Richard Miller (London, Jonathan Cape, 1975).

— *The Pleasure of the Text*, tr. Richard Miller (London, Cape, 1976).

Belsey, C., *Critical Practice* (London, Methuen, 1980).

Harland, B., *Superstructuralism* (London, Methuen, 1987).

Harari, J.V., ed., *Textual Strategies: Perspectives in Post-Structuralist Criticism* (Ithaca, NY, Cornell University Press 1979; London, Methuen, 1980).

Hawthorn, J. *Criticism and Critical Theory* (London, Edward Arnold, 1984).

Leitch, V., *Deconstructive Criticism: An Advanced Introduction* (London, Hutchinson, 1983).

Lentricchia, F., *After the New Criticism* (London, Athlone Press, 1980).

Marks, E. and Courtivron, I. de, eds, *New French Feminisms* (Brighton, Sussex, Harvester, 1980).

Norris, C., *The Contest of Faculties: Philosophy and Theory after Deconstruction* (London and New York, Methuen, 1985).

Sturrock, J., ed. *Structuralism and Since: From Lévi-Strauss To Derrida* (Oxford, Oxford University Press, 1979).

Young, R., ed. *Untying the Text: a Post-Structuralist Reader* (Boston, Mass., and London, Routledge & Kegan Paul, 1981).

The Subject

Belsey. C., *The Subject of Tragedy* (London, Methuen, 1985).

Coward, R. and Ellis, J., *Language and Materialism: Developments in Semiology and the Theory of the Subject* (London, Routledge & Kegan Paul, 1977).

Felman, S. ed., Literature and Psychoanalysis: The Question of Reading: Otherwise. *Yale French Studies* 55/56, 1977.

Flax, J., *Thinking Fragments: Psychoanalysis, Feminism and Postmodernism in the Contemporary West* (Berkeley, California University Press, 1980).

Grosz, E., *Sexual Subversions: Three French Feminists* (Sydney, Allen & Unwin, 1989).

Lacan, J., *Ecrits: a Selection*, tr. A. Sheridan (London, Tavistock, 1977).

— *The Four Fundamental Concepts of Psychoanalysis*, tr. A. Sheridan (London, Hogarth Press, 1977).

Wright, E., *Psychoanalytic Criticism: Theory and Practice* (London, Methuen, 1984).

Language and Textuality

Attridge, D., *Peculiar Language: Literature as difference from the Romantics to James Joyce* (London, Methuen, 1988).

Derrida, J., *Of Grammatology*, tr. G. Spivak (Baltimore, MD, and London, Johns Hopkins University Press, 1976).

— *Writing and Difference*, tr. A Bass (London, Routledge & Kegan Paul, 1978).

Hartman, G., ed. *Deconstruction and Criticism* (London, Routledge & Kegan Paul, 1979).

Norris, C., *Deconstruction: Theory and Practice* (London, Methuen, 1982).

Ryan, M., *Marxism and Deconstruction: A Critical Articulation* (Baltimore, MD, and London, Johns Hopkins University Press, 1982).

History and Discourse

Bakhtin, M.M., *The Dialogic Imagination: Four essays*, tr. M. Holquist and C. Emerson (Austin, University of Texas Press, 1981).

— *Rabelais and his World* (Cambridge, Mass., MIT Press, 1986).

Diamond, I. and Quilby, L., *Feminism and Foucault: Reflections on Resistance* (Boston, Mass., Northwestern University Press, 1988).

Dollimore, J. and Sinfield, A., eds, *Political Shakespeare: New Essays in Cultural Materialism* (Ithaca, NY, Cornell University Press, 1985).

Foucault, M., *The Order of Things* (London, Tavistock, 1970).

— *Technologies of the Self*, ed. L.H. Martin, H. Gutman, P.H. Hutton (London, Tavistock Press, 1988).

Goldberg, J., *James I and the Politics of Literature: Jonson, Shakespeare, Donne, and their Contemporaries* (Baltimore, MD, and London, Johns Hopkins, 1983).

Greenblatt, S., *Renaissance Self-Fashioning: From More to Shakespeare* (Chicago, Chicago University Press, 1980).

Levinson, M. *et al. Rethinking Historicism: Critical Readings in Romantic History* (Oxford, Blackwell, 1989).

McGann, J., *The Beauty of Inflections: Literary Investigations in Historical Method and Theory* (Oxford, Clarendon, 1988).

Said, E., *Orientalism* (London: Routledge & Kegan Paul, 1978).

Stallybrass, P. and White, A. *The Politics and Poetics of Transgression* (London, Methuen, 1986).

Volosinov, V.N. *Marxism and the Philosophy of Language*, tr. L. Matejka and I.R. Titunik (London and New York, Seminar Press, 1973).

Weimann, R., *Structure and Society in Literary History: Studies in the History and Theory of Historical Criticism* (London, Lawrence & Wishart, 1977).

Postmodernism and Postcolonialism

Postmodernism

Baudrillard, J. *Simulations* (New York, Semiotext(e), 1983).

— *In the Shadow of the Silent Majorities* (New York, Semiotext(e), 1983).

Foster, H., ed., *Postmodern Culture* (London, Pluto Press, 1985).

Jameson, F., *The Ideologies of Theory: Essays 1971–86* (New York, 1989).

Lyotard, J-F., *The Postmodern Condition* (Manchester, Manchester University Press, 1985).

Rorty, R., *Contingency, Irony and Solidarity* (Cambridge, Cambridge University Press, 1989).

Waugh, P., *Practising Postmodernism/Reading Modernism* (London, Edward Arnold, 1992).

Postcolonialism

Adam, Ian and Tiffin, Helen, eds, *Past the Last Post: Theorising Post-Colonialism and Postmodernism* (Hemel Hempstead, Harvester, 1987).

Ahmad, Aijaz, *In Theory: Classes, Nations, Literatures* (London, Verso, 1992).

Bennington, Geoff, Bowlby, Rachel, and Young, Robert, eds, *Oxford Literary Review: Colonialism and Other Essays*, 9/1–2, 1987.

BhaBha, Homi, ed., *Nation and Narration* (London and New York, Routledge, 1994).

hooks, bell, *Ain't I a Woman: Black Women and Feminism* (London, Pluto, 1982).

Spivak, Gayatri Chakravorty, *The Post-Colonial Critic* (New York and London, Routledge, 1990).

Young, Robert, *Writing History and the West* (London and New York, Routledge, 1990).

INDEX

Adorno, T. 161, 329
aesthetics of reception: *see* Iser; Jauss
Althusser, L. 51, 53–61, 64, 101, 124, 161, 292, 304, 305
Aristotle 24, 25, 83, 230
Artaud, A. 132, 136, 243, 304, 377
author 1, 33–4, 46, 57, 63, 65, 90, 95–7, 98, 106–7, 117, 118–22, 191–7, 202, 203, 204, 229, 236–9, 245–8, 256, 257, 259, 284, 286, 300, 333

Bakhtin, M. 226–30, 230–9, 275
Balibar, E. 61–9
Barthes, R. 22, 23, 25, 26, 29, 32, 41–50, 52, 101, 114, 115, 118–22, 166, 168–9, 175, 202, 329
Bataille, G. 193, 243
Baudelaire, C. 66, 86, 97, 119, 121, 332
Baudrillard, J. 290
Beauvoir, S. de 98, 145–7, 149–50, 156–8
Belsey, C. 5, 17
Benjamin, W. 161
Benveniste, E. 43
BhaBha, H. 291, 360–7
Bloom, H. 95–7, 175, 215, 218–21
Brecht, B. 64, 66, 72, 120, 161
Butler, J. 145–52
Butler, M. 229

Caillois, R. 128
Cixous, H. 125, 137–44
Culler, J. 26, 31, 115, 218, 369
cultural capital 52

Deleuze, G. 300, 308
Derrida, J. ix, 114, 115, 117, 118, 162, 165, 173–5, 176–91, 216, 300, 368–78
Dollimore, J. 125, 159–72, 229

Eagleton, T. 16, 17, 52, 69–72, 111, 166
Eco, U. 22
empiricism 3, 119, 163, 186, 253, 267

Fanon, F. 301, 302, 350, 363, 365
feminism 3, 4, 98–113, 125, 135, 290, 322–41

Fish, S. 73, 213
formalism 16–21, 26–7, 252, 276, 370, 374
Foucault, M. 4, 114, 117, 118, 125, 154, 155, 162, 165–6, 168, 226–30, 239–51, 289, 291, 295, 322, 355, 363, 366
Freud, S. 6, 75, 89, 95, 96, 123, 125, 133, 140–2, 168, 179, 334, 337

Gadamer, H-G. 74–5
gender 109–13, 125, 145–52, 215–25
Genette, G. 22, 26, 33–4, 183, 204
Gramsci, A. 4, 25, 37, 202, 208, 291
Greenblatt, S. 228–30, 268–88
Greimas, A. 25, 37, 202, 208, 291, 302

Habermas, J. 295, 300, 301, 325, 334
Hartman, G. 215, 216–17
Hassan, I. 329, 331
Hawkes, T. 8, 115
Heidegger, M. 179, 202, 329, 376
Hillis Miller, J. 215, 217–18
Hjelmslev, L. 252, 253
hooks, bell 290, 341–8
humanism 16–17, 116, 122, 159–72, 253, 304, 333, 334, 367
Husserl, E. 92

Ideological State Apparatuses 51–2, 53–61, 62–9
Ingarden R. 76–82
interpretation 53–61, 74–5, 80, 82, 83, 91, 124, 362
intertextuality 195–6
Iser, W. 73–4, 76–82, 212

Jakobson, R. 16, 27–8, 42, 82, 203, 254
Jameson, F. 290, 292–322, 326, 375
Jauss, R. 73–4, 82–9, 212
Johnson, B. 174, 175, 21–6
jouissance 142, 197, 328, 334

Kant, I. 164–5, 202, 253, 259, 307, 334, 372
Kermode, F. 25, 323
Kristeva, J. 124, 131–7, 157, 324, 331
Kroker, A. 340

Lacan, J. 4, 101, 113, 114, 117, 123–5, 126–31, 133, 141, 158, 193, 300, 331, 334, 365
Lentricchia, F. 166–7, 311
Lévi-Strauss, C-L. 6, 25, 179–90, 253
literariness 16–17, 204–5
Lodge, D. 23, 24–41
logocentrism 141, 173–5, 375
Lubbock, P. 27
Lukács, G. 71, 295
Lyotard, J-F. 289, 290, 325, 330, 331, 355

Macherey, P. 51, 61–9, 101, 109, 110
Man, P. de 174, 175–6, 198–214, 215, 221–3, 371
Marx, K. 161, 206, 305
Marxism 3, 6, 51–72, 89, 93, 109–13, 162, 192, 202, 226, 272, 275, 301, 302, 319, 321, 370, 374, 377
McGann, J. 228–30, 251–68
meaning 117, 122, 132, 133, 137, 173–5, 244–5, 272
    indeterminacy of, 76–82, 116, 208–11
metalanguage 116, 196–7
metaphor and metonymy 27–41, 177, 276, 364–6
mirrorstage 123–5, 126–31
multiaccentuality 226–8, 230–9

New Criticism 1, 16, 27, 119, 201, 212, 256, 267, 271, 335, 376
New Historicism ix, 228–30, 268–88, 374, 375, 376, 377
Nietzsche, F. 178, 179, 202, 243, 272, 290, 322, 331, 335

Oedipus complex 130, 133, 141

phallocentrism 140, 142, 334, 372
Plato 57, 241, 242, 284, 376

positivism 119
Postcolonialism ix, 3, 117, 291, 341–67
Postmodernism 3, 117, 289–348
Post-structuralism 3, 114–18, 123, 124, 173–5, 289, 295, 333, 373, 374, 375, 376
presence, metaphysics of 117, 173–5, 178–90
Propp, V. 25, 253
psychoanalysis 62, 93, 124, 126–31, 132, 192, 240, 302, 334

realism 24–41, 64–5, 71, 110, 333
reception theory 3, 73–97, 118–22, 196–7, 212
rhetoric 41, 49, 119, 196, 207–9, 211, 222
Ricoeur, P. 74–5, 89–94
Rifaterre, M. 212, 222
Rorty, R. 290, 300

Said, E. 291, 348–60, 365
Sartre, J-P. 145–90, 201, 296, 300, 303, 338
Saussure, F. de 3, 6–15, 43, 114, 115, 116, 173, 174, 203, 252, 300, 310
semiotics 22–3, 42, 114, 300
Shklovsky, V. 16–21
Showalter, E. 99–108
Spivak, G. 215
Structuralism 3, 22–50, 51, 92, 114, 176–90, 192, 201, 300, 303, 304, 325
subject 3, 44–5, 51–2, 57–60, 64–9, 118, 120, 123–72, 273, 300, 303, 325, 327, 328, 333, 337, 338, 345, 357, 361
symbolic order 124, 133–4, 300, 312

Todorov, T. 22, 25

Williams, R. 166, 229, 292
Wittgenstein, L. 290, 332